GENERAL PRINCIPLES OF STROKE ORDER

1. Top to bottom.

three 

word 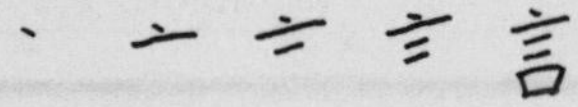

guest 

2. Left to right.

province 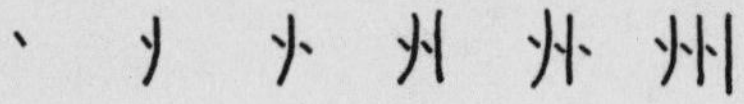

faction 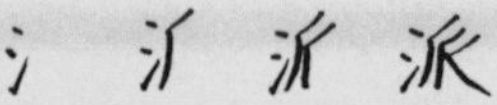

example 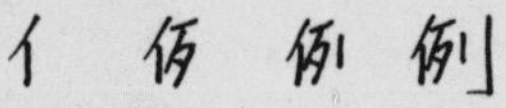

3. Horizontal strokes usually precede vertical strokes when crossing.

ten 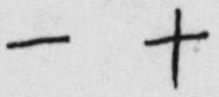

earth 

till 

4. However, in a few cases vertical strokes precede horizontal ones.

king 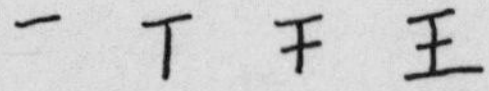

field 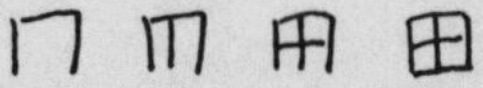

bend 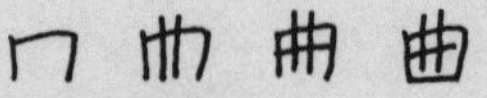

5. Center usually precedes left and right where latter do not exceed two strokes each.

small 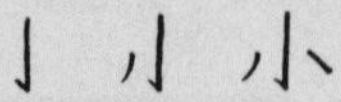

water 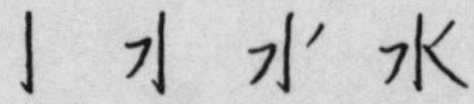

receive 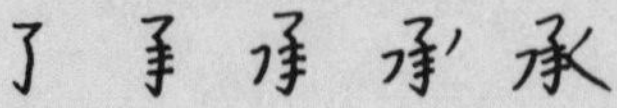

Note that the two exceptions are the heart radical 忄 (八 忄) and fire 火 (丷 火).

6. Outer frame first, but bottom line last.

country　　　冂　囯　国

sun　　　　冂　日　日

moon　　　　冂　月　月

Note the order of 匚 , with the left hand stroke joined to the bottom (e.g. 一 兀 匠).

7. Right-to-left diagonal stroke precedes left-to-right.

person　　　丿　人

father　　　　少　父

again　　　　フ　又

8. Central vertical line last.

middle　　　口　中

vehicle　　　一　亘　車

thing　　　　一　弓　事

9. Strokes which cut through come last.

woman　　　彑　女

child　　　　了　子

boat　　　　自　舟

Note that the only exception is 世 (一 廿 世).

The following pointers should also be observed.

a. squares are written with three strokes not four (丨 冂 口)
b. vertical strokes should not slope (e.g. 中 not 中)
c. horizontal strokes may slope, but should be parallel (e.g. 羊)
d. characters should be of uniform size.

A GUIDE TO REMEMBERING
JAPANESE CHARACTERS

A GUIDE TO REMEMBERING JAPANESE CHARACTERS

by Kenneth G. Henshall

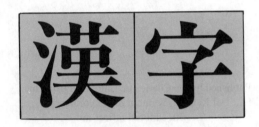

CHARLES E. TUTTLE COMPANY
Rutland, Vermont & Tokyo, Japan

Published by the Charles E. Tuttle Company, Inc.
of Rutland, Vermont & Tokyo, Japan
with editorial offices at
2-6 Suido 1-chome, Bunkyo-ku, Tokyo 112

© 1988 by Charles E. Tuttle Publishing Co., Inc.

LCC Card No. 88-50325
ISBN 0-8048-2038-4

First edition, 1988
Eleventh printing,1998

Printed in Singapore

CONTENTS

Acknowledgements   vii

Preface   ix

Introduction   xiii

    The History of Kanji   xiii

    Types of Kanji   xv

    The Structure of Kanji   xix

    General Principles of Stroke Order   xxi

Explanatory Notes   xxiv

FIRST-GRADE CHARACTERS   1

SECOND-GRADE CHARACTERS   22

THIRD-GRADE CHARACTERS   64

FOURTH-GRADE CHARACTERS   127

FIFTH-GRADE CHARACTERS   189

SIXTH-GRADE CHARACTERS   254

GENERAL-USE CHARACTERS   316

Appendices and Indices   623

    Elements Appendix   624

    Kana Appendix   627

    Non-General-Use Character Index   631

    Stroke Count Index   636

    Readings Index   646

ACKNOWLEDGEMENTS

I am greatly indebted to Tomoko Aoyama, of the Japanese Studies Unit of the University of Western Australia, for the calligraphy in this book. I am also greatly indebted to Professor Jim Everett, of the Department of Management, University of Western Australia, for his invaluable technical guidance in the computer-assisted preparation of camera-ready copy. In addition, my thanks are due to the Charles E. Tuttle Company for their guidance and support, and to my wife Carole for her many hours of proofreading.

In the research for this book I have been especially guided by the work of three of Japan's most highly regarded scholars in the field of kanji etymology, namely Tsunekata Kato, Katsumi Yamada, and Hideyuki Shindo. Those readers wishing to pursue further study of kanji are recommended to consult in particular their joint work Jigen Jiten (Etymological Dictionary of Kanji, Kadokawa, Tokyo, 2nd edition 1985), together with Katsumi Yamada's Kanji no Gogen (The Etymology of Kanji, Kadokawa, Tokyo, 1976).

With regard to stroke count, and in some cases arrangement of characters within a given grade, I have been guided by the reference work Kanji Kakijun Jiten (Dictionary of Kanji Stroke Order, edited by Hiroshi Fujiwara, Daiichi Hoki Publishing, Tokyo, revised edition 1982).

British spelling has been retained throughout.

PREFACE

The main aim of this book is to help students of the Japanese language overcome the obstacle presented by characters -- or kanji, to use the Japanese term. Without a sound knowledge of kanji it is impossible to acquire a proper command of the language, and yet so many students seem to spend years gaining merely a vague knowledge of no more than a few hundred of the two thousand kanji in general use. For every one student who feels confident in reading and writing kanji, there are dozens who seem daunted and full of despair.

For students accustomed to Western writing systems kanji can indeed be a daunting proposition. Mastering the twenty-six simple symbols in the English alphabet, even allowing for difficulties with their pronunciation, seems like child's play compared with tackling two thousand kanji of up to twenty or so strokes. It should be realised that there is no magic way to set about this task. Even Japanese nationals themselves often have problems learning and remembering kanji, despite the great advantage of constant exposure. There are, however, ways to make the task a lot easier.

I believe that for Western students the key to successful study of kanji lies not in rote learning, as favored by the Japanese themselves, but in breaking down the barrier of unfamiliarity. Once one can appreciate how a character is made up, how it acquired its shape and how and why it came into existence, then one is a long way towards achieving this end. Something that is understood and therefore familiar is far less daunting than something unknown, and far more easily remembered. A character that once seemed merely a lifeless and anonymous jumble of lines and dots becomes a 'character' in a different sense; that is, with a distinctive personality of its own.

Once a character is essentially understood, the proper use of mnemonics (memory aids) is a useful adjunct, though for the serious scholar it can be misleading to rely on mnemonics alone. That is, there is no harm in a student remembering the character used for 'east' (see # 184) by conveniently interpreting its elements as the sun rising behind a tree, provided the student also remembers that that is not the real meaning. Misunderstanding the origin of a character or element can in some cases lead to serious misconceptions regarding its connotations, its role in compounds, and its role as a window on the society of the day.

In this book I have explained the origin and subsequent evolution of each of the characters

ix

in general use, and where relevant have given the ancient forms. There are a few cases where the exact origin is obscure, and here, after clearly stating that the character is obscure, I have given the most authoritative theories and occasionally some thoughts of my own. I have also made frequent reference to Chinese character usage, since the kanji are -- with a handful of exceptions -- Chinese in origin (see Introduction). The elements forming each character are analysed and explained in detail, with cross-referencing to indicate where a recurring element is first introduced. Where relevant I have also added socio-historical comment to clarify the meaning and role of a character. Each character's usage is illustrated by three compound terms, alongside its modern readings and meanings. At the end of each explanation I have given a suggested mnemonic using the key elements in that character. Where possible I have tried in the mnemonic to use the elements in exactly the same way that they are used in the character itself, but since so many characters have changed their original meaning due to borrowing and/or miscopying this is usually not feasible. The suggested mnemonics are ones which I personally have found useful, but each reader may prefer to make up their own.

The characters are listed systematically in the order determined by the Japanese Ministry of Education (see Introduction). That is, the first 996 kanji, the so-called Educational Kanji which are prescribed for the six grades of elementary school, are set out in their respective grades (76 for Grade One, 145 for Grade Two, etc. etc.), followed by the remaining 949. Since these gradings approximately correspond to frequency of usage, the reader who wishes to learn only a few hundred kanji will be able to concentrate on the early grades confident in the knowledge that these will contain the most useful characters.

In the course of explaining the kanji in general use it has often been necessary to refer to characters outside the general use category, as well as to characters found in Chinese but to all intents and purposes no longer used in Japanese. For the reader's convenience I have listed these in an index under stroke count. The general use kanji are listed in both a stroke count index and a readings index. I have also added an appendix of the key elements found in kanji, and for the reader's interest an appendix showing the characters from which the two kana syllabaries have evolved. In the Introduction I have briefly outlined the history, structure, and types of kanji, together with a guide to general principles of stroke order. Following the Introduction there are Explanatory Notes which clarify the conventions and terms used in the text. The reader should consult both the Introduction and the Explanatory Notes before proceeding to the main text.

It is my hope and belief that the book will be of value not only to students tackling the entire corpus of the Japanese language, but also to those with more moderate aims, such as secondary students with a target of just two or three hundred kanji and private individuals wishing for an introduction to the Japanese writing system. In all cases, I will be happy if the book goes some way towards removing the mystique surrounding kanji.

K. G. Henshall,
Perth, Australia,
February 1988

INTRODUCTION

The characters from which kanji are ultimately derived originated between 2000 - 1500 B.C. in the Yellow River region of China. About 3000 characters have been discovered from this early period, mostly inscribed on bones and tortoise shells and often connected with divination. At the outset they were mostly simple pictographs, but with the passage of time became increasingly complex and abstract. Pictographs were combined to form ideographs, symbolic characters were also devised, and, as standardisation of form started to prevail, certain characters also acquired a more or less fixed phonetic role (see Types of Kanji below). A considerable degree of standardisation is evident in highly stylised characters from the third century B.C., while the square style forming the real prototype of today's characters (known in Japanese as kaisho 楷書) was established by about 200 A.D. By this stage the number of characters had grown to approximately 50,000.

Characters were first brought to Japan around the third or fourth century A.D. by migrating Chinese and Koreans, and became established during the following four centuries. (The word kanji 漢字 means literally 'symbols from Han China', the Han Period extending from 206 B.C. to 220 A.D.) At that stage the Japanese language existed only in spoken form, and Chinese characters were borrowed to enable it to be expressed in writing. For example, the Chinese character for mother, 母, pronounced BO (for the sake of illustration: its actual pronunciation at the time was different) was used to express the spoken Japanese word for mother, pronounced haha. Its own Chinese pronunciation also entered the Japanese language, and was generally favored in compounds. Thus many compounds using 母 take its Chinese reading of BO, such as BOSEI 母性(motherhood) and BOKOKU母国 (mother country). The Chinese reading is known as the on reading and the Japanese reading the kun reading. KOKU 国 of BOKOKU above is, as a further example, the on reading of the character for country, which has a kun reading of kuni. (Note that the convention usually followed is to romanise on readings in upper case and kun readings in lower case.)

As seen from the above examples, the adoption of the Chinese script presented no particular problems with simple lexical items and indeed contributed to the enrichment of the Japanese language, leading to the formation of many new terms (especially compounds) and in some cases new concepts and modes of expression. Its role has often been likened to that of Latin in the case of English. However, as a result of fundamental differences between the monosyllabic Chinese language and the polysyllabic, highly inflected Japanese language, the Chinese writing system proved decidedly unsuitable in the case of inflected items such as verbs. In practice a principal character was used for its meaning to represent the stem of a Japanese verb of similar meaning, while other characters were used for their sound to represent the variable ending of the verb. The potential for confusion was obviously considerable, even more so in view of the fact that a whole range of characters could be used to express a given sound, and it became necessary to use various methods to distinguish between the semantic characters and the phonetic characters. At one stage, for example, the latter were written smaller and/or to one side (script being vertical). Eventually, by about the ninth century, standardised characters used as phonetics were simplified into syllabaries known as kana (仮名 : literally 'assumed names'). There are two such syllabaries: hiragana, which generally derives from highly stylised cursive forms of full characters, and katakana, which generally uses just one part of a character (see Kana Appendix). Katakana symbols are now used primarily for expressing words borrowed from English or other Western languages, and hiragana used for inflections. For example, the Japanese verb meaning to go, iku, uses the Chinese character with that meaning, 行 (see # 118), to express its unchangeable stem i-. -ku is then expressed by means of hiragana, giving 行く. Not go, ikanai, is written with the kana symbols for ka, na, and i, giving 行かない. Thus i- is the principal <u>kun</u> reading of 行, while its <u>on</u> readings -- usually KŌ or GYŌ -- are generally used in compounds, e.g. ryokō 旅行 meaning travel.

Over the ensuing centuries the characters brought into Japan evolved in their own particular way, acquiring nuances and connotations not necessarily found in Chinese, and in most cases undergoing phonetic modification. Many characters were borrowed for their sound to express entirely different meanings, and in not a few cases miscopying also led to the acquisition of new meanings. Periods of renewed contact with China, such as around the ninth and thirteenth centuries, also tended to bring newly evolved Chinese readings and meanings, and thus the potential range of meanings and readings for any one character became quite considerable. The typical kanji now has two or three <u>on</u> readings and two or three <u>kun</u> readings, while some of the commoner kanji, such as life 生 42 and below 下 7, can have as many as ten fundamentally different readings. Not all readings are in common use, however. In a handful of cases new characters were created in Japan using Chinese elements, such as dry field 畑 369 and frame 枠 1943, and some of these have since been borrowed for use in Chinese (such as work 働 558). These 'made in Japan' characters usually -- but not necessarily -- have <u>kun</u> readings only.

Shortly after the end of World War Two the Japanese Ministry of Education attempted to rationalise the characters used in Japan by designating 1850 of them as the Tōyō Kanji 当用漢字(literally 'Temporary Use Kanji'), which were felt to represent the commonest and most important of the kanji. Of these 1850, 881 were designated as Kyōiku Kanji 教育漢字 (Educational Kanji), these being seen as particularly important and forming the basic requirement for the six years of elementary education. Accordingly the Kyōiku Kanji were divided into six grades to correspond to the elementary grades, with the grading also approximately corresponding to frequency of usage and/or degree of importance (though certain anomalies do appear to exist, such as in the omission of the characters for differ 違 1006 and sharp/ bitter 辛 1432). Readings were also prescribed, including the point in the syllabus at which a particular reading should be taught.

Theoretically no characters outside the Tōyō Kanji were supposed to be used except in proper nouns (for which there were an additional 92 approved characters in the case of personal names) and special circumstances such as the writing of literature. However, in practice these limitations were not infrequently ignored, and persons or companies involved in work related to printing and publishing sometimes appear to have followed their own guidelines. In this regard it might be of interest to the reader to note that a Japanese typewriter produced by a well known manufacturer as late as 1979 has, while containing several thousand characters, omitted no fewer than 35 of the Tōyō Kanji from its standard range (a fact which has caused considerable inconvenience in the preparation of the manuscript for this book!). The same typewriter also uses a number of old and variant forms, which is similarly not in keeping with the guidelines for the Tōyō Kanji.

In 1981 a revision of the Tōyō Kanji took place, resulting in the establishment of the Jōyō Kanji 常用漢字(which can be interpreted either as 'General Use Kanji' or 'Permanent Use Kanji'). The Jōyō Kanji comprise 1945 characters, of which 996 are designated as Kyōiku Kanji (the six grades containing 76, 145, 195, 195, 195, and 190 kanji respectively). However, the reader should still be prepared to encounter occasional characters outside the prescribed range.

Types of Kanji

Since as early as the second century A.D., when the first Chinese dictionary was produced, characters have traditionally been classified into six categories. However, in many cases the categorisation is open to difference of opinion, and similarly in many cases one character can legitimately belong to more than one category. Moreover, the categories are of questionable validity as classifications since they are based upon different criteria, the first four relating to character composition while the other two relate to character usage. In practice these traditional categories are unimportant to all but the specialist scholar, and may even be misleading. They are listed below for the reader's convenience, and do shed considerable light on the nature of kanji, but at the same time the reader should treat the the categories per se as no more than rough guides.

1. **The Pictograph** (象形文字 Shōkei Moji). Essentially a picture of a physical object, and usually quite simple. For example, tree 木 69 (from 米), or eye 目 72 (from ∅). Some of these have become highly stylised and to all intents and purposes unrecognisable as pictographs, such as horse 馬 191 (from 𢒁) or woman 女 35 (from 㞢). Some have also been turned on their axis, such as moon 月 16 (from 𝄐).

2. **The Sign** or **Symbol** (指事文字 Shiji Moji). Essentially a symbol expressing an abstract concept, and usually quite simple. For example, above 上 37 (from 二) or rotational motion 回 86 (from ⊙). There is some confusion as to whether certain characters are symbols or pictographs, with considerable evidence of miscategorisation. For example, one 一 1 is treated by many scholars as a symbol, but in fact it seems more appropriate to treat it as a pictograph, since it originally depicted a single finger.

3. **The Ideograph** (会意文字 Kaii Moji). Essentially a meaningful combination of two or more pictographs or symbols, and usually quite simple. For example, mountain pass 峠 1663, combining up 上 37, down 下 7, and mountain 山 24. See servant 僕 1820 for an unusually complex example, made more so by a high degree of stylisation. In many cases the ideograph category has a considerable overlap with the semasio-phonetic category (see 4 below).

4. **The Phonetic-Ideograph** or **Semasio-Phonetic** (形声文字 Keisei Moji). The largest of the categories, theoretically containing about 85% of all the characters, but at the same time a rather confused one. Essentially a combination of a semantic element with a phonetic element, the former usually indicating the general nature of the item to be represented and the latter usually giving more specific information by lending its sound to express the pronunciation of a descriptive word (which word typically has a character of its own too complex to be used easily in combination). For example, pour 注 344 has a semantic element water 氵 40, and a phonetic element 主 299 which expresses the sound of a word meaning continuous (specifically continue 続 536, both 536 and 299 having the same pronunciation at the time). Thus continuous (flow of) water, a reference to pouring. Since it could also be said that at the same time 主 necessarily acts phonetically to express the word pour itself, there is clearly an etymological link between pour and continui-

ty, and thus an analysis of semasio-phonetic characters sheds considerable light on the etymology of words and not just characters (cf. similar etymological/ phonetic links in English between birch, beech, bark, book etc.).

The element used as a phonetic was usually chosen from a range of similarly pronounced characters on the basis of its also lending relevant semantic connotations of its own. In the case of the example above it is almost certain that 主 was chosen as the phonetic because its original meaning was long stemmed lamp, thus suggesting connotations of column and hence column of water, thereby reinforcing the idea of continuous flow of water. Thus it is also possible to consider such semasio-phonetics as ideographs, and whether they are categorised as ideographs or semasio-phonetics then becomes a matter of degree, i.e. depending on whether the semantic role is felt to outweigh the phonetic or vice-versa. In the case of pour 注 it is clear that the sound is the more important and thus it is classified as a semasio-phonetic, but classification is not always so easy. The matter is made more complex since even in the case of seemingly obvious ideographs one of the elements also lends its sound, and could therefore be said to be a phonetic element expressing its own meaning through its own sound. For example, blind 盲 1852 combines die 亡 973 and eye 目 72, and is treated in this book as an ideograph meaning dead eyes. However, some scholars make out a case that it is technically a semasio-phonetic, with 亡 acting phonetically to express die and thus giving the same result of dead eyes.

This treatment of seemingly obvious ideographs as semasio-phonetics may seem unnecessarily complex, and in this book has been avoided where at all possible. However, the problem in attempting to attribute a semantic role to a phonetic element is that the present-day scholar is frequently reduced to speculation, since most of the principal ancient sources used in etymological research (such as the writings of the tenth century scholar Jokai 徐鍇) generally tend to state the phonetic role of an element but do not necessarily refer to any semantic role. The reason for this is not clear, since some of the characters treated as semasio-phonetics in Jokai's writings are treated as ideographs in still earlier writings. As a result of this relative wealth of information regarding phonetic roles the present-day scholar can be sure that, despite enormously convoluted changes in pronunciation over the centuries (for example en changing by degrees to soku and shi changing to ten), at a given point in time a particular element had a particular reading and served a particular phonetic role. With regard to semantic role, however, from today's perspective it is not at all easy to know with certainty what particular meaning an element had at a given point in time two thousand or more years ago (such as for instance at what precise point in time long stemmed lamp 主 in the example above ceased to mean long stemmed lamp and came to mean master). Thus in most cases comments regarding semantic roles must be expressed with varying degrees of tentativeness and qualification.

Some of the simpler elements do appear to have been used purely as phonetics in some cases, such as 工 113 in nape of neck 項 1262 (expressing rear/back, in place of 後 111), but in general one must reasonably assume that any element with more than a few strokes was chosen for its connotations as well as its sound. If this were not the case, one would surely see a more or less fixed pattern in which a given sound was expressed by the same (simple) element. One can however only ever say 'more or less fixed', since there is evidence to suggest that in some cases complex characters were chosen as a phonetic despite their complexity, or even because of it, in order to display erudition and/or to lend a degree of visual substance or elegance to a character. (See also borrowings in Category 5 below.)

A further type of semasio-phonetic which is treated by some scholars as a distinct category is the onomatopoeic character. For example, in the case of mosquito 蚊 1056 the element 文 68 is used purely for its sound BUN, combining with insect 虫 56 to give 'insect that makes a BUN sound'. There are only a few of these onomatopoeic characters, however.

5. **Characters of borrowed meaning and pronunciation** (転注文字 Tenchū Moji). A rather vague category which has never been properly defined, but essentially kanji whose meanings and/or pronunciations have changed as a result of borrowing. Some scholars take the category to include extended and associated meanings, while others restrict it simply to pure borrowings. Since the majority of characters have undergone some change of meaning, now often displaying extended or associated meanings in addition to or in place of their original meanings (such as a sword meaning by association to cut -- see 181), and since a very large number have also experienced a change of pronunciation, any category based upon such changes is now in effect pointless, though it may have had some relevance in the second century.

The confusing vagueness of the category is perhaps typified by the fact that it is traditionally illustrated by the character for music and enjoyment 楽 218, which is popularly said to have pictographically depicted a drum and then to have acquired its present meanings by association and/or borrowing. This is a very poor example since in fact the character is not a pictograph at all, but essentially an ideograph which originally meant oak tree, and it is not really clear how it came by its present meanings. Nevertheless, it still serves as an example of how a character can acquire new meanings and pronunciations, though not for the reasons popularly cited. A better example is 占 1491, which originally meant divination but has now also acquired a major meaning of occupy as a result of its being used instead of a similarly pronounced but more complex character of that meaning (in very similar fashion to many of the phonetic elements in the semasio-phonetic characters of Category 4). See domination 覇 1683 for an example of a rare case where a more complex character was deliberately borrowed.

6. **Phonetically borrowed characters** (仮借文字 Kasha Moji or Kashaku Moji). Somewhat confused with the preceding category, but essentially characters borrowed phonetically in what is in effect a kanji alphabet (in that sense very similar to the origins of the kana syllabaries). For example, the four kanji used to express one syllable each of A-me-ri-ca, namely 亜米利加.

In addition to the above six categories, some scholars treat as a seventh category the dozen or so characters made in Japan, known as Kokuji (国字 , literally National Characters). They are mostly ideographic, as for example mountain pass 峠 used to illustrate Category 3, but do include extremely unusual characters such as monme 匁 1858, which is a strange graphic amalgam devised for phonetic reasons and does not readily fit into any recognised category.

The Structure of Kanji

Though some of the simpler kanji, such as the pictographs and symbols seen in Categories 1 and 2 above, are essentially single element characters, most kanji comprise two or more elements. In almost all cases there is one key element, known as the radical, which indicates the general nature of the character . This radical combines with one or more other elements which give more specific information, either semantically or phonetically (see Categories 3 and 4 above). For example, earth 土 60 is often used as a radical, usually at the bottom of the composite character or in slightly stylised form 土 on the left, and indicates that the character relates in some way to earth, or soil, or ground (though its present meanings may have changed through borrowing or extension). For example, 城 903 originally meant earthen ramparts and now means castle (成 primarily acting phonetically to express pile up), while 型 468 originally meant a clay mold and now usually means model in a broad sense (刑 primarily acting phonetically to express make). There are about two hundred of these radicals, most of which are listed in the Elements Appendix towards the end of this book. Most character dictionaries list their characters under radicals, but unfortunately such listings can be misleading from an etymological point of view as they sometimes use graphic similarity as an expedient. For example, leave 去 258 is listed in many dictionaries under the earth radical 土 due to the presence of the shape 土, but in fact 土 derives from a double lid 㚢 and has nothing to do with earth.

introduction

There are seven basic positions in which a radical can be used, as listed below.

1. On the left (hen or -ben). For example, person 亻 39 in rank 位 421 (combining with standing person 立 73 to give person standing in position in a line), or tree/ wood 木 69 in timber 材 485 (in which 才 primarily acts phonetically to express cut down). Person on the left is known as ninben and tree/ wood on the left is known as kihen.

2. On the right (tsukuri or -zukuri). For example, sword/ cut 刂 181 in divide 割 823 (with 害 primarily acting phonetically to express dismember), or strike/ coerce 攵 101 in government 政 724 (combining with correct 正 41 to give an original meaning of enforce correctness/ make correct). Sword on the right is known by the special term rittō ('standing sword'), while strike/ force on the right is known as bokuzukuri (boku meaning strike).

3. On the top or crown (kanmuri). For example, bamboo 竹 170 in pipe/ tube 管 443 (in which 官 primarily acts phonetically to express pierce), or hole 穴 849 in sky/ space 空 15 (with 工 primarily acting phonetically to express open). Bamboo crown is known as take kanmuri and hole crown is known as ana kanmuri.

4. At the base or foot (ashi or shita-). For example, heart/ feelings 心 147 in endure 忍 1677 (in which blade 刃 1446 acts phonetically to express bear and also lends connotations of something painful), or fire 灬 8 in fierce/ intense 烈 1929 (in which 列 primarily acts phonetically to express destroy, to give an original meaning of destructive fire). Heart at the base is known as shitagokoro, while fire at the base is known by the special term rekka ('fire in a row').

5. The outside or frame (kamae or -gamae). For example, enclosure 囗 123 in country 国 123 (with 玉 being a simplification of delineated area 或 809), or gate 門 211 in space 間 92 (combining with sunlight 日 62), or container 匚 225 in craftsman 匠 1388 (combining with ax 斤 1176 to give an original meaning of tool box). Enclosure frame is known as kunigamae, gate frame is known as kadogamae, and container frame is known as kakushigamae ('hiding frame').

6. Hanging or trailing (tare or -dare). For example, building 广 114 in store 店 178 (in which 占 primarily acts phonetically to express display), or sickness 疒 381 in epidemic 疫 1019 (combining with strike 殳 153). Hanging building is known as madare (being named after the character hemp [pronounced ma] 麻 1829), while hanging sickness is known as yamaidare.

7. L-shaped (nyō). For example, movement 辶 129 in advance 進 326 (combining with bird 隹 216 to give move like a bird, i.e. forwards), or run 走 161 in proceed 赴 1751 (with 卜 acting phonetically to express announce and giving an original meaning of run to announce something). L-shaped movement is known as shinnyō or shinnyū, while L-shaped run is known as sōnyō.

Of these seven basic positions, on the left (hen) is the most common.

General Principles of Stroke Order

Though there are inevitably a number of exceptions, most characters are written according to established principles of stroke order. A knowledge of these principles is important in order to achieve the proper shape and to write in the cursive style or semi-cursive style, in which normally separate strokes flow into one another. The basic principles listed below were issued by the Ministry of Education in 1958, and are considered the most authoritative. The guidelines apply either to individual strokes or to the arrangement of component elements as the case may be. The first two are especially important.

1. Top to bottom.

three 23

word 274

guest 252

2. Left to right.

province 304

faction 955

example 605

3. Horizontal strokes usually precede vertical strokes when crossing.

ten 33

earth 60 　一　十　土

till 673 　三　丰　未　耒　耕

4. However, in a few cases vertical strokes precede horizontal ones.

king 5 　　　一　丁　干　王

field 59 　　　冂　冊　田　田

bend 261 　　冂　曲　曲　曲

5. Center usually precedes right and left where latter do not exceed two strokes each.

small 36 　　　丨　小　小

water 40 　　　丨　丬　水　水

receive 713 　　了　丮　丞　承　承

Note that the two exceptions are the heart radical 忄(⺗ 忄) and fire 火(⺨ 火).

6. Outer frame first, but bottom line last.

country 123 　　冂　囯　国

sun 62 　　　冂　日　日

moon 16 　　　几　月　月

Note the order of 匚 , with the left hand stroke joined to the bottom (e.g. 一 丆 匠).

7. Right-to-left diagonal stroke precedes left-to-right.

person 39 　　　丿　人

father 197 　　　丷　父

again 1835　　ㄱ 又

8. Central vertical line last.

middle 55　　口 中

vehicle 31　　一 亘 車

thing 293　　一 吾 事

9. Strokes which cut through come last.

woman 35　　ㄥ 女

child 25　　ㄱ 子

boat 1354　　凡 舟

Note that the only exception is 世 (一 卅 世).

The following pointers should also be observed.

a. squares are written with three strokes not four (｜ 冂 口)

b. vertical strokes should not slope (e.g. 中 not 中)

c. horizontal strokes may slope, but should be parallel (e.g. 羊)

d. characters should be of uniform size.

EXPLANATORY NOTES

Characters are set out according to the conventions established by the Ministry of Education, that is with the first 996 characters (the Kyōiku Kanji or Educational Kanji) divided into six grades corresponding to the six grades of elementary school, followed by the remaining 949. There is slight potential for confusion in that the latter are usually referred to as general use kanji, while General Use Kanji is also the generic term for the whole set of 1945 characters comprising the Jōyō Kanji.

Within each grade characters are arranged in the gojūonjun (a-i-u-e-o order) according to their principal reading, with a 'hard' sound following the unmodified sound (e.g. GA after KA, JI after SHI). Where two or more characters within a given grade share the same reading they are listed in ascending order according to their stroke count. Where characters in a given grade share both the same readings and the same stroke count there is no real convention regarding order, and this book has simply followed the order of printing in Ministry of Education lists. On readings take precedence over kun readings of the same sound. That is, the 15 stroke KA 樛 (1055) comes after the 14 stroke KA 箇 (1054) but before the 10 stroke ka 蚊 (1056). Principal readings are usually on, but not necessarily so (e.g. ka 蚊 above, which is listed under its kun reading ka but also has an on reading BUN).

There are a few dozen characters which are the subject of difference of opinion as to which of their readings is the principal one, and accordingly kanji lists arranged by some scholars do not neccessarily follow the same order as the Ministry of Education lists (though gradings etc. are unaffected). After surveying a range of such lists I have made the following six alterations to the order given in the Ministry of Education lists: 楽 218 listed under RAKU not GAKU; 象 533 under ZŌ not SHŌ; 治 544 under CHI not JI; 興 652 under KYŌ not KŌ; 率 803 under RITSU not SOTSU; and 矢 981 under its kun reading ya not its on reading SHI. I have also made a number of alterations which do not affect order, such as listing 大 53 as TAI, DAI rather than DAI, TAI. The Ministry of Education recognises the right of scholars to make such alterations to arrangement within a given grade and in no way claims its own arrangement to be definitive. No alteration should be made to actual gradings themselves, however.

On readings are given in upper case, kun readings in lower case. Word stems are given in bold type, with italics being used to indicate variable endings (i.e. the part of the word which should be expressed in kana, known in this case as okurigana), such endings being separated from one another by an oblique (/). The use of okurigana is very vague, and the reader should not be alarmed at the frequent discrepancy between the okurigana given in the readings block, which usually follows strict theory, and examples given in the compounds block, which usually follow actual practice. For example, jibiki (dictionary) can be written either as 字引き or 字引, though technically the former is correct. With regard to theory I have generally followed the conventions found in Ministry of Education publications, while with regard to practice I have been guided by such widely used dictionaries as Nelson's <u>Japanese-English Character Dictionary</u> (Tuttle, Tokyo, 1962) and Kenkyusha's <u>New Japanese-English Dictionary</u> (Kenkyusha, Tokyo, 4th edition 1974).

The reader should similarly expect minor graphic discrepancies between the form of the character given in brush and the typed form in the compounds block. The latter occasionally uses slightly old forms (e.g. 挾 for 挟 1165) or even variant forms (e.g. with upturned dish 襾 instead of west 西 in the case of 覇 1683, though it should be noted that even the more usual west 西 is in any case a simplification/ variant of rain 雨). Since these were the forms supplied with a typewriter manufactured as late as 1979 it is clear that they are still widely used, and thus the reader should be prepared to recognise them. One should similarly be prepared to encounter any form of character described in the explanation as 'formerly written.....', which usually indicates a form that was standard until shortly after World War Two, whereas forms described as 'ancient', 'still earlier', 'once written....', or 'original' are almost without exception no longer found in Japanese (though they may be in Chinese).

Characters which lie outside the General Use/ Jōyō Kanji but are still found in Japanese (usually in the Nelson dictionary cited above, which lists 5446 characters in total) are referred to in this book as NGU characters, standing for Non General Use. Characters found in Chinese (in Mathews' <u>Chinese-English Dictionary</u> [Harvard U.P., Massachusetts, 1966], which lists 7773 characters) but not normally in Japanese are referred to as CO characters, standing for Chinese Only. It should however be noted that, with the possible exception of the very modern simplified forms, any Chinese character can theoretically be used in Japanese in an NGU capacity (some of the pre-war Japanese dictionaries listing as many as 50,000 characters). Some 400 NGU/CO characters occur incidentally in the course of the Jōyō Kanji explanations given in this book, and for the reader's convenience are listed under stroke count in a separate index. It should be appreciated, however, that there is no systematic explanation of them nor any listing of their readings.

As a general principle, when seeking characters in any stroke count index the reader should always be prepared to check one or two strokes either side of the estimated number. Some characters are legitimately permitted to be written in slightly different ways, which can affect the stroke count, and some variant forms also result in a slightly different stroke count. In some dictionaries, it seems that there are also occasional cases of honest miscounts!

Obliques have been used in the explanations with considerable frequency, partly as a stylistic expedient and partly in order to aid flexibility of conceptualisation. It is a serious error to assume that each word in Japanese corresponds exactly to a word in English, and the same applies to characters and their component elements. For example, 貝 90 means shell when used as an independent character, but as an element usually means money, and occasionally means valuable item or asset in a broad sense. Thus it is usually referred to as shell/ money rather than just shell. Similarly 示 695 is used as an independent character to mean show, but as an element sometimes has its literal meaning of altar and generally has its associated meaning of 'relating to the gods'. Thus it is usually referred to as altar/ show or altar/ of the gods etc.

The question of classification into nouns, verbs, adjectives etc. should similarly be treated with considerable conceptual flexibility. For this reason the readings and compounds blocks have omitted (o/ to) suru (and its variant jiru), meaning to do, on the grounds that so many nouns can be made into verbs (especially in their on readings) by adding suru/ jiru that it is in effect pointless to list each one (e.g. KAN feeling 感 246 giving kanjiru/ to feel, or BATSU punishment 罰 1709 giving bassuru/ to punish). Similarly almost any adjective can be made into a verb by adding suru to its adverbial form (e.g. TAI/ ō big 大 53 giving ōkiku suru/ to enlarge).

The main text is generally written in semi-note style. I have deliberately kept the explanations in the early grades relatively brief and simple, while those in the later grades go into greater detail in the expectation of a more specialised readership.

In one or two cases I have used the adjective 'authoritative' in front of the term 'scholars'. This is in no way intended to imply that scholars not so described lack authority, but in most cases is simply used to indicate that an explanation which may possibly seem unlikely to the general reader is in fact supported by scholars whose views are particularly highly respected in their field.

Examples used in the compounds block are chosen to illustrate a variety of readings and meanings. The vast majority of the terms can be found in the Nelson dictionary and/ or Kenkyusha dictionary mentioned above, but a few are reasonably rare and will only be found in large Japanese-Japanese dictionaries. Where such terms contain a character outside the Jōyō Kanji, kana has been used. Asterisks denote irregular readings.

Generally only principal readings and meanings have been given, particularly in the early grades, though specific minor meanings/ readings have been given where important to a proper understanding of the evolution of a particular character. It should be appreciated that where a character has multiple readings and multiple meanings, it does not necessarily follow that each reading can be used to express each meaning.

Finally, as a convenient reference I give below a simple summary explanation of key terms with which some readers may not be completely familiar:

CO character:	found in Chinese only
connotation(s):	suggested or implied meaning
etymology:	the history/ evolution of a word or character
ideograph:	combination of meaningful elements to express a new idea
lexical:	relating to vocabulary
mnemonic:	relating to memory; as a noun, memory aid
NGU character:	found in Japanese but not in general use
phonetic:	relating to sound/ pronunciation
pictograph:	picture-drawing
q.v.	quod vide/ which see (by way of cross reference)
semantic:	relating to meaning
semasio-phonetic:	combination of meaning-element and sound-element
syllabary:	form of alphabet

THE 76 FIRST GRADE CHARACTERS

1　一

ICHI, ITSU, hito-
ONE
1 stroke

一月	ICHIGATSU	January
均一	KINITSU	uniformity
一人	HITORI	one person

The easiest character of all. A pictograph of a **single** extended finger 一.

Mnemonic: **ONE FINGER**

2　右

U, YŪ, migi
RIGHT
5 strokes

右派	UHA	rightist faction
右岸	UGAN	right bank
右手	MIGITE	right hand

Originally , showing a **right hand** ⊃ over a **mouth** 口 20. The right hand symbolised **strength/support**, and the original meaning of 2 was **support verbally** (still occasionally found in Chinese). This meaning was later assumed by an NGU character 佑 that adds **person** 亻 39, while 2 itself came to mean simply **right hand.** The retention of mouth 口 may have been influenced by a popular interpretation of the elements as **hand favored for feeding**.

Mnemonic: **RIGHT HAND TO THE MOUTH**

3　雨

U, ame, ama-
RAIN
8 strokes

雨季	UKI	rainy season
大雨	ŌAME	heavy rain
雨雲	AMAGUMO	rain cloud

Ancient form 𩂳 or 𩃀. **Raindrops** ∴ falling from **clouds** ⊓ beneath a symbol of the **heavens** ⁻. Some scholars feel that ⊓ alone is cloud, and that | is a symbol of **falling**.

Mnemonic: **RAIN FROM HEAVENLY CLOUDS**

1

4	円	EN, marui	円形	ENKEI	circle
		ROUND, YEN	円高	ENDAKA	strong yen
		4 strokes	百円	HYAKUEN	hundred yen

Formerly 圓. □ indicates **roundness**, while 員 is **round kettle** 228 q.v., here emphasising roundness and also lending its sound to express **circle**. The meaning **coin** (**yen** in Japan) stems from an association of shape. A simpler if facetious mnemonic is to see the character as a **bank-teller's window,** from which **round coins** are issued.

Mnemonic: **ROUND COINS FROM BANK-TELLER'S WINDOW**

5	王	Ō	王子	ŌJI	prince
		KING, RULER	女王	JOŌ	queen
		4 strokes	王様	ŌSAMA	king

Usually explained as a symbol of the three orders of **heaven, earth,** and **man** 三 united by an **all-pervading force** |, to give a meaning of **great potentate** or **king**. A useful mnemonic, but incorrect. 王 was once written 玊 and 大, depicting the **blade of a large battle ax**. Over the years, rather like the English terms 'big gun' and 'big shot', it came to mean **powerful figure,** and eventually **king.**

Mnemonic: **KING WITH AX RULES HEAVEN, EARTH AND MAN**

6	音	ON, IN, oto, ne	音楽	ONGAKU	music
		SOUND	子音	SHIIN	consonant
		9 strokes	発音	HATSUON	pronunciation

Once written 𩒣. The old form of **speak** 言 274 q.v., 言, with the addition of **tongue** - inside the mouth 口 to show greater **vocalisation**, i.e. **shout/sing**. This led to just **sound**. Suggest taking 立 as **rise/stand** 73, and 日 as **sun** 62.

Mnemonic: **SOUND OF RISING SUN**

2

7 下 KA,GE,shita,shimo,moto, 低下 TEIKA decrease

kuda*saru/ru,* sa*garu, o*riru 下車 GESHA alighting

BASE, UNDER, LOWER 川下 KAWASHIMO

3 strokes downstream

Symbol indicating an area **below** a given line. Originally 〓 , with a vertical line added later for emphasis. The downwards tilt of the short third stroke is also believed to be for emphasis.

Mnemonic: **T-BAR WITH DROOPY LOWER HANDLE**

8 火 **KA, hi** 火曜日 KAYŌBI Tuesday

FIRE 火山 KAZAN volcano

4 strokes 火花 HIBANA spark

Stylised derivative of pictograph of **fire** with **flames** and **sparks** . As a radical often occurs as ⺌⺌ .

Mnemonic: **FLAMES OF FIRE**

9 花 **KA, hana** 花弁 KABEN petal

FLOWER, BLOSSOM 花火 HANABI fireworks

7 strokes 花見 HANAMI

blossom viewing

Grass/plant ⺾ (derived from a pictograph of growing plants to ⺿ to ⾋ to ⺾) plus **change** 化 238 q.v., to give a meaning of **change in state of plants**, i.e. blossoming.

Mnemonic: **FLOWERS APPEAR WHEN PLANTS UNDERGO CHANGE**

3

10 学	GAKU, mana*bu* **LEARNING** 8 strokes	学校 GAKKŌ 化学 KAGAKU 学者 GAKUSHA	school chemistry scholar

Somewhat obscure. Formerly 學, and originally ⺉. ⺉/𦥑 represents **hands**. 爻 is a CO character meaning **intertwine**, and shows interwoven sticks. Since the sticks had to be matched it has connotations of **match** and by extension **emulate**. Thus 𢲵 means **emulate manually**. An old form 斈 suggests that ⼍ derives from a **roof/ building** 宀, but some scholars maintain that 宀 was originally merely a stylisation of 爻, and cite another old form 斅. **Child** 子 25 is a later addition, presumably from a natural association of children with the idea of manual emulation (i.e. learning by imitation to use the hands, symbolic of **learning** in general). Suggest taking ⺍ as an **ornate roof.**

Mnemonic: **CHILD LEARNING UNDER ORNATE ROOF**

11 気	KI, KE **SPIRIT** 6 strokes	気分 KIBUN 天気 TENKI 電気 DENKI	mood, feeling weather electricity

Formerly written 氣. 米 is **rice** 201, while 气 is a representation of **vapors** 𠂉. 11 originally meant **vapors rising from (cooked) rice**, and eventually came to mean **invisible movement/ unseen force/ spirit** etc. Suggest taking ㄨ as **X**.

Mnemonic: **SPIRIT-LIKE VAPORS FROM SOURCE X**

12 九	KYŪ, KU, kokono- **NINE** 2 strokes	十九 JŪKYŪ 九日 KOKONOKA 九月 KUGATSU	nineteen ninth day September

Originally written 㐅, depicting a **bent elbow**. In ancient times a bent elbow was used to indicate the number **nine** when counting with only one arm. The commonly heard explanation that it is the character for **ten** 十 33 with a hook on the cross stroke to represent the concept of **subtraction** is incorrect, but is useful as a mnemonic.

Mnemonic: **LESS THAN PERFECT TEN: WORTH ONLY NINE**

13	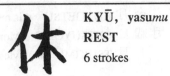	KYŪ, yasu*mu*	休日 KYŪJITSU	holiday
		REST	休戦 KYŪSEN	truce
		6 strokes	夏休み NATSUYASUMI	
				summer vacation

亻 is **person** 39 and 木 is **tree** 69. 木 is used partly phonetically to express **stop/stay**, and partly semantically as **tree**, i.e. a shady place where **people stop to rest**. Now means **stop** or **rest** in general.

Mnemonic: **PERSON RESTS AGAINST TREE**

14		KIN, KON, kane, kana-	金曜日 KINYŌBI	Friday
		GOLD,MONEY,METAL	金色 KONJIKI	gold color
		8 strokes	金持 KANEMOCHI	
				rich person

Once written 金. The four dots ∷, now reduced to two, represent **nuggets** buried in the **ground** 土 60. There is a range of opinion regarding 스/仝. Some scholars take it to show a **mound** ○, others an element indicating **covering** (see 87), which also lent its sound to express **shine**. The latter theory seems more likely.

Mnemonic: **TWO GOLD NUGGETS UNDER COVER OF EARTH**

15		KŪ, sora, kara, a*ku*	空気 KŪKI	air
		SKY, EMPTY	空色 SORAIRO	sky-blue
		8 strokes	空箱 KARABAKO	empty box

Hole 穴 849 (literally **open space under roof**) and **work upon** 工 113. The latter is used for its sound to express **opening** as well as its meaning. Originally 15 meant to **work upon** the digging out of a **hole** that would then be covered with a **roof** to form a primitive dwelling. Since the roof was domed the idea of (**empty**) **space** within the dwelling naturally became particularly associated with the central vaulted area, and eventually the concept of **upper space** extended to the **sky** itself.

Mnemonic: **WORK TO OPEN HOLE IN ROOF TO SEE EMPTY SKY**

5

16 月 GETSU, GATSU, tsuki   今月 KONGETSU this month
    MOON, MONTH   月曜日 GETSUYŌBI Monday
    4 strokes   月見 TSUKIMI moon viewing

From a pictograph of a **crescent moon** with **pitted surface** gradually tilted on its axis in the course of stylisation (〇 to 〇 to 月). Popularly interpreted as a **crescent moon behind wispy clouds**, but this appears incorrect. See also 44.

Mnemonic: **PITTED CRESCENT MOON SHINING DOWN**

---

17 犬 KEN, inu   猟犬 RYŌKEN hunting-dog
    DOG   犬小屋 INUGOYA kennel
    4 strokes   小犬 KOINU puppy

Stylised derivative of a pictograph showing a **dog** with pointed ears standing on its hind legs barking . As a radical found as 犭 (also symbolising **beast**). Suggest remembering by association with **big** 大 53, with ` as a **spot**.

Mnemonic: **BIG SPOTTED DOG REARING UP**

---

18 見 KEN, mi*ru/seru/eru*   発見 HAKKEN discovery
    LOOK, SEE, SHOW   見物 KENBUTSU sightseeing
    7 strokes   見物 MIMONO spectacle

Eye 目 72 and **bent legs** 儿, the latter deriving from a pictograph of **a person kneeling** 人 39 (to **stare** at something).

Mnemonic: **BENDING DOWN TO LOOK CLOSELY WITH SEEING EYE**

---

19 五 GO, itsu-   五月 GOGATSU May
    FIVE   五人 GONIN five people
    4 strokes   五日 ITSUKA fifth day

Five was once shown by **five fingers** . However, from ancient times a **thread-reel** 〇 (〇 to 五) was used as a substitute, both for its sound and the fact that it replaced the **five fingers** when winding yarn.

Mnemonic: **A REEL IS BETTER THAN FIVE FINGERS**

20 口	KŌ, KU, kuchi MOUTH, OPENING 3 strokes	人口 JINKŌ	population
		口実 KŌJITSU	pretext
		出口 DEGUCHI	exit

A pictograph of an **open mouth**, originally written ⊌. Can also symbolise **speech**.

Mnemonic: **OPEN MOUTH**

21 校	KŌ SCHOOL, CHECK 10 strokes	校正 KŌSEI	proof reading
		高校 KŌKŌ	high school
		校長 KŌCHŌ	school principal

木 is **tree/wood** 69. 交 is **crossed legs** 115. 21 originally meant **wooden shackles** (i.e. wooden item to encumber the legs). However, owing to the similarity in both meaning and depiction to **crossed sticks** 爻 in Character 10 q.v., reinforced by a similarity in pronunciation at the time, it took on the latter's meanings of **collate/match/ emulate**. In fact, at one stage the two characters seem to have been virtually interchangeable. Eventually 10 came to mean **learning** while 21 became **checking** and also **place of learning**. Suggest taking 六 as **six** 76 and 乂 as a **cross**.

Mnemonic: **CHECK SIX WOODEN CROSSES FOR SCHOOL**

22 左	SA, hidari LEFT 5 strokes	左派 SAHA	leftist faction
		左側 HIDARIGAWA	left side
		左手 HIDARITE	left hand

Left hand ナ and **work upon** 工 113 q.v. Rather like the right hand, the left hand also symbolised **support**, but with connotations of **reserve/auxiliary** as opposed to the strength of the right (see 2). Thus 22's original meaning was **assist someone at work** (still found in Chinese). Again like 2, its original meaning was later taken over by a character adding **person** イ 39, giving **assist** 佐 1283, while 22 itself came to mean simply **left hand**, with 工 retained though redundant. Suggest taking 工 literally as **carpenter's square**.

Mnemonic: **LEFT HAND STEADIES CARPENTER'S SQUARE**

23 三	SAN, mi- THREE 3 strokes	三月 SANGATSU	March
		三日 MIKKA	third day
		三角 SANKAKU	triangle

Three extended fingers 三 .

Mnemonic: **THREE FINGERS**

24 山	SAN, yama MOUNTAIN 3 strokes	氷山 HYŌZAN	iceberg
		沢山 TAKUSAN	a lot
		山場 YAMABA	peak, climax

A range of **mountains** with a prominent central peak 山 .

Mnemonic: **TRIPLE-PEAKED MOUNTAIN**

25 子	SHI, SU, ko CHILD 3 strokes	電子 DENSHI	electron
		子供 KODOMO	child
		様子 YŌSU	look, situation

An **infant** wrapped in swaddling clothes waving its arms ♀ .

Mnemonic: **LONG-ARMED CHILD IN SWADDLING CLOTHES**

26 四	SHI, yon, yo- FOUR 5 strokes	四月 SHIGATSU	April
		四日 YOKKA	fourth day
		四回 YONKAI	four times

Four was once shown by **four fingers** 三 , while 四 originally meant **breath** (that which emerges 八 66 from a mouth 口 20). 四 was later used as a phonetic substitute for 三, but may also have been chosen since its shape was a rough approximation of the **four fingers** of a **fist** held palm side down 四.

Mnemonic: **FOUR FINGERS IN CLENCHED FIST**

8

27		SHI, ito	製糸	SEISHI	silk making
		THREAD	毛糸	KEITO	woolen yarn
		6 strokes	糸巻き	ITOMAKI	thread-reel

From a pictograph of a **skein of yarn** 臾, originally doubled 臾臾.

Mnemonic: **SKEINS OF TWISTED THREAD**

28		JI	字引き	JIBIKI	dictionary
		LETTER, SYMBOL	赤字	AKAJI	'the red', deficit
		6 strokes	数字	SŪJI	digit, number

Roof 宀 (from 冂), symbolising **house/home**, and **child** 子 25. It originally meant a **house where children are raised** (still found in Chinese in the minor meanings **suckle/nourish/bring forth**). This came to symbolise **proliferation** and, fanciful as it may seem, came to be figuratively applied to **written symbols**, which like children became increasingly numerous and complex.

Mnemonic: **CHILD AT HOME STUDYING LETTERS**

29		JI, mimi	耳科	JIKA	otology
		EAR	耳鳴り	MIMINARI	tinnitus
		6 strokes	耳飾り	MIMIKAZARI	earring

Stylised derivative of the pictograph of an **ear** 目.

Mnemonic: **POINTED EAR**

30	七	SHICHI, nana-	七月	SHICHIGATSU	July
		SEVEN	七日	NANOKA*	seventh day
		2 strokes	七晩	NANABAN	seven nights

Originally 十, with a longer lateral line than the character for **ten** 十 33, to represent and mean a line **cutting** another. It was one of several characters used phonetically to express **seven**, and was probably especially favored since it roughly resembled a **bent finger under a fist**, an old way of signaling **seven**.

Mnemonic: **BADLY WRITTEN TEN AGAIN: NOW WORTH ONLY SEVEN**

| 31 車 | SHA, kuruma
VEHICLE, CHARIOT
7 strokes | 電 車 DENSHA   train
発 車 HASSHA   departure
口 車 KUCHIGURUMA
               cajolery |

From a pictograph of a long-shafted **two-wheeled chariot**, viewed from above .

Mnemonic: **CHARIOT WITH TWO WHEELS**

| 32 手 | SHU, te
HAND
4 strokes | 手 段 SHUDAN   means
手 本 TEHON   model, standard
上 手 JŌZU*   skill |

From a semi-stylised pictograph of a **hand** with **five fingers** (one bent), a **palm**, and **wrist** ⅏ . As a radical usually found as 扌 .

Mnemonic: **HAND WITH FINGERS SPREAD**

| 33 十 | JŪ, tǒ
TEN
2 strokes | 十 月 JŪGATSU   October
十 日 TŌKA   tenth day
十 字 JŪJI   a cross |

Usually explained as **two lines crossing** to symbolise the **four main directions**, which in turn expressed the concept of **completeness** and by association **all the fingers**, i.e. **ten**. However, this seems a confused version of its actual origin. It derives from a depiction of a **sewing needle** ✝, and was used purely as a substitute for the more complex character **ten** 拾 305 q.v. (literally **hands together**).

Mnemonic: **ALL POINTS CONSIDERED, TEN OUT OF TEN**

| 34 出 | SHUTSU, deru, dasu
EMERGE, PUT OUT
5 strokes | 出 発 SHUPPATSU   departure
思 い 出 OMOIDE   memory
引 き 出 し HIKIDASHI   drawer |

Once written ⿺, with **foot** 止 129 q.v. and ∪. Some scholars take ∪ to indicate a **cover**, i.e. **shoe**, to symbolise **going out**, while others take it to be a **line of containment**, beyond which the foot has **emerged**. Another theory sees the character as derived from a pictograph of an **emerging plant** ⿻ (see 42), but this is not widely supported. Suggest taking it as two **mountains** 山 24.

Mnemonic: **MOUNTAIN EMERGING ATOP ANOTHER**

10

| 35 | JŌ, NYŌ, NYO, onna, me
WOMAN
3 strokes | 女性 JOSEI
女房 NYŌBŌ
女の子 ONNA-NO-KO | woman
wife
girl |

From a pictograph of a **kneeling woman** with outstretched arms 乙.

Mnemonic: **KNEELING WOMAN**

| 36 | SHŌ, ko-, o-, chiisai
SMALL
3 strokes | 小人 SHŌJIN/KOBITO
小牛 KOUSHI
小川 OGAWA | dwarf
calf
brook, stream |

Commonly but erroneously explained as a **person standing with their arms at their side**, i.e. **looking small**. The error is no doubt attributable to the pictographic origin of the opposite **big** 大 53 q.v. (literally a person with arms outstretched). 小 is actually a stylised representation of **three small points**, as is clear from the older version ハ. Some scholars feel the lengthening of the middle stroke serves to express the concept of **one large** item being **divided** into **two small ones**.

Mnemonic: **A STROKE DIVIDED INTO TWO SMALL ONES**

| 37 上 | JŌ, ue, kami, uwa-,
noboru, agaru/geru
UP,TOP,OVER,GO UP
3 strokes | 以上 IJŌ
川上 KAWAKAMI
値上げ NEAGE | over, above
upstream
price rise |

Symbol indicating an area **above** a line. Originally written 二, with a vertical line added later for clarity.

Mnemonic: **BAR WITH HANDLE, STICKING UP OVER BASELINE**

| 38 | SHIN, mori
WOODS
12 strokes | 森林 SHINRIN
森厳 SHINGEN na
森閑 SHINKAN | forest
solemn
silence |

An ideograph showing **many trees** 木 69. See also **forest** 林 75.

Mnemonic: **THERE ARE MANY TREES IN THE WOODS**

39

人

JIN, NIN, hito
PERSON, PEOPLE
2 strokes

日本人 NIHONJIN　　Japanese
人間 NINGEN　　human being
人出 HITODE　crowd, turn-out

From a pictograph of a **standing person** viewed side-on 人 , though in compounds often
a bending or stooping person 𠆢/𠆢 . As a radical usually found as 亻 , but occasionally 𠆢/𠂉 , or even 𠆢 . Better taken as **headless, armless person**.

Mnemonic: **HEADLESS, ARMLESS PERSON**

40

水

SUI, mizu
WATER
4 strokes

水曜日 SUIYŌBI　　Wednesday
水素 SUISO　　hydrogen
大水 ŌMIZU　　flood

From a pictograph of a **river** 川, the central stroke showing **current** and the dots **ripples**.
Since ancient times blurred with **river** 川 48. As a radical, usually found as 氵, best remembered as **falling droplets**. Suggest taking フく as **narrow banks**.

Mnemonic: **WATER SQUEEZES BETWEEN BANKS**

41

正

SEI,SHŌ,masa,tada*shii/su*
CORRECT, PROPER
5 strokes

正解 SEIKAI　　correct answer
正月 SHŌGATSU　New Year
正直 SHŌJIKI na　　honest

Often explained as **foot/stop** 止 129 q.v. and a **bar** 一, to indicate **stopping at the
right place**, i.e. being **correct**. A useful mnemonic, especially in view of the English
term **toe the line**, but in fact old forms such as 㞢 show it to be a variant of **lower leg**
足 51, which was **straight** and by figurative extension **proper/correct**.

Mnemonic: **TO STOP AT THE LINE IS TO DO THE CORRECT THING**

42

生

SEI, SHŌ, nama,
ikiru, u*mu/mareru*, ha*eru*
LIFE, BIRTH, GROW
5 strokes

学生 GAKUSEI　　student
一生 ISSHŌ　one's whole life
生き物 IKIMONO　　living thing

From a pictograph of a **growing plant** 生, symbolising **vitality**. Note that there is a
character-element 止, derived from a differently written **plant** 止, which confusingly is
identical to **foot/stop** 止 129.

Mnemonic: **GROWING PLANT IS A SYMBOL OF LIFE**

| 43 青 | SEI, SHŌ, ao*i*
BLUE, GREEN, YOUNG
8 strokes | 青年 SEINEN
青空 AOZORA
青物 AOMONO | a youth
blue sky
greens |

Also written 靑 . 㞢 is a simplified version of **growing plant/life** 生 42. 円/月 is a simplified version of 丼 . Now an NGU character meaning **receptacle/bowl**, 丼 originally depicted a **well** 井 1470 with a mark to indicate **water** in it. Here it has that original meaning, and combines with 㞢 to express **growth around a full well**, which is **fresh** and **green**. Green overlaps conceptually with **blue**, and also has a figurative association with **immature** and **young** (as in English). Suggest taking 月 as **moon 16**.

Mnemonic: **YOUNG BLUE-GREEN PLANTS LIVE ON THE MOON**

| 44 夕 | SEKI, yū
EVENING
3 strokes | 今夕 KONSEKI this evening
夕食 YŪSHOKU evening meal
夕日 YŪHI setting sun |

To all intents and purposes derived from the same pictograph of a **crescent moon** as moon 月 16 q.v., but without the pitted surface. The **unpitted,** only semi-tilted **crescent moon** of 44 came to symbolise **evening**.

Mnemonic: **CLEAR MOON INDICATES EVENING**

| 45 石 | SEKI, SHAKU, ishi
STONE, ROCK
5 strokes | 化石 KASEKI fossil
小石 KOISHI pebble
石油 SEKIYU petroleum |

A slightly modified **cliff** 厂 (to 厂) and a **boulder** 口 . Usually explained as a **boulder having rolled down a cliff**, but it is more likely a **boulder hewn from a cliff-face**.

Mnemonic: **ROUND STONE AT BASE OF CLIFF**

| 46 赤 | SEKI, SHAKU, aka*i*
RED
7 strokes | 赤道 SEKIDŌ equator
赤面 SEKIMEN blush
赤ん坊 AKANBŌ infant |

Usually explained as an ideograph combining **earth** 土 60 and **fire** 小(variant 灬 8), with a meaning of **fired earth/terracotta**. However, an old form 交 clearly shows that 土 is a variant of **big** 大 53, giving a meaning of **big blaze** with a **ruddy glow**.

Mnemonic: **BIG FIRE MAKES EARTH GLOW RED**

13

47 千	SEN, chi THOUSAND 3 strokes	千円 SENEN	thousand yen
		五千 GOSEN	five thousand
		千鳥 CHIDORI	plover

A combination of **person** イ 39 and **one** 一 1. Possibly partly for phonetic reasons, in ancient times the **body** symbolised a **thousand**, with one thousand being written ４, two thousand ４, and so on.

Mnemonic: **THAT ONE PERSON IS WORTH A THOUSAND OTHERS**

48 川	SEN, kawa RIVER 3 strokes	川口 KAWAGUCHI	rivermouth
		川端 KAWABATA	riverside
		江戸川 EDOGAWA	Edo River

Once written , showing **water** ⟨ **flowing between two banks** ⟩ ⟩. See also 40.

Mnemonic: **RIVER FLOWING BETWEEN BANKS**

49 先	SEN, saki PREVIOUS,PRECEDE,TIP 6 strokes	先生 SENSEI	teacher
		先月 SENGETSU	last month
		指先 YUBISAKI	fingertip

A combination of 止 and 儿. As an old form clearly reveals, 止 derives from **foot/stop** 止 129 and 儿 derives from **person** 人 39. **Stop** came to mean by extension **cease to be/ die**, and the whole character meant **dead people/ancestors**. By association of ideas it later acquired meanings such as **precede, lead, tip**, and so on. Suggest taking 止 as a variant of **life** 生 42.

Mnemonic: **THOSE DEAD PEOPLE PRECEDED US IN LIFE**

50 早	SŌ, hayai EARLY, PROMPT, FAST 6 strokes	早急 SŌKYŪ	immediately
		早口 HAYAKUCHI	rapid speech
		早死に HAYAJINI	early death

Sun 日 62 and **cutting/opening** 十 (see 30), to give a meaning of the **sun breaking through** (the darkness). The popular theory that 十 represents a **plant**, to give a meaning of the **sun just rising through the plants**, is incorrect. **Fast** is an associated meaning with **early**. Suggest taking 十 as **ten** 33.

Mnemonic: **SUN SHOWS TEN BUT IT'S STILL EARLY**

| 51 | | SOKU, ashi, ta*riru*
LEG, FOOT, SUFFICIENT
7 strokes | 不足 FUSOKU insufficiency
足首 ASHIKUBI ankle
足音 ASHIOTO footsteps |

Foot 止 (variant 止 129) and a **kneecap** 口 , giving **(lower) leg**. Borrowed phonetically to express **suffice**, though it may also have lent an idea of **able** (i.e. not maimed).

Mnemonic: **ROUND KNEE AND FOOT SUFFICE TO SHOW LEG**

| 52 | | SON, mura
VILLAGE
7 strokes | 村長 SONCHŌ village head
農村 NŌSON farming village
村人 MURABITO villager |

Surprisingly obscure. Of confused etymology, though its elements are clearly **tree** 木 69 and **hand/measure** 寸 909. According to one theory 村 is a simplification of 梳 , a CO character comprising **tree** 木 and **encampment** 屯 1669 q.v. and meaning **lacquer tree**, with 屯 felt to be used partly for its original meaning of **shoot** and partly phonetically for the name of the tree (寸 had the same pronunciation). 梳 became confused with 阯 , a CO character meaning **village** (composed of **encampment** 屯 and **village** β 355). Thus at one stage both 梳 and 阯 were used for **village**. 村 then replaced 梳 in this meaning, and 梳 went back to meaning **lacquer tree**.

Mnemonic: **MEASURE TREES IN VILLAGE**

| 53 | 大 | TAI, DAI, ō*kii*
BIG
3 strokes | 大会 TAIKAI assembly
大学 DAIGAKU university
大声 ŌGOE loud voice |

A **person standing with arms and legs spread out** to look as **large** as possible 大 . Occasionally used to indicate **person**, as well as **big**.

Mnemonic: **PERSON LOOKING BIG AS POSSIBLE**

| 54 | | DAN, NAN, otoko
MAN, MALE
7 strokes | 男子 DANSHI boy
長男 CHŌNAN eldest boy
男気 OTOKOGI gallantry |

Usually explained as the **strength** 力 74 out in the **fields** 田 59, though there is also a theory that 田 was used purely phonetically to express a word **reliable**, to give a meaning of **reliable strength**.

Mnemonic: **MAN PROVIDES STRENGTH IN FIELD**

15

| 55 | | CHŪ, naka
MIDDLE, INSIDE, CHINA
4 strokes | 中立 CHŪRITSU neutrality
中国 CHŪGOKU China
真ん中 MANNAKA very middle |

Once written 𠂤. Some scholars take this to be a stylised depiction of a **flagpole** reinforced by a **second pole** running through its **center**, while others take it to show an **arrow piercing the center of a target**. In Chinese it can still mean **hit center**, suggesting the latter theory is correct. Also refers to **China**, the **middle kingdom**. See also 496.

Mnemonic: **CHINESE ARROW PIERCES MIDDLE OF TARGET**

| 56 | | CHŪ, mushi
INSECT, WORM
6 strokes | 寄生虫 KISEICHŪ parasite
害虫 GAICHŪ harmful insect
虫歯 MUSHIBA decayed tooth |

From a pictograph of a **partly coiled snake**. The earliest form ℓ suggests a **large-headed snake**, whereas a later form Φ suggests a **hooded snake (cobra)**. In ancient times **snakes** and **insects** were treated much alike. Suggest taking 中 as **inside** 55.

Mnemonic: **COILED HOODED SNAKE: SIMILAR INSIDE TO INSECT**

| 57 | | CHŌ, machi
TOWN, BLOCK
7 strokes | 町民 CHŌMIN townspeople
町長 CHŌCHŌ town mayor
下町 SHITAMACHI downtown |

Field 田 59 q.v. and **nail** 丁 346. The latter was used phonetically to express **walk**, and also lent its T-shape to suggest **junction of paths**. 57 originally meant **paths through the fields**, and by extension **place where fields join**, then **area/community**.

Mnemonic: **TOWN AT T-JUNCTION OF PATHS THROUGH FIELDS**

| 58 | 天 | TEN, ama-
HEAVEN, SKY
4 strokes | 天使 TENSHI angel
天皇 TENNŌ emperor
天下り AMAKUDARI
descent from heaven |

Originally written 𠀡, showing **person** 大 53 with an **exaggerated head** symbolising **uppermost/ upper part**. By association it came to mean **that up above**.

Mnemonic: **PERSON'S HEAD IS CLOSEST PART TO HEAVEN**

59	田	DEN, ta RICE FIELD 5 strokes	田園 DENEN 田植え TAUE 田舎 INAKA*	rural district rice planting countryside

A pictograph of a **rice field** □ crossed by **ridges/paths** 十.

Mnemonic: **RICE FIELD CROSSED BY PATHS**

60	土	DO, TO, tsuchi EARTH, SOIL, GROUND 3 strokes	土曜日 DOYŌBI 土地 TOCHI 土臭い TSUCHIKUSAI	Saturday land cloddish

From a pictograph of a **clod of earth** on the ground ⊴. The popular theory that it shows a **plant** 十 growing in the **earth** ﹣ is incorrect but a useful mnemonic.

Mnemonic: **PLANT GROWS IN EARTH**

61		NI, futa- TWO 2 strokes	二月 NIGATSU 二十 NIJŪ 二人 FUTARI	February twenty two people

Two extended fingers ⸗.

Mnemonic: **TWO FINGERS**

62	日	NICHI, JITSU, hi, -ka SUN, DAY 4 strokes	日曜日 NICHIYŌBI 本日 HONJITSU 二日 FUTSUKA*	Sunday today second day

A pictograph of the **sun with a sunspot** ⊝. Also indicates **day**, and **light**.

Mnemonic: **SUN WITH SPOT**

63		NYŪ, hairu, ireru/ru ENTER, PUT IN 2 strokes	輸入 YUNYŪ 入り口 IRIGUCHI 入れ物 IREMONO	import entrance container

Popularly said to show a person **bending down** ∧ to **enter** a primitive dwelling. However, old forms such as 人, ∧ and ∧ show it to be the **entrance** itself.

Mnemonic: **ENTER THROUGH INVERTED V OPENING**

64 年 **NEN, toshi**
YEAR
6 strokes

来年	RAINEN	next year
五年生	GONENSEI	fifth grader
年寄	TOSHIYORI	old person

Stylised derivative of ideograph 𠇙, showing **rice-plant** 禾 81 q.v. and **bending person** 𠆢 39. Some scholars take it to show a **person bending to cut rice**, others as simply showing the relationship between **man** and **rice**, while yet others feel that 𠆢 was used phonetically to express **abundant**. The first view is the most likely, but all involve the **annual harvest**, which symbolised the **cycle of a year**. Suggest taking ⺊ as **person**, and 㐄 as variant of **well** 井 1470.

Mnemonic: **PERSON VISITS WELL EVERY YEAR**

65 白 **HAKU, shiro*i***
WHITE
5 strokes

白書	HAKUSHO	White Paper
面白い	OMOSHIROI	interesting
白人	HAKUJIN	Caucasian

From a **pointed thumbnail** 白 (some forms such as 白 show the exaggerated length in vogue in ancient China), used phonetically to express **white**, and also suggesting **paleness** (relative to the skin). However, there is also some evidence to support a popular belief that 白 shows an **acorn**, whose inside is **whitish** (see 218), suggesting that two pictographs may have coexisted at one stage. See also 67. Suggest taking 日 as **sun** 62, with ノ as a **stroke**.

Mnemonic: **SUNSTROKE LEAVES ONE WHITE?!**

66 八 **HACHI, ya-**
EIGHT
2 strokes

八月	HACHIGATSU	August
八百屋	YAOYA*	greengrocer
八つ当り	YATSUATARI	outburst of anger

Once written)(, symbolising **splitting/dividing**. Some scholars feel it was later used for **eight** since it is a **readily divided number**, others that its shape was close to the old way of showing **eight** by bending down the three middle fingers and extending the **thumb** and **little finger**. In compounds, often found as ハ or 丷, with a meaning of **divide/ disperse/ away/ out**.

Mnemonic: **EIGHT CAN BE EASILY DIVIDED**

67

HYAKU
HUNDRED
6 strokes

百倍 HYAKUBAI hundred-fold
百性 HYAKUSHŌ   farmer
百貨店 HYAKKATEN
                    department store

One 一 1 and **white** 白 65 q.v., here used for its meaning of **thumbnail**. In ancient times the **thumb** was used to indicate a **hundred**, and two hundred was written 𦣞 , five hundred 䎛 (see 19), and so on.

Mnemonic: **SCORE ONE HUNDRED WITH ONE WHITE THUMBNAIL**

68

BUN, MON, fumi
WRITING, TEXT
4 strokes

文学 BUNGAKU   literature
文字 MO(N)JI   character
文部省 MONBUSHŌ
                Ministry of Education

Originally written 𡥳, depicting a **beautifully/ intricately patterned overlaid collar** (it can still mean stripe/pattern in Chinese). The core meaning of **intricate pattern** was eventually extended to **writing**. Suggest taking ㄨ as **cross** and 亠 as a **top**.

Mnemonic: **CROSS IS BASIC FORM OF WRITING: TRY TO TOP IT**

69

BOKU, MOKU, ki, ko-
TREE, WOOD
4 strokes

木曜日 MOKUYŌBI   Thursday
木目 KIME   grain, texture
木立ち KODACHI   grove

Pictograph of a **tree** with **sweeping branches** 朩. Often indicates **wood(en)**.

Mnemonic: **TREE WITH SWEEPING BRANCHES**

70

HON, moto
ROOT,TRUE,BOOK,THIS,
CYLINDER-COUNTER
5 strokes

日本 NIHON/NIPPON   Japan
本屋 HONYA   bookstore
本店 HONTEN
                head office, this store

Usually explained as an ideograph showing the **base** 一 of a **tree** 木 69, but an old form 夲 shows it to be a pictograph of the **roots**. Numerous extended meanings have evolved from this concept, usually involving **essence/origin**. Also used for counting cylindrical objects.

Mnemonic: **TREE WITH ONE CENTRAL ROOT**

| 71 | | MEI, MYŌ, na
NAME, FAME
6 strokes | 有名 YŪMEI
名人 MEIJIN
名前 NAMAE | famous
expert
name |

Mouth/say 口 20 and **evening** 夕 44. The latter also lends its sound to express **call**. That is, in the dim light of evening it was necessary to identify people verbally, calling their **names**.

Mnemonic: **MOUTH CALLS NAME AT NIGHT**

| 72 | | MOKU,BOKU,me,ma-
EYE,ORDINAL SUFFIX
5 strokes | 一つ目 HITOTSUME
注目 CHŪMOKU
一目 HITOME de | first one
attention
at a glance |

Pictograph of an **eye**, originally written ⌀. Sometimes found as ∞, but usually tilted on its axis to 目. Borrowed to express ordinals.

Mnemonic: **UPRIGHT EYE**

| 73 | 立 | RITSU,RYŪ, ta**tsu**/**teru**
STAND, RISE, LEAVE
5 strokes | 自立 JIRITSU
立場 TACHIBA
目立つ MEDATSU | independence
standpoint
stand out |

From a pictograph of a **person standing on the ground** 仚. Originally it meant to **stand still**, then to **stand up**, and by extension came to mean **leave**.

Mnemonic: **PERSON STANDING**

| 74 | | RYOKU, RIKI, chikara
STRENGTH, EFFORT
2 strokes | 能力 NŌRYOKU
人力車 JINRIKISHA
力試し CHIKARADAMESHI | ability
rickshaw

test of strength |

From a pictograph of an **arm with bulging biceps** ⼒, simplified to ⼒ and later 力, pushing down and symbolising **strength/ effort/ force**.

Mnemonic: **HAND PRESSING DOWN WITH STRENGTH**

75 林	RIN, hayashi	林学 RINGAKU	forestry
	FOREST	小林 KOBAYASHI	a surname
	8 strokes	密林 MITSURIN	dense forest

As with **woods** 森 38 q.v., an ideograph showing plural **trees** 木 69. In comparison to 38 the trees are fewer, but taller and more stately, which some may feel to be the difference between **forest** and **woods**.

Mnemonic: **FOREST CONTAINS TALL STATELY TREES**

76 六	ROKU, mu-	六月 ROKUGATSU	June
	SIX	六日 MUIKA*	sixth day
	4 strokes	六角 ROKKAKU	hexagon

One popular theory claims that an early form ᐱ shows **two hands** of which the **thumbs** and **index fingers** are joined in a circle and the remaining **three fingers** are pointed downwards. However, ᐱ is simply a stylistic variation of a still earlier form 六. This was in fact a **roof**, and originally had that meaning before being used as a phonetic substitute for a complex character meaning **clenched fist**, which was an old way of showing **six**. Suggest taking ハ as **eight** 66 and ⊥ as a **top**.

Mnemonic: **EIGHT TOPPED BY SIX?!**

END OF FIRST GRADE

21

THE 145 SECOND GRADE CHARACTERS

77 IN, hik*u*   引力 INRYOKU   gravitation
PULL, DRAW   字引 JIBIKI   dictionary
4 strokes   取り引き TORIHIKI   dealings

Bow 弓 836 and a line |. Some scholars interpret the line as the bow string, i.e. **that which is pulled**, while others see it simply as an abstract symbol representing **stretching**.

Mnemonic: **BOW WITH STRING WAITING TO BE DRAWN**

78 UN, kumo   雲母 UNMO*   mica
CLOUD   星雲 SEIUN   nebula
12 strokes   浮き雲 UKIGUMO drifting cloud

Originally written 𠃌, later inverted to 乙 and eventually 云, representing **billowing vapors.** This was later used as an NGU character to mean **speak**, so **rain** 雨 3 was added to emphasise **cloud**. Suggest taking 云 as **two** = 61 **noses** ム 134.

Mnemonic: **BILLOWING RAIN-CLOUDS LOOK LIKE TWO NOSES**

79 遠 EN, tō*i*   遠足 ENSOKU   excursion
DISTANT   遠回り TŌMAWARI   detour
13 strokes   遠視 ENSHI   longsighted

Movement 辶 129 and 袁. The latter is a CO character meaning **long robe**, to all intents and purposes combining a variant of **clothing** 衣 420 with 口, meaning **encircling** and by extension **spacious** and **big**, leading by association to **long**. Here 袁 acts phonetically to express **long**, and also lends similar connotations of its own. Thus **long movement**, i.e. **distance/ distant**.

Mnemonic: **LOOSE CLOTHES FOR TRAVELING ANY DISTANCE**

80 KA, nani, nan
WHAT? HOW MANY?
7 strokes

何回 NANKAI　　how often?
何者 NANIMONO　　who?
何人 NANNIN
　　　　how many people?

Person イ 39 and **can** 可 816 q.v., here acting phonetically to express **bear** and also lending its own connotations of **bending**. Thus **person bending bearing (heavy load)**, still retained as a minor meaning in Chinese. In Japanese this meaning has been entirely taken over by 荷 239 q.v., while 80 itself has come to be used purely phonetically to express **what?** Suggest taking ロ as **mouth/say** 20 and 丁 as a variant of **to a T/ exactly** 丁 346.

Mnemonic: **WHAT EXACTLY CAN A PERSON SAY?**

81 KA
COURSE, SECTION
9 strokes

科学 KAGAKU　　science
学科 GAKKA　　school subject
研究科 KENKYŪKA
　　　　research section

Rice plant 禾 (from a pictograph 禾), symbolising **grain**, and **measure** 斗 1633, to give a meaning of **measure grain**. By extension this came to mean **sift/sort** and then **category**, which by further extension came to mean **section**. **Course** is an associated meaning. See also 599.

Mnemonic: **COURSE TO CATEGORIZE RICE MEASURES**

82 KA, GE, natsu
SUMMER
10 strokes

初夏 SHOKA　　early summer
真夏 MANATSU　midsummer
夏祭 NATSUMATSURI
　　　　summer festival

Originally written 憂, showing a person **dancing** (symbolised by stopping and starting 夂 438 q.v.) **holding** (symbolised by hands ヒ彐) a **mask** (represented by head 酉 93 q.v.). How exactly it came to mean **summer** is not clear. Some scholars claim it was borrowed purely phonetically, but its complexity suggests otherwise. Presumably summer was associated with a particular dance or festival. Suggest remembering 夂 as the shape of **crossed legs**.

Mnemonic: **MASKED HEAD AND CROSSED LEGS IN SUMMER DANCE**

83 家 | KA, KE, ie, ya | 農家 NŌKA | farmhouse
HOUSE, SPECIALIST | 武家 BUKE | warrior family
10 strokes | 作家 SAKKA | writer

Roof/building 宀 28 and pig 豕 1670. Long believed to refer to supposed ancient practice of keeping pigs in house. However, many scholars now take 豕 to be used phonetically to express **leisure/relax**, giving **building for relaxing**. The pig may also have been associated with **not working,** as opposed to a working animal such as a horse. Ironically, 83 has now also come to mean **(house of) a specialist.**

Mnemonic: **HOUSE LOOKING LIKE PIG-STY**

---

84 歌 | KA, uta, uta*u* | 歌手 KASHU | singer
SONG, SING | 短歌 TANKA | short verse
14 strokes | 数え歌 KAZOEUTA | counting-rhyme

Lack/ **gaping mouth** 欠 471 q.v. and 哥. The latter is an NGU character that doubles **can** 可 816 q.v. It can mean elder brother (presumably associated with permission or potential), but here acts phonetically to express the sound KA doubled, i.e. KA-KA. This was the ancient Chinese equivalent of (TRA-)LA-LA, and indicated **singing.** From its literal meaning of **emerge from the mouth** 可 may also act to reinforce **gaping mouth** 欠. Thus **KA-KA from a wide open mouth.**

Mnemonic: **GAPING MOUTH SINGS THE CAN-CAN**

---

85 画 | GA, KAKU | 映画 EIGA | movie
PICTURE, STROKE | 画面 GAMEN | screen
8 strokes | 計画 KEIKAKU | plan

Formerly . 聿 shows a **hand** ⺕ applying a **brush** 夫 142. 田 is **rice field** 59. ⎵/— indicates **partitioning.** Thus to **partition fields with a brush,** i.e. on a map. By extension it also came to mean **strokes** or **diagram/picture.**

Mnemonic: **FIELD IN PICTURE PARTITIONED BY STROKES**

---

86 回 | KAI, mawa*ru*/*su* | 回転 KAITEN | revolution
TURN, ROTATE | 回数 KAISŪ | frequency
6 strokes | 言い回し IIMAWASHI | turn of phrase

From a symbol of **rotational motion** .

Mnemonic: **COAXIAL ROTATION**

---

87 **KAI, E, a***u* 　　　　　会社　KAISHA　　company
　　　　　　MEET　　　　　　　会釈　ESHAKU　　greeting
　　　　　　6 strokes　　　　　　国会　KOKKAI　　the Diet

Formerly 會 , and in ancient times 曾 . 曾 is a **pot** for steaming rice, and 亼 is its **lid**. Putting the lid on the pot came to mean **put together** in general, and eventually became the intransitive **come together/ meet**. The simplification using **speak** 云 78 may possibly stem from confusion with **put together** 合 121 (literally mouth/say and lid), compounded by confusion of the lower part of the pot 曰 with an old NGU character meaning **say**, 曰 (see 688) . However, an intermediate form 𠆢 suggests it may result merely from a graphic simplification. Suggest taking 云 as **two** = 61 **noses** 厶 134, with 亼 as a **roof**.

Mnemonic: **TWO NOSES MEET UNDER ROOF**

---

88 **KAI, umi**　　　　　海軍　KAIGUN　　　　navy
　　　　　　SEA　　　　　　　日本海　NIHONKAI　Japan Sea
　　　　　　9 strokes　　　　　　海辺　UMIBE　　　seaside

Water 氵 40 and **every** 毎 206, which may also act phonetically to express **salty**. Thus **every (drop of) (salty?) water.** All waters finish in the **sea**.

Mnemonic: **EVERY DROP OF WATER GOES INTO SEA**

---

89 **KAI, E**　　　　　絵画　KAIGA　　picture,painting
　　　　　　PICTURE　　　　口絵　KUCHIE　　frontispiece
　　　　　　12 strokes　　　　絵本　EHON　　picture book

Formerly 繪 . **Thread** 糸 27 and **put together/meet** 會/会 87. Originally **embroidered picture**, now **picture** in general.

Mnemonic: **THREADS MEET IN EMBROIDERED PICTURE**

---

90 貝 **kai**　　　　　　帆立貝　HOTATEGAI　scallop
　　　　SHELL, SHELLFISH　貝殻　KAIGARA　　seashell
　　　　7 strokes　　　　　貝類　KAIRUI　　shellfish

Usually claimed to be derived from a pictograph of a **cone-shell** or similar with **feelers** protruding. A useful mnemonic, but old forms such as 𦥑/𦘒 show that it derives from an exaggeratedly pointed **bivalve**. Shells were once used as **money** and symbolised **valuable items** or **assets**. In compounds 90 is generally used in such an extended sense.

Mnemonic: **SHELLFISH WITH PROTRUDING FEELERS**

91 GAI,GE,soto,hoka,hazu*su*   外人 GAIJIN   foreigner

OUTSIDE,OTHER,UNDO   外科 GEKA   surgery

5 strokes   外側 SOTOGAWA   exterior

Crescent moon 夕 44 and ﾄ . The latter shows a **crack** (in a turtle shell used in divination), and is in fact an NGU character meaning **divination** . 夕 is used phonetically to express **split open**, and also lends its crescent shape to suggest a **turtle shell**. Since the cracks generally appeared on the **outside** (convex) surface of the shell, 91 came to mean **outside/outer**. **Other** and **undo** are associated meanings.

Mnemonic: **CRESCENT MOON WITH CRACK ON OUTSIDE**

---

92 KAN, KEN, aida, ma   時間 JIKAN   hour, time

SPACE, GAP   人間 NINGEN   human being

12 strokes   間違い MACHIGAI   mistake

Door/gate 門 211 with **sun(light)** 日 62 showing through, indicating a **gap** or **space**. In olden times **moon** 月 16 could be used instead of sun with no change of meaning.

Mnemonic: **GATE WITH SPACE TO LET SUN SHINE THROUGH**

---

93 顔 GAN, kao   顔面 GANMEN   face

FACE   顔色 KAOIRO   complexion

18 strokes   顔付き KAOTSUKI   features

頁 is an NGU character now used to mean **page**, but in Chinese can still be used in its original meaning of **head.** It derives from 覓, showing person ㅅ39 with exaggerated head 凹. 彦 is an NGU character meaning **handsome.** 立 is a variant of intricate/ elegant collar 文 68, here meaning **attractive**, while 彡 is a CO character meaning **hair,** showing three delicate hairs and sometimes meaning **delicate** and by extension **attractive** . 厂 is cliff 45, here used largely phonetically to express **forehead** but probably also suggesting **brow** in itself. Thus 彦 means literally **attractive forehead**, with **head** 頁 reinforcing this. It then came to mean attractive face, then just **face.** Suggest taking 产 as a variant of **stand** 立 73.

Mnemonic: **ONLY THREE HAIRS STAND ON HEAD: GLUM FACE**

---

94 KI   汽車 KISHA   steam train

STEAM, VAPOR   汽船 KISEN   steamship

7 strokes   汽圧 KIATSU   steam pressure

Water 氵 40 and vapor 气 11.

Mnemonic: **STEAM COMPRISES WATERY VAPORS**

95

記

KI
ACCOUNT, CHRONICLE
10 strokes

記者 KISHA   journalist
記事 KIJI   article
日記 NIKKI   diary

Words 言 274 and self/thread 己 855 q.v., used both for its sound to express **account** and for its idea of **from end to end**. Thus **thorough verbal account**, now also of written accounts.

Mnemonic: **WORDY ACCOUNT OF ONESELF**

96

KI, kae*ru*
RETURN
10 strokes

帰化 KIKA   naturalisation
帰省 KISEI   homecoming
帰り道 KAERIMICHI   way back

Formerly 歸. 帚 is an NGU character meaning **broom** (from a hand ⺕ holding a broom 巾), and by extension meant (house-)**wife** (see also 779). 𠂤 is a variant of **follow** 追 350. Thus **wife following**. In ancient China it was the custom for a groom to spend some time at his new bride's home, before **returning** to his own home with his wife following. Suggest taking simplified リ as **sword** 181.

Mnemonic: **RETURN WITH WIFE CARRYING BROOM AND SWORD**

97

牛

GYŪ, ushi
COW, BULL
4 strokes

牛肉 GYŪNIKU   beef
牛乳 GYŪNYŪ   milk
牛飼い USHIKAI   cowherd

From a stylised pictograph of a **cow's head and horns** 半. Opinion is divided as to whether the lower cross-stroke depicts **ears** or represents the crown of the head.

Mnemonic: **COW WITH EARS AND BROKEN HORN**

98

魚

GYO, uo, sakana
FISH
11 strokes

金魚 KINGYO   goldfish
魚つり UOTSURI   fishing
魚屋 SAKANAYA   fishmonger

From a pictograph of a **fish** . Suggest remembering by association with **fire** ⺍⺌ 8.

Mnemonic: **FISH WITH FIERY TAIL**

---

99 京	KYŌ, KEI CAPITAL 8 strokes	東京 TŌKYŌ	Tokyo
		上京 JŌKYŌ	going to capital
		京浜 KEIHIN	
			Tokyo-Yokohama

Often explained as deriving from a pictograph of a **stone lantern** at the gate of the emperor's palace in the **capital**. A useful mnemonic, but incorrect. It derives from a pictograph 余. Some scholars see this as a **tower** of the emperor's palace, others as a **house on a hill** . In ancient China nobles generally lived on hilltops, with commoners on the flatland. Since nobles also spent much of their time in the **capital** (to be near the emperor), the idea of the **place where nobles live** is felt to have eventually become associated with the capital. It can still mean **height** in Chinese.

Mnemonic: **STONE LANTERN AT EMPEROR'S PALACE IN CAPITAL**

100 強	KYŌ, GŌ, tsuyoi STRONG 11 strokes	勉強 BENKYŌ	study
		強化 KYŌKA	strengthening
		強味 TSUYOMI	strongpoint

Formerly 強 . 虫 is **insect** 56. (also 弘) is an NGU character meaning **big/strong**, and is technically a simplification of the NGU character 彊, also **big/strong**. This comprises **bow** 弓 836 and **big** 畺 (actually large area of delineated fields, similar to 85 q.v.), giving **big, strong bow.** In the case of 100 it acts phonetically to express **pierce,** and also lends an idea of **big** and **strong.** Thus **big, strong insect that pierces,** a reference to the **horsefly.** This came to represent **strength,** possibly via an intermediate meaning of **persistent.** Suggest taking ㄙ as **nose** 134.

Mnemonic: **STRONG INSECT DRAWS BOW WITH ITS NOSE**

101 教	KYŌ, oshieru TEACH 11 strokes	教会 KYŌKAI	church
		教室 KYŌSHITSU	classroom
		教え子 OSHIEGO	pupil

Formerly 教 and originally 斈, showing that 孝 is not **filial piety** 孝 860 q.v. 爻 (now 耂) is the same **crossed sticks/ emulation** as in 10 q.v., while 孚/子 is **child** 25. 攴/攵 shows a **hand holding a cane** or stick, and means **strike/ coerce/ cause to do** (sometimes interchanged with 攵/攴 , showing a hand holding a **whip**). Thus **force a child to emulate,** i.e. **teach.** See also 197.

Mnemonic: **CANE IN HAND TEACHES CHILD STICK ARRANGING**

102		GYOKU, tama JEWEL, BALL 5 strokes	玉杯 GYOKUHAI	jade cup
			玉突き TAMATSUKI	billiards
			目玉 MEDAMA	eyeball

From a pictograph of a **string of beads** 𢀖, probably originally jade discs. **Ball** is an extended meaning. The extra point ` was added to distinguish it from **king** 王 5, but is dropped in the radical 𤣩.

Mnemonic: **STRING OF JEWELS FIT FOR KING**

103		KIN, chikai NEAR 7 strokes	近所 KINJO	neighborhood
			最近 SAIKIN	recently
			近道 CHIKAMICHI	shortcut

Movement 辶 129 and **ax** 斤 1176, here used phonetically to express **short** and probably also lending an idea of **chop/make small**. Thus **short movement**, indicating **near**.

Mnemonic: **DISTANCE TO MOVE CHOPPED, MAKING IT NEAR**

104		KEI, GYŌ, kata, katachi SHAPE, PATTERN 7 strokes	形式 KEISHIKI	form
			人形 NINGYŌ	doll
			形作る KATACHIZUKURU	
				form

Once written 𢆶 . 井 is not **well** 井 1470, but a **grille** or **lattice window**, here meaning **pattern** or **frame**. 彡 is **hairs** 93, here also suggesting **pattern** and reinforcing 井. Thus **pattern/shape**. Some scholars feel 彡 indicates a **brush**, to give a meaning of **write down/copy a pattern**.

Mnemonic: **PUT HAIRS INTO PATTERN OF WELL-FRAME**

105		KEI, hakaru MEASURE 9 strokes	合計 GŌKEI	total
			計算 KEISAN	calculation
			寒暖計 KANDANKEI	
				thermometer

Words 言 274 and **ten** 十 33, meaning to **count in tens** and later just **count/measure**.

Mnemonic: **COUNTING IN TENS IS A WAY OF MEASURING**

106 GEN, GAN, moto
ORIGIN, SOURCE
4 strokes

元気 GENKI　　　good health
元来 GANRAI　　　originally
元通り MOTODŌRI　as before

Once written 兀, showing a **person** 人 39 with the **head** exaggerated. As in English, the head symbolised **upper part** or **prime part**, and by extension **origin**. An extra top stroke was added later for emphasis. Suggest taking 二 as **two** 61.

Mnemonic: **TWO PERSONS OF SAME ORIGIN**

107 GEN, hara
PLAIN, ORIGIN
10 strokes

原子 GENSHI　　　atom
原文 GENBUN　　original text
草原 KUSAHARA grassy plain

厂 is **cliff** 45. 泉 is a variant of **spring** 泉 915 q.v. Thus **cliffside spring**, and by extension **source** or **origin**, often with connotations of **primary/primitive/natural**. **Plain/moor** is felt by some scholars to be a borrowed meaning, and by others to stem from the idea of primitive and undeveloped land.

Mnemonic: **ORIGINALLY CLIFF WITH FUNNY SPRING, NOW A PLAIN**

108 KO, to
DOOR
4 strokes

戸外 KOGAI　　　outdoor
戸主 KOSHU　　head of house
戸口 TOGUCHI　　doorway

From a pictograph of a **door** 戸, being one half of **door/gate** 門 211.

Mnemonic: **ONE DOOR FORMS HALF A GATE**

109 KO, furu*i*
OLD
5 strokes

復古 FUKKO　　　restoration
考古学 KŌKOGAKU archeology
古本 FURUHON
　　　　　secondhand book

Somewhat obscure. Commonly explained as mouth/**say** 口 20 and **ten** 十 33, with the latter meaning **many**, to give **something told many times** and therefore **old**. A useful mnemonic, but shown to be incorrect by old forms such as 古. Some scholars take this to indicate a **skull-like mask** (sometimes an actual skull) worn at festivals honoring **ancestor-gods**. Since the ancestor-gods were people of old, the mask itself came to symbolise **antiquity** and hence **old**.

Mnemonic: **AN OLD STORY, TOLD AT LEAST TEN TIMES**

110	午	GO NOON 4 strokes	午前 GOZEN	a.m., morning
			午後 GOGO	p.m., afternoon
			正午 SHŌGO	noon

From a pictograph of a **pestle** 𝙸. It was borrowed to express the **central zodiac/ horary sign**, i.e. the **middle part of the day**, partly because a pestle was associated with striking the **center** of a mortar. Pestle itself is now represented by an NGU character adding wood 木 69, 杵. Distinguish **cow** 牛 97.

Mnemonic: **NOON STRIKES, KNOCKING TOP BIT OFF COW**

111	後	GO, KŌ, ushiro, ato, nochi, okureru BEHIND, AFTER, DELAY 9 strokes	以後 IGO	after
			後半 KŌHAN	second half
			後味 ATOAJI	aftertaste

Road/movement 彳 118 q.v., **inverted foot** 夂 438, and 幺, a CO character meaning **small** and to all intents and purposes a **short** version of **thread** 糸 27. 彳 normally combines with <u>uninverted</u> foot 止 to give **normal progress/movement** (see 129), but here, in combination with <u>inverted</u> foot, indicates **abnormal progress**. 幺 acts phonetically to express **go** but also lends its meaning of **little**. Thus to **make (abnormally) little progress**, indicating **delay** and by extension **coming after/behind**. Suggest taking 夂 as **sitting crosslegged**.

Mnemonic: **SIT CROSSLEGGED ON THREADING ROAD, FALL BEHIND**

112	語	GO, kataru TELL, SPEAK, TALK 14 strokes	語調 GOCHŌ	tone
			物語 MONOGATARI	saga
			日本語 NIHONGO	
				Japanese language

Words 言 274 and 吾. The latter is an NGU character meaning **I/me**, but in Chinese can also mean **resist**. It was originally written 㖦, showing **two identical reels** 㐅 19. This expressed the idea of **being equal** and **well matched**, leading both to **resist** and to its use as a first person pronoun: that is, **one who is a person just like anyone else**. Note that not all first person references were depreciatory (see also 817). 112 originally meant **match someone verbally**, i.e. in an argument or similar, but later came to mean **speak well** and later **tell/speak** in a broad sense. Suggest taking 五 as **five** 19 and 口 as **mouth** 20.

Mnemonic: **FIVE MOUTHS SPEAK MANY WORDS**

113	KŌ, KU WORK 3 strokes	工場 KŌJŌ	factory
		人工 JINKŌ	manmade
		大工 DAIKU	carpenter

A **carpenter's adze-cum-square**, originally written 工. Symbolises **work**.

Mnemonic: **WORK WITH CARPENTER'S SQUARE**

114	KŌ, hiro*i/geru* WIDE, SPACIOUS 5 strokes	広大 KŌDAI	vast
		広島 HIROSHIMA	place name
		広告 KŌKOKU	advertisement

Formerly 廣, and originally 圙. 𠆢/广 shows a **roof/building**. 食/黄 is **yellow** 120 q.v., here used phonetically to express **space** but possibly also lending an idea of **big area** from its original meaning of flaming arrow, with its connotations of illuminating an area. 114 originally referred to a **spacious building**, and now means **spacious** in a broad sense. Suggest taking the modern ム as an **elbow**.

Mnemonic: **SPACIOUS BUILDING WITH ELBOW-ROOM**

115	KŌ, maji*ru*, kawa*su* MIX, EXCHANGE 6 strokes	交通 KŌTSŪ	traffic
		外交 GAIKŌ	diplomacy
		交換 KŌKAN	exchange

From a pictograph of a **person sitting with crossed legs** 𡘾. Crossing gave rise to various extended meanings such as **intermingle, mix, change, exchange**. Suggest taking 六 as **six** 76 and ㄨ as a **cross**.

Mnemonic: **MIX SIX CROSSES**

116 光	KŌ, hika*ru*, hikari LIGHT, SHINE 6 strokes	日光 NIKKŌ	sunlight
		光年 KŌNEN	light year
		光学 KŌGAKU	optics

Old forms such as 𤇾 show 业 to be a variant of **fire** 火 8, with 儿 being **bending person** 39. Some scholars feel 儿 is used purely phonetically to express **big**, giving **big fire** and by extension **light**. However, the positioning of the components suggests a fire carried overhead, i.e. a **torch**.

Mnemonic: **PERSON CARRIES FIRE THAT SHINES LIGHT**

| 117 考 | KŌ, kangaeru CONSIDER 6 strokes | 考案 KŌAN idea 参考 SANKŌ reference 考え事 KANGAEGOTO concern |

Once written 𠤏. 𠤎 (now 耂) is a rather awkward ideograph showing a **bent figure** 人 39 and **long hair** 耂 (the same form as hair 毛/毛 210), both of which were associated with **old age**. 丁/ㄅ (also ㄎ) is **twisting waterweed** 281, emphasising the idea of **bending**. Thus an **old man bent with age**, a meaning still found in Chinese. Some scholars feel **consider** is a borrowed meaning, others see it as stemming from the wisdom associated with old age. Suggest remembering old man 耂 by association with **earth** 土 60, with / representing something **half-buried**, i.e. ready for grave.

Mnemonic: **BENT OLD MAN CONSIDERS BURIAL IN EARTH**

| 118 行 | KŌ, GYŌ, AN, iku, yuku, okonau GO,CONDUCT,COLUMN 6 strokes | 実行 JIKKŌ carrying out 行列 GYŌRETSU procession 行方 YUKUE * whereabouts |

From a pictograph of **crossroads** 𢌍. Has a range of extended meanings, such as **go, travel, column**, and **act**. As a radical, simplified to 彳. Often combined with **foot** 止 129 q.v. to produce 辶 or 廴, both indicating **movement**.

Mnemonic: **COLUMN GOES ALONG TO CROSSROADS**

| 119 高 | KŌ, taka, takai TALL, HIGH, SUM 10 strokes | 高原 KŌGEN plateau 最高 SAIKŌ highest 高値 TAKANE high price |

Also 髙. From a pictograph of a **tall watchtower** . **Sum** derives from the idea of **build up**.

Mnemonic: **TALL WATCHTOWER**

| 120 黄 | KŌ, Ō, ki*iro* **YELLOW** 11 strokes | 黄葉 KŌYŌ yellow leaves 黄金 ŌGON gold 黄色 KIIRO yellow |

Formerly 黃 , and in ancient times 奎 or 𡞴. 奎 shows an **arrow**, while ⊖ is **combustible material** bound to it (some scholars claim a **weight** to counterbalance combustible material at tip). The exact meaning of ㅂ (earliest form ㅂ) is not clear, but it is known to be associated with **burning** and is possibly a stylised variant of an early form of fire 火 8. The original meaning of 120 was **flaming arrow**. Yellow was the color of the light given off, and came to prevail as a meaning. Suggest remembering flaming arrow by association with **grass** 艹 9 and **field** 田 59.

Mnemonic: **ARROW BURNS YELLOW WITH GRASS FROM FIELD**

| 121 合 | GŌ, KATSU, a*u/waseru* **MEET, JOIN, FIT** 6 strokes | 合理 GŌRI rationality 合戦 KASSEN battle 話し合い HANASHIAI discussion |

Originally 合 . 亼 is a **lid** or **cover**. Some scholars see 口 as a **container**, to give a similar meaning to that of 87, while others see it as **mouth** /say 20, to give a meaning similar to the English term **cap off a remark**, i.e. **reply fittingly**. The role of 121 in **reply** 答 185 q.v. supports the latter theory. It now means **fit** or **join** in a broad sense.

Mnemonic: **CAP FITS MOUTH**

| 122 谷 | KOKU, tani, ya **VALLEY, GORGE** 7 strokes | 幽谷 YŪKOKU deep ravine 谷底 TANIZOKO valley bottom 長谷川 HASEGAWA* surname |

Opening 口 20 and **splitting** 八 66, doubled for emphasis. Thus **deeply/ widely split opening**, i.e. **valley** or **gorge**.

Mnemonic: **VALLEY IS DOUBLY SPLIT OPENING**

| 123 国 | KOKU, kuni **COUNTRY, REGION** 8 strokes | 外国 GAIKOKU overseas 四国 SHIKOKU Shikoku 国家 KOKKA state |

Formerly 國 . 或 is **delineated area** 809 q.v., while 口 indicates **enclosed**. The modern form uses **jewel** 玉 102, though **king** 王 5 might have been a more logical choice.

Mnemonic: **ONE'S COUNTRY IS AN ENCLOSED JEWEL**

124 黒	KOKU, kuroi BLACK 11 strokes	黒人 KOKUJIN	negro
		黒字 KUROJI	(in) 'the black'
		黒死病 KOKUSHIBYŌ	
			black death

Formerly 黑, and originally 燹 . 炎 is **flame** 1024. ⊕ represents a **grille** or **window** ⊕ with marks ∵ on it resulting from its position over the flames, i.e. **soot** . Soot symbolises **black**. Suggest following the popular but incorrect theory that 田 is **field** 59 and 土 is **ground** 60, with ⺍⺍ as **fire** 8, giving the **color of the ground in a burnt field**.

Mnemonic: **GROUND IN BURNT FIELD IS BLACK**

125 今	KON, KIN, ima NOW 4 strokes	今週 KONSHŪ	this week
		今度 KONDO	this time
		今年 KOTOSHI*	this year

Somewhat obscure. Once written 亼 and 仝. 亼 is **cover** 87. ㇈ is felt to mean **put in a corner** /**conceal** (variant L 349). Thus to **cover/hide**. Some scholars feel it was borrowed to express **sudden**, which came to mean **imminent** and finally **now**.

Mnemonic: **COVER THE CORNER, RIGHT NOW**

126 才	SAI TALENT, YEAR OF AGE 3 strokes	天才 TENSAI	genius
		才能 SAINŌ	talent
		五才 GOSAI	five years old

Originally 𢦏, later 才, depicting a **dam** ▽ across a **stream** 丨. Its current meanings result from borrowing.

Mnemonic: **FUNNY DAM BUILT BY TALENTED ONE-YEAR-OLD**

127 作	SAKU, SA, tsukuru MAKE 7 strokes	製作 SEISAKU	production
		作品 SAKUHIN	a work
		動作 DŌSA	action

亻 is **person** 39. 乍 is an NGU character now borrowed phonetically to express **while** but it originally meant **make**. It derives from 㐅, with ㇄ being a type of **adze** and 木 being **wood** 69, giving **adze on wood** and thus **make/construct** something. Here it lends its early meaning of **make**, and also acts phonetically to express **deceive** . Thus a **made/ constructed person used to deceive**, i.e. a **dummy** or by extension stand-in. Over the years the elements became reinterpreted as **person who makes**, rather than **person who is made**, and finally came to mean just **make**. Suggest taking 乍 as a **saw**.

Mnemonic: **PERSON WITH SAW ABOUT TO MAKE SOMETHING**

128	算	SAN RECKON, COUNT 14 strokes	計算 KEISAN	calculation
			予算 YOSAN	budget
			算数 SANSŪ	arithmetic

竹 is **bamboo** 170. 昇 derives from 昇, showing **two hands** 𦥑 holding what is felt to be an **abacus** 目. Thus **use a bamboo abacus**.

Mnemonic: **COUNT BY USING BAMBOO ABACUS WITH BOTH HANDS**

129	止	SHI, to*meru*/*maru* STOP 4 strokes	中止 CHŪSHI	suspension
			止め処 TOMEDO	end
			止まり木 TOMARIGI	perch

From a pictograph of a (left) **footprint** , later Ⱳ. Originally meant **foot**, but also came to mean **stop**, from the idea of **planting the foot**. Confusingly, it can also be used in compounds to mean **move**, from the idea of a **trail of footprints**, but when used in this sense it is almost always used in combination with **road** 彳 118 to give 辵 and hence 辶 / 辶 / 辶. Also confusingly, the shape 止 is virtually identical with 屮, a rarely encountered variant of **growing plant** 生 42. Suggest remembering by association with **above** 上 37.

Mnemonic: **FOOTPRINTS STOP ABOVE LINE**

130	市	SHI, ichi CITY, MARKET 5 strokes	吹田市 SUITASHI	Suita City
			市場 SHIJŌ	market
			魚市 UOICHI	fishmarket

Originally 𠂔. 止 is **stop** 129.) (indicates **confines** and by extension **delineated area**. 丁 is a variant of **waterweed** 丂 281, which normally indicates **bending** but confusingly can occasionally mean **flat** (from the idea of the weed twisting up to the surface and then spreading out flat). Thus **place where things flatten out and stop**. Fanciful as it may seem, this was a reference to the abstract idea of the leveling of opposed interests of buyer and seller, which took place in a **market**. Markets were usually held in **large towns**. Suggest taking 巾 as **cloth** 778 and 亠 as a **top hat**.

Mnemonic: **GO TO CITY MARKET TO BUY CLOTH TOP HAT**

131 思	SHI, omou THINK 9 strokes	思想 SHISŌ 思考 SHIKŌ 思い出す OMOIDASU	ideology thought recall

Usually explained as **heart/feelings** 心 147 q.v. and **field** 田 59, to the effect that people of old were constantly thinking of their fields and crops. A useful mnemonic, but incorrect. Old forms such as show that 田 is a **brain** (from a depiction of a brain with crenellations ᗡ). Thus the **feelings in one's brain**, i.e. **thoughts**.

Mnemonic: **ALWAYS THINKING OF ONE'S FIELD IN ONE'S HEART**

132 紙	SHI, kami PAPER 10 strokes	表紙 HYŌSHI 和紙 WASHI 手紙 TEGAMI	book-cover Japanese paper letter

 糸 is **thread** 27, here meaning **silk** thread. 氏 is **spoon/ladle** 495 q.v., here used phonetically to express **smooth** and possibly also lending similar connotations (the surface of a spoon usually being smooth). 132 originally referred to **smooth silk**, and by extension **smooth cloth**. In ancient times cloth was used as writing material, and thus 132 came to mean **writing material** and hence **paper**.

Mnemonic: **POUND THREADS WITH SPOON TO MAKE PAPER**

133 寺	JI, tera TEMPLE 6 strokes	竜安寺 RYŌANJI 寺院 JIIN 山寺 YAMADERA	Ryoan Temple Buddhist temple mountain temple

Once written 寺 , leading to long-standing belief that 止 is **stop** 止 129. However, an earlier form 坐 shows that it is in fact the confusingly similar variant of **growing plant** 生 42 q.v. It is used here to symbolise **activity** (an extended meaning from living growth as opposed to inanimate inertia), and combines with **measure/hand** 寸 909, which here means **regular and methodical use of the hands**, to give **active and methodical use of the hands** (rather than stationary work with hands when 止 is taken to mean **stop**). This was a reference to **clerical work** (the English use of the term manual labor to mean physical labor being somewhat misleading), and by extension **place of work/ government office**. It can still have this meaning in Chinese, but generally came to mean **temple** since temples were often associated with clerical work. Suggest taking 土 as **ground** 60.

Mnemonic: **TEMPLE HAS MEASURED GROUNDS**

134 JI, SHI, mizuka*ra*
SELF
6 strokes

自 分 JIBUN   self
自 然 SHIZEN nature
自 信 JISHIN self-confidence

From a stylised depiction of the **nose** 凸, for some reason showing what appears to be a ridge ⸗. **Self** stems from the Oriental practice of pointing to the nose to refer to oneself, as opposed to the chest as in the West. **Self** is sometimes expressed by ム, an NGU character and a common element in compounds. Its early form is 𠂤, the same form as **plow** 419 q.v. Some scholars see these as one character, plow, with **self** stemming from a phonetic borrowing, while others see it as depicting a **nose** seen side-on and thus by association **self**. Suggest remembering by association with **eye** 目 72, taking ノ as a **stroke**.

Mnemonic: **NOSE IS JUST A STROKE FROM EYE, SYMBOLISING SELF**

---

135 JI, toki
TIME, HOUR
10 strokes

時 代 JIDAI era, period
二 時 NIJI two o'clock
時 時 TOKIDOKI sometimes

Surprisingly obscure. Originally written 𣅔, showing **stop** 㞢/止 129 and **sun** /**day** 日 62, and possibly having a meaning such as **end of the day** and thus symbolising the **passage of time**. However, at a very early stage **stop** 止 appears to have become confused with **growing plant** 㞢/生 42 q.v., giving 㞢, which possibly meant **emergence of the sun**. At a later stage 㞢 was replaced by **temple** 寺 133 q.v., used phonetically to express **move** and probably also lending connotations of **regularity**. Thus **regular movement of the sun**, i.e. **time**. **Hour** is an associated meaning.

Mnemonic: **TELL TIME BY SUN ON TEMPLE**

---

136 SHITSU, muro
ROOM, HOUSE
9 strokes

室 内 SHITSUNAI indoors
居 室 KYOSHITSU living room
室 津 MUROTSU place-name

宀 is **roof** 28. 至 is **arrive** 875 q.v., here acting phonetically to express **stop** and also lending a similar idea of **arrive and stop** (from an arrow sinking in). Thus **place under roof where one can stop**, i.e. a **room**. By extension it is sometimes used to mean **house** or **household**.

Mnemonic: **ARRIVE AT ROOFED ROOM**

137	SHA, yashiro SHRINE 7 strokes	社会 SHAKAI society 神社 JINJA shrine 社員 SHAIN company employee

Formerly 社. 示/ネ is **altar** 695 q.v. 土 is **ground** 60. The ground around an altar was sacred, and thus a **shrine**.

Mnemonic: **ALTAR GROUND IS SHRINE**

138	JAKU, yowai WEAK 10 strokes	弱点 JAKUTEN weak point 弱小 JAKUSHŌ puniness 弱虫 YOWAMUSHI weakling

Formerly 弱 and earlier 弱, showing a doubling of **bow** 弓 836, here meaning **bending**, and **delicate hairs** 彡 93. Thus **something bent easily as delicate hair**, i.e. **weak**.

Mnemonic: **WEAK HAIRS BEND LIKE BOWS**

139	SHU, kubi HEAD, NECK, CHIEF 9 strokes	首領 SHURYŌ leader 首輪 KUBIWA necklace 首切り KUBIKIRI decapitation

Originally 首, showing an **eye** with exaggerated eyebrow and indicating the eye area of the face. However, later forms such as 首 show confusion with **head** 囟/頁 93, with **hair** 川 added. Can also be used figuratively as **chief**. **Neck** is an associated meaning. Suggest taking 自 as a variant of 93, with 丷 as **hair**.

Mnemonic: **CHIEF HAS HAIR ON HEAD**

---

140 秋	SHŪ, aki AUTUMN 9 strokes	晩秋 BANSHŪ late autumn 秋分 SHŪBUN autumn equinox 秋空 AKIZORA autumn sky

Rice plant 禾 81 and **fire** 火 8. Some scholars feel 火 is used purely phonetically to express **gather**, thus referring to the autumn harvest. However, it may also lend a meaning of **dry** (after the heat of summer) or refer literally to the **autumn crop-fires** caused by the Foehn Wind.

Mnemonic: **RICE PLANTS CAN GET BURNED IN AUTUMN**

141 春	SHUN, haru SPRING 9 strokes	青春 SEISHUN — youth 売春 BAISHUN — prostitution 春着 HARUGI — spring clothes

Originally 萅, showing the **vigorous growth of a mulberry plant** 米 (see 1518) in the **sunshine** 日 62. Vigorous growth symbolises **spring**. Suggest taking 夫 as **three** 三 23 **people** 人 39.

Mnemonic: **THREE PEOPLE ENJOY SPRING SUN**

142 書	SHO, ka*ku* WRITE 10 strokes	書記 SHOKI — secretary 教科書 KYŌKASHO — textbook 葉書 HAGAKI — postcard

書 shows a **hand** 彐 holding a **brush** 人. 曰 is a simplified form of **thing** 者 298, which also lends its sound to express **copy**. Thus **copy a thing by brush**, i.e. **write**. Suggest taking 曰 as **day** 62.

Mnemonic: **TAKE BRUSH IN HAND DAILY AND WRITE**

143 少	SHŌ, suko*shi*, suku*nai* FEW, A LITTLE 4 strokes	少年 SHŌNEN — a youth 少数 SHŌSŪ — minority 多少 TASHŌ — more or less

Originally 小. As **small** 小 36 but with four points instead of three, to suggest smaller size. It originally meant **tiny size** but is now generally applied to quantity rather than size.

Mnemonic: **SMALL WITH JUST A LITTLE EXTRA**

144 場	JŌ, ba PLACE 12 strokes	会場 KAIJŌ — meeting place 入場 NYŪJŌ — admission 広場 HIROBA — open space

土 is **ground** 60. 易 is a CO character now meaning **bright** and **open out**. Its early form 昜 shows the **sun** 日 62 rising high and shining down (represented by a symbol 丂 conveniently thought of as **rays**), and in compounds it often lends a meaning of **rise**. **Sun rising and shedding light** led by association to **bright** and to the idea of **opening something up to the light**. Here it lends a meaning of **open** and also lends its sound to express **clear**. Thus **clear open ground**, now used to mean **place**.

Mnemonic: **PLACE WHERE SUN SHINES DOWN ON GROUND**

145		SHOKU, SHIKI, iro COLOR, SENSUALITY 6 strokes	好色 KŌSHOKU amorousness 色素 SHIKISO pigment 銀色 GINIRO silver color

Once written . カ/ヘ shows a **person bending**. 乙/巴 also shows a **person bending** (originally kneeling, but used to indicate bending body in general). Thus one person bending over another bending person, which was a reference to the **sex act**. It still retains strong sexual connotations, especially in Japanese. It is not completely clear how it came to mean **color**. However, many scholars feel that it was used to refer to **sexual partner**, especially from a male perspective, and that it then came to mean **sexually attractive**, leading in time to **attractive/ pretty** in a general sense and then by association to **colorful**.

Mnemonic: **COLORFUL TALE ABOUT BODIES BENT IN SEX ACT**

146		SHOKU, ta*beru*, ku*u* FOOD, EAT 9 strokes	食事 SHOKUJI meal 食べ物 TABEMONO food 食い物 KUIMONO food, victim

Originally 皀, showing **food piled in a long-stemmed dish** and essentially the same prototype as vessel 豆 1640. At an early stage the piled food ∧ became a **lid** ∧ 87, giving **covered food in dish**. Thus **food** and by association **eat**. Suggest remembering by association with **good** 良 598. As a radical, usually 食 , 食 , or 皀 .

Mnemonic: **COVERED FOOD GOOD FOR EATING**

147	心	SHIN, kokoro HEART, FEELINGS 4 strokes	中心 CHŪSHIN core 心臓 SHINZŌ heart 真心 MAGOKORO sincerity

From a pictograph of a **heart** 心. Also used figuratively as **feelings** or **mind**. As a radical usually 忄 . Suggest remembering as a heart whose **strokes** have been '**damaged**' by stylisation.

Mnemonic: **HEART SHOWS STROKE DAMAGE**

41

148

SHIN, atara*shii*, ara*ta*
NEW
13 strokes

新年	SHINNEN	New Year
新品	SHINPIN	new article
新人	SHINJIN	newcomer

Originally 𣂎, showing **ax** 𣂆/斤 1176 and **needle/sharp** 䇂/辛 1432. Thus **sharp ax**. At an early stage the barbs of the needle became merged or confused with **tree** 木 69 and its branches, giving 𣂎 and a meaning of **chop down a tree**. The idea of cutting wood is retained in **firewood** 薪 1445, that adds plant 艹 9. (Note also that 枼 exists as a CO character meaning thorn-tree, but does not act in that capacity here.) How exactly 148 came to mean **new** is not clear. Some scholars feel it was borrowed phonetically, but its complexity suggests otherwise. More likely, the idea of chopping down trees was associated with building, i.e. **new** construction, or else **newly cut** wood requiring seasoning. Suggest taking 立 as **stand** 73.

Mnemonic: **STAND OF TREES NEWLY CUT DOWN BY SHARP AX**

149

SHIN, shita*shii*, o*ya*
INTIMATE, PARENT
16 strokes

両親	RYŌSHIN	parents
親類	SHINRUI	relatives
親子	OYAKO	parent and child

Somewhat obscure. Originally 𢌞, showing **see** 見 18 and **needle/sharp** 䇂/辛 1432. The latter acted phonetically to express **kin**, giving **kin one sees** (all the time), i.e. one's **immediate family**. Possibly because of the similarity to 148 q.v., 149 similarly (but at a later stage) replaced needle 䇂 with needle-tree 亲, though the sound value was unaffected. Suggest taking 立 as **stand** 73 and 木 as **tree** 69.

Mnemonic: **PARENT SEES ALL FROM STAND OF TREES**

150

ZU, TO, haka*ru*
PLAN, DIAGRAM
7 strokes

地図	CHIZU	map
図画	ZUGA	drawing
図書館	TOSHOKAN	library

Formerly 圖. 囗 is an **enclosure**. 啚 is to all intents and purposes a variant of the **fields and sections** seen in **picture** 画 85 q.v. In fact, 150 and 85 are very similar in their basic meaning of **partitioning fields on a map**. Suggest taking 乂 as **X** and ` as **two pointers**.

Mnemonic: **DIAGRAM WITH SPOT MARKED BY X AND TWO POINTERS**

158		SEN, fune, funa- BOAT, SHIP 11 strokes	船長 SENCHŌ	captain
			こぎ船 KOGIBUNE	rowboat
			船便 FUNABIN	sea-mail

舟 is **boat** 1354. 公 is a CO character now meaning water at base of hill, but it originally meant **hollowed out** (from split/out ハ 66 and opening ロ 20), and was virtually a lesser version of valley 谷 122. Thus a **hollowed out boat**. Opinion is divided as to whether this initially referred to a primitive dug-out or rather to the carrying capacity of a boat (cf. English **vessel**). Suggest taking ハ as **eight** and ロ as **hole**.

Mnemonic: **BOAT WITH EIGHT PORTHOLES IS SHIP**

159		ZEN, mae BEFORE, FRONT 9 strokes	前者 ZENSHA	the former
			空前 KŪZEN	unprecedented
			前払い MAEBARAI	prepayment

Formerly 歬, and earlier 歬. 刂/刀 is **sword/cut** 181. 歬/歬 is a now defunct character meaning **advance**, comprising foot 止 129 (now ⺊), here meaning **go**, and **boat** 月/舟 1354, which from its connotations of **hollowed out (wood)** was occasionally used, as here, to refer to a primitive type of **clog**. Thus 歬 meant literally **put on one's shoes and go**, thus coming to mean **go ahead/ advance**. In combination with **cut** it lent its sound to express **trim/ arrange** and also lent an idea of **progress**, to mean **make progress in trimming with a cutting tool**. However, eventually 歬 reverted to the meaning of 歬, i.e. **advance** and by extension **front/ before**. The idea of trimming with a cutting tool is now conveyed by an NGU character **prune** 剪, that adds an extra **cut** 刀 181. (Note also that adding **hand** 扌 32 gives the NGU character **arrange** 揃.) Suggest taking 月 as **meat** 365, with ⺊ as **horns**.

Mnemonic: **BEFORE CUTTING MEAT CUT HORNS**

160	組	SO, kumi, ku*m*u GROUP, ASSEMBLE 11 strokes	組織 SOSHIKI	organisation
			組合 KUMIAI	union
			組み立て KUMITATE	assembly

Thread 糸 27 and **furthermore/ cairn** 且 1091 q.v., here used in its early meaning of **build up**. **Build up threads** meant to **braid**, and by extension **assemble**. **Group** is an associated meaning.

Mnemonic: **FURTHERMORE, THREADS CAN BE ASSEMBLED IN GROUP**

45

161	走	SŌ, hashir*u* RUN 7 strokes	競走 KYŌSŌ	race
			走行 SŌKŌ	traveling
			走り書き HASHIRIGAKI	scrawl

Originally 夵, showing foot 止/止 129, here meaning **move**, and a **man moving frantically** 大. Thus **frantic movement with the feet**, i.e. **running**. Suggest taking 土 as **ground** 60.

Mnemonic: **FOOT RUNNING ALONG GROUND**

162	草	SŌ, kusa GRASS, PLANT 9 strokes	雑草 ZASSŌ	weed
			草書 SŌSHO	cursive script
			草地 KUSACHI	grassland

Grass/plant 艹 9 and **early** 早 50 q.v. The latter is used phonetically to express **plant**, and possibly also lends an idea of a **seed splitting open** and thus being about to develop into a **plant** . (Though the 十 of 50 can conveniently be taken as the crossed lines/cut of seven 七 30, it also overlaps with the crossed cuts 十 of the early forms 田 and 十 of shell 甲 1243 q.v., depicting a seed splitting open. 50 and 1243 were in fact sometimes confused.) **Plant** and **grass** are less clearly differentiated than in English.

Mnemonic: **GRASS IS EARLY PLANT**

163	多	TA, ō*i* MANY 6 strokes	多数 TASŪ	majority, mass
			多面 TAMEN	many sides
			多過ぎる ŌSUGIRU	too many

Evening 夕 44 doubled to indicate plurality. Thus **many evenings/ often**, finally just **many**.

Mnemonic: **MANY EVENINGS**

164	太	TAI, TA, futo*i/ru* FAT, BIG 4 strokes	太子 TAISHI	prince
			太陽 TAIYŌ	sun
			太字 FUTOJI	bold type

A simplification of 夳, showing **two** 二 61 and **big** 大 53, which was in turn a simplification of 夵, being a doubling of 大 for emphasis. Thus **very big**, now often used for **fat**.

Mnemonic: **FAT IS A BIT MORE THAN JUST BIG**

| 165 体 | TAI, TEI, karada
BODY
7 strokes | 体格 TAIKAKU physique
風体 FŪTEI appearance
体付き KARADATSUKI figure |

Formerly also 體, showing **bone** 骨 867 and **plentiful** 豊 790. Thus, **that in which bones are plentiful**, meaning the **entire body** as opposed to a limb. The form using **person** イ 39 and **root** 本 70, to give the **root of a person**, has been used for several centuries as a substitute, but is technically a separate character with an early meaning of crude (presumably **basic person** or similar).

Mnemonic: **ROOT OF A PERSON IS THE BODY**

| 166 台 | DAI, TAI
STAND, PLATFORM
5 strokes | 土台 DODAI base
台風 TAIFŪ typhoon
台所 DAIDOKORO kitchen |

In Japanese formerly also written 臺, but this is a separate character and is generally treated as such in Chinese. 臺 is the correct character for **platform**, and comprises **tall** 冖 (variant 高 119), **earth** 土 (variant 土 60), and **peak/arrive** 至 875, which also acts phonetically to express stop/be stationed. Thus **mound of earth on the top of which one is stationed**, i.e. look-out rampart and hence **platform**. 台 is used in Chinese to mean **self** (confusingly both as I and you), and comprises **self** ム 134 and **mouth/say** 口 20, giving **name oneself** and finally just **self**. It was borrowed phonetically as a simple substitute for 臺.

Mnemonic: **I MOUNT STAND TO SAY SOMETHING**

| 167 地 | CHI, JI
GROUND, LAND
6 strokes | 地方 CHIHŌ region
地下 CHIKA underground
生地 KIJI* cloth, texture |

土 is **ground** 60. 也 is an NGU character now borrowed to express **to be**, but originally meant **twisting creature** (opinion is divided as to whether early forms such as 𠃌 and 𠃌 depict a scorpion, snake, or some type of insect, though snake seems most likely), and often lends an idea of **twisting**. Here it means **undulating**, giving **undulating ground** and eventually just **ground/land/region** with various extended usages. Unfortunately there is no easy mnemonic for 也.

Mnemonic: **LAND WITH ODD TWISTING CREATURES ON GROUND**

168	CHI, ike	用水池 YŌSUICHI	reservoir
	POND, LAKE	電池 DENCHI	battery
	6 strokes	古池 FURUIKE	old pond

Water 氵 40 and **twisting creature** 也 167. The latter is used phonetically to express **bank**, and probably also lends an idea of **coiling** and thus joining with itself. Thus **water encircled by banks**.

Mnemonic: **WATERS OF POND CONTAIN TWISTING CREATURES**

169	CHI, shiru	知識 CHISHIKI	knowledge
	KNOW	知性 CHISEI	intellect
	8 strokes	知り合い SHIRIAI	acquaintance

Mouth/say 口 20 and **arrow** 矢 981, to give a meaning of **speak with speed of arrow** , thus indicating **thorough knowledge**. Suggest taking 口 as a **hole**.

Mnemonic: **KNOW ARROW HOLE**

170	CHIKU, take	竹材 CHIKUZAI	bamboo
	BAMBOO	竹田 TAKEDA	a surname
	6 strokes	竹やぶ TAKEYABU	
			bamboo grove

Often believed to show bamboo segments 𝍓, but in fact early forms such as ↑↑ depict **stems of dwarf bamboo with spiky leaves**. Now **bamboo** in general.

Mnemonic: **TWO BAMBOO STEMS**

171	CHA, SA	茶わん CHAWAN	teabowl
	TEA, ANNOY	茶茶 CHACHA	interruption
	9 strokes	茶菓 SAKA	tea and cakes

Formerly also 茶, incorrectly showing tree 木 69. 艹 is **plant** 9, while 朶 is a simplification of **ample** 余 800. The latter is used phonetically to express **bitter**, but its semantic role is unclear. **Bitter plant** is a reference to **tea**. The very occasional use of 171 to mean **annoy** or similar may derive from **bitter**.

Mnemonic: **AMPLE TEA PLANTS**

172 昼	CHŪ, hiru NOON, DAYTIME 9 strokes	昼食 CHŪSHOKU	lunch
		昼行性 CHŪKŌSEI	diurnal
		昼間 HIRUMA	daytime

Formerly written 畫, and earlier as 晝. Very similar to early form of **picture** 画 85 q.v., 畫 (also earlier as 晝), except field 田 59 is replaced by **sun/day** 日 62. 畫/畫 still acts to indicate **section off/ partition**, and also lends its sound to express **bright**. Thus the **bright section of the day**, i.e. **daytime** or **noon**. Suggest taking ― as **horizon** and the modern simplification 尺 as **measure in feet** 尺 884, of which it may in fact be a deliberate borrowing.

Mnemonic: **MEASURE IN FEET NOON SUN OVER HORIZON**

173 長	CHŌ, nagai LONG, SENIOR 8 strokes	成長 SEICHŌ	growth
		会長 KAICHŌ	chairperson
		長生き NAGAIKI	long life

Also 长. From a depiction of an **old man with long flowing hair** (a sign of age), bent with age and leaning on a stick (see also old 老 609). This gave rise to **long, grow,** and **senior**, with associated meanings such as **excel** and **chief**.

Mnemonic: **LONG HAIRED OLD MAN WITH STICK IS VERY SENIOR**

174 鳥	CHŌ, tori BIRD 11 strokes	白鳥 HAKUCHŌ	swan
		野鳥 YACHŌ	wild bird
		鳥居 TORII	shrine gate

From a pictograph of a **bird** .

Mnemonic: **BIRD WITH WINGS AND TALONS**

175 朝	CHŌ, asa MORNING, COURT 12 strokes	朝食 CHŌSHOKU	breakfast
		朝日 ASAHI	morning sun
		朝廷 CHŌTEI	imperial court

Formerly 朝, and earlier as 勦, showing that 月 is not moon 16 but a derivative of **river** 川 48. 草/草 shows the **sun** 日 62 **rising** through **plants** 十 9, lending a meaning of **rise** to give **rising river**. This is still found in **tide** 潮 941, which adds **water** 氵 40. In the case of 175 the rising sun element came to prevail in its own right, leading to **morning**. **Court** is felt to derive from figurative association with the idea of **source of light**. Suggest taking 月 as **moon**.

Mnemonic: **MORNING SUN RISES ON PLANTS, DISPLACING MOON**

---

176 通 TSŪ, tŏru/su, kayou   通行 TSŪKŌ   passage
PASS, WAY, COMMUTE   通勤 TSŪKIN   commuting
10 strokes   大通り ŌDŌRI   main road

辶 is **movement** 129. 甬 is a CO character meaning **raised**. It was originally written 甬, showing the **sun** ⊙ / 日 62 rising above a **brushwood fence** 甶/用 215, and also has connotations of **break clear** or **emerge**. In combination with 辶 it gives a meaning of **uninterrupted movement**, giving **pass through**, a **road/way**, and **commute** (i.e. go directly). Suggest taking 用 in its modern sense of **use**, with マ as a **bent figure**.

Mnemonic: **BENT FIGURE USES EXTRA MOVEMENT TO PASS**

---

177 弟 TEI, DAI, DE, otŏto   子弟 SHITEI   sons
YOUNGER BROTHER   弟子 DESHI   pupil
7 strokes   兄弟 KYŌDAI   brothers

Once written 弟. 弋 is a **stake**, still technically listed as an NGU character 弋 with that meaning but now usually found as an NGU character **stake** 杙 that adds wood 木 69. 乙 shows **binding**, which was necessary as a grip since stakes were used as weapons (弋 overlaps with 弋, the prototype of lance/halberd 493). There was a set **order** to the manner of binding, and hence 177 also came to mean **sequence** or **order**. It can still be used in this sense in Chinese, though it is generally replaced by **order** 第 339, that adds **bamboo** 竹 170. By association the idea of order was also applied to **sons** in a family, especially those other than the eldest, since **age-order** was an important factor in **ranking**.

Mnemonic: **YOUNG BROTHERS PUT IN ORDER AS BINDING ON STAKE**

---

178 TEN, mise, tana   店員 TENIN   store clerk
STORE, PREMISES   夜店 YOMISE   night stall
8 strokes   店立て TANADATE   eviction

广 is **building** 114. 占 is **divination** 1491 q.v., here acting phonetically to express **arrange/ display** and probably also lending its own idea of **arrange and announce**. Thus **building where goods are arranged on display (and announced?)**, i.e. a **store**. It is sometimes used of **premises** in general. Suggest taking 占 in its commoner meaning of **occupy**.

Mnemonic: **STORE OCCUPIES BUILDING**

179		TEN	点線	TENSEN	dotted line
		POINT, MARK	得点	TOKUTEN	points
		9 strokes	重点	JŪTEN	emphasis

Formerly 點 . 黑 is **black** 124. 占 is **divination** 1491 q.v., here acting phonetically to express **small** and also lending an idea of **meaningful sign**. Thus **small black sign**, i.e. **point/ mark**, also used as in English to mean **score**. Suggest taking 占 in its commoner meaning of **occupy**, and 灬 as **fire** 8.

Mnemonic: **MARK LEFT AFTER OCCUPATION BY FIRE**

180		DEN	電話	DENWA	telephone
		ELECTRICITY	電球	DENKYŪ	light bulb
		13 strokes	電流	DENRYŪ	electric current

Once written 電 , and earlier 電 . 雨 is **rain** 3, here meaning **sent down from the heavens**. 臼/电/电 is the prototype of **lightning** 申 322 q.v. 180 can still occasionally mean lightning, but is usually used nowadays to refer to **electricity**. Suggest taking 电 as **field** 田 59 with **lightning bolt** 乚.

Mnemonic: **LIGHTNING STRIKES FIELD IN ELECTRIC RAIN STORM**

181		TŌ, katana	大刀	DAITŌ	long sword
		SWORD	軍刀	GUNTŌ	military sword
		2 strokes	小刀	KOGATANA	pocket knife

From a pictograph of a **curved sword** 丿, broader than the typical Japanese katana. As a radical usually found as 刂 . Often symbolises **cut**.

Mnemonic: **BROAD-BLADED SWORD**

182		TŌ, fuyu	冬眠	TŌMIN	hibernation
		WINTER	冬季	TŌKI	winter season
		5 strokes	冬将軍	FUYUSHŌGUN	
					'Jack Frost'

Obscure. Formerly also 冬 , and earlier 夊 and 夊 . The exact meaning of 夊 is unclear, though it is known to have acted phonetically to express **gather together/become compact**. There is some evidence to support a view that it represents **hanging ropes tied together** (see 306), said by some scholars to be ropes from which cured meat was hung during **winter**. 夂/冫is the prototype of **ice** 氷 378. Thus **when ice becomes compact**, i.e. **winter**. Suggest taking 夂 as **sitting crosslegged**.

Mnemonic: **SITTING CROSSLEGGED ON WINTER ICE**

51

183

TŌ, *ataru/teru*
**APPLY, HIT MARK,
APPROPRIATE, THIS**
6 strokes

相当 SŌTŌ　　appropriate
当人 TŌNIN　person concerned
手当て TEATE　　allowance

Formerly 當. 田 is **field** 59. 尚 is a variant of **furthermore** 尚 1392 q.v., used phonetically to express **in proportion** and possibly also lending its own connotations of **appropriate** (from its depiction of a house with window **appropriately** facing north to avoid the sun from the south). 183 originally referred to offering a field -- or by extension property -- as surety for a loan, the amount of land to be pledged being determined **in proportion** to the sum advanced and being therefore deemed **appropriate**. (More exactly, the surety was usually the right to farm the land, since private ownership was very limited.) It still retains **pledge** as a lesser meaning in Chinese. **Apply**, **this**, and **hit mark/ be accurate** are associated meanings. Suggest taking modern form as **small** \|⁄ (variant 小 36) and **hand** ∃ (see 96).

Mnemonic: **SMALL HAND APPROPRIATELY HITS MARK**

184 東

TŌ, *higashi*
EAST
8 strokes

東洋 TŌYŌ　　　　Orient
中東 CHŪTŌ　　Middle East
東側 HIGASHIGAWA east side

Usually explained incorrectly as **sun** 日 62 **rising** behind **trees** 木 69 to indicate **dawn** and thus **east**, an error of many centuries' standing. Very old forms such as 柬 reveal that it is a **tied sack** 柬 with a **pole thrust through** to facilitate carrying, and in that regard it is in the same group as **bundle** 束 1535 and **select/ open bundle** 柬 608 (see also **ridge-pole** 棟 1653). The error appears to stem from a reasonably early form 東 in which the ends of the binding have become separated from the sack, thus suggesting the early form of tree/wood. It is not clear whether this is a simple copying error, an attempt to refer to the wooden nature of the pole, or a mistaken interpretation of the elements as sun and tree. In any event, from an early stage 184 was borrowed phonetically to express **east**. Some scholars feel that it also lent an idea of **thrusting through** (i.e. the pole through the binding) and thus by extension suggested the **sun thrusting up through the horizon**, giving **dawn** and hence **east**. The usual theory is useful as a mnemonic.

Mnemonic: **SUN RISING THROUGH TREES IN EAST**

185 答 TŌ, kota*eru*
ANSWER
12 strokes

解答 KAITŌ — solution
答案 TŌAN — answer paper
口答え KUCHIGOTAE — retort

Fit 合 121 q.v. and **bamboo** 竹 170. If 121 is taken to mean **lid on container** then this would give **bamboo lid**, but no such meaning has been discovered. It is thus assumed that 121 is **cap off a remark**, i.e. **reply fittingly**, and that, most unusually for a radical, 竹 is used phonetically, to express **firm**. Thus **fitting, firm answer**.

Mnemonic: **BAMBOO GIVES FITTING ANSWER**

186 頭 TŌ, ZU, atama, kashira
HEAD, TOP, START
16 strokes

頭骨 TŌKOTSU — skull
頭痛 ZUTSŪ — headache
頭打ち ATAMAUCHI — top

Head 頁 93 and **bean/ vessel** 豆 1640, giving **vessel which is the head**. Also used figuratively as **brain, chief, top** or **start**.

Mnemonic: **HEAD IS A BEAN-LIKE VESSEL**

187 同 DŌ, ona*ji*
SAME
6 strokes

同様 DŌYŌ — similar
同時 DŌJI — same time
同意 DŌI — agreement

Somewhat obscure. Once written . Taken by some scholars to indicate a **round hole** 凵 in a **board** 片, a round hole having the **same** diameter from all angles. However, 片 is more likely to be a variant of **boat** 片/舟 1354, used phonetically to express **together** and also lending an idea of **convey**, with 凵 being **mouth/say** 20. Thus **convey verbally together**, meaning **say the same thing**, and hence **same**. Suggest taking 冂 as a **hoop**, 口 as an **opening**, and — as **single** 1.

Mnemonic: **ALL HOOPS HAVE SAME SINGLE OPENING**

188 道 DŌ, TŌ, michi
WAY, ROAD
12 strokes

鉄道 TETSUDŌ — railway
神道 SHINTŌ — Shinto
道端 MICHIBATA — roadside

 is **movement** 129. 首 is **head/chief** 139, here acting phonetically to express **direct** and also lending an idea of **chief/main**. Thus **chief means of direct movement**, meaning a **main road**. Also used figuratively as an abstract **way** (to enlightenment etc.).

Mnemonic: **HEAD MOVES, SHOWING WAY ALONG ROAD**

189

DOKU, TOKU, *yomu*
READ
14 strokes

読者 DOKUSHA　　　reader
読本 TOKUHON reading-book
読み方 YOMIKATA　　reading

Formerly 讀．言 is **words** 274. 賣 is to all intents and purposes a variant of the old form of **sell** 賣 / 売 192, which had connotations of **calling out** (one's wares). Thus **call out words**, i.e. **read**.

Mnemonic: **SELL WORDS TO READ**

190

NAN, minami
SOUTH
9 strokes

東南 TŌNAN　　　south-east
南極 NANKYOKU South Pole
南側 MINAMIGAWA
　　　　　　　south side

Somewhat obscure. Originally 𩵋, later 𡴋 and 𢆶 Some scholars feel ㄨ depicts a primitive tepee-like tent, and take 凵 to be the prototype of **red** 丹 1563 used phonetically to express **warm**. Thus, the **warm side of a tent**, i.e. the **south** side. Suggest taking 十 as **ten** 33, 冂 as a **hoop**, and ¥ as the sign for **yen**.

Mnemonic: **GET A HOOP FOR TEN YEN DOWN SOUTH**

191

BA, uma, ma
HORSE
10 strokes

馬術 BAJUTSU　　　equitation
馬車 BASHA　　horse carriage
馬乗り UMANORI　　　riding

From a pictograph of a **horse** 𢒅, stylised to 馬.

Mnemonic: **REARING HORSE**

---

192 売

BAI, uru/reru
SELL
7 strokes

売買 BAIBAI　　　　dealing
売店 BAITEN　　　　stall
売り物 URIMONO　item for sale

Formerly 賣．買 is **buy** 193 q.v. 士 is a simplification of **put out** 出 34. Thus **put out for buying**, i.e. **sell**. Suggest taking 士 as **samurai** 494, with 冗 as **legs behind a counter**.

Mnemonic: **SAMURAI STANDS BEHIND COUNTER SELLING**

193 買	BAI, ka*u* BUY 12 strokes	買収 BAISHŪ	purchase
		買い物 KAIMONO	shopping
		買い手 KAITE	buyer

Once written 買. 貝/貝 is **shell/money** 90. 网/网 is a **net**, though there is disagreement over its role. Some scholars see it as acting phonetically to express **exchange**, giving **exchange money (for goods)**. Others see it as indicating a **bagful** of money, suggesting someone about to **buy**. It may serve both roles.

Mnemonic: **NET FULL OF SHELL-MONEY CAN BUY A LOT**

194	BAKU, mugi BARLEY, WHEAT 7 strokes	麦芽 BAKUGA	malt
		麦茶 MUGICHA	barley tea
		小麦 KOMUGI	wheat

Formerly 麥. 夾 derives from a pictograph of a **wheat plant** 夾. 夂 is **inverted foot** 438 q.v., acting phonetically to express **sharp/spiky** and possibly also lending an idea of **slow progress**. Thus (**slow growing?**) **wheat plant with spiky ears**. Suggest taking 夂 as **sitting crosslegged**, with 主 as a variant of **growing plant/life** 生 42.

Mnemonic: **SITTING CROSSLEGGED WATCHING WHEAT PLANT GROW**

195 半	HAN, naka*ba* HALF, MIDDLE 5 strokes	半分 HANBUN	half
		半島 HANTŌ	peninsula
		半年 HANTOSHI	half-year

Formerly 半, and earlier 半. 八 is **split** 66, while 半 is a variant of **cow** 牛 97. 195 originally referred to butchering a cow by splitting it in **half**, i.e. down the **middle**. Now used in a broader sense.

Mnemonic: **HALF A HORNLESS COW, SPLIT DOWN MIDDLE**

196	BAN TURN,NUMBER,GUARD 12 strokes	順番 JUNBAN	order, turn
		番人 BANNIN	watchman
		一番 ICHIBAN	number one

Once written 番, showing **field** 田 59 and **rice** 米 201. At some stage 米 became 釆, apparently a confusion with **rice plant** 禾 81. The planting of rice in the fields followed a **set order** and also involved working by **roster**, i.e. in **turn**. **Roster** also led by association to **guard** (duty).

Mnemonic: **RICE SOWN IN FIELDS BY NUMBER, IN TURNS**

197 **FU, chichi**
FATHER
4 strokes

父 母 FUBO parents
お 父 様 OTŌSAMA Father
父 親 CHICHIOYA father

Once written 又, showing a **hand holding a stick** (as strike 攵 101), indicating a **stern figure**.

Mnemonic: **FATHER HAS CANE IN HAND**

---

198 **FŪ, kaze**
WIND, STYLE
9 strokes

風 船 FŪSEN balloon
神 風 KAMIKAZE divine wind
和 風 WAFŪ Japanese style

Somewhat obscure. Felt to be a simpler form of 鳳, an NGU character meaning **phoenix**. This comprises **bird** 鳥 174 and 凡, a variant of **common** 凡 1827. The latter is thought to be used phonetically to express **big**, but may also be used in a sense of **common** since the phoenix was a very common motif. The phoenix was believed by the ancients to **ride the wind** and hence came to symbolise it. **Wind** itself represented abstract concepts such as **invisible force** and **spirit**, with **manner** and **style** being extended meanings from **spirit**. **Insect** 虫 56 appears to have been used as a simple substitute for bird 鳥. The popular explanation using **sail** 帆 1711 q.v., giving **insect blown by wind against sail**, is incorrect but a useful mnemonic.

Mnemonic: **INSECT BLOWN AGAINST SAIL BY WIND**

---

199 **BUN, FUN, BU, wa**karu/keru
DIVIDE, MINUTE,
UNDERSTAND
4 strokes

分 子 BUNSHI molecule
一 分 IPPUN one minute
一 分 ICHIBU one tenth

Split 八 66 and **sword/cut** 刀 181, giving **cut and split**, and hence **divide**. This has led to numerous extended meanings, such as **fraction, minute** (now of time, but originally meaning small portion, in similar fashion to the English term), and **understand** (i.e. something which is able to be divided/broken down).

Mnemonic: **UNDERSTAND ONE DIVIDES BY SPLITTING WITH SWORD**

200 BUN, MON, ki*ku*/ko*eru*   新聞 SHINBUN   newspaper
HEAR, ASK, LISTEN   聴聞 CHŌMON   listening
14 strokes   聞き取る KIKITORU   catch, hear

Usually taken as an **ear** 耳 29 **listening** at a **gate** 門 211, though some scholars feel 門 also lends its sound to express **distinguish**. Thus **distinguish through ear (at gate)**. **Ask** is an associated meaning.

Mnemonic: **EAR LISTENING AT GATE HEARS A LOT**

201 BEI, MAI, kome   米価 BEIKA   price of rice
RICE, AMERICA   米国 BEIKOKU   America
6 strokes   白米 HAKUMAI   polished rice

From a **grain-laden ear of rice** 米. Later appears to have become confused with rice plant 禾/禾 81, resulting in central grains becoming joined as if a stalk, and in the variant 米. In Japanese also borrowed phonetically to refer to **AMErica** (from old reading ME).

Mnemonic: **GRAIN-LADEN EAR OF AMERICAN RICE**

202 HO, aru*ku*, ayu*mu*   進歩 SHINPO   progress
WALK   歩行者 HOKŌSHA   pedestrian
8 strokes   歩き出す ARUKIDASU
   start walking

Formerly also 歩, and earlier 歩, showing a doubling of **foot** 止 129 q.v. (the lower one being a right foot, the upper a left) to indicate **putting one foot in front of the other**. Suggest taking stylised 少 as **few** 143.

Mnemonic: **FEW FEET WALK NOWADAYS**

203 母 BO, haha   母性 BOSEI   maternity
MOTHER   お母様 OKĀSAMA   Mother
5 strokes   母親 HAHAOYA   mother

Variant 母 of **woman** 女 35 with **nipples** ⠄ exaggerated to suggest **suckling** and **motherhood**. In compounds usually 毋.

Mnemonic: **MOTHER IS WOMAN WITH PROMINENT NIPPLES**

204 方

HŌ, kata
SIDE, WAY, SQUARE, DIRECTION, PERSON
4 strokes

方角	HŌGAKU	direction
親方	OYAKATA	boss
見方	MIKATA	way of looking

Surprisingly obscure. Popularly felt to derive from a pictograph of a **tethered boat** 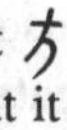 swinging in the **direction** of the current. There is evidence to support the view that it shows a boat (see 1815), though technically it is probably two boats tethered together to form a **square** (square being the main meaning of 204 in Chinese). However, many scholars feel that 204 in fact derives from a **plow**, and cite an old form  as well as the similarity to sword/blade 力/刀 181. **Direction** can then be taken as an associated idea, from the line of the plowed furrow. **Side** and **way** can be taken as extended meanings from **direction** (from the idea of **over that way**), as also **person** (originally an indirect and usually polite reference). No one interpretation seems to satisfy all meanings, though some of these may have been borrowed. The most likely explanation is that there were two separate pictographs in existence, one being boats tethered to form a square, the other a plow.

Mnemonic: **BOTH BOAT AND PLOW CAN POINT THE WAY**

205 北

HOKU, BOKU, kita
NORTH, FLEE
5 strokes

東北	TŌHOKU	north-east
敗北	HAIBOKU	defeat
北風	KITAKAZE	north wind

Originally 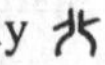, showing **two persons sitting back to back**. Turning one's back expressed the idea both of **fleeing** and of the **north**, the coldest direction and hence shunned.

Mnemonic: **PEOPLE FLEE, TURNING THEIR BACKS ON THE NORTH**

206 毎

MAI, -goto
EACH, EVERY
6 strokes

毎日	MAINICHI	daily
毎度	MAIDO	each time
日毎	HIGOTO	daily

Formerly 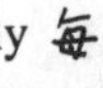. Usually interpreted as **every person** ト/イ 39 has a **mother** 母 203, which is a useful mnemonic. However, old forms such as  show that the upper part is not person but a **plant** ψ 9. **Mother** symbolised **fertility**, and the original meaning of 206 was **richly growing plant**. It is not clear how exactly it came to mean **every**. Some scholars feel it was borrowed, others that the idea of fertile growth led to **reproduction** and hence **repetition/ cycle**, with **every** being an associated idea.

Mnemonic: **EVERY PERSON HAS A MOTHER**

207		MAI, imōto YOUNGER SISTER 8 strokes	姉妹 SHIMAI	sisters
			妹分 IMŌTOBUN	'sister'
			令妹 REIMAI	your sister

Woman 女 35 and **immature** 未 794 q.v.

Mnemonic: **YOUNGER SISTER IS IMMATURE WOMAN**

208		MEI, MYŌ, akarui, akeru CLEAR, OPEN, BRIGHT 8 strokes	明白 MEIHAKU	clarity
			明日 MYŌNICHI	tomorrow
			明け方 AKEGATA	dawn

Sun 日 62 and **moon** 月 16, both symbolising **light**. Thus **very light/bright**. **Open** is an associated idea.

Mnemonic: **BRIGHT SUN AND MOON GIVE CLARITY**

209		MEI, naku/ru NON-HUMAN CRY 14 strokes	鳴動 MEIDŌ	rumbling
			鳴き声 NAKIGOE	animal cry
			鳴り物 NARIMONO	music

Mouth 口 20 and **bird** 鳥 174. Originally **bird-call**, later sound from a range of non-human sources including insects and inanimate objects.

Mnemonic: **BIRD'S MOUTH PRODUCES NON-HUMAN CRY**

210		MŌ, ke HAIR 4 strokes	羊毛 YŌMO	wool
			毛皮 KEGAWA	fur
			毛虫 KEMUSHI	caterpillar

From a pictograph of a **tuft of hair** 𣬛.

Mnemonic: **TUFT OF HAIR**

211	門	MON, kado GATE, DOOR 8 strokes	正門 SEIMON	main gate
			門番 MONBAN	doorman
			門出 KADODE	departure

From a pictograph of a **double-doored gate** 門.

Mnemonic: **DOUBLE-DOORED GATE**

212

YA, yo, yoru
NIGHT
8 strokes

本夜	HONYA	tonight
夜明け	YOAKE	dawn
夜顔	YORUGAO	moonflower

Once written 夾. ㅂ is the old form of **moon** 月 16 (ancient forms show **moon/ evening** 夕 44). 亦 is a variant of 亦, the old form of the NGU character **again** 亦 (literally both sides ハ of a person 大 53). 亦 is used phonetically to express **clear**, but its semantic role is not known. Thus **when the moon is clear**, i.e. **night**. Suggest taking イ as **person** 39, ⊥ as a **top hat**, and 夊 simply as a variant of **moon**.

Mnemonic: **AT NIGHT, PERSON PUTS ON TOP HAT TO VIEW MOON**

213

YA, no
MOOR, WILD
11 strokes

野性	YASEI	wild
野球	YAKYŪ	baseball
野原	NOHARA	moor, field

里 is **village** 219. 予 is **already** 403 q.v., here with its early meaning of **ample space**. Thus **ample space around a village**, meaning the outer parts still not fully developed. Hence **moor** and **wild**.

Mnemonic: **VILLAGE ALREADY BUILT ON WILD MOOR**

214

YŪ, tomo
FRIEND
4 strokes

友人	YŪJIN	friend
友情	YŪJŌ	friendship
友達	TOMODACHI	friend

Often thought to be a **left hand** 大 22 reaching out to grasp a **right hand** 又 2 in **friendship**. A useful mnemonic, but in fact old forms such as 𠂇 show **two right hands**, indicating **togetherness** and also both lending their sound to express **support** (i.e. **mutual support**).

Mnemonic: **HANDS REACHING OUT IN FRIENDSHIP**

215

YŌ, mochiiru
USE
5 strokes

用事	YŌJI	business
用意	YŌI	preparation
悪用	AKUYŌ	abuse

Once written 拼 and 朋, showing crude **fencing**. It was borrowed to express **use**, but, since fencing was **used** to enclose pasture land, it may also have suggested something **useful** in its own right.

Mnemonic: **USE FENCE**

216 曜 YŌ
DAY OF WEEK
18 strokes

曜日 YŌBI day of week
火曜 KAYŌ Tuesday
七曜 SHICHIYŌ days of week

日 is **sun** 62. 羽 is **wings** 812. 隹 is **bird**, from a pictograph 隹. 翟 is a CO character meaning **bird's plumage**, and in combination with 日 means **dazzling** (i.e. plumage of the sun). This is still 216's meaning in Chinese. In Japanese it can very occasionally mean dazzling, but has generally had its elements reinterpreted as **sun winging like a bird**, giving the **passing of a day**.

Mnemonic: **SUN WINGS ITS WAY LIKE A BIRD, AND SO DAY PASSES**

---

217 来 RAI, ku*ru*
COME
7 strokes

来月 RAIGETSU next month
新来者 SHINRAISHA newcomer
出来る DEKIRU be possible

Formerly 來, from a pictograph of a **wheat plant** 来 (see 194). It still retains **wheat** as a minor meaning in Chinese. It is used to express **come** instead of **come** 徠, listed in Japanese as an old form of 217 but in Chinese as a separate character. 徠 comprises **road/movement** 彳 118 and **wheat** 来 217, which is used for its sound to express **move towards** but also lends its own connotations of **emerge** or **come out** (from the idea of a plant growing). Suggest taking as **ten** 十 33 **grains of rice** 米 201.

Mnemonic: **WHEAT COMES TO BE TEN GRAINS OF RICE?!**

---

218 RAKU, GAKU,
tano*shii/shimu*
PLEASURE, MUSIC
13 strokes

気楽 KIRAKU comfort
楽しみ TANOSHIMI pleasure
楽器 GAKKI musical instrument

Popularly said to be one of the easiest characters to explain but in fact one of the most difficult. The common explanation that it derives from a pictograph of a **tasseled drum-like musical instrument on a stand**, with **music** coming to mean **pleasure**, is incorrect, though a useful mnemonic. The earlier form 樂 shows **threads** 絲 111, **white** 白 65 q.v., and **tree/wood** 木 69, while the earliest form 𣕱 shows only threads and tree. It originally referred to a type of **oak**, whose leaves were eaten by silk worms (symbolised by thread 絲). The role of the later addition 白 is not clear. No phonetic use has been

61

identified. On the other hand, neither its early meaning of **thumb nail** nor its later meanings of **hundred** or **white** seem obviously relevant, unless white reinforced the idea of silk. It is also possible that thumb lent an idea of **principal** (as in 1694), to mean principal type from among a variety of oaks. However, it seems more likely that there existed a second prototype for white, the pictograph of an **acorn**. In any event, the original meaning of 218 was **oak tree**, now conveyed by an NGU character that adds an extra tree. How it came to mean **pleasure** and **music** is not clear. Its complexity suggests it was not merely borrowed for its sound. It may possibly have symbolised the joy of a silk worm breeder upon finding such a type of oak, with music being an associated meaning of joy, or its shape may indeed have suggested a musical instrument, with pleasure being the associated meaning.

Mnemonic: **TASSELED DRUM ON STAND MAKES PLEASING MUSIC**

219	里	RI, sato **VILLAGE, LEAGUE** 7 strokes	一里 ICHIRI	one league
			里人 SATOBITO	rustic
			古里 FURUSATO	home town

Field 田 59 and **earth/ground** 土 60. The latter lent its sound to express **path**, and also lent an idea of the raised earthen ridges separating the fields. Thus **ground with fields and dividing paths**, indicating a **settlement**. Also used as a unit of distance (2.44 miles), i.e. **league**.

Mnemonic: **GROUND TILLED INTO FIELDS, INDICATING VILLAGE**

220	理	RI **REASON, RATIONAL** 11 strokes	理性 RISEI	reason
			無理 MURI	unreasonable
			心理学 SHINRIGAKU	
				psychology

王 is **jewel** 102. 里 is **village** 219 q.v., here acting phonetically to express **split** and also lending its own loose connotations of **divide** (from paths dividing the fields). 220 originally meant to **split a jewel** (still retained as a minor meaning in Chinese). This involved splitting along the natural line of cleavage, which required considerable **attention**. Thus 220 came to mean **act carefully/ handle/ manage** (also still retained in Chinese), and also came to indicate **concentration**, leading to the idea of **using the mind** and hence the associated meaning **reason(ing)**.

Mnemonic: **KEEPING JEWELS IN VILLAGE IS REASONABLE**

221		WA, hanashi, hana*su*	会話	KAIWA	conversation
		SPEECH, TALK	話題	WADAI	talking point
		13 strokes	小話	KOBANASHI	tale

Usually explained as **words** 言 274 and **tongue** 舌 732 q.v., giving **articulated words** and hence **speak**. A useful mnemonic, but incorrect. Old forms such as 話 show that 舌 is not tongue but the early form of **hollowed out space** 𠙵 244 q.v. Here it lends its sound to express **good**, and may also lend an idea of **booming/echoing**, or else **coming out from the space that is the mouth**. Thus **good words**, giving **speech**.

Mnemonic: **TONGUE CONTROLS WORDS WHEN TALKING**

END OF SECOND GRADE

THE 195 THIRD GRADE CHARACTERS

222　悪　AKU, O, warui
BAD, HATE
11 strokes

悪意 AKUI　　　　　malice
悪寒 OKAN　　　　　chill
悪者 WARUMONO　　rascal

Formerly 惡. 心 is **heart/feelings** 147. 亞/亜 is **sub-** 997 q.v., here acting phonetically to express **ugly** and also lending its own connotations of **ugly and twisted**. Thus **ugly, twisted feelings**. 222 originally referred to someone twisted with hatred, and can still occasionally be used in this sense, but in general it has come to mean **bad** in a broad sense.

Mnemonic: **SUB-HUMAN, UGLY, TWISTED FEELINGS ARE BAD**

223　安　AN, yasui/maru
RESTFUL, EASE, CHEAP
6 strokes

不安 FUAN　　　　　unease
安心 ANSHIN　　　　relief
安物 YASUMONO cheap item

Woman 女 35 q.v. and **building/home** 宀 28. Usually explained as a woman at home representing the idea of **peaceful normality**. However, old forms such as reveal that 女 does not derive from the normal <u>kneeling</u> woman 㞢, but a woman <u>sitting</u> on a thin, flat item 几. It referred to a woman using a **napkin** during **menstruation**. At such times a woman was left alone to **rest quietly** in a corner of the house, and did no work. That is, she was **at her ease**. **Cheap** is an associated meaning, related to the idea of giving no cause for concern.

Mnemonic: **WOMAN AT HOME, RESTING AT EASE**

224　暗　AN, kurai
DARK, GLOOMY
13 strokes

明暗 MEIAN　　light and dark
暗殺 ANSATSU　assassination
真暗 MAKKURA　　pitch dark

日 is **sun** 62. 音 is **sound** 6 q.v., here acting phonetically to express **shade** and possibly also lending connotations of **indistinctness** (from its stress on volume of sound rather than articulateness or clarity). Thus **shaded sun**, i.e. **darkness** and **gloom**.

Mnemonic: **SUN GOES DARK, ACCOMPANIED BY SOUND**

64

| 225 | | I , iyas*u*
HEAL, MEDICAL
7 strokes | 医者 ISHA
外科医 GEKAI
医学 IGAKU | doctor
surgeon
medical science |

Formerly 毉. 殳 is **striking hand** 153, while 矢 is an **arrow** 981 in its **quiver** ㄷ, giving a now defunct character 医殳 meaning to **attack**. 酉 is a **wine jar** 302, here indicating **alcohol**. Thus to **attack with alcohol**, which refers to the ancient practice of using alcohol as a medicine and possibly also anesthetic. By extension this came to refer to **healing** and **medical practice**.

Mnemonic: **DOCTOR'S BAG CONTAINS ARROW, USED FOR HEALING**

| 226 | 意 | I
MIND, THOUGHT, WILL
13 strokes | 注意 CHŪI
決意 KETSUI
意見 IKEN | attention, care
resolution
opinion |

心 is **heart/feelings** 147. 音 is **sound** 6. Some scholars feel the latter is used to mean **state aloud**, to give **voicing one's feelings** and hence **opinion** or similar. Others feel it is used phonetically to express **full**, to give **that of which the heart is full**, i.e. **concerns** or **thoughts**. Some feel it may also lend an idea of sound but in a figurative sense, i.e. **'the sound of the heart'**. A combination of the last two theories seems the most likely, i.e. a **heart full of thoughts which are its 'sounds'**. **Will** and **mind** are extended meanings.

Mnemonic: **A THOUGHT IS A SOUND FROM THE HEART**

| 227 | | IKU, soda*tsu*/*teru*
RAISE, EDUCATE
8 strokes | 教育 KYŌIKU
育児 IKUJI
育て親 SODATEOYA | education
childcare
foster parent |

Originally 㐬, showing a **woman** ㄐ / 女 35 q.v. (but sitting rather than kneeling) and inverted **child** 𠫓 / 子 25. The inversion indicates a **newborn infant**, emphasised by the **amniotic fluid** '。' (see also 409). In a later form 㐬 the drops of fluid became stylised as 川, and in a still later form 㐬 became replaced by 肉/月. Some scholars see this as **meat** 365 used purely phonetically to express **birth** (replacing woman 女, which similarly represented birth), but it may just be a stylisation of 川. 227 can still mean birth in Chinese, but it is generally used to mean **raise children** in a broad sense.

Mnemonic: **EDUCATE CHILD UPSIDE-DOWN LIKE PIECE OF MEAT**

228		IN	会員	KAIIN	group member
		MEMBER, OFFICIAL	全員	ZENIN	all members
		10 strokes	動員	DŌIN	mobilisation

Old forms such as 鼎 show that 貝 is not shell 90 but a simplification of **round three legged kettle** 鼎 (now an NGU character with that meaning), which in itself symbolised **roundness** but is here reinforced by a **circle** 口 . Thus the original meaning was **round kettle**. This led to **round** (still found in Chinese). **Member** and **official** are felt to derive from the idea of a group of persons gathered **around** (a superior) in a meeting. Suggest taking 貝 as shell-**money** and 口 as mouth/**say** 20.

Mnemonic: **OFFICIAL MEMBERS ALWAYS TALK OF MONEY**

229	院	IN	病院	BYŌIN	hospital
		INSTITUTE	寺院	JIIN	temple
		10 strokes	議院	GIIN	the House

阝 is from a pictograph of a **terraced slope** 皀 , and often means **hill, mound,** or **embankment** (as here). It is the forerunner of the NGU character **hill** 阜. 完 is **complete** 440 q.v., which originally meant **building with surrounding fence/wall** and as such is the prototype of 229. The addition of embankment 阝 suggests an important building with solid surrounding walls. It can still mean **large building,** but generally indicates an **institute** or similar. Suggest remembering 阝 in its commonest sense of **hill**.

Mnemonic: **INSTITUTE COMPLETE WITH SURROUNDING HILLS**

230		IN, nom*u*	飲用水	INYŌSUI	drinking water
		DRINK, SWALLOW	飲み物	NOMIMONO	drinks
		12 strokes	飲み屋	NOMIYA	tavern

Though nowadays written with the **food/eat** radical 食 146, old forms such as 𩚁 show clearly that this is a substitute for **wine jar /alcohol** 酉 302. 欠 is **lack** 471, used here in its early sense of **gaping mouth**. Thus to **quaff alcohol with gaping mouth**, now to **drink** in general, as well as **swallow** (without chewing).

Mnemonic: **LACK FOOD, SO SWALLOW DRINK**

231	**UN,** hako*bu*	運動 UNDŌ	movement
	TRANSPORT,LUCK,MOVE	不運 FUUN	misfortune
	12 strokes	運送 UNSŌ	transportation

⻌ is **movement** 129. 軍 is **army** 466 q.v. Some scholars take the latter in a literal sense, giving **army on the move** and by association **transportation** and the **fortunes** of war. Others take it to act phonetically to express **round**, as well as lending its own connotations both of **circle** and **vehicle** (from a circle of vehicles), thus giving a meaning of **vehicles rolling along**, and hence t**ransport**. **Luck** is then felt to stem from an association between fortune and circular/cyclic movement.

Mnemonic: **ARMY ON MOVE NEEDS LUCK AND TRANSPORT**

232	**EI,** oyog*u*	水泳 SUIEI	swimming
	SWIM	背泳 HAIEI	backstroke
	8 strokes	平泳ぎ HIRAOYOGI	breaststroke

氵 is **water** 40. 永 is **long** 615 q.v., here used phonetically to express **float** and also lending its original connotations of **flowing water**. 232 originally meant to **float with the current**, but has now broadened to mean **swim**.

Mnemonic: **LONG SWIM IN WATER**

233	**EKI**	駅長 EKICHŌ	stationmaster
	STATION	駅弁 EKIBEN	station lunch
	14 strokes	東京駅 TŌKYŌEKI	Tokyo Station

Formerly 驛 . 馬 is **horse** 191. 睪 is a CO character meaning **spy on** and **lead**. It was once written 睪 , showing an **eye** ⌀ 72 and 幸 (also 夆), a type of shackle used on **prisoners** and hence symbolising them. Thus 睪 is an ideograph meaning to **keep watch over prisoners**. Since the prisoners were chained together in a line it often also has connotations of **line** or **succession**, as here. Thus 233 means literally a **succession of horses**, and referred to the **relay stations** at which imperial messengers changed their horses. It now means **station** in a broader sense. Suggest taking the simplified form 尺 as a **person** 人 39 with a **pack** ⊐ on their back.

Mnemonic: **LADEN PERSON MOUNTS HORSE AT RELAY STATION**

234		EN, sono	公園 KŌEN	park
		GARDEN, PARK	動物園 DŌBUTSUEN	zoo
		13 strokes	花園 HANAZONO	
				flower garden

Enclosure □ 123 and **spacious** 袁 79. The latter also lends its sound to express **fence**. Thus **spacious fenced enclosure**. Suggest remembering 袁 by association with **distant** 遠 79.

Mnemonic: **SPACIOUS PARK ENCLOSES CONSIDERABLE DISTANCE**

235	横	Ō, yoko	横断 ŌDAN	crossing
		SIDE, CROSSWAYS	横行 ŌKŌ	strutting
		15 strokes	横顔 YOKOGAO	profile

Wood 木 69 and **yellow** 黄 120. The latter acts phonetically to express **bar/block**, and may also lend connotations of **wooden shaft** from its original meaning of flaming arrow. 235 originally referred to a piece of wood laid across a gate to prevent its being opened, leading to **crossways** and by extension **on its side** and **side**. It also occasionally has connotations of defiance (from prevent) and perversity (a figurative extension from not upright).

Mnemonic: **YELLOW PIECE OF WOOD LAID ON ITS SIDE**

236	屋	OKU, ya	屋上 OKUJŌ	roof
		STORE, BUILDING	小屋 KOYA	hut
		9 strokes	パン屋 PANYA	baker(y)

尸 is an NGU character meaning **corpse**, derived from a slumped figure 尸. In compounds it can also mean **buttocks** or, as here, slump in the sense of **relax**. 至 is **arrive (and stop)** 875, which also acts phonetically to express **room** (in fact, some scholars feel it is used as a simplified form of room 室 136). Thus a **room where, having arrived, one can relax**. This came by extension to mean **house** or **building**, and in Japanese is also used of **store** and by extension **storekeeper**.

Mnemonic: **ARRIVE AND FIND CORPSE IN STORE BUILDING**

237 温	ON, atatakai/meru WARM 12 strokes	温泉 ONSEN	spa
		温情 ONJŌ	kindness
		温室 ONSHITSU	hothouse

Formerly 溫 . There is some difference of opinion as to its origins. Some scholars take it to refer to an act of **kindness** in giving a **prisoner** 囚 1353 a **bowl** 皿 1307 of **water** 氵 40, with the figurative sense of **warm** unusually preceding the physical one. Other scholars interpret 囚 as a variant of **vapors** 囚 26, with **watery vapors from a bowl** indicating steam and thus **heat.** Though the latter theory seems the more logical, 昷 is listed (though without examples) as a CO character meaning **feed a prisoner**, suggesting that the former theory is in fact accurate. For the modern form, suggest taking 日 as **sun** 62.

Mnemonic: **SUN WARMS WATER IN A BOWL**

238 化	KA, KE, bakeru CHANGE, BEWITCH 4 strokes	変化 HENKA	change
		化粧 KESHŌ	make-up
		化け者 BAKEMONO	'spook'

亻 shows a <u>standing</u> person 39, while 匕 shows a <u>fallen</u> person, thus indicating a **change of state**. Some scholars feel that 匕 also acts phonetically to express **deceive**, leading to deceitful change and hence **bewitch**, while others see bewitch simply as an associated meaning of change.

Mnemonic: **BEWITCHED PERSON CHANGES AND FALLS**

239 荷	KA, ni LOAD, BURDEN 10 strokes	出荷 SHUKKA	consignment
		船荷 FUNANI	ship's cargo
		荷物 NIMOTSU	baggage

艹 is **plant** 9. 何 is **what?** 80 q.v. The latter is almost certainly used in its early sense of **bear a heavy load**, though its precise role is unclear. The original meaning of 239 was **lotus** (still retained in Chinese as a significant meaning). The idea of bearing a heavy load may possibly have been used to refer to the large head of the lotus. In any event, **bearing a load** came to prevail as the main meaning in Chinese and the sole meaning in Japanese.

Mnemonic: **WHAT A BURDEN THE LOTUS PLANT CAN BE!**

240	**KAI** **AREA, BOUNDARY** 9 strokes	世界 SEKAI 境界 KYŌKAI 政界 SEIKAI	world boundary political world

Field 田 59 and **come between** 介 1059. Thus **division of land**, leading to both **boundary** and **area**.

Mnemonic: **BOUNDARY BETWEEN FIELDS MARKS AREAS**

241	**KAI, hira**ku, **a**keru **OPEN** 12 strokes	開発 KAIHATSU 開始 KAISHI 開き綱 HIRAKIZUNA	development inception rip-cord

Once written 開, showing a **gate** 門 211 and two **hands** 廾 reaching out to remove the **bar** ― that is keeping it closed, thereby **opening** it.

Mnemonic: **HANDS REMOVE BAR AND OPEN GATE**

242	**KAI** **STORY, GRADE, STEP** 12 strokes	階段 KAIDAN 二階 NIKAI 階級 KAIKYŪ	stairs upstairs class, grade

阝 is **terraced hill** 229. 皆 is **all** 1064, here acting phonetically to express **row** and also lending similar connotations from its literal meaning of **row** (of people talking). Thus **row of terraces on a hillside**, now used to mean **step** or **graduation** in a broad sense.

Mnemonic: **ALL THE STEPS OF A TERRACED HILL**

243	**KAKU, tsuno, kado** **HORN, ANGLE, CORNER** 7 strokes	角度 KAKUDO 角笛 TSUNOBUE 町角 MACHIKADO	angle horn, bugle street corner

From a pictograph of a **horn** 角. Now has a range of extended meanings such as **corner**, **angle**.

Mnemonic: **ANGULAR HORN**

244　**KATSU**　生活 SEIKATSU　　　life
ACTIVITY, LIFE　活気 KAKKI　　liveliness
9 strokes　活動 KATSUDŌ　　activity

Usually explained as a **moist** 氵 (water 40) **tongue** 舌 732, which is a sign of **life**. A useful mnemonic, but old forms such as 澗 show that 舌 is in fact a derivative of 㕊, an element combining opening 口 20 and scoop 乃 495 and meaning **hollowed out space**. 244 originally referred to **water rushing** into such a space. By extension it came to mean **activity** and, perhaps because of the life-giving property of water, **life**. Note that in Chinese it still retains a minor meaning of **sound of (rushing) water**.

Mnemonic: **WET TONGUE IS SIGN OF LIFE**

245　**KAN, samu**i　寒波 KANPA　　cold wave
COLD　寒気 SAMUKE　　　chill
12 strokes　寒暖計 KANDANKEI
　　　thermometer

Somewhat obscure. Formerly 寒, and in ancient times 𡨄. ∩/宀 is **roof/building** 28. 人/冫 is **ice** 378, possibly symbolising winter. 卄 (also 茻) appears to be **plants** 9. 245 thus appears to be a reference to the custom of binding straw or rushes to the outside of a house to insulate it against the **cold** of winter. Suggest taking 卄 as **well** 1470 and 𠆢 as a variant of **six** 六 76.

Mnemonic: **BUILDING'S SIX WELLS ICE OVER IN COLD**

246　**KAN**　感心 KANSHIN　admiration
FEELING　感覚 KANKAKU　　sense
13 strokes　感情 KANJŌ　　feeling

Heart/feeling 心 147 and 咸. The latter is a CO character meaning **unison**. It comprises **trimming tool/ sharp weapon** 戉 (variant 戊 515 q.v.), which symbolised trimming and making correct and by extension **harmonising**, and **mouth/say** 口 20, thus giving harmony of expression and unison. Here it acts phonetically to express **sway**, and probably also lends an idea of **all together**. Thus **all hearts swayed together**, indicating intense **emotion** or **feeling**. Suggest taking 戊 as a variant of **halberd** 弋 493, with 一 as **one** 1.

Mnemonic: **ONE HALBERD IN MOUTH CAUSES FEELING IN HEART**

71

247		KAN LARGE BUILDING, HALL 16 strokes	会館 KAIKAN	hall
			旅館 RYOKAN	inn
			美術館 BIJUTSUKAN	art gallery

Eat 食 146 and **official** 官 441 q.v., here with its original meaning of **official in a building.** 247 originally referred to a building where traveling officials could eat, i.e. an **inn**, but then came to mean **building** in a broader sense, usually with connotations of size and quality.

Mnemonic: **OFFICIAL EATS IN HALL**

248		GAN, kishi BANK, SHORE 8 strokes	海岸 KAIGAN	coast
			対岸 TAIGAN	far bank
			川岸 KAWAGISHI	riverbank

山 is **mountain** 24, here meaning **high ground.** 厂 is **cliff** 45. 干 is **dry** 825 q.v., here acting phonetically to express **high** and also lending an idea of **thrusting** from its original meaning of **thrusting weapon.** Thus **tall thrusting cliffs**, and by extension **shore** or **bank**.

Mnemonic: **MOUNTAINOUS CLIFF FORMS DRY SHORE**

249		GAN, iwa ROCK, CRAG 8 strokes	岩石 GANSEKI	rock
			岩屋 IWAYA	cave
			火成岩 KASEIGAN	igneous rock

Mountain 山 24 and **stone/rock** 石 45.

Mnemonic: **STONY MOUNTAIN SHOWS ROCKY CRAGS**

250		KI, okiru/koru/kosu ARISE, CAUSE 10 strokes	起原 KIGEN	origin
			早起き HAYAOKI	early rising
			起動力 KIDŌRYOKU	motive power

Formerly 起. 走 is **run** 161. 巳 is an NGU character meaning **serpent**, and derives from a pictograph 𠃌. Here it acts phonetically to express **stop**, and also lends an idea of **rearing up.** Thus to **stop running and rear up**, such as an animal at bay. The idea of rearing came to prevail, leading to associated meanings such as **rise**, **arise**, **occur**, and **cause.** Suggest taking 己 as **thread/self** 855.

Mnemonic: **CAUSE ONESELF TO RUN**

258	去	KYO, KO, sa*ru* GO, LEAVE, PAST 5 strokes	去年 KYONEN 過去 KAKO 立ち去る TACHISARU	last year the past depart

Once written 盍, showing a **double-lid on a rice container**. The double-lid indicated security, indicating in turn the importance of rice. Though a lidded container might logically be expected to suggest fullness, as indeed it does in the case of joy 吉 1142 q.v., in the case of 258 it seems that since the rice was looked upon as vital rations its rate of **consumption** was of paramount importance. Consumption led to **used up** and **gone**, with **past** being a figurative extension. Suggest taking ム as **nose** 134 and 土 as **ground** 60.

Mnemonic: **NOSE TO GROUND SUGGESTS ONE'S GONE TOO FAR**

259	橋	KYŌ, hashi BRIDGE 16 strokes	鉄橋 TEKKYŌ 陸橋 RIKKYŌ 石橋 ISHIBASHI	steel bridge overpass stone bridge

木 is **wood** 69. 喬 is an NGU character meaning **tall**. In effect it is a variant of tall 高 119 q.v., showing a watchtower 髙/冏 but surmounted by a person with bent neck 夭 279, symbolising **bent at the tip/top**. Thus **tall arched wooden structure**, now used of **bridges** in general.

Mnemonic: **TALL ARCHED WOODEN STRUCTURE IS BRIDGE**

260	業	GYŌ, GŌ, waza PROFESSION, DEED, KARMA 13 strokes	産業 SANGYŌ 罪業 ZAIGŌ 仕業 SHIWAZA	industry sin act, deed

Once written 業, depicting a base and notched board of a **musical instrument**. Crosspieces were slotted into the notches and bells hung from them. Opinion differs as to how this pictograph of a musical instrument came to acquire its present meanings. Some scholars feel that there was a similar device from which wooden tablets inscribed with characters were hung, these tablets apparently being used as teaching aids. Thus the pictograph became associated with **learning**, leading to **profession** and hence to **work**, with work giving rise to **deed/act**, which in turn became associated with **karma** (the effect of a person's actions on the sum of their existence). Other scholars see the instrument as symbolising **intricacy** and **complexity**, and by extension something demanding much **study** in order to master. From **study**, the evolution of meaning is seen as similar to that of the first theory. Suggest remembering partly by association with **wood** 木 69.

Mnemonic: **STUDY COMPLEX WOODEN INSTRUMENT AS PROFESSION**

261 KYOKU, ma*garu*/*geru*   曲線 KYOKUSEN   curve
BEND, MELODY   作曲 SAKKYOKU songwriting
6 strokes   曲げ物 MAGEMONO   round box

Somewhat obscure. Originally ㇄ , and later ㇇ and ㇈. Some scholars see this as a **carpenter's tool** used in cutting **curves** and **angles**, while others see it as a crude **receptacle** made by **bending** softened wood. There is in fact evidence to support both views. **Melody** is an associated meaning, from the idea of **convoluted**. Suggest taking as a 'multi-pathed' variant of **field** 田 59.

Mnemonic: **FIELD HAS MANY BENDING PATHS**

262 KYOKU   局面 KYOKUMEN   situation
OFFICE, SECTION, END,   結局 KEKKYOKU   finally
CIRCUMSTANCES   郵便局 YŪBINKYOKU
7 strokes   post office

Obscure. Once written 局 and 局. Some scholars see 尸 as the prototype of **measure** 尺 884 q.v. and 口 as an **area**, giving **measured area** and by extension **prescribed section**, leading on the one hand to **division** and by figurative extension interruption and thence **termination/end**, and on the other to appropriate **part** of a larger unit, such as a specialised branch/office of a government ministry. However, such a theory does not easily explain the meaning **circumstances**. Other scholars see 尸/尸 as a slumped figure symbolising **bending** (essentially **corpse** 尸 236), plus the prototype 句 of **phrase** 句 655 q.v., used for its idea of **interlocking**, thus giving a meaning of interlocking and bending, i.e. **convoluted**. **Circumstances** is an associated meaning from convolutions. **Office** is seen as stemming from 262's replacement of a now defunct character of which it was an element in combination with **building** 宀 28, 宮, which meant **complicated building** such as one housing many government offices. The **office** was a **section** of the maze-like building, which one **finally** found. (Similarly a **court lady's chamber**, which is a further minor meaning of 262.) A further theory is that 尸 is merely a variant of **large building** 广 114. The later use of corpse 尸 236 is consistent with the occasional use of 尸 as a simplification of **building** 屋 236. This gives **interlocking** (i.e. **complicated**) **building**, and then follows the second theory, but does not account for **circumstances**. It seems possible that 262 may in fact be a confusion of several characters. Suggest taking it as **corpse** and a variant of **phrase**.

Mnemonic: **OFFICE CORPSE USES ODD PHRASE IN CIRCUMSTANCES**

263	銀	GIN, shirogane	銀行 GINKŌ	bank
		SILVER	銀河 GINGA	Milky Way
		14 strokes	銀貨 GINKA	silver coin

金 is metal 14. 艮 is an NGU character meaning stop. It was once written 艮, showing an eye on twisted legs (as opposed to eye on bent legs in look 見 18), and indicated a person turning round and staring. Here it is used primarily for its sound, to express white, but also lends an idea of take a second look , i.e. scrutinise. That is, it required a careful examination to distinguish silver from similar but less precious metals. Thus white, carefully examined metal. Suggest remembering 艮 as stop and stare, distinguishing it from good 良 598. Note that shirogane means literally 'white metal'. See also 353.

Mnemonic: STOP AND STARE AT SILVERY METAL

264	苦	KU, kuru*shii*/*shimu*, nigai	苦心 KUSHIN	pains, trouble
		PAINFUL, BITTER	苦痛 KUTSŪ	pain, agony
		8 strokes	苦味 NIGAMI	bitterness

Plant 艹 9 and old 古 109, here used phonetically to express bitter but possibly also lending an extended idea of lingering. Thus plant with (lingering?) bitter taste. Bitter is also used figuratively.

Mnemonic: OLD PLANT LEAVES BITTER TASTE

265	具	GU, sona*eru*	具合 GUAI	condition
		EQUIP(MENT), MEANS	用具 YŌGU	appliance
		8 strokes	道具 DŌGU	tool

Formerly 具, and in ancient times 𤔔, showing hands 𠂇乂 holding up a kettle 鼎 228. Kettle symbolised utensil. Thus offer a utensil, meaning to equip with the wherewithal. Some later forms such as 具 suggest that kettle became confused with shell/money 貝 90, but the core meaning (provide wherewithal) remained unchanged. Suggest taking 目 as eye 72 and 八 as a table.

Mnemonic: KEEP AN EYE ON TABLE: IT'S VALUABLE EQUIPMENT

266

KUN, kimi
LORD, YOU, MR
7 strokes

暴君 BŌKUN   tyrant
細君 SAIKUN   wife
山田君 YAMADAKUN
                              (Mr) Yamada

口 is **mouth/say** 20. ⺻ is a CO character meaning **govern**, deriving from **hand holding a stick** ⺻ (see also 101). Thus to **govern by mouth**, i.e. command and by extension **commander/lord**. Also used as what was originally a very polite form of address (now informal).

Mnemonic: **LORD HOLDS STICK NEXT TO MOUTH**

267

KEI, KYŌ, ani
ELDER BROTHER
5 strokes

父兄 FUKEI   guardians
兄様 NIISAMA * Elder Brother
兄弟愛 KYŌDAIAI brotherly love

Once written 兄, showing a **person crouching** ⌐39 and a **mouth** 口 20, indicating **speaking**. There is some disagreement over the role of crouching figure. Many scholars claim that it was used phonetically to express **big** and also lent similar connotations of its own (i.e. a big person bending to be on a level with other persons), and that 267 originally meant **big words/ exaggeration** before coming to mean **big** in general and finally **big brother**. However, there is little obvious evidence to support this claimed early meaning, and no explanation as to why big (person) 大 53 was not used. It seems equally if not more likely that the ideograph indicated a **person associated with speaking**, namely an **elder brother** whose role was to advise and represent his younger siblings. The occasional use of 267 to indicate big can then be seen as deriving from big brother, rather than vice-versa.

Mnemonic: **ELDER BROTHER IS ALL MOUTH AND LEGS**

268

KEI, kakari
INVOLVEMENT
9 strokes

関係 KANKEI   relationship
係争 KEISŌ   contention
係員 KAKARIIN
                          clerk in charge

Person 亻 39 and **joined threads** 糸 844 q.v., here meaning simply **connected**. Thus **person connected**, i.e. **involved** or **concerned**. Also used nowadays of **connection** in general.

Mnemonic: **PERSON INVOLVED WITH JOINING THREADS**

| 274 | | GEN, GON, koto, *iu*
WORD, SAY, SPEAK
7 strokes | 発言 HATSUGEN statement
無言 MUGON silence
言葉 KOTOBA word |

Formerly 𧮯 and originally 𧮫 . 口 is **mouth/say** 20. ▽ / 辛 is **needle/sharp** 1432. Some scholars see the latter as acting purely phonetically to express **heart/ feelings**, to give **oral expression of feelings**, but this does not explain why the character for heart itself (147) was not used. Other scholars see sharp as lending an extended meaning of **articulate**, to give **articulate use of the mouth**. Still others see needle as representing **teeth**, which were considered necessary for good enunciation. The second theory seems the most likely, with 辛 possibly also having a secondary phonetic role of expressing **feelings**. Suggest taking the modern form 言 as **three** 三 23 and a **bit** 丶 .

Mnemonic: **MOUTH SPEAKS THREE AND A BIT WORDS**

| 275 | | KO
STOREHOUSE
10 strokes | 車庫 SHAKO garage, depot
倉庫 SŌKO warehouse
冷蔵庫 REIZŌKO refrigerator |

Large building 广 114 and **vehicle** 車 31. Some scholars feel that 275 once meant literally **large building for housing vehicles** (especially war-chariots), while others feel that by extension vehicle indicated the **goods** carried on a cart, giving **large building for cart-load of goods**, i.e. **storehouse**.

Mnemonic: **STOREHOUSE IS BUILDING CONTAINING VEHICLES**

| 276 | | KO, mizuumi
LAKE
12 strokes | 十和田湖 TOWADAKO Lake Towada
湖岸 KOGAN lakeshore
湖水 KOSUI lake |

Somewhat obscure. 氵 is **water** 40. 胡 is an NGU character now borrowed to express a range of meanings such as barbarian, but its original meaning was **beard** and by extension **old person** (both meanings still retained in Chinese). It comprises **old** 古 109 q.v., possibly used in an assumed early sense of skull but more likely in an extended sense of old person, and 月 (once 肉), which is felt to derive from a pictograph of a beard (a symbol of an old person). Here 胡 is used phonetically to express **big**. It may also have lent some meaning, possibly **long time** or similar, though this is not clear. Thus **big body of water** (taking a long time to cross?). Suggest taking 月 as **moon** 16.

Mnemonic: **OLD MOON SEEN IN WATERS OF LAKE**

277 公

KŌ, ōyake
PUBLIC, FAIR, LORD
4 strokes

公共 KŌKYŌ	public
公平 KŌHEI	fairness
紀州公 KISHŪKŌ	Lord Kishu

Once written 㕣. ロ is an **enclosure**, indicating **private property**.)(is **split/away** 66, indicating **dissolution**. Thus the **dissolution of private property**, giving **public property**. It also led to the idea of belonging to the **state/government** as opposed to private individuals. Government conceptually overlapped with **royal household**, leading by association to **member of royal household** such as **prince** and eventually **lord**. **Fair** is an associated meaning of public and open. It is not clear whether ム is merely a graphic simplification of ロ or a deliberate use of **self** ム 134. Suggest taking ム as **nose** 134 and ハ in its meaning of **eight**.

Mnemonic: **EIGHT LORDS SHOW NOSE IN PUBLIC**

278 向

KŌ, *muku/keru/kō/kau*
FACE TOWARDS, BEYOND
6 strokes

向上 KŌJŌ	improvement
意向 IKŌ	intention
前向き MAEMUKI	forward looking

From a pictograph of a **house with a window** 向. The **direction** the window **faced** was considered important (usually north, since the southern sun was generally too hot). As in English, **facing** could also mean being **opposite**, leading to **other side** and by further extension to **beyond**.

Mnemonic: **HOUSE WINDOW FACES ONE**

279 幸

KŌ,saiwa*i*,shiawa*se*,sachi
HAPPINESS, LUCK
8 strokes

幸運 KŌUN	good fortune
不幸 FUKŌ	misery, bad luck
幸い SAIWAI ni	fortunately

Once written 𡴘. 夭 is an NGU character meaning **death or calamity**, and derives from a figure 大 53 with a slumped head ㇀. 屰 is an inverted stylisation 大 of figure 53, the inversion indicating the **reversal** of the calamity. A reversal of calamity means **happiness** and **good fortune**. See also 646. Suggest remembering by association with needle/**sharp** 辛 1432, 279 having an extra stroke.

Mnemonic: **EXTRA SHARP STROKE BRINGS HAPPINESS**

280		KŌ, minato	空港 KŪKŌ	airport
		HARBOR, PORT	入港 NYŪKŌ	port entry
		12 strokes	港町 MINATOMACHI	
				port town

Also written 港. 氵 is **water** 40. 巷 is an NGU character meaning **streets of a settlement**. It was once written 巷, showing the early forms of **village** 邑/阝 355 and **together** 戓/共 460, and referred to the coming together of roads near a village. Confusingly, though it usually means point of <u>convergence</u> of roads and hence **settlement**, from a different perspective it can also mean point of <u>divergence</u> and hence **forking road**. Some scholars take 巷 to mean settlement and thus assume 280 means simply **waterside settlement**, but usage in Chinese, where 280 can also mean **creek**, suggests that 氵 represented **river**, that 巷 meant **forking road**, and that 280 originally meant **forking river**. That is, it presumably then came to refer to a **delta** (characterised by branching) and hence **rivermouth**, the site of most **ports**. Suggest taking 共 as **together** and 己 as **self** 855.

Mnemonic: **FIND ONESELF TOGETHER WITH WATER IN PORT**

281	号	GŌ	番号 BANGŌ	number
		NUMBER, CALL, SIGN	号令 GŌREI	command
		5 strokes	号泣 GŌKYŪ	wailing

Formerly 號. 虎 is an NGU character meaning **tiger**. Though it looks like a variant of skin 皮 374 it is in fact derived from an extremely stylised pictograph of a tiger that appears to have accentuated the fangs 虍 (to 虎 to 虎), and to all intents and purposes represents a mass of claw and fang. 八/儿 is felt to be **legs** 39 used ideographically, and is dropped in most cases in compounds. 口 is **mouth/say** 20. 丂 is a CO character meaning **seeking an exit**, and shows a **waterweed twisting** up to the surface before spreading out flat. Thus 号 indicates a call that is loud and/or drawn out, i.e. that is preceded by a certain build-up such as the gathering of breath. 281 originally referred to a **tiger's call**, then came to mean **loud call** in general. **Number** is an extended meaning from calling out a person's name or number, as in the army, and **sign** is a similar extension from designation.

Mnemonic: **MOUTH CALLS NUMBER OF TWISTING WEED**

282		**KON, ne** **ROOT, BASE** 10 strokes	根本 KONPON 大根 DAIKON 屋根 YANE	basis giant radish roof

Tree 木 69 and **stopping and staring** 艮 263. The latter acts phonetically to express **root/base** and also lends an idea of 'rooted' to the spot. Thus **root which fixes tree in place**, now also **root/base** in a figurative sense.

Mnemonic: **STOP AND STARE AT TREE ROOT**

283		**SAI, matsuru, matsuri** **FESTIVAL, WORSHIP** 11 strokes	祭日 SAIJITSU 祭壇 SAIDAN 雪祭 YUKIMATSURI	holiday altar snow festival

Once written 祭, clearly showing a **hand** 又 placing **meat** 月 365 on an **altar** 示 695, thus indicating a sacrifice during a religious **ceremony**. **Festival** and **worship** are associated meanings.

Mnemonic: **HAND PUTS MEAT ON ALTAR IN FESTIVAL OF WORSHIP**

284		**SAI, hosoi, komakai** **SLENDER, FINE** 11 strokes	細工 SAIKU 細長い HOSONAGAI 細か KOMAKA ni	craftsmanship slender minutely

Once written 細, showing **thread** 🔾 / 糸 27 and **brain** 🔾 / 田 131. 田 acts phonetically to express **thin**, and also lends an idea of **fine** crenellations. Thus **fine, thin thread(s)**. Suggest taking 田 as **field** 59.

Mnemonic: **SLENDER PATH THREADS THROUGH FIELD**

285	仕	**SHI, JI, tsukaeru** **SERVE, WORK, DO** 5 strokes	仕事 SHIGOTO 仕方 SHIKATA 仕組み SHIKUMI	work way, means arrangement

Person イ 39 and **samurai** 士 494. A samurai was a person who **served** his master. **Do** and **work** are associated meanings.

Mnemonic: **SAMURAI IS PERSON WHO WORKS AND SERVES**

| 286 | | **SHI, shi***nu*
DEATH
6 strokes | 死体 SHITAI
死去 SHIKYO
若死に WAKAJINI | corpse
death
early death |

Once written 𣦵. 冎 (now 歹) is a variant of **bone** 骨 867 q.v., its 'meatlessness' indicating **bare bone**(s) and hence **skeleton/ death**. 人 is **person** 39, now replaced by **fallen person** ヒ 238 which reinforces the idea of death. Thus **death of a person**, now **death** in general.

Mnemonic: **PERSON FALLS IN DEATH, SOON BARE BONES**

| 287 | | **SHI, tsuka***u*
USE, SERVANT
8 strokes | 使用 SHIYŌ
大使 TAISHI
小使 KOZUKAI | use
ambassador
servant |

Once written 𠈮. イ is **person** 39. 㬥 is the early form of **thing** 事 293 q.v., here with its original meaning of **work**. Thus 287 originally meant **working person**. In time it also acquired a causative meaning, i.e. to **make a person work**, and **employ/use** eventually became extended to inanimate objects also. See also **official** 吏 1894, and suggest taking 吏 as this.

Mnemonic: **OFFICIAL PERSON USES SERVANT**

| 288 | 始 | **SHI, haji***meru/maru*
BEGIN, FIRST
8 strokes | 始終 SHIJŪ
始動機 SHIDŌKI
仕始める SHIHAJIMERU | throughout
starter
start to do |

Somewhat obscure. Once written 𡥆 and earlier as 𡥈. The later forms clearly show **name oneself** 台 166 q.v. The early form appears to use just **self/nose** 㠯/厶 134 without the **mouth/say** element 口 20. 女 is **woman** 35. 厶/台 is known to have acted phonetically to express **start**, giving **start of females** and by extension **first-born daughter**. Opinion differs, however, over its semantic role. Some scholars take 㠯/厶 to be **plow** 419 q.v., used in its meaning of **starting point** and thus reinforcing the phonetic **start**, and take 台 to be a miscopying. However, it seems questionable whether plow had acquired this meaning at the time of the form 𡥈. Other scholars take 㠯 to be **self** 134, with an associated meaning of **first person**, and take 台 to be a later deliberate use of 166 in its meaning of **announce oneself**, since the first born daughter would have spoken on behalf of all the daughters of a family. In any event, from **beginning of female line** 288 came to mean **first** and **beginning** in a broad sense. Suggest taking 台 in its modern meaning of **platform**.

Mnemonic: **FIRST WOMAN BEGINS TO MOUNT PLATFORM**

289 指 SHI, yubi, sasu
FINGER, POINT
9 strokes

指示 SHIJI — indication
親指 OYAYUBI — thumb
指図 SASHIZU — directions

扌 is hand 32. 旨 is good 1312, here used phonetically to express branch and possibly also lending an idea of good in the sense of skilful or useful. Thus (useful?) branches of the hand, i.e. fingers. Point is an associated meaning. Suggest taking 旨 as person sitting ヒ 238 and sun 日 62.

Mnemonic: PERSON SITS POINTING AT SUN WITH FINGER

290 歯 SHI, ha
TOOTH
12 strokes

歯根 SHIKON — dental root
歯医者 HAISHA — dentist
歯車 HAGURUMA — gear

Formerly 齒, and earlier 齒. The earliest form 𦥑 is a pictograph of teeth in a mouth ꕼ 20. Stop 止 129 was added later largely for its sound, to express row, but may also have lent an extended meaning of clamp. Its bottom stroke became fused with the upper stroke of mouth. Suggest taking the modern form as rice 米 201.

Mnemonic: TEETH ENSURE RICE STOPS IN MOUTH

291 詩 SHI
POETRY
13 strokes

詩人 SHIJIN — poet
詩的 SHITEKI — poetic
詩情 SHIJŌ — poetic feeling

言 is word 274. 寺 is temple 133 q.v., here used largely phonetically to express feeling but probably also lending connotations of regular, i.e. in this case rhythmic. Thus rhythmic words of feeling.

Mnemonic: WORDS FROM TEMPLE ARE PURE POETRY

292 次 JI, SHI, tsugi, tsugu
NEXT, FOLLOW
6 strokes

三次 SANJI — tertiary
次第 SHIDAI ni — gradually
相次いで AITSUIDE — in succession

Once written 二人, showing that 冫 derives from two 二 61. 欠 is lack/ gaping mouth 471 q.v., here meaning yawn. When one person yawns, a second invariably follows suit. Thus sequence. Suggest taking 冫 as ice 378.

Mnemonic: LACK OF ICE FOLLOWS NEXT

| 293 | 事 | JI, ZU, koto
THING, MATTER, ACT
8 strokes | 大事 DAIJI
好事 KŌZU
出来事 DEKIGOTO | importance
curiosity
event |

Once written 𝌗, and earlier as 𝌗. 乑 is a **hand**, but the precise meaning of 屮 is unclear. It appears to show a **flag on a pole** 屮 (see 333), with some scholars taking ⼝ to be an outer support for the flagpole (see 55) and others taking it to be a placard or **signboard**. In any event it seems likely that 293 originally showed a hand holding aloft some form of identification, taken to indicate a guild or similar engaged in a particular type of **work** (not unlike the distinctive pole once seen outside a barber's shop in the West). Certainly its early meaning was **work** and by extension **worker/servant**, and in Chinese it still retains servant as a reasonably major meaning. It is also the prototype of servant 使 287 q.v. (and see also official 吏 1894). Its present meanings are all felt to be extensions of **work**. Suggest taking the modern form as a mix of **ten** 十 33, **box** ⼝, and **hand** 彐.

Mnemonic: **HANDLING TEN BOXES IS NO SMALL THING**

| 294 | | JI, motsu
HOLD,HAVE,MAINTAIN
9 strokes | 持参 JISAN
持ち主 MOCHINUSHI
長持ち NAGAMOCHI | bringing
owner
durability |

扌 is **hand** 32. 寺 is **temple** 133 q.v., here acting phonetically to express **use** and also lending its early meaning of **use of the hands**. Thus to **use the hands**. Though somewhat vague, this appears to have originally meant to **hold** something up, leading to the present meanings of **support/ maintain** and **hold/ have**. Hold is also found in the extended sense of hold out, i.e. **last/ endure**.

Mnemonic: **HOLD HANDS AT TEMPLE**

| 295 | 式 | SHIKI
CEREMONY, FORM
6 strokes | 新式 SHINSHIKI
方式 HŌSHIKI
開会式 KAIKAISHIKI | new style
formula
opening ceremony |

工 is **carpenter's square** 113, here meaning **measure**. 弋 is a **stake** 177. 295 originally referred to stakes planted in the ground at measured intervals, giving **scale**. Scale then came to mean **set format** or **order**, leading to **pattern**, **style** etc. In Japanese it also refers by association to a **formal ceremony**.

Mnemonic: **CARPENTER'S SQUARE IS A FORM OF STAKE**

296 実 **JITSU, mi, minoru** 　　　実行 JIKKŌ 　　carrying out
(BEAR) FRUIT, TRUTH, 　　事実 JIJITSU 　　　fact
REALITY 　　　　　　　　　実入り MIIRI 　　crop, gains
8 strokes

Formerly 實 and originally 𡧊 . 田 is **field full of ripe crops** 504, with **shell/money** 貝 90 emphasising the value of the crop. ⼧ is **building** 28. 296 originally referred to a house made prosperous through bumper crops. The idea of house has now disappeared, leaving such meanings as **crop, fullness, substance, ripen**, and by extension **bear fruit** and **reality**. Unusually, the semi-abstract idea of bumper crop was also extended to the physical crop, giving **fruit, nut**, etc. The use of **threaded money** 貫 1102 is a longstanding miscopying, though it still gives a meaning of prosperous house. Suggest taking 夫 as a **big man** 大 53 with **six arms**.

Mnemonic: **IN REALITY, A BIG SIX-ARMED MAN IS IN THE HOUSE!**

---

297 写 **SHA, utsusu/ru** 　　　写真 SHASHIN 　photograph
COPY, TRANSCRIBE 　　写実 SHAJITSU 　　realism
5 strokes 　　　　　　　　複写機 FUKUSHAKI 　copier

Somewhat obscure. Formerly 寫 . ⼧ is **building** 28. 舄 is a CO character now used in a number of rather unhelpful meanings such as **shoe** and **large**. It comprises 𦥑, which is a simplified form of **bird** 鳥 174, and **mortar** 臼 648, and this appears to be a variant of a similar combination of bird and mortar (with the latter used purely phonetically) found in **owl** 舊 648 q.v. Thus presumably 舄 also originally meant owl, which is a <u>large</u> bird (though how it came to mean shoe is not clear). In the case of 297 it is known to have acted phonetically to express **transfer**, to give a meaning of **transfer from one building to another**. Its semantic role is not clear, though some scholars feel it could also mean **magpie**, a bird associated with removing items. It is also possible that 舄 suggested talons, and by extension seizing and **removing**. Transfer from one building to another came to mean **transfer** in a broader sense, and for some unclear reason later became particularly associated with transferring written items, i.e. **transcribing** or **copying**. The modern form uses **convey** 与 1873, partly as a graphic simplification and partly for its meaning.

Mnemonic: **CONVEY COPY OF BUILDING**

298 SHA, mono
PERSON
8 strokes

作者 SAKUSHA　　　author
後者 KŌSHA　　　the latter
若者 WAKAMONO

young people

Formerly 者 and earlier 𡆥. 日 is a **storage box** (container 口 plus contents -), while
米 is **kindling** (felt to be a combination of fire 丷/ 火 8 and wood 木 69). Thus **box
for storing kindling**. This became **box for storing odds and ends**, and eventually
just **odds and ends** or **various things**. Thing later became used as a somewhat unflat-
tering reference to certain **persons**, and later became **person** in a general sense. Suggest
taking 土 as **buried in the ground** 117, with 日 as **day** 62. Note that in compounds
298 often lends an idea of **many** (from **various things**).

Mnemonic: **PERSON WILL BE BURIED IN GROUND ONE DAY**

299 主 SHU, nushi, omo
MASTER,OWNER,MAIN
5 strokes

主人 SHUJIN master, husband
地主 JINUSHI　　　landowner
主要 SHUYŌ　　　principal

From a pictograph of an **ornately stemmed burning oil lamp** 𤔔 . It became a symbol of the **master** of the house, who issued the command for the lamp to be lit. Master led
to extended meanings such as **lord, owner, chief/main** etc. Suggest taking as **king** 王
5 and a **bit** 丶.

Mnemonic: **KING WITH BIT EXTRA IS REAL MASTER**

300 SHU, SU, mamor*u*
PROTECT, KEEP
6 strokes

保守 HOSHU　　　conservatism
留守番 RUSUBAN　　caretaker
子守 KOMORI *　　nursemaid

Building/house 宀 28 and **hand/measure** 寸 909, here meaning **regulate** or **administer**. Thus **looking after a house**, later to **keep** or **protect** in general.

Mnemonic: **TAKE MEASURES TO PROTECT HOUSE**

301 SHU, to*ru* 取得 SHUTOKU acquisition
TAKE, CONTROL 取り出す TORIDASU take out
8 strokes 牛取る GYŪJIRU* control

A **hand** 又 **taking hold** of an **ear** 耳 29. Usually explained as seizing a person by the ear, with the explanation often extended to ripping off the ear of a prisoner of war as a symbol of capture. Ripping off an ear by hand would be no easy matter, but it should be noted that there is a CO character 刵, using ear and cut 刂 181, which means cutting off a prisoner's ear. This was actually a punishment rather than a symbol of capture, but it may account for the popular misinterpretation of 301. It seems more likely that the ear actually represented an animal's ear. When **seizing** an animal that may bite or gore the ear is the safest part to **take hold** of. It is also a tender part, both for animals and humans, and thus an important part when attempting to **control** or subdue these. Thus **hand holding ear** represented both **seize/take** and **control**, though the latter is now a minor meaning.

Mnemonic: **HAND TAKES CONTROL OF EAR**

302 SHU, sake, saka- 飲酒 INSHU drinking
ALCOHOL, SAKE 酒場 SAKABA tavern
10 strokes 酒飲み SAKENOMI hard drinker

酉 is a pictograph of a **wine jar**, and symbolises **alcohol** in general. (It now exists as a minor NGU character indicating a zodiac sign, deriving from the fact that a particular type of spirit was brewed [actually from millet] at a fixed point [the eighth month] of the year.) 氵 is **water** 40, here indicating **liquid**. Thus **liquid in wine jar**, i.e. **alcohol**. In Japanese it also refers to **sake**.

Mnemonic: **WATERY ALCOHOL IN WINE JAR**

303 JU, u*keru* 受験者 JUKENSHA examinee
RECEIVE 受取 UKETORI receipt
8 strokes 受付 UKETSUKE reception

Once written 受, showing a **hand reaching down** 爫 (now an NGU character meaning claws/ talons), a **hand reaching up** 又, and 冖, the prototype of boat 舟 1354 q.v. which was often used as a symbol of **conveyance**. Thus to **convey from one hand to another**. 303 came to indicate the **receiving** hand, whereas the **giving** hand is now expressed by 授 702, which adds a further hand 扌 32. Suggest taking 冖 as a **baton**.

Mnemonic: **ONE HAND RECEIVES BATON FROM ANOTHER HAND**

304

SHŪ, su
PROVINCE, SANDBANK
6 strokes

本州 HONSHŪ   Honshu
砂州 SASU   sandbank
州議会 SHŪGIKAI
                     state parliament

Once written 州 and earlier as 州, showing a **sandbank** o in a **river** 川 48. The idea of small amount of land surrounded by water gave rise to **separate area**, i.e. a **state** or **province**.

Mnemonic: **SANDBANK IN RIVER IS SEPARATE PROVINCE**

305

SHŪ, JŪ, hiro*u*
PICK UP, GATHER,
TEN
9 strokes

収拾 SHŪSHŪ   control
拾い物 HIROIMONO   bargain
拾壱 JŪICHI   eleven

Hand 扌 32 and **join** 合 121, to give the idea of **using both hands** to **gather** or **pick up**. It also came to express **ten**, i.e. the **fingers of two hands**, and was in fact the precursor of ten 十 33.

Mnemonic: **JOINED HANDS CAN GATHER OR COUNT TO TEN**

---

306 終

SHŪ, owaru/eru
FINISH
11 strokes

終点 SHŪTEN   end, terminus
終止 SHŪSHI   termination
終わり OWARI ni   finally

Formerly 終, and once 夂 and 𢎨. 𢎨 is felt to be a pictograph of **ropes** with a **knot** in each **end** (to prevent fraying), and 夂 to be **ropes tied together**. Ropes tied together also led to **knot**, which by association meant **tying off** and thus **finishing**. **Thread** 糸 27 was added later for clarity. Suggest taking 冬 as **winter** 182.

Mnemonic: **THREADS FINISH IN WINTER**

307		SHŪ, narau LEARN, TRAIN 11 strokes	練習 RENSHŪ	practice
			習字 SHŪJI	penmanship
			見習い MINARAI	apprentice

Somewhat obscure. Once written 習 , and originally 習 . The upper part is **wings** 羽 812. The meaning of the lower part is unclear, but it is known to have acted phonetically to express **repeat**, giving **repeated (flapping of the) wings**. This was a reference to a **fledgling learning** to fly. Some scholars take 臼 / 白 to be a simplification of **self** 自 134 q.v., used to symbolise **proper being** and thus giving an idea of the fledgling learning to become a proper (i.e. mature) bird. However, the earlier form ○ does not support this view. It may be **mouth** 口 20 (later **say** 曰 688 or a variant of it?), thus suggesting a fledgling learning to become a bird through using its wings and mouth. Suggest taking 白 as **white** 65, which may even have been used deliberately at a later point since it has connotations of innocence, youth, and **amateurishness** (cf. shirōto, though technically this uses a different character for shiro).

Mnemonic: **WHITE WINGS LEARNING TO FLY**

308		SHŪ WEEK 11 strokes	先週 SENSHŪ	last week
			週間 SHŪKAN	week
			二週目 NISHŪME	second week

Movement 辶 129 and **around** 周 504. It originally meant to **go around**, giving both **cycle/ circuit** and **walk around** (both still retained in Chinese). Cycle eventually came to mean **cycle of time** and was used to mean **week**, especially in Japanese where it is now the sole meaning of 308.

Mnemonic: **ANOTHER WEEK ROLLS AROUND**

309		SHŪ, atsumeru/maru GATHER, COLLECT 12 strokes	集団 SHŪDAN	group
			編集 HENSHŪ	editing
			集中 SHŪCHŪ	concentration

Formerly 雧 , showing **birds** 隹 216 **gathered** in a **tree** 木 69. Now **gather** or **assemble** in general, including transitively.

Mnemonic: **BIRDS GATHER IN TREE**

310 JŪ, sum*u*
RESIDE, LIVE
7 strokes

住所 JŪSHO — address
住宅 JŪTAKU — dwelling
住み手 SUMITE — occupant

イ is **person** 39. 主 is **master** 299 q.v., here used for its literal meaning of oil **lamp** lit by master of house. Thus **where a person is master of the lamp**, i.e. the **house** where he **lives**.

Mnemonic: **WHERE PERSON LIVES IS WHERE HE IS MASTER**

---

311 重 JŪ, CHŌ, kasa*neru*/*naru*,
omo*i*, e
HEAVY, PILE, -FOLD
9 strokes

重大 JŪDAI — seriousness
重さ OMOSA — weight
三重 MIE — threefold

Once written 𤿤, showing **person** 人 39, **ground** 土 60, and **east** 東/東 184 q.v., here used for its literal meaning of (heavy) **sack**. Thus **person standing on ground carrying heavy sack**, leading to **heavy** in general including figuratively as **grave**. **Pile** (up) and **-fold** are felt to derive from the idea of adding to the weight being carried. 311 is unusual in that, although it is an ideograph and not a pictograph, it shows three elements arranged vertically, whereas one might have expected 俥 or similar in the interests of balanced appearance (see also 363). Suggest taking it as a **'double wheeled' vehicle** 車 31.

Mnemonic: **HEAVY VEHICLE HAS DOUBLE WHEELS**

---

312 所 SHO, tokoro
PLACE, SITUATION
8 strokes

場所 BASHO — place
所有 SHOYŪ — possession
居所 IDOKORO — address

Door 戸 108 and **ax/chop** 斤 1176. Usually explained as the doorway being the **place** where wood was chopped, which is a useful mnemonic but almost certainly incorrect. 戸 was used purely for its sound, which was originally KO (cf. English CUt) before changing to CHO (cf. English CHOp) and finally SHO (cf. English SHEar/SHOre/SHOrn). Thus the **KO (CHO/SHO) sound of something being chopped**. It is not fully clear how it came to mean **place**. Some scholars feel it was borrowed phonetically as a substitute for SHO place 處 896, but it may also have derived from a particular place associated with chopping (wood). Thus there may be some slight support for the 'chopping in a doorway' theory. **Place** has also come to be used figuratively to mean **situation** or **circumstances**.

Mnemonic: **CHOP DOWN DOOR WITH AX TO GET INTO PLACE**

93

313		SHO, atsui HOT (WEATHER) 12 strokes	酷暑 KOKUSHO	intense heat
			避暑地 HISHOCHI	cool resort
			暑さ ATSUSA	heat

Formerly 暑. 日 is sun 62. 者/者 is **person** 298 q.v., here acting phonetically to express **burn** and possibly also lending loose connotations of **much** (much/many being an occasional connotation lent by 298, felt to derive from its idea of various bits and pieces). Thus (**much?**) **burning sun**, i.e. **heat**.

Mnemonic: **PERSON UNDER HOT SUN**

314		JO, tasukeru/karu ASSIST, HELP 7 strokes	助手 JOSHU	assistant
			助力 JORYOKU	help, support
			助け合い TASUKEAI	mutual aid

Strength 力 74 and **furthermore/ cairn** 且 1091 q.v., here used for its original meaning of **build up/ add**. Thus **added strength**, i.e. **help**.

Mnemonic: **FURTHERMORE, HELP BY ADDING STRENGTH**

315		SHŌ BRIGHT, LIGHT 9 strokes	昭和 SHŌWA	Showa Period
			昭昭 SHŌSHO	brightness
			昭代 SHŌDAI	enlightened era

日 is **sun** 62, here indicating **brightness**. 召 is **summon** 1387, here acting phonetically to express **clear** and probably also lending an idea of **muster**. Thus (**a mustering of?**) **clarity** and **brightness**.

Mnemonic: **SUMMON SUN, AND LET THERE BE LIGHT**

316		SHŌ, kesu, kieru EXTINGUISH, VANISH, CONSUME 10 strokes	消費 SHŌHI	consumption
			消しゴム KESHIGOMU	eraser
			消火器 SHŌKAKI	fire extinguisher

Formerly 消. シ is **water** 40. 肖/肖 is **be like** 1391 q.v., here acting phonetically to express **few/ little** and also lending an idea of **reduced** from its original meaning of **miniature version**. The original meaning appears to have been **reduced to little water**, leading to the idea of **consuming** and hence **vanishing**. Suggest taking ⺌ as a variant of **little** 小 36 and 月 as **moon** 16.

Mnemonic: **WATER HAS VANISHED FROM OUR LITTLE MOON**

317

SHŌ, akina*u*
TRADE, DEAL, SELL,
SHANG CHINA
11 strokes

商業 SHŌGYŌ   commerce
商人 SHŌNIN   merchant
商売 SHŌBAI   business

Obscure. Owing to its similarity in meaning and shape to **sell** 売 192 q.v. it is often felt to be a variant of the latter, with **mouth/say** ㅂ 20 indicating **hawking**. However, the old forms of both characters show clearly that there is no connection. The oldest forms of 317 are 弄 and 喬. 丙 is almost certainly **spread thighs** (see also 1103), the plumpness indicating female thighs, with **opening** ㅂ 20 added to indicate **vagina**. 辛 is the early form of needle 辛 1432, which was often used to symbolise **pierce/ penetrate**. Thus 317 appears to have originally meant **vaginal penetration**, i.e. copulation. From this point the link with **trade** seems clear, i.e. the world's oldest trade of **prostitution**. A number of authoritative Japanese scholars, however, while accepting that 丙 is vagina, take 辛 to be used purely phonetically to express **birth**, giving **opening in female thighs that gives birth** and thus reinforcing the meaning **vagina**. That is, they feel that 317 meant simply vagina and not copulation, and that it was then borrowed purely phonetically as a substitute for a complex character meaning to **peddle**. This does not seem especially convincing. Even less convincing is the obviously incorrect but often heard explanation that 317 is a variant of **tall/high** 高 119, to the effect that it meant high plateau and that this name was given to dwellers of the high plains who were noted traders and who also became the ancient **Shang** dynasty. Certainly, however, the Shang period was associated with trade (and not prostitution or vaginas, though the apparent contemporaneity of the Shang period [c.1500-c.1000 B.C.according to some sources, and 1766-1122 B.C. according to others] and the early forms given above [c.1500 B.C.] might be felt to leave some room for doubt). Suggest taking 立 as a variant of **stand** 立 73, 冖 as a **counter**, ハ as **legs** 39, and 口 as **mouth** 20.

Mnemonic: USE MOUTH AND LEGS TO TRADE, STANDING AT COUNTER

318

SHŌ
BADGE, CHAPTER
11 strokes

記章 KISHŌ   medal, badge
文章 BUNSHŌ   writing, prose
章句 SHŌKU   chapter, passage

Once written 辛. 辛 is **needle** 辛 1432. The exact meaning of ⊖ is not clear, but it is felt to be a stylisation influenced by needle 十 33 q.v., which was originally written 十 with • indicating the eye. Whereas 33 was a sewing needle, 1432 was a **tattooist's needle**, and was used in particular for tattooing slaves (usually on the forehead). The **tattoo** was an **identifying mark**. This gave rise to the meaning **sign** or **badge**. It also came to mean **pattern**, and even ornamental and beautiful (still retained in Chinese), which was then applied to a **piece of writing** (not unlike pattern/text 文 68). Suggest taking as **stand** 立 73 and **quickly** 早 50. See also 340.

Mnemonic: BADGE QUICKLY STANDS OUT

| 319 勝 | SHŌ, ka*tsu*, masa*ru*
 WIN, SURPASS
 12 strokes | 勝利 SHŌRI
 勝負 SHŌBU
 勝ち気 KACHIKI | victory <br> outcome <br> spiritedness |

Formerly 勝 . 力 is **strength/effort** 74. 朕/朕 is a variant of **royal we** 朕 1603 q.v., here lending its sound to express **raise** and also lending similar connotations of its own. 319 originally referred to **exerting oneself in order to raise something.** This came to mean **succeed,** leading to **win** and **surpass.** Suggest taking 月 as **moon** 16, and 关 as **two** ニ 61 **fires** 火 8.

Mnemonic: **WITH EFFORT, TWO FIRES CAN SURPASS MOON**

| 320 | JŌ, no*ru*/*seru*
 RIDE, MOUNT, LOAD
 9 strokes | 乗船 JŌSEN
 乗数 JŌSŪ
 乗り物 NORIMONO | embarkation <br> multiplier <br> vehicle |

Formerly 乘 and earlier 椉, while the oldest form is 枽, showing a **person** 大 53 on top of a **tree** 木 69. Thus to **climb a tree,** with climb giving **mount** and thus **ride,** and **load** being the transitive form. The intermediate form 椉 shows person 人 39, tree 木, and **opposed feet** 舛 422, indicating a firm position in the treetop. Suggest remembering by association with **come** 来 217, taking ∠ as a variant of **two** ニ 61.

Mnemonic: **TWO COME RIDING**

| 321 | SHOKU, u*eru*
 PLANT
 12 strokes | 植物 SHOKUBUTSU
 田植え TAUE
 植民地 SHOKUMINCHI | flora <br> rice planting <br> colony |

Tree 木 69 and **straight** 直 349 q.v., meaning to **make a tree straight,** i.e. **plant.**

Mnemonic: **STRAIGHT TREE IS PROPERLY PLANTED**

| 322 申 | SHIN, mō*su*
 SAY, EXPOUND
 5 strokes | 申告 SHINKOKU
 申し込む MŌSHIKOMU
 申し訳 MŌSHIWAKE | report <br> apply <br> excuse |

Once written 𡴋 and 𦥒, showing a jagged bolt of **forked lightning.** It is in fact the prototype of lightning/ electricity 電 180 q.v. How exactly it came to mean **say/ expound** is not clear. Some scholars feel it was borrowed purely phonetically, others feel that it (also) lent a meaning of **speaking with the impact of lightning,** i.e. a forceful or dramatic speech, while still others feel that lightning was considered the **voice** of the gods (see also 324). It usually means **speak in detail.** Suggest taking as a pierced | **sun** 日 62.

Mnemonic: **SUN IS PIERCED: WHAT CAN ONE SAY?!**

323		SHIN, mi BODY 7 strokes	身体 SHINTAI	body
			自身 JISHIN	oneself
			身分 MIBUN	status

Once written 𠂤, showing a side-on view of the **body of a pregnant woman**. It originally meant pregnant body, but later came to mean **body** in a broad sense.

Mnemonic: **PREGNANT WOMAN HAS CONSPICUOUS BODY**

324		SHIN, JIN, kami GOD, SPIRIT 9 strokes	精神 SEISHIN	spirit
			神父 SHINPU	priest
			女神 MEGAMI*	goddess

Formerly 神. 示/礻 is **altar** 695, here in its extended sense of **related to the gods**. 申 is **say** 322 q.v., here in its literal sense of **lightning**. Lightning was thought to be a manifestation of the **gods** (some scholars feel **voice of the gods**). **Spirit** is an associated meaning.

Mnemonic: **GODS SAY SOMETHING SPIRITED AT ALTAR**

325		SHIN, fukai/meru DEEP, DEEPEN 11 strokes	深遠 SHINEN	profundity
			深海 SHINKAI	deep sea
			深入り FUKAIRI	going deeply

Once written 𣲽. 川/氵 is **water** 40. 罙 is an element showing **hole** 穴 849, **hand** 又, and **fire** 火 8. It originally referred to a hand reaching into a chimney to remove the soot, then came to mean **chimney-like hole**. Thus **hole in water**, indicating a **deep** part of a river or similar. The modern form has mistakenly used **tree** 木 69, with 冖 being a variant of hole 穴.

Mnemonic: **FIND DEEP WATERHOLE NEAR TREE**

326		SHIN, susumu/meru ADVANCE 11 strokes	前進 ZENSHIN	advance
			進化 SHINKA	evolution
			進言 SHINGEN	proposition

Movement 辶 129 and **bird** 隹 216, giving **move like a bird**, i.e. **forwards**.

Mnemonic: **ADVANCE LIKE MOVING BIRD**

327		SEI, SE, yo WORLD, GENERATION 5 strokes	世紀 SEIKI 世話 SEWA 世の中 YONONAKA	century care the world

Once written 卋 and 𠀍, both being stylised versions of **three tens** 十 33. **Thirty years** was the norm for a **generation**, and this later came to mean **the times** and **the world at large**. See also 405.

Mnemonic: **ODD WORLD OF THE THIRTIES' GENERATION**

328		SEI, totono*u/eru* ARRANGE 16 strokes	整理 SEIRI 整備 SEIBI̅ 微調整 BICHŌSEI	arrangement maintenance fine tuning

正 is **proper/ correct** 41. 敕 is **edict** 1600 q.v., here with its literal meaning of **enforcing correct action**. Thus to **make someone act correctly**, giving **bring order** and thus **arrange**. Suggest taking 敕 literally as **bundle** 束 1535 and **stick in hand/ force** 攵 101.

Mnemonic: **FORCE CORRECT ARRANGEMENT OF BUNDLES**

329		SEN LINE 15 strokes	脱線 DASSEN 光線 KŌSEN 直線 CHOKUSEN	derailment light ray straight line

糸 is **thread** 27. 泉 is **source/ spring** 915, here acting phonetically to express **slender** and also lending a similar idea (from a **thin** stream of water). Thus **slender thread**, eventually giving **line**.

Mnemonic: **TRACE THREAD-LIKE LINE TO SOURCE**

330	全	ZEN, matta*ku* WHOLE, COMPLETE(LY) 6 strokes	全部 ZENBU 全身 ZENSHIN 安全 ANZEN	all whole body safety

𠆢 is a **cover** 87. 王 is **jewel** 102. Thus **jewel under cover**, indicating a protected and therefore precious jewel. A precious jewel was a **perfect**, unblemished one, and the idea of perfect eventually came to mean **whole** or **complete**. Suggest taking 王 as **king** 5.

Mnemonic: **KING COMPLETELY UNDER COVER**

331	SŌ, oku*ru*	放送 HŌSŌ	broadcast
送	SEND	送金 SŌKIN	remittance
	9 strokes	見送る MIOKURU	see off

辶 is **movement** 129. 关 is the right hand part of **royal we** 朕 1603 q.v., with its meaning of **raise repeatedly**. Here it lends an extended idea of **following on** (from repeat), and also lends its sound to express **follow**. Thus **move and follow**. This originally referred to a **servant following** his master. Then, in very similar fashion to servant following/ send 遣 1220 q.v., it came to mean **servant sent on errands** and then just **send**. Suggest taking 天 as **heaven** 58 and ゛as **away** 66.

Mnemonic: **SENT AWAY FROM HEAVEN**

332	SOKU, iki	休息 KYŪSOKU	rest
息	BREATH,REST,CHILD	ため息 TAMEIKI	sigh
	10 strokes	息子 MUSUKO*	son

自 is **self** 134 q.v., here with its literal meaning of **nose**. 心 is **heart** 147, here meaning **essence of life**. The essence of life associated with the nose is **air that one breathes**. It is not fully clear how this also came to mean **rest** and **child**, but it is possible that rest is an associated meaning of breath (cf. English [take a] breather).

Mnemonic: **HEART BREATHES THROUGH NOSE**

333	ZOKU	家族 KAZOKU	family
族	CLAN, FAMILY	民族 MINZOKU	race
	11 strokes	種族 SHUZOKU	tribe

Once written 㫃, showing an **arrow** 夨 / 矢 981 under a **streaming banner** 〰 tied to a crude **pole** 丫. There is some disagreement over the exact role of these elements, but many scholars take them to indicate a mustering or rallying of arms under a banner, with the idea of **people forming a group** eventually leading to **clan** and **family**. It can also occasionally mean **gather**. The modern form of streaming banner, 方, derives from a rather confusing stylisation 㫃. Suggest taking it as **side** 方 204 and **person** 𠂉 39.

Mnemonic: **PERSON WITH ARROW IN SIDE IS ONE OF THE CLAN**

334 他	TA, hoka	他人 TANIN	stranger
	OTHER	他国 TAKOKU	foreign land
	5 strokes	他所 YOSO*	elsewhere

Person ｲ 39 and **twisting creature** 也 167. Some scholars take the latter to mean **twisting**, which could sometimes mean by extension **unusual** (see also 1041), thus giving **unusual person** and hence **stranger** or **person from other parts**. Other scholars take twisting creature (either snake or scorpion) as a symbol of something dangerous, giving **dangerous person**, which was also a reference to an **unusual person** and hence person from other parts. Person from other parts came to mean **other** in general.

Mnemonic: **OTHER PERSON IS LIKE TWISTING CREATURE**

335 打	DA, *utsu*	打者 DASHA	batter
	HIT, STRIKE	打撃 DAGEKI	blow
	5 strokes	打ち返す UCHIKAESU	hit back

扌 is **hand** 32. 丁 is **nail** 346, acting phonetically to express **strike** and possibly also lending an idea of **something to be struck**. Thus to **strike with the hand**, now **strike** in a broader sense.

Mnemonic: **HAND HITS NAIL**

336 対	TAI, TSUI	反対 HANTAI	opposition
	OPPOSE, AGAINST,	対象 TAISHŌ	object
	PAIR	対句 TSUIKU	couplet
	7 strokes		

Formerly 對. 丵 is the same complex **musical instrument** seen in profession 業 260 q.v. 寸 is **measure/hand** 909, here with its meaning of **regulate**. Thus 336 originally referred to adjusting the complex instrument. This involved balancing the crosspieces from which the bells were hung, leading to an idea of **counterbalance**. This eventually came to mean **be set in an opposed position**, usually of items in a **pair**. Suggest taking 文 as a variant of **text** 文 68.

Mnemonic: **MEASURE OPPOSITION TO TEXT**

337　待　TAI, ma*tsu*　　　待機 TAIKI　　awaiting chance
　　　　　　WAIT　　　　　　招待 SHŌTAI　　invitation
　　　　　　9 strokes　　　　　待ち伏せ MACHIBUSE　　ambush

Movement along a road 彳 118 and temple 寺 133 q.v. The latter acts phonetically to express **stop**, to give **stop moving** and hence **wait**. It is not clear why 寺 was used instead of the simpler stop 止 129, but it may possibly lend an idea of **being active** (with the hands), thus suggesting **occupying oneself** while **waiting**.

Mnemonic: **WAIT AT TEMPLE BESIDE ROAD**

338　代　DAI, TAI, ka*waru/eru*, yo　　世代 SEDAI　　generation
　　　　　　REPLACE, WORLD,　　　交代 KŌTAI　　alternation
　　　　　　GENERATION, FEE　　　部屋代 HEYADAI　　room rent
　　　　　　5 strokes

彳 is **person** 39. 弋 is **stake** 177, here acting phonetically to express **replace** and possibly loosely lending similar connotations since stakes were generally of a set size and thus **interchangeable**. Thus **replacement person**, meaning a representative or stand-in. This gradually broadened to mean **generation**, i.e. people who replace others, and by extension **the times/world**, and also to mean **exchange** in a general sense. **Fee** is an associated idea, being exchanged for goods or services.

Mnemonic: **PERSON REPLACED BY STAKE**

339　第　DAI　　　　　　　第二課 DAINIKA　　Chapter Two
　　　　　　GRADE, ORDER　　次第書 SHIDAISHO　　program
　　　　　　11 strokes　　　　　及第 KYŪDAI　　making grade

竹 is **bamboo** 170, here meaning **bamboo tablets** used for keeping records. 弔 is a variant of **younger brother** 弟 177 q.v., here with its literal meaning of **order/ sequence**. Thus to **put bamboo tablets in order**, leading to **order/ sequence** in general. See also 361.

Mnemonic: **BAMBOO TOPS YOUNG BROTHER IN ORDER OF THINGS**

340 題	DAI SUBJECT, TITLE 18 strokes	問題 MONDAI problem, issue 題名 DAIMEI title 話題 WADAI topic

頁 is **head** 93. 是 is **proper** 910, here used phonetically to express **hairless** and possibly also loosely lending an idea of **straight** and by extension **flat**. The (flat?) hairless part of the head is the **forehead**, the original meaning of 340 (a meaning still listed in some Chinese dictionaries). Some scholars make a direct link between **forehead** and **title** in the same way as the English term **heading**. This is a useful mnemonic, but it seems more likely the evolution was somewhat similar to badge/chapter 章 318 q.v. That is, slaves were tattooed on the forehead with identifying marks, with **identifying mark** coming to mean **title** or **subject**. Suggest taking 是 as **day** 日 62 and **correct** 正 41.

Mnemonic: **GET SUBJECT HEADING CORRECT ON THE DAY**

341 炭	TAN, sumi CHARCOAL, COAL 9 strokes	石炭 SEKITAN coal 炭素 TANSO carbon 炭火 SUMIBI charcoal fire

Somewhat obscure. Popularly explained as **combustible material** (from fire 火 8) taken from the **side** (from cliff 厂 45) of a **hill (mountain)** 山 24. This is a useful mnemonic for the modern form, but the older form 炭 shows that 厂 is not cliff, but a simplification of 屮. This appears to be **hand**, with 灰/灰 seeming to be **ash** 818 q.v. Thus **ash and hill**, presumably a reference to **charcoal burning** that was normally carried out in the hills. However, some scholars maintain that 屵 is used as a purely phonetic element meaning **return**, giving **fire that returns (to fire)**, i.e. **charcoal**. **Coal** and **charcoal** are associated in meaning.

Mnemonic: **FIERY MATERIAL FROM MOUNTAIN CLIFF IS COAL**

342 短	TAN, mijika*i* SHORT 12 strokes	短所 TANSHO shortcoming 短気 TANKI short temper 手短か TEMIJIKA brief

Arrow 矢 981 and **food vessel** 豆 1640. Arrows were generally of a fixed length and were occasionally used as crude **measures** (cf. English measures rod, perch, pole etc., and note that the addition of big/ carpenter's square 巨 1153 gives the NGU character rule/ measuring square 矩). 豆 acts phonetically to express **small**, and almost certainly lends a similar idea of generally **fixed dimensions**. (Though in many cases 豆 is used in characters in a rather vague sense to mean food vessel in general, technically it refers to a small one-legged table for one person [takatsuki], of a more or less fixed height.) Thus **small measurement** (comparable to arrow and food vessel), i.e. **short**.

Mnemonic: **BOTH ARROW AND FOOD VESSEL ARE SHORT**

| 343 | | CHAKU, tsu*ku*, ki*ru*
ARRIVE, WEAR
12 strokes | 到着 TŌCHAKU
着物 KIMONO
船着き FUNATSUKI | arrival
clothing
anchorage |

A variant of remarkable/show/**wear**/**arrive** 著 937, q.v. Suggest taking 䒑 as **sheep** 986, 目 as **eye** 72, and ／ as a **line**.

Mnemonic: **SHEEP ARRIVES WEARING EYE-LINER!**

| 344 | | CHŪ, sosog*u*
POUR, NOTE
8 strokes | 注目 CHŪMOKU
注射 CHŪSHA
注釈 CHŪSHAKU | attention
injection
notes |

氵 is **water** 40. 主 is **master** 299 q.v., acting phonetically to express **continuous** and almost certainly also lending an idea of **column** from its literal meaning of long stemmed lamp (see also 345). Thus **continuous column of water**, giving **pour**. Also used figuratively as pour one's thoughts, i.e. **pay attention**.

Mnemonic: **MASTER POURS WATER**

| 345 | 柱 | CHŪ, hashira
COLUMN, PILLAR
9 strokes | 柱石 CHŪSEKI
電柱 DENCHŪ
氷柱 TSURARA* | pillar
telegraph pole
icicle |

木 is **wood** 69. 主 is **master** 299 q.v., acting phonetically to express **firm** and also lending an idea of **column** from its original meaning of long stemmed lamp. Thus **firm wooden column**, now **column** or **pillar** in a broader sense including the figurative.

Mnemonic: **MASTER WOODEN PILLAR**

| 346 | | CHŌ, TEI
BLOCK, EXACT
2 strokes | 丁度 CHŌDO
丁寧 TEINEI
丁目 CHŌME | exactly
civility
city block |

Once written 丁, depicting a **nail**. This meaning has now been taken over by an NGU character that adds metal 金 14, 釘, while 346 itself has come to be borrowed widely, both for its sound and its shape. **Block** comes from the idea of intersecting paths/ lines suggested by the shape (see also town/ block 町 57), while **exact** may, like the English term **to a T**, come from a suggestion of a carpentry joint.

Mnemonic: **BLOCK IS EXACT TO A T**

347 帳

CHŌ
REGISTER, DRAPE
11 strokes

手帳	TECHŌ	notebook
帳場	CHŌBA	counter, desk
蚊帳	KAYA*	mosquito net

巾 is **cloth** 778. 長 is **long** 173, here also acting phonetically to express **spread**. Thus **long spread cloth**, giving **drape**. It is not fully clear how it came to mean **register**, but it seems likely that records were kept on (rolls of) cloth before (scrolls of) paper became common.

Mnemonic: **LONG CLOTH DRAPE USED AS REGISTER**

---

348 調

CHŌ, shira*beru*, totono*eru*
ADJUST, INVESTIGATE, TONE, TUNE
15 strokes

調整	CHŌSEI	adjustment
調査	CHŌSA	investigation
調子	CHŌSHI	tone, condition

Words/speak 言 274 and **around** 周 504. The original meaning was **discuss comprehensively** (i.e. talk all around a topic). From this it acquired meanings such as **examine, adjust** (one's views), and **overall situation** (leading to **condition**). Adjustment and condition were also applied to music, giving **tone** and **melody** (cf. English tune, etymologically the same word as tone).

Mnemonic: **INVESTIGATE BY TALKING AROUND**

---

349 直

CHOKU, JIKI, nao*ru/su*, su*gu*, tada*chi*
DIRECT,UPRIGHT,FIX
8 strokes

直接	CHOKUSETSU	direct
正直	SHŌJIKI	honesty
直立	CHOKURITSU	erect

Once written [illegible], and earlier as [illegible]. θ / 目 is **eye** 72, here meaning **look.** | / 十 is **needle** 33, here acting phonetically to express **direct** as well as lending an idea of **pierce.** Thus **direct, piercing stare.** The later addition 乚 is a **corner**, felt by some scholars to indicate the object of the stare being **fixed in place**, and by others to indicate (attempted) **concealment**, giving **stare at something supposed to be hidden**. In very similar fashion to the English term **fix,** which can mean fix with a stare or make straight and/or firm, the meaning of 349 broadened from **fix with direct stare** to fix in the sense of **mend**, while **direct** also came to mean **straight** and **proper** and by extension **upright/ honest**. Suggest taking 十 in its modern sense of **ten.**

Mnemonic: **TEN EYES FIXED DIRECTLY ON CORNER**

350		TSUI, *ou* **CHASE, PURSUE** 9 strokes	追究 TSUIKYŪ	inquiry
			追放 TSUIHŌ	banishment
			追い払う OIHARAU	drive off

辶 is **movement** 129. 㠯 has long been confused with **terraced hill** 阝 / 阝 229, and even exists as a CO character meaning pile or heap, but the oldest forms such as 㠯 show that it is in fact a pair of **buttocks**. Here it acts phonetically to express **chase**, and almost certainly lends an idea of **person's rear**. Thus to **move in pursuit of a person**. Though it originally meant chase in the sense of pursue, it can now also mean **chase off**. Pursue can also be used in the sense of **conduct** (investigations etc.).

Mnemonic: **PURSUE MOVING BUTTOCKS**

351		TEI, JŌ, sada*meru* **FIX, ESTABLISH** 8 strokes	定期 TEIKI	fixed term
			不定 FUTEI	indefinite
			決定 KETTEI	decision

Roof/building ウ 28 and **correct** 疋 / 正 41. 351 originally referred to the correct erection of the framework of a building, then came to mean **establish** or **fix** in a broader sense.

Mnemonic: **FIX ROOF CORRECTLY**

352		TEI, niwa **GARDEN, COURTYARD** 10 strokes	家庭 KATEI	household
			庭園 TEIEN	garden
			庭師 NIWASHI	
				master gardener

广 is **large building** 114, here meaning **palace**. 廷 is **court** 1610 q.v., here with its literal meaning of **people standing around at court**. People generally did their waiting at the palace/ court in the **courtyard** or **garden**.

Mnemonic: **PALACE COURTYARD IS FINE GARDEN**

353

TETSU, kurogane
IRON, STEEL
13 strokes

鉄板 TEPPAN   steel plate
地下鉄 CHIKATETSU   subway
国鉄 KOKUTETSU
                  (former) National Railway

Formerly 鐵. 金 is **metal** 14. 𢧜 (also 𢦏') is an element known to have meant **big**, though for unclear reasons it is listed in some Chinese dictionaries (without illustration) as a character meaning scrape or advantageous. It was once written 𢧜, showing that 𢦏 is not the usual cut 𢦏 872, which is to all intents and purposes a variant of cut/ halberd 戈 493, but 493 plus big 大 53. 呈 is offer 1611. Thus 𢧜 presumably originally meant **cut up a big offering**. In the case of 353 it acts phonetically to express **black**, and presumably also lends an idea of **big** (i.e. **massive**). Thus **massive black metal**, a reference to **iron** and by extension **steel**. Note that kurogane literally means **black metal**. Suggest taking the modern simplification 失 as **lose** 501. See also 263.

Mnemonic: **LOST METAL PROVES TO BE IRON**

354

TEN, koro*geru/garu/gasu/bu*
ROTATE, ROLL, TUMBLE
11 strokes

転送 TENSŌ   forwarding
運転 UNTEN   driving
自転車 JITENSHA   bicycle

Formerly 轉. 車 is **vehicle** 31. 專 is the old form of exclusive 専 914 q.v., here acting phonetically to express **move** and also lending an idea of **rotating** from its literal meaning of spinning weight. Thus **rotational movement of vehicle**, i.e. **roll**. It is also used to mean **rotate** and **tumble**. Suggest taking 云 as **two** 二 61 **noses** 厶 134.

Mnemonic: **VEHICLE ROLLS OVER TWO NOSES**

355

TO, TSU, miyako
CAPITAL, METROPOLIS
11 strokes

都市 TOSHI   city
首都 SHUTO   capital
都合 TSUGŌ   circumstances

阝 is not hill 229 but an element meaning **village**, deriving from the NGU character village 邑 (once 㕞, felt to show an enclosure 口 and a sitting person 㔾, indicating at ease). 者 is **person** 298 q.v., acting phonetically to express **gather** and also lending its connotations of **many** and **various** in addition to **person**. Thus **village where many and various persons are gathered**, i.e. a **big town**.

Mnemonic: **METROPOLIS IS VILLAGE OF MANY PERSONS**

106

356 DO, TAKU, tabi 程度 TEIDO degree
DEGREE, TIMES 温度 ONDO temperature
9 strokes 一度 ICHIDO once

庐 is an abbreviation of **various** 庶, 1381, and also acts phonetically to express **measure**. 又 is **hand**, which was often used for **measuring** things. Thus to **measure various things with the hand**, finally giving **measurement** in a range of senses. It is not clear why measure/hand 寸 909 was not used instead of just hand. Suggest taking 广 as **building** 114, with 廿 as **two tens** 十 33 and **one** 一 1, i.e. **twenty-one**.

Mnemonic: **HAND MEASURES TWENTY-ONE DEGREES IN BUILDING**

357 TŌ, na*geru* 投手 TŌSHU pitcher
THROW, CAST 投票 TŌHYŌ vote
7 strokes 投げ出す NAGEDASU abandon

Hand 扌 32 and **strike with ax** 殳 153. The latter also acts phonetically to mean **throw**. Thus **throw a weapon**, then just **throw**.

Mnemonic: **HAND STRIKES BY THROWING AX**

358 TŌ, shima 列島 RETTŌ archipelago
ISLAND 島民 TŌMIN islanders
10 strokes 島国 SHIMAGUNI
island nation

Formerly 嶋 and 㠀, clearly showing **bird** 鳥 174 and **mountain** 山 24. **Mountains where birds alight** is a reference to **islands in the sea**. Some scholars feel that 鳥 also acts phonetically to express **tide** and by extension **sea**, thus clarifying the interpretation of the character.

Mnemonic: **BIRD ALIGHTS ON MOUNTAINOUS ISLAND**

359 湯 TŌ, yu 銭湯 SENTŌ public bath
HOT WATER 湯気 YUGE steam
12 strokes 茶の湯 CHANOYU tea ceremony

氵 is **water** 40. 昜 is **rising sun** 144, indicating **becoming hot**. Thus **heated water**.

Mnemonic: **RISING SUN HEATS WATER**

107

360 TŌ, TO, nobor*u*
CLIMB
12 strokes

登場 TŌJŌ　　appearance
登山 TOZAN　　mountaineering
木登り KINOBORI　tree climbing

Somewhat obscure. Once written 登, showing **two feet** 129, **hands** , and **food vessel** 豆 1640 q.v. It is not fully clear how these elements combined. Some scholars see them as as a virtual pictograph depicting a child or similar clambering onto the food vessel (this being taken in its literal meaning of a single legged table that could be several feet high). Others take 豆 to be used purely phonetically to express **climb**, giving **climbing feet (and hands)**. Still others take the hands to be **offering** up the food vessel (here meaning just dish of food), and take the element to be used phonetically to express **climb** as well as lending connotations of **raise/ rise**, thus giving **climbing (and rising) feet**. The last theory seems the most likely, though the first is perhaps the simplest to remember.

Mnemonic: **TWO FUNNY FEET CLIMB FOOD VESSEL**

---

361 等 TŌ, hito*shii*, na*do*
CLASS, EQUAL,
ETCETERA
12 strokes

一等 ITTŌ　　first class
上等 JŌTŌ　　high class
等圧線 TŌATSUSEN　isobar

Bamboo 竹 170, here meaning **bamboo tablets** used for keeping records, and **temple** 寺 133 q.v., which acts phonetically to express **arrange** and also lends its idea of **work with the hands**. Thus to **arrange bamboo tablets** (with the hands). This is very similar to order/ arrange bamboo tablets 第 339, but whereas 339 means putting in <u>sequential</u> order, 361 means putting in <u>**equal groups**</u>. Group of equal or similar items led to **class, equal**, and by extension **etcetera**.

Mnemonic: **BAMBOO TABLETS AT TEMPLE ARE ALL EQUAL**

---

362 DŌ, ugo*ku/kasu*
MOVE
11 strokes

動物 DŌBUTSU　　animal
自動車 JIDŌSHA　vehicle
動き出す UGOKIDASU　move off

力 is **strength** 74. 重 is **heavy** 311, which also acts phonetically to express **sway**. Thus to **apply strength and cause something heavy to sway**, leading to **move**.

Mnemonic: **STRENGTH MOVES HEAVY OBJECT**

363

童

DŌ, warabe
CHILD
12 strokes

童話 DŌWA　　　nursery tale
児童 JIDŌ　　　children
童心 DŌSHIN　　child's mind

Somewhat obscure. Once written , possibly the most esthetically unbalanced of all the characters in that it combines four elements vertically. The elements are, in descending order, **needle** 辛 / 辛 1432, **eye** ⌀ / 目 72, east/ **sack** 東 /東 184, and **ground** 土 60. The original meaning is known to have been **slave**, and it seems likely that it is the early form of **heavy** 重 / 重 311 q.v., namely **person standing on the ground carrying heavy sack**, with person 𠆢 replaced by the combination of eye and (tattooist's) needle. (This substitution would partly explain the awkward vertical alignment.) Slaves had an identification mark tattooed on the forehead (see 340), i.e. above the eye, and it therefore seems probable that 辛 indicates slave. Thus <u>slave</u> **standing on ground carrying heavy sack**. How this came to mean **child** is not clear. Child slaves were far from uncommon so it may have been an associated meaning, though this is unlikely. Some scholars feel it was used instead of a CO character meaning **child**, 僮, comprising person 亻 39 and slave 童 363, in which 童 is believed to lend a meaning to the effect of **person not having full rights as a citizen** as well as lending its sound to express **growing up**. Suggest taking the modern form of 363 as **stand** 立 73 and **village** 里 219.

Mnemonic: **CHILD STANDS IN VILLAGE**

364

内

NAI, DAI, uchi
INSIDE
4 strokes

内部 NAIBU　　　inner part
家内 KANAI　　　　wife
内気 UCHIKI　　　shyness

Formerly 內, and earlier , showing **enter** 𠆢 / 入 63 q.v. and a **dwelling** ∩/冂. Once entered, one is **inside**. Suggest taking 人 as **person** 39 and 冂 as a **hoop**.

Mnemonic: **PERSON TRIES TO GET INSIDE HOOP**

365

肉

NIKU
MEAT, FLESH
6 strokes

馬肉 BANIKU　　　horsemeat
肉屋 NIKUYA　　　butcher
肉眼 NIKUGAN　　　naked eye

From a pictograph of a **fillet of meat** showing the graining of the flesh 肉. As a radical usually 月, and often having a meaning of **relating to the body**. Suggest remembering as **inside** 内 364 q.v. and **person** 人 39.

Mnemonic: **INSIDE PERSON THERE IS MEAT**

| 366 | | NŌ
FARMING
13 strokes | 農場 NŌJŌ
農民 NŌMIN
農業 NŌGYŌ | farm
farmers
agriculture |

辰 is now an NGU character used for dragon, but its original meaning was **clam** (now conveyed by an NGU character 蜃, that adds insect 虫 56). It derives from a pictograph of a clam with fleshy feelers protruding 𝅘. The clam shell was used as a crude cutting tool, and so 辰 occasionally symbolises **cutting**, as here. 曲 is not **bend** 曲 261, though it may be helpful to remember it as such. One early form of 366 shows it as 𝅘, which clearly reveals hands 𝅘 held to a brain/head 𝅘 131. This has been interpreted by some scholars as **racking one's brains**, and has resulted in some intriguing theories attempting to link clam, racking one's brains, and farming. However, still older forms such as 𝅘 and 𝅘 show that 𝅘 is a miscopying of **field** 田 59 and either **plants/grass** ⼗⼗9 or **trees** 木 69. Thus the original meaning of 366 was **cutting grass/trees to clear fields**, giving **working on the land** and hence **farming**.

Mnemonic: **FARMING UNEARTHS BENT CLAM SHELL**

| 367 | | HA, nami
WAVE
8 strokes | 周波 SHŪHA
音波 ONPA
波乗り NAMINORI | frequency
sound wave
surfing |

氵 is **water** 40. 皮 is **skin** 374 q.v., here acting phonetically to express **rise and fall** and probably also lending an idea of **peeling off**. Thus **water which rises and falls** (and peels off?), i.e. **wave**.

Mnemonic: **WAVES FORM SKIN OF WATER**

| 368 | 配 | HAI, kubaru
DISTRIBUTE
10 strokes | 心配 SHINPAI
配達 HAITATSU
配り手 KUBARITE | worry
delivery
(card) dealer |

Somewhat obscure. Once written 酉乁, showing **wine jar** 酉 302 and a **kneeling person** 八 39, but the role of these elements is not clear as there is almost no example of historical usage. In the absence of evidence to the contrary it is assumed to indicate a person pouring -- i.e. **distributing** -- wine. Suggest taking 己 as **self** 855.

Mnemonic: **DISTRIBUTE WINE TO ONESELF**

| 369 | | hata, hatake
(DRY-)FIELD
9 strokes | 茶畑 CHABATAKE tea field
田畑 TAHATA field, estate
麦畑 MUGIBATAKE
wheat field |

A 'made in Japan' character comprising field 田 59 and fire 火 8, giving **field that is burned off** (as opposed to a paddy field).

Mnemonic: **BURNED FIELD IS A DRY FIELD**

| 370 | | HATSU, HOTSU
DISCHARGE, START,
LEAVE
9 strokes | 発表 HAPPYŌ announcement
発足 HOSSOKU inauguration
発電機 HATSUDENKI generator |

Formerly 發. 癶 is two (planted) feet 360, here indicating standing firm. 弓 is bow 836. 殳 is strike/ hand holding weapon 153. Thus to take up firm stance and shoot arrow from bow. This has led to a range of derived meanings such as discharge, leave, and by extension start. Suggest taking 尢 as two 二 61 bent legs 儿 39.

Mnemonic: **DISCHARGED WITH TWO BENT LEGS AND FUNNY FEET**

| 371 | | HAN, TAN, soru/rasu
OPPOSE,ANTI,REVERSE,
BEND,CLOTH,MEASURE
4 strokes | 反応 HANNŌ* reaction
反核 HANKAKU anti-nuclear
反物 TANMONO textiles |

又 is a hand. 厂 is cliff 45, acting phonetically to express turn over, and probably also lending an idea of abrupt (an occasional connotation of cliff, from the idea of abrupt rise). 371 originally meant suddenly turn the hand over. This led to a range of derived meanings, such as go against or oppose, reverse, and twist or bend. In Japanese it is also used of cloth, from the idea of a draper flicking out a roll of cloth, and can mean a measure of cloth (a roll of some 10m), as well as a measure of area.

Mnemonic: **CLIFF OPPOSES HAND**

372

HAN, saka
SLOPE
7 strokes

急坂 KYŪHAN　　steep slope
坂道 SAKAMICHI　　slope
下り坂 KUDARIZAKA downhill

Ground 土 60 and oppose 反 371. The latter is used primarily for its sound, to express **slanting**, but may also lend an idea of **reverse** (i.e. a slope can be either an upgrade or a downgrade) or of **opposition/ resistance** (i.e. an upgrade). Thus **slanting ground**.

Mnemonic: **SLOPE IS OPPOSED GROUND**

373

HAN, BAN, ita
BOARD, PLATE
8 strokes

黒板 KOKUBAN　　blackboard
板紙 ITAGAMI　　cardboard
板前 ITAMAE　　chef

Wood 木 69 and oppose 反 371. The latter is used primarily for its sound, to express **thin (and flat)**, but may also lend an idea of **reverse** (i.e. a board is reversible). Thus **thin, flat piece of wood**, i.e. **board**, now also used of non-wooden **sheets** or **plates**.

Mnemonic: **OPPOSED TO WOODEN BOARDS**

374

HI, kawa
SKIN, LEATHER
5 strokes

皮膚 HIFU　　skin
皮肉 HINIKU　　sarcasm
木の皮 KINOKAWA　　bark

From a pictograph 皮, showing a hand 又 pulling the **hide** off an animal with its head still attached 厂. Suggest remembering by association with **oppose** 反 371, with ノ as **one stroke**.

Mnemonic: **OPPOSED TO SKINNING WITH ONE STROKE**

375

HI, kana*shii/shimu*
SAD
12 strokes

悲劇 HIGEKI　　tragedy
悲鳴 HIMEI　　shriek, wail
悲しさ KANASHISA　　sadness

心 is **heart/feelings** 147. 非 is **not** 773 q.v., acting phonetically to express **sad** and also lending connotations of **splitting open** (from its literal meaning of wings opening in opposite directions). Thus **sad feelings which rend the heart**.

Mnemonic: **BROKEN HEART DOES NOT WANT TO BE SAD**

112

376

BI, utsuku*shii*
BEAUTIFUL, FINE
9 strokes

美人 BIJIN　　　a beauty, belle
美術 BIJUTSU　　　fine arts
美学 BIGAKU　　　esthetics

Sheep 羊 986 and **big** 大 53. A **big** (i.e. fat) **sheep** was highly prized and **desirable**. **Desirable appearance** eventually led to **beautiful** in a broad sense.

Mnemonic: **BEAUTIFUL BIG SHEEP**

377

BI, hana
NOSE
14 strokes

鼻音 BION　　　nasal sound
鼻先 HANASAKI　　tip of nose
鼻薬 HANAGUSURI　　bribe

Formerly 鼻 . 自 is **self/nose** 134. 畀 is a CO character meaning **give**, but is also known to lend a meaning here of **prominent**. (Its old form 畁 suggests that 廾 is not derived from hands offering ㄨㄨ [the usual origin], but represents a table. ⊕ presumably represents an item, giving a meaning of item intended as gift <u>prominently</u> displayed on table.) Thus **prominent nose**, now just **nose**. Suggest taking 田 as **field** 59 and 廾 as **two tens** 十 33, i.e. **twenty**.

Mnemonic: **OWN NOSE FOLLOWS TRAIL THROUGH TWENTY FIELDS**

378

HYŌ, kŏri
ICE
5 strokes

氷原 HYŌGEN　　　ice floe
氷点 HYŌTEN　　freezing point
氷水 KŌRIMIZU　　ice water

Formerly 冰 , and originally 仌仌. 川/水 is **water** 40, while 仌 (now ㇀) represents the **cracks in ice**.

Mnemonic: **ICE IS FROZEN WATER**

379

HYŌ, arawa*su*, omote
SHOW, SURFACE, LIST
8 strokes

表面 HYŌMEN　　　surface
表現 HYŌGEN　　expression
時刻表 JIKOKUHYŌ　　timetable

Once written 裊, combining the early form 仌 of **clothing** 衣 420 and **hair/fur** 毛 210. **Fur clothing** was worn on the outside, thus giving **outer surface** and by association **manifest/ show** and **list** (cf. English term ship's manifest). Suggest remembering by association with **long** 長 173.

Mnemonic: **SHOWN LONG-LOOKING LIST**

113

380		BYŌ SECOND (OF TIME) 9 strokes	二秒 NIBYŌ	two seconds
			秒針 BYŌSHIN	second hand
			秒速 BYŌSOKU	speed per second

禾 is **rice plant** 81, here meaning **grain plant**. 少 is **few/little** 143 q.v., here with its original meaning of **miniscule**. 380 originally referred to the **tip of the ear of a grain plant,** but then came to mean **tiny bit** and eventually something even smaller than minute, i.e. **second**.

Mnemonic: **LITTLE RICE, EATEN IN A MERE SECOND**

381		BYŌ, HEI, ya*mu*, yamai ILLNESS 10 strokes	病気 BYŌKI	illness
			病人 BYŌNIN	sick person
			らい病 RAIBYŌ	leprosy

疒 is an element indicating **sickness**. It was once written 疒人, showing **bed** 爿 1389 and **person** 人 39 and indicating **someone 'laid up'**. 丙 is **third rate** 1773 q.v., here acting phonetically to express **increase**, giving **illness that increases (in severity)**. There is some disagreement as to the semantic role of 丙. Its original meaning was **big altar**, leading some scholars to assume that it lends an idea of **big**, giving **major illness**. Others take it to suggest **rigidity** and **immobility**, since the altar was sturdy and rigid, giving **crippling illness**. Still others take it to symbolise **about to die**, from the idea of sacrifice associated with the altar, giving **fatal illness**. In any event, 381 originally meant **serious illness**, but is now used of **illness** in general. Suggest taking 丙 in its modern sense of **third rate**.

Mnemonic: **THIRD RATE HEALTH LEADS TO ILLNESS**

382	品	HIN, shina GOODS,QUALITY,KIND 9 strokes	商品 SHŌHIN	commodity
			品質 HINSHITSU	quality
			品物 SHINAMONO	goods

Three **mouths** 口 20, indicating a **group of people**. This came to mean **assemblage**, and eventually specifically **group of things** rather than people. **Quality** and **kind** are associated ideas. Note that 382 has switched from meaning person to thing, while 者 298 has switched from thing to person. Suggest taking as three **boxes**.

Mnemonic: **QUALITY GOODS COME IN BOXES**

383 FU, ma*keru*/*kasu*, *ou*
DEFEAT, BEAR
9 strokes

負傷 FUSHŌ wound
負担 FUTAN burden
負け嫌い MAKEGIRAI unyielding

Somewhat obscure. Once written 負 , showing a **bending person** ∧ 39 and **shell/money** 貝 90. (The variant form 負 using sword/cut 刀 181 is a miscopying.) There is some disagreement as to the role of these elements. Some scholars take 貝 to be used phonetically to express **back** (as well as having its own loose idea of back as an extension of shell), giving **(on) a bending person's back** and hence **bear**, leading to ideas such as **suffer an imposition** and hence **defeat**. Other scholars take 貝 to be used in its sense of **valuables**, as well as possibly also acting phonetically to express **back**, to give an idea of a **person bent under a load of valuables** (on their back). This later came to symbolise being **defeated** or routed, i.e. fleeing with one's valuables. Note that 383 can also occasionally be used causatively, giving **to defeat**.

Mnemonic: **DEFEATED PERSON FLEES BEARING MONEY**

384 BU, BE
PART, SECTION, CLAN
11 strokes

部分 BUBUN part
部族 BUZOKU tribe
部屋 HEYA* room

Obscure. Once written 㕻. 㐆/阝 is **village** 355. 㕻/咅 is not **say** 㝵/言 274 but a CO character meaning **spit**. Its etymology is unclear, though 口 is presumably **mouth** 20. There is some support for a view that 咅 is a variant of 又, the old form of **not**不 (read FU) 572 q.v. The latter originally indicated a bud **emerging** from a whorl of leaves, and may thus indicate **coming out**, giving 咅 a meaning of **that coming out of the mouth**. It should be noted that in compounds 咅 often seems to be associated both with **dividing** and **growing**, both of which can be interpreted as derived meanings of 又 though not, strictly speaking, of 咅 itself. It should also be noted that a combination of **not** and **mouth** definitely exists as the character **deny** 否 962 q.v., which literally means **make the negating sound 'fu' with the mouth**. Thus, if the 立 part of 咅 is a variant of 不, this would mean that 咅 is ipso facto a variant of 否, raising the possibility that **spit** similarly derives from **making the sound 'fu' with the mouth**. Unfortunately not only is the etymology of 咅 unclear, its role here (both semantic and/or phonetic) is also unclear. Some scholars claim that it lends a meaning of **division**, giving **division or part of a village** and hence **clan**. However, 384 is known to have once referred to a specific clan in ancient China, thus suggesting that the clan was associated with a **village called FU** . From this point opinion is further divided, some scholars claiming that the meaning **division** and hence **section /part** is the result purely of borrowing or miscopying (involving **divide** 咅刂 1813), while others take the village in question to be a division or part of a larger administrative district. Still others see it as a village of outcasts (from spit out/ reject). Suggest taking 立 as **stand** 73 and 口 as **(open) mouth**.

Mnemonic: **CLAN STANDS OPEN MOUTHED IN PART OF VILLAGE**

115

385 服	**FUKU** **CLOTHES, YIELD, SERVE** 8 strokes	服装 FUKUSŌ clothing 服従 FUKUJŪ submission 服部 HATTORI* a surname

Somewhat obscure. Once written 𦝄, showing a **boat** 月 / 舟 1354 q.v., a **person bending** 勹 39, and a **hand** 又. Still older forms such as 𦥑 show boat and a hand holding a **weapon** or **tool**, suggesting that the hand is **working**, and also suggesting that the later bending person may be a miscopying. The early meaning of 385 is known to have been **work**, and some scholars feel that it meant literally bend down in order to work on (building or repairing) a boat. **Yield/ serve** is felt to derive from a combined idea of bending down and performing work. How exactly it came to mean **clothes**, however, is not clear. It is assumed to be a borrowed meaning, though it is also possible that 385 once came by extension to indicate a **servant's livery**. Suggest taking 月 as **moon**, 又 as a **hand**, and 卩 as a **clothes hoist**.

Mnemonic: **SERVILE HAND PUTS CLOTHES ON HOIST UNDER MOON**

386 福	**FUKU** **GOOD FORTUNE** 13 strokes	幸福 KŌFUKU happiness 福引き FUKUBIKI lottery 福音書 FUKUINSHO Gospels

Formerly 福. 示 / 礻 is **altar/ of the gods** 695. 畐 is a CO character meaning **full**, and derives from a pictograph of a **(full) wine jar** 畐. 386 originally referred to wine blessed by the gods and used in religious ceremonies. The idea of **blessed by the gods** then came to mean **blessed** or **fortunate** in general. Suggest taking 畐 as **single** — 1 **entrance** 口 20 to **field** 田 59.

Mnemonic: **ALTAR AT SINGLE ENTRANCE TO FIELD -- GOOD FORTUNE**

387 物	**BUTSU, MOTSU, mono** **THING** 8 strokes	人物 JINBUTSU person 食物 SHOKUMOTSU food 食べ物 TABEMONO food

牛 is **cow** 97. 勿 is an NGU character now used to mean **not**, but it originally depicted a **variety of streamers** ⿹ (still listed as a minor meaning in Chinese). Here it lends a meaning of **variety**, thus giving **variegated cow**, a reference to a type of cow with a mottled hide. 387 then came to mean **creature**, and then **thing** in a broad (but usually tangible) sense. Suggest taking 勿 as a 'thing' with **four legs**.

Mnemonic: **COW IS A THING WITH FOUR LEGS**

388 HEI, BYŌ, tai*ra*, hira*tai*   平気 HEIKI   calmness
FLAT, EVEN, CALM   平等 BYŌDŌ   equality
5 strokes   平手 HIRATE   palm of hand

Possibly because 388 can mean **set of scales** or **balance** in Chinese it is often explained as deriving from a supposed pictograph of scales, and some scholars even refer to a mysterious 'pictograph' 平 . However, old forms such as 屮 in fact appear to show a combination of **twisting water weed** 丁 / 丂 281 and **small** 小 36. 丁 usually has a meaning of bending but can occasionally, as here, mean **flat**, since the weed **flattens** out across the surface of the water (see also 130). 小 is felt to be added for clarity, to distinguish the water weed in question from a larger type less suited to symbolising flatness. Similarly a lateral stroke 一 was added to later forms to emphasise flatness, giving 平 and hence the modern form. **Scales** is felt to derive from **flatness**, not vice-versa. Note that scales is conveyed in Japanese by an NGU character that adds rice (plant) 禾 81, 秤 (i.e. an even measure of rice). Note also that waterweed is now conveyed by a CO character that adds plant 艹 9, 苹 , and by an NGU character that adds plant and water 氵 40, 萍. In view of the symmetrical shape of 388, suggest using the scales theory as a mnemonic.

Mnemonic: **BALANCED SCALES ARE FLAT AND EVEN**

389 HEN, kae*su/ru*   返事 HENJI   reply
RETURN   返済 HENSAI   repayment
7 strokes   仕返し SHIKAESHI retaliation

辶 is **movement** 129. 反 is **oppose** 371, here meaning **reverse**. Thus **reverse movement**, i.e. **return**. Now often used in the transitive sense, i.e. **give back**.

Mnemonic: **REVERSE MOVEMENT AND RETURN**

390 BEN   勉強 BENKYŌ   study
STRIVE   勤勉 KINBEN   diligence
10 strokes   勉学 BENGAKU   study

力 is **effort** 74. 免 is **avoid** 1849 q.v., here used in its literal meaning of **woman striving to give birth**. Thus **woman striving with great effort to give birth**, now just **strive/ try hard** in general. Give birth is now conveyed by an NGU character 娩 that uses woman 女 35 instead of effort 力 , and a CO character 㝃 that uses child 子 25.

Mnemonic: **STRIVE TO AVOID EFFORT?!**

117

391 放	HŌ, hanasu/tsu RELEASE, EMIT 8 strokes	解放 KAIHŌ	liberation
		放射 HŌSHA	radiation
		手放す TEBANASU	let go

Usually explained as **direction** 方 204 and **stick in hand/ strike** 攵 101, giving **driving off in all directions** and thus **radiate** and hence **release**. A useful mnemonic, but not quite correct. Old forms such as 𠬝 show 方 to be a miscopying of **person** 人 39. Thus **drive off a person**, leading to **discharge** and then **release** and **emit**.

Mnemonic: **STRIKING IN ALL DIRECTIONS IS A FORM OF RELEASE**

392 万	MAN, BAN TEN THOUSAND, MYRIAD 3 strokes	五万 GOMAN	fifty thousand
		万事 BANJI	everything
		万年筆 MANNENHITSU	fountain pen

Often thought to be a simplification of 萬, which tended to be used until recently to express **ten thousand**, but in fact they are separate characters. 万 was once written 丂, and is felt by some scholars to be a variant of **twisting waterweed** 丂 281 borrowed for its sound. Other scholars feel it is a simplification of the ancient **swastika** symbol 卐 or 卍 (both NGU characters), which has connotations of **all encompassing** and by association **myriad**. 萬 derives from a pictograph of a **scorpion** 𧒽 with the addition of nine/**bent elbow** 九 12 q.v. to emphasise the curling tail, and originally meant (striking) **scorpion**. It is not clear how it came to represent ten thousand. Certainly it was used partly for its sound, but its complexity suggests some additional significance. It may have been that scorpions were **extremely numerous**. Suggest remembering 万 by association with **direction** 方 204, taking it to be a 'wrong' version of this.

Mnemonic: **TEN THOUSAND MARCH IN WRONG DIRECTION**

393 味	MI, aji, ajiwau TASTE, RELISH 8 strokes	意味 IMI	meaning
		興味 KYŌMI	interest
		味見 AJIMI	tasting

口 is **mouth** 20. 未 is **unfinished** 794, here acting phonetically to express **good** and also lending an idea of **lingering**. Thus **something good lingering in the mouth**, i.e. **nice taste**. It can now be used of **taste** in general, but at times still retains connotations of **appreciation**. It is also sometimes used of an **attribute** or **quality**.

Mnemonic: **TASTE LINGERS UNFINISHED IN THE MOUTH**

394		MEI, MYŌ, inochi	命令 MEIREI	order
		LIFE, ORDER	生命 SEIMEI	life
		8 strokes	命取り INOCHITORI	fatal

Order 令 603 with a **mouth /say** 口 20 added to emphasise the **issuing** of the order. The issuing of an order came to symbolise the expression of will of those superiors who govern one's life, including the gods, and thus 394 also came to mean **one's lot** or **fate**, and eventually **life**.

Mnemonic: **LIFE CAN HINGE ON A SPOKEN ORDER**

395		MEN, omote, omo, tsura	外面 GAIMEN	exterior
		FACE, ASPECT, MASK	仮面 KAMEN	mask
		9 strokes	鼻面 HANAZURA	muzzle

Once written 圆 . 㫃 is **face** 93, while 口 indicates **enclosing** or **covering**. Thus **that which encloses the face**, i.e. a **mask**. This led to the idea of **external appearance**, giving **aspect**. 395 is also used for the **face** itself. Suggest remembering by partial association with **eye** 目 72.

Mnemonic: **MASK ENCLOSES FUNNY FACE WITH BIG EYE**

396		MON, tou	質問 SHITSUMON	question
		ASK	学問 GAKUMON	scholarship
		11 strokes	問屋 TOIYA/TONYA*	dealer

Usually explained simply as a **mouth** 口 20 asking at a **door/gate** 門 211, but some scholars feel that 門 acts largely phonetically to express **question**.

Mnemonic: **MOUTH ASKING AT GATE**

397		YAKU, EKI	役人 YAKUNIN	functionary
		ROLE, SERVICE, DUTY	役者 YAKUSHA	actor
		7 strokes	兵役 HEIEKI	military service

Movement along road 彳 118 and **weapon in hand** 殳 153. 397 originally referred to soldiers **going off to fight** (still occasionally used in this meaning), then came to mean **service**, **duty**, and by extension **role**.

Mnemonic: **MOVE OFF WITH WEAPON IN HAND TO DO ONE'S DUTY**

398		YAKU, kusuri	薬局	YAKKYOKU	pharmacy
		MEDICINE, DRUG	火薬	KAYAKU	gunpowder
		16 strokes	薬指	KUSURIYUBI	
					ring finger

サ is plant 9. 楽 is pleasure 218, acting phonetically to express cure and also lending an idea of soothing. Thus curative, soothing plant, i.e. a medicinal herb.

Mnemonic: **MEDICINAL PLANT GIVES PLEASURE**

399		YU, YŪ, yoshi	由来	YURAI	derivation
		REASON, MEANS, WAY	理由	RIYŪ	reason
		5 strokes	自由	JIYŪ	freedom

From the same pictograph of a basket /wine press 甴 as west 152 q.v. Whereas 152 focussed on the falling drops, 399 focussed on the abstract idea of the drops falling from the basket. From came by association to mean cause, i.e. reason, and by extension also came to mean significance, means, and way. Suggest remembering by association with field 田 59, taking | as a derrick (and see oil 油 400).

Mnemonic: **THERE'S A REASON FOR DERRICK IN FIELD**

400		YU, abura	油田	YUDEN	oil field
		OIL	灯油	TŌYU/TŌYU	kerosene
		8 strokes	油絵	ABURAE	oil painting

Basket/ wine press 由 399 q.v. and water/liquid 氵 40. Originally the liquid from the press, later viscous fluid, eventually oil. Suggest taking 由 as a field 田 59 with a derrick | .

Mnemonic: **LIQUID FROM FIELD WITH DERRICK IS OIL**

401	有	YŪ, U, aru	所有者	SHOYŪSHA	owner
		HAVE, EXIST	有無	UMU	existence
		6 strokes	有り難う	ARIGATŌ*	thank you

Once written 有, showing a (right) hand ナ 2 holding a piece of meat 月 365. This symbolised possession or having, which also came by association to mean existing.

Mnemonic: **HAVE MEAT IN YOUR HAND**

402 遊 **YŪ, YU, aso*bu***
PLAY, RELAX
12 strokes

遊覧	YŪRAN	sightseeing
遊山	YUSAN	excursion
遊び場	ASOBIBA	playground

Often explained as **children** 子 25 **gathering** under a **flag** 㫃 333 (symbolising **gathering**) and **moving about** 辶 129, i.e. **playing**, with **relax** being an extension of **play**. A useful mnemonic, but incorrect. 斿 is a CO character meaning the **billowing shape of a waving flag** (from fluttering flag 㫃, with child 子 used to mean small part, and originally referring to the small scalloped parts formed as the flag waves). In combination with movement (along a road) 辶 it meant **moving in a wave-like and hence indirect fashion**, giving saunter and the idea of **acting in an unhurried fashion**. Thus **relax** (or more exactly, **not work**) is the earlier meaning, with **play** being the extension. Suggest taking 㫃 as **person** 𠂉 39 and **side** 方 204.

Mnemonic: **CHILDREN PLAY AT MOVING PERSON'S SIDE**

403 予 **YO, kane*te***
ALREADY, PRIOR, I
4 strokes

予約	YOYAKU	booking
予想	YOSŌ	expectation
予定	YOTEI	schedule

Formerly also 豫, though technically this is a separate character. Old forms such as 𠨑 show a combination of symbol and pictograph, namely a **weaving shuttle** ロ (from 0) being **pushed** | **to one side** 𠨑. This came to represent the idea of doing one action as part of a sequence, i.e. **prior** to doing the next action. The idea of **doing something in advance** also came to mean leaving a **margin**. Elephant 象 533 was added to give an idea of **big** margin, though it is not clear why such a complex character was chosen. Thus at one stage 403 had a secondary meaning similar to ample/margin 余 800, and it is interesting that both 403 and 800 have been borrowed to express **I/me**. This has always been assumed to be for purely phonetic reasons, but the coincidence of meaning may suggest some additional but now unclear semantic connection. Margin has now faded as a major meaning, leaving the earlier idea of **acting in advance** and hence **already**.

Mnemonic: **I'VE ALREADY PUSHED THE SHUTTLE**

404 洋	YŌ	西洋人 SEIYŌJIN	Westerner
	OCEAN, WESTERN	大西洋 TAISEIYŌ	Atlantic
	9 strokes	洋食 YŌSHOKU	Western food

Water 氵 40 and sheep 羊 986. Usually explained to the effect that a sheep indicates white, giving whitecaps and hence suggesting a large body of water (i.e. an ovine version of the English term white horses). Some scholars feel that 羊 was used in an unknown phonetic role and that 404 once referred to a specific river in ancient China (details unclear) before coming to be applied by extension to the ocean. The former theory seems the more helpful. Ocean came to symbolise from across the ocean, i.e. foreign and especially Western.

Mnemonic: OCEAN OF WHITE SHEEP, NOT WHITE HORSES

405 葉	YŌ, ha	針葉樹 SHINYŌJU	conifer
	LEAF	葉巻き HAMAKI	cigar
	12 strokes	葉書 HAGAKI	postcard

Somewhat obscure. Often assumed to be generation 世 327 q.v. of plant-life ⺿ 9 on a tree 木 69, which is an excellent mnemonic. Since it is also possible that, through early forms such as 世, 327 may have become somewhat confused graphically with a growing plant and hence life and generation (see also 42), as opposed to its literal origin of three tens (thirty years) and hence generation, it would seem quite reasonable to assume that 枼 means generation/ plant growth on a tree and that ⺿ is used merely to reinforce this. This is especially so in view of the fact that 枼 does indeed exist as a CO character meaning leaf. However, 枼 also means flat piece of wood/ writing tablet, and some scholars feel that this is its main meaning (from wood 木, with 世 suggesting grouping together, as of wooden tablets bound together) and that its meaning of leaf results from its later being used as a simple version of 葉. Thus, according to the latter view, 405 means plant-life resembling a group of flat wooden tablets, i.e. leaves.

Mnemonic: LEAVES ARE GENERATION OF PLANTS ON TREE

406 陽	YŌ, hi	陽極 YŌKYOKU	anode
	SUNNY, MALE,	陽気 YŌKI	gaiety, season
	POSITIVE	太陽系 TAIYŌKEI	solar system
	12 strokes		

Hill 阝 229 and sun shining down 昜 144, to give sunny (side of) hill. This has led to various extended meanings, primarily the concept of yang (as opposed to yin 陰 1013).

Mnemonic: SIDE OF HILL IS POSITIVELY SUNNY

407 様 YŌ, sama, zama   仕様 SHIYŌ   way, means
SITUATION, APPEARANCE, 有様 ARISAMA   situation
WAY, POLITE SUFFIX   皆様 MINASAMA   everyone
14 strokes

Somewhat obscure. Formerly 樣, and incorrectly as 樣. 木 is **tree** 69. 羕 is a now defunct character meaning **tributary**, comprising tributary/ long 永 615 and **sheep** 羊 986 (the latter presumably used for its literal meaning of branching horns). It acts here phonetically to express **resemble**, giving **tree that resembles**. This was a reference to the **horse chestnut**, which resembles the edible chestnut. The reason for such a complex character occurring as a phonetic is possibly that it was initially confused with elephant / **resemble** 象 533, which had the same pronunciation at the time (SHŌ) and which is also combined with tree 木 to give the NGU character horse chestnut 橡. It is not clear how 407 came to acquire its present meanings. Some scholars feel they are purely borrowed meanings, while others feel 407 was confused with **image** 像 740, from which many of the present meanings can be taken to have derived. In Japanese 407 can also be used as a **polite suffix**, though again the process of acquisition of this meaning is unclear. Suggest taking 羕 as a combination of **sheep** 羊 / 羊 and **water** 水 40.

Mnemonic: **SHEEP APPEARS TO WATER TREE -- AWKWARD SITUATION**

408 RAKU, *ochiru/tosu*   落下 RAKKA   fall, descent
FALL, DROP   落ち葉 OCHIBA   fallen leaf
12 strokes   落とし物 OTOSHIMONO
     dropped item

艹 is **plant** 9. 洛 is an NGU character now used to refer to the **old capital** (Kyoto), but in Chinese it refers to a certain river and originally meant **falling water**. It comprises **water** 氵 40 and **each** 各 438 q.v., here with its early meaning of **descend** (and stop). Thus **plants falling like water**, which was a reference to **falling leaves**. It now means **fall** in a broad sense.

Mnemonic: **FROM EACH PLANT, LEAF FALLS LIKE DROP OF WATER**

409

流

RYŪ, RU, naga*reru/su*
FLOW, STREAM
10 strokes

流行 RYŪKŌ   fashion
流布 RUFU   spread
流れ木 NAGAREGI   driftwood

Once written 水㐬. 㐬 is an inverted (indicating **newborn**) **infant** 子 25 in **amniotic fluid** 巛, to all intents and purposes the same element as birth/ raise children 育 227 q.v. ⺡ is **water** 40, emphasising the fluid. Thus the **flow of fluid at birth**, later **flow** in a broad sense. There is also a theory that 巛乚 represents the dangling **hair** of the infant, and that this serves to emphasise the idea of flowing (down). This is a useful mnemonic, but in view of the clear use of amniotic fluid in 227 almost certainly incorrect. The element 㐬 often lends an idea of **dangle** in compounds, but this is felt to be an extended meaning from flow and not hair. It also exists as a minor CO character confusingly listed in some dictionaries (but without illustration) as meaning **cap with pendants**. This appears to be a popular mnemonic interpretation with no academic basis.

Mnemonic: **HAIR AND WATER FLOW AS CHILD IS BORN**

410

旅

RYO, tabi
JOURNEY
10 strokes

旅行 RYOKŌ   trip
旅人 TABIBITO   traveler
旅費 RYOHI   travel expenses

Once written 㫃, showing **two (i.e. plural) persons** 亻 39 gathered under a **streaming banner** 㫃 333. It originally referred to warriors rallying under a banner prior to **setting out** on a campaign. On the one hand this came to mean simply **set out** or **make a journey**, and on the other came to mean a group of warriors (specifically five hundred). The latter meaning is retained in Chinese but has disappeared in Japanese. Suggest taking 方 as **side** 方 204, and 衣 as an 'odd' variant of **clothes** 衣 420.

Mnemonic: **PUT ODD CLOTHES ON ONE SIDE FOR JOURNEY**

411

両

RYŌ
BOTH, PAIR, COIN
6 strokes

両方 RYŌHŌ   both sides
両手 RYŌTE   both hands
両替え RYŌGAE   money change

Formerly 兩, and earlier 𠕒. Popularly taken to be a set of **scales** symbolising **equality**, which is a useful mnemonic but almost certainly incorrect. It seems more likely to be a **gourd** (with a wrinkled membraneous inside) split into **two equal halves**. The role of the later addition ⁻ is not clear, but it may symbolise unity, i.e. the **equality** between the two halves. 411 was also used for a **measure of silver** (in Japan the old ryo coin), which probably did derive from association with weighing on scales and may account for the popular theory mentioned above.

Mnemonic: **SCALES WEIGH BOTH PARTS OF A PAIR**

412 RYOKU, ROKU, midori　常 緑 樹 JŌRYOKUJU　evergreen
GREEN　　　　　　　　 緑 青 ROKUSHŌ　verdigris
14 strokes　　　　　　　 緑 色 MIDORIIRO　green

Formerly 綠. 糸 is **thread** 27. 彔 is an element depicting **liquid** 氺 (originally drops
 and a symbol of falling |, but probably stylised under the influence of **water** 氺 40)
falling from a basket used as a crude wine press 彐 (inverted version of 甾 399). That
is, it is very similar to oil 油 400. It came to mean **ooze** or **exude** (a meaning it still retains in some compounds), and was used with metal 金 14 to give 録 611 q.v., now
meaning inscription or record but originally meaning **verdigris** (the **green** rust which
'oozes' out of copper). 彔 itself thus became associated with **green**, and usually lends
such a meaning in compounds, as indeed here. Thus **green threads**, and now **green** in
general. Note that 彔 exists as a minor CO character, confusingly listed in some Chinese
dictionaries (but without illustration) as meaning to carve wood. This is presumably a
meaning ascribed or assumed under the influence of 611's later meaning of inscription.
Suggest taking 糸 as **strand**.

Mnemonic: **WATERY GREEN LIQUID OOZES IN THREAD-LIKE STRANDS**

---

413 REI　　　　　　　　　 失 礼 SHITSUREI　rudeness
PROPRIETY, BOW　 礼 服 REIFUKU　full dress
5 strokes　　　　　　　 敬 礼 KEIREI　bow

Formerly also written 礼 and 禮, though technically the two are separate characters. 示/
ネ is **altar** 695. 乚 is a **kneeling figure**, not a simplification of 豊. Thus **kneeling at
the altar**, meaning to pray and thus **act with propriety**. 豊 is plentiful 790 q.v., literally meaning full vessel, giving 禮 a meaning of offer a full vessel (of sacred wine) at the
altar and thus similarly **act with propriety**.

Mnemonic: **PRAYING AT ALTAR IS ACT OF PROPRIETY**

---

414 列 RETSU　　　　　　 列 車 RESSHA　train
ROW, LINE　　　　　 列 次 RETSUJI　sequence
6 strokes　　　　　　　 前 列 ZENRETSU　front row

Denuded bone 歹 286 and **cut** 刂 181. Thus **cut to the very bone**, which was
originally a reference to **butchery**. The meaning of **row** is felt to stem from the fact that
there was a set **sequence** for dismembering a carcass (sequence/ order is still a strong
meaning in Chinese).

Mnemonic: **CUT UP BONES LINED UP IN A ROW**

415	RO, ji ROAD, ROUTE 13 strokes	道路 DŌRO	road
		線路 SENRO	rail track
		旅路 TABIJI	journey

足 is **foot** 51. 各 is **each** 438 q.v., here used in its early meaning of **stop and start** and by extension **move slowly**. 415 originally referred to moving slowly forward, testing the ground with one's foot. This came to mean **path**, and eventually **route** or **road** in a broader sense.

Mnemonic: **EACH FOOT FOLLOWS SAME ROUTE**

416	WA,O,yawa*ragu*,nago*yaka* PEACE, SOFT, JAPAN 8 strokes	平和 HEIWA	peace
		大和 YAMATO*	Japan
		和食 WASHOKU	
			Japanese food

Formerly also sometimes written 咊. **Rice plant** 禾 81 and **mouth/say** 口 20. The rice plant was often a symbol of **pliancy** and **softness**, and lends such connotations here to mean **pliant in speech**, i.e. accommodating and **harmonious**. This eventually came to mean **peaceful**. It is also used to refer to **Japan**.

Mnemonic: **RICE SOFTENED IN THE MOUTH IN PEACEFUL JAPAN**

END OF THIRD GRADE

THE 195 FOURTH GRADE CHARACTERS

417		AI LOVE 13 strokes	愛情 AIJŌ 母性愛 BOSEIAI 愛国者 AIKOKUSHA	love maternal love patriot

Obscure. Often explained as a hand reaching down/ **convey** 〈ハ 303, a **cover** ⌐, **heart** 心 147, and **stop and start** 夂 438 q.v., to give a meaning of **convey something to the heart and (hesitantly) keep it hidden there**, i.e. a **secret love** that one frequently almost reveals. A useful mnemonic, but an old form 𢙩 shows that 〈ハ is not in fact a hand. Some scholars take 𢙩 to be the prototype of a now defunct character 㤅 meaning a **charitable feeling** of wishing to give food and hence **kindness** and **warm feelings**. It comprises heart/feelings 心 and **satiated person** 旡 688, the latter also acting phonetically to express **give**. Thus feeling of giving food to a person till they become satiated. In the case of 417 𢙩 is felt to have acted phonetically to express **hidden**, though its semantic role (if any) is unclear. Stop and start 夂 is felt to have been used in a sense of **move hesitantly**. Thus the original meaning is believed to have been **move forward hesitantly and furtively,** with the idea of **warm kind feelings** contained in 𢙩 eventually prevailing and replacing move furtively. Still others see 𢙩 as encircled/ **enveloped heart** (see 655), and 夂 as opposed feet 422 q.v., the latter lending its meaning of **all around.** Thus **that which completely envelops the heart.** The last theory seems the most likely, but suggest taking the modern form as **hand** 〈ハ **covering** ⌐ **heart** 心, with 夂 as **sitting crosslegged.**

Mnemonic: **SIT CROSSLEGGED, HAND ON HEART, IN LOVE**

418		AN PLAN,CONCERN,TABLE 10 strokes	提案 TEIAN 案外 ANGAI 案上 ANJŌ	proposal unexpectedly on the table

Wood 木 69, here indicating item made of wood, and **restful** 安 223 q.v. The latter acts phonetically to express **put down and leave,** and may possibly also lend similar connotations of **being left** from its original meaning of a woman being left to rest quietly. 418 originally referred to a **wooden table on which eating utensils were set out and left,** i.e. by way of preparation. It is still occasionally used to mean **table**, especially in Chinese. However, rather like the English term **table a proposal**, it also came to mean something put carefully on a table, and by extension a **proposal** or **plan. Concern** is an associated idea, i.e. something obliging consideration.

Mnemonic: **CONSIDER PLAN AROUND RESTFUL WOODEN TABLE**

127

419	**I, mot*te*** **STARTING POINT, MEANS,** **USE, THROUGH, BECAUSE** 5 strokes	以下 IKA 以内 INAI 以外 IGAI	below within outside, except

Once written 𠃊, also 乙 or ㄥ, depicting a **person** 人 39 behind a **plow** ㄥ. It is not clear how it came to acquire its present meanings. Some scholars assume them to be borrowed, but it seems possible that **plow** came to symbolise **utensil** and hence something **used** as a **means through** which an end is achieved. **Starting point** is possibly an associated idea with **through**, both overlapping with the concept of **from**. **Because** is an extension of through. See also 134.

Mnemonic: **PERSON USES PLOW AS STARTING POINT**

420	**I, koromo** **CLOTHING** 6 strokes	衣服 IFUKU 衣類 IRUI 衣替え KOROMOGAE	clothing clothing change of clothes

Originally 𧘇, showing a **collar** ∧ and **sleeves** 以 and thus ideographically expressing **clothing**. As a radical usually found as 衤, and sometimes split as 衣 or 衣.

Mnemonic: **COLLAR AND SLEEVES SYMBOLISE CLOTHING**

421	**I, kurai** **RANK, EXTENT** 7 strokes	地位 CHII 学位 GAKUI 十二位 JŪNIGURAI	position, rank academic degree about twelve

Person 人 39 **standing** 立 73. This referred to a person standing in a row, their **position** determined by order of precedence, i.e. **rank**. By association position came to mean **extent**, which as in English also became used of **approximation**.

Mnemonic: **PERSON STANDS ACCORDING TO RANK**

---

422   I, kako*mu/u*   周囲 SHŪI   perimeter
SURROUND   範囲 HANI   range
7 strokes   囲い込む KAKOIKOMU   enclose

Formerly 圍. 囗 is an **enclosure** (see 123). 韋 is a CO character now confusingly used to mean leather/ hide (probably through graphic confusion with leather/hide 革 821), but its original meaning was essentially **patrol**. Once written 韋, it shows **opposed feet** 𠂤 /㐄 (variants of feet 𡕒/止 129) **around a central point** ○ (abstract symbol), and can mean **be opposed, move all around, guard all quarters** and so on. Here it acts phonetically to express **surround**, and also lends an idea of **moving all around**. Thus an **enclosure that emphatically surrounds**. Suggest taking 井 as **well** 1470.

Mnemonic: **ENCLOSURE SURROUNDS WELL**

---

423   I, yuda*neru*   委員会 IINKAI   committee
ENTRUST   委任 ININ   entrustment
8 strokes   委託金 ITAKUKIN   trust money

禾 is **rice plant** 81, here symbolising **softness** and **pliancy**. 女 is **woman** 35, also a symbol of softness and pliancy. Thus to **be soft and pliant,** which came by extension to mean be pliant in one's affairs and then leave decisions to others, eventually leading to **entrust**. The popular explanation that gathering the rice crop was entrusted to women is incorrect but a useful mnemonic. See also 416.

Mnemonic: **ENTRUST RICE PLANTS TO WOMAN**

---

424   I   胃液 IEKI   gastric juice
STOMACH   胃袋 IBUKURO   stomach
9 strokes   胃弱 IJAKU   dyspepsia

From a pictograph of the **stomach** ⊛ (showing folds and possibly hairs), reinforced by **flesh/ of the body** 月 365. Suggest taking 田 as **field** 59.

Mnemonic: **FLESHY STOMACH SEEN IN FIELD**

---

425   IN, shirushi   印刷 INSATSU   printing
SEAL, SIGN, SYMBOL   印判 INBAN   seal
6 strokes   目印 MEJIRUSHI guiding mark

Originally 𢑤, showing a **hand pressing down** ⺈ on a **bending person** 卩 39. The original meaning of **press down** then came to be used of pressing down on a **seal**, with seal giving rise to **sign** or **symbol**. 425 is also borrowed for the IN of **India** (Indo).

Mnemonic: **HAND PRESSES DOWN ON PERSON AS ON SEAL**

| 426 | 英 | EI
SUPERIOR, ENGLAND
8 strokes | 英才 EISAI
英国 EIKOKU
英語 EIGO | talent
England
English language |

艹 is **plant** 9. 央 is **center** 429 q.v., here acting phonetically to express **bloom** and possibly also lending an idea of **blocked off at the head** from its assumed original meaning of person yoked at the neck. 426 originally meant a **flower that blossomed but lacked seed**, such a flower being **exceptionally beautiful**. It can still mean beautiful flower in Chinese. Exceptionally beautiful came to mean **superior**, with extended meanings such as **talented** or **brave**. It is also used for the first syllable of **England**, largely under the influence of Chinese in which 426 is pronounced YING and is a closer approximation to ENG.

Mnemonic: **ENGLAND HAS SUPERIOR PLANTS IN ITS CENTER**

| 427 | 栄 | EI, saka*eru*, ha*eru*
GLORY,FLOURISH,SHINE
9 strokes | 光栄 KŌEI
栄養 EIYŌ
繁栄 HANEI | glory, honor
nutrition
prosperity |

Formerly 榮 . It originally indicated a **tree** 木 69 **covered** 冖 with flowers as dazzling as **flame** 火 8, specifically a type of paulownia. Eventually the idea of **blossoming into something dazzling** came to prevail, being used in a range of extended senses such as **flourish** and **shine**. Suggest taking ⺍ as **ornate cover**.

Mnemonic: **TREE FLOURISHES GLORIOUSLY UNDER ORNATE COVER**

| 428 | 塩 | EN, shio
SALT
13 strokes | 食塩 SHOKUEN
塩水 SHIOMIZU
製塩所 SEIENSHO | table salt
saltwater
saltworks |

Formerly 鹽 or 鹽 . The latter is a modified combination of supervise/ **look carefully** 監 1111 and 鹵, an NGU character meaning **salt** (from a pictograph of a basket 㢰 [essentially the same as an early form of basket/west 西 152 q.v.] used as a primitive salt shaker). The exact role of 監 is not clear, but it is felt to have acted phonetically to express **salty taste** and possibly also to have lent an idea of **careful** (salt being a precious commodity in certain areas, and thus something used carefully). The shaker 鹵 was also used for things other than salt, thus necessitating the clarification given by 監. The later use of **ground** 土 60 may be a simplification of 臣 , but may also be a deliberate reference to a principal source of salt, the **salt pan**. Suggest taking 塩 as **person** 卜 39, **mouth** 口 20, and **dish** 皿 1307.

Mnemonic: **PERSON THROWS SALTY DISH FROM MOUTH TO GROUND**

429

央

Ō
CENTER
5 strokes

中央 CHŪŌ center
中央部 CHŪŌBU central part
中央口 CHŪŌGUCHI central exit

Somewhat obscure. Once written 𡈼, showing a **person** 大 53 with what many scholars take to be a **yoke** 𠄎 on the **neck**. It is felt to have originally meant **restrained at the neck**, with the idea that the neck represented the **central line of the body** later coming to prevail. Other scholars feel that 𠄎 is not a yoke but an abstract symbol indicating **confines** and thus focusing on what lies (centrally) within the confines, i.e. in this case the **neck/ central line**. (Some scholars take ㇒ ㇏ as the confines and 大 as man 573.) The use of 央 in 426 q.v. seems to support the yoke theory. Suggest taking 大 in its usual sense of **big**, and 央 as a combination of 大 and **opening** 口 20.

Mnemonic: **BIG OPENING IN CENTER**

430

億

OKU
HUNDRED MILLION
15 strokes

二億 NIOKU 200 million
十億 JŪOKU billion
億万長者 OKUMANCHŌJA billionaire

亻 is **person** 39. 意 is **thought** 226 q.v., here lending its literal meaning of **heart full of thoughts and feelings**. 430 originally referred to a person brimming over with thoughts and feelings, then came to mean **brimming over** in general. This eventually came to mean **too numerous to contain**, giving the idea of a **very large number**. It became particularly associated with a hundred thousand, and still represents this number in Chinese, but in Japanese, from the medieval period on, it gradually came to mean a **hundred million** (i.e. a squaring of ten thousand 万 392).

Mnemonic: **PERSON WITH HUNDRED MILLION THOUGHTS**

431

加

KA, kuwaeru/waru
ADD, JOIN
5 strokes

増加 ZŌKA increase
参加 SANKA participation
加え算 KUWAEZAN addition

Mouth/say 口 20 and **strength** 力 74. It originally meant **add strength to an argument by adding one's own words**, then came to mean **add** or **join** in general.

Mnemonic: **STRENGTHENED BY ADDED MOUTH**

131

| 432 | | KA
GOODS, MONEY
11 strokes | 貨物船 KAMOTSUSEN freighter
硬貨 KŌKA currency
雑貨 ZAKKA sundry goods |

Shell/**money** 貝 90 and **change** 化 238, giving **that which can be exchanged for money**, i.e. **goods**. It then came to mean **assets** and later also **money**.

Mnemonic: **CHANGE GOODS FOR MONEY AND VICE-VERSA**

| 433 | | KA
SECTION,LESSON,LEVY
15 strokes | 課税 KAZEI taxation
課長 KACHŌ section head
第二課 DAINIKA Lesson Two |

言 is **word** 274. 果 is **fruit/perform** 627 q.v., here acting phonetically to express **consider** and probably also lending a meaning of **carry out**. 433 originally meant to consider a person's words, and by extension **carry out an investigation** (still a major meaning in Chinese). It became particularly associated with investigating with a view to levying a tax or amount of work, and hence eventually came to mean **levy**. It also came to acquire connotations of order and ranking, and some scholars feel that **lesson** and **section** both derive from the idea of being part of a sequence, but it seems more likely that they stem from the idea of **that which is levied**, i.e. a **task** or **section** of a task or by extension **lesson** to be worked on.

Mnemonic: **SECTION OF LESSON CONTAINS FRUITFUL WORDS**

| 434 | | GA, me
BUD, SPROUT, SHOOT
8 strokes | 発芽 HATSUGA sprouting
新芽 SHINME bud, sprout
芽生える MEBAERU bud, sprout |

艹 is **plant** 9. 牙 is an NGU character meaning **fang** (from a pictograph of interlocking fangs 𠁡). Thus **fang-like plant**, i.e. a **shoot**.

Mnemonic: **PLANT WITH FANG-LIKE SHOOTS**

| 435 | | KAI, arata*meru*/*maru*
REFORM
7 strokes | 改革 KAIKAKU reform
改正 KAISEI amendment
改めて ARATAMETE once again |

Often explained as **strike/force** 攵 101 and **twisting thread/self** 己 855, to give **enforce (the straightening of) something twisted** and hence **reform**. A useful mnemonic, but incorrect. Old forms such as 𢻳 show that 己 is actually the same variant of **serpent** 巳 as in arise 起 250 q.v. 435 originally meant **drive off serpents** (a symbol of undesirable things), and thus **clear an area** and hence by extension **reform**. Suggest taking 己 as **self**.

Mnemonic: **FORCE ONESELF TO REFORM**

436		KAI	器械 KIKAI	apparatus
		DEVICE	機械 KIKAI	machine
		11 strokes	機械化 KIKAIKA	mechanisation

木 is **wood** 69. 戒 is **admonish** 1060. Thus **wooden item for admonishing**, a reference to **shackles**. This meaning is still very occasionally encountered in Japanese, and with more frequency in Chinese. Wooden shackles came to mean **wooden device** and then **device** in general.

Mnemonic: **WOODEN DEVICE FOR ADMONISHING**

437		GAI	損害 SONGAI	damage, loss
		HARM, DAMAGE	殺害 SATSUGAI	murder
		10 strokes	妨害 BŌGAI	obstruction

Once written 𠔿, showing **old** 古 109 q.v., here felt to be used for its assumed literal meaning of **skull** and by extension **head**, and an inverted **basket** 甶 399. Thus to **cover a head with a basket**. It is not clear how this came to mean **harm**. Some scholars feel it meant cover, and that harm is a purely borrowed meaning that replaced cover. Others feel it meant **smother a person**, then **kill** or **cause harm** in general. Suggest taking 口 as **mouth** 20, 宀 as a roof and by extension **cover** (see 28), and 主 as a variant of **life** 生 42.

Mnemonic: **COVERING LIVE MOUTH CAN CAUSE HARM**

438		KAKU, ono-ono	各駅 KAKUEKI	each station
		EACH	各国 KAKKOKU	each country
		6 strokes	各自 KAKUJI	each

Originally 𠙹, showing a **mouth** 口 20 and an **inverted foot** 夂 / 止 129 q.v. Just as 止 can mean either stop or go, the inverted form can have a similar range of often confusing meanings, but usually indicates <u>abnormal</u> progress in the sense of **stopping and starting**. It is listed as a CO character meaning **follow**, and can also mean **go somewhere and then stop**, or **fall over**, or **come down from above**. Here it is felt to mean **come down from above and stop**, with 口 acting phonetically to express the reinforcing meaning of **descend**. This referred to visits by high ranking dignitaries, who would visit one place, stop for a while, then move to another place. Thus **stop at each place**, eventually giving just **each**. Other scholars feel that **each** is a purely borrowed meaning (that replaced descend). Suggest taking 夂 as **sitting crosslegged**.

Mnemonic: **EACH PERSON SITS CROSSLEGGED AND OPEN MOUTHED**

133

439 KAKU,obo*eru*, sa*meru*/*masu* 自覚 JIKAKU self-awareness
REMEMBER, WAKE 目覚め MEZAME awakening
12 strokes 覚え書き OBOEGAKI memorandum

Formerly 覺. 與 is **emulate manually** 10, here meaning **emulate/learn**. 見 is **look** 18. Thus **learn by looking**, giving **remember** on the one hand and **be alert** and hence **wide awake** on the other. Suggest remembering by association with **learning** 学 10.

Mnemonic: **REMEMBER TO BE AWAKE WHEN LEARNING BY LOOKING**

440 KAN 完成 KANSEI completion
COMPLETE 未完 MIKAN incomplete
7 strokes 完全 KANZEN perfection

宀 is **roof/building** 28. 元 is **origin** 106 q.v., here acting phonetically to express **fence/wall** and probably also lending connotations of **round** (from its depiction of an exaggerated head, which occasionally symbolised roundness). Thus **building with fence/wall around**. Some scholars feel that **complete** comes from the idea of the fence **completely** surrounding the building, others from the idea that the building is truly **completed** when the fence is erected.

Mnemonic: **COMPLETELY ORIGINAL BUILDING**

441 KAN 警官 KEIKAN policeman
GOVERNMENT,OFFICIAL 官僚 KANRYŌ bureaucracy
8 strokes 官庁 KANCHŌ
government office

宀 is **roof/building** 28. 目 is **buttocks** 350, here acting phonetically to express **work** and almost certainly also lending an idea of **sedentary**. Thus **person doing sedentary (i.e. clerical) work in a building**, which came to have particular associations with an **official** doing work for the **government**.

Mnemonic: **GOVERNMENT OFFICIAL IN BUILDING SITS ON BACKSIDE**

| 442 漢 | KAN
HAN CHINA, MAN
13 strokes | 漢字 KANJI character
悪漢 AKKAN rogue
漢詩 KANSHI Chinese poetry |

Ironically one of the most obscure of the kanji. Formerly 漢 , and earlier 𤆄 and 𤇾. 氵 is **water** 40, here meaning **river**. 𦰩 is known to have acted phonetically to express the name of a river, specifically the **Han River** from which the Han Dynasty took its name. However, as an element it is obscure. It shows strong similarities to the early forms of **flaming arrow/ yellow** 黄 120 q.v. (unconnected with the Yellow River), possibly suggesting **Han River gleaming (in the sunset) like a flaming arrow**. However, some scholars have interpreted it as a **beast being roasted** (see 949 and then 842, 1281 and 821), though what connotations such a meaning might lend here are not clear. It also shows strong similarities to **rare/few/violet** 菫 (see 842), which is itself of obscure origin and is indeed taken by some scholars to be a variant of 𦰩. However, variant or not, it is still not clear what meaning it might have lent. Han China became a reference to **China** in general, and by association **belonging to China** and hence **Chinese man** and finally just **man** (a lesser meaning). Suggest remembering by association with **man** 夫 573, **grass** 艹 9, and **mouth** 口 20.

Mnemonic: **MAN FROM MOUTH OF HAN RIVER IN GRASSY HAN CHINA**

| 443 | KAN, kuda
PIPE, CONTROL
14 strokes | 管理 KANRI control
気管 KIKAN wind pipe
管楽器 KANGAKKI
wind instrument |

⺮ is **bamboo** 170. 官 is **official** 441, here acting phonetically to express **pierce** and probably also lending an idea of **control**. 443 originally referred to **pierced bamboo which controlled sound**, i.e. a **wind instrument**. It then came to mean on the one hand any type of **pipe** and on the other **control**.

Mnemonic: **BAMBOO PIPE UNDER CONTROL**

---

444 **KAN, seki**
BARRIER, CONNECTION
14 strokes

関東 KANTŌ   Kanto area
関心 KANSHIN   interest
関の山 SEKINOYAMA   utmost

Formerly 關. 門 is **gate** 211. 絲 is a CO character now meaning **thread/ weave**, but it originally referred specifically to a **treadle on a loom**, and derives from (short) threads 幺 111 and crossed pieces of wood 屮(once ††). Here 絲 acts phonetically to express **bar** and also lends its idea of **crossed pieces of wood**. Thus **crossed pieces of wood barring a gate**, i.e. **barrier**. **Connection** is an associated idea, since a barrier also represents the point of contact between the areas either side of it. Suggest taking 关 as **heaven** 天 58 and **away** `' 66 (and see **send** 送 331).

Mnemonic: **HEAVEN'S GATES ARE IMPASSABLE BARRIER: SENT AWAY**

---

445 **KAN**
WATCH, OBSERVE
18 strokes

観光 KANKŌ   sightseeing
観察 KANSATSU observation
観客 KANKYAKU   spectator

Formerly 觀. 見 is **look** 18. 雚 is a CO character meaning **heron**, comprising **bird** 隹 216 and a **crest** 拓 (once 艸向). (Note that in Japanese the addition of an extra bird 鳥 174 gives the NGU character stork 鸛.) Here it acts phonetically to express **turn**, giving **turn and look (around)**, and may possibly also lend an idea of a heron's habit of looking around as it wades. The idea of turning as such has now disappeared, but the connotations of **observing widely** are retained. Suggest remembering 隹 as **crested bird**.

Mnemonic: **LOOK AND OBSERVE CRESTED BIRD**

---

446 **GAN, nega***u*
REQUEST, WISH
19 strokes

志願者 SHIGANSHA   applicant
願望的 GANBŌTEKI   wishful
願い事 NEGAIGOTO   prayer

頁 is **head** 93. 原 is **spring/origin** 107, here acting phonetically to express **big**. Thus **big head**. It is not clear why such a complex character was chosen for the phonetic. Some scholars feel that a big head was seen as a **source** of **intellectual ability**, and that 446 originally meant therefore **big ideas (from a big head)**. This may serve to explain how it later came to mean **wish**. Others see wish as a pure borrowing.

Mnemonic: **WISH SPRINGS FROM HEAD NOT HEART**

136

447		**KI, KE** **DESIRE, SCANTY, RARE** 7 strokes	希望 KIBŌ	hope
			希求 KIKYŪ	desire
			希薄 KIHAKU	thinness

Once written 帛, showing **interweave** 乂 10 and **cloth/ threads** 巾 778. 447 original-ly meant **weaving threads,** i.e. **embroidery,** and its current meanings all result from borrowings.

Mnemonic: **INTERWOVEN CLOTH THREADS DESIRABLE BUT RARE**

448		**KI** **SEASON, YOUNG** 8 strokes	季節 KISETSU	season
			四季 SHIKI	four seasons
			季女 KIJO	youngest daughter

Rice plant 禾 81 and **child** 子 25, and originally meaning **young rice plant.** This came to mean **young** in a broader sense, and is especially applied to the **youngest of a line** (and hence very occasionally has an associated meaning of **end**). Some scholars feel that **season** is a borrowed meaning, others that it stems from association between young rice and a particular time of the year.

Mnemonic: **RICE PLANTS IN SEASON GROW LIKE YOUNG CHILDREN**

449		**KI** **CHRONICLE, START** 9 strokes	紀元 KIGEN	epoch, era
			紀行 KIKŌ	travelogue
			二十世紀 NIJŪSEIKI	20th century

Thread 糸 27 and **self/ twisting thread** 己 855, meaning **thread from end to end.** On the one hand this gave rise to **end/start,** and on the other to the idea of an **account** or **chronicle** (which threads from one end of an episode to the other).

Mnemonic: **CHRONICLE OF SELF THREADS FROM BEGINNING TO END**

450	喜	**KI, yorokob**u **REJOICE, HAPPY** 12 strokes	喜劇 KIGEKI	comedy
			歓喜 KANKI	delight
			大喜び ŌYOROKOBI	great joy

口 is **mouth** 20. 豈 was once written 壴 and 喜, showing a **plant** 屮 / 凷 (9 and vari-ant 42) and a **food vessel** 豆 / 豆 1640, and essentially means **edible plant.** Here it also acts phonetically to express **soft.** 450 originally meant **putting soft plants in the mouth,** i.e. **eat cooked vegetables.** This came to mean simply **eat,** which in turn sym-bolised **pleasure.** Suggest taking 士 as **samurai** 494.

Mnemonic: **FOOD POT AT MOUTH MAKES SAMURAI HAPPY**

137

---

451 KI, hata   国旗 KOKKI   national flag
FLAG   旗持ち HATAMOCHI flag bearer
14 strokes   旗魚 KAJIKI*   billfish

Somewhat obscure, though its elements are clearly **fluttering flag** 㫃 333 and **winnowing device/ that** 其 251 q.v. The latter is felt by some scholars to act phonetically to express **gather**, giving **flag under which one gathers** (i.e. warriors rallying). Since winnowing symbolised the arrival of a specific time of year it may also lend an idea of **the time having arrived** (to assemble and go off to fight). Suggest taking 㫃 as **person** ㇃ 39 and **side** 方 204.

Mnemonic: **PERSON AT SIDE OF WINNOWING DEVICE HOLDS FLAG**

---

452 KI, utsuwa   器具 KIGU   utensil
VESSEL,UTENSIL,SKILL 食器 SHOKKI   tableware
15 strokes   器用 KIYŌ   adroitness

Somewhat obscure. Formerly 㗊 and earlier 㗊, showing **dog** 犬 17 and what appears to be **four mouths** 口 20. The exact role of these elements is not clear. The positioning of the mouths suggests a **dog wheeling with open mouth (i.e. barking?) to face all quarters** (see also 1522), though some scholars feel 452 originally had a meaning of a dog panting (i.e. open mouthed). It is believed that the **four mouths** eventually dominated the original meaning and came to suggest a **collection of openings/ receptacles**, leading to **vessel** and thus **utensil**. **Skill** is felt to be an associated meaning with utensil, both sharing an idea of enabling a function to be carried out. Suggest taking 犬 as **big** 53, and 㗊 as **four boxes**. Note that a sometimes encountered simplified form 㗊 is unconnected with **work** 工 113.

Mnemonic: **FOUR BIG BOX-LIKE VESSELS ARE USEFUL UTENSILS**

---

453 KI, hata   機能 KINŌ   function
LOOM, DEVICE,   機会 KIKAI   opportunity
OCCASION   機織り HATAORI   weaving
16 strokes

木 is **wood** 69. 幾 is **how many** 1129 q.v., here used in its original meaning of **loom**. Thus **wooden loom**, now also **device** in general. This gave rise to the idea of the **wherewithal/ means** to perform a function, leading to associated ideas such as **opportunity** and **occasion**.

Mnemonic: **ON HOW MANY OCCASIONS IS WOODEN LOOM USED?**

454 議	GI DISCUSSION 20 strokes	議論 GIRON	discussion
		会議 KAIGI	conference
		議会 GIKAI	the Diet

言 is words/speak 274. 義 is righteousness 645, acting phonetically to express mutual (exchange) and also lending an idea of propriety. Thus proper mutual exchange of words.

Mnemonic: **DISCUSSION INVOLVES RIGHTEOUS USE OF WORDS**

455 求	KYŪ, motomeru REQUEST, SEEK 7 strokes	要求 YŌKYŪ	demand
		追求 TSUIKYŪ	pursuit
		求職 KYŪSHOKU	
			seeking work

Once written , known to represent the **skin/fur of a fanged creature**, though it is not clear whether it is a pictograph of the body with legs attached or an ideograph combining the head and body ψ with bristles 朱, possibly under the influence of fur/hair 毛 210 q.v. 455 originally meant **fur coat**, which was a highly **desirable** object. Some scholars feel its present meanings stem from such an object being much **sought after,** while others feel they result from borrowings. Suggest remembering by association with **water** 水 40, taking 一 as a **cross** (stroke) and ` as a **spot.**

Mnemonic: **CROSS WATER TO SEEK SPOTTED FUR COAT**

456 救	KYŪ, sukuu RESCUE, REDEEM 11 strokes	救命ブイ KYŪMEIBUI	lifebuoy
		救援 KYŪEN	relief, rescue
		救い出す SUKUIDASU	extricate

求 is seek/ request 455. 攵 is threaten/ coerce 101. 456 originally meant to **request threateningly,** i.e. **demand.** Some scholars feel 求 also acts phonetically to express **cease,** giving **demand a cessation.** It is not fully clear how it came to mean **rescue.** Some scholars see it as a borrowed meaning, others as an extended meaning from the idea of demanding the release of a prisoner or similar.

Mnemonic: **RESCUE BY COERCIVE REQUEST**

| 457 | | KYŪ, tama*u*
SUPPLY, BESTOW
12 strokes | 供給 KYŌKYŪ
月給 GEKKYŪ
来給え KITAMAE | supply
monthly pay
Come! |

Thread 糸 27 and **join** 合 121, giving **join threads**. The idea of joining threads to achieve a desired length came to mean **furnish by whatever means**, later **supply/ bestow** in a broad sense. It is also used as a verbal suffix (originally polite).

Mnemonic: **SUPPLY JOINED THREADS**

| 458 | | KYO, a*geru*, kozo*tte*
OFFER, RAISE, ACT,
PERFORM, TOGETHER
10 strokes | 挙手 KYOSHU
選挙 SENKYO
一挙 IKKYO ni | raising hands
election
at a stroke |

Formerly 擧 . 與 is the old form of **give** 与 1873 q.v., here used both in its early sense of **(hands) working together to perform a task** and in its later sense of **give/ raise/offer**. The additional **hand** 手 32 emphasises the idea of doing something with the hands. Suggest taking 兴 as a **laden table**.

Mnemonic: **RAISE LADEN TABLE BY HAND: SOME ACT!**

| 459 | | GYO, RYŌ
FISHING
14 strokes | 漁船 GYOSEN
漁師 RYŌSHI
漁業 GYOGYŌ | fishing boat
fisherman
fishery |

Fish 魚 98 with **water** 氵 40 added to indicate **fish in water**, i.e. in the natural state and not yet caught. This came to mean **fish waiting to be caught** and eventually (professional) **fishing**.

Mnemonic: **FISHING REQUIRES BOTH FISH AND WATER**

| 460 | | KYŌ, tomo
TOGETHER
6 strokes | 共通 KYŌTSŪ
共食い TOMOGUI
共産主義 KYŌSANSHUGI | commonality
cannibalism
communism |

Originally 𢆶 and later 㒸 , showing **two hands** 𦥑 **offering a jewel** 〇 /廿 . The idea of **offering** was later conveyed by a character adding person イ 39, i.e. offer 供 839, while 460 came to focus on the idea of doing something with **both** hands and by extension **jointly/ together**. Suggest taking 艹 as **plant** 9 and 六 as a **table**.

Mnemonic: **PLANT AND TABLE GO TOGETHER**

461		KYŌ COOPERATE 8 strokes	協定 KYŌTEI	agreement
			協力 KYŌRYOKU	cooperation
			協会 KYŌKAI	association

協 is a trebling of **strength** 74. 十 is **ten** 33, here acting phonetically to express **gather** and also lending an idea of **many**. Thus **many persons' strength**, i.e. **cooperation**.

Mnemonic: **THIRTEEN STRONG ARMS COOPERATING**

462		KYŌ, kagami MIRROR 19 strokes	望遠鏡 BŌENKYŌ	telescope
			鏡台 KYŌDAI	dresser
			手鏡 TEKAGAMI	hand mirror

金 is **metal** 14. 竟 is an NGU character meaning **finish**, comprising **sound** 音 6 q.v. and a **bent figure** ㇄ 39 and originally indicating the conclusion of a musical recital (some scholars taking the bent figure to indicate the performer bowing, others taking it to be used phonetically to express finish). Here 竟 is used phonetically to express **scene**. Its semantic role is unclear, though it may possibly suggest **transitoriness** (i.e. soon finished). Thus **metal which shows (transitory?) scene**, i.e. a **bronze mirror**, later **mirror** in general. Suggest taking 音 literally as **shout aloud**, and ㇄ as **bent legs**.

Mnemonic: **SHOUT ALOUD AT BENT LEGS IN METAL MIRROR**

463		KYŌ, KEI, kisou, seru COMPETE, BID 20 strokes	競争 KYŌSŌ	competition
			競馬 KEIBA	horse race
			競り売り SERIURI	auction

Formerly written 競, showing that 誩 derives from 誩, the old form of a CO character 誩 meaning **argue/ wrangle** (comprising **words** 言 274 q.v. set against each other). ㄦㄦ shows **two persons** 亻 39, emphasising the adversaries in the dispute. (Note that 从 is a CO character now used largely to mean **follow**, but its original meaning is simply two persons.) Thus **two persons vying against each other**. Suggest taking as a doubling of **elder brother** 兄 267 and **stand** 立 73.

Mnemonic: **TWO ELDER BROTHERS COMPETE IN STAND-OFF**

---

464 KYOKU,GOKU,kiwa*meru*　　北極　HOKKYOKU　North Pole
EXTREME, POLE　　　　　　至極　SHIGOKU　　extremely
12 strokes　　　　　　　　　消極　SHŌKYOKU

negative pole

木 is **wood** 69. 亟 is a CO character meaning **urgency**. Its exact etymology is unclear, but an early form 𠳏 shows a **hand** ⟨ appearing to **push a person** 𠂊 39 between **two lines** 二 (indicating **constraint** or **pressure**) into an **opening** 口 20. Here it acts phonetically to express **extreme**, and almost certainly lends similar connotations of its own. 464 originally meant **wood in an extreme position**, and was a reference to the **ridgepole** (the highest beam of a house), but later came to mean **extreme** in general. Suggest taking 二 as **poles**, with a play on the word pole.

Mnemonic: **PERSON PUSHED INTO OPENING BETWEEN WOODEN POLES**

---

465 KU　　　　　　　区別　KUBETSU　　distinction
WARD, SECTION　　地区　CHIKU　　　　district
4 strokes　　　　　　北区　KITAKU　　Kita Ward

Formerly 區 . ⊏ is an **enclosure**. 㕚 is now clearly associated with **three mouths** 口 20 (see 1034), but probably originally meant three smaller **enclosures**, indicating **partitioning within partitioning** and thus **section**. A **ward** is a section of a city.

Mnemonic: **ENCLOSED SECTION X IS A WARD**

---

466 GUN　　　　　　　空軍　KŪGUN　　　　airforce
ARMY, MILITARY　　軍人　GUNJIN　　military man
9 strokes　　　　　　米国軍　BEIKOKUGUN

US Forces

Popularly explained as a **covered** ⌐ **vehicle** 車 31, namely a **supply wagon** symbolising an **army** on the move. A useful mnemonic, but incorrect. Old forms such as 𤰔 and 𤰖 show a vehicle with a protective encircling arm ⟩ or womb ⟨⟩ (see 655). 466 actually referred to **carts drawn into a circle** to form a protected encampment, an ancient military practice long before the days of the Wild West. The circle of carts symbolised the **army**.

Mnemonic: **COVERED WAGONS ENCIRCLE ARMY CAMP**

467 **GUN, kōri**
COUNTY, DISTRICT
10 strokes

郡部 GUNBU　　rural district
郡山 KŌRIYAMA a placename
和気郡 WAKEGUN

Wake County

阝 is **village** 355. 君 is **governor/ lord** 266. Usually explained as **villages under the same governership** and thus forming an **administrative district**. Some scholars feel that 君 also acts phonetically to express **gather**, giving a **gathering/ grouping of villages**.

Mnemonic: **VILLAGE BELONGS TO LORD OF COUNTY DISTRICT**

468 **KEI, kata**
TYPE, MODEL, MOLD
9 strokes

元型 GENKEI　　prototype
大型 ŌGATA　　large size
典型的 TENKEITEKI　　typical

土 is **earth** 60. 刑 is **punish** 1193 q.v., here acting phonetically to express **make** and also lending its idea of **frame**. Thus to **make an earthen frame**, i.e. a **clay mold**. This later came to mean **pattern, type, model**, and so forth.

Mnemonic: **MODEL PUNISHMENT FOR EARTHY TYPES**

469 **KEI, KE**
SCENE, VIEW, BRIGHT
12 strokes

光景 KŌKEI　　scene
景気 KEIKI liveliness, business
景色 KESHIKI　　scenery

日 is **sun** 62. 京 is **capital** 99 q.v., here acting phonetically to express **clear and open** and almost certainly lending connotations of **exposed** from its literal meaning of **building on a hill**. Thus **open to the sun** (as a hilltop), i.e. **bright**. In Chinese this is still a major meaning, whereas in Japanese it is usually found in the figurative sense of **lively**. Scene/ view is an extension of **open to the light**.

Mnemonic: **SUNNY CAPITAL IS A BRIGHT SCENE**

| 470 芸 | GEI
ART, SKILL, PLANT
7 strokes | 芸術 GEIJUTSU
種芸 SHUGEI
芸者 GEISHA | art
planting
geisha |

Formerly 藝. 埶 derives from 坴丸 of which 木 is **tree** 69, 土 is **earth** 60, and 丸 is a **person kneeling** ⼄ 413 with **arms outstretched** ⺬. Thus 埶 depicts a person kneeling to **plant** a tree in the ground. It was later enforced by the addition of **plant** ⾋ 9. Both 埶 and 蓻 still exist as CO characters interchangeable with 藝. Speak/ **vapors** 云 78 was added later in a phonetic capacity to express **cultivate**, but it should be noted that 芸, the de facto simplified form of 藝, is not a mere graphic simplification. It still exists in Chinese as a separate character from 藝, with a meaning of **fragrant plant** (i.e. plant giving off fragrant vapors). Thus 云 may have been chosen partly with this in mind, i.e. to link up with the other addition ⾋ and lend an elegant connotation of **plant a fragrant tree**. The idea of planting a tree properly came to mean **horticultural skill** and then **skill** in a broader sense, usually in relation to **artistic accomplishment**. Suggest taking 云 as **two** ⼆ 61 **noses** ⼛ 134.

Mnemonic: **TWO NOSEY PEOPLE EXAMINE ART OF PLANTING**

| 471 欠 | KETSU, ka*ku*/ke*ru*
LACK
4 strokes | 欠席者 KESSEKISHA
欠点 KETTEN
欠け目 KAKEME | absentee
fault
break |

From a pictograph of a **person yawning** 欠 (person ⼈ 39 with gaping mouth フ). **Gaping mouth** came to mean **be wide open**, then **be vacant**, then **be lacking**. The character 缺 is often assumed to be an old form of 471 of which 欠 is assumed to be a simplification, but in fact it is a separate character of similar meaning. It comprises container /bottle 缶 1095 and open 夬 271, and originally meant **open container**.

Mnemonic: **PERSON WITH GAPING MOUTH LACKS DIGNITY**

| 472 結 | KETSU, musu*bu*, yu*u*
BIND, JOIN, END
12 strokes | 結婚 KEKKON
結果 KEKKA
結び目 MUSUBIME | marriage
result
knot |

糸 is **thread** 27. 吉 is good luck 1142 q.v. Some scholars take the latter to act phonetically to express **entwine**, giving **entwine threads** and thus **join** them. Others take it to lend its early meaning of **lidded container**, giving **bind lid on container**. It may in fact combine both phonetic and semantic roles, giving **bind lid on container by entwining it with thread**. **End/ conclusion** is an associated meaning, as in the English term **tie up**. Suggest taking 吉 as **samurai** ⼠ 494 and **mouth** ⼝ 20.

Mnemonic: **BIND SAMURAI'S MOUTH WITH THREAD**

---

473   KEN, KON, ta*tsu*/*teru*   建設 KENSETSU   building
BUILD, ERECT   建立 KONRYŪ   erection
9 strokes   建物 TATEMONO   building

Movement 又 129 and **hand holding brush** 聿 142. 473 originally referred to the **movement of a brush** when writing. The brush was held **erect**, leading to **make erect** and then, as in English, to **build**.

Mnemonic: **HAND HOLDS PEN ERECT**

---

474   KEN, suko*yaka*   健康 KENKŌ   health
HEALTHY   健全 KENZEN   soundness
11 strokes   健筆家 KENPITSUKA
                                               prolific writer

Person イ 39 and **erect** 建 473. A **person standing erect** is a sign that they are **healthy**. Some scholars feel that 建 also lends its sound to express **strong**.

Mnemonic: **HEALTHY PERSON STANDS ERECT**

---

475   KEN   試験 SHIKEN   examination
EXAMINE   実験 JIKKEN   experiment
18 strokes   経験 KEIKEN   experience

Formerly 驗. 馬 is **horse** 191. 僉 is a CO character meaning **whole/all**. It derives from 僉 showing **two talking persons** 吅 267, here representing **plurality of opinion**, and **cover** 亼 87, here meaning **bringing together**. Thus **synthesis of opinions**, leading to unity and hence its modern meanings. In compounds it often lends connotations such as overview, arbitrate, combine, discuss, examine, and so forth. In the case of 475 it essentially means **examine**, giving **examine horses** and eventually **examine** in a broad sense, including **try out**. Suggest taking 兄 in its more common meaning of **elder brother**.

Mnemonic: **ELDER BROTHER EXAMINES HORSE COVER**

---

476   KO, katai/*meru*/*maru*   固体 KOTAI   solid state
HARD, FIRM, SOLID   強固 KYŌKO   solidity
8 strokes   固まり KATAMARI lump, mass

口 is **enclosure** 123. 古 is **old** 109, here acting phonetically to express **solid** and probably also lending an extended idea of **long in place** and thus **firmly established**. 476 originally referred to **solid walls surrounding a castle**, then came to mean **solid** in a general sense.

Mnemonic: **SOLID OLD ENCLOSURE**

477	KŌ, KU	成功 SEIKŌ	success

KŌ, KU
MERIT, SERVICE
5 strokes

成功 SEIKŌ — success
功罪 KŌZAI — pros and cons
功労 KŌRŌ — distinguished service

Strength/ effort 力 74 and work 工 113, giving **dedicated work**.

Mnemonic: **MERITORIOUS SERVICE ENTAILS EFFORTFUL WORK**

478

KŌ, sōrō
WEATHER, SIGN, ASK,
POLITE SUFFIX, SERVE
10 strokes

気候 KIKŌ — climate
候補 KŌHO — candidacy
候文 SŌRŌBUN — polite style

Somewhat obscure, having become etymologically confused with marquis 侯 1256 q.v. 亻 is **person** 39. 㑽 is a variant of 矦, a now defunct character meaning **meet/ greet**. It derives from **bending person** 勹 (originally ᄂ) and 矦 . The latter is a now defunct character meaning **target range** (矢 being arrow 981 and 厂 being a leather curtain hung down to protect the judges, though some scholars feel it indicated the target itself) and by extension **target**. Thus 矦 is **target person**, meaning a **person one wishes to meet/ greet**. In the case of 478 a further **person** 亻 was added for clarity, while the bent person 勹/ᄀ, which originally seems to have applied to the <u>person being met</u>, came through its bent posture (apparently actually just a stylisation) to be taken as the <u>person instigating the meeting</u>, whose bent posture was taken as a symbol of **humility**. Thus at this stage 478 meant **humbly await/request a meeting or visit**. It can still mean **request** or **greet** (or **await** in Chinese), which all stem from this early meaning. In Japanese its use as a **polite suffix** and its meaning of **serve** also stem from its early connotations of humility. **Sign** is an associated meaning, from the idea of having an audience with a superior, stating one's business, and watching for **signs** indicating the superior's response. In Japanese **sign** has extended to **weather**. Unfortunately there is no easy mnemonic for the entire character, but suggest remembering by partial association with **arrow** 矢 and **person** 亻 , perhaps taking | as a pointer symbolising **point**.

Mnemonic: **PERSON POINTS TO WEATHER SIGNS WITH ARROW**

479		KŌ SAIL, VOYAGE 10 strokes	航空 KŌKŪ 航海 KŌKAI 航路 KŌRO	flight sea voyage route

舟 is **boat** 1354. 亢 is an NGU character now meaning **high**, but in Chinese it can mean **neck** and does in fact derive from 亢, showing a person 人 39 and an exaggerated neck held erect 几. In Chinese it can also mean stiff, prim and proper, erect, straight, and haughty, and often lends such meanings in compounds. Here it acts phonetically to express **side** (by side), and also lends a meaning of **straight**. 479 originally referred to **lashing boats together (side-on) in a straight line** to form a pontoon bridge. This came to mean **cross water**, and eventually **voyage**. Suggest taking ⊥ as a **top** and 几 as a **desk** 832.

Mnemonic: **DESKTOP BOAT VOYAGE**

480		KŌ PEACE, HEALTH 11 strokes	小康 SHŌKŌ 不健康 FUKENKŌ 健康体 KENKŌTAI	respite ill health healthy body

Originally written 康, showing **hands** 丱 holding a **pestle** 干 110 pounding cereals/rice, with **bran** ⠒ being produced. 480 originally meant **rice-bran**. This meaning is now conveyed by an NGU character 糠 that adds rice 米 201, while 480 itself has become used as a substitute for a complex character meaning **peace**. **Health** is an associated meaning from the idea of nothing to cause concern. Suggest remembering 隶 as hand holding pestle, i.e. **pound**, with 广 as **building** 114.

Mnemonic: **HAND POUNDS HEALTHY BRAN FLAKES IN BUILDING**

481	告	KOKU, tsugeru PROCLAIM, INFORM 7 strokes	抗告 KŌKOKU 公告 KŌKOKU 広告 KŌKOKU	complaint public notice advertisement

Formerly written 告, leading to the popular explanation that it is cow/**bull** 牛 97 and **mouth/say** 口 20 to give **roar like a bull**, i.e. **proclaim**. A useful mnemonic, that may in fact have been believed for many centuries, but incorrect. Very ancient forms such as 告 and 告 show that 屮 derives from a variant of **growing plant** 生 42, which acts phonetically to express **advance/ proffer** and may also lend an idea of **emerge** (a growing plant emerging from the ground). Thus to **proffer from the mouth, i.e. verbally**, meaning to **make a statement** and hence **proclaim** or **inform**.

Mnemonic: **PROCLAIM WITH BULL-LIKE ROAR FROM MOUTH**

| 482 | | SA, sasu
DIFFERENCE, THRUST
10 strokes | 時差 JISA　　　　　time lag
差別 SABETSU discrimination
差し込む SASHIKOMU　　insert |

Once written 羍. 釆 is a **plant with new side-shoots/ leaves hanging down** (see 907). 𠂇 is **left hand** 22, acting phonetically to express **uneven/ unequal**. Some scholars feel that it also lends a similar connotation of unequal by implied comparison with the right hand, to which it was considered inferior in terms of strength. Thus 482 originally appears to have referred to the **uneven lengths of the new shoots on a plant**, though some scholars feel rather that it indicated the **uneven length of fingers on a hand**, before coming to mean **unevenness** and thus **difference** in general. It is not fully clear how it came to mean **thrust**, but it is assumed to be an extended meaning from the idea of the new shoots (or fingers) thrusting out. Suggest taking as a modified combination of **sheep** 羊 986 and **left** 左 22.

Mnemonic: **SHEEP ON LEFT IS DIFFERENT**

| 483 | | SAI, na
VEGETABLE, RAPE
11 strokes | 野菜 YASAI　　　　vegetables
菜種 NATANE　　　rape-seed
菜食主義 SAISHOKUSHUGI
　　　　　　vegetarianism |

采 is an NGU character meaning **take/gather/pluck**, and shows a **reaching hand** 爫 303 and **tree/shrub** 木 69. Some scholars take it to be a hand plucking a shrub, others a hand plucking fruit from a tree or bush. 艹 is **plant** 9, giving **gather/pluck plants**. 483 means **edible plants** in general, i.e. **vegetables**, but has particular associations with the **rape plant**.

Mnemonic: **HAND PLUCKS VEGETABLES NEAR TREE**

| 484 | | SAI, mottomo
MOST, -EST
12 strokes | 最大 SAIDAI　　　　　biggest
最後 SAIGO　　　　　　last
最新式 SAISHINSHIKI
　　　　　　latest style |

Once written 㝡, showing that 日 is not sun 日 62 but a variant of warrior's helmet 冃 1812 q.v., here symbolising **attack** (and to all intents and purposes a simplification of attack 冒 1812). 取 is **take** 301. Thus to **attack and take**, i.e. **seize by force**. This meaning is now conveyed by seize 撮 1305, that adds hand 扌 32, although in Chinese 484 itself still has the related minor meaning of gather. How exactly 484 came to mean **most** is not clear. Some scholars assume it to be a borrowed meaning, others see it as an associated meaning from the idea of **extreme** force/behavior. Suggest taking 日 as **sun**.

Mnemonic: **TAKE MOST SUN WHEN IT'S AT ITS HIGHEST POINT**

485 ZAI
TIMBER, RESOURCE
7 strokes

材木 ZAIMOKU   timber
材料 ZAIRYŌ   material, data
人材 JINZAI   talented person

木 is **tree** 69. 才 is **dam** 126, acting phonetically to express **cut down** (some scholars feel **use**) and probably also lending an idea of **fallen trees**. Thus **felled trees** (i.e. **trees cut for use/ timber**). It later came to mean **material** or **resource** in a wider sense, including the figurative idea of **resourcefulness**.

Mnemonic: **LOTS OF TIMBER IN DAM OF FELLED TREES**

---

486 SAKU
YESTERDAY, PAST
9 strokes

昨日 SAKUJITSU   yesterday
昨夜 SAKUYA   last night
昨年 SAKUNEN   last year

日 is **day** 62. 乍 is **make** 127, here acting phonetically to express **accumulate** and probably also lending an idea of **build up**. Thus **accumulated days**, indicating the **passage of time** and by extension the **past**. It became particularly associated with **yesterday**, according to some scholars because its sound could also express **removed one unit of distance**.

Mnemonic: **PAST MADE UP OF YESTERDAY AND OTHER DAYS**

---

487 刷 SATSU, su*ru*
PRINT, RUB
8 strokes

印刷所 INSATSUSHO   printery
刷新 SASSHIN   reform
校正刷り KŌSEIZURI   proofs

Etymologically somewhat indelicate. Originally the idea of rubbing was conveyed by a character 刷, which in Chinese is interchangeable with 487. It shows **buttocks** 尸 236, **cloth** 巾 778, and a **hand** 又 , and first meant **wipe the buttocks with a cloth**. It then came to mean **rub/wipe** in a broader sense, including the idea of rubbing in order to **print** (an early technique). As the association with printing became stronger, hand 又 was replaced by **cut** 刂 181, to refer to **printing by engraving**. However, it still retains the idea of **rubbing**, though as a minor meaning.

Mnemonic: **'BUTTOCK CLOTH' HAS FINELY CUT PRINT**

488 殺

SATSU, SETSU, koro*su*
KILL
10 strokes

殺人 SATSUJIN		murder
自殺 JISATSU		suicide
殺し屋 KOROSHIYA		killer

Once written 殺, showing that 杀 is a corruption of **pig** 豕 1670. 殳 is **strike/ weapon in hand** 153. Thus 488 originally meant **kill a pig**, then **kill** in general. Suggest taking 杀 as a **wooden** 木 69 **cross** 乂.

Mnemonic: **KILL BY STRIKING WITH WOODEN CROSS**

489 察

SATSU
JUDGE, SURMISE, REALISE
14 strokes

警察 KEISATSU		police
察知 SATCHI		inference
観察 KANSATSU		observation

Somewhat obscure, though its elements are clearly **roof/ building** 宀 28 and **worship** 祭 283 q.v. Most scholars feel that from its literal meaning of **sacrifice** 祭 had strong connotations of **purify**, i.e. **make clean**, which came by association to mean **open up.** 宀 is taken here to mean **cover**. Thus **open up that which is covered**. By figurative extension this came to mean **realise**, leading to **surmise** and **judge**.

Mnemonic: **SURMISE WHY ONE WORSHIPS UNDER ROOF**

490 参

SAN, mai*ru*
ATTEND, GO, BE IN LOVE, BE AT A LOSS, THREE
8 strokes

参加 SANKA		participation
参考 SANKŌ		reference
参議 SANGI		Councilor

Formerly 參, and in ancient times [illegible], showing a kneeling **woman** 女 (see 35) wearing either a tiara or, more likely, **three ornamental hairpins**. The original meaning was **attractive woman**. **Three hairs** 彡 93 was added later for its reinforcing meaning of **delicate** and **attractive**, giving [illegible]. At an early stage the character was used to express **three**, both for its sound and for its **trios** of pins and hairs. How it came to acquire its other meanings is not fully clear. Some scholars take them to be borrowed, others to be extended meanings from the idea of suitors **flocking around** an attractive woman, **falling in love**, and **losing their sense of reason**. Still others feel that it acquired an idea of **cluster** from the three hairpins, that **cluster** came to mean on the one hand **gather** and thence **attend** and on the other **too many to choose from** and thus **confusion**, and that **falling in love** is an associated idea with confusion. Suggest taking 大 as **big** 53 and 厶 as **nose** 134.

Mnemonic: **GO TO GET BIG NOSE WITH THREE HAIRS ATTENDED TO**

491		SAN, u*mu* **BIRTH, PRODUCE** 11 strokes	生産 SEISAN	production
			産物 SANBUTSU	product
			出産 SHUSSAN	birth

Somewhat obscure. 生 is **birth/life** 42. 产 appears to be a simplification of handsome/ attractive (forehead) 彦 93. 产 is known to have acted here phonetically to express **birth/ growth**, thus reinforcing 生 , but any semantic role is unclear. **Produce** is an extended meaning from **bear**. Suggest taking 产 as a combination of **stand** 立 73 and **cliff** 厂 45.

Mnemonic: **LIVE BIRTH STANDING ON CLIFF**

492		SAN, chiru/rasu **SCATTER** 12 strokes	散歩 SANPO	stroll
			散文 SANBUN	prose
			散らし CHIRASHI	leaflet

Once written 瞉 and earlier just 㪔, showing that 枯 is derived from a doubling of **wood/shrub** 木 69, in fact indicating **hemp** (see 1829). 攵 is **strike with stick** 101. 492 originally meant **beat hemp with sticks** (to make cloth). This led to **pulverise** and hence **break into little pieces** and **scatter**. **Meat** 夕 / 月 365 was added later, to give a meaning of **shred meat**, but has now become redundant. Suggest remembering 枯 as **two tens** 十 33 and **one** 一 1, i.e. **twenty-one**.

Mnemonic: **HAND STRIKES MEAT, SCATTERING TWENTY-ONE PIECES**

493	残	ZAN, noko*ru*/*su* **LEAVE, CRUEL, HARM** 10 strokes	残金 ZANKIN	balance
			残念 ZANNEN	regret
			残忍 ZANNIN	brutality

Formerly 殘. 歹 is **bare bone/ death** 286. 戋 is an NGU character meaning **lance/ halberd**, deriving from a pictograph 戈 (essentially an elaboration of stake 弋 177), here doubled for emphasis. 戈 often means **cut, pierce, kill, menace**, or similar. Here it means **cut and kill**, giving **kill someone cruelly by cutting them to the bone**. Thus the meanings of **cruel, harm**, etc., which are still 493's main meanings in Chinese. **Remain/ leave** is felt by some scholars to be a borrowed meaning, by others to derive from the idea of hacking a person till only the bare bones **remain**. Suggest taking 戋 as **halberd** 戈 and **two** 二 61.

Mnemonic: **TWO CRUEL HALBERDS LEAVE ONLY BARE BONE**

494 士	SHI, samurai	武士 BUSHI samurai, warrior
	WARRIOR,SCHOLAR,MAN	士官 SHIKAN military officer
	3 strokes	修士 SHŪSHI Master (degree)

Often explained as a stylised simplification of **man standing** 立 73, but this is incorrect. Very old forms such as ⊥ show a symbol indicating **being erect**, a reference to the **erect male organ**. The later cross-stroke is seen by some scholars as an esthetic embellishment to give balance to the character, by others as a stylised indication of the glans. The erect male organ symbolises **masculinity**, and hence **man**. **Samurai/ warrior** is felt by some scholars to be a borrowed meaning from serving man 仕 285 q.v., but this is something of a circular argument and unconvincing. It is more likely that the warrior was seen as the epitome of masculinity. **Scholar** is an associated meaning.

Mnemonic: **SAMURAI STANDS ERECT**

495	SHI, uji	氏名 SHIMEI full name
	CLAN, FAMILY, MR	氏族 SHIZOKU clan
	4 strokes	加とう氏 KATŌSHI Mr Kato

Once written 𠂉, showing a utensil that was essentially a **ladle** with a cutting edge. **Clan/ family** stems from 495's becoming confused with (or deliberately being substituted for) **hill** 𨸏 (now 阝) 229. Since noble families invariably lived on hilltops 氏 then became used as a reference to a **particular noble family**. It is now used of **family** regardless of social rank. **Mr** similarly relates to reference to a family.

Mnemonic: **MR HILL BORROWS FAMILY LADLE**

496 史	SHI	歴史 REKISHI history
	HISTORY, CHRONICLER	女史 JOSHI Miss, Mrs
	5 strokes	史上 SHIJŌ in history

Often thought to be associated with official 吏 1894, but old forms such as 㞢 reveal a **hand** 彐 holding 中. The latter is thought to be a combination of a **counting-stick** | and **mouth/say** 口 20, to give a meaning of **person counting out loud** or **tallying** and by extension **recording things**. 中 is confusingly the same shape as middle 中 55 q.v., and indeed some scholars feel that the graphic evolution of the latter was influenced by the 中 of 496. Suggest taking 中 as a variant of **middle/ center**.

Mnemonic: **HAND OF MAN CENTRAL TO HISTORY**

497   **SHI, tsukasadoru**   司法 SHIHŌ   judicature
ADMINISTER, OFFICIAL   司令部 SHIREIBU   headquarters
5 strokes   司会者 SHIKAISHA
   master of ceremonies

Once written 司 , being a mirror image of **anus** 后 858 q.v., i.e. an **opening** 口 20 under **buttocks** 尸 /尸 236. (Just as the elements of characters were sometimes repositioned [e.g. 416], so also mirror images were not unknown, though it is not clear whether they had any particular significance.) It is not clear how 497 came to mean **administer/ official**. Some scholars feel it results from borrowing or confusion with chronicler 史 496, but in view of the fact that buttocks in a building 官 441 q.v. came to mean sedentary work and hence government/ official, it is not impossible that anus/ posterior similarly came to symbolise **sedentary work** and hence **official**. Suggest taking 冂 as **entrance**, 一 as **one 1**, and 一 as a **corner**.

Mnemonic: **ONE OFFICIAL ADMINISTERS CORNER ENTRANCE**

498   **SHI, ane**   姉さん NEESAN*   elder sister
ELDER SISTER   姉上 ANEUE   Elder Sister
8 strokes   姉妹都市 SHIMAITOSHI sister city

Formerly 姉. 女 is **woman 35**. 市 is confusingly similar to binding on a stake/ order/ younger brother 弟 177 q.v., but is taken to be a **vine winding round a stake** to symbolise **growth** and by association **starting point**. It also acts phonetically to express **start**. Thus **female starting point**, meaning the first born daughter and hence **elder sister** (see also 288). 市 later became confused with **city** 市 130, which lends no meaning but still acts phonetically to express **start**.

Mnemonic: **ELDER SISTER WORKS IN CITY**

499   **SHI, kokoromiru, tamesu**   試合 SHIAI   match
TRIAL, TEST   試験官 SHIKENKAN examiner
13 strokes   試み KOKOROMI   trial, test

言 is **words 274**. 式 is **form 295**, which also acts phonetically to express **observe**. 499 originally referred to **observing which form of words was most effective**, leading to **test**.

Mnemonic: **TEST FORMS OF WORDS**

| 500 辞 | JI, *yameru*
WORD, DECLINE, LEAVE
13 strokes | 辞書 JISHO
辞職 JISHOKU
修辞学 SHŪJIGAKU | dictionary
resignation
rhetoric |

Somewhat obscure. Formerly written . derives from 𤔔, showing **hands** 𦥑 **untying a knot** 𢆶, and came by extension to mean **unravel, solve, perceive, judge** and so forth. 辛 is **(tattooist's) needle/ sharp** 1432. Some scholars take the latter to symbolise a **prisoner** (who, like a slave, was tattooed [see 318]), and take 500 to have originally meant **judge a prisoner**. All its modern meanings are taken to be essentially borrowed. However, **words** may possibly have evolved from the idea of a judge's **pronouncement**, or else simply from confusion between the simplified form 舌 and **tongue** 舌 732, i.e. giving **sharp tongue/ incisive words**. Other scholars in fact feel that from the outset 辛 meant **sharp**, giving 𤔔辛 a meaning of **sharp insight**. This is felt to have come to mean **be to the point**, then **speak to the point**, with 舌 thus being a later deliberate use of tongue (symbolising **speak**) and not a mere graphic simplification. In view of the fact that the words in 500 came to have a particular association with **refusal** (which might be considered a form of speaking to the point), the latter theory seems the more helpful. **Leave** is an associated meaning of refuse.

Mnemonic: **DECLINE WITH WORDS FROM SHARP TONGUE**

| 501 失 | SHITSU, *ushinau*
LOSE
5 strokes | 失敗 SHIPPAI
失敬 SHIKKEI
失業 SHITSUGYŌ | failure
rudeness
unemployment |

Once written . 𠂆 is **hand** 32. ㇋ is a variant of **odd** 乙 1041, here acting phonetically to express **lose** but also felt by many scholars to suggest the idea of **slipping** by its shape. Thus to **lose by slipping from the hand**. Suggest taking 夫 as **man** 573 and ノ as a **baton**.

Mnemonic: **MAN ABOUT TO LOSE BATON**

| 502 借 | SHAKU, *kariru*
BORROW, RENT
10 strokes | 借金 SHAKKIN
借家 SHAKUYA
借り主 KARINUSHI | debt
rented house
borrower |

亻 is **person** 39. 昔 is **past** 1481 q.v., here acting phonetically to express **imitate** and probably also lending an idea of **duplicate** from its original meaning of succession of days. 502 originally meant **imitate a person**, the idea of deception still being found in its minor Chinese meaning of **make a pretext of**. From this it came to mean **not the real thing**, which by association came to mean something **not really one's own**, i.e. something **borrowed** or **rented**.

Mnemonic: **PERSON WHO HAS BORROWED IN THE PAST**

154

503 SHU, tane
SEED, KIND
14 strokes

一 種	ISSHU	a kind, sort
人 種	JINSHU	humankind
種 無 し	TANENASHI	seedless

禾 is **rice plant** 81. 重 is **heavy** 311, here acting phonetically to express **slow** and probably also lending an idea of **ponderous**. 503 originally referred to a **particular type** of late ripening rice, then came to mean **type/ kind** in general. **Seed** is felt to derive from a reinterpretation of 503's elements as **heavy part of the rice (or grain) plant**, namely the **seed**-bearing head.

Mnemonic: **KIND OF RICE PLANT HEAVY WITH SEED**

504 SHŪ, mawari
CIRCUMFERENCE,
AROUND
8 strokes

周辺	SHŪHEN	perimeter
周到	SHŪTŌ	circumspect
一 周	ISSHŪ	a lap, circuit

Formerly 圕 and once 圍 or 圕, showing a **field** 田 59 **completely full of crops** ∴ (i.e. in all corners). This gave rise to the idea of **complete**, leading by association to completion of a **cycle** and hence **around**. The later element 口 appears to be a **circle**, reinforcing the idea of **round** (as 228). However, some scholars feel that 口 is actually mouth 20, giving what was originally full mouth (or, according to one view, a completely closed mouth, with 冉 acting essentially phonetically to express close) before it was borrowed to express **around**. Suggest taking 口 as **mouth**, 土 as **earth** 60, and 冂 as a **hoop**.

Mnemonic: **EARTH AROUND MOUTH OF HOOP**

505 SHUKU, yado, yadoru
LODGE, SHELTER,
HOUSE
11 strokes

宿題	SHUKUDAI	homework
宿屋	YADOYA	inn
下 宿人	GESHUKUNIN	boarder

Once written 宿, showing **building** 冂/宀 28, **person** 儿/亻 39, and a **rush mat** (bedding, symbolising **resting**) 囹. Thus **building in which a person can rest**, i.e. **house** or **inn**. The use of **hundred** 百 67 results from a long-standing miscopying.

Mnemonic: **HUNDRED PEOPLE LODGING IN ONE HOUSE**

155

| 506 | JUN
SEQUENCE,COMPLIANCE
12 strokes | 順序 JUNJO
従順 JŪJUN
順調 JUNCHŌ ni | sequence
obedience
favorably |

頁 is **head** 93. 川 is **river** 48, here acting phonetically to express **comply** and also lending an idea of **flowing down** and by association not being upright (i.e. **bowing**). 506 originally referred to a **person bowing their head in compliance**. This gave rise to **follow** and hence **order** or **sequence**, the latter meanings probably also influenced by the strong presence of river/ **flow**. Note that the English word **order** similarly has associations both with sequence and compliance (but the latter from the causative rather than passive perspective).

Mnemonic: **COMPLIANT HEADS IN SEQUENCE LIKE FLOWING RIVER**

| 507 | SHO, hatsu-, haji*me*
BEGINNING, FIRST
7 strokes | 最初 SAISHO
初めて HAJIMETE
初恋 HATSUKOI | first
first time
first love |

衤 is **clothing** 420. 刀 is **cut** 181. Thus to **cut cloth to make clothes**. This came to mean **set about doing something,** as well as **new** and therefore **for the first time**.

Mnemonic: **CLOTHES MUST FIRST BE CUT**

| 508 | SHŌ, tona*eru*
RECITE, PREACH
11 strokes | 提唱 TEISHŌ
合唱 GASSHŌ
唱え値 TONAENE | advocacy
chorus
asking price |

口 is **mouth/say** 20. 昌 is an NGU character meaning **bright** or **intense**, comprising two **suns** 日 62, which also acts phonetically to express **raised**. (Some scholars feel that originally 昌 was actually a symbol showing the position of the sun higher than its earlier position, and that it therefore meant **high/ raised**, though it soon became interpreted as double sun in the sense of bright/ intense.) Thus to **speak in a raised and intense voice,** as when **reciting** or **preaching**. Suggest taking 日 in its meaning of **day**.

Mnemonic: **PREACHER'S MOUTH RECITES FOR TWO DAYS**

156

509 SHŌ, yaku/keru 燃焼 NENSHŌ combustion
BURN, ROAST 焼け跡 YAKEATO burnt remains
12 strokes 焼き立て YAKITATE fresh baked

Formerly 燒. 火 is **flames/fire** 8. 堯 is a CO character meaning **high** (literally raised earth, from a trebling of **earth** 土 60 and 兀, an NGU character meaning **high** that is to all intents and purposes a variant of **upper part** 元 106). Thus **high flames**, indicating **burning**. Suggest taking 圭 as **three tens** 十 33 and **one** 一 1, and 儿 as **legs**.

Mnemonic: **ROAST THIRTY-ONE LEGS ON FIRE**

510 SHŌ, teru/rasu 参照 SANSHŌ reference
ILLUMINATE, SHINE 対照 TAISHŌ contrast
13 strokes 照明 SHŌMEI illustration

Bright light 昭 315 with **fire** ⺣ 8 emphasising **brightness**. Thus **shine/ illuminate**.

Mnemonic: **ILLUMINATE BY BRIGHT LIGHT OF FIRE**

511 SHŌ 賞品 SHŌHIN prize
PRIZE, PRAISE 賞讃 SHŌSAN praise
15 strokes 一等賞 ITTŌSHŌ first prize

貝 is **shell** 90, here meaning **money** or **valuable item**. 业 is a variant of **furthermore** 尚 1392 q.v., here acting phonetically to express **bestow** and also lending connotations of **esteem**. Thus **bestow valuable item as token of esteem**, leading to **prize** and **praise** (note that the English terms are etymologically the same word).

Mnemonic: **MOREOVER, SHELLS ARE PRIZES**

512 SHIN, JIN 臣下 SHINKA vassal
RETAINER, SUBJECT 臣民 SHINMIN subjects
7 or 6 strokes 大臣 DAIJIN minister

Once written 𦣹, showing an **eye** with deliberate exaggeration of the pupil to symbolise **wide eyed alertness** (cf. English keep an eye out). This came to mean **guard**, and by extension **retainer, servant, public servant**, and **subject**. Distinguish huge 巨 1153.

Mnemonic: **RETAINER KEEPS WATCHFUL EYE OUT**

157

---

513 信 **SHIN**
TRUST, BELIEVE
9 strokes

信用 SHINYŌ   trust
迷信 MEISHIN   superstition
確信 KAKUSHIN conviction

Word 言 274 and person イ 39. A person's word is something which can be **believed** and **trusted**.

Mnemonic: **PERSON'S WORD IS BELIEVED AND TRUSTED**

---

514 真 **SHIN, ma**
TRUE, QUINTESSENCE
10 strokes

真実 SHINJITSU truth
写真機 SHASHINKI camera
真っ白 MASSHIRO* pure white

Formerly and earlier 眞. ヒ is **fallen person** 238. 臭/眞 derives from an **inverted head** 首 139 (see also 273). 514 originally meant **person upside-down** and then **upside-down** or **overturn** in a broader sense. This meaning is now conveyed by an NGU character 顛 that adds a further **head** 頁 93. It is not clear how it came to mean **truth/essence**. It is generally assumed to result from borrowing, but it is probable that upside-down person meant **dead** person, and therefore possible that this led to the idea of **soul** or **spirit**, giving in turn **essence** and eventually **truth**. It should be noted that in Chinese 514 has strong connotations of the human soul or spirit. Suggest taking as **equipment** 具 265 and **ten** 十 33.

Mnemonic: **IT'S TRUE THAT EQUIPMENT IS IN TEN PIECES**

---

515 成 **SEI, JŌ, naru/su**
BECOME, MAKE,
CONSIST
6 strokes

成分 SEIBUN   component
成人 SEIJIN   adult
成り立ち NARITACHI formation

Once written 戓, showing **exact** 丁 346 and 戊. The latter derives from 戈, showing **halberd** 戈/戈 493 with an exaggerated **blade** ▷/ト. The large blade was also used for shaving wood and fine trimming, and in compounds often lends an idea of **making just so**. It lends such a meaning in 515, reinforced by 丁. It meant **exactly right**, giving **make right** or **be right**. **Consist** is an associated meaning from the idea of **being properly formed**. Note that there is a range of half a dozen or so CO and NGU characters based upon 戊, chiefly being used either for zodiac signs or for concepts involving cutting or weapons. They appear to have become somewhat confused etymologically. For example, 戉 is a CO character meaning halberd or battle ax, while 戊 is listed as a zodiac sign, but they are clearly essentially the same character. Suggest treating them all as variants of **halberd** 戈.

Mnemonic: **BECOME EXACT AFTER TRIMMING WITH HALBERD BLADE**

516 SEI, SHŌ, habu*ku*, kaeri*miru* 反省 HANSEI reflection
MINISTRY, OMIT, 省略 SHŌRYAKU omission
EXAMINE 厚生省 KŌSEISHŌ
9 strokes Welfare Ministry

Somewhat obscure, though its elements are clearly **eye** 目 72 and **few/ little** 少 143. Some scholars take the latter to act phonetically to express **obstructed**, as well as lending a meaning of **small**, to give **reduced vision**, and take all the modern meanings to be borrowings. However, most scholars take the elements to be used ideographically to give a meaning of **narrowing one's eyes** in order to **scrutinise**. Scrutinise led to **examine**, and became particularly associated with the idea of scrutinising in order to **trim to an optimum**, i.e. by **removing** unnecessary elements. This led to **omit**. Examining also appears to have become associated with **government**, leading by association to **government ministry** (and **administrative district** in Chinese). Note that a different positioning of the same elements gives the NGU character 眇, which means both minute and squint.

Mnemonic: **FEW EYES EXAMINE MINISTRY: AN OMISSION**

517 SEI, SHŌ, kiyo*i/meru* 清潔 SEIKETSU cleanliness
PURE, CLEAN 清浄 SEIJŌ/SHŌJŌ purity
11 strokes 清水 SHIMIZU* spring water

氵 is **water** 40. 青 is **blue/ green** 43 q.v., here acting phonetically to express **clear/ clean** and also lending an idea of **fresh**. **Fresh clear water** came to mean **pure** in general.

Mnemonic: **BLUE WATER IS PURE AND CLEAN**

518 SEI, ikio*i* 勢力 SEIRYOKU power
POWER, FORCE 大勢 ŌZEI multitude
13 strokes 勢いよく IKIOIYOKU vigorously

力 is **strength** 74. 埶 is **kneeling to plant a tree** 470, here meaning **plant** in general. Planting requires great strength, thus the **strength required for planting** indicates considerable **power**. Suggest taking 埶 as **round** 丸 830 and **mounds of earth** 坴 597.

Mnemonic: **STRONG POWER FORCES UP ROUND EARTHEN MOUNDS**

519 静	SEI, JŌ, shizuka/maru QUIET, CALM 14 strokes	静止 SEISHI	stillness
		静けさ SHIZUKESA*	quietude
		静脈 JŌMYAKU	vein

Formerly 靜 . Somewhat obscure, though its elements are clearly **green** 青/青 43 q.v. and **conflict** 争/爭 529 q.v. Some scholars take the latter to act phonetically to express **beautiful**, giving **beautiful green color**, and take **quiet/ calm** to be a borrowed meaning. However, if 519 did indeed originally mean beautiful green, then it might be felt that quiet/ calm is an associated meaning (from the apparently universal interpretation of green as a **restful color**). Other scholars take 青 to indicate **clear** (partly phonetically, partly from its own idea of fresh [and clean]), and take 争 in its meaning of **conflict,** to give **clear of conflict.** Still others take 青 to mean **fresh/ pure** and take 争 to mean **stop/ stay** (from its assumed literal meaning of one arm stopping another), to give **staying pure.** Quiet/ calm is then taken to be an associated meaning from the idea of **desirable lack of movement.** It should be noted that 519 has a lesser meaning of **pure** in Chinese, and that it also has connotations of **lack of movement,** suggesting that the last theory is the most likely.

Mnemonic: **CONFLICT QUIETENED BY SIGHT OF CALMING GREEN**

520 席	SEKI SEAT, PLACE 10 strokes	出席 SHUSSEKI	attendance
		欠席 KESSEKI	absence
		空席 KŪSEKI	empty seat

A much changed character. Originally written 囮, showing a **rush mat** (see 505) used as crude **seating** or bedding. Cliff 厂 45 was added as a phonetic to express **spread**, giving 庿, later being replaced by 庶. The latter is an abbreviation of **various** 庶 1381, used in a similar phonetic role to 厂 and presumably also used to lend an idea of **plurality.** Finally rush mat 囮 was replaced by **cloth** 巾 778, presumably indicating an improvement in the quality of the seating. Suggest taking 广 as **building** 114 and 廿 as **two tens** 十 33 and **one** 一 1, i.e. **twenty-one.**

Mnemonic: **BUILDING WITH TWENTY-ONE CLOTH SEATS**

521 積	SEKI, tsumu/moru PRODUCT, PILE 16 strokes	面積 MENSEKI	dimensions
		積雪 SEKISETSU	snow depth
		積もり TSUMORI	intention

禾 is **rice plant** 81. 責 is **blame** 728 q.v., here acting phonetically to express **gather/ accumulate** and possibly also lending its own similar connotations of **accumulate.** 521 originally referred to the **rice crop being gathered and heaped in a pile. Product** is an extended idea from **pile/ total.**

Mnemonic: **TAKE BLAME FOR PILE UP OF RICE PLANTS**

522		SETSU, ori, *oru/reru* BEND, BREAK, OCCASION 7 strokes	屈折 KUSSETSU	refraction
			折り目 ORIME	fold, crease
			折り紙 ORIGAMI	origami

扌 is **hand** 32. 斤 is **ax/chop** 1176. Usually explained as **'chopping' with the hand**, i.e. **bending** or **breaking**. In fact, while an old form 𣂐 shows hand ㄓ, the earliest forms such as 𣏒 show **two plants** Ψ 9. Plant Ψ was occasionally used to mean **tree**, instead of the normal 木 69, and in fact 522 originally meant to **chop down trees**. However, the miscopying is of very long standing, and the original meaning has long since disappeared. It is not clear how 522 also came to mean **occasion** (Japanese only).

Mnemonic: **HAND-AX CAN BREAK OR BEND**

523		SETSU, SECHI, fushi SECTION, JOINT, PERIOD, POINT, TUNE, RESTRAIN 13 strokes	調節 CHŌSETSU	adjustment
			関節 KANSETSU	joint
			節穴 FUSHIANA	knothole

⺮ is **bamboo** 170. 即 is **namely** 1534 q.v., here acting phonetically to express **division** and also lending an idea of **order** (from seating order at a table). Thus **ordered division of bamboo**, a reference to (the **ordered arrangement of**) its **nodes and sections**. This gave rise to a wide range of extended meanings, including a section of time (**period**), a section of a song (originally a **stanza** or **verse**, now **tune**), and even the idea of keeping oneself in order (giving **restraint** and **integrity**).

Mnemonic: **BAMBOO HAS JOINTS, NAMELY SECTIONS**

524	説	SETSU, *toku* PREACH, EXPLAIN 14 strokes	説明 SETSUMEI	explanation
			小説 SHŌSETSU	novel
			学説 GAKUSETSU	theory

言 is **words/speak** 274. 兌 is an NGU character meaning exchange or barter (or **issue** in Chinese), comprising **speaking person** 兄 267 and **away/out/disperse** ⺍ 66 and literally meaning a **person dispersing words**. Here 兌 means **issuing words**, and also acts phonetically to express **construct**. Thus **speak while issuing constructive words**, i.e. **preach** or **explain**. Suggest taking 兄 in its modern meaning of **elder brother**.

Mnemonic: **ELDER BROTHER DISPERSES WORDS, PREACHING AWAY**

525		SEN, asa*i*	浅薄 SENPAKU	shallowness
		SHALLOW, LIGHT	浅瀬 ASASE	shallows
		9 strokes	浅黄 ASAGI	light yellow

Formerly 淺 . ⺡ is **water** 40. 戔 is **two halberds** 493, here acting phonetically to express **small (amount)** and also lending an idea of **cut away** and thereby **reduce**. Thus **water reduced to a small amount**, giving **shallow**. **Light** is an associated meaning.

Mnemonic: **WATER SHALLOW: DEPTH OF TWO HALBERDS**

526		SEN, tataka*u*, ikusa	大戦 TAISEN	major war
		FIGHT, WAR	戦場 SENJŌ	battleground
		13 strokes	作戦 SAKUSEN	strategy

Formerly 戰 , and originally just 戔 , namely **two halberds** 493. In later times the halberds were reduced to one, while **simple** 罩 / 単 542 q.v. was added in its literal sense of **forked thrusting weapon**. Thus **two (i.e. many) weapons**, indicating **fighting** and **war**.

Mnemonic: **FIGHT WAR WITH SIMPLE HALBERD**

527		SEN, era*bu*, yo*ru*	当選 TŌSEN	election
		CHOOSE	選手 SENSHU	player
		15 strokes	選び出す ERABIDASU	pick out

Formerly 選 . ⻌ is **movement (along a road)** 129. 巽 / 巺 is somewhat obscure. It exists as a CO character with a current meaning of bland, while its core meaning appears to be **arrange in sequence**, giving rise to extended meanings such as follow and comply (hence bland). It appears to comprise **twisting threads** 己 855 (or twisting serpents 巳 250), indicating a **line or sequence**, and **together** 共 460. Here it acts phonetically to express **follow** (after someone), and almost certainly lends similar connotations of its own. Thus 527 originally meant **follow someone along a road**. Some scholars see **choose** as being an extension of this, i.e. choosing a leader, while others see it as a borrowed meaning.

Mnemonic: **CHOOSE TO MOVE TOGETHER LIKE TWISTING THREADS**

528	ZEN, NEN, shika*ru/shi*	当然	TŌZEN	rightly
	DULY, THUS, SO, BUT	天然	TENNEN	nature
	12 strokes	然るべく	SHIKARUBEKU	duly

Fire ⺍ 8, **meat** 月 365, and **dog** 犬 17. 528 originally meant to **roast dog meat**, then came to mean **roast** or **burn** in a broad sense. It can still occasionally mean roast or burn in Chinese, but in Japanese this meaning has been entirely assumed by 燃 765, that adds an extra fire 火 8. It was later borrowed phonetically to express **thus/ duly/ as things should be** (but derives from an inflexion of this term [shikaru to shikashi], to the effect of **be that as it may**). It is not clear why such a complex character was chosen as a phonetic, but it is possible that 528 had connotations of **contentment**, and was thus considered appropriate to express **as things should be**.

Mnemonic: **DULY EAT ROAST DOG MEAT, BUT...**

529	SŌ, arasou	戦争	SENSŌ	war
	CONFLICT, VIE	言い争い	IIARASOI	quarrel
	6 strokes	競争者	KYŌSŌSHA	competitor

Formerly 爭 , and earlier ⺈. This clearly shows a **hand reaching down** ⺈ 303 and another **hand** ⺺ holding an **item** /, for possession of which the hands are presumably **vying**. However, still older forms such as 𠂹 reveal that ⺈ is a miscopying of a **hand** ⺺ **seizing an arm** with bulging biceps 𠂆 (the prototype of strength 力 74). 529 originally meant to **take hold of someone** and **restrain** them, indicating a **conflict**. **Vie** is an associated meaning. Suggest taking ⺈ as **bent person** 145, and 尹 as **hand holding stick**.

Mnemonic: **VIE WITH BENT OLD MAN, STICK IN HAND**

530	SŌ, SHŌ, ai-	相談	SŌDAN	discussion
	MUTUAL, MINISTER,	相手	AITE	other party
	ASPECT	首相	SHUSHŌ	Prime Minister
	9 strokes			

Somewhat obscure, though its elements are clearly **tree** 木 69 and **eye** 目 72. Most scholars assume it to refer to an eye watching from behind a tree, symbolising **cautious observation**. It still means **observe carefully** in Chinese. **Mutual** is taken by some scholars to be an associated meaning, since the observer might himself be under observation (as in two adversaries carefully weighing each other up). Others take it to be a borrowing. Similarly some scholars take **minister** to be an associated meaning from the idea of **examining** or **keeping alert**, as in the case of examine/ ministry 省 516 or keep alert/ public servant 臣 512, while others take it to be a borrowing. **Aspect**, in the sense of the **appearance of a situation**, appears to stem from **careful observation**.

Mnemonic: **MINISTERS EYE EACH OTHER FROM TREES**

163

---

531 SŌ, kura
WAREHOUSE, SUDDEN
10 strokes

船倉 SENSŌ   ship's hold
倉皇 SŌKŌ   bustle
倉荷 KURANI

warehouse goods

Formed from a **cover** 亼 87, here indicating **preserving**, and 昃 . The latter is a now defunct character meaning **door** (comprising opening/ **entrance** 口 20 and a variant 尸 of **door** 尸 108). Thus **that which is covered and behind a door**, a reference to **goods in a storehouse**. Some scholars feel that 昃 also lent its sound to express **smell**, being a reference to the smell of stored grain. The minor meaning **sudden** is assumed to be a borrowing, but may possibly relate to the idea of hurrying to put crops in storage.

Mnemonic: **WAREHOUSE HAS COVER AND DOORED ENTRANCE**

---

532 SŌ, SO
IDEA, THOUGHT
13 strokes

着想 CHAKUSŌ   concept
理想 RISŌ   ideal
愛想 AISO/AISŌ   affability

心 is **heart/ feelings** 147. 相 is **mutual** 530 q.v., here used for its literal meaning of **observe carefully** and by extension **examine**. Thus **examine carefully in one's heart**, i.e. **cogitate**.

Mnemonic: **THOUGHTS CAN BE MUTUAL FEELINGS**

---

533 ZŌ, SHŌ
ELEPHANT, IMAGE
12 strokes

象げ ZŌGE   ivory
印象 INSHŌ   impression
象徴的 SHŌCHŌTEKI symbolic

From a pictograph of an **elephant** 𧰨 . The elephant has a dramatic **form**, and thus 533 also acquired connotations of **form, shape,** and **image**. By association it can also occasionally mean **resemble**. Suggest remembering by association with **pig** 豕 1670, perhaps taking 吅 as **two big ears** and 勹 as a curled **trunk**.

Mnemonic: **ELEPHANT RESEMBLES PIG WITH BIG EARS AND TRUNK**

534	**SOKU, hayai, sumiyaka** 速記 SOKKI shorthand **SPEED, FAST** 時速 JISOKU speed per hour 10 strokes 高速道路 KŌSOKUDŌRO freeway

辶 is **movement** (along a road) 129. 束 is bundle/ **manage** 1535, acting phonetically to express **hurry** and also probably lending an idea of **control**. Thus **(controlled?) hurrying movement**.

Mnemonic: **MANAGE FAST MOVEMENT**

535	**SOKU, kawa, gawa, soba** 側面 SOKUMEN side, flank **SIDE** 右側 MIGIGAWA right side 11 strokes 側仕え SOBAZUKAE valet

亻 is **person** 39. 則 is rule/ **model** 742. The role of the latter is disputed. Some scholars feel it acts phonetically to express **lean** and that 742 meant **leaning person**, i.e. a cripple, before coming to mean **leaning to one side** in general and hence **side**. Other scholars feel that 則 did express **lean**, but that this was used in the figurative sense of **tend /incline**, and that it also lent its own meaning of **model**. Thus a **person whom one looks upon as a model and towards whom one inclines**. One is always at the **side** of such a person.

Mnemonic: **BE AT SIDE OF MODEL PERSON**

536	**ZOKU, tsuzuku/keru** 続続 ZOKUZOKU successively **CONTINUE, SERIES** 連続 RENZOKU continuity 13 strokes 手続き TETSUZUKI procedure

Formerly 續. 糸 is **thread** 27. 賣/売 is **sell** 192, here acting phonetically to express **join** and also lending an idea of **equivalence** (from the idea of exchanging goods for an equivalent amount of money). Thus to **join threads of equal length**, giving the idea of **continuity** and **succession**.

Mnemonic: **CONTINUE TO SELL THREADS**

165

537		SOTSU	卒業 SOTSUGYŌ	graduation
		SOLDIER, END	兵卒 HEISOTSU	soldier
		8 strokes	卒去 SOKKYO	death

Once written 衾. 衾 is the early form of **clothing** 衣 420 q.v., with the lower stroke lengthened in order to accommodate ╱, a CO character meaning **dash** or **mark**. 537 originally referred to **marked clothing**, indicating a slave or, later, a **soldier**. The lesser meaning of **end** is borrowed. Suggest taking ⊥ as a **top hat**, 从 as persons/ **men** 39, and ┼ as **ten** 33.

Mnemonic: **TEN SOLDIER-MEN IN TOP HATS**

538		SON, mago	子孫 SHISON	descendants
		DESCENDANTS,	孫引き MAGOBIKI	requotation
		GRANDCHILDREN	孫娘 MAGOMUSUME	
		10 strokes		granddaughter

Originally 웃8, showing **child** ㄗ/子 25 and **short thread** 8/幺 111. The latter symbolised **very small**, giving **very small child**, a reference to **grandchildren**. **Descendants** is an associated meaning. The modern form uses **joined threads/ lineage** 系 844.

Mnemonic: **DESCENDANTS ARE CHILDREN IN THREAD-LIKE LINEAGE**

539		TAI, obi, *obiru*	地帯 CHITAI	zone
		BELT, OBI, WEAR,	帯地 OBIJI	obi material
		ZONE	熱帯魚 NETTAIGYO	tropical fish
		10 strokes		

Formerly 帶, combining **cloth** 巾 778 and a pictograph of a **belt/ obi** with items attached to it 㡀. Also used figuratively as a **belt/ zone** of land. Suggest remembering by association with **mountain** 山 24.

Mnemonic: **FIND CLOTH BELT IN MOUNTAIN ZONE**

540		TAI	兵隊	HEITAI	soldier
		CORPS, UNIT	軍隊	GUNTAI	army
		12 strokes	部隊	BUTAI	troop

Hill β 229 and (group of) **pigs moving** 㒸 1458 q.v. The latter acts phonetically to express **come down** and almost certainly also lends an idea of **moving in an ungainly fashion**. 540 originally meant **fall down a hill** (still retained as a minor meaning in Chinese). It is not fully clear how it came to acquire its present meaning. Some scholars feel it is purely the result of borrowing, but since hills were often associated with **troop encampments** there may be some loose semantic connection such as **commotion on a hillside** or similar.

Mnemonic: **UNIT OF PIG-LIKE SOLDIERS ON HILL**

541		TATSU, -tachi	発達	HATTATSU	development
		ATTAIN, PLURAL SUFFIX	達人	TATSUJIN	expert
		12 strokes	人達	HITOTACHI	people

辶 is **movement** 129. 羍 was once written 㚎, comprising **sheep** 羊 986 and **big** 大 53, and refers to the **ease** with which sheep are born and grow big (note that a different arrangement of the same elements big and sheep gives beautiful 美 376). Here 羍 acts phonetically to express **pass**, and also lends connotations of **ease**. Thus **easy movement**, indicating the **attainment of a goal** without difficulty. In Japanese it was later borrowed as a **plural suffix**, though the exact reason for this is not clear. In Chinese 541 can also be used to mean lamb. Suggest taking 土 as **ground** 60.

Mnemonic: **SHEEP MOVE ON GROUND TO ATTAIN GOAL**

542		TAN	単位	TANI	unit
		SIMPLE, SINGLE, UNIT	単純	TANJUN na	simple
		9 strokes	単独	TANDOKU	solo

Formerly 單 and in ancient times 𓎤, showing a **forked thrusting weapon** Y (see also 825) with guard — and exaggerated binding ⊖. It was borrowed essentially phonetically to express **simple** -- with **single** and **unit** being associated meanings of this -- but as a primitive weapon may also have had its own connotations of simple. Suggest remembering by association with **ten** 十 33 and **field** 田 59.

Mnemonic: **SIMPLE UNIT OF TEN FIELDS**

167

543   **DAN**   相談役 SŌDANYAKU   adviser
              CONVERSATION, TALK   会談 KAIDAN   conference
              15 strokes   談話 DANWA   conversation

Words 言 274 and **leaping flames** 炎 1024, indicating a **spirited discussion**.

Mnemonic: **CONVERSATION OF FIERY WORDS**

---

544   **CHI, JI, osa***meru*, **nao***su*   政治 SEIJI   politics
              GOVERN, RULE, CURE   治安 CHIAN   public order
              8 strokes   治療 CHIRYŌ   remedy

Somewhat obscure. 氵 is **water** 40, while 台 is **platform/ self** 166. Some scholars feel that 544 originally referred to a certain river in ancient China and that its present meanings result from borrowing. Others feel that it meant to **bring water to oneself**, i.e. by irrigation, and that this symbolised **control** over the environment, with its present meanings being extensions of control.

Mnemonic: **GOVERN FROM A WATERY PLATFORM**

---

545   **CHI, o***ku*   放置 HŌCHI   leaving as is
              PUT, PLACE   置き物 OKIMONO   ornament
              13 strokes   置き場 OKIBA   repository

罒 is **net** 193. 直 is **direct** 349, here acting phonetically to express erect/ **set up** and also lending connotations of **directly**. Thus to **set up a net directly** (in something's path), leading to **put in place**.

Mnemonic: **PUT NET DIRECTLY IN PATH**

---

546   **CHO, takuwa***eru*   貯金 CHOKIN   savings
              STORE, SAVE   貯蔵 CHOZŌ   storage
              12 strokes   貯水池 CHOSUICHI   reservoir

Once written 宁, showing a frame for **storing** yarn (now simplified to 宁). Shell/ **money** 貝 90 was added later to give the idea of **storing assets/ wealth**. Suggest taking 宀 as **roof** 28 and 丁 as **exactly** 346.

Mnemonic: **STORED WEALTH FITS EXACTLY UNDER ROOF**

547		CHŌ, harawata INTESTINE(S) 13 strokes	腸線 CHŌSEN	(cat) gut
			腸炎 CHŌEN	enteritis
			大腸 DAICHŌ	large intestine

月 is **flesh/ of the body** 365. 易 is **rising sun** 144, here acting phonetically to express **long** and probably also lending an extended idea of path/ **passage** (i.e. the course of the sun). Thus **long passage in the body**. Note that long itself, 長 173, combines with 易 to give distend 脹 1593.

Mnemonic: **FLESHY INTESTINES EXPOSED TO RISING SUN**

548		TEI, hiku*i* LOW 7 strokes	最低 SAITEI	lowest
			低利 TEIRI	low interest
			低落 TEIRAKU	decline

イ is **person** 39. 氐 is **bottom of a hill**, comprising **scoop/ hill** 氏 495 q.v. and a **base line** 一. Thus **people at bottom of hill**, i.e. **lowly** commoners as opposed to the nobles who lived on top of the hill (see 99). Lowly person later came to mean **low position** and then **low** in general.

Mnemonic: **PERSON SCOOPS LOW, DOWN TO BASE LINE**

549		TEI, soko BOTTOM, BASE 8 strokes	海底 KAITEI	seabed
			奥底 OKUSOKO	depths
			底流 TEIRYŪ	undercurrent

广 is **building** 114, and 氐 is **bottom of hill** 548. Thus **building at bottom of hill**, later **bottom** or **base** in general. Suggest taking 氐 literally as hill/ **scoop** 氏 495 and a **base** 一.

Mnemonic: **SCOOP OUT BASE OF BUILDING**

550		TEI STOP 11 strokes	停止 TEISHI	stoppage
			停車所 TEISHAJO	station
			停電 TEIDEN	power cut

Person イ 39 and **inn** 亭 1614, giving **inn where person stays** and eventually **stay/ stop** in general.

Mnemonic: **PERSON STOPS AT INN**

169

551		TEKI, mato TARGET, -LIKE, ADJECTIVAL SUFFIX 8 strokes	目的 MOKUTEKI	purpose
			理想的 RISŌTEKI	ideal
			的外れ MATOHAZURE	off the mark

White 白 65, here meaning **conspicuous**, and **ladle/** scoop 勺 1342, here meaning **select** and by extension **set apart**. Thus **something conspicuous and set apart**, i.e. a **target**. (Some old forms such as ⊖勺 show sun/bright 日 62 instead of white 白, but the meaning of conspicuous is unaffected.) Setting something apart also gave rise to the idea of **classification**, which in turn gave rise to **likeness**. The idea of **-like** became a common way of forming adjectives.

Mnemonic: **WHITE LADLE MAKES GOOD TARGET**

552		TEN, nori CODE, RULE, PRECEDENT 8 strokes	辞典 JITEN	dictionary
			典拠 TENKYO	authority
			典型 TENKEI	type, model

Originally 興. ⧻ is the prototype of **books** 冊 874 q.v., namely a collection of writing tablets bound together, while 丌 is a table/ **desk**. Thus **collection of written material on a desk**, i.e. reference material, leading to **codex, code, law** etc. Suggest remembering by association with **bend** 曲 261 and **six** 六 76.

Mnemonic: **BEND SIX RULES**

553		DEN, tsuta*eru/waru* CONVEY, TRANSMIT 6 strokes	伝説 DENSETSU	legend
			伝記 DENKI	biography
			伝染病 DENSENBYŌ	
				contagious disease

Formerly 傳. イ is **person** 39. 專 is the old form of exclusive 專 914 q.v., here used for its literal meaning of spinning weight to give an idea of **rotating**. Thus to **rotate amongst people**, i.e. **convey** or **transmit**. Suggest taking 云 as **two** 二 61 and **nose** ム 134.

Mnemonic: **TWO PEOPLE NOSE TO NOSE CONVEYING SOMETHING**

554

TO, ada, itazura
FOLLOWER, FUTILITY
10 strokes

生徒 SEITO   pupil
徒歩者 TOHOSHA   pedestrian
徒花 ADABANA wasted effort

Usually explained as **movement along a road** 彳 118 and **run** 走 161 q.v., giving **run along a road** and by extension **pursue** and **follow**. A useful mnemonic, but old forms such as 㣙 show that 走 is not run but literally **foot** 止 129 and **ground** 土 60. 554 originally meant **someone who went on foot**, especially foot soldiers (still a meaning in Chinese) but also crowds and **followers**. Follower later came to prevail as the main meaning. It is not clear how 554 also came to mean **futility**, though it may be an idea associated with the difficulty of traveling on foot (as opposed to horseback).

Mnemonic: **FOLLOWER RUNS FUTILELY ALONG ROAD**

555

DO, tsuto*meru*
ENDEAVOR, TRY
7 strokes

努力 DORYOKU   effort
努力家 DORYOKUKA 'worker'
努めて TSUTOMETE
               to best of one's ability

Strength/ **effort** 力 74 and **slave** 奴 1638, giving **work like a slave**, i.e. **try hard**.

Mnemonic: **TRY WITH SLAVE-LIKE EFFORT**

556

TŌ, hi
LIGHT, LAMP
6 strokes

灯台 TŌDAI   lighthouse
電灯 DENTŌ   electric light
灯船 TŌSEN   lightship

Formerly 燈. 火 is **fire** 8. 登 is climb 360 q.v., here with its literal meaning of **atop a pedestal**. Thus fire atop a pedestal, i.e. a **beacon** or **lamp**. Exactly 丁 346 was used partly as a graphic simplification and partly for its stand-like shape.

Mnemonic: **LAMP'S FLAME IS EXACT**

---

557 堂

DŌ
HALL, TEMPLE
11 strokes

講堂 KŌDŌ   auditorium
食堂 SHOKUDŌ dining hall
堂堂 DŌDŌ   grandly, fairly

Furthermore 尚 1392 q.v., here with its original meaning of **tall building** (with window), and **ground** 土 60, here meaning **mound**. Thus **tall building on raised ground**, indicating an important and stately building.

Mnemonic: **FURTHERMORE, HALL IS ON RAISED GROUND**

171

558		DŌ, hataraku WORK 13 strokes	労働 RŌDŌ	labor
			働き手 HATARAKITE	worker
			働き者 HATARAKIMONO	
				hard worker

A 'made in Japan' character, though it is now also used in Chinese, ideographically combining **person** 亻 39 and **move** 動 362 to express the idea of **being busy** and **working**.

Mnemonic: **WORKING PEOPLE ON THE MOVE**

559	毒	DOKU POISON 8 strokes	有毒 YŪDOKU na	poisonous
			気の毒 KINODOKU	sorry
			食中毒 SHOKUCHŪDOKU	
				food poisoning

Somewhat obscure. 主 is generally seen as a simplification of **growing plant/ life** 生 42, and 毋 as **mother** 203. It is not fully clear how these elements differ from the similar elements of every 毎 206 q.v. Some scholars feel that 毋 acts phonetically to express **harm**, giving either **harmful to life** or **harmful plant** depending on the semantic role ascribed to 主. However, it would seem unlikely that the character for mother, with such benign and life-giving connotations, would be borrowed for such a negative phonetic role, and perhaps more likely that 559 originally meant **life-giving plant**, then **powerful herb/drug**, then somehow acquired the sinister connotations of **drug able to control/ take away life**.

Mnemonic: **MOTHER LIVES ON, DESPITE POISON**

560		NETSU, atsui HEAT 15 strokes	熱心 NESSHIN	fervor
			熱帯 NETTAI	tropics
			熱力学 NETSURIKIGAKU	
				thermodynamics

.... is **fire** 8. 埶 is person bending to plant tree 470 q.v., here meaning by association **person kneeling holding a stick**, as in early methods of making fire. According to some scholars 埶 also acts phonetically to express **rising heat**. Suggest remembering by association with **round** 丸 830 and **mound of earth** 坴 597.

Mnemonic: **EARTHEN MOUNDS ROUND FIRE BECOME HOT**

561	NEN	念力 NENRIKI	will
	THOUGHT, CONCERN	念入り NENIRI na	careful
	8 strokes	念仏 NENBUTSU	
			Buddhist prayer

心 is **heart/ feelings** 147. 今 is **now** 125 q.v., here used in its early sense of **cover/ hide** and also acting phonetically to express **firmly possess**. Thus **something firmly possessed and hidden in the heart**, such as a religious conviction or similar. It has now broadened to mean **profound thought**, and in Chinese can also mean remember.

Mnemonic: **HAVE THOUGHTS IN HEART EVEN NOW**

562	HAI, yabu*reru*	敗戦 HAISEN	lost fight
	DEFEAT	敗走 HAISŌ	rout
	11 strokes	敗北主義 HAIBOKUSHUGI	
			defeatism

貝 is **shell/money** 90, here meaning **asset** or property. 攵 is **striking hand** 101, here meaning **attack and damage**. Thus to **attack and damage someone's assets**, meaning to **defeat/ destroy**. It has now generally come to be used in the passive sense of **be defeated**.

Mnemonic: **SHELL 'DEFEATED' BY STRIKING HAND**

563	BAI	五倍 GOBAI	five-fold
	DOUBLE, -FOLD	倍加 BAIKA	doubling
	10 strokes	倍数 BAISŪ	multiple

亻 is **person** 39. 咅 is the obscure element **spit** 384 q.v., here acting phonetically to express **turn against** and probably also lending an idea of **division** and/or **rejection**. 563 originally referred to two persons turning their back on each other. This came to symbolise **division into two,** and by extension the idea of a mathematical **multiple**. Suggest taking 咅 as **stand** 立 73 and **open mouth** 口 20.

Mnemonic: **PERSON STANDS OPEN MOUTHED WITH DOUBLE**

173

564 HAKU, BAKU   博士 HAKASE*   Ph.D.
EXTENSIVE, SPREAD,   博徒 BAKUTO   gambler
GAIN, GAMBLE   博物館 HAKUBUTSUKAN
12 strokes   museum

Though confusingly similar to **exclusive** 専 914, 尃 is a different element. It can also be written 尃, and as such is a CO character meaning **spread** (interchangeable with spread 敷/敷 1756). It comprises **(crude) start** 甫 970 q.v. and **measure/hand** 寸 909, a crude start to measuring being to **spread** the fingers of the hand. 尃 also acts phonetically to express **big/ extensive**. 十 is **ten** 33, here used to mean **numerous** and also lending connotations of **acquire** from its associations with the fingers of both hands and thus to **pick up** (see ten/ gather 拾 305). Thus the overall idea of **spreading and making numerous/ extensive gains**, with **gamble** being an associated meaning. Suggest using **exclusive** 専 as a mnemonic, taking the extra stroke ` as a **point**.

Mnemonic: **GAIN TEN EXCLUSIVE POINTS BY EXTENSIVE GAMBLING**

565 HAN, meshi   御飯 GOHAN   rice, food
COOKED RICE, FOOD   昼飯 HIRUMESHI   lunch
12 strokes   飯田 IIDA*   a surname

食 is **food/ eat** 146. 反 is **oppose** 371 q.v., here acting phonetically to express **eat** and almost certainly also lending its literal meaning of **turn the hand over**. Thus to **eat food** (turning the hand over in so doing). It can still mean eat in Chinese, but has generally come to refer to the **food** being eaten (especially **rice**) rather than the act of eating.

Mnemonic: **OPPOSED TO EATING COOKED RICE**

566 HI, tobu   飛行機 HIKŌKI   airplane
FLY   飛語 HIGO   wild rumor
9 strokes   飛び出す TOBIDASU   jump out

Once written 飛, showing a **long-necked crane with spread wings**, soaring upwards in **flight**. Suggest taking as **two 'streamlined' cranes** with particularly slim bodies and **long beaks** 飛 skimming low through tall **reeds** 川.

Mnemonic: **TWO LONG BEAKED CRANES FLY THROUGH TALL REEDS**

567		HI, tsuiyasu SPEND 12 strokes	費用 HIYŌ	costs
			消費者 SHŌHISHA	consumer
			生活費 SEIKATSUHI	
				cost of living

貝 is shell/ money 90. 弗 is a CO character meaning not. It shows binding 弓 (see 177) being undone ﾉ\ (see 66), and originally meant undo/ remove/ disperse. Thus to disperse money until none is left, i.e. spend (heavily).

Mnemonic: UNWIND AND SPEND MONEY

568		HITSU, kanarazu NECESSARILY 5 strokes	必要 HITSUYŌ	need
			必死 HISSHI no	desperate
			必然 HITSUZEN no	inevitable

Once written)刈｜, showing a halberd/ lance ㄎ 493 between two poles)｜. The poles were strapped to the lance to prevent the possibility of the latter's breakage while not in use. It is not fully clear how this came to mean necessarily, but some scholars feel that the idea of keeping something safe and secure led to the idea of sureness, with this eventually leading to surely and hence by association necessarily. Suggest remembering by association with heart 心 147, taking ／ as a bent lance.

Mnemonic: LANCE THROUGH HEART IS NECESSARILY BENT

569		HITSU, fude WRITING BRUSH 12 strokes	鉛筆 ENPITSU	pencil
			筆者 HISSHA	writer
			筆使い FUDEZUKAI	penmanship

Bamboo ⺮ 170 and brush in hand 聿 142. Originally bamboo writing brush.

Mnemonic: TAKE BAMBOO WRITING BRUSH IN HAND

570		HYŌ VOTE, LABEL, SIGN 11 strokes	票決 HYŌKETSU	vote
			投票 TŌHYŌ	voting
			伝票 DENPYŌ	chit, slip

Once written 燹. 火 is flames/ fire 8. 臾 is often taken to be a variant of waist 臾 593 (literally hands ㇆ ㇇ 'gathering in' a backbone 又), but it seems more likely that ㅿ is brain/ head 131 and that 臾 therefore means neck rather than waist. Here it acts phonetically to express leap and probably also lends an idea of upper tapered part. Thus leaping (tongues of?) flame. 570 was later used as a simpler substitute for mark/ sign 標 571 q.v., and by association also came to acquire connotations of vote. Suggest taking as west 西 152 and show 示 695.

Mnemonic: VOTE SHOWS WEST IS BEST

571
HYŌ, shirushi
SIGN(POST), MARK
15 strokes

標準 HYŌJUN — standard
里程標 RITEIHYŌ — milestone
標識 HYŌSHIKI — signal

木 is **tree** 69. 票 is **sign** 570 q.v., here acting phonetically to express **tip** and almost certainly lending an idea of **upper tapered part**. Thus the **tip of a (particularly tall) tree**, which by extension came to mean **landmark** and then **mark** or **sign** in general. Suggest taking 票 as **west** 西 152 and **show** 示 695.

Mnemonic: **TREE IS A SIGNPOST SHOWING WEST**

572
FU, BU
NOT, UN-, DIS-
4 strokes

不明 FUMEI na — unclear
不平 FUHEI — complaint
不気味 BUKIMI na — weird

Originally 夬 (later 杲), showing a **calyx** (**bud** ▽ surrounded by a **whorl of leaves** 朳). It was later borrowed purely for its sound FU, this being a sound of **denial** and **negation** (cf. English Huh, Phooey etc.). Suggest remembering as **one** 一 1 and **three down**-strokes 朳.

Mnemonic: **PUT DOWN ONCE, THEN THRICE, FOR EMPHATIC 'NOT SO'**

573
FU, FŪ, otto
HUSBAND, MAN
4 strokes

人夫 NINPU — laborer
夫人 FUJIN — wife, Mrs -
夫婦 FŪFU — married couple

Originally 夫, showing a **big (i.e. adult) male** 大 53 with an ornamental **hairpin** 一 through his hair (a sign of **adulthood** in ancient China).

Mnemonic: **BIG MAN WITH PIN THROUGH HEAD IS GOOD HUSBAND**

574
FU, tsuku/keru
ATTACH, APPLY
5 strokes

付着 FUCHAKU — adhesion
付き合う TSUKIAU — associate
名付ける NAZUKERU — name, call

Originally 𠂔, showing **person** 亻 39 and a **hand** reaching out holding something 又. The original meaning was to **reach out and give something to someone**. The idea of **give to** later came by association to mean **add to** or **attach**. Later forms use **hand/ measure** 寸 909, which appears to be a miscopying.

Mnemonic: **HAND ATTACHES MEASURE TO PERSON**

176

575 **FU**   政府 SEIFU   government
              GOVERNMENT CENTER,   府県 FUKEN   prefectures
              URBAN PREFECTURE   京都府 KYŌTOFU
              8 strokes   Kyoto Prefecture

广 is **large building** 114. 付 is **attach** 574 q.v. The original meaning of 575 was **storehouse** (still retained in Chinese). Some scholars argue that this meaning stems from **that attached to a large building**, i.e. an annex and by extension storehouse, others that it stems from **large building for that attached to one**, i.e. one's belongings. Some also feel that 付 acts phonetically to express **accumulate**. The present meanings are felt to derive from the extended idea of **large building belonging to the government** (though there is no specific element referring to government: see also 273), and hence eventually just **attached/ belonging to the government** (including an **administrative district**).

Mnemonic: **LARGE BUILDING ATTACHED TO GOVERNMENT CENTER**

---

576 **FUKU**   副業 FUKUGYŌ   side-job
              DEPUTY, VICE-, SUB-   副詞 FUKUSHI   adverb
              11 strokes   副領事 FUKURYŌJI vice-consul

刂 is **sword/ cut** 181. 畐 is **full** 386, used phonetically to express **cut open** and probably also lending an idea of **wide open** from its original meaning of wide-lipped jar. Thus to **cut wide open/ split**. Splitting led to the idea of **duplicating** (i.e. making one large item into two smaller parts similar to each other), which by association led to **substituting** and hence the present meanings. Suggest taking 畐 as **single** 一 1 **entrance** 口 20 to **field** 田 59.

Mnemonic: **DEPUTY CUT DOWN AT SINGLE ENTRANCE TO FIELD**

---

577 粉 **FUN, kona, ko**   花粉 KAFUN   pollen
              POWDER   粉粉 KONAGONA   fragments
              10 strokes   麦粉 MUGIKO   wheat flour

Rice 米 201 and **divide/ cut into minute pieces** 分 199. Originally **reduce rice to powder**, now **powder** in a wider sense. Still occasionally used to mean **fragments**.

Mnemonic: **MINUTELY DIVIDED RICE BECOMES POWDER**

578	**HEI, HYŌ** **SOLDIER** 7 strokes	兵士 HEISHI 歩兵 HOHEI 兵器 HEIKI	soldier infantry weapon

Originally 𠔉, showing an **ax** 勹 / 斤 1176 being held with **both hands** 廾 and indicating a **fighting man**. Suggest taking 𠆢 as a **table**.

Mnemonic: **SOLDIER PUTS AX ON TABLE**

579	**BETSU, waka**reru **DIVERGE, SPLIT,** **DIFFER, SPECIAL** 7 strokes	別名 BETSUMEI 特別 TOKUBETSU 別れ WAKARE	alias special parting

Once written 𪜈. 刀/刂 is sword/ **cut** 181. 冎/𠭇 is a variant of **bone** 冎 867. Thus to **cut through a bone**, leading to **chop up** and **divide** in a broad sense. **Differ** and **diverge** are extended meanings, while **special** is an associated meaning (i.e. something set apart). Suggest taking 𠮷 as **mouth** 口 20 with 刀 as a variant of **cut** 刀 181.

Mnemonic: **TWO CUTS TO THE MOUTH MEAN SPLIT LIP**

580	**HEN, atari, be** **VICINITY, BOUNDARY** 5 strokes	辺境 HENKYŌ 近辺 KINPEN 川辺 KAWABE	frontier vicinity riverside

Formerly 邊. 辶 is **movement** 129. 臱 is an element meaning **blind** (of unclear etymology, but apparently comprising nose/self 自 134, hole 穴 849, and direction 方 204, and presumably having a meaning such as heading blindly into a trap/hole). 臱 is used here phonetically to express edge/ **boundary**, and almost certainly lends an idea of **with uncertainty**. Thus to **move with uncertainty along a boundary**, i.e. reach the limits of known territory. Boundary came by association to mean **that included within**, i.e. **general area**. This in turn came to mean **vicinity**, which, like the English term, can also be used of approximation. Suggest taking the modern form 刀 as sword/ **cut** 181.

Mnemonic: **MOVEMENT CUTS THROUGH BOUNDARY**

| 581 | | HEN, kaeru/waru
CHANGE, STRANGE
9 strokes | 変成 HENSEI metamorphosis
大変 TAIHEN very
変わり者 KAWARIMONO eccentric |

Formerly 變, showing that 夂 is not stop and start 夊 438 but a variant of **striking hand/ coerce** 攵 101. 戀 is a CO character meaning **tied together** (threads 糸 27 put together like words 言 274), and acts phonetically to express **reverse** as well as lending an idea of **complicated**. Thus to **coerce someone into reversing something complicated**. This became **cause to change** in a wider sense, and eventually the causative aspect faded to leave just **change**. Suggest taking 亦 as a 'sort of' variant of **red** 赤 46. Suggest taking 夂 as **sitting crosslegged**.

Mnemonic: **CHANGE TO A SORT OF RED AS ONE SITS CROSSLEGGED**

| 582 | | BEN, BIN, tayori
CONVENIENCE,
SERVICE, MAIL
9 strokes | 便利 BENRI na convenient
便所 BENJO toilet
郵便 YŪBIN mail |

亻 is **person/man** 39. 更 is **change** 1248, here acting phonetically to express **servant** and also lending an idea of **bring about a result**. 582 originally meant **efficient servant**, but later came to mean **service** and hence **convenience**. As with the English term convenience, it also has euphemistic associations with bodily waste. **Mail** is an associated idea from service/ servant.

Mnemonic: **CHANGE OF MAIL MAN LEADS TO CONVENIENT SERVICE**

| 583 | | HŌ, tsutsumu
WRAP, ENVELOP
5 strokes | 小包み KOZUTSUMI parcel
包囲 HŌI encircle
包み紙 TSUTSUMIGAMI
wrapping paper |

Formerly 包, and originally (ᴂ). ⌒ is a **womb** 655, while ᇈ, though having the same shape as **serpent** ᇈ / 己 250, is a human **embryo**. The idea of carrying a child in the womb broadened to **envelop** in a general sense.

Mnemonic: **SERPENT-LIKE EMBRYO ENVELOPED IN WOMB**

179

| 584 | | HŌ, HATSU
LAW
8 strokes | 法学 HŌGAKU jurisprudence
文法 BUNPŌ grammar
不法 FUHŌ illegal |

シ is **water** 40. 去 is **leave** 258 q.v., here used in its early sense of **tight-lidded container** and also acting phonetically to express **envelop/ hold securely**. Thus a **tight-lidded leak-proof container holding water**. This was later applied figuratively to the **law**, which similarly **contains/ constrains** human behavior.

Mnemonic: **CONSTRAINED BY LAW TO LEAVE WATER**

| 585 | | BŌ, MŌ, nozomu
WISH, HOPE, GAZE
11 strokes | 失望 SHITSUBŌ despair
願望 GANMŌ/GANBŌ wish
望見 BŌKEN watch from afar |

Once written 𦥑, showing a **person** 𠆢 39 standing on the **ground** 土 60 **gazing with wide open eyes** 臣/臣 512 at the **moon** 夕/月 16. Rather like the English terms staring into space or wishing on a star this symbolised **wishful thinking**, though it can also be used literally as **gaze**. Suggest taking 亡 as **death** 973 and 王 as **king** 5.

Mnemonic: **KING GAZES AT MOON, WISHING FOR DEATH**

| 586 | | BOKU, maki
PASTURE
8 strokes | 牧場 BOKUJŌ pasture
放牧 HŌBOKU grazing
牧場鳥 MAKIBATORI meadowlark |

Cow 牛 97 and **strike with stick** 攵 101, a reference to **herding cattle** and by association **grazing ground/ pasture**.

Mnemonic: **HAND WITH STICK MAKES COW GO INTO PASTURE**

| 587 | | MATSU, BATSU, sue
END, TIP
5 strokes | 週末 SHŪMATSU weekend
末っ子 SUEKKO* youngest child
世紀末 SEIKIMATSU fin de siecle |

Originally the same character as **immature** 未 794 q.v., with both deriving from a pictograph showing the **top of a tree** 朱 (**tree** 木 69 with an additional cross-stroke 一 indicating the **topmost branches**). Whereas the short cross-stroke in 794 came to indicate fresh/young growth, the fuller cross-stroke of 587 came to indicate the **treetop** proper, and by extension **extremity** or **tip**. There is still some overlap between the two characters.

Mnemonic: **TIP OF TREE**

588		MAN, michiru/tasu FULL, FILL 12 strokes	満月 MANGETSU full moon 満足 MANZOKU satisfaction 満潮 MANCHŌ/ MICHISHIO full tide

Formerly 滿 . 氵 is **water** 40. 㒼 is known to have meant **join both halves of a gourd**, with 兩/両 clearly being **both** (halves of a gourd) 両 411 and ⺾ assumed to be a symbol of **joining** (though the latter is somewhat unclear). 㒼 also acts phonetically to express **full/ overflowing**. Thus a **gourd full of water to the point of overflowing**. Suggest taking ⺾ as **grass** 9.

Mnemonic: **BOTH GRASS AND WATER CAN BE FILLING**

589		MYAKU VEIN, PULSE 10 strokes	脈管 MYAKKAN blood vessel 鉱脈 KŌMYAKU ore-vein 山脈 SANMYAKU mountain range

Formerly also 脉. 月 is **flesh/ of the body** 365. 永/𠂢 derives from a depiction of a **tributary** 𣲖 (see also 955 and 615). Thus **tributaries of the body**, i.e. **veins**. **Pulse** is an associated meaning. As in English, vein is also used figuratively to mean branch or line.

Mnemonic: **VEINS ARE TRIBUTARIES OF THE BODY**

590		MIN, tami PEOPLE, POPULACE 5 strokes	国民 KOKUMIN nation 民間 MINKAN no private 民主主義 MINSHUSHUGI democracy

Somewhat obscure. Once written 𤰔. 十/七 is **needle** 十 33, but there is some difference of opinion as to whether ᐟ is a **handle**, making 𤰔 a pictograph of a **gimlet** (i.e. needle with handle), or a variant of **eye** 𠃑 / 目 72, making 𤰔 an ideograph meaning **blind** (i.e. needle in the eye). Scholars of the latter view feel that blinded person symbolised **slave** (blinding being a common punishment), which later came to mean **lowly people** or **commoners** in general. Scholars of the former view feel that 590 was borrowed as a simple substitute for a more complex character meaning **outcast**, with outcast then coming to mean lowly people or commoners. 590 is unconnected with the graphically similar **clan** 氏 495 q.v. (though it is remotely possible that there was some mutual influence in the graphic evolution of the modern forms, especially of 495 upon 590), but it may be useful to take 590 as a more 'substantial' version of 495.

Mnemonic: **POPULACE IS MORE SUBSTANTIAL THAN CLAN**

591 **YAKU**　　　　　　　　約束 YAKUSOKU　　promise
PROMISE, SUMMARIZE,　節約 SETSUYAKU economise
APPROXIMATELY　　約五十人 YAKUGOJŪNIN
9 strokes　　　　　　　　　　　　about fifty people

Formerly also 約 . 糸 is **thread** 27. 勺/勹 is **ladle**/ measure 1342, here used phonetically to express **tie tightly**. Thus to **tie threads tightly (into a knot)**. On the one
hand this came by figurative association to be applied to **binding agreements**, and on the
other to mean **tighten up** in the sense of remove non-essential elements, i.e. **summarize**.
By further association summary/ gist led to **approximation**.

Mnemonic: **KNOTTED THREAD REMINDS OF PROMISE ABOUT LADLE**

592 **YŪ**, *isamu/mashii*　　　勇者 YŪSHA　　　hero
BRAVE, SPIRITED　　　勇気 YŪKI　　　courage
9 strokes　　　　　　　勇み足 ISAMIASHI　rashness

Once written 勈, showing **break through/ emerge** 甩/甬 176 and **strength** 力/力
74, and expressing the idea of having enough determination to succeed. The modern form,
which uses 甬 instead of 甬, may have been influenced by **man** 男 54. Suggest using
this as a mnemonic, taking ヌ as a **bent figure** (see 176), i.e. bent with age.

Mnemonic: **OLD MAN BENT WITH AGE BUT STILL BRAVE**

593 **YŌ**, *iru*, **kaname**　　不必要 FUHITSUYŌunnecessary
NEED, VITAL, PIVOT　　要点 YŌTEN　　　gist
9 strokes　　　　　　　　重要 JŪYŌ　　important

Originally 㺪, showing **hands** 臼 holding in a **waist** 8 (some scholars see this as a
waist itself, others as a backbone), with 八 being **legs**. **Woman** 女 35 later replaced
legs to emphasise the focus on the **waist**, which was the original meaning of 593. Waist
then came by association to mean **middle part**, leading to **pivot** and the idea of **being
essential**. Waist itself is now conveyed by 腰 1879, a character that adds flesh/ of the
body 月 365. Suggest taking 襾 as **west** 152.

Mnemonic: **EVERY WESTERN HAS VITAL NEED FOR WOMAN IN IT**

594

YŌ, yashina*u*
REAR, SUPPORT
15 strokes

養成 YŌSEI — training
栄養士 EIYŌSHI — dietitian
教養 KYŌYŌ — culture

Sheep 兰 986 and **food/ eat** 食 146. Originally to **rear sheep for food**, now **rear** in a broader sense.

Mnemonic: **REAR SHEEP FOR FOOD**

595

YOKU, *abiru*
BATHE
10 strokes

浴室 YOKUSHITSU bathroom
日光浴 NIKKŌYOKU sunbathing
水浴び MIZUABI bathing

氵 is **water** 40. 谷 is **valley** 122 q.v., here acting phonetically to express **spray** and also lending an idea of **cleave open**. Thus to **cleave open water and send up spray**, as in plunging into a river in order to **bathe**.

Mnemonic: **VALLEY WATER IS GOOD FOR BATHING**

596

RI, ki*ku*
PROFIT, GAIN, EFFECT
7 strokes

利益 RIEKI — profit, gain
利用 RIYŌ — utilisation
利き目 KIKIME — efficacy

Rice plant 禾 81 and **sword/ cut** 刂 181. The idea of **reaping the harvest** led to **profit** and **gain** on the one hand, and on the other to the idea of cutting the plants with the sharpest and thus most **effective** tool possible (presumably to maximise gain).

Mnemonic: **EFFECTIVE SHARP TOOL CUTS RICE FOR PROFIT**

597

RIKU
LAND
11 strokes

陸軍 RIKUGUN — army
上陸 JŌRIKU — landing
大陸 TAIRIKU — continent

阝 is **hill** 229. 坴 is a CO character meaning **mound(s) of earth/ hill(s)**. It was originally written 坴, showing **earth** 土 60 piled up like **houses** 仌 (see 76), and later 坴 and finally 坴. Thus 597 means **numerous hills**, i.e. **land** as opposed to sea.

Mnemonic: **HILLS AND EARTHEN MOUNDS INDICATE LAND**

| 598 | | RYŌ, yoi
GOOD
7 strokes | 良心 RYŌSHIN conscience
改良 KAIRYŌ improvement
良さ YOSA worth, quality |

Once written , showing a **sieve** ◎ into which material was **poured** ⅼⅼ and from which **sifted** material **flowed** ⅼⅼ. Sifting led by association to **selecting the good**. Suggest remembering the modern form as **eat/ food** 食 146 without the **lid** ∧.

Mnemonic: **TAKE LID OFF FOOD -- LOOKS GOOD**

| 599 | | RYŌ
MATERIALS, MEASURE,
CHARGE
10 strokes | 原料 GENRYŌ raw material
料金 RYŌKIN charge, fee
料理 RYŌRI cooking |

Rice 米 201 and **measure** 斗 1633, and originally meaning **measure rice**. In that regard it is similar to measure 料 81 q.v., but whereas 81 came to connote sorting, 599 generally came to connote rather the **substance** itself, as well as the **quantity**. **Charge** is felt to be an associated meaning, from the idea of apportionment.

Mnemonic: **MEASURE OF RICE HAS FIXED CHARGE**

| 600 | 量 | RYŌ, hakaru
MEASURE, QUANTITY
12 strokes | 重量 JŪRYŌ weight
分量 BUNRYŌ quantity
大量生産 TAIRYŌSEISAN
mass production |

Once written . is the prototype of heavy /重 311 q.v., but minus person ∧ to leave just **heavy sack on the ground** . ◎ is a vessel ◯ full of something ‾, reinforcing . Thus a **heavy (i.e. full) sack of something left on the ground**, indicating a **completed measure** or **quantity**. Suggest taking as **village** 里 219, **one** —, 1, and **day** 日 62.

Mnemonic: **VILLAGE GETS MEASURED QUANTITY, FOR ONE DAY**

| 601 | | RIN, wa
WHEEL, HOOP
15 strokes | 車輪 SHARIN vehicle wheel
三輪車 SANRINSHA tricycle
輪投げ WANAGE quoits |

車 is **vehicle** 31. 侖 is a CO character meaning **arrange/ align neatly**, and derives from a bundle of bamboo tablets bound together and stacked on end 冊 874, **capped** with a lid ∧ 121 to indicate being neatly finished off. It also acts here phonetically to express **roll**. Thus **aligned rolling parts of a vehicle**, i.e. the **wheels**.

Mnemonic: **VEHICLE HAS ALIGNED AND CAPPED WHEELS**

184

602		RUI **RESEMBLE, VARIETY,** **SORT** 18 strokes	種類 SHURUI	sort, kind
			分類 BUNRUI	classification
			類似 RUIJI	resemblance

Formerly 類, clearly showing **rice** 米 201, **dog** 犬 17, and **head** 頁 93. Rice and head once formed a now defunct character 頪, meaning **close resemblance** (i.e. as heads of rice). This was then borrowed -- largely for its sound but also for its meaning of resemble -- and combined with dog 犬 to give 類, which originally referred to a mythical raccoon-like creature (a meaning still occasionally found in Chinese). Somewhat unusually, 類 replaced the simpler character 頪, acquiring the latter's meaning of **resemble**. **Variety** and **sort** are associated meanings. The modern form uses **big** 大 53 as a simplification of dog 犬.

Mnemonic: **VARIETY OF RICE WITH BIG HEAD**

603		**REI, RYŌ** **ORDER, RULE** 5 strokes	令状 REIJŌ	warrant
			命令法 MEIREIHŌ	imperative
			司令官 SHIREIKAN	commander

Also 令, and originally 㑴. へ is a **kneeling person** 39 (see also 425). 亼 is cover/ **cap** 87/121, here acting phonetically to express **summon** and probably also lending an idea of **imposing from above**. 603 originally referred to people summoned to hear the orders of their lord, but now means **order** or **rule**.

Mnemonic: **KNEELING PERSON ORDERED TO DON CAP**

604		**REI, tsumetai, hieru/yasu,** *sameru/masu* **FREEZE, COLD** 7 strokes	冷蔵 REIZŌ	refrigeration
			冷静 REISEI na	cool-headed
			冷え性 HIESHŌ	sensitivity to cold

Also 冷. 冫 is **ice** 378. 令/令 is order/ **rule** 603, here acting phonetically to express **tremble** and also lending an idea of **prevail/** dominate. Thus **tremble as a result of prevailing ice**, now **freeze** or **ice-cold**.

Mnemonic: **ICE RULES IN FREEZING COLD**

605 **REI, tato***eru* 例外 REIGAI   exception
EXAMPLE, LIKEN, 例年 REINEN   normal year
PRECEDENT 例えば TATOEBA   for example
8 strokes

Person 亻 39 and **line/ row** 列 414. 605 originally referred to **people lined up in proper order**, but gradually changed to a meaning of **comparison** (cf. **compare** 比 771). This led in turn to its present associated meanings.

Mnemonic: **PEOPLE IN LINE SHOW EXAMPLE OF PRECEDENT**

606 **REKI** 歴史家 REKISHIKA   historian
HISTORY, PATH 経歴 KEIREKI   past career
14 strokes 遍歴 HENREKI   travels

Formerly written 歷 , in ancient times 秝 , and nowadays sometimes simply as 厂. 中/止 is **footprint** 129 q.v., here used in the sense of **trail**. 秝 is a doubling of **rice plant** 81, meaning plural rice plants. Thus 秝 meant a **trail of rice plants**, a reference to rice plants in an ordered, **regularly spaced row**. The role of the later addition 厂 is not clear. It appears to be cliff 45, possibly used in some unclear phonetic role, but may possibly be an abbreviation of **large building** 广 114, indicating a building in which rice seedlings were planted. In any event, **regular row of rice plants** came to mean **regular row** or **path** in a wider sense, and was eventually applied figuratively to **history** and to a **career path** or similar. Suggest taking 止 in its usual sense of **stop**.

Mnemonic: **HISTORY STOPS WITH INDOOR RICE PLANTS?!**

607 **REN, tsu***reru*, **tsura***neru* 連絡船 RENRAKUSEN   ferry
ACCOMPANY, ROW 連中 RENCHŪ/ RENJŪ party
10 strokes 連想 RENSŌ
                                      thought association

Movement 辶 129 and **vehicle** 車 31, giving **(succession of) moving vehicles**. This came to mean **row** on the one hand, and **be part of a group/ accompany** on the other.

Mnemonic: **ACCOMPANIED BY ROW OF MOVING VEHICLES**

608

REN, *neru*
REFINE, KNEAD, TRAIN
14 strokes

訓練 KUNREN   training
洗練 SENREN   refinement
練り粉 NERIKO   dough

Formerly 練. 糸 is **thread** 27. 柬 is a CO character now meaning **select**, and is felt to derive from a combination of bundle 束 1535 and disperse/ away ヽ ノ 66 (i.e. remove selected items from a bundle). 柬 also lends its sound to express **soften by boiling**. Thus to **soften selected threads by boiling**, which was a reference to the glossing of raw silk. This led to associated ideas such as **kneading, improving,** and by extension **training**. Suggest taking 東 as **east** 184.

Mnemonic: **REFINED THREADS FROM THE EAST**

609

RŌ, *oiru*, f*ukeru*
OLD, AGED
6 strokes

老人 RŌJIN   old person
老練 RŌREN na   veteran
老齢年金 RŌREINENKIN

    old age pension

Originally 耂, showing an **old man** 𠆢 / ≠ 117 q.v. leaning on a **stick** ├ / ヒ. As with 117, suggest taking ≠ as **half buried / in ground** 土 60, with ヒ as **fallen person** 238.

Mnemonic: **OLD MAN FALLS, READY FOR BURYING IN GROUND**

610

RŌ
LABOR, TOIL
7 strokes

労働者 RŌDŌSHA   laborer
苦労 KURŌ   pains, trouble
労働関係 RŌDŌKANKEI

    labor relations

Formerly 勞. 火火 is **covered in flame** 427 while 力 is **strength/ effort** 74. The original meaning was to **do physical work under torchlight**, which came to mean **work hard and long** in a general sense. Suggest taking 冖 as an **ornate roof**.

Mnemonic: **LABOR WITH EFFORT UNDER ORNATE ROOF**

| 611 | **ROKU** **RECORD, INSCRIBE** 16 strokes | 記録 KIROKU record 実録 JITSUROKU true record 録音 ROKUON sound recording |

Formerly 錄. 金 is **metal** 14, while 彔 is **exude** 412 q.v. 611 originally referred to the 'green rust' or verdigris which is 'exuded' from copper. Having largely had this meaning taken over by 412, 611 came to mean **marks on metal** in a broad sense, and later became particularly associated with **inscriptions**. A metal inscription is an enduring **record**. Suggest remembering by association with **green** 緑 412.

Mnemonic: **RECORD ON GREEN METAL**

END OF FOURTH GRADE

THE 195 FIFTH GRADE CHARACTERS

612 **ATSU**   圧力 **ATSURYOKU**   pressure

PRESSURE   電圧 **DENATSU**   voltage

5 strokes   圧倒的 **ATTŌTEKI**

                                  overwhelming

Formerly 壓 . 土 is ground/ **earth** 60. 厭 is an NGU character meaning **satiated/ weary**. It derives from **roof** 厂 (variant 广 114), here meaning cover and by figurative extension smother, **dog** 犬 17, **meat** 月 365, and 曰 , a simplification of **sweet** 甘 1093, and its original meaning was be smothered in sweet dog meat (i.e. have a surfeit of/ **be satiated with sweet dog meat**). This came to mean be bloated, with connotations of **ready to burst** and therefore **pressure**. In the case of 612 厭 also acts phonetically to express **push/ press**. Some scholars feel 612 originally meant **earth pressing as if to burst**, as in a cave-in, while others feel it meant **push with earth**, as in attempting to reinforce defensive earthworks. The idea of earth gradually faded, leaving **press/ pressure** in general.

Mnemonic: **ROOF UNDER PRESSURE FROM EARTH**

613 移 **I, utsuru/su**   移住 **IJŪ**   migration

TRANSFER, MOVE   移民 **IMIN**   migrant

11 strokes   移動 **IDŌ**   move

Rice plant 禾 81 and **much/ many** 多 163, with the latter also lending its sound to express **sway**. 613 originally referred to a field full of (i.e. many) rice plants swaying (in the breeze), but later became confused with 迻 , a CO character interchanged with 613 and clearly meaning **much movement** (see movement 辶 129).

Mnemonic: **TRANSFER MANY RICE PLANTS**

189

614		**IN,** yoru	原因 GENIN	cause
		CAUSE, BE BASED ON,	死因 SHIIN	cause of death
		DEPEND ON	因果関係 INGAKANKEI	
		6 strokes		cause-and-effect

Of disputed etymology, though its elements are clearly (**big**) **man** 大 53 and **enclosure** □ 123. Some scholars take it to be an **enclosed man,** i.e. a prisoner, which by association raises the question of the **cause** of his imprisonment, with **based on/ depend on** being extensions of cause. Other scholars see □ as symbolising a **territory** (or even house), and take 大 to act phonetically as well as semantically, lending its sound to express **visit/ stay.** Thus a man visiting and staying in a certain territory/ house, meaning that he is **based** there and is also **dependent upon** the goodwill of the host. **Cause** is seen as an extension from dependent. A combination of the two theories seems possible, in that enclosed man might suggest protected man, who is **dependent** upon his protector, with **based upon** and **cause** being associated meanings.

Mnemonic: **ENCLOSED MAN HAS CAUSE TO DEPEND ON OTHERS**

615		**EI,** nagai	永遠 EIEN	eternity
		LONG, LASTING	永続 EIZOKU	perpetuity
		5 strokes	永住者 EIJŪSHA	
				permanent resident

From a pictograph of the **confluence of a tributary and main river** 㳄 (see also 589 and 955). 615 originally meant **long distance** (presumably from the idea of an extensive river-system), but eventually came rather to mean **long** in the sense of **enduring** (possibly because a confluence of rivers was a lasting source of water). Suggest remembering by association with **water** 水 40 and **ice** 氷 378, from which distinguish.

Mnemonic: **WATER LOOKS ICY FOR A LONG TIME**

616		**EI,** itonamu	経営 KEIEI	management
		CONDUCT, BARRACKS	営業 EIGYŌ	business
		12 strokes	営所 EISHO	barracks

Formerly 營 . 𤇾 is covered in flame/ light 427, here meaning **surrounded by torches.** 呂 is **joined rooms** 256, here indicating a **large building/ encampment.** Thus **large building/ encampment surrounded by torches,** a reference to **military barracks.** It was later also used to express **conduct,** partly through confusion with conduct 爲 1003. Suggest taking 宀 as an **ornate roof.**

Mnemonic: **ORNATELY ROOFED BARRACKS WITH JOINED ROOMS**

617

EI

GUARD, PROTECT

16 strokes

衛生 EISEI　　　　　hygiene

守衛 SHUEI　　　　　guard

自衛 JIEI　　　　self-defense

A combination of **guard all directions** 韋 422 and **go** 行 118, giving **patrol/ guard thoroughly**. Suggest taking 𠃋 as **'almost' five** 五 19, 牜 as **'almost' year** 年 64, and 口 as **opening** 20.

Mnemonic: **OPENING TO GO ON GUARD FOR ALMOST FIVE YEARS**

618

易

EKI, I, yasu*i*, yasa*shii*

EASY, CHANGE,

DIVINATION

8 strokes

貿易 BŌEKI　　　　　trade

易者 EKISHA　　　fortuneteller

安易 ANI na　　　easy-going

Once written 𨈒 , showing a **big-eyed lizard** 𦑣 and **rays of the sun** ⸜ . 618 originally referred to the sun's rays reflecting off a lizard's (iridescent) skin. This led to the idea of **readily changing**, giving both **change** and **readily/ easy**. **Divination** is an associated meaning, from the idea of interpreting changes. The graphic evolution of the character may have been influenced by sun shining down 昜 144, though some scholars feel that the sunrays ⸜ became misinterpreted as the lizard's legs. Suggest taking 日 as **sun** 62, and 勿 as **legs**.

Mnemonic: **SUN BOUNCES EASILY OFF LIZARD'S CHANGING LEGS**

619

EKI, YAKU, masu

GAIN, PROFIT,

BENEFIT

10 strokes

有益 YŪEKI　　　　profitable

益益 MASUMASU increasingly

利益配当 RIEKIHAITŌ　dividend

Formerly 𥁅 . 皿 is **dish** 1307. 八 derives from 氺 , a variant of **water** 氵/水 40. Thus **dish full of water**, leading to **overflowing** and by association **profit** and **gain**. Suggest taking ⸜ as a variant of **eight** 八 66, and 六 as a **table**.

Mnemonic: **MAKE PROFIT ON EIGHT SETS OF TABLEWARE**

---

620 EKI
LIQUID
11 strokes

液体 EKITAI   liquid
液化 EKIKA   liquefaction
血液型 KETSUEKIGATA
                blood type

氵 is **water** 40, here meaning **liquid**. 夜 is **night** 212, here acting phonetically to express **immerse** and possibly also lending a loose idea of **engulfing**. Thus **liquid in which things are immersed (and engulfed?)**, eventually **liquid** in general.

Mnemonic: **NEED FOR LIQUID, EVEN WATER AT NIGHT**

---

621 EN
ACT, PERFORM
14 strokes

演出 ENSHUTSU   production
出演 SHUTSUEN   performance
演説 ENZETSU   speech

氵 is **water** 40, here meaning **river**. 寅 is an NGU character now borrowed to refer to a zodiac sign. However, it was originally written 𡨈, showing two hands 𦥑 straightening an arrow 矢 120/981, and meant **straighten an arrow**. This came by association to mean **lengthen/ extend**, and when combined with 氵 meant **long/ extensive river**. The river element eventually faded, leaving just **extensive**. This is still one of 621's meanings in Chinese, but in Japanese it has given way entirely to derived meanings such as **extended performance**, and even simply **performance** and **act**. Suggest taking 宀 as roof / **building** 28, and 更 as a variant of **yellow** 黄 120 q.v.

Mnemonic: **PERFORM IN BUILDING BY YELLOW RIVER**

---

622 Ō
RESPOND, REACT
7 strokes

応答 ŌTŌ   response
反応 HANNŌ*   reaction
応用 ŌYŌ   application

Formerly 應. 心 is **heart/ feelings** 147. 雁 is the prototype of the NGU character hawk 鷹 (which adds an additional bird 鳥 174). It now comprises roof 广 114, here meaning by extension shelter (formerly illness 疒 381, suggesting care for), person 亻 39, and bird 隹 216, to give **bird sheltered by person,** i.e. taken in hand. In the case of 622 雁 lends its sound to express **respond**, and possibly also lends an idea of **taking in**. Thus to **(take in a situation and?) respond with one's heart**, now simply **react/ respond**.

Mnemonic: **REACT WITH FEELING TO BUILDING**

623 Ō

GO, GONE, PAST

8 strokes

往復 ŌFUKU　　　round trip

往事 ŌJI　　　　things past

往来 ŌRAI　　coming and going

Once written 徃 , and earlier as 些 , showing **king** 太 / 王 5 and **foot** 山 / 止 129. The latter is used in its sense of **move**, while 王 is used both for its sound, to express **go**, and for its idea of **leading person**. 些 meant **person going in front**, with **go/ movement** 彳 118 added later for emphasis. Rather like precede 先 49 q.v., this idea eventually led to that of **things past**. It is not clear whether the later use of **master** 主 299 is a purely graphic simplification or one that purposely keeps an idea of leading person.

Mnemonic: **MASTER GOES OFF**

624 ON

FAVOR, KINDNESS

10 strokes

恩人 ONJIN　　　　benefactor

恩知らず ONSHIRAZU　　　ingrate

恩返し ONGAESHI　return favor

心 is **heart/ feelings** 147. 因 is **cause** 614 q.v., which acts phonetically to express **pity**. The exact semantic role of the latter is unclear due to its unclear origins, but it would presumably lend either supporting connotations of **pity** (for an imprisoned man) or **charity** (for a man needing protection and/or lodgings). Thus **feelings of pity**, leading to its present meanings.

Mnemonic: **FEELINGS ARE CAUSE OF KIND FAVOR**

625 KA, KE, kari

TEMPORARY, FALSE

6 strokes

仮説 KASETSU　　　hypothesis

仮に KARI ni　　　provisionally

仮病 KEBYŌ　　feigned illness

Formerly 假 , and earlier 叚 . The latter, which is still found as a CO character meaning **false**, was still earlier written 叚 . This reveals **two hands** 彐彐 and 戸 , a variant of **cliff** 厂 45 (possibly showing terracing or steps ：). The two hands are felt to show **manual dexterity** and by extension **emulation** (see 10), while 戸 acts phonetically to express **false/ deceive**. Thus 叚/ 叚 (the latter apparently a graphic confusion) means literally to **emulate skillfully and deceitfully**. **Person** 亻 39 was added to give the idea of a **skilled impersonator**, leading by extension to the present meanings of **temporary** and **false**. The modern form replaces 叚 with **oppose** 反 371 q.v., partly for its idea of **change** and partly for the fact that it uses essentially the same components of cliff and hand but in simpler form.

Mnemonic: **PERSON OPPOSED TO EVEN TEMPORARY FALSEHOOD**

193

626 価 **KA, atai**
PRICE, VALUE, WORTH
8 strokes

価値	KACHI	value
価格	KAKAKU	price
物価	BUKKA	price of goods

Formerly 價. 賈 is an NGU character technically meaning **trader** (perhaps best thought of as a variant of the old form 賣 of sell 売 192), though it appears from an early stage to have developed strong connotations of the **act of buying and selling** and of the **items being traded** and their **value** rather than the person doing the trading. It retained these connotations despite the later addition of **person** 亻 39, and in particular became associated with **value** and **price**. Suggest taking 覀 as **west** 152.

Mnemonic: **PERSON FROM WEST HAS PRICE ON HEAD**

627 果 **KA, ha*te*, ha*tasu***
FRUIT, RESULT,
CARRY OUT
8 strokes

成果	SEIKA	result
果物	KUDAMONO*	fruit
果たして	HATASHITE	as expected

Originally , showing **fruit**  on a **tree** 木 69. From an early stage  was replaced by full rice field  504 to give the idea of **abundant crop**, and later this was simplified to just **field** 田 59. As in English, fruit was used figuratively to mean **outcome/ result**, and by extension also came to mean **bring about an outcome, i.e. carry out/ perform.**

Mnemonic: **TREE, LIKE FIELD, PRODUCES FRUITFUL RESULTS**

628 河 **KA, kawa**
RIVER
8 strokes

河口	KAKŌ	rivermouth
河豚	FUGU*	globefish
河馬	KABA	hippopotamus

氵 is **water** 40, here meaning **river**. 可 is **can** 816 q.v., here with its literal meaning of **coil (slowly) to a mouth** and also lending its sound to express **twist/ meander**. Thus **river meandering to the sea**, now used of **rivers** in general.

Mnemonic: **WATER CAN FORM RIVER**

629

KA, sugiru/gosu, ayamachi   通過 TSŪKA   passage
PASS, EXCEED, ERROR   過去形 KAKOKEI   past tense
12 strokes   言い過ぎ IISUGI   exaggeration

⻌ is **movement** 129. 冎 is **bone/ vertebrae** 867, here lending an idea of flexibility and suppleness and by extension **ease of movement**. Opinion is divided as to whether ⼝ represents another vertebra (see 256) or mouth 20 (thus giving twisted mouth or similar). In any event, 咼 is known to have acted phonetically to express much/ **substantial**. Thus 629 originally referred to **making easy and substantial movement/ progress**. As well as leading to the idea of **slip by** and **pass**, it also led by extension to the idea of **going too far**, including in the sense of **making an error**. Suggest taking ⼝ as **mouth**.

Mnemonic: **EXCESSIVE MOVEMENT MAKES BACKBONE PASS MOUTH!**

630

GA   賀詞 GASHI   congratulations
CONGRATULATIONS   年賀状 NENGAJŌ New Year Card
12 strokes   祝賀会 SHUKUGAKAI   celebration

加 is **add** 431. 貝 is **shell/ money** 90, here used to mean **valuable item**. To **add valuable items** was a reference to adding one's gift to a number of other gifts, indicating an occasion for **congratulations**.

Mnemonic: **CONGRATULATIONS ON ADDING TO ONE'S MONEY**

631

KAI, kokoroyoi   不愉快 FUYUKAI   unpleasant
PLEASANT, CHEERFUL   快楽 KAIRAKU   pleasure
7 strokes   快活 KAIKATSU   cheerful

Heart/ **feelings** ⼼ 147 and **open up** 夬 271, giving to be in an **expansive mood** and hence **cheerful**. **Pleasant** is an associated meaning. Suggest remembering 夬 by association with a **'waterless'** (see water ⺡ 40) **decide** 決 271.

Mnemonic: **NO WATER, BUT DECIDEDLY CHEERFUL FEELINGS**

632

KAI, GE, toku
UNRAVEL, EXPLAIN,
SOLVE
13 strokes

解説 KAISETSU   commentary
理解 RIKAI   understanding
分解 BUNKAI   break-up

刀 is sword/ **cut** 181, 牛 is **cow** 97, and 角 is **horn** 243. Some scholars feel that 刀 and 牛 combine to give **cut up/ butcher a cow**, with 角 acting purely phonetically by way of emphasis to express **dissect**, while others feel that the three elements combine ideographically to convey the idea of **cutting off a cow's horn to disentangle it**. The present meanings are extensions of either cut up or disentangle.

Mnemonic: **SOLVE PROBLEM BY CUTTING OFF COW'S HORN**

633

KAKU, KŌ
STANDARD, STATUS
10 strokes

資格 SHIKAKU   qualification
性格 SEIKAKU   character
所有格 SHOYŪKAKU   genitive

木 is **tree** 69. 各 is **each** 438 q.v., here acting phonetically to express **tall** and possibly also lending its own connotations of **descending from a height**. 633 originally meant **tall tree**, leading to various extended and associated meanings such as **reach a height** (still a meaning in Chinese) and therefore **achieve status** as well as **set a standard**. It can also mean **case** (in grammar).

Mnemonic: **EACH TREE SETS A STANDARD**

634

KAKU, tashika/kameru
ASCERTAIN, FIRM
15 strokes

正確 SEIKAKU   precise
確認 KAKUNIN   confirmation
確実 KAKUJITSU   reliable

Once written 石崔. 石 is **rock** 45. 崔/隺 is a crested 冖 bird 隹 216, specifically a **crane** (now conveyed by an NGU character 鶴 that adds an extra bird 鳥 174: distinguish heron 藋/隺 445). Here 隺 acts phonetically to express **hard**, and is also felt by some scholars to lend an associated idea of **white** (cranes being predominantly white). Thus **hard (white?) rock**, a reference to **granite**. This came to mean **hard** or **firm** and by association **reliable**. Note that the occasionally encountered variant form 碻 is a miscopying. However, it may be usful to remember 冖 as a variant of **roof** 宀 28, with a pun on **rock** and **roc** (a mythical bird).

Mnemonic: **ASCERTAIN THAT BIRD UNDER ROOF IS A ROC**

| 635 | | GAKU, hitai
SUM, PLAQUE,
FRAME, FOREHEAD
18 strokes | 金 額 KINGAKU sum of money
額 面 GAKUMEN face value
額 際 HITAIGIWA hairline |

Formerly also written 頟 (still found in Chinese). 頁 is **head** 93. 各 is **each** 438 q.v., while 客 is **visitor** 252 q.v. Both 各 and 客 act phonetically to express **shave**, and both may also lend extended connotations of **attend** from their original meaning of **visit and stay**. Thus **shaven part of the head (to which one attends?)**. This was a reference to the **forehead**, which in ancient China was often exaggerated by shaving back the hairline. **Frame** (of picture etc.) and **plaque** are felt to be associated meanings, from the idea of **clear, angular area** (though it is not impossible that there might be some connection with the ancient practice of tattooing/ identifying slaves on the forehead -- see 340). It is not clear how 635 also came to mean **sum**, though some scholars feel it may stem from the idea of **high point** (cf. taka 高 119, meaning both height and sum).

Mnemonic: **VISITOR'S FOREHEAD LOOKS LIKE PLAQUE**

| 636 | | KAN
PUBLISH, ENGRAVE
5 strokes | 刊 行 KANKŌ publication
日 刊 NIKKAN daily issue
発 刊 HAKKAN launching |

刂 is **sword/ cut** 181. 干 is **dry** 825 q.v., here acting phonetically to express **carve/ engrave** and also lending an idea of **cut** from its original meaning of **thrusting weapon**. The original meaning was simply **engrave**, but it then came to be associated with engraving as part of the **printing** process. It now means **publish** in a broad sense.

Mnemonic: **PUBLISH BOOK ON HOW TO KEEP SWORD DRY**

| 637 | | KAN, miki
TRUNK, MAIN
13 strokes | 幹 線 KANSEN trunk line
幹 部 KANBU leaders
幹 事 KANJI manager |

Once written 榦. 木 is **tree** 69. 𠦝 is a variant of 倝, a CO character meaning **sunrise** (comprising **rising sun** 卓 175 and a **person** 人 39 presumably watching it, though the exact role of 人 is unclear). 倝 acts phonetically to express **base/ support**, and almost certainly also lends an extended idea of **rising straight up**. Thus the **base of a tree that rises straight up**, i.e. the **trunk**. **Main** is an associated meaning. The modern form uses **dry** 干 825 q.v., which is generally assumed to be a miscopying but may in fact make deliberate use of 825's literal meaning of **thrusting wooden item**. Suggest taking 卓 literally as **sun** 日 62 rising through **grass** 十 9.

Mnemonic: **PERSON DRIES TRUNK AS SUN RISES THROUGH GRASS**

638

KAN, na*reru*
BECOME USED TO
14 strokes

習慣 SHŪKAN habit, custom
慣例 KANREI   convention
世慣れた YONARETA worldly-wise

忄 is **heart/ feelings** 147. 貫 is **pierce** 1102 q.v., here acting phonetically to express **accumulate** and also lending similar connotations from its literal meaning of threaded amount of money. Thus **accumulate feelings**, a reference to **increasing familiarity**.

Mnemonic: **BECOME USED TO HAVING HEART PIERCED**

639

KAN, yoroko*bu*
REJOICE, MERRY
15 strokes

歓迎 KANGEI   welcome
歓楽 KANRAKU   pleasure
交歓 KŌKAN fraternisation

Formerly 歡 . 萑/雈 is **crested bird/ heron** 445 q.v., acting phonetically to express **banquet** and possibly also loosely lending similar connotations since the heron was a delicacy at banquets. 欠 is **lack** 471 q.v., here with its literal meaning of **gaping mouth**. Thus to **gorge oneself at a banquet**, symbolising **making merry**.

Mnemonic: **MERRIMENT IS GAPING MOUTH FULL OF CRESTED BIRD**

640

GAN, manako
EYE
11 strokes

双眼鏡 SŌGANKYŌ binoculars
肉眼 NIKUGAN naked eye
血眼 CHIMANAKO
            bloodshot eyes

目 is **eye** 72. 艮 is **stop and stare** 263, here also acting phonetically to express **round**. Thus to **stop and stare with round eyes**, i.e. **wide eyed**. Wide eyed eventually led to just **eye**.

Mnemonic: **STOP AND STARE WITH WIDE EYES**

641

KI, moto, moto*zuku*
BASE
11 strokes

基本 KIHON   basis, standard
基金 KIKIN   foundation
基地 KICHI base (army etc.)

Formed from **winnowing device** 其 251 q.v., which is itself set on a **base/ stand** 丌 and here lends such connotations, and **earth/ ground** 土 60. Thus **earthen base/ foundation**, now **base** in a broad sense.

Mnemonic: **WINNOWING DEVICE BASED ON FIRM GROUND**

---

642 **KI**, *yoru/seru* 寄 与 KIYO contribution
DRAW NEAR, SEND, 寄 せ 波 YOSENAMI surf
VISIT 立 ち 寄 る TACHIYORU visit, call
11 strokes

宀 is **roof/ house** 28. 奇 is **strange/ unfamiliar** 1123, which also acts phonetically to express **seek protection**. 642 originally referred to **seeking protection in a stranger's house**. This gave rise to a range of extended and associated meanings, particularly **visit** and by association **draw near**. **Send** is the causative form of visit.

Mnemonic: **DRAW NEAR TO STRANGE HOUSE**

---

643 **KI** 規 則 KISOKU rule
STANDARD, MEASURE 定 規 JŌGI rule(r)
11 strokes 大 規 模 DAIKIBO large scale

夫 is (person becoming) **adult male** 573 q.v., used here to indicate attainment of a certain **standard** and thus something to be **measured** against, while 見 is **look** 18 q.v. Some scholars see the two elements as combining ideographically to give **adult male looked upon as a standard**. Others see 見 as being used essentially phonetically to express **round**, though it would almost certainly also lend an idea of **observe carefully** (from its literal meaning of person kneeling to stare). Thus a **round measure (which is observed)**, i.e. a **compass**. The fact that 643 can mean compass in Chinese suggests strongly that the latter theory is correct, though the former may be more helpful as a mnemonic.

Mnemonic: **ADULT MALE LOOKED UPON AS STANDARD**

---

644 **GI, waza** 技 術 GIJUTSU technique
CRAFT, SKILL 技 師 GISHI engineer
7 strokes 演 技 ENGI acting

支 is **support** 691 q.v., here lending both its literal meaning of **hold in hand** and its sound to express **work**. 扌 is **hand** 32, the additional hand giving **both hands**. Thus to **work with both hands**, suggesting an **intricate task**. By association this came to mean **skill** and **craft**.

Mnemonic: **SUPPORT FROM SKILLED HANDS FACILITATES CRAFT**

645		GI RIGHTEOUSNESS 13 strokes	主義 SHUGI	principle, ism
			義理 GIRI	justice
			意義 IGI	significance

Somewhat obscure, though its elements are clearly **sheep** 羊 986 q.v. and **I/ self** 我 817 q.v. Some scholars feel that sheep is used in its extended sense of **praiseworthy**, to give the idea of **being able to consider oneself praiseworthy** (i.e. through one's **righteousness**). Others see 我 as being used purely phonetically to express **ceremony**, giving **praiseworthy ceremony**, i.e. one that is performed **properly** (with righteousness being an extension of proper). Still others agree that it meant proper and praiseworthy ceremony, but arrive at this through interpreting the elements ideographically as **slaughter** (i.e. **sacrifice**) **a sheep** (我 literally meaning to **kill with a lance/ halberd**). The first theory is perhaps the most helpful.

Mnemonic: **I AM LIKE A SHEEP, FULL OF RIGHTEOUSNESS**

646		GYAKU, sakarau REVERSE, OPPOSE 9 strokes	逆行 GYAKKŌ	retrogression
			逆説 GYAKUSETSU	paradox
			反逆 HANGYAKU	treason

辶 is **movement** 129. 屰 derives from 屰, a stylised and inverted variant of **(big) man** 大 53, the inversion indicating **opposite to normal**. Thus a **man going backwards**, leading to **reverse** and by association **oppose**.

Mnemonic: **BIG UPSIDE-DOWN MAN MOVES IN REVERSE**

647	久	KYŪ, KU, hisashii LONG TIME, LASTING 3 strokes	永久 EIKYŪ	permanence
			久遠 KUON*	eternity
			久し振り HISASHIBURI	
				for the first time in ages

Somewhat obscure. Early forms such as 入 have been interpreted as a **person** 𠂉 39 **held in place** (indicated by the abstract sign 乀), with this leading by extension to **stay in place** and hence **last a long time**. Suggest taking ク as a **stooping person** and 乀 as a **prop**.

Mnemonic: **STOOPING PERSON PROPPED UP FOR A LONG TIME**

200

648　旧

KYŪ

OLD, PAST

5 strokes

旧友 KYŪYŪ	old friend
旧派 KYŪHA	old school
旧式 KYŪSHIKI	old style

Formerly 舊 and 舊. 萑 is not the CO character reed 萑 (literally bird-grass, from bird 隹 216 and grass 艹 9). Old forms such as 萑 show that it is a **crested bird**, though different from crested bird/ heron 鷺 /雚 445 and crested bird/ crane 寉 634. It is in fact a white-horned owl (see below). 臼 is an NGU character meaning **mortar**, taken by some scholars to show a bowl with bits in it (from a stylised old form ㄩ) but more likely originally a mouth with grinding teeth (old form ㅌ). Here 臼 is used purely for its sound **KYŪ**, to give 舊 a meaning of **crested bird with a cry of KYŪ**, which was a reference to the **(white-horned) owl**. (Note that 舊 was once interchanged with 鵂, a CO character which combines bird 鳥 174 with KYŪ rest 休 13 and which similarly means white-horned owl/ bird that cries KYŪ.) 舊 was then drastically simplified to 旧 and used as a phonetic alternative to **KYŪ long time** 久 647, eventually acquiring its own particular connotations of **old** and **past**. It is not clear why any need was felt for an alternative to the already simple 久, but it is possible that 日 was seen as **day** 62 and ｜ as **draw** (bowstring 77), giving the **drawing out of days** or similar. Suggest taking 日 as **day** and ｜ as **one**.

Mnemonic: **ONLY ONE DAY OLD, BUT OLD NONETHELESS**

649　居

KYO, *iru, oru*

BE, RESIDE

8 strokes

居住 KYOJŪ	dwelling
住居 JŪKYO	dwelling
居所 IDOKORO	whereabouts

尸 is **person sitting slumped** 236. 古 is **old** 109, here acting phonetically to express **crouch** and possibly also lending an idea of **the passing of time**. 649 originally referred to a **person staying in a crouched position**. This came to mean **be immobile** and **stay in one place**, leading to the idea of **residing** and by extension **being/ existing**.

Mnemonic: **OLD PERSON SITTING SLUMPED IS AT HOME**

650		KYO, yuru*su*, moto PERMIT, FORGIVE, PLACE, HOME 11 strokes	許可 KYOKA	permission
			特許 TOKKYO	patent
			手許 TEMOTO	at hand

言 is **word/ speak** 274. 午 is **noon** 110 q.v., here acting phonetically to express **approve/ forgive** and according to some scholars also possibly lending an idea of **pounding** (a table or similar) as a sign of **hearty endorsement** (from its literal meaning of pestle, which could symbolise pounding). Thus to **approve/ forgive someone's words.** It is not clear how it acquired the meaning of **place/ home**, but it may possibly have been used as a phonetic alternative to **reside** (and by extension residence) KYO 居 649.

Mnemonic: **PERMIT SPEECH AT NOON**

651		KYŌ, KEI, sakai BOUNDARY, BORDER 14 strokes	国境 KOKKYŌ	frontier
			境内 KEIDAI	precinct
			境界線 KYŌKAISEN	
				boundary line

士 is **ground** 60. 竟 is **finish** 462. Thus **finish of a piece of ground**, i.e. a **boundary.** Suggest taking 立 as **stand** 73, 日 as **sun** 62, and ル as **legs.**

Mnemonic: **STAND ON SUNNY GROUND, LEGS ASTRIDE BOUNDARY**

652	興	KYŌ, KŌ, okosu/ru RISE, RAISE, INTEREST 16 strokes	興奮 KŌFUN	excitement
			復興 FUKKŌ	revival
			興味深い KYŌMIBUKAI	
				very interesting

Once written 興, showing **raise/ hands working together** 𦥑 458/1873 and **same** 同 187, here also meaning **together/ in unison.** Thus to **raise up together**, giving **raise** and **rise. Interest/ excitement** is an associated meaning, from the idea of raised feelings. Suggest taking ⼧ ヨ as **hands** and 八 as **table.**

Mnemonic: **SAME HANDS RAISED AT TABLE -- HOW INTERESTING**

653

KIN, hito*shii*
AVERAGE, LEVEL,
ALIKE
7 strokes

平均 HEIKIN average
均等 KINTŌ uniformity
不均衡 FUKINKŌ imbalance

Somewhat obscure. 土 is **ground** 60. 勹 is often thought to be a variant of **ladle**/ measure 勺/ 勺 1342, but in fact old forms such as 勽 and 圴 show **coiling** (some scholars take the latter form to derive from a pictograph of a snake coiled on the ground, but it is safer to think of both forms simply as symbols of coiling -- see 655). 勹 is known to have acted phonetically to express **flat**, and presumably it also lent similar connotations from the idea of coiling (coils lying flat). Thus **flat ground**, leading to **level** and by figurative extension **average**. **Alike** is an associated meaning, from the idea of **norm**. Suggest taking 勺 as a combination of **ladle** 勹 and **one** — 1.

Mnemonic: **LEVEL GROUND WITH ONE LADLE?!**

654

KIN
BAN, FORBID
13 strokes

禁止 KINSHI prohibition
禁煙 KINEN 'No Smoking'
厳禁 GENKIN
strictly prohibited

示 is **show**/ **altar** 695 q.v., here with its connotations of **religious**/ of the gods. 林 is **forest** 75, used purely phonetically to express **abstain**. Thus **abstain for religious reasons**, leading to **abstain/ taboo/ ban/ forbid** etc. in a wider sense.

Mnemonic: **ALTAR IN FORBIDDEN FOREST**

655

KU
PHRASE, CLAUSE
5 strokes

字句 JIKU phraseology
句切り KUGIRI punctuation
文句 MONKU words, complaint

口 is **mouth/say** 20, here meaning **word**. 勹 is an element generally meaning **cover/ wrap/ encircle**. Strictly speaking, in the case of 655 its old form is 乛, showing interlocking strokes to convey the idea of **intertwining/ wrapping around**. However, the graphic evolution of 乛 into 勹 seems to have been influenced by a number of other forms of similar meaning, such as encircling arm ㇆/勹, womb ㇆/勹, and possibly also coiled snake 勽/勺. **Intertwining words** led to **phrase, clause**, etc.

Mnemonic: **MOUTH WRAPS ITSELF AROUND PHRASE**

203

656

KUN
LESSON, RULE,
KUN READING
10 strokes

訓読み KUNYOMI kun reading
訓練士 KUNRENSHI trainer
教訓的 KYŌKUNTEKI edifying

言 is **words/** speak 274. 川 is **river** 48, here acting phonetically to express **order** and also lending an idea of **flowing in a given way**. 656 originally meant **logical argument**, then came to mean **teaching** and by association **lesson**, **standard** or **rule**. It is also used for the **kun reading** of a character (i.e. the Japanese as opposed to Chinese).

Mnemonic: **WORDS FLOW LIKE RIVER IN LESSON**

657

GUN, mura, mure/reru
GROUP, FLOCK
13 strokes

群集 GUNSHŪ crowd
魚群 GYOGUN school of fish
群居 GUNKYO gregarious

羊 is **sheep** 986. 尹 is **lord** 266 q.v., here acting phonetically to express **assemble** and also lending its literal connotations of **command (with a stick)**. 657 originally referred to **herding sheep**, but then came to focus rather on the **group of animals**. Now also used of humans.

Mnemonic: **LORD OF SHEEP FLOCK**

658

KEI, KYŌ, heru, tatsu
PASS, SUTRA,
LONGITUDE
11 strokes

経済 KEIZAI economy
経線 KEISEN meridian
経過 KEIKA passage

Formerly 經 . 巠 is **lengthwise threads on a loom (warp)** 269, reinforced by **thread** 糸 27. **Pass (through)** and **longitude** are associated meanings. Since the warp threads act as **guides** for the crosswise weft threads, 658 also came to represent **guiding principles**, including the **sutras**. Suggest taking 巠 as **ground** 土 60 and **hand** 又 .

Mnemonic: **GUIDING HAND PASSES THREADS TO GROUND**

659 **KETSU, isagiyo**i   潔白 KEPPAKU na   immaculate
CLEAN, PURE   潔癖 KEPPEKI na   fastidious
15 strokes   潔く ISAGIYOKU   valiantly

Formerly 潔. 丯 is a **tally**, namely a piece of wood with serrations that was interlocked with another serrated piece (i.e. the matching other half) upon the proper fulfilment of a contract or similar. Sword/ **cut** 刀 181 emphasises the idea of cutting notches. As with the English term, **tally** also has connotations of making things **right and proper**. When combined with **thread** 糸 27, giving the CO character 絜 , it originally meant to **adjust threads and make them right**, though it presently came to mean simply to **correct**. The addition of **water** 氵 40 gave to **correct with water**, i.e. to **purify by ablution**. This came to mean **clean** or **pure**, including in the figurative sense of honorable. See also 1195. Suggest taking 丯 as a variant of **master** 主 299.

Mnemonic: **MASTER CUTS THREADS, WASHES CLEAN IN WATER**

---

660 **KEN**   事件 JIKEN   incident
ITEM, MATTER   用件 YŌKEN   business
6 strokes   条件 JŌKEN   condition, term

Person 亻 39 and **cow** 牛 97. 660 originally referred to a **person leading a cow away** from a herd, having **selected** and **purchased** it. It was later used of sorting out items for business in a general sense (including slaves, an early meaning of 660), and thus came to mean **something to be attended to**. Note that in Chinese it can still mean to separate.

Mnemonic: **PERSON LEADING AWAY COW IS A SERIOUS MATTER**

---

661 **KEN**   旅券 RYOKEN   passport
TICKET, PASS, BOND   証券 SHOKEN   bond
8 strokes   定期券 TEIKIKEN commuter pass

刀 is sword/ **cut** 181. 米 is an element once written 龸 , showing **rice** (plant) 禾/朱 81, and **two hands** 八. It originally meant to roll rice. It acts here phonetically to express **notched pledge/ tally** (see 659), but it is not clear whether it also lends any meaning. Thus **cut/ notched tally**, which in addition to being a symbol of a contract or pledge was also used as a symbol of official business or authority, and hence a **guarantee of safe conduct**, i.e. **pass** or **ticket** (cf. English term tally). Suggest taking 米 as **two** 二 61 **fires** 火 8.

Mnemonic: **START TWO FIRES WITH CUT UP TICKETS**

662

KEN, kewa*shii*
STEEP, SEVERE,
PERILOUS
11 strokes

険悪　KENAKU na　dangerous
保険　HOKEN　insurance
険そ　KENSO na　precipitous

Formerly 險 . β is **hill** 229. 僉/僉 is synthesised opinion 475 q.v., here acting phonetically to express **combine** and also lending similar connotations of its own. Thus **combined hills**, a reference to **particularly hilly terrain** and hence the present meanings. Suggest taking 僉 as a modified combination of cover/ **cap** ∧ 87/121 and **elder brother** 兄 267.

Mnemonic: **ELDER BROTHER DONS CAP TO CLIMB STEEP HILL**

663

KEN
INVESTIGATE
12 strokes

検討　KENTŌ　enquiry
探検　TANKEN　exploration
検査員　KENSAIN　inspector

Formerly 檢 . 僉/僉 is synthesised opinion 475 q.v., here acting phonetically to express **store safely** and also lending its meaning of **examine**. 木 is **wood** 69, here meaning wooden tablet upon which records were kept. Thus to **examine wooden records**, now **investigate** in a broad sense. Suggest taking 僉 as a modified combination of cover/ cap ∧ 87/121 and **elder brother** 兄 267.

Mnemonic: **ELDER BROTHER INVESTIGATES WOODEN COVER**

664

KEN, kinu
SILK
13 strokes

絹布　KENPU　silk cloth
人絹　JINKEN　rayon
絹物　KINUMONO　silk goods

糸 is **thread** 27. 肙 is a CO character meaning **small worm** or **coil** (coil/ circle/ **round** ▱ and **flesh** 月 365), here acting phonetically to express the color **cream** and almost certainly also lending connotations of **silkworm**. Thus **cream colored thread (from a worm)**, i.e. **silk**.

Mnemonic: **SILK THREADS FROM ROUND FLESHY WORM**

665

GEN, kagi*ru*
LIMIT
9 strokes

限度　GENDO　limit
限界　GENKAI　boundary
無限　MUGEN　infinity

β is **hill** 229. 艮 is **stop and stare** 263 q.v., acting phonetically to express **difficult** and almost certainly also lending an idea of **turning round**. Thus to reach a difficult hill, stop, and turn to look back, suggesting that one has reached the **limits** of familiar territory.

Mnemonic: **STOP AND STARE FROM HILL, HAVING REACHED LIMITS**

666

GEN, arawa*reru*/*su*
APPEAR, EXIST, NOW
11 strokes

発現 HATSUGEN   revelation
現象 GENSHŌ   phenomenon
現実 GENJITSU   reality

Jewel 玉 102 and see 見 18. Thus to **see a jewel**. On the one hand this came to refer to its luster (still listed as a minor meaning in Chinese), and on the other to the idea of **being visible/ appear**. **Exist** and **now** are associated meanings, from the idea of being before one's very eyes.

Mnemonic: **SEE JEWEL THAT NOW APPEARS**

667

GEN, he*ru*/*rasu*
DECREASE
12 strokes

減少 GENSHŌ   decrease
加減 KAGEN   extent, state
目減り MEBERI   weight loss

氵 is **water** 40. 咸 is unison 246 q.v., here acting phonetically to express **small amount**. In view of its complexity 咸 must presumably also have lent some meaning, possibly the idea of cutting away/ **reducing** from its trimming/ halberd element 戊 515. Thus a **small amount of water**, symbolising **reduction** and **decrease**. Suggest remembering by association with **feeling** 感 246, taking 咸 as a 'heartless' version (see heart 心 147).

Mnemonic: **DECREASED WATER BRINGS ON HEARTLESS FEELING**

---

668 故

KO, yue
PAST, REASON
9 strokes

事故 JIKO   accident
故事 KOJI   history
故山田氏 KOYAMADASHI
   the late Mr Yamada

Stick in hand/ coerce 攵 101, here acting as a causative element, and **old** 古 109, here indicating **the past**. Thus to **make something a thing of the past**. This led on the one hand to **past/ deceased**, and on the other to the idea of **causality/ reason**, i.e. with past events influencing the present/ future.

Mnemonic: **OLD STICK IN HAND A THING OF THE PAST**

669

KO
INDIVIDUAL, COUNTER
10 strokes

個人 KOJIN   individual
個性 KOSEI   individuality
一個 IKKO   one item

Person 亻 39 and **hard** 固 476. 669 originally referred to a person wearing armor (i.e. made hard), but from an early stage became confused with 箇 1054 q.v., which was a **counter** for bamboo slats. Probably because of the presence of person 亻, 669 has strong associations with the idea of **individuality**.

Mnemonic: **THAT INDIVIDUAL IS A HARD PERSON**

670 護	GO **DEFEND, PROTECT** 20 strokes	弁護士 BENGOSHI	lawyer
		保護 HOGO	protection
		護衛 GOEI	guard, escort

言 is **words** 274. 蒦 is crested bird 隹 648 in hand 又, here lending a meaning of **seize/ snare** and according to some scholars also acting phonetically to express **spin/ make dizzy**. Thus to **snare with words** (making the other party dizzy?), a reference to **proving an argument**. This came to have particular associations with **defence** against an accusation. Eventually the idea of words faded, leaving just **defend/ protect**. Suggest taking 蒦 as **bird** 隹 216 and **grass** 艹 9.

Mnemonic: **WORDILY DEFEND HAND SEIZING BIRD IN GRASS**

671 効	KŌ, ki*ku* **EFFECT, EFFICACY** 8 strokes	効果 KŌKA	effect
		有効 YŪKŌ na	valid
		効き目 KIKIME	effect

Formerly 效. 交 is **exchange** 115, here meaning **interchange** and by extension **match/ emulate** (see also 21). 攵 is **strike/ coerce** 101, here acting as a causative element. Thus to **make someone emulate**, i.e. **make them learn to perform** a given task. Eventually the causative aspect faded, leaving just **ability to perform** a given task, i.e. **efficacy**. In modern popular usage coerce 攵 has been replaced by **strength** 力 74. Note that in Chinese both forms now exist as separate characters, with 效 meaning emulate/ effect and 効 meaning toil/ effect.

Mnemonic: **EXCHANGE OF STRENGTH PROVES MOST EFFECTIVE**

672 厚	KŌ, atsu*i* **THICK, KIND** 9 strokes	部厚 BUATSU na	bulky, thick
		厚生 KŌSEI	welfare
		厚情 KŌJŌ	courtesy

Once written and later 厚. 厂 is **cliff** 45. 昆/厚/厚 is an inversion of 畬/富, a tall watchtower that is the prototype of **tall** 高 119. 672 originally meant **tall cliff**. The reason for the inversion is not clear, though it is possible that the original meaning had specific connotations of <u>descending</u> a tall cliff. Tall cliff eventually came to mean simply **substantial**, leading to **thick**. **Kind** is an associated meaning, from the idea of depth of feeling. Suggest taking 昆 as **day** 日 62 and **child** 子 25.

Mnemonic: **KIND BUT 'THICK' CHILD PLAYS DAILY BY CLIFF**

---

673 耕

KŌ, tagaya*su*
TILL, PLOW
10 strokes

耕地 KŌCHI — arable land
耕作 KŌSAKU — farming
耕うん機 KŌUNKI — cultivator

Formerly 耕. 耒 is a CO character meaning **plow** (of unclear etymology, but once written 耒, suggesting tree/shrub 木 69 and possibly serrated wood 丰 659, here representing a saw or similar cutting device, to give an idea of cutting away shrubs and thus preparing ground). 井 is **well** 1470, acting phonetically to express **conquer** and possibly also lending an associated idea of **fertile**. Thus to **conquer with a plow (and make fertile?)**, i.e. **till**. Suggest remembering 耒 as a **many branched tree** 木 69.

Mnemonic: **TILL AROUND WELL AND MANY BRANCHED TREE**

---

674 鉱

KŌ
MINERAL, ORE
13 strokes

鉱物 KŌBUTSU — mineral
鉱石 KŌSEKI — ore
炭鉱 TANKŌ — colliery

Formerly 鑛, and earlier 礦. The early form shows **rock** 石 45 and **yellow** 黄/黄 120, giving **yellow rock** and hence **mineral/ ore**. Yellow 黄 was later replaced by **wide/ extensive** 廣 / 広 114, possibly as a result of a miscopying influenced by the cliff part 厂 of 石 but possibly also for semantic reasons, and rock itself was replaced by **metal** 金 14.

Mnemonic: **EXTENSIVE METAL ORE**

---

675 構

KŌ, kama*u/eru*
BUILD, MIND
14 strokes

構成 KŌSEI — construction
結構 KEKKŌ — structure, fine
心構え KOKOROGAMAE — mental readiness

木 is **wood** 69. 冓 is a CO character meaning **large amount** or **accumulation**. It was originally written 冓, showing two bamboo (storage) **baskets piled up** (one inverted). Here 冓 acts phonetically to express **interweave** and also lends a meaning of **accumulate/ build up**. Thus to **build up by interweaving wood**, a reference to erecting the timber frame of a building. This came to mean **build** in a broader sense. **Mind/ care** is an associated meaning, from the idea of building up thoughts/ worries. Suggest remembering 冓 as **build with baskets**.

Mnemonic: **DO YOU MIND IF IT'S BUILT WITH WOODEN BASKETS?**

676		KŌ	講義	KŌGI	lecture
		LECTURE	講演	KŌEN	address
		17 strokes	講師	KŌSHI	lecturer

言 is **words** 274. 冓 is accumulation 675 q.v., here meaning **build up** and according to some scholars also acting phonetically to express **clarify**. Thus **something built of (clarifying?) words**, i.e. an **argument, speech, lecture**, or similar. Suggest taking 冓 literally as **build with baskets**.

Mnemonic: **LECTURE BUILT WITH 'BASKETS' OF WORDS**

677		KON, ma*jiru/zeru*	混血	KONKETSU mixed blood
		MIX, CONFUSION	混乱	KONRAN	confusion
		11 strokes	混ぜ物	MAZEMONO	mixture

氵 is **water**. 昆 is multitude 1276 q.v., here acting phonetically to express **spin/ swirl** and also lending its own idea of **confusion** (from people milling around). 677 originally referred to **water rushing and swirling** with no fixed course, as in a flood (still a meaning in Chinese). **Confused waters** then came to mean **confused** in a broader sense. **Mix** is an associated meaning, from the idea that in a state of confusion sundry impure elements can become mixed in. Suggest taking 昆 as **sun** 日 62 and **compare** 比 771.

Mnemonic: **COMPARE SUN AND WATER -- A CONFUSING MIX**

678	查	SA	検査	KENSA	inspection
		INVESTIGATE	審査	SHINSA	investigation
		9 strokes	査問	SAMON	inquiry

Wood 木 69, here meaning **timber**, and furthermore 且 1091 q.v., here with its literal meaning of **build up** and according to some scholars also acting phonetically to express **crosswise**. Thus to **build something with timber (laid crosswise?)**. In Chinese it can still be used in associated meanings, such as raft, but in Japanese it has come to be used purely in the borrowed meaning of **investigate**.

Mnemonic: **FURTHERMORE, WOOD SHOULD BE INVESTIGATED**

| 679 | | SAI, SA, futatabi
AGAIN, TWICE, RE-
6 strokes | 再生 SAISEI　　　regeneration
再刊 SAIKAN　　　reprint
再来年 SARAINEN year after next |

冉 is the lower part of accumulate/ **build with baskets** 冓 675, namely an inverted **basket. One** 一 1 was added to indicate **one further basket** being added to the pile. The idea of **one more** led to the present meanings.

Mnemonic: **ADD ONE BASKET AGAIN**

| 680 | | SAI, wazawai
CALAMITY
7 strokes | 災難 SAINAN　　　calamity
災害 SAIGAI　　　disaster
火災 KASAI　　　conflagration |

Once written 灾, showing **river** 川 48, here meaning **flood**, and **fire** 火 8. **Fire** and **flood** were symbols of **calamity**.

Mnemonic: **FIRE AND FLOODING RIVER ARE POTENTIAL CALAMITIES**

| 681 | | SAI, tsuma
WIFE
8 strokes | 後妻 GOSAI　　　second wife
夫妻 FUSAI husband and wife
人妻 HITOZUMA
　　　　married woman |

女 is **woman** 35. 妻 derives from 㞢, showing a **hand** ∂ **holding a broom** Ψ (to all intents and purposes a variant of hand holding broom 帚 96). See also 779.

Mnemonic: **WIFE HOLDS BROOM IN HAND**

| 682 | | SAI, toru
TAKE, GATHER
11 strokes | 採用 SAIYŌ　　　adoption
採集 SAISHŪ　　　collection
採取 SAISHU　　　harvesting |

Hand plucking (fruit) from a tree 釆 483, with an extra **hand** 扌 32. Suggest taking 釆 literally as (reaching) **hand** 爫 303 and **tree** 木 69.

Mnemonic: **GATHER FRUIT FROM TREE WITH TWO HANDS**

211

683   SAI, kiwa   実際 JISSAI   actuality
           OCCASION, EDGE,   国際 KOKUSAI   international
           CONTACT   窓際 MADOGIWA
           14 strokes   beside window

阝 is **hill** 229 q.v., here meaning **earthen rampart**. 祭 is **festival** 283, acting phonetically to express **meet/ come into contact** and possibly also loosely lending similar connotations of its own (from the idea of meeting associated with a festival). Thus **earthen ramparts meeting**, i.e. the junction of walls. This later came to mean **meet/ come into contact** in general. **Edge** is an associated meaning from that which comes into contact. **Occasion** is also felt to be an associated meaning, i.e. when one can come into contact with others.

Mnemonic: **FESTIVAL AT EDGE OF HILL IS QUITE AN OCCASION**

---

684   ZAI, aru   存在 SONZAI   existence
           BE LOCATED, DWELL, 在留 ZAIRYŪ   residence
           COUNTRYSIDE, BE   在所 ZAISHO   country home
           6 strokes

才 is a variant of talent 才 126 q.v., here used in its literal meaning of **dam** and by extension **barrier**. 土 is **earth** 60. Thus **earthen dam/ barrier**. The idea of substantial/ solid barrier led to the idea of **being firmly in place**, eventually giving **be located** and simply **be**. **Dwell/ reside** is an extension of be located. It is not fully clear how 684 also came to mean **countryside**, but it is assumed to be an associated meaning of dwell, i.e. one's **country home**.

Mnemonic: **FUNNY DAM IS LOCATED NEAR COUNTRYSIDE DWELLING**

---

685   ZAI, SAI   財産 ZAISAN   wealth, assets
           WEALTH, ASSETS   財団 ZAIDAN   foundation
           10 strokes   財政的 ZAISEITEKI   financial

貝 is **shell/ money** 90, here meaning **wealth/ assets**. 才 is talent 126 q.v., here acting phonetically to express **accumulate** and also lending a similar idea from its literal meaning of **dam** (i.e. that which causes a build-up). Thus **accumulated wealth/ assets**.

Mnemonic: **DAM FULL OF MONEY MEANS GREAT WEALTH**

686 罪 ZAI, tsumi   犯罪 HANZAI   crime
         CRIME, SIN   罪悪 ZAIAKU   vice
         13 strokes   罪深い TSUMIBUKAI   sinful

Somewhat obscure. 罒 is **net** 193, here with connotations of **catching**. 非 is **not** 773 q.v. Some scholars feel the latter acts purely phonetically to express **catch**, giving **catch in a net**, while others feel that it lends its literal meaning of **going in opposite directions** to refer by extension to **rebels**, thus giving **catch rebels in a net**. It is also not clear whether **crime/ sin** is a borrowed meaning or an associated meaning from the idea of that which results in one being caught, though the latter seems more likely.

Mnemonic: **NOT A NETWORK, BUT STILL CRIMINAL**

687 雑 ZATSU, ZŌ   雑談 ZATSUDAN   chitchat
         MISCELLANY   雑音 ZATSUON   noise, static
         14 strokes   雑兵 ZŌHYŌ   rank and file

Formerly 襍 . 衣 is **cloth** 420 q.v. 椎 is a variant of 集 , an element showing **tree** 木 69 and **bird** 隹 216 and meaning **birds gathering in a tree**. Here 椎 acts phonetically to express **gather** and also lends a similar meaning. 687 originally referred to **gathering bits of cloth** and making up a **patchwork** garment from them. Rather like the English term patchwork, it came to mean **miscellany** in a broad sense. Cloth 衣 was later replaced with **nine** 九 12, presumably to indicate plurality/ **many** (i.e. gather many bits). It is somewhat surprising that the cloth radical 衤 was never used, to give 襍 .

Mnemonic: **NINE MISCELLANEOUS BIRDS GATHERED IN TREE**

688 SAN, kaiko   蚕業 SANGYŌ   sericulture
         SILKWORM   養蚕 YŌSAN   sericulture
         10 strokes   蚕豆 SORAMAME* broad bean

Formerly 蠶 . 蚰 is **insect** 虫 56 doubled for emphasis. 朁 is a CO character meaning **if/ supposing**. It comprises the CO character **not/ without** 旡 (of unclear etymology, but derived from 旡, felt to show a person kneeling [at a table] with head turned, indicating that they are **unable** to eat any more), and the NGU character **say** 曰 (often written as 日 and confused with sun/day 日 62, but in fact the cross-stroke is only threequarter size and indicates a tongue - inside a mouth 口 20, not unlike the lower element of sound 音 6), thus giving a meaning of **not actually stated** and by extension (but) **if/ supposing** (that). In the case of 688 朁 acts phonetically to express **swollen**, to give **swollen insect**, a reference to a **silkworm full of silk threads**. In view of its complexity 朁 probably also lent some meaning, but this is unclear. It may have lent connotations of swollen/ bloated from the satiated person element 旡 , or may have lent some idea of hypotheticality, as in a silkworm which <u>should</u> produce silk. Suggest taking 天 as **heaven** 58.

Mnemonic: **SILKWORM IS A HEAVENLY INSECT**

689		SAN, *sui/ppai* **ACID, BITTER** 14 strokes	酸素 SANSO	oxygen
			酸性 SANSEI	acidity
			塩酸 ENSAN	hydrochloric acid

酉 is wine jar/ **alcohol** 302, here meaning **alcohol-like liquid**. 夋 is a CO character meaning **linger/ dawdle** (of unclear etymology, but showing stop and start 夂 438 q.v, meaning slow progress, and 允, which appears to be self 厶 134 and legs 儿). Here 夋 acts phonetically to express **sharp**, and almost certainly also lends its meaning of **linger**. Thus **sharp alcohol-like liquid (that lingers in the mouth?)**, leading to **bitter taste** and eventually also **acid**. Suggest remembering 夋 as **linger**.

Mnemonic: **ALCOHOL HAS LINGERING BITTER ACID TASTE**

690		SAN **PRAISE** 15 strokes	賛成 SANSEI	approval
			賛美歌 SANBIKA	hymn
			賛辞 SANJI	eulogy

Formerly 贊. 貝 is shell/ **money** 90, here meaning **valuable object**. 兟 is precede/ **advance** 先 49 doubled for emphasis. The latter lends its sound to express **offer**, and may also lend an associated transitive meaning of **advance/ proffer**. 690 originally meant to **offer someone a valuable object**, leading to the idea of **reward** and **praise**. Suggest taking 夫 as **male** 573.

Mnemonic: **TWO MALES PRAISED AND GIVEN MONEY**

691	支	SHI, *sasaeru* **BRANCH, SUPPORT** 4 strokes	支店 SHITEN	branch office
			支持 SHIJI	support
			支点 SHITEN	fulcrum

Once written 攴, showing a **hand** ⇒ holding up a **branch**/ section of bamboo 个 (see 170). It originally meant **break off a branch**/ small section/ offshoot. The physical branch is now represented by 枝 1315, that adds wood/tree 木 69, whereas 691 has come to refer to **branch** in the figurative sense (as in branch office etc.) **Support** derives from the idea of holding up.

Mnemonic: **HAND SUPPORTS CROSS-SHAPED BRANCH**

692		SHI,kokoroza*su*,kokorozashi	意志 ISHI	will
		WILL, INTENT	志望 SHIBŌ	aspiration
		7 strokes	有志 YŪSHI	voluntary

Usually explained as the **heart** 心 147 of a **warrior** 士 494. A useful mnemonic, but incorrect. Old forms such as 㞢 and 㞢 show that 士 derives from **emerging plant** 㞢/生 42, here acting phonetically to express **move** and also lending similar connotations of its own (from growth/ emerge). Thus **movement of the heart**, indicating **intent** or **will**.

Mnemonic: **WARRIOR'S HEART SHOWS WILL**

693		SHI	教師 KYŌSHI	teacher
		TEACHER,MODEL,ARMY	師表 SHIHYŌ	paragon
		10 strokes	師団 SHIDAN	army division

Somewhat obscure. 𠂤 is shown in some early forms to be **hill** 229 q.v. and in others to be **buttocks** 350 q.v., though in both cases the meaning is known to be **swelling/ rising**. 帀 is an inverted form of 㞢, itself a variant of **growing plant** 生 42 q.v., which acts phonetically to express **hill** and also lends a similar meaning of **rising** (from the idea of growing up from the ground). Thus **prominent hill**. Hills were often associated with **troop encampments** (see 540), and 693 eventually came to acquire such associations itself, leading to the present meaning of **army**. **Teacher** results from confusion with **commander/ leader** 帥 1454 q.v., of which it is an extended meaning, while **model** is an associated meaning with teacher. Suggest taking 𠂤 as **buttocks**, and 帀 as **cloth** 巾 778 and **one** 一 1.

Mnemonic: **MODEL TEACHER HAS ONE BIT OF CLOTH OVER BUTTOCKS**

694		SHI	資本 SHIHON	capital
		CAPITAL, RESOURCES	資料 SHIRYŌ	raw materials
		13 strokes	資金 SHIKIN	funds

貝 is shell/ **money** 90. 次 is **next** 292 q.v., here acting phonetically to express **possess** and almost certainly also lending an idea of **continuity**. Thus to **possess** (a continuity of?) **money**, i.e. **capital/ resources**.

Mnemonic: **NEXT SUM OF MONEY PROVIDES CAPITAL**

695

JI, SHI, shime*su*
SHOW
5 strokes

暗示 ANJI — hint
展示 TENJI — display
示教 SHIKYŌ — guidance

Once written 示 or 不. 丅 is a primitive **altar**. ✓/✓ is **drops** of blood (or possibly sacrificial wine). A top stroke 一 was added later to indicate a **sacrifice**/ item placed on the altar. Though as an independent character 695 is no longer used to mean altar, as a radical (usually 礻) it frequently has a meaning of **related to the gods**. **Show** is an extended meaning, from the idea of the outcome of a sacrifice showing the will of the gods.

Mnemonic: **DROPS FROM ALTAR SACRIFICE SHOW WILL OF GODS**

696

JI, ni*ru*
RESEMBLE
7 strokes

類似品 RUIJIHIN — imitation
似非 ESE-* — false, sham
似合う NIAU — be suited

亻 is **person** 39. 以 is **starting point**/ means 419, acting phonetically to express **resemble** and possibly also lending an idea of **starting point**. Thus to **resemble a person** (whom one takes as a starting point?). Now used of **resemble** in a broad sense.

Mnemonic: **STARTING POINT FOR PERSON IS TO RESEMBLE ONE**

697 児

JI, NI, ko
CHILD
7 strokes

孤児 KOJI — orphan
小児 SHŌNI — infant
児童文学 JIDŌBUNGAKU — juvenile literature

Formerly 兒, and earlier as 兒. 八/儿 shows a **person kneeling** (i.e. **not standing**) 39, while 臼 is mortar 648. Some scholars feel the latter is used purely phonetically to express **weak**/ **helpless**, giving **helpless person (unable to stand)**, that could originally apply to a very aged or sick person as well as a very young one. Others feel that 臼 is used in its literal sense of **grinding teeth**, referring to **young children during the teething stage**, and take 儿 to refer to **crawling**. Thus **crawling, teeth-grinding person**. The latter theory seems the more likely. (Note also similar English slang terms for a teething, crawling infant, such as anklebiter.) Suggest taking 旧 as **old** 648.

Mnemonic: **OLD PERSON IS REALLY A CHILD**

698   **SHIKI**   常識 JŌSHIKI   common sense
         KNOWLEDGE   意識 ISHIKI   awareness
         19 strokes   知 識 人 CHISHIKIJIN intellectual

言 is **words** 274, 音 is **sound** 6, and 戈 is **lance/ halberd** 493, though there is some disagreement as to how these elements are grouped. 戈 is known to have acted to mean **marker** or **sign**. (A lance was sometimes thrust into the ground -- in some cases with a banner attached -- as a crude marker or pointer [note also the graphic and semantic overlap with stake 弋 177].) Some scholars take 䜱 as the NGU character **memorise**, ascribing a meaning to 698 of **memorise signs** and therefore **possess knowledge**. Others take 戠 as meaning **marker**. (It is in fact a CO character with a range of borrowed meanings, but its original meaning is felt to have been lance that produces 'sound', i.e. conveys a message. This was a reference to the fact that messages as well as banners were sometimes attached to marker lances.) Thus **marker that produces words**, i.e. with words 言 re-inforcing the message-conveying role discussed above. Conveying information then came by association to mean **intelligence/ knowledge**. Since 音 and 戈 have become com-bined to 戠, suggesting that they are treated as one element, and since the element occurs with some frequency in compound characters, the latter theory seems the more likely.

Mnemonic: **HAVE KNOWLEDGE OF A WORD SOUNDING LIKE LANCE**

---

699   **SHITSU, SHICHI, CHI**   品 質 HINSHITSU   quality
         QUALITY, PAWN   質屋 SHICHIYA   pawnshop
         15 strokes   人 質 HITOJICHI   hostage

貝 is **shell/ money** 90. 斦 is **ax** 1176 doubled for emphasis, acting phonetically to ex-press **equivalence** and almost certainly lending an idea of **chop up** (figuratively) and hence analyse/**understand** (see 199). Thus **something whose monetary equivalence is understood**, leading on the one hand to **quality** and on the other to **pawn/** pledge.

Mnemonic: **TWO AXES CHOP PAWNED SHELL TO ASCERTAIN QUALITY**

---

700   **SHA**   宿舎 SHUKUSHA   lodgings
         HOUSE, QUARTERS   舎営 SHAEI   billet
         8 strokes   田舎者 INAKAMONO*   yokel

Formerly 舍, and earlier 舍. 口 is **mouth** 20, here meaning by extension **breathe**. 余/ 亼 / 仐 is margin 余 800 q.v., here lending its connotations of **easily**. Thus **breathe easily/ relax**. Possibly because of the **roof/ building** element 𠆢 in 仐, 700 presently came (like 800) to mean **building where one can relax**, i.e. one's **house** or **quarters**. Suggest taking 𠆢 as **roof**, 土 as **ground** 60, and 口 as opening/ **entrance**.

Mnemonic: **QUARTERS WITH ROOF AND ENTRANCE BELOW GROUND**

217

701 SHA, ayama*ru*
APOLOGIZE, THANK
17 strokes

謝罪 SHAZAI apology
謝礼 SHAREI honorarium
感謝 KANSHA gratitude

言 is **words** 274. 射 is **shoot** 882 q.v., here acting phonetically to express **leave** and almost certainly lending similar connotations (from an arrow leaving the bow, and cf. English slang 'shoot off' meaning leave). Thus **words said upon leaving**.

Mnemonic: **WORDS OF APOLOGY AND THANKS AS ONE SHOOTS OFF**

---

702 JU, sazu*keru*
CONFER, TEACH
11 strokes

授業 JUGYŌ tuition
授与 JUYO conferment
教授 KYŌJU
teaching, professor

Receive 受 303 q.v., here in its literal sense of **convey**, with an extra **hand** 扌 32. Whereas 303 came to mean receive, 702 came rather to mean **confer/ bestow**, including in the sense of confer knowledge / **teach**.

Mnemonic: **TEACHER'S HAND CONFERS RECEIPT**

---

703 SHŪ, osa*meru/maru*
OBTAIN, STORE,
SUPPLY
4 strokes

収入 SHŪNYŪ income
収益 SHŪEKI gains
収容力 SHŪYŌRYOKU capacity

Formerly 收. 攵 is **striking hand/ coerce** 101, here used as a **causative** element. 丩 derives from 乚乚, showing **intertwined threads** and meaning put together/ **assemble**, and by extension **gather**. Some scholars feel 丩 also acts phonetically to express **seek out**. Thus to **cause threads to be (sought out and?) gathered together**. This came to mean simply **gather** and by extension **obtain**, with **store** being an associated meaning. **Supply** is felt to be in turn an associated meaning with store. The modern form uses **hand** 又 instead of striking hand 攵. Suggest taking 丩 as a **pitchfork**.

Mnemonic: **HAND OBTAINS PITCHFORK FROM SUPPLY STORE**

704 SHŪ, SHU, osa*meru*/*maru*   修理 SHŪRI   repair

PRACTICE, MASTER   修正 SHŪSEI   amendment

10 strokes   修業 SHUGYŌ /SHŪGYŌ

study

彡 is **delicate hairs** 93 q.v., here lending an idea both of **elegant** and of **brush.** 攸 comprises **stick in hand/ strike** 攵 101, a further **stick** 丨, and **person** 亻 39, and means to **strike a person with a stick**. 704 originally referred to 'striking' a person with a brush in order to make them appear elegant, i.e. brushing specks of dust/ dirt off their clothes. It then came to mean **make something just so**, leading by association to **practice** and **master**.

Mnemonic: **PERSON PRACTICES TO MASTER STRIKING WITH BRUSH**

---

705 SHŪ, SHU   公衆 KŌSHŪ   public

MULTITUDE, MASS   大衆 TAISHŪ   the masses

12 strokes   合衆国 GASSHŪKOKU   USA

Formerly 衆. An early form 𤶈 shows that 血 derives from **eye** 𥅀/目 72 tilted on a horizontal axis, while the oldest form 𤷾 shows that it is in fact a miscopying of **sun** ⊙/ 日 62. 𠈓 shows **person** 亻 39 trebled to indicate a **large number**. Thus a **large number of people gathered (working?) under the sun**, later presumably misinterpreted as a large number of people gathered under a **watchful eye**. The reason for the later addition of ノ over the eye is not clear, but suggest taking it as an **eyelash**, with a play on the word **lash**.

Mnemonic: **MASS OF ODD PEOPLE UNDER WATCHFUL EYE WITH LASH**

---

706 SHUKU, SHŪ, iwa*u*   祝賀 SHUKUGA   celebration

CELEBRATE   祝辞 SHUKUJI congratulations

9 strokes   祝い事 IWAIGOTO   happy event

Formerly 祝. 示/ネ is **altar** 695. 兄 is **elder brother** 267 q.v., here used in its literal sense of **person speaking (and crouching/ bending?)**. Thus **person (kneeling?) at altar**, i.e. **giving thanks**.

Mnemonic: **ELDER BROTHER CELEBRATES AT ALTAR**

707

JUTSU, no*beru*
STATE, RELATE
8 strokes

前述　ZENJUTSU no　　the said
述語　JUTSUGO　　　predicate
叙述　JOJUTSU　　　description

Originally 術, showing **movement** 化/辶 129 and a **hand** ㄓ with **bits** (of glutinous rice) ⼞ **sticking** to it. ㄓ/朮 thus has a meaning of **stick/ adhere**, and 707 originally referred to 'sticking' to a person as they moved, i.e. **following** them. This came to mean 'shadow' a person in a broad sense, including **repetition** of their words. Repeat then came to mean simply **relate** or **state**. Suggest taking 朮 as a **'funny' tree** 木 69.

Mnemonic: **STATE HOW ONE MOVED AROUND FUNNY TREE**

708

JUTSU, sube
MEANS, TECHNIQUE
11 strokes

技術的　GIJUTSUTEKI　technical
芸術的　GEIJUTSUTEKI　artistic
手術　SHUJUTSU　　operation

彳 is **go** 118, here also lending its literal connotations of **roads**. 朮 is **adhere** 707 q.v., here acting phonetically to express **twisting** and almost certainly lending its meaning of adhere/ follow. Thus **twisting road/ path to which one adheres**, a reference to the **means/ technique** to be followed in order to achieve one's goal. Suggest taking 朮 as a **'funny' tree** 木 69.

Mnemonic: **GO AROUND FUNNY TREE WITH CERTAIN TECHNIQUE**

709

JUN
LEVEL, CONFORM,
QUASI-
13 strokes

準備　JUNBI　　　preparation
水準　SUIJUN　　　standard
準決勝　JUNKESSHŌ semifinals

Formerly also 準, with **ice** ⼎ 378 replacing **water** 氵 40. 隼 is a CO character meaning hawk, deriving from **bird** 隹 216 and either talons or a branch 十. 隼 is used here phonetically to express **level**, and possibly also lends connotations of **settled** from the idea of a hawk settled on a branch. Thus 709 meant **water (settled?) at a level**. **Quasi-** and **conform** both stem from the idea of more or less attaining a level. Suggest taking 十 as **ten** 33. See also 1376.

Mnemonic: **TEN BIRDS ON WATER, ALL AT SAME LEVEL**

710

序

JO, tsuide

BEGINNING, ORDER

7 strokes

序文 JOBUN   preface

序列 JORETSU   order

序数 JOSŪ   ordinal number

广 is **building** 114. 予 is **already/ in advance** 403. Thus **that which one does in advance of (erecting) a building**, namely lay the foundations. Thus the **beginning** of something, and by extension (proper) **order**.

Mnemonic: **BUILDING ALREADY BEGINNING TO SHOW ORDER**

711

除

JO, JI, nozoku

EXCLUDE, REMOVE

10 strokes

除去 JOKYO   removal

免除 MENJO   exemption

掃除 SŌJI   cleaning

阝 is **mound/ hill** 229 q.v. 余 is **margin/ surplus** 800 q.v. Some scholars feel the latter lends its literal meaning of **open up** to give **open up hilly ground**, i.e. by **removing** obstacles. Others feel that 阝 is used in its sense of **terracing/ steps** with 余 acting purely phonetically to express **order/ sequence**, giving **sequence of steps**, and that the present meanings are borrowed. The fact that in Chinese 711 has a lesser meaning of **steps** suggests that the latter theory is correct, though the former may be a useful mnemonic.

Mnemonic: **SURPLUS HILLS MUST BE REMOVED**

712

招

SHŌ, maneku

INVITE, SUMMON

8 strokes

招待 SHŌTAI   invitation

招集 SHŌSHŪ   convocation

手招く TEMANEKU   beckon

Hand 扌 32 and **summon** 召 1387 q.v., giving **summon with the hand/ beckon**. Now **invite** in a broad sense.

Mnemonic: **INVITE BY SUMMONING WITH HAND**

221

713

承

SHŌ, uketamawa*ru*
RECEIVE, HEAR, KNOW
8 strokes

承知 SHŌCHI   consent
承認 SHŌNIN   recognition
継承者 KEISHŌSHA   successor

Originally 發, showing a **hand** ♨/手 32 and **two hands holding up an object** 𦥑. The latter is to all intents and purposes the prototype of together 共 460 q.v., but confusingly, the same pictograph can also indicate (as here) **receiving**, since the formal manner of receiving is to hold the item up level with the forehead. The extra hand ♨ is theoretically for clarity, though it might be argued that it would have been better added to 460 than to 713. Possibly because the object ○ was misinterpreted as **mouth/ say** 20, 713 also came to acquire connotations of **receiving spoken information**, leading to **hear** and **know**. Suggest taking 秉 as a **baby** 子 25 with **bristles** ≡, and ⊃< as a variant of **water** 水 40.

Mnemonic: **HEAR ABOUT A BRISTLY WATER-BABY**

714

称

SHŌ
PRAISE, NAME, CHANT
10 strokes

称号 SHŌGŌ   title
称賛 SHŌSAN   praise
名称 MEISHŌ   name

Formerly 稱. 禾 is **rice plant** 81. ⌒ is **hand reaching down** 303. 冉 is **basket** 675. Thus **hand reaching down to (pluck) rice plants and put same in basket**. This work was invariably accompanied by singing and **chanting**, and thus 714 later came to mean **chant**. **Name** is an associated meaning. **Praise** is also felt by some scholars to be an associated meaning, and by others to be a borrowing. Suggest remembering 尔 by partial association with **bamboo** 竹 170 and **eight** ハ 66.

Mnemonic: **PRAISE EIGHT BAMBOO-LIKE RICE PLANTS**

715

証

SHŌ
PROOF
12 strokes

証人 SHŌNIN   witness
論証 RONSHŌ   demonstration
証明 SHŌMEI   proof

Formerly also 證, though technically they are separate characters. 言 is **words** 274. 登 is climb 360, acting phonetically to express **clear/ clarify** and possibly also lending an idea of **offer up**. Thus (to offer up?) **clarifying words**, i.e. **prove/ proof**. 登 has now been replaced with **correct** 正 41, though 証 is actually a character of long standing that originally meant remonstrate/ counsel against.

Mnemonic: **CORRECT WORDS ARE PROOF**

716 JŌ   無条件 MUJŌKEN unconditional
CLAUSE, ITEM, LINE   条約 JŌYAKU   treaty
7 strokes   条鉄 JŌTETSU   bar-iron

Formerly 條, showing **wood/tree** 木 69 and **hand striking person with stick** 攸 704. Thus **wooden stick/ branch for striking**. On the one hand **stick** led to the idea of something straight and thus **line**, including in the figurative sense of a line of argument, and on the other **branch** led to the idea of something small broken off from the main part, and thus acquired connotations of **small part** and hence **item/ detail**. The two meanings overlapped to give a detailed line of argument, leading to **clause**. Suggest taking 夊 as **sitting crosslegged**.

Mnemonic: **ITEM ABOUT SITTING CROSSLEGGED IN TREE**

---

717 JŌ   状態 JŌTAI   situation
CONDITION, LETTER   現状 GENJŌ   status quo
7 strokes   招待状 SHŌTAIJŌ
     letter of invitation

Formerly 狀. 犬 is **dog** 17. 爿 is **bed** 1389, here used purely phonetically to express **appearance**. Thus **appearance/ condition of a dog**. This later came to mean **condition/ situation** in a broad sense, and also extended to the idea of writing a **report** about a situation, hence **letter**. Suggest taking 丬 as a **bar |** of **ice** 冫 378.

Mnemonic: **DOG EATS BAR OF ICE, NOW IN BAD CONDITION**

---

718 常 JŌ, tsune   非常 HIJŌ   emergency
USUAL, ALWAYS   常例 JŌREI   convention
11 strokes   日常 NICHIJŌ   daily

巾 is **cloth/ threads** 778. 尚 is **furthermore** 1392 q.v., here acting phonetically to express **long** and probably also lending an idea of **trailing** from its original meaning of smoke trailing upwards from a window. Thus **long trailing threads**, later used figuratively to describe something **ongoing** and hence **usual/ always**.

Mnemonic: **FURTHERMORE, THE USUAL CLOTH, AS ALWAYS**

719	JŌ, SEI, nasake	同情	DŌJŌ	sympathy
	FEELING, PITY, FACT	情勢	JŌSEI	situation
	11 strokes	情け無い	NASAKENAI	wretched

忄 is **heart/ feeling** 147. 青 is **blue/ green** 43 q.v., here lending its connotations of **fresh** and **pure**. Thus **pure heart,** leading by association to **compassion** (cf. English 'heart'). **Fact/ situation** stems from the idea of a heart with nothing to hide, i.e. exposing the truth.

Mnemonic: **HEART MADE BLUE WITH FEELING OF PITY**

720	SHOKU, SHIKI, oru	織機	SHOKKI	loom
	WEAVE	組織的	SOSHIKITEKI	systematic
	18 strokes	織り物	ORIMONO	textiles

糸 is **thread** 27. 戠 is **marker-lance** 698. Some scholars see 720 as an ideographic combination of these elements to give **marker threads**, used at a certain stage in **weaving**. Others feel that 戠 acts phonetically to express **straight/ upright**, as well as lending similar connotations of its own (from a lance thrust upright in the ground), to give **upright threads**, a reference to the warp threads that symbolise the start of **weaving**. Suggest taking 戠 literally as **lance** 戈 493 and **noise** 音 6.

Mnemonic: **WEAVE THREADS WITH NOISE LIKE A LANCE**

721	SHOKU	職人	SHOKUNIN	artisan
職	EMPLOYMENT, JOB	職業	SHOKUGYŌ	profession
	18 strokes	職員	SHOKUIN	staff

耳 is **ear** 29, here used figuratively to mean **flap/ attached item**. 戠 is **marker-lance** 698 q.v., here used in its literal sense of pole stuck in ground to indicate something. Thus 721 originally meant **marker-pole with something (flag or similar) attached to it**. This was a reference to tradesmen's practice of erecting outside their premises a flagpole bearing a flag which indicated the nature of their business. Hence 721 came to refer to **employment**. Suggest taking 戠 literally as **lance** 戈 493 and **noise** 音 6.

Mnemonic: **JOB AS LANCER LEAVES NOISE IN EARS**

722		SEI **SYSTEM, CONTROL** 8 strokes	制度 SEIDO	system
			制止 SEISHI	restraint
			強制 KYŌSEI	compulsion

Once written 𣂁, showing sword/ **cut** 刀 / 刂 181 and a **many branched tree** 朱 (variant tree 木 69). 722 originally meant **prune a tree**, leading by extension to **put in order** and thence **control**, with **system** being an associated meaning. Suggest remembering 牜 by partial association with **cow** 牛 97.

Mnemonic: **TREE CUT IN SHAPE OF COW SHOWS SYSTEM OF SORTS**

723		SEI, SHŌ **NATURE, SEX** 8 strokes	男性 DANSEI	male
			性的 SEITEKI	sexual
			性分 SHŌBUN	disposition

Heart/ feeling 忄 147 and **birth** 生 42, giving the **heart one is born with**, i.e. one's **nature**. **Gender**/ sex is an associated meaning.

Mnemonic: **ONE'S NATURE IS THE HEART ONE IS BORN WITH**

724		SEI, SHŌ, matsurigoto **GOVERNMENT** 9 strokes	行政 GYŌSEI	administration
			政治家 SEIJIKA	politician
			中央政府 CHŪŌSEIFU	
				central government

正 is **correct** 41. 攵 is **strike**/ **force** 101, here acting as a causative element. Thus to **make something correct**, leading to **govern** and **government**.

Mnemonic: **GOVERNMENT FORCES CORRECTNESS**

725	精	SEI, SHŌ **SPIRIT, VITALITY,** **REFINE, DETAIL** 14 strokes	精力 SEIRYOKU	vitality
			精密 SEIMITSU	precision
			不精 BUSHŌ	indolence

米 is **rice** 201. 青 is **blue**/ **green** 43 q.v., here lending its connotations of **fresh** and **pure**. Thus **pure rice**. This led by extension to **refine**, with **detail** being an associated meaning (i.e. going into detail by removing even the tiniest impurity). **Spirit** is an associated meaning with purity (cf. English quintessence), leading by extension to **vitality** (cf. English spirit).

Mnemonic: **REFINED GREEN RICE FILLS ONE WITH SPIRIT**

---

726 製

SEI
MANUFACTURE
14 strokes

製造 SEIZŌ manufacture
精製 SEISEI refining
日本製 NIHONSEI made in Japan

衣 is **clothing** 420. 훼 is **system/ control** 722 q.v., here lending its meaning of **cut to shape**. Thus **cut clothes to shape**, i.e. **make clothes**, later **make/ manufacture** in a broad sense.

Mnemonic: SYSTEM FOR MANUFACTURING CLOTHING

---

727 税

ZEI
TAX, TITHE
12 strokes

税金 ZEIKIN tax
税務所 ZEIMUSHO tax office
所得税 SHOTOKUZEI income tax

禾 is **rice (plant)** 81. 兌 is **exchange** 524 q.v., here acting phonetically to express **divide** and also lending connotations of disperse/ **give away**. Thus to **divide up rice and give (part of) it away**, a reference to paying a **tithe/ tax**. Suggest taking 兌 literally as **elder brother** 兄 267 and **away** ヽ 66.

Mnemonic: ELDER BROTHER GIVES AWAY RICE-TAX

---

728 責

SEKI, se*meru*
LIABILITY, BLAME
11 strokes

責任 SEKININ responsibility
自責 JISEKI self-reproach
責務 SEKIMU duty

Popularly explained to the effect that 貝 is **shell/ money** 90 and 圭 is a variant of **growth** 生 42, giving a meaning of **growing/ accumulating money** and by association growing **responsibilities / liabilities**. A useful mnemonic, but old forms such as 𠧪 show that 圭 is in fact a variant of **taper** 朿 873. Here it acts phonetically to express **demand**, and may possibly also lend connotations of **sharp**. Thus **money which can be demanded** (sharply/ promptly?), i.e. a **loan/ debt** (still retained in Chinese, and see also debt/ loan 債 1292). A debt necessarily involves the idea of **liability**. **Blame** is felt to stem from an associated idea of culpability. Since 728 often seems to lend a meaning of accumulate in compounds (e.g. 521and 729) it is possible that the 'growing money' interpretation is of long standing, though it is also possible that accumulation is a concept associated with debt/ liability.

Mnemonic: GROWING MONEY DEBTS MEAN GROWING LIABILITY

729		**SEKI** **ACHIEVEMENT, SPIN** 17 strokes	成績 SEISEKI	result
			業績 GYŌSEKI	achievement
			紡績 BŌSEKI	spinning

糸 is **thread** 27. 責 is **blame**/ liability 728 q.v., here used phonetically to express **join** and possibly also lending an idea of **accumulate**. 729 originally referred to **joining threads by spinning**, and also had strong connotations of the **amount** of thread spun. Amount led to the figurative **achievement**.

Mnemonic: **BLAME THREADS FOR POOR ACHIEVEMENTS IN SPINNING**

730	接	**SETSU, tsug***u* **CONTACT, JOIN** 11 strokes	面接 MENSETSU	interview
			接続 SETSUZOKU	connection
			接ぎ目 TSUGIME	joint

扌 is **hand** 32. 妾 is an NGU character meaning concubine. It was once written 妾, showing that 立 is a variant of (tattooist's) **needle** 辛 1432, while 女 is **woman** 35. Some scholars interpret needle 立 as symbolising tattooed **slave** (see 340), giving **slave woman,** but as it could also symbolise penetration and by extension **copulation** 妾 may simply mean **woman with whom one copulates**. In fact, in view of its strong connotations of **join** (e.g. with tree 木 69 it gives the CO character graft 椄) the latter explanation seems the more likely. In the case of 730 妾 acts phonetically to express **take** and almost certainly also lends a meaning of **join**, giving **take someone by the hand/ join hands** and hence eventually **join/ contact** in a broad sense. Suggest taking 立 as **stand** 73.

Mnemonic: **JOIN HANDS WITH WOMAN STANDING ALONE**

731	設	**SETSU, m***ō**keru* **ESTABLISH, BUILD** 11 strokes	設置 SETCHI	founding
			設計 SEKKEI	design
			設立 SETSURITSU	founding

Once written 設, but earlier still as 𝌀, showing that **words** 言/言 is in fact a miscopying of 丫, which is assumed to be a wedge or **stake**. 攴/殳 is a **striking hand holding a utensil** (see 153), in this case a mallet or **hammer**. 731 originally meant to **set about laying foundations by driving in stakes**, and hence came to mean **build, found,** and so forth.

Mnemonic: **BUILD WITH WORDS, DESPITE HAMMER IN HAND**

| 732 | | ZETSU, shita
TONGUE
6 strokes | 舌戦 ZESSEN war of words
舌足らず SHITATARAZU lisping
弁舌 BENZETSU eloquence |

Once written 舌, showing **mouth** 口 20 and **dry/ forked thrusting weapon** ¥/干
825 q.v. The latter acts phonetically to express **emerge**, and also lends its own connotations of **thrusting out**. It may also be felt to lend an idea of **fork**, a forked tongue being a distinctive symbol of a tongue in general. Thus **that (forked item?) which thrusts forth from the mouth**, i.e. the **tongue**.

Mnemonic: **TONGUE SHOWS DRY MOUTH**

| 733 | | ZETSU, ta*eru*, ta*tsu*
CEASE, SEVER, END
12 strokes | 絶望 ZETSUBŌ despair
絶対的 ZETTAITEKI absolute
絶えず TAEZU unceasingly |

Formerly 絶 and earlier 𢇁, showing that 色 is not color 色 145 but a miscopying of
bending body 乚/巴 145 and **sword/ cut** 刀/刀 181. 糸 is **thread** 27. 色 acts phonetically to express **bend/ break** and almost certainly lends similar bending connotations of its own (bend and break conceptually overlapping). Thus to **cut and break threads**, leading to **sever** and **cease** in a broad sense. However, suggest taking 色 as **color**.

Mnemonic: **SEVER COLORFUL THREADS**

| 734 | 銭 | SEN, zeni
SEN, COIN, MONEY
14 strokes | 小銭 KOZENI small change
金銭 KINSEN money
さい銭 SAISEN offertory |

Formerly 錢 , showing **gold/ metal/ money** 金 14 and two **halberds** 戔 493 q.v.
Since the latter often has connotations of **cutting away / reducing** and by extension
small amount it is often assumed that 734 simply means **small amount of money**.
This is a useful mnemonic, but not quite correct. 戔 also has connotations of **sharp**, and
in the case of 734 not only lends such a meaning but also acts phonetically to express **taper**. 金 is used in the sense of **metal** rather than money. The character originally meant
sharp tapered piece of metal, and referred to a **plowshare**. Note that it still retains
this meaning in Chinese. Since one of the ancient Chinese **coins** (of small value) resembled the shape of the plow 734 came by association to be applied to this coin, though it is
possible that this process may also have been influenced to some extent by a popular reinterpretation of the elements of the character (or at least of 金 as money). In Japanese it is
applied by further association to the sen coin, equivalent to one hundredth of a yen. Suggest taking 戔 as **two** = 61 **halberds** 戈 493.

Mnemonic: **TWO GOLD HALBERDS REDUCED TO MERE COIN**

735 **ZEN,** *yoi*
GOOD, VIRTUOUS
12 strokes

善意 ZENI — good faith
親善 SHINZEN — friendship
善後策 ZENGOSAKU — remedy

Once written 𦎫 , and earlier as 譱. 羊 is **sheep** 986 q.v., here lending its connotations of **fine** and **praiseworthy**. 誩 is the old form of **argue** 諍 463 (literally words 言 274 set against each other). Thus a **praiseworthy argument**, i.e. a **fine debate**. This later came to mean **fine** or **praiseworthy** in a broad sense. Suggest taking as a combination of **sheep** 𦍌 , **one** 一 1, **small** 小 36, and **mouth** 口 20.

Mnemonic: **SHEEP HAS ONE SMALL BUT GOOD MOUTH**

736 **SO**
ANCESTOR
9 strokes

祖先 SOSEN — ancestors
先祖 SENZO — ancestors
祖父母 SOFUBO — grandparents

Formerly 祖 . 示/礻 is **altar** 695, here indicating **(worship) gods**. 且 is **furthermore/ cairn** 1091, here indicating **accumulation** and also felt by some scholars to act phonetically to express **beginning**. Thus **(worship) an accumulation of gods (going back to the beginning?)**. **Gods** conceptually overlapped with **ancestors**.

Mnemonic: **FURTHERMORE, AT ALTAR ONE WORSHIPS ANCESTORS**

737 **SO, SU,** *moto*
ELEMENT, BASE, BARE
10 strokes

元素 GENSO — element
要素 YŌSO — factor
素足 SUASHI — bare feet

Once written 𩃬 , showing **thread** 𢆶 / 糸 27 and the prototype 𡿧 of **droop** 垂 907. The latter acts phonetically to express **white** and almost certainly also lends connotations of **soft**. Thus **soft white threads** (i.e. **silk**), leading to **white silkcloth**. White silkcloth came to represent something **unpatterned** and therefore **undeveloped/ pristine** in a broad sense, giving **elemental, basic, bare**, etc. Suggest taking 主 as a variant of life/ **raw** 生 42.

Mnemonic: **RAW THREADS ARE BARE AND BASIC ELEMENTS**

229

738

SŌ, sube*te*
WHOLE, TOTAL
14 strokes

総額 SŌGAKU　total amount
総合 SŌGŌ　synthesis
総理大臣 SŌRIDAIJIN
prime minister

Formerly 總 . 糸 is **thread** 27. 悤 is an old variant of **window** 窓 919, here acting phonetically to express **gather** and possibly also lending an idea of **widely** (wide/ sweeping being an associated concept with window). Thus to **gather threads (widely?)**, eventually leading to the idea of **assembling every item** in a category and hence **whole/ total**. Suggest taking 公 as **public** 277 and 心 as **heart/ feeling** 147.

Mnemonic: **THREAD RUNS THROUGH PUBLIC FEELING**

739

ZŌ, tsuku*ru*
MAKE, BUILD
10 strokes

造船 ZŌSEN　shipbuilding
木造 MOKUZŌ　wooden
人造 JINZŌ　manmade

Once written 艁, showing **boat** 月/舟 1354 and **proclaim** 告/告 481 q.v. The latter acts phonetically to express **reach** and may also lend its own loose connotations of reach (from the idea of reaching a point where words emerge from the mouth). Thus to **reach somewhere by boat**, with boat 月 later being replaced by **movement** 辶 129 to give just **reach/ arrive** and by extension **attain**. Note that 739 still retains these meanings in Chinese. It is not clear how it came to mean **make/ build**. Some scholars assume it to be a borrowing, while others see it as an associated idea with traveling by boat, i.e. building a boat in order to reach the other side of a body of water, leading to the general idea of making something in order to attain a goal. The fact that in Chinese 739 has strong connotations of acting with haste and expediency suggests the latter theory is correct.

Mnemonic: **PROCLAIM THAT ONE HAS MADE A MOVE**

740

ZŌ
IMAGE
14 strokes

想像 SŌZŌ　imagination
木像 MOKUZŌ　wooden statue
現像 GENZŌ　developing (film)

Person/ man イ 39 and **elephant/ image** 象 533. 740 originally referred to the **image of a person**, but is now used of **image** in a broad sense.

Mnemonic: **IMAGE OF ELEPHANT MAN**

741

ZŌ, masu, fueru/yasu | 増大 ZŌDAI | increase
INCREASE, BUILD UP | 増税 ZŌZEI | tax increase
14 strokes | 増幅 ZŌFUKU | amplification

Formerly 增 . 土 is **earth** 60. 曾/曽 is an NGU character now used to express **formerly**, but it originally meant **build up** (symbolically expressed as steam issuing forth 八 66 from a rice cooker 曰 87, indicating a build up of steam/ pressure). Thus 741 originally meant a **build up/ accumulation of earth**, as in a rampart or dam, but now means **build up** or **increase** in general. Suggest taking 曽 as **eight** 丶/ 66, **field** 田 59, and **day** 日 62.

Mnemonic: **BUILD UP EARTH IN FIELD OVER EIGHT DAYS**

742

SOKU, nori, nottoru | 規則的 KISOKUTEKI | regular
RULE, MODEL, | 法則 HŌSOKU | law
STANDARD | 原則 GENSOKU | principle
9 strokes

Once written 鼎刂, showing that 貝 is not shell/ **money** 貝 90 but a simplification of **kettle** 鼎 228. 刀/刂 is sword/ **cut** 181. 貝 acts phonetically to express **mark/ cut** (notches), and may also lend similar connotations (i.e. the kettle may have been marked with a series of notches as a scale of capacity). Thus **cut marks**, a reference to a **scale** or **measure**, leading to the present meanings. Suggest taking 貝 as **money**.

Mnemonic: **RULES REGARDING THE CUTTING OF MONEY**

743

SOKU, hakaru | 測定 SOKUTEI | measurement
MEASURE, FATHOM | 測知 SOKUCHI | inference
12 strokes | 測り難い HAKARIGATAI |
| | hard to fathom

氵 is **water** 40. 則 is **rule** 742 q.v., here used in its sense of **measure**. Thus **measure (the depth of) water**, i.e. **fathom**. Like the English term, fathom is now used in a broad sense.

Mnemonic: **MEASURE WATER WITH FATHOM-RULE**

231

744 **ZOKU**　　　　　　　　　　金属 KINZOKU　　　metal
BELONG, GENUS　　　付属 FUZOKU　　　attached
12 strokes　　　　　　　　属名 ZOKUMEI　generic name

Somewhat obscure. Formerly written 屬. 尸 is a variant of **tail** 尾 1734 q.v., while 蜀 is an NGU character meaning **caterpillar** (specifically, a large eyed 罒 72 coiled 勹 655 insect 虫 56). Beyond this point opinions diverge. Some scholars take tail 尸 in its euphemistic role of **genitals**, specifically **vagina** (though it should be noted that it is more commonly used of testicles), and take 蜀 to act phonetically to express **continually emerge**. Thus **that which continually emerges from a vagina**, namely a **succession of children**. The children all **belong** to the same mother, and thus form a **category** (the latter leading to **genus**). Others take **tail** literally, and take 蜀 similarly to act literally as **caterpillar** as well as acting phonetically to express **immovable**. The character is then seen as a reference to the habit of the caterpillar of coiling itself head to tail in what is in effect an immovable position. **Belong** is seen as deriving from the idea of the tail being **firmly joined** to the head in such a position, and **genus** is seen as an associated meaning from the idea of belonging (together). Suggest taking 尸 as **buttocks** 236, and 禹 as **insect** 虫 56 with long **legs** 冂 and **head** ╱.

Mnemonic: **INSECT WITH BUTTOCKS, LEGS, AND HEAD BELONGS TO WHICH GENUS?**

745　　**SON, soko*nau***　　　　損失 SONSHITSU　　　loss
LOSS, SPOIL, MISS　　損害高 SONGAIDAKA damages
13 strokes　　　　　　　　言い損い IISOKONAI
　　　　　　　　　　　　　　　　　　　　　slip of the tongue

扌 is **hand** 32. 員 is **member** 228 q.v., here acting phonetically to express **remove** and also lending its literal connotations of **round vessel**. Thus to **remove with a round (i.e. cupped) hand**. Removing some part led to the idea of being **less than complete/ full**, i.e. having **something missing**, hence **loss** and **spoil**.

Mnemonic: **MEMBER HAS HAND MISSING -- SERIOUS LOSS**

746		TAI, shirizo*ku*/*keru* **RETREAT, WITHDRAW** 9 strokes	後退 KŌTAI	retreat
			退職 TAISHOKU	retirement
			退位 TAII	abdication

Often explained as **movement** 辶 129 and **stop and stare** 艮 263, the latter with its connotations of **turning back**, to give **move back**. A useful mnemonic, but incorrect. Old forms such as 迟 reveal that 艮 is actually derived from **sun** 日 62 and **inverted foot** 夂 438 q.v., the latter lending its idea of **coming down from above**. Thus 746 originally referred to the **movement of the setting sun**, i.e. **declination** and by extension **withdrawal** and **retreat**. The graphic evolution of 夛 into 艮 (as opposed to 早 or 夏) suggests a longstanding confusion with stop and stare 艮.

Mnemonic: **STOP AND STARE, THEN MOVE BACK IN RETREAT**

747		TAI, ka*su* **LEND, LOAN** 12 strokes	貸費 TAIHI	loan
			貸し金 KASHIKIN	loan
			貸し家 KASHIYA	house to let

Shell/ **money** 貝 90 and **replace** 代 338, to express the idea of **providing money against a surety**.

Mnemonic: **LOAN IS REPLACEMENT MONEY**

748		TAI, waza, zama **APPEARANCE, INTENT** 14 strokes	態度 TAIDO	attitude
			態勢 TAISEI	position
			態態 WAZAWAZA	purposely

Somewhat obscure, though its elements are clearly **heart/ feelings** 心 147 and **ability** 能 766 q.v. Some scholars take the latter to lend connotations of **speed**, giving **quickly changing feelings** and by extension **feelings/ attitude/ intent/ appearance of the moment**. Of the moment is then assumed to have faded with time, leaving just **appearance** and **intent**. Others take 能 to be used primarily phonetically to express **praiseworthy**, as well as lending an extended idea of **dependable**, thus giving **praiseworthy dependable heart/ spirit**. **Appearance** and **intent** are then assumed to be borrowed meanings.

Mnemonic: **HAVE APPEARANCE OF ABLE HEART**

749		DAN, TON GROUP, BODY, MASS, BALL, ROUND 6 strokes	団体 DANTAI	group
			布団 FUTON	bedding
			団結 DANKETSU	solidarity

Formerly 團. 口 is a **circle** and/or a symbol of **rotation** (see rotate 回 86). 専 is the old form of exclusive 專 914 q.v., here lending connotations both of **round** and **force** from its literal sense of **spinning weight** and also felt by some scholars to lend its sound to express **round**. 749 originally referred to **something made round**, i.e. a **ball**. By extension this came to mean **lump, mass, body,** etc. **Group** is also generally seen as an extension of the idea of compressing, though some scholars see it rather as deriving from **circle** (of people). The modern form uses just the **measure/ hand** element 寸 909 of 專.

Mnemonic: **MEASURED CIRCLE PRODUCES WELL ROUNDED GROUP**

750		DAN, kotowa*ru*, ta*tsu* CUT, DECLINE, WARN, JUDGE, BE DECISIVE 11 strokes	切断 SETSUDAN	amputation
			断言 DANGEN	affirmation
			断り書 KOTOWARIGAKI	
				proviso

Formerly 斷. 斤 is **ax** 1176, here indicating **cutting cleanly**. 𢇍 is an element indicating **cut threads** (truncated threads 幺 111 and a symbol of cutting/ compartmenting ㄴ). Thus to **cut threads cleanly**, later **cut cleanly** in general. This gave rise to a range of extended and associated meanings, such as to **be decisive** and hence **judge, decline,** etc. (cf. the cutting connotations of the English de<u>cis</u>ive). Suggest taking the modern form 迷 as **rice** 米 201 in a **corner** ㄴ.

Mnemonic: **DECISIVELY DECLINE RICE CUT WITH AX IN CORNER**

751		CHIKU, kizu*ku* BUILD 16 strokes	建築 KENCHIKU	building
			建築家 KENCHIKUKA	architect
			築き直す KIZUKINAOSU	rebuild

木 is **tree/ wood** 69. 筑 is an NGU character meaning **percussion instrument**. It comprises **bamboo** 竹 170 and 凡, which was originally written 𢀎. This shows a hand holding a plectrum/ stick or similar 又 and the instrument itself 工 (possibly a string), and referred to a stringed instrument struck with bamboo. Here 筑 acts phonetically to express **pound** and lends similar connotations of **striking**. 751 originally referred to a **wooden stamper** used for tamping down ground prior to building, and later came to refer to the act of **building** itself. Suggest taking 工 as **work** 113 and 凡 as **mediocre** 1827.

Mnemonic: **MEDIOCRE WORK WITH WOOD AND BAMBOO IN BUILDING**

---

752 張

CHŌ, har*u*
STRETCH
11 strokes

主張　SHUCHŌ　　　assertion
拡張　KAKUCHŌ　　extension
見張る　MIHARU　　　guard

弓 is **bow** 836. 長 is **long** 173, here acting phonetically to express **swell/ curve out-wards** and also lending its connotations of **drawn out**. Thus to **draw out bow till it curves**, i.e. **stretch**.

Mnemonic: **DRAW LONGBOW TO FULL STRETCH**

---

753 提

TEI, CHŌ, sa*geru*
HOLD, CARRY, OFFER
12 strokes

提出　TEISHUTSU presentation
前提　ZENTEI　　　　premise
提灯　CHŌCHIN*　　　lantern

扌 is **hand** 32. 是 is **proper** 910 q.v. The latter acts phonetically to express **hold**, but its semantic role is not clear. It is possible that it lends its later meaning of **proper**, to give **hold properly in the hands** (as when formally **offering/ presenting** something), but also possible that from its literal meaning of **spoon** it lends an extended meaning of **scoop up**, giving **scoop up with the hands**. **Offer/ present** can then be taken as an extend-ed meaning of **hold/ carry**. Somewhat confusingly, 753 is now also used for dangling something from the hands, such as a bucket or similar (see also sageru 下 7).

Mnemonic: **HOLD PROPERLY IN HAND**

754

TEI, hodo
EXTENT, ABOUT,
ORDER
12 strokes

程度　TEIDO　　　　degree
過程　KATEI　　　　process
程近い　HODOCHIKAI　near

Somewhat obscure. 禾 is **rice plant** 81. 呈 is **present (verbal report)** 1611. Some scholars feel that 754 originally meant **present a verbal report concerning the rice crop**, and that this involved **estimation/ approximation**, thus leading to the present meanings (cf. English **in the order of**). Others feel that 呈 acts purely phonetically to express **arrange in order**, giving **pile up harvested rice in an orderly fashion**. **Order** is then felt to have given rise to the associated meaning of **degree/ extent**. Suggest taking 呈 as **mouth** 口 20 and **king** 王 5.

Mnemonic: **TO AN EXTENT, RICE ENDS UP IN KING'S MOUTH**

235

755

TEKI
SUITABLE, FIT, GO
14 strokes

適当 TEKITŌ na — suitable
適性 TEKISEI — aptitude
適帰 TEKKI — leading, following

辶 is **movement** 129. 啇 is a CO character meaning **base/ starting point**. The latter is of somewhat unclear etymology, though it is known that 啇 is a variant of **emperor/ altar** 帝 1616 q.v. Some scholars take this in its early sense of **altar** and take 口 as a **block** at the **base** of same. Others take 帝 as **emperor** and take 口 to be **mouth/ say** 20, giving **emperor's words**, which were seen as the **basis/ starting point** of all actions. In compounds 啇 often lends a meaning of **appropriate**, suggesting that the latter theory is correct. Here it lends such a meaning, and also acts phonetically to express **proceed**. Thus to **proceed in an appropriate fashion**, leading to **go about one's business** and eventually **go** in a broad sense (now a minor meaning in Japanese, but reasonably major in Chinese). **Suitable** is felt by some scholars to result from confusion with **match** 敵 756 q.v., and by others to be an extension from proceeding in an appropriate fashion. 755 also occasionally has a meaning of **by chance**, which is felt to stem from the idea of things happening by chance to be suitable. Suggest taking 啇 as a combination of **emperor** 帝 and **old** 古 109.

Mnemonic: **MOVE IN MANNER BEFITTING OLD EMPEROR**

756

TEKI, kataki
MATCH, ENEMY
15 strokes

敵意 TEKII — hostility
無敵 MUTEKI no — matchless
敵討ち KATAKIUCHI — vendetta

攵 is **strike** 101, here meaning **attack/ fight**. 啇 is **base/ starting point** 755 q.v., here acting phonetically to express **equivalence** as well as lending its connotations of **appropriate**. Thus to **fight with someone appropriately matched**, leading to both **enemy** and **match**. Suggest taking 啇 as a combination of **emperor** 帝 1616 and **old** 古 109, as well as remembering by association with **suitable** 適 755.

Mnemonic: **OLD EMPEROR STRIKES SUITABLY MATCHED ENEMY**

757

TŌ, suberu
SUPERVISE, LINEAGE
12 strokes

伝統 DENTŌ — tradition
統計 TŌKEI — statistics
大統領 DAITŌRYŌ — president

糸 is **thread** 27. 充 is **full** 1362 q.v., here acting phonetically to express **beginning** and also lending similar connotations from its literal meaning of newborn babe (i.e. at the beginning of its life). Thus the **beginning of a thread**. Since this is also the same as its **end** 757 came to mean **thread from end to end**, and by extension **lineage**. The idea of following a thread from end to end led to **overview** and **supervise**.

Mnemonic: **SUPERVISE LINEAGE FULL OF THREADS**

758 銅

DŌ, akagane
COPPER
14 strokes

銅像　DŌZŌ　bronze statue
銅貨　DŌKA　copper coin
青銅　SEIDŌ　bronze

金 is **metal** 14. 同 is **same** 187, used phonetically to express **red** and possibly also being chosen as a phonetic due to its similarity to **red** 丹 1563. **Red metal** is a reference to **copper** (akagane meaning literally red metal).

Mnemonic: **COPPER IS SAME METAL AS RED METAL**

---

759 導

DŌ, michibi*ku*
GUIDE, LEAD
15 strokes

指導　SHIDŌ　guidance
主導権　SHUDŌKEN　initiative
伝導　DENDŌ　conduction

Hand/ measure 寸 909, here meaning **careful use of the hand**, and **road/ way** 道 188. Thus to **lead someone carefully along the road by hand**, now **lead/ guide** in a broader sense.

Mnemonic: **MEASURED GUIDING HAND LEADS ALONG WAY**

---

760 特

TOKU
SPECIAL
10 strokes

特長　TOKUCHŌ　forte
特有 TOKUYŪ no　peculiar
特色　TOKUSHOKU
　　　characteristic

Somewhat obscure, though its elements are clearly **cow/bull** 牛 97 and **temple** 寺 133. Some scholars take the elements to be used ideographically, giving **cow/bull in temple grounds**. Such a creature, which was kept for sacrifice, was usually a **bull**, moreover a bull of outstanding and thus **special** quality (see also sacrifice 犠 1140). Others take 寺 to be used purely phonetically to express **male** (as an alternative to male/warrior 士 494, both characters having the same pronunciation SHI at the time), thus giving **male cow**, i.e. **bull**. **Special** is then taken to be a borrowed meaning. However, this theory does not account for the difference between 特 and the NGU character bull/male 牡, which does use male 土, nor is it clear why there should be any need to replace the three stroke character 土 with the six stroke 寺, especially since the latter has no intrinsic semantic relevance to the concept of male. Note that in Chinese 760 can still mean bull and male (the latter presumably being an associated meaning of bull if the former theory is followed).

Mnemonic: **SPECIAL BULL SENT TO TEMPLE**

761 得	TOKU, *eru*, *uru* GAIN, POTENTIAL 11 strokes	得点 TOKUTEN marks, score 所得 SHOTOKU income 有り得る ARIURU possible

Originally 㝵, showing shell/ money/ **valuable item** 㝵/貝 90 and a **hand** ㄨ, and indicating **obtaining something valuable**. Hand ㄨ was later replaced by **measure/ hand** 寸 909, presumably lending an idea of **handle carefully**. **Go/ move** 彳 118 was added at a still later stage to give a meaning of **go somewhere to obtain something valuable**. This led to **do something (potentially) to one's gain**. Suggest taking 昙 as **day** 日 62, **one** 一 1, and **measure** 寸.

Mnemonic: **MEASURE POTENTIAL GAINS IN MOVEMENT OVER ONE DAY**

762 徳	TOKU VIRTUE 14 strokes	道徳 DŌTOKU morality 徳義 TOKUGI integrity 徳利 TOKKURI* sake bottle

Formerly 德 and earlier 悳 . 心 is **heart/ feeling** 147. 直 is a variant of direct/ **upright** 直 349. Thus **upright heart**, meaning **virtue**. **Go/ move** 彳 118 was added later, with 直 being used phonetically to express **lofty** and also lending connotations of **steep**, to give **go to a steep and lofty place**, but eventually the meaning reverted to that of 悳 , i.e. **virtue**. Suggest taking 十 as **ten** 33 and 罒 as **eye** 72.

Mnemonic: **MOVE THAT VIRTUOUS HEART IS WORTH TEN EYES**

763	DOKU, hito*ri* ALONE, GERMANY 9 strokes	独英 DOKUEI Anglo-German 独り言 HITORIGOTO soliloquy 独立 DOKURITSU independence

Formerly 獨 . 犭 is **dog** 17. 蜀 is **caterpillar** 744 q.v., here acting phonetically to express **fight** and probably also lending a meaning of **join firmly together**. 763 originally referred to **dogs locked together in a fight** so tightly that they are **inseparable** and **as if one body**. This later came to mean **as if one** in a broad sense, leading to **alone**. 763 is also used to refer to **Germany** (Deutschland/ Doitsu). The modern form uses **insect** 虫 56.

Mnemonic: **INSECT-RIDDEN GERMAN SHEPHERD DOG IS LEFT ALONE**

238

764		NIN, maka*seru* **DUTY, ENTRUST** 6 strokes	任命 NINMEI	appointment
			任意 NINI no	optional
			責任者 SEKININSHA	
				person in charge

亻 is **person** 39. 壬 derives from 工, a spindle on which thread is wound. The latter acts phonetically to express **burden** and also lends similar connotations of carrying/ **bearing**. Thus the **burden borne by a person**, leading to **duty** and by association **giving/ entrusting** a duty to a person. Suggest taking 壬 as a variant of **jewel** 王 102.

Mnemonic: **ENTRUST JEWELS TO PERSON ON DUTY**

765		NEN, moeru/yasu **BURN** 16 strokes	燃料 NENRYŌ	fuel
			燃焼 NENSHŌ	combustion
			燃え付く MOETSUKU	ignite

Originally the same as **duly/ roast dog meat** 然 528 q.v.(literally **fire** 灬 8, **dog** 犬 17, and **meat** 月 365), but with an extra **fire** 火 8 added when 然 underwent a change in meaning.

Mnemonic: **DOG MEAT DULY BURNS WITH EXTRA FIRE**

766	能	NŌ, atou **ABILITY, CAN, NOH** 10 strokes	可能性 KANŌSEI	possibility
			能力 NŌRYOKU	ability
			能面 NŌMEN	Noh mask

Originally 能, showing **claws and chest** 比, **head** or **body** 𠂤, and **flesh/ of the body** 月 / 月 365. Later forms such as 能 show **nose** 乙 / ム 134 instead of body/ head 𠂤. Thus **creature with fleshy body, claws, and prominent head/ nose**, a reference to the **bear**. (Some scholars feel that 肖 also acts phonetically to give **black**, i.e. **black bear**.) Bear is now conveyed in practice by the NGU character 熊 , that adds fire 灬 8, but it should be noted that 能 technically means raging fire (literally a fire as strong and fierce as a bear), a meaning still found by association in the lesser meaning of bright/ glare that 熊 has in Chinese. **Ability/ can** is assumed by some scholars to be a borrowed meaning, and by others to be an associated meaning stemming from the attributes of a bear (strength, agility, etc.). In Japanese 766 also refers to **Noh drama**, which appears to be an extension from ability.

Mnemonic:**FLESHY BEAR WITH CLAWS AND NOSE CAN PERFORM NOH**

767	HA, yaburu/reru	破産 HASAN	bankruptcy
	BREAK, TEAR	破損 HASON	damage
	10 strokes	破れ目 YABUREME	tear

石 is **rock** 45. 皮 is **skin** 374 q.v., here acting phonetically to express **small piece** and also lending an idea of **pulling/breaking apart**. Thus to **break a rock into small pieces**, later **break** in a general sense. Possibly because of the presence of skin, which may be felt to suggest clothing or material, it has also acquired particular connotations of **tearing**.

Mnemonic: **SKIN A ROCK!? MUST MEAN BREAK IT**

768	HAN, okasu	犯人 HANNIN	criminal
	CRIME, VIOLATE,	犯意 HANI	malice
	COMMIT, ASSAULT	犯罪学 HANZAIGAKU	
	5 strokes		criminology

犭 is **dog** 17. 㔾 is a **slumped/prone figure** (to all intents and purpose a variant of slumped figure ヒ 238), which is felt by some scholars to lend its sound to express **injure** as well as lending its own idea of **injured person**. Thus **person injured by dog**, leading to **assault** and a number of associated and derived meanings such as **crime** and **commit**.

Mnemonic: **DOG COMMITS CRIME OF ASSAULTING PRONE PERSON**

769	HAN, BAN	判断 HANDAN	judgment
	JUDGE, SEAL, SIZE	判事 HANJI	judge
	7 strokes	判子 HANKO	personal seal

刂 is **sword/cut** 181. 半 is **half** 195 q.v., here used in its literal sense of **cut in two** and by extension **dissect**. Not unlike divide/ understand 分 199, this came by association to mean **analyse**, **judge**, etc. The idea of cutting finely also led to **engraving** and hence **seal**. It is not clear how it also came to mean **size** (in printing), but this is assumed to stem from the idea of cutting to size.

Mnemonic: **CUT IN HALF -- A JUDGMENT WITH SOLOMON'S SEAL**

240

| 770 | | HAN
PRINT, BOARD
8 strokes | 出版者 SHUPPANSHA publisher
版画 HANGA woodcut print
版権 HANKEN copyright |

片 is **thin piece of wood** 969. 反 is **oppose** 371 q.v., here acting phonetically to express **cut thinly** and possibly also lending an idea of **reversible** (a board being reversible). Thus **thin wooden board**. 770 is very similar to board 板 373, but has come to acquire particular connotations of an **engraved plate** or block used in printing, and by extension **printing** and **print**.

Mnemonic: **OPPOSED WOODEN BOARD MAKES PRINT**

| 771 | | HI, kura*beru*
COMPARE, RATIO
4 strokes | 比例 HIREI proportion
比較 HIKAKU comparison
比べ物 KURABEMONO
comparison |

Once written ᎡᎡ , showing **two figures sitting next to each other**. This led to the idea of **comparison**, while **ratio** is an associated meaning with compare.

Mnemonic: **COMPARE TWO PERSONS SITTING SIDE BY SIDE**

| 772 | | HI, koeru/yasu
FATTEN, ENRICH
8 strokes | 肥料 HIRYŌ fertiliser
肥満 HIMAN corpulence
肥え土 KOETSUCHI rich soil |

月 is **flesh/of the body** 365. 巴 is **bending body** (i.e. **person not standing**) 145. Some scholars take the elements to be used ideographically, to convey the idea of a **person too fleshy (i.e. fat) to stand up properly**. Others take 巴 to be used phonetically to express increase/ **add**, to give **added flesh** (or possibly **that added to the body**), i.e. **layer of fat**. A combination of both theories seems possible. **Enrich** is an associated meaning with fat/ fatten.

Mnemonic: **FLESHY BENDING BODY HAS BEEN FATTENED**

773

非

HI
NOT, UN-, FAULT
8 strokes

非人　HININ　'non-person'
非合理的　HIGŌRITEKI　irrational
非行　HIKŌ　misdemeanor

Originally 𣏟, depicting the **wings of a bird spreading apart** as it flies off. 773 orig-inally meant to **move in opposite directions**, then, not unlike oppose 反 371 q.v., came to mean **anti-** and by extension **un-** and **not**. Going in opposition to something led by association to **misdemeanor** or **fault**, i.e. going against the rules.

Mnemonic: **WINGS UNFOLD -- NOT A FAULT**

774

備

BI, sona*eru/waru*
EQUIP, PREPARE
12 strokes

設備　SETSUBI　facilities
準備中　JUNBICHŪ in preparation
備え付け　SONAETSUKE
equipment

Somewhat obscure. 亻 is **person** 39. 𤰔 is felt by many scholars to derive from 𢎜, a **quiver with arrows in it**. Thus a **person equipped with arrows**, i.e. **prepared** to fight. Later forms such as 𤰆 and 𤰇 appear to show confusion with **use** 用/用 215, presumably because of the similarity both graphically and semantically. Suggest tak-ing 𤰔 as **use** 用, **grass** 艹 9 and **roof** 厂 (variant 广 114).

Mnemonic: **PERSON EQUIPPED WITH GRASS USES IT FOR ROOF**

775

俵

HYŌ, tawara
SACK, BAG
10 strokes

一俵　IPPYŌ　one bag
米俵　KOMEDAWARA ricesack
土俵　DOHYŌ
sandbag, sumo ring

A somewhat obscure character of relatively late origin, comprising **person** 亻 39 and **list/ show** 表 379. Some scholars feel the latter acts purely phonetically to express **light/ nimble**, giving **light and nimble person**, and that its present meanings (including **dis-tribute** in Chinese) are borrowed. However, the Chinese meaning of distribute (its sole meaning) suggests the possibility that persons to whom distributions were made were re-corded on a list, i.e. that the elements acted ideographically to give **listed persons**. Dis-tributions might also have been made in **sacks** and **bags**, though it is not clear why these meanings are not also found in Chinese.

Mnemonic: **LISTED PERSONS RECEIVE SACKS**

776 HYŌ 評価 HYŌKA appraisal
CRITICISM, COMMENT 評判 HYŌBAN reputation
12 strokes 悪評 AKUHYŌ notoriety

Words 言 274 and flat/ even 平 388, giving **even/ balanced words**, i.e. **fair appraisal/ comment**.

Mnemonic: **EVEN WORDS ARE FAIR COMMENT**

777 HIN, BIN, mazu*shii* 貧血 HINKETSU anemia
POOR, MEAGER 貧困 HINKON poverty
11 strokes 貧乏人 BINBŌJIN pauper

貝 is shell/ **money** 90, here meaning **wealth**. 分 is cut up/ **divide** 199 q.v., here meaning **reduce to miniscule pieces**. Thus **wealth reduced to a miniscule amount**, giving both **poor** and by association **meager**.

Mnemonic: **MONEY DIVIDED, SO NOW POOR**

778 FU, nuno 配布 HAIFU distribution
CLOTH, SPREAD 毛布 MŌFU blanket
5 strokes 布地 NUNOJI cloth

Once written 𠁁. 朮/巾 is an NGU character now meaning towel but clearly showing **threads** and generally having a meaning of **cloth** in compounds, as here. 又 is **hand holding stick/ strike** 101, simplified in the modern form to just **hand** ナ 2. Thus **hand beating cloth**, i.e. hemp or similar, now **cloth** in general. **Spread/ stretch** is an associated meaning.

Mnemonic: **HAND WORKS ON SPREAD OF CLOTH THREADS**

779 FU 婦人 FUJIN woman
WOMAN, WIFE 主婦 SHUFU housewife
11 strokes 婦長 FUCHŌ chief nurse

Woman 女 35 and **hand holding broom** 帚 96 q.v. See also wife/ woman holding broom 妻 681. Some scholars feel that 帚 acts purely phonetically to express **elegant**, giving **elegant woman**, but this is not convincing in view of 96 and 681.

Mnemonic: **WOMAN HOLDING BROOM MAY BE WIFE**

780

富

FU, FŪ, tomi, to*mu*
WEALTH, RICHES
12 strokes

富裕 FUYŪ   wealth
富くじ TOMIKUJI   lottery
富士山 FUJISAN   Mount Fuji

Roof/ **house** 宀 28 and **full** 畐 386. The latter acts phonetically to express **rich** and also lends its own connotations of full. Thus **house full of riches**, later just **riches/ wealth**. Suggest taking 畐 as **single** 一 1 **entrance** 口 20 to **field** 田 59.

Mnemonic: **HOUSE AT SINGLE ENTRANCE TO FIELD GROWS WEALTHY**

781

武

BU, MU
MILITARY, WARRIOR
8 strokes

武士道 BUSHIDŌ   warrior code
武器 BUKI   weapon
武者 MUSHA   warrior

Once written 𢧤 . 止 is **foot** 129, here meaning **advance (on foot)**. 戈 is **halberd** 493. Thus **advance on foot with a halberd**, a reference to a **warrior** and by extension **things military**. The reason for the change of stroke arrangement in the modern form (戈 going to 弋) is not clear, but it is assumed to be a stylistic variation.

Mnemonic: **WARRIOR ADVANCES ON FOOT WITH HALBERD**

782

復

FUKU
AGAIN, REPEAT
12 strokes

復活 FUKKATSU   revival
回復 KAIFUKU   recovery
復習 FUKUSHŪ   revision

复 is a CO character meaning **go back**. It derives from a food container of **reversible** shape 畐 (now 旨), indicating **reverse**, and inverted foot 夂 438 q.v., here in its sense of **go somewhere and stop**. Thus to **go somewhere and then reverse** (one's steps), an idea reinforced in the case of 782 by the addition of **go** 彳 118. It is still occasionally found in the sense of **return**, but in general has come to mean **redo/ repeat** in a broad sense. Suggest taking 复 as **person** 𠂉 39, **sun** 日 62, and **sitting cross-legged** 夂.

Mnemonic: **PERSON GOES REPEATEDLY TO SIT CROSSLEGGED IN SUN**

783		**FUKU** **DOUBLE, AGAIN** 14 strokes	重複 CHŌFUKU repetition
			複製 FUKUSEI reproduction
			複雑 FUKUZATSU complexity

Clothing 衤 420 and go back 复 782 q.v., here with connotations of **duplicate**. Thus to **duplicate clothing**, i.e. wear **double** layers. Clothing gradually faded to leave just **duplicate/ do something again/ double**. Suggest taking 复 as **person** ├ 39, **sun** 日 62, and **sitting crosslegged** 夊.

Mnemonic:**PERSON CROSSLEGGED IN SUN WITH DOUBLE CLOTHING!**

784		**BUTSU, FUTSU, hotoke**	仏教 BUKKYŌ Buddhism
		BUDDHA, FRANCE	成仏 JŌBUTSU death
		4 strokes	のど仏 NODOBOTOKE
			Adam's apple

Formerly 佛 . 亻 is **person** 39, while 弗 is unwind/ disperse/ **not** 567 q.v. The latter acts phonetically to express **resemble**, and may also lend an idea of **not**. Thus 784 originally meant **resemble a person (but not really a person?)**. It was then borrowed to express the BU of **Buddha** (possibly also being considered to have an appropriate sense of **he who resembles a [normal] person but is not**), and also to express the FU of Furansu/ **France**. Suggest taking 厶 as **nose** 134.

Mnemonic: **BUDDHA HAS PROMINENT NOSE**

785		**HEN, a***mu*	編集者 HENSHŪSHA editor
		EDIT, KNIT, BOOK	編成 HENSEI compilation
		15 strokes	編み物 AMIMONO knitting

糸 is **thread** 27. 扁 is an NGU character now meaning level or small, but its original meaning was **doorplate** (still retained in Chinese). It comprises **door** 戸 108 and **book/ bundle of bound writing tablets** 冊 /冊 874 q.v., the latter indicating **writing tablet**. Thus writing tablet at the door. Its present meanings are presumably extensions, since the tablet was flat -- giving level -- and small. It should also be noted that in compounds 扁 occasionally appears to lend an idea of to one side, presumably because the doorplate was to one side of the door. In the case of 785 扁 seems to be misused, lending a meaning of **bind together** that is properly conveyed by 冊 rather than 扁, and also acts phonetically to express **arrange in order**. Thus to **bind together in ordered arrangement using threads**, leading to **knit** on the one hand and **edit/ compilation** on the other.

Mnemonic: **BOOKS BOUND WITH THREAD LEFT AT EDITOR'S DOOR**

786 BEN
SPEECH, KNOW, VALVE,
PETAL, BRAID
5 strokes

弁当 BENTŌ　　packed lunch
弁論 BENRON　　argument
弁膜 BENMAKU　　valve

An awkward character in that it is actually four separate characters, being the modern form of **speech** 辯 , **knowledge** 辨 , **valve/petal** 瓣 , and **braid** 辮 . In all cases the key element is 辡 , which is a doubling of **needle/ sharp** 辛 1432 and basically means **great sharpness** or **penetration**. In the case of speech 辯 it combines with **words/ speak** 言 274 q.v. (itself formed from needle and mouth), to give **very penetrative/ articulate words**. In the case of knowledge 辨 it combines with sword/ **cut** 刂 181, here used in the sense of **incisiveness/ analysis** (see also 199 and 769), to give **penetrative analysis**. In the case of valve/ petal 瓣 it combines with **melon** 瓜 1229 to give **cut open a melon cleanly**, leading by extension to **that which opens cleanly**, such as a **petal and valve**. In the case of braid 辮 it almost certainly acts in the literal sense of **needle** and by extension **sew**, combining with **thread** 糸 27 to give **sew threads**. 弁 itself derives from 𠬞 , showing **two hands** ㅆ offering up a **cap (of office)** 𠆢 , and originally indicated someone being **raised to a certain rank or position** (a meaning still retained in Chinese). It was then borrowed as a simple phonetic substitute for the above four characters. Suggest taking ㄥ as **nose** 134 and 廾 as **two tens** 十 33, i.e. **twenty**.

Mnemonic: **SPEECH ABOUT TWENTY NOSES!?**

787 HO, HŌ, tamo*tsu*
PRESERVE, MAINTAIN
9 strokes

確保 KAKUHO　　security
保存 HOZON　　preservation
生命保険 SEIMEIHOKEN
　　　　life insurance

Once written 伃 and later 保. 亻 is **person** 39 (here **mother** or **nursemaid**) and 呆 / 子 is **child** 25. ノ indicates a **carrying blanket** by which the child was strapped to the mother's back. The reason for the later stroke ノ is unclear, but it is assumed to represent the idea of the blanket **thoroughly** wrapping the child (i.e. **on all sides**). A mother with a child strapped to her back came to symbolise **care** and **protection**, with **maintain** being an extended meaning. Wrapped child 呆 later became graphically confused with tree/ **wood** 木 69. Suggest taking 呆 as **wood** 木 and **box** 口 .

Mnemonic: **PERSON PRESERVED IN WOODEN BOX**

788 BO, haka   墓地 BOCHI   graveyard
GRAVE   墓標 BOHYŌ   grave marker
13 strokes   墓参り HAKAMAIRI grave visit

土 is **earth** 60. 莫 is an NGU character now mostly used to express **not**. It derives from 𦰌, showing **sun** 日 62 and **grass/plants** 艸 9. Confusingly, whereas sun among plants 草 / 卓 175 means sun rising, this **sun among (many) plants** 𦰫 / 莫 means **sun setting** (a meaning seen most clearly in sunset 暮 1789, that adds an extra sun 日). As a result it often lends a meaning in compounds of **sinking out of sight, disappearing, hidden, ceasing to exist** (from which it takes its present meaning of **not**), and occasionally extended meanings from hidden of **obscure** and **vague**, leading by further extension to **undefined** and even **unlimited** and **vast**. Here it acts phonetically to express **cover** and also lends such connotations as **covered, out of sight**, and **ceasing to exist**. Thus to **cover with earth that which has ceased to exist**, i.e. **bury the dead**, leading to **grave**. Suggest taking 艹 as **grass**, 日 as **sun**, and 大 as a variant of **big** 大 53.

Mnemonic: **SUN SHINES ON BIG, GRASS COVERED, EARTHEN GRAVE**

789 HŌ, muku*iru*   報告 HŌKOKU   report
REPORT, REWARD   電報 DENPŌ   telegram
12 strokes   報酬 HŌSHŪ   compensation

幸 is not **good fortune** 幸 279, though it may be useful to remember it as such, but **prisoner/ criminal** 233 q.v. 𠬝 derives from 𠬝, showing a **hand** 又 **seizing** a person 卩 (actually bending person/ buttocks 236, indicating being seized from behind). 789 originally referred to **seizing a criminal**, leading by extension to pronouncing judgment and **meting out justice**. Thus to **give someone that which they deserve**, i.e. **reward** in the full (not just positive) sense. **Report** is felt by some scholars to be a borrowed meaning, and by others to be an associated meaning connected with the judicial process.

Mnemonic: **BY GOOD FORTUNE SEIZE PERSON, REPORT FOR REWARD**

| 790 | 豊 | HŌ, yutaka
ABUNDANT, RICH
13 strokes | 豊作 HŌSAKU good harvest
豊富 HŌFU na rich
豊満 HŌMAN na corpulent |

Formerly 豐 , and earlier 壴 and 豐. 豐 shows **food vessel plus edible plant** 壴 450, with additional **plants** ⺫ (variant growing plant 生 42). Thus **food vessel full of edible plants**, indicating **abundance** and **plenty**. Later forms appear to have confused plant 屮 with a further vessel ⊔ / ⊔, and to have used **food vessel** 豆 1640 in its modern form (i.e. with the extra top stroke ⁻, giving 豆 as opposed to 旦). 丰 is also a variant of plant 生 . Suggest taking 曲 as **bend** 261.

Mnemonic: **FOOD VESSEL BENDS UNDER WEIGHT OF RICH CONTENT**

| 791 | 防 | BŌ, fusegu
PREVENT, DEFEND
7 strokes | 予防 YOBŌ prevention
防水 BŌSUI waterproof
防衛 BŌEI defense |

Hill/ **embankment** 阝 229 and **side** 方 204. Thus a **hill/ embankment to one side**, which came to symbolise **defense** and by extension **prevention**.

Mnemonic: **DEFENSIVE HILL TO ONE SIDE PREVENTS ATTACK**

| 792 | | BŌ
TRADE, EXCHANGE
12 strokes | 貿易業 BŌEKIGYŌ trading
貿易風 BŌEKIFŪ trade wind
貿易者 BŌEKISHA trader |

貝 is shell/ **money/ valuable item** 90. ㋔ derives from 丣, showing a **horse's bit**. Here it acts phonetically to express **exchange**, and almost certainly also lends its own idea of **controlled change** (from the role of the bit). Thus **controlled exchange of items for money (or other valuable items)**, i.e. **trade**. Suggest taking 刀 as **sword** 181 and 𠂉 as a symbol of **bending**.

Mnemonic: **EXCHANGE BENT SWORD FOR MONEY IN TRADE DEAL**

793 BŌ, BAKU, aba*reru/ku*   暴力 BŌRYOKU   violence
VIOLENCE, EXPOSE   暴露 BAKURO   exposure
15 strokes   暴れ者 ABAREMONO roughneck

Once written , showing **rice** 米 201, **sun** 日 62, and 𦨶, the prototype of **offer** 奉 1793 comprising two hands 𦥑 offering up a thickly growing plant 𡴌 (variant growing plant 生 42). 793 originally meant **expose rice to the sun** (to dry it), then came to mean **expose** in general. **Violence** is popularly believed to be an associated meaning related to torture by exposure to the sun. Though useful as a mnemonic, this is almost certainly incorrect. The word abaku can mean both **divulge** and **violate a grave,** suggesting strongly that violence stems from violate, which in turn stems from **laying bare/ open** (disturbing privacy/ sanctity). Suggest taking 共 as **together** 460, and 氺 as an **'insufficient'** variant of **water** 水 40.

Mnemonic: **EXPOSED TO VIOLENT SUN TOGETHER WITH INSUFFICIENT WATER**

---

794 MI, mada   未来 MIRAI   future
IMMATURE, NOT YET   未知 MICHI   unknown
5 strokes   未未 MADAMADA   still

Tree 木 69 with additional **branches** 一 at the top. Originally the same as end/tip 末 587 q.v., but in time the shorter tip of 794 came to indicate **still growing/ immature/ not yet complete.**

Mnemonic: **GROWTH OF IMMATURE TREE NOT YET FINISHED**

---

795 務 MU, tsuto*meru*   義務 GIMU   duty
(PERFORM) DUTY   事務所 JIMUSHO   office
11 strokes   職務 SHOKUMU   job duties

敄 is a CO character now meaning **perform a task/ work.** It comprises **lance/halberd** 矛 1843 q.v. and **strike/ force** 攵 101, and originally meant **force someone at lance- point to do something.** In time both lance-point and the causative faded to leave just **do something/ perform a task.** Here it is reinforced by strength/ **effort** 力 74, giving **perform a task/ duty with effort.**

Mnemonic: **LANCE FORCES EFFORT IN PERFORMING DUTY**

249

796		MU, BU, nai/*shi*	無料	MURYŌ	free of charge
		NOT, NONE,	無事	BUJI na	safe
		CEASE TO BE	無くなる	NAKUNARU	vanish
		12 strokes			

Of somewhat confused and obscure etymology. 無 derives from 𣴎 later stylised to 𣴎, showing a **dancer** 大 (person 53) with exaggeratedly **tasseled sleeves** 夶/林. The original meaning was **dance** (with flapping sleeves), a meaning now conveyed by **dance** 舞 1761 q.v. 無 was then borrowed phonetically to express **not/ cease to be**, though it is not clear why such a complex character should have been chosen. **Cease to be/ die** 亡 973 was added later for clarity, though confusingly its modern much abbreviated form 灬 is identical to **fire** 灬 8. Further confusion is caused by an intermediate form 𣴎, in which the tasseled sleeves look very similar to **trees** 林/林 69. In fact, 舞 does exist in Chinese as a corrupt variant of 無, causing some scholars to evolve convoluted theories linking trees, dance, and cease to exist. Suggest taking 灬 as **fire/ burn** and 無 as a **sheaf of wheat**.

Mnemonic: **WHEATSHEAF BURNED, NOW NONE LEFT**

797		MEI, mayo*u*	迷路	MEIRO	maze
		BE LOST, PERPLEXED	迷夢	MEIMU	illusion
		9 strokes	迷い子	MAYOIGO	lost child

辶 is **movement** 129. 米 is **rice** 201, acting here phonetically to express **uncertain**. Thus **uncertain movement**, as when one is **lost** or **perplexed**. It is not clear why 米 was chosen as a phonetic, but it is possible that it was at one stage confused with **not yet (finished)** 未 794 q.v., giving movement unable to be completed (due to uncertainty). 未 may in turn have been intended as a simpler version of 昧 or 眛, NGU characters meaning dark/ obscure and hence uncertain (combining not yet 未 with sun/light 日 62 and eye/see 目 72 respectively).

Mnemonic: **RICE IS MOVED AND LOST -- HOW PERPLEXING**

798		MEN, wata	木綿	MOMEN*	cotton
		COTTON, COTTON WOOL	綿毛	WATAGE	down, fluff
		14 strokes	綿菓子	WATAGASHI	candy floss

Formerly 緜. 帛 is **white** 白 65 and **threads** 巾 778, indicating **cotton** (though some scholars feel that it originally indicated silk), while 糸 is **joined threads** 844. Thus **many joined white threads**. The modern form simply uses **thread** 糸 27.

Mnemonic: **MANY WHITE THREADS OF COTTON MAKE COTTON WOOL**

799 輸

YU
TRANSPORT, SEND
16 strokes

輸出	YUSHUTSU	export
輸送	YUSŌ	transportation
運輸	UNYU	transportation

Formerly also written 輸, though 巜 is merely a misleading variant of sword/ **cut** 刂 181. 俞 is a CO character now used to express affirmation, but it originally meant **convey**. It comprises **cut** 刂, **boat** 舟/月/月 1354, and **cap** 亼 121 q.v., here used in the sense of **cap off** or **finish** and by extension **succeed**, and originally referred to **succeeding in cutting timber in order to make a boat to convey goods** (note that boat and convey conceptually overlapped, as seen in 303 etc.). In the case of 799 俞 also acts phonetically to express **transfer** as well as lending its meaning of **convey**. **Vehicle** 車 31 was added to give a meaning of **convey (goods) by vehicle**, i.e. **transport**. **Send** is an associated meaning. Suggest taking 月 as **meat** 365 and 𠆢 as **cover** (see 87).

Mnemonic: **TRANSPORT CUT MEAT UNDER COVER IN VEHICLE**

800 余

YO, ama*ri/ru/su*
EXCESS, AMPLE, I
7 strokes

余分	YOBUN	surplus
余計	YOKEI	superfluity
五十余り	GOJŪAMARI	fifty plus

Formerly also 餘, and in ancient times 余. 亼 is **cover** 87, here meaning **roof**, while 朩 is a **wooden crossframe** supporting it. The spread of the upper beams indicated that the building was large, leading to **'roomy'** and **ample**, with **excess** being an associated meaning. 800 was also borrowed to express **I/me**. The reasons for this are not clear, but it should be noted that **already** 予 403, which also had a secondary meaning of margin/ **ample**, was similarly borrowed to express I/me, suggesting the possibility of some now unknown semantic connection. **Food** 食 146 was added at one stage, giving an idea of **ample food**. This has now disappeared in Japanese, but in Chinese 餘 is used to express ample and 余 to express I. Suggest taking 禾 as **dry** 干 825 and **eight** 八 66.

Mnemonic: **EIGHT EXCESSIVELY DRY BEAMS UNDER AMPLE ROOF**

801 預

YO, azu*karu/keru*
DEPOSIT,
LOOK AFTER
13 strokes

預金	YOKIN	deposit
預かり人	AZUKARININ	trustee
預かり証	AZUKARISHŌ	receipt

頁 is **face** 93. 予 is **already** 403 q.v., here acting phonetically to express **relax** and probably lending similar connotations from its early meaning of ample/ margin (i.e. lack of pressure/ constraint). 801 originally referred to a **facial expression of relaxation and comfort**, and it can still mean comfort in Chinese. Its present meanings are borrowed.

Mnemonic:**ALREADY FACED WITH HAVING TO LOOK AFTER DEPOSITS**

802

YŌ, *ireru*
CONTAIN, LOOKS
10 strokes

美容院 BIYŌIN — beauty parlor
内容 NAIYŌ — contents
形容詞 KEIYŌSHI — adjective

宀 is **roof/ building** 28. 谷 is **valley** 122 q.v., here acting phonetically to express **ample** and also lending its own connotations of **ample capacity**. Thus **building of ample capacity**, i.e. which can **contain** many things or people. **Looks/ appearance** is essentially a borrowed meaning, but it may be felt that **contain** led to **content** and that **looks** is an associated meaning with this.

Mnemonic: **ROOFED VALLEY LOOKS ABLE TO CONTAIN A LOT**

803

RITSU, SOTSU, hiki*iru*
RATE, COMMAND
11 strokes

能率 NŌRITSU — efficiency
統率 TŌSOTSU — command
税率 ZEIRITSU — tax rate

Once written ⠃⠃, showing **short thread** 8 / 幺 111 and **bits** ∷ and originally meaning **bits of thread**. 十 was added later, representing two **devices used to twist threads into rope**. Twisting bits of thread into rope led to the idea of **put in order** and hence **control/ command**. Some scholars take **rate** to be a borrowed meaning, while others see it as an associated meaning with order. Suggest taking 亠 as a symbol of **top**, and 十 as **ten** 33.

Mnemonic: **TEN BITS OF THREAD COMMAND TOP RATE**

804

RYAKU
ABBREVIATE, OUTLINE
11 strokes

略語 RYAKUGO — abbreviation
略説 RYAKUSETSU — summary
略図 RYAKUZU — sketch

Formerly also 畧. 田 is **field** 59. 各 is **each** 438, here acting phonetically to express **separate/ divide** and also lending its own idea of **separateness**. Thus **that which divides and separates fields**, namely a **boundary**. Boundary led to **outline**, with **summarise/ abbreviate** being a figurative extension of this.

Mnemonic: **ABBREVIATED OUTLINE OF EACH FIELD**

805 RYŪ, RU, to*maru*/*meru*   留守番 RUSUBAN   caretaker
STOP, FASTEN   留め金 TOMEGANE   clasp
10 strokes   留学生 RYŪGAKUSEI
    overseas student

Formerly 畱. 丣/𠃊刀 derives from **horse's bit** 丣 792. 田 is a simplification of **reason/ means** 由 399 q.v., here acting phonetically to express the word for the **linkage between the bit and the reins**, and possibly also lending an idea of **connection** or **means**. **Fasten to the bit** came to mean **fasten/ stop** in a very broad sense. Suggest taking 刀 as **sword** 181, 𠃊 as a symbol of **bending**, and 田 as **field** 59.

Mnemonic: **STOP IN FIELD TO FASTEN ON BENT SWORD**

806 RYŌ   領事 RYŌJI   consul
CONTROL, POSSESS,   領土 RYŌDO   territory
CHIEF, TERRITORY   要領 YŌRYŌ   gist
14 strokes

Also 領. 頁 is **head** 93. 令/⽒ is **order/ rule** 603, here felt by many scholars to act phonetically to express **neck** though it almost certainly also lends a meaning of **rule**. Thus the **head and neck**. As with **head/ neck/ chief** 首 139 q.v., 806 came from an early stage (in the view of some scholars, from the outset) to mean **chief** and by extension **that which (or he who) rules**, with **possess** and **territory** being associated meanings.

Mnemonic: **HEAD RULES, CONTROLLING POSSESSED TERRITORY**

END OF FIFTH GRADE

THE 190 SIXTH GRADE CHARACTERS

807 異 **I, koto*naru***
DIFFER, STRANGE
11 strokes

異様	IYŌna	strange
異常	IJŌ	abnormality
異人	IJIN	foreigner, alien

A misleading early form  has led to the popular explanation that hands  are placing something special (i.e. **different** from usual) ⊕ on a table or altar . However, still earlier forms such as  show this to be incorrect, and show a **person** 大 53 **putting on**  a **mask** ⊕ (see also 1128). This led to associated meanings such as **being different from normal** and of **strange appearance**, eventually giving just **differ** and **strange**. Suggest taking 田 as **field** 59 and 共 as **together** 460.

Mnemonic: **TOGETHER AGAIN IN DIFFERENT FIELD -- HOW STRANGE**

808 遺 **I, YUI**
LEAVE,BEQUEATH,LOSE
15 strokes

遺伝	IDEN	heredity
遺失	ISHITSU	loss
遺言	YUIGON/ IGON	will

辶 is **movement** 129. 貴 is **precious** 834, here acting phonetically to express **lose** and probably also lending its meaning of **precious item**. Thus to **lose something (precious) while on the move**. It then also came to mean **leave behind**, which, like the English term, included the idea of **bequeath**.

Mnemonic: **MOVE ON AND LEAVE BEHIND SOMETHING PRECIOUS**

809 域 **IKI**
AREA, LIMITS
11 strokes

領域	RYŌIKI	domain
地域	CHIIKI	region
区域	KUIKI	limits, zone

土 is **ground** 60. 或 is an NGU character meaning **a certain** -. It comprises **lance/halberd** 戈 493, here used in its sense of **marker** (see 698), and 彐, which is to all intents and purposes a simplification of 亘 depicting the **boundaries** 二 of a **field** 田 59 (see also 85). 809 thus referred to **ground in a field delineated by markers**, leading to **area** and **limits** in a broad sense. Suggest taking 口 as **entrance** 20 and 一 as **one/sole** 1.

Mnemonic: **LANCE IN GROUND AT SOLE ENTRANCE -- OFF LIMIT AREA**

810

ICHI
ONE
7 strokes

壱万円 ICHIMANEN 10,000 yen
壱千 ISSEN　　　one thousand
弐拾壱 NIJŪICHI　　twenty-one

Formerly 壹 and earlier 𡐀, showing a **double-lidded** 大 258 **food vessel** 豆 1640, which had connotations of **fullness**. Its use as the formal character for **one** is the result of phonetic borrowing, though it is remotely possible that its choice as a phonetic was influenced by the fact that full vessel suggested completeness and by association being whole/ one. Suggest taking 士 as **samurai** 494, 冖 as **cover**, and ヒ as a **prone figure** 238.

Mnemonic: **ONE SAMURAI STANDS COVERING PRONE FIGURE**

811

U
EAVES, ROOF, HEAVEN
6 strokes

宇宙 UCHŪ　　　universe
堂宇 DŌU　　　　hall
宇頂天 UCHŌTEN　ecstasy

宀 is **roof** 28. 于 is an NGU character meaning from/ emerge/ go. It was originally written 㞢, showing twisting waterweed/seek an exit 㞢 281 q.v. and a symbol 一 of unclear meaning, and it also has connotations of twisting. Here it acts phonetically to express **complete cover**, and may possibly also lend a loose idea of **extensive** from the lengthy and convoluted waterweed element 㞢. Thus 811 originally meant **roof that completely covers**, leading to **eaves** and by extension **firmament/ heaven**. Suggest facetiously taking 于 as a 'stiff' (i.e. dead) **child** 子 25.

Mnemonic: **CHILD LIES STIFF UNDER ROOF, SET TO GO TO HEAVEN**

812

U, ha, hane
WING, FEATHER,
BIRD COUNTER
6 strokes

羽毛 UMŌ　　　plumage
羽織 HAORI　　haori coat
一羽 ICHIWA　　one bird

Formerly 羽. A pictograph of a **bird's wings**.

Mnemonic: **FEATHERED WINGS**

813

EI, utsuru/su, haeru
REFLECT, SHINE
9 strokes

映画館 EIGAKAN　　cinema
反映 HANEI　　　reflection
夕映え YŪBAE　　sunset glow

日 is **sun** 62. 央 is **center** 429, here acting essentially phonetically to express **bright** but probably also lending its meaning. Thus **bright (center of?) sun**, giving **shine** and by association **reflect**.

Mnemonic: **CENTER OF SUN SHINES BRIGHTLY**

255

814		EN, no*biru*/*beru*/*basu* **EXTEND, POSTPONE** 8 strokes	延長 ENCHŌ	extension
			延期 ENKI	postponement
			延び延び NOBINOBI	delay

Somewhat confused. Once written 延, showing **foot/ movement** 止 / 止 129 q.v. and **go/ move** ㇇ / 彳 118 q.v. 延 is in fact the prototype of 廴 itself, showing that a further foot 止 has been added in the case of the modern form. The extra stroke ノ is felt by some scholars to symbolise **dragging** and thus **lengthening** and **protraction** , while others see it as the CO character mark ノ 537, used purely phonetically to express **lengthen**. Lengthy, protracted movement led to **extend** and **postpone**.

Mnemonic: **DRAG FEET IN EXTENDED MOVEMENT**

815		EN, s*ou* **GO ALONGSIDE** 8 strokes	沿岸 ENGAN	coast
			沿道 ENDŌ	roadside
			沿線 ENSEN	railside

氵 is **water** 40, here meaning **river**. 㕣 is hollowed out 158, here acting phonetically to express **follow** and probably also lending an idea of **from a source** (from a different interpretation of its literal elements from/away ハ 66 and source/opening 口 20). Thus **follow a river (from its source?)**, leading to **follow/ go alongside** in a broader sense. Suggest taking 口 as **opening** and ハ in its commoner meaning of **eight.**

Mnemonic: **GO ALONGSIDE OF WATER, THROUGH EIGHT OPENINGS**

816		KA, -be*ki*/*shi*/*ku* **APPROVE,CAN,SHOULD** 5 strokes	可能 KANŌ na	possible
			可決 KAKETSU	approval
			言う可き IUBEKI	should say

Once written 叮, showing **mouth/say** ㅂ / 口 20 and **twisting waterweed/ seek an exit** 丂 / 丂 / 丁 281. That is, the components are the same as drawn out call 号 281 q.v., but in this case they refer rather to a statement that is finally made after considerable hesitation (symbolised by the waterweed twisting its way to the surface), such as **grudging approval**. Some scholars feel that 丂 /丁 also acts here phonetically to express **approve**. Approval led to the idea of **that which can be done**, and by extension **that which should be done**. Suggest taking 丁 as a variant of **exact** 丁 346.

Mnemonic: **SAY EXACTLY WHAT CAN AND SHOULD BE APPROVED**

817 　　　GA, ware, wag*a*　　　自我 JIGA　　　　　self
　　　　　　　　　I, SELF, MY　　　　我まま WAGAMAMA selfishness
　　　　　　　　　7 strokes　　　　　我我 WAREWARE　　　we

Once written 㦮 and 㦱, showing a **broadbladed halberd** 戈/戊 515 q.v. and **tassels** 丿. The tassels were hung on weapons to indicate a **killing**, rather like notches being scored on a gun handle in the West. Thus 817 originally meant to **kill with a halberd**. It was later borrowed phonetically to express **I/me/my** and by extension **self**. Why a character with such an unpleasantly aggressive meaning should be chosen as a phonetic is a matter of some conjecture, but it is in line with the 'being as good as anyone else' first person pronoun 吾 112 q.v. It may indeed be appropriate to draw again a parallel with the gun in the West, which was seen as the great equaliser.

Mnemonic: **I HAVE A TASSELED HALBERD, A SYMBOL OF ME MYSELF**

818　　　　　　　KAI, hai　　　　　石灰 SEKKAI　　　　lime
　　　　　　　　　ASHES　　　　　　灰色 HAIRO　　　　　gray
　　　　　　　　　6 strokes　　　　　火山灰 KAZANBAI volcanic ash

Formerly 灰 and earlier 㶹, showing a **hand** ㇇/ナ and **fire** 火 8. Some scholars take ナ to be used phonetically to express **use up**, giving **used up fire**, while others take the elements to be used ideographically to give **fire that one can hold in the hand**. The latter theory seems more convincing. Suggest taking the simplified 厂 as **cliff/ hillside** 45.

Mnemonic: **HILLSIDE ABLAZE -- REDUCED TO ASHES**

819 　　　GAI, KAI, machi　　市街 SHIGAI　　　　town, city
　　　　　　　　　ROAD, TOWN, AREA　　街道 KAIDŌ　　　　　highway
　　　　　　　　　12 strokes　　　　　商店街 SHŌTENGAI
　　　　　　　　　　　　　　　　　　　　　　　shopping street

A combination of **go** 行 118 q.v., here with its literal meaning of **crossroads**, and 圭. The latter is an NGU character meaning **edge/ angle/ jewel**. It comprises **earth** 土 60 doubled to indicate **raised earth**, and originally referred to the **raised earthen paths** that formed edges/ boundaries between fields (a meaning now conveyed by the NGU character 畦, that adds field 田 59). The idea of raised edges/ ridges also led by association to facets on a jewel (now conveyed by the NGU character 珪, that adds jewel 玉 102), and to angle. In the case of 819 圭 is used phonetically to express **diverge**, and also lends an idea of **multiple paths**. Thus **many diverging roads**, which by association also necessarily meant **many converging roads** (see also 280), leading to such meanings as **town**, **road**, and **area/ hub of activity**.

Mnemonic: **ROAD-TOWN IS JUST CROSSROADS OF RAISED EARTH**

820	**KAKU** **SPREAD** 8 strokes	拡大 KAKUDAI magnification 拡散 KAKUSAN dissemination 拡声器 KAKUSEIKI loudspeaker

Formerly 擴 . 扌 is **hand** 32, while 廣/広 is **wide** 114. Thus **make the hands wide**, i.e. **spread**.

Mnemonic: **SPREAD HANDS WIDE**

821	**KAKU, kawa** **LEATHER, REFORM** 9 strokes	革命 KAKUMEI revolution 革新 KAKUSHIN reform 革工場 KAWAKŌBA tannery

Once written 革 , apparently showing **hands** ㇇ ㇈ pulling the **skin** off a **horned creature** 화 in similar fashion to skin/ leather 皮 374 q.v. However, still earlier forms such as 革 and 革 show that the later 'hands' are a miscopying of **flaps of skin** ⋲⋺ . Unlike 374, 821 came to be used only of **hairless hide** (usually **tanned leather**), and its connotations of **processing** eventually led to **change/ reform**. Suggest taking 中 as a combination of **middle** 中 55 and **ten** 十 33, with 廾 as a **horned head**.

Mnemonic: **GET LEATHER FROM MIDDLE OF TEN HORNED CREATURES**

822	**KAKU** **CABINET, CHAMBER** 14 strokes	閣下 KAKKA Your Excellency 内閣 NAIKAKU Cabinet 閣僚 KAKURYŌ Cabinet member

門 is **door/ gate** 211, here meaning by extension a **place with a door/ gate** and by further extension a **place sealed off for privacy**. 各 is **each** 438 q.v., here used in its sense of **visit by a dignitary**. Thus a **private place which dignitaries visit**, such as a **council chamber** or **Cabinet**.

Mnemonic: **EACH GATE LEADS TO CABINET**

823	**KATSU, wari, waru** **DIVIDE, RATE** 12 strokes	分割 BUNKATSU division 割引 WARIBIKI discount 割合 WARIAI rate

刂 is **sword/ cut** 181. 害 is **harm** 437, acting phonetically to express **dismember** and probably also lending an idea of damage/ destroy. 823 originally meant **cut up/ dismember**, leading by extension to **divide**. **Rate** is an associated meaning (cf. English pro rata).

Mnemonic: **SWORD HARMS BY DIVIDING**

258

| 824 |  | kabu
STOCK, SHARE, STUMP
10 strokes | 切り株 KIRIKABU　stump
株式 KABUSHIKI　stocks
株主 KABUNUSHI stockholder |

木 is **tree** 69. 朱 is **red** 1346 q.v., here acting phonetically to express **firm** and also lending its literal meaning of **central part of a tree**. Thus **that central part of a tree which stands firm**. This originally referred to its **base** but later came to mean **stump/ stock**, i.e. the part left standing firm after the tree proper is cut down. In Japanese, but not Chinese, the idea of firm base extended to include **stocks/ shares** in a company (cf. English stock).

Mnemonic: **RED TREE STUMP PROVIDES FIRM STOCK**

| 825 | 干 | KAN, ho*su*, hi*ru*
DRY, DEFENSE
3 strokes | 干潮 KANCHŌ　ebb/ low tide
干城 KANJŌ　bulwark
干し肉 HOSHINIKU dried meat |

Originally ㄓ, depicting a primitive **forked thrusting weapon** Y with either a large **hand-guard** — or, to judge from some almost contemporaneous forms such as ㄓ, **sturdy binding** ●. The weapon was used both for defense and attack. It thus acquired a large range of extended meanings, such as **attack, defend, thrust**, and **fork**, and was also borrowed widely as a phonetic due its simplicity. It was borrowed for its sound to express **dry**, although some scholars feel that technically it is an abbreviation of the NGU character drought 旱, which has the same pronunciation and which uses 干 both for its sound to express dry and for its connotations of attack, combining it with sun 日 62 to give attack from the sun that causes dryness.

Mnemonic: **FLATTENED FORKED POLE FOR DRYING WASHING**

| 826 | | KAN, maki, ma*ku*
ROLL, REEL, VOLUME
9 strokes | 第一巻 DAIIKKAN Volume One
巻き物 MAKIMONO　scroll
糸巻き ITOMAKI　bobbin |

Formerly 卷 and occasionally 巻, though the latter appears to be a confusion with settlement 巷 280. 关 is **hands rolling rice** 661, with the idea of **rolling** emphasised by **curled body** ㄷ 768 or **bent body** 己 (from ㄹ 145). Thus **roll and curl**, giving **roll** and **reel** and leading by extension to **scroll** and hence **volume**. Suggest taking ㄹ as **self** 855 and 关 as **two** 二 61 **fires** 火 8.

Mnemonic: **LIGHT TWO FIRES BY ONESELF WITH ROLLED VOLUMES**

827		KAN WATCH 9 strokes	看護婦 KANGOFU	nurse
			看板 KANBAN	signboard
			看守 KANSHU	warder

Hand 手 32 above eye 目 72, to give a meaning of **place hand above eye**. This was a reference to shading the eyes in order to **gaze intently**.

Mnemonic: **PUT HAND ABOVE EYE TO WATCH BETTER**

828		KAN, susu*meru* ENCOURAGE, ADVISE 13 strokes	勧告 KANKOKU	advice
			勧奨 KANSHŌ	encouragement
			勧誘 KANYŪ	persuasion

Formerly 勸 . 力 is **strength/ effort** 74. 藿/隺 is **crested bird/ heron** 445, acting phonetically to express **strong** and possibly also lending its own loose idea of **persistence** (from a heron persistently searching for food). 828 originally meant to **make great and determined efforts** to achieve something. This later came to include the idea of **exhorting others** to make similar efforts, leading to **encourage**. **Advise** is an associated meaning with encourage.

Mnemonic: **ENCOURAGED BY EFFORTS OF CRESTED BIRD**

829		KAN SIMPLE, BRIEF, LETTER 18 strokes	簡単 KANTAN na	simple
			書簡 SHOKAN	letter
			簡略 KANRYAKU	
				conciseness, simplicity

Formerly also 簡 . 竹 is **bamboo** 170, here indicating **bamboo tablet used for records**. 閒/間 is **space** 92. Thus **bamboo record with space (left)**, indicating that the record is a **simple** and **brief** one. Brief text later came to include **letter** (cf. English brief), while **simple** and **brief** came to be used in a general sense.

Mnemonic: **SPACE LEFT ON BRIEF AND SIMPLE BAMBOO LETTER**

830		GAN, maru, marui ROUND, CIRCLE, BALL, SHIP'S MARK 3 strokes	丸薬 GANYAKU	pill
			丸味 MARUMI	roundness
			日本丸 NIPPONMARU	
				Vessel Nippon

Originally 𝍅. ⼁ is a **bending/ hunched person** (mirror image of ⼈ 39). ⼂ is a **cliff/ hillside** (mirror image of ⼚ 45), acting phonetically to express **roll** as well as lending its meaning of **slope**. Thus a **person hunched as they roll down a slope**, leading to **ball** and by association **round** and **circle**. 830 is also used of a **ship's mark**, said to derive from the ancient practice of licensing vessels with a round seal. It is not clear why the elements in 830 are in mirror image form. Suggest taking as **nine** 九 12 with an **extra stroke** ⼂ .

Mnemonic: **NINE ROUNDED OFF WITH EXTRA STROKE**

831		KI, abunai, ayaui DANGEROUS 6 strokes	危機 KIKI	crisis
			危険 KIKEN	danger
			危害 KIGAI	harm

Once written 𝍅 , showing a **person crouching** ⼓ 145 on the edge of a **cliff** ⼚ 45, fearful of the **danger**. This came to symbolise a **dangerous** situation. A further **bending figure** 𝍅 145 was added later for emphasis, giving 𝍅 , but in time this apparently became confused with **prone/ fallen figure** ⼂ 768, leading to the popular interpretation of the modern form as a person kneeling on the edge of a dangerous cliff looking down at his companion who has fallen over the edge. This explanation is technically incorrect but is a useful mnemonic. See also **misfortune** 厄 1859.

Mnemonic: **CROUCH ON EDGE OF DANGEROUS CLIFF -- MATE FALLEN**

832		KI, tsukue DESK, TABLE 6 strokes	机上 KIJŌ no	theoretical
			机辺 KIHEN	around table
			事務机 JIMUTSUKUE	office desk

⼏ is an NGU character pictographically representing a **small table** or armrest (or occasionally stool), while 木 is tree/ **wood** 69. Thus **small wooden table**. Now used for **table/ desk** in a broader sense.

Mnemonic: **USE WOODEN TABLE FOR DESK**

261

833	**挥**	**KI**	発揮 HAKKI	display
		WIELD,SHAKE,COMMAND	指揮 SHIKI	command
		12 strokes	揮発性 KIHATSUSEI	volatility

扌 is **hand** 32. 軍 is **army** 466, here acting phonetically to express **agitate** and possibly also lending loose connotations of agitation/ commotion. 833 originally meant to **shake the hands wildly**, leading to **brandish/ wield** and by extension **command**.

Mnemonic: **ARMY HAND WIELDS COMMAND**

834	**貴**	**KI, tattoi/bu, tōtoi**	貴族 KIZOKU	aristocrat
		PRECIOUS, REVERED	貴重 KICHŌ na	precious
		12 strokes	貴方 KIHŌ/ ANATA*	you

貝 is **shell/ money/ valuable item** 90. 虫 is a simplification of 臾, the prototype of the NGU character 臾. The latter is now used to mean **urge**, but has a core meaning of **gather**, and in Chinese can mean **basket**. It is not clear whether 臾 derives from a pictograph of a **basket** (symbolising gathering) or an ideograph of **hands gathering** something in. In the case of 834 虫 acts phonetically to express **accumulate** and also lends a meaning of **gather**. Thus **gather and accumulate valuable items**, leading to **something of great value** and hence **precious**. **Revered** is an associated meaning. Suggest taking 虫 as **middle** 中 55 and **one** 一 1, with 貝 literally as **shell**.

Mnemonic: **ONE PRECIOUS SHELL IN MIDDLE OF COLLECTION**

835	**疑**	**GI, utagau**	質疑 SHITSUGI	question
		DOUBT, SUSPECT	疑問 GIMON	doubt
		14 strokes	疑似 GIJI	false

Etymologically and graphically somewhat confused. Once written 毕. As very early forms such as 矣 show, ヒ is not **sitting person** ヒ 238 but a confusing stylisation of an **(old) man's stick** 卜 (see 609). 矣 is similarly an extreme and confusing stylisation (through an intermediate form 矣) of a pictograph of an **(old) man** 矢, whose long hair (a symbol of age) is trailing as his head moves from side to side 牛. The fact that his head is moving indicates that he is **in doubt**, and looking about him wondering where to turn. At a later stage two further elements were added, **child** 孑 /子 25 and **foot/ stop** 止/止 129, and in fact in some versions replaced stick 卜 /ヒ , thus giving 疑 and hence the modern 疑. This originally referred to a child becoming lost, standing still and looking about him not knowing which way to turn. Both 疑 and 毕 became blurred, and resulted in a meaning of **not knowing what to do**, which eventually led by association to **doubt** and **suspicion**. Suggest taking ヒ as **sitting person**, ㄏ as a **bending person** (thus giving **two 'felled' persons**), 矢 as **arrow** 981, and 疋 as **correct** 41.

Mnemonic: **TWO PEOPLE FELLED BY ONE ARROW? DOUBT IF CORRECT**

836

KYŪ, yumi
BOW, ARCHERY
3 strokes

弓道 KYŪDŌ   archery
弓状 KYŪJŌ   arch
弓取り YUMITORI   archer

From a pictograph of **bow** β / ℟ , **minus the string**. Note that 836 can also be used of an **arc** or **bend** (cf. English bow, and etymological connection between arc, arch, archery).

Mnemonic: **STRINGLESS BOW**

837

KYŪ, su*u*
SUCK, INHALE
6 strokes

吸収 KYŪSHŪ   absorption
吸血鬼 KYŪKETSUKI   vampire
吸い取る SUITORU   soak up

口 is **mouth** 20. 及 is **reach** 1148 q.v., here acting phonetically to express **pull** and probably also lending connotations of **draw towards oneself**. Thus to **pull/ draw with the mouth**, i.e. **suck/ inhale**.

Mnemonic: **IF IT REACHES MOUTH, THEN SUCK IT IN**

838

KYŪ, na*ku*
WEEP, CRY
8 strokes

泣訴 KYŪSO   imploring
泣き虫 NAKIMUSHI   crybaby
泣き出す NAKIDASU
    burst into tears

氵 is **water** 40. 立 is **stand** 73, here acting phonetically to express **tear** and almost certainly also lending an idea of **verticality** and by association **falling** (see also pour 注 344). Thus **falling drops of 'tear-water'**.

Mnemonic: **PERSON STANDS WEEPING WATERY TEARS**

---

839 供

KYŌ, KU, tomo, sona*eru*
OFFER, ATTENDANT
8 strokes

提供 TEIKYŌ   offer
供回り TOMOMAWARI   retinue
供養 KUYŌ   memorial service

亻 is **person** 39. 共 is **together** 460 q.v., here with its literal meaning of **offer**. Thus **offer something to a person**, later just **offer**. It is not fully clear how the meaning of **attendant** evolved. Some scholars take it to be an extension of offer to a person, i.e. a **person who offers** something to another person, while others take it to stem from a reinterpretation of the elements as **together with a person**, i.e. **companion** and hence **attendant**.

Mnemonic: **ATTENDANT OFFERS TOGETHERNESS TO PERSON**

840		KYŌ, mune, muna-	胸部 KYŌBU	thorax
		CHEST, BREAST, HEART	胸毛 MUNAGE	chest hair
		10 strokes	度胸 DOKYŌ	heart, courage

Once written simply as 囪, and earlier as 囱. 勹/勹 is womb 655, here indicating **container**, while 凶 is **empty container** 1159. Some scholars feel that 凶 also acts phonetically to express **air**. Thus **empty container (associated with air?)**, a reference to the **lungs**. 匈 does in fact exist as an NGU character that once meant lung (and still has this meaning in Chinese), but is now used largely as a phonetic to represent Hungary (easily remembered by a facetious association with 'hungry', i.e. referring to an empty container of a different kind). **Lungs** led by extension to the **chest area** in general. **Flesh/ of the body** 月 365 was added later for clarity. Suggest taking 勹 as **encircle**, and 凶 as a **scarred** ✕ **container** 凵.

Mnemonic: **FLESH ENCIRCLING SCARRED 'CONTAINER' IS THE CHEST**

841		KYŌ, GŌ	望郷 BŌKYŌ	homesickness
		VILLAGE, RURAL	郷士 GŌSHI	squire
		11 strokes	郷土 KYŌDO	local

Of somewhat confused graphic origin. Formerly written 鄉 or 鄉, and in ancient times as 鄉 and 鄉. 皀/皀/皀/艮 are **food** 食 146 q.v., while 卯 clearly shows **two persons** sitting either side of the food. On the one hand this led to the idea of **meeting over dinner**, which just as in the modern West often indicated meeting with a **superior** to discuss something. This meaning is still retained in the NGU character 卿/卿, which means lord, minister, or you, and is etymologically the same character as 841. On the other hand it led to the idea of **feasting** and holding a **get-together**, indicating a **community event** and by extension the **community/ village** itself. This in turn led to the replacement of 卯 with 幺幺, being the prototype 呂 of **village** 阝 355 q.v. and its mirror image. It is not clear whether this substitution was done deliberately or in error. Suggest taking 幺 as a variant of short thread 幺 111, taking this by extension as **string**.

Mnemonic: **ODD STRINGY FOOD SERVED IN VILLAGE**

---

842 **KIN, tsuto*meru***
WORK, DUTIES
12 strokes

出勤 SHUKKIN — attendance
勤勉性 KINBENSEI — diligence
勤め先 TSUTOMESAKI — place of work

Somewhat obscure due to the obscure nature of 堇, which was formerly written 堇 and earlier 菫. 堇 is an NGU character with the unhelpful meaning of **violet** (the flower). In Chinese it can mean **yellow loam** or **season** as well as **rare** and **few,** the last two meanings of which are also found in a number of compounds in Japanese (such as few words/ circumspect 謹 1180 q.v. [言 being word 274] and the NGU character few 僅 [亻 being person 39]). Some scholars take the early form 堇 to show **earth** 土 60 plus a combination 英 of **horned beast** 芽 (see 821) and **fire** 火 8, to give a meaning of **roast a beast in an earthen firepit,** but it is not clear how any of the present meanings came about. In any event, in the case of 842 堇 is known to have acted phonetically to express **muscle,** combining with **strength/effort** 力 74 to convey the idea of **making a great physical effort.** It is also possible that 堇 lends an idea of **rare,** to give **make a rare (i.e. outstanding) physical effort.** Make a physical effort eventually came to mean **do one's work/ duties** in a broad sense. Suggest taking 堇 as a combination of **plants** 艹 9, **grow** 主 (variant 生 42), and **(seed-)box** 口 .

Mnemonic: **WORK WITH EFFORT TO GROW PLANTS FROM SEED-BOX**

---

843 **KIN, suji**
MUSCLE,SINEW,THREAD
12 strokes

筋肉 KINNIKU — muscle
筋道 SUJIMICHI — logic
筋書き SUJIGAKI — synopsis

竹 is **bamboo** 170. 肋 is an NGU character meaning **rib,** namely that which gives **strength** 力 74 to the **flesh** 月 365. The ribs of a bamboo plant are its **fibers,** the original meaning of 843. In time this came to mean **thread,** with **sinew** and **muscle** being associated meanings (probably also influenced by the presence of flesh 月).

Mnemonic: **BAMBOO HAS STRONG FLESHY SINEWS**

---

844 **KEI**
LINEAGE, CONNECTION
7 strokes

家系 KAKEI — lineage
系統 KEITŌ — system, line
系列 KEIRETSU — succession

Once written 絲, showing a **hand** 爪 holding **two threads** 𠮷/糸 27. This indicated **twisting/ intertwining** them, with intertwined threads being used figuratively to describe a **lineage** or **connection.** Suggest taking ／ as a symbol of **twisting.**

Mnemonic: **LINEAGE COMPOSED OF TWISTED CONNECTED THREADS**

265

845

KEI
PATH, DIRECT
8 strokes

直径 CHOKKEI　　　diameter
しょう径 SHŌKEI　　　shortcut
直情径行 CHOKUJŌKEIKŌ
　　　　　　　　　impulsiveness

Formerly 徑 . 彳 is go/ road 118. 巠 is **lengthwise threads on a loom** 269 q.v., here acting phonetically to express **small** and also lending an idea of **direct** (from going in a straight line, though confusingly the stylised 巛 shows unstraight threads). Thus **small, direct road**, leading both to **path** and **direct**. Suggest taking 圣 as **hand** 又 and **ground** 土 60.

Mnemonic: **DIRECT PATH ENTAILS MOVING WITH HANDS ON GROUND**

846

KEI, uyamau
RESPECT
12 strokes

尊敬 SONKEI　　　　respect
敬語 KEIGO　　polite language
い敬 IKEI　　　　　　awe

攵 is strike/ **force** 101, here acting as a causative element. 苟 is an NGU character now used to convey insignificance, but a very early form 口茍 shows a **person bending** (in a position of **humility**) へ 39 and **speaking** ⼝ (mouth/say 20), and it originally meant **speak respectfully**. The exact meaning of ⼝ / ⼧ is not clear, but other early forms such as 苟 and 苟 support the theory that it shows a minor chieftain's headdress (of sheep's horns), to give a specific meaning of minor chieftain speaking respectfully to his lord. The addition of force 攵 gave **force someone to speak respectfully**, but this has now faded to leave just **show respect** in a broad sense. The graphic evolution of the character may have been influenced by **phrase** 句 655, which may be useful as a mnemonic. Suggest taking ⼧ as **plants** 9.

Mnemonic: **FORCE PERSON TO USE RESPECTFUL PHRASES OF PLANTS**

847

KEI
WARN, REPROACH
19 strokes

警官 KEIKAN　　police officer
警告 KEIKOKU　　　　warning
警報 KEIHŌ　　warning, alarm

言 is **words/ speak** 274. 敬 is **respect** 846, here lending connotations of acting **cautiously** as well as **respectfully**. 847 originally meant **speak cautiously and respectfully**, but later came to mean **be cautious** as well as **counsel caution**, i.e. **warn**. As with the English term, warn later came to be used in the sense of **reproach** as well as counsel.

Mnemonic: **WARN WITH RESPECTFUL WORDS**

266

848 **GEKI** 劇場 GEKIJŌ theater
DRAMA, INTENSE 劇的 GEKITEKI dramatic
15 strokes 劇痛 GEKITSŪ intense pain

刂 is **sword/ cut** 181, 虎 is **tiger** 281, and 豕 is **pig** 1670. Though there is some disagreement over the interpretation of these elements, the character is generally seen as an ideograph meaning **attack with a sword in the manner of a tiger attacking a pig**, i.e. **fiercely**, with **intense** being an extended meaning. Some scholars take **drama/ dramatic** to be a borrowed meaning, while others take it to stem from the idea of **exciting** and **intense** (cf. English drama/ dramatic).

Mnemonic: **TIGER ATTACKS PIG WITH SWORD?! -- WHAT DRAMA!**

849 **KETSU, ana** 穴居人 KEKKYOJIN troglodyte
HOLE 穴子 ANAGO conger eel
5 strokes 穴埋め ANAUME stopgap

宀 is **roof/ cover** 28. ハ is **disperse/ away** 66, here meaning **open up** and according to some scholars also acting phonetically to express **dig**. 849 originally referred to a **space being opened up (in the ground) and covered**, a primitive method of forming a dwelling (see also 15). It later came to mean **hole** in general.

Mnemonic: **TAKE COVER AWAY AND EXPOSE HOLE**

850 **KEN, ka**neru 兼業 KENGYŌ side business
COMBINE, UNABLE 兼用 KENYŌ dual purpose
10 strokes 為兼ねる SHIKANERU cannot do

Once written 兼, showing a **hand** ⇒ holding **two rice plants** 禾 81 and symbolising **doing two things at once**. Its use as a verbal suffix to express being **unable** to do something is felt to stem from the idea that in trying to do two things at once one is unable to do either thing properly. Suggest remembering 禾 as **combined rice plants**.

Mnemonic: **HAND REALLY UNABLE TO HOLD COMBINED RICE PLANTS**

267

851 **KEN, GON**
RIGHT, AUTHORITY,
BALANCE
15 strokes

権利 KENRI — right, claim
権衡 KENKŌ — balance
権化 GONGE — embodiment

Formerly 權. 木 is **tree**/ wood 69. 蔧/雈 is **crested bird**/ heron 445, here acting phonetically to express **cream** (color) but of unknown semantic role. 851 originally referred to a certain **tree whose flowers were cream**. As a result of miscopying it was later used instead of a now defunct character 㩲. This comprised heron 蔧, used phonetically to express **stone** but of unknown semantic role, and **hand** 扌 32, and referred to stones of a more or less given size -- just able to be held in one hand-- which were used as **weights** in a primitive **set of scales/ balance**. **Right** and **authority** are felt to be associated meanings, from the fact that the person doing the weighing had the right to provide his own weighing-stones and thereby possibly gain some slight advantage. **Balance** is now a very minor meaning.

Mnemonic: **CRESTED BIRD HAS RIGHT TO BALANCE IN TREE**

852 **KEN**
LAW, CONSTITUTION
16 strokes

憲法 KENPŌ — constitution
憲章 KENSHŌ — charter
憲兵 KENPEI — military police

Somewhat obscure. Once written 㝣, showing an **inverted basket** 冄/由 399 and an **eye** 𦣝/目 72. Some scholars feel that inverted basket 冄/宀 acted purely phonetically to express **quick/ sharp**, to give a meaning of **sharp eyed**. When **heart/ feelings** 心 147 was added later the meaning changed to **quick with feelings**, i.e. **emotional/ sensitive**. Its present meaning of **legal authority** is then assumed to be borrowed. Other scholars feel that inverted basket symbolised **covering**, giving **covered eye** and by extension **acting blindly**. The later addition of heart/ feeling 心 is then felt to extend the meaning to **acting blindly and without emotion**, in other words **doing something without question**. The **law/ constitution** is something that should be obeyed in this fashion. The fact that in Chinese 852 can also mean **ruler** and **complacent** supports the latter theory, since both meanings can be interpreted as stemming from a core concept of **acting or obeying without question**. Suggest taking 宀 as **cover**, and 𰀱 as a variant of **life** 生 42.

Mnemonic: **CONSTITUTIONAL LAW COVERS ALL ONE SEES AND FEELS IN LIFE**

853		**GEN, minamoto** **SOURCE, ORIGIN** 13 strokes	資源 SHIGEN 源泉 GENSEN 源氏 GENJI	resources source Minamoto Clan

原 is **plain/ origin** 107 q.v., here in its early sense of **spring. Water** ⟩ 40 was added after 107 started to lose its original meaning. 853 is now often used in the figurative sense of **origin**, though it can still mean specifically a **water source**.

Mnemonic: **WATER SOURCE IS IN ORIGINAL SPRING ON PLAIN**

854		**GEN, GON, kibi**shii, ogoso*ka* **SEVERE, STRICT,** **SOLEMN** 17 strokes	厳格 GENKAKU 厳秘 GENPI 壮厳 SŌGON	strictness strictly secret solemnity

Formerly 嚴, and earlier 嚴. 厂 is **cliff** 45. 敢 is **daring** 1106 q.v., here acting phonetically to express **gape** and possibly also lending connotations of **remove** and by extension **be missing.** 厰 originally referred to **holes in a cliffside**, i.e. **fissures** or **caves**, but gradually came to mean just **cliff.** In an attempt to shift the focus back to the holes in the cliff the element ʋʋ was added. It technically shows a doubling of **mouth/ say** 口 20 and means **noisy**, but was used here for its idea of **two openings** (also 20) as well as for its sound, which like 敢 expressed **gape**. However, once again **cliff** came to prevail. Ironically, cliff is now conveyed by the NGU character 巌, which adds **mountain** 山 24, while 854 became used to express **severe/ strict/ solemn** instead of the NGU character 儼. This adds **person** イ 39 and means literally **person as firm as a cliff/ rock.** Suggest taking 产 as an **ornate building** (see 10 and 114).

Mnemonic: **DARINGLY ORNATE BUILDING IS STRICTLY SOLEMN!**

855		**KO, KI, onore** **I, ME, YOU, SELF** 3 strokes	自己 JIKO 知己 CHIKI 利己 RIKO	self friend selfishness

From a pictograph of a **twisting thread** ⟨, which was its original meaning. Its use as a **first person pronoun** is felt by some scholars to be a purely phonetic borrowing, but it seems highly likely that it became graphically confused with the early form 乞 of **I/ self** ム 134. Confusingly, 855 is also occasionally used as a **second person pronoun**, a usage that is felt to stem from generalisations involving the concept of **self** (cf. English use of **you** instead of **oneself**).

Mnemonic: **I MYSELF FOLLOW THE THREAD -- WHAT ABOUT YOU?**

856	KO, yobu	呼吸 KOKYŪ	breathing
	CALL, BREATHE	点呼 TENKO	roll call
	8 strokes	呼び物 YOBIMONO	drawcard

口 is **mouth/ say** 20. 乎 is an NGU character now used to indicate a question or exclamation, but was originally a symbol of **exhalation**, being written 乎. This shows **seeking an exit** 丂 281, **away** ⼃ 66, and a further symbol of **expulsion** ⼃. Rather like call 号 281 q.v. (and see also 816), 856 originally referred to something **emerging from the mouth**, and was applied both to **breathing** (especially exhaling) and **vocalising**. Suggest taking 乎 as an **'odd' hand** 手 32.

Mnemonic: **ODD HAND BY MOUTH STOPS BREATHING OR CALLING**

857	GO, ayamaru	誤解 GOKAI	misunderstanding
	MISTAKE, MIS-	誤判 GOHAN	mistrial
	14 strokes	誤訳 GOYAKU	mistranslation

Formerly 誤. 吳/吴 is **give** 1237 q.v., here used in its literal sense of brag/ **deviate from the truth**, with **words/ speak** 言 274 added after 1237's meaning became vague. Words which deviate from the truth led to **mistake** and the idea of **not saying/doing something properly**.

Mnemonic: **MISTAKEN WORDS GIVEN**

858	KŌ, GO, kisaki	皇后 KŌGŌ	empress
	EMPRESS, BEHIND,	后妃 KŌHI	queen
	LATER	午后 GOGO	afternoon
	6 strokes		

⼃ is a variant of **buttocks** 尸/尸 236, while 口 is **opening** 20. **Opening in the buttocks** was a reference to the **anus**, the original meaning of 858. Not unlike the English term **behind**, this later also came to be used in the prepositional sense, including of time. **Empress** is felt by some scholars to be a borrowed meaning, but it seems far more likely to stem from a practice of referring to the empress indirectly as the **one who follows behind** (the emperor). Suggest remembering ⼃ by partial association with **ax** 斤 1176. See also 497.

Mnemonic: **EMPRESS COMES BEHIND, CUTTING OPENING WITH AX**

859	KŌ, su*ku*, kono*mu*/*mashii*	好意 KŌI	goodwill
	LIKE, GOOD, FINE	好き SUKI na	nice, liked
	6 strokes	好男子 KŌDANSHI	
			handsome man

Popularly explained as the **liking** a **woman** 女 35 has for a **child** 子 25, symbolising a **fine** and **loving** relationship. However, some authoritative Japanese scholars feel that child 子 is used essentially phonetically to express **beautiful**, as well as probably lending connotations of **that which one wishes to embrace** and/or **that towards which one feels tender**, to give a meaning of **beautiful woman (to whom one feels tender?)**. Beautiful/ attractive then came to mean **fine** and **good** in a broader sense, with **like** being seen as an associated meaning. It is possible, however, that the evolution of the meaning **like** was influenced by the above popular interpretation of the elements as **woman liking child**, which is a useful mnemonic.

Mnemonic: **WOMAN LIKES CHILD -- WHAT A FINE THING**

860	KŌ	孝子 KŌSHI	dutiful child
	FILIAL PIETY	孝行 KŌKŌ	filial piety
	7 strokes	不孝 FUKŌ	filial impiety

Popularly explained as an **old man** 耂 117 q.v. and **child** 子 25 symbolising the **relationship between the generations**, with **filial piety** being an associated meaning. However, some authoritative Japanese scholars feel that child 子 is used essentially phonetically to express **care for**, as well as probably lending a meaning of **offspring**, to give a meaning of **(offspring?) caring for an old person**. The fact that at one stage child 子 was interchanged with food 食 146, as seen in an early form 𩙿, supports this theory (i.e. with food 食 playing a similar phonetic role and also semantically suggesting look after/ provide for). However, suggest using the popular explanation as a mnemonic, and rembering 耂 as **old man** by partial association with **earth** 土 60.

Mnemonic: **FILIAL PIETY IS CHILD CARING FOR EARTHY OLD MAN**

861	KŌ, Ō	皇太子 KŌTAISHI	crown prince
	EMPEROR	法皇 HŌŌ	monk-emperor
	9 strokes	明治天皇 MEIJI TENNŌ*	
			Emperor Meiji

Once written 𝌏, showing **king** 王 5 and a **crown** 𦥑. 861 originally referred to a **king's crown** or **ceremonial headpiece** (still a meaning in Chinese), but later came to refer to the person wearing such an item, i.e. the **ruler/ emperor**. Suggest taking 白 as **white** 65.

Mnemonic: **EMPEROR IS WHITE KING**

271

| 862 | KŌ, KU, kurenai, beni
RED, CRIMSON, ROUGE
9 strokes | 紅葉 KŌYŌ
真紅 SHINKU
紅茶 KŌCHA | red leaves
crimson
brown tea |

糸 is **thread** 27. エ is **work** 113, here acting phonetically to express **pink** and possibly also lending an idea of **process**. Thus (**processed?**) **pink threads**. This later came to mean pink in general, then **red/ crimson/ rouge**. As with the English term rouge, it is also used to refer to cosmetics, including lipstick.

Mnemonic: **WORK WITH CRIMSON THREADS**

| 863 | KŌ, furu, oriru/rosu
FALL, ALIGHT,
DESCEND
10 strokes | 降雨 KŌU
降伏 KŌFUKU
乗り降り NORIORI | rainfall
surrender
getting on and off |

阝 is **hill** 229. 夅 was once written 𠁨, showing **two inverted feet** 夂 (夂 438 and ヰ 422). Inverted feet is used in its sense of **come down from above** (see 438), giving **come down a hill** and hence the present meanings. Suggest taking 夂 as **sitting crosslegged** and ヰ as a variant of **well** 井 1470.

Mnemonic: **DESCEND HILL AND SIT CROSSLEGGED BY WELL**

| 864 | KŌ, hagane
STEEL
16 strokes | 鋼鉄 KŌTETSU
製鋼所 SEIKŌJO
鋼色 HAGANEIRO | steel
steelworks
steel blue |

岡 is an NGU character meaning **hill**. It was once written 𡉵, showing **hill** 凵/山 24 and net 冂/网 193, the latter lending a meaning of **draw in/up**. Thus **hill that is drawn up**, i.e. one that is **towering** and **formidable**. Here it lends an idea of **formidable** as well as acting phonetically to express **strong**, combining with **metal** 金 14 to give **strong/ formidable metal**. It is now used particularly of **steel**.

Mnemonic: **METAL IN HILLS PROVES TO BE STEEL**

865 **KOKU, kiza***mu*   時刻 JIKOKU   time, hour
CHOP, MINCE,   刻印 KOKUIN   engraved seal
ENGRAVE   刻み目 KIZAMIME   notch
8 strokes

刂 is sword/ **cut** 181. 亥 is an NGU character used as the zodiac sign **hog**, and is to all intents and purposes a variant of **pig** 豕 1670. Here it acts phonetically to express **carve**, and possibly also lends similar connotations of **cutting/ carving** from the idea of butchering (e.g. see 195). Thus to **cut and carve**, leading both to **engrave** and to the idea of **cutting twice over**, i.e. **mince**. Suggest taking 亠 as a symbol of **top** and 乂 as a variant of (short) **thread** 幺 111.

Mnemonic: **MINCE THREADS BY CUTTING TOPS OFF**

---

866 **KOKU**   穀物 KOKUMOTSU   cereals
GRAIN, CEREALS   穀類 KOKURUI   cereals
14 strokes   穀倉 KOKUSŌ   granary

Formerly 穀. 禾 is **rice plant** 81, here meaning **food plant**. 殼 is a variant of shell/ **husk** 殼 1075. Thus **husked food plant**, i.e. **grain/ cereal**. Suggest taking 殳 as **beat/ strike** 153, 士 as **samurai** 494, and 冖 as **cover**.

Mnemonic: **SAMURAI BEATS RICE UNDER COVER TO MAKE CEREALS**

---

867 **KOTSU, hone**   骨折 KOSSETSU   fracture
BONE, FRAME   老骨 RŌKOTSU   old person
10 strokes   骨折る HONEORU   strive

冎 derives from 咼, showing **skull and vertebrae** and meaning **bone(s)**. **Flesh/ of the body** 月 365 was added later, to give **bones in the body/ skeleton**. This is still seen occasionally in the lesser meaning of **frame**, but generally 867 has come to mean simply **bone(s)** in a broad sense. Suggest remembering by partial association with **cover** 冖.

Mnemonic: **FLESH COVERED BONES**

868

KON, koma*ru*

BE IN DIFFICULTY

7 strokes

困 難 KONNAN   trouble

困 苦 KONKU   hardship

困 ら せ る KOMARASERU   annoy

Widely interpreted as a **tree** 木 69 in a **confined area** or **box** 口 (see 123), to symbolise being **constrained** or **in difficulty**. However, some scholars feel that 木 acts rather in its meaning of **wood**, as well as lending its sound to express **barrier**, and that 口 is **opening/ entrance** 20. Thus **wooden barrier barring entrance**, leading by association to the idea of a place that is **difficult to enter** and eventually just **difficult/ difficulty**. Suggest following the former theory.

Mnemonic: **TREE IN DIFFICULTY, TRAPPED IN BOX**

869

SA, SHA, suna

SAND, GRAVEL, GRAIN

9 strokes

砂 金 SAKIN   gold dust

砂 利 JARI*   gravel

砂 浜 SUNAHAMA sandy beach

石 is **stone** 45, while 少 is **little/ few** 143 q.v., here used in its literal sense of **tiny points**. Thus **tiny stones**, leading to the present meanings. Note that 869 is to all intents and purposes interchangeable with the NGU character SA/SHA sand 沙 , which uses **water/ river** 氵 40 instead of stone 石 to give tiny items in a river.

Mnemonic: **SAND COMPRISES LITTLE STONES**

870

ZA, suwa*ru*

SEAT, SIT, GATHER

10 strokes

座 席 ZASEKI   seat

座 談 会 ZADANKAI symposium

銀 座 GINZA   the Ginza

Formerly also written 坐 , showing **two persons** 人 39 on the **ground** 土 60. Though the use of <u>standing</u> persons as opposed to <u>sitting</u> persons (e.g. 卩 236 or ヒ 238) is somewhat confusing, 870 does in fact refer to **persons sitting on the ground**. **Building / roof** 广 114 was added later, giving persons **sitting on the ground under a roof**, suggesting a **gathering**.

Mnemonic: **PERSONS SIT ON GROUND UNDER ROOF AT GATHERING**

871

SAI, SEI, su*mu/masu*　経済学 KEIZAIGAKU economics
SETTLE, FINISH　返済 HENSAI　repayment
11 strokes　済まない SUMANAI　be improper

Formerly 濟 . 氵 is **water** 40. 齊/斉 is alike 1473 q.v., here acting phonetically to express **clear** and probably also lending its own connotations of **pure** (from items prepared for offering to the gods). Thus **clear pure water**, which by extension is **settled** water. This meaning is now conveyed by 澄 1597, while 871 has come to mean settled in the sense of **concluded** and **put in order** (note the various meanings of the verb sumu). Suggest taking 斉 as writing/ **text** 文 68 and an **'odd' moon** 月 16.

Mnemonic: **TEXT ABOUT ODD MOON SEEN IN SETTLED WATER**

---

872 裁

SAI, saba*ku*, ta*tsu*　裁判 SAIBAN　trial
JUDGE, DECIDE, CUT 裁ちくず TACHIKUZU　shreds
12 strokes　裁ち方 TACHIKATA　cut, fit

衣 is **clothing/ cloth** 420. 戈 is a CO character meaning wound/ **cut,** and is to all intents and purposes a **'fancy'** variant of **lance/ halberd/ cut** 戈 493. (Some scholars see 戈 as a variant of trim/ broad bladed halberd 戊 515, but old forms such as 裁 suggest rather that it is technically a variant of tasseled lance/ halberd 我 817.) Thus to **cut cloth** (into clothing). As with judge/ cut 断 750, cutting came to represent **being decisive** and hence **judging**.

Mnemonic: **JUDGE DECIDES TO CUT CLOTH WITH FANCY HALBERD**

---

873 策

SAKU　政策 SEISAKU　policy
POLICY, PLAN, WHIP　対策 TAISAKU　counterplan
12 strokes　策動家 SAKUDŌKA　schemer

⺮ is **bamboo** 170, here meaning **thin stem of wood.** 朿 is an NGU character meaning **thorn** (see also thorn 刺 1314). It derives from a combination of **tree/ wood** 木 69 and a symbol of **tapering** △, giving 本 and later 朿 and hence 朿. Here it acts phonetically to express **beat** and also lends its meaning of **sharply tapered piece of wood**. Thus 873 originally meant **sharply tapered thin piece of wood for beating**, and referred to a **horsewhip**. It is still occasionally used in this sense, especially in Chinese. **Policy/ plan** is felt to stem from confusion with **book/ bamboo records** 冊 874 q.v., which has the same pronunciation and shares common semantic ground of thin piece of bamboo/wood. Keeping a written record of something led by association to the idea of formulating a detailed policy/ plan. Suggest taking 朿 as a **tree with droopy branches**.

Mnemonic: **PLAN TO FIX DROOPY TREE BRANCHES WITH BAMBOO**

874				
	SATSU	冊子	SASSHI	booklet
	BOOK, VOLUME	二冊	NISATSU	two volumes
	5 strokes	短冊	TANZAKU	
				paper strip for poem

Formerly 丹丹 and earlier 丹丹丹, depicting a **bundle of thin bamboo tablets (used for records) bound together**. Hence **collection of written material**.

Mnemonic: **STACKED BOUND TABLETS RESEMBLE VOLUMES OF BOOKS**

875				
	SHI, itaru/ri	至急	SHIKYŪ	emergency
	GO, REACH, PEAK	夏至	GESHI	summer solstice
	6 strokes	至らない	ITARANAI	imperfect

From a pictograph ꝺ , showing an **arrow** ꝺ (probably with something bound to its stem) **falling to the ground** _ . While this occasionally lends connotations of upside-down, it usually connotes **reaching a point (and stopping)**, that point being the **maximum** edge of its range. You may prefer to see the arrow the other way up, i.e. ꝺ , or else take 至 as **ground** ± 60, **nose** 厶 134, and a symbol of **flatness** ⁻ .

Mnemonic: **NOSE FLAT TO GROUND AS ONE REACHES ONE'S PEAK**

876				
	SHI, wata[ku]shi	私立	SHIRITSU	private
	I, PRIVATE, PERSONAL	私達	WATASHITACHI	we
	7 strokes	私事	SHIJI	personal affairs

Rice plant 禾 81 and **self** 厶 134, to give **one's own rice** and by extension **private, personal**, and **things pertaining to oneself** (i.e. **I/ me/ my**).

Mnemonic: **RICE IS PRIVATE AND BELONGS TO ME MYSELF**

877				
	SHI, sugata	姿勢	SHISEI	posture
	FORM, FIGURE	容姿	YŌSHI	form
	9 strokes	姿見	SUGATAMI	full mirror

女 is **woman** 35. 次 is **next** 292 q.v., acting phonetically to express **voluptuous** and probably also lending a literal idea of **people standing open mouthed**. 877 originally referred to a **woman of stunning attractiveness**, and later came to mean **fine figure** and eventually just **figure/ form** in a broad sense.

Mnemonic: **NEXT WOMAN HAS A GOOD FIGURE**

276

878		SHI, mi*ru* SEE, LOOK, REGARD 11 strokes	視力 SHIRYOKU	eyesight
			視覚 SHIKAKU	vision
			無視 MUSHI	disregard

Formerly 視 . 示/ネ is **show** 695. 見 is **look** 16. Some scholars feel 見 also lends its sound to express **stop/ fix in place**. Thus **look at something on show (and fix one's gaze on it?)**, later **look/ regard** in a broader sense.

Mnemonic: **LOOK AND SEE WHAT'S ON SHOW**

879		SHI, kotoba WORD, PART OF SPEECH 12 strokes	動詞 DŌSHI	verb
			歌詞 KASHI	lyrics
			詞書 KOTOBAGAKI	foreword

言 is **word** 274. 司 is **administer/ official** 497 q.v., acting phonetically to express **join** and almost certainly also lending a meaning of **control**. Thus words **which join (other words) (and control them?)**, a reference to **parts of speech** and by extension **words** in a broader sense.

Mnemonic: **PARTS OF SPEECH ARE OFFICIAL WORDS**

880		SHI RECORD, JOURNAL 14 strokes	本誌 HONSHI	this journal
			雑誌 ZASSHI	magazine
			週間誌 SHŪKANSHI	a weekly

言 is **word** 274. 志 is **will/ intent** 692, acting phonetically to express **record** and almost certainly also lending an idea of **intent**. Thus to **record words (with intent?)**, giving **record** and by extension **journal**. Suggest taking 志 as **samurai** 士 494 and **heart/ feeling** 心 147.

Mnemonic: **SAMURAI'S HEARTFELT WORDS RECORDED IN JOURNAL**

881	磁	JI MAGNET, PORCELAIN 14 strokes	磁石 JISHAKU	magnet
			磁器 JIKI	porcelain
			磁力 JIRYOKU	magnetism

Formerly 磁 . 石 is **stone** 45. 玆 is an NGU character now used to convey **this/ here**. Its semantic evolution is somewhat unclear, but it is a doubling of **twisted thread/ occult/ invisible** 玄 1227 q.v. It acts here phonetically to express **draw/ pull**, and probably also lends similar connotations from its literal meaning of threads drawn together by a twisting device, and/or connotations of invisibility/ mystery. Thus **stone that draws/ pulls (mysteriously/ invisibly?)**, i.e. a **magnet**. **Porcelain** is a borrowed meaning.

Mnemonic: **ROCK HAS INVISIBLE MAGNETIC THREADS**

882

SHA, *iru*
SHOOT
10 strokes

注射器 CHŪSHAKI syringe
射倒す ITAOSU shoot down
射撃場 SHAGEKIJŌ rifle range

Originally ᑽᏳ , a pictograph showing a **bow** ᒣ 836 and **arrow** ↤ 981. A **hand** ᘇ was added later to draw attention to the **shooting** of the arrow, giving ᑽᏳᘇ, and this was then replaced with **measure/ hand** 寸 909 q.v., with its connotations of **careful use of the hand**. The use of **body** 身 323 (early form ᑎ) instead of bow and arrow ᑽᏳ results from a miscopying.

Mnemonic: **HAND SHOOTS MEASURED ARROW INTO BODY**

883

SHA, *suteru*
ABANDON
11 strokes

喜捨 KISHA charity
捨て子 SUTEGO foundling
捨て置く SUTEOKU leave alone

扌 is **hand** 32. 舎 is house/ **quarters** 700 q.v., here acting phonetically to express **put down (and leave)** and possibly also lending its literal meaning of **relax/ not worry**. Thus to **put something down with the hand and leave it (without worrying?)**, leading to **abandon**.

Mnemonic: **FIND ABANDONED HAND IN ONE'S QUARTERS!**

884

SHAKU, SEKI
MEASURE, FOOT
4 strokes

尺度 SHAKUDO scale, gauge
尺八 SHAKUHACHI flute
尺地 SEKICHI strip of land

Once written ᒋ . ᒑ depicts the **elbow** and **lower arm** down to an **extended finger tip**, while ᑕ depicts a **spread hand**. 884 thus referred to the **span of a hand**, which became a measuring unit roughly equivalent to one **foot** (actually 30.3 cms, as opposed to 30.48 for the Western foot). It also came to represent **measure** in a broad sense. See also 1415. Suggest taking 尸 as a 'topless' variant of **door** 戸 108 and 乀 as a **prop**, with a pun on 'foot'.

Mnemonic: **MEASURE PROP FOR FOOT OF TOPLESS DOOR**

885 SHAKU, to*ku* 解釈 KAISHAKU interpretation
EXPLAIN, RELEASE 釈放 SHAKUHŌ release
11 strokes 釈明 SHAKUMEI explanation

Formerly 釋. 釆 is the same apparent confusion of **rice** 米 201 and **rice plant** 禾 81 seen in 196 q.v., and similarly has connotations of **planting**. 睪 is **keep watch over prisoners** 233 q.v., here acting phonetically to express **scatter** and probably also lending an idea of **succession**. Thus to **scatter rice (seeds) (in succession?)**. This came to mean **scatter/ disperse** in a broad sense, including such ideas as **release** and **undo,** and eventually acquired connotations of **undoing/ solving** a problem, i.e. **explaining**. Suggest taking the modern form 尺 as **person** 人 39 with a **pack** ⊐ on their back.

Mnemonic: **PERSON EXPLAINS, IS RELEASED AND GIVEN RICE PACK**

886 若 JAKU, wak*ai*, mo*shi* 若年 JAKUNEN youth
YOUNG, IF 若しくは MOSHIKUWA or
8 strokes 若者 WAKAMONO youth

Very old forms such as 𦰩 show a **person kneeling** attending to their **long flowing hair**. Ironically, long hair is generally a symbol of old age (e.g. see 173), but here it symbolised **wavy/ pliant**. It combined with mouth/ say 口 20 to give a meaning of **pliant words**, i.e. **agreement**. This meaning is now conveyed by agree 諾 1557, which added words 言 274 after the meaning of 886 became vague. Softness and pliancy also symbolised **weakness** (e.g. see 138), and eventually 886 itself acquired this meaning. **Young** is an associated meaning with weak. **If** is a borrowed meaning. The present form results from an early miscopying of 𦰩 (variant 𦱳) as 𦱶, i.e. showing a hand 又/ナ 2 and plants 屮屮 9. Suggest taking 右 as **right** 2 and 艹 as **plants** 9.

Mnemonic: **PLANTS ON RIGHT ARE YOUNG**

887 JU 需要 JUYŌ demand
NEED, DEMAND 必需品 HITSUJUHIN necessities
14 strokes 需給 JUKYŪ supply and demand

雨 is **rain** 3. 而 is an NGU character now used to convey **however**, but it derives from a stylised pictograph of a **beard** 而 and originally had that meaning (still in fact a minor meaning in Chinese). Here it acts phonetically to express **wet**, to give a **beard soaked by the rain**. (Note that **become soaked** is now expressed by the NGU character 濡, which adds water 氵 40.) Some scholars feel that **need/ demand** is a purely borrowed meaning, while others see it as convolutedly deriving from the idea of waiting to avoid becoming soaked and hence waiting for something better, leading to **desire** and hence **need/ demand**. Suggest taking 而 as a **rake**.

Mnemonic: **RAIN FALLS ON RAKE -- NEED NEW ONE**

888	**JU, ki** **TREE, STAND** 16 strokes	樹脂 JUSHI 樹立 JURITSU 樹皮 JUHI	resin founding bark

Once written 尌 . 壴 is **edible plant** 450, while 寸 is **hand/ measure** 909 q.v., here meaning **careful use of the hands**. The food vessel element 豆 1640 q.v. of 壴 also acts phonetically to express **stand/ erect**, as well as lending similar connotations of its own (from the fact that the vessel had a long upright stem). Thus to **erect an edible** (i.e. **food-bearing) plant with care**, i.e. **carefully plant it upright**. **Tree** 木 69 was added later to enforce the idea of upright flora, and presently 888's meaning changed to **plant a tree**, and eventually **tree** itself. It is however still occasionally used in the sense of **erect/ stand**. Suggest taking 壴 as **food pot** 豆 / 豆 1640 and **samurai** 士 494.

Mnemonic: **SAMURAI'S HAND STANDS FOOD POT NEXT TO TREE**

889	**SHŪ, SŌ** **RELIGION, MAIN** 8 strokes	宗教 SHŪKYŌ 宗家 SŌKE 宗派 SHŪHA	religion main family sect

Roof/ building 宀 28 and **altar** 示 695, to give **building with altar**, i.e. shrine or in some cases mausoleum. By association this also came to symbolise **religion**. **Main** is felt to stem from the fact that such a building was the main building in a community.

Mnemonic: **BUILDING WITH ALTAR IS MAIN CENTER OF RELIGION**

890 就	**SHŪ, JU, tsuku** **TAKE UP,** **BE INVOLVED** 12 strokes	成就 JŌJU に就いて NITSUITE 就職 SHŪSHOKU	accomplishment concerning finding employment

京 is **capital** 99 q.v., here in its literal sense of **(aristocrat's) house on a hill**. 尤 is an NGU character meaning **outstanding**. Its origin is somewhat unclear, but old forms such as 㞤 suggest a person with long hair, which was usually associated with old age and by association sometimes with excellence (see 173). Here 尢 lends connotations of **prominence**, and also acts phonetically to express **arrive**. 890 originally meant **prominent person arriving at a prominent house on a hill**, a reference to a dignitary arriving at a town to **take up a new post**. Taking up a post led to the idea of **becoming involved**. Suggest taking 尤 as a **dog** 犬 17 with a **crooked leg**.

Mnemonic: **TAKE UP ISSUE OF CRIPPLED DOGS IN CAPITAL**

---

891 JŪ, shitaga*u*
FOLLOW, COMPLY
10 strokes

従業員 JŪGYŌIN　　employee
従者 JŪSHA　　follower
従って SHITAGATTE
　　　　　　accordingly

Formerly 從 . 彳 is **road/ move** 118 q.v. and 止 is **foot/ move** 止 129 q.v., with the combination in fact being the prototype of **move** 辶 129. 从 is **follow** 463 (literally **two persons** 人 39). Thus **two persons moving along (a road)**, with one **following** the other. Follow also came to be used in the figurative sense of **comply**. Suggest taking 辶 as **correct** 疋/正 41 and **eight** ヅ/八 66.

Mnemonic: **FOLLOW EIGHT ROADS CORRECTLY**

---

892 JŪ, tate
VERTICAL, SELFISH
16 strokes

縦線 JŪSEN　　vertical line
放縦 HŌJŪ　　self-indulgence
縦書き TATEGAKI vertical script

Formerly 縱 . 糸 is **thread** 27, here meaning **cord/ binding**. 從/従 is **follow** 891 q.v., here acting phonetically to express **slacken** and possibly also lending an idea of **movement** from its literal meaning of one person moving along after another. 892 originally meant **slacken binding (thus permitting movement?)**. It is still very occasionally used in this sense, but more often in the associated sense of **selfish** (i.e. from **lax** and **unconstrained** behavior). Its most common meaning of **vertical**, in which it often replaces lengthwise/ warp threads 経 658, is felt to stem from a popular reinterpretation of its elements as **threads to follow**, i.e. the generally **vertical** warp.

Mnemonic: **THREADS TO FOLLOW ARE THE VERTICAL ONES**

---

893 SHUKU, chiji*mu/meru*
SHRINK, REDUCE
17 strokes

縮小 SHUKUSHŌ　reduction
短縮 TANSHUKU　contraction
縮み止め CHIJIMIDOME
　　　　　　shrinkproof

糸 is **thread** 27. 宿 is **lodge** 505 q.v., here acting phonetically to express **arrange** and possibly also lending an idea of **gather** from its connotations of a gathering place for travelers. Thus to **arrange threads (by gathering them in?)**. Some scholars see its present meaning as borrowed, others as an extension of drawing together loose/ slack threads and thus making them **tight** and **compact**.

Mnemonic: **REDUCED TO THREADBARE LODGINGS**

281

894

熟

JUKU
RIPE, MATURE, COOKED
15 strokes

成熟 SEIJUKU   maturity
半熟 HANJUKU   half-boiled
熟練 JUKUREN   mastery

Somewhat obscure. Formerly 孰. This now exists as an NGU character used to convey who/ where, but it was originally written 孰, showing a **person bending and holding something** 丮, **woman** 丸/女 35, and what appears to be a **lidded cooking pot** 𠱸 (possibly variant 會 87), and its original meaning was **cook by boiling**. 𠱸 appears to have become confused with **receive** 𠱸/享 1162, while 丮 has become confused with **round** 丸 830 (see also 470). **Fire** 灬 8 was added later for clarity, when 孰 itself started to become semantically vague, and it should be noted that 烹 also exists as an NGU character meaning boil. Something that is boiled is ready for eating, leading by association to **ripe**, with **mature** being a figurative extension. Suggest taking 享 as **lid** 亠, **child** 子 25, and **mouth** 口 20.

Mnemonic:**MATURE CHILD PUTS ROUND LID OVER MOUTH OF FIREPIT**

895

純

JUN
PURE
10 strokes

純粋 JUNSUI   purity
純毛 JUNMŌ   pure wool
純益 JUNEKI   net profit

糸 is **thread** 27. 屯 is encampment 1669 q.v., here acting phonetically to express **superior** and also lending connotations of **fresh/ pure** from its literal meaning of **sprout** (i.e. fresh growth). 895 originally meant **superior pure (silk) threads**, but now means **pure** in a broad sense. Suggest remembering 屯 by association with **hair** 毛 210.

Mnemonic: **PURE THREADS LOOK LIKE HAIR**

896

処

SHO
DEAL WITH, PLACE
5 strokes

処理 SHORI   management
処置 SHOCHI   measure
処処 SHOSHO   here and there

Once written 処, showing **table/ rest/ stool** 几 832 and **inverted foot** 夂/夂/夂 438 q.v., here in its sense of **visit and stop**. Thus to **visit somewhere and stop, sitting on a stool**. This came to mean **be settled down**, leading on the one hand to **place** (where one is settled) and on the other to settle in a broader figurative sense, i.e. **conclude** or **deal with**. 896 was formerly also written 處, though technically this is a separate character of somewhat obscure etymology. It is generally interpreted as 処 with the addition of **tiger** 虍 281, which is felt to act phonetically to express **sit casually**. However, old forms such as 𠩄 and 𠩄 suggest strongly that it was in fact a highly stylised pictograph showing a person 𠱸 sitting down on a stool 几 before becoming confused with early forms of tiger such as 虎 and 虎. Suggest taking 夂 as **sit crosslegged**.

Mnemonic: **SIT CROSSLEGGED ON STOOL TO DEAL WITH SITUATION**

897 署 **SHO**
GOVERNMENT OFFICE, SIGN
13 strokes

署名	SHOMEI	signature
署員	SHOIN	official
警察署	KEISATSUSHO	police station

Formerly 署. 罒 is **net** 193. 者/者 is **person** 298, here also acting phonetically to express **put**. 897 originally referred to **persons given the task of putting the net in place** during a hunt. It then came to mean **employed person**, then **official**, then **place where officials work**. **Sign** is generally assumed to be a borrowed meaning, but it is possible that it is an idea associated with government office.

Mnemonic: **PERSON NETTED, SIGNS UP FOR GOVERNMENT OFFICE**

898 諸 **SHO, moro**
VARIOUS, MANY
15 strokes

諸島	SHOTŌ	island group
諸君	SHOKUN	'my friends'
諸手	MOROTE	both hands

Formerly 諸. 言 is **words** 274. 者/者 is **person** 298 q.v., here acting phonetically to express **many** and also lending similar connotations of its own from its early meaning of **many various things**. 898 originally meant **many/ various words**, but then came to mean **many/ various** in general.

Mnemonic: **PERSON'S WORDS ARE MANY AND VARIOUS**

899 将 **SHŌ, masa**
COMMAND, ABOUT TO
10 strokes

将来	SHŌRAI	future
将軍	SHŌGUN	generalissimo
将に	MASA ni	on the point of

Formerly 將 and earlier [illegible], showing that **measure/ hand** 寸 909 is a miscopying of/ substitution for **two hands** 廾 (indicating **offering**) and that **hand reaching down** ⺤ 303 is a miscopying of/ substitution for **meat** 夕/月 365. 爿/丬/冫 is **bed** 1389, here acting phonetically to express **offer up** and possibly also lending a meaning of **litter**. 899 originally meant **offer meat to a superior** (the latter reclining on a litter?). Some scholars feel that its present meaning of **command** is borrowed, while others see it as stemming from the idea of the superior rank of the person being offered meat, i.e. that person being a commander or a person who has commanded that meat be brought. It is not clear how it also came to mean **be about to**, although it is possible that this may also have evolved from the idea of offering meat, i.e. with the person being offered the meat **being about to** receive/ eat it. Suggest taking 丬 as a **bar** 丨 of **ice** 冫 378.

Mnemonic: **COMMANDER'S HAND ABOUT TO REACH FOR BAR OF ICE**

900

SHŌ, war*au*, e*mu*   苦笑 KUSHŌ   wry smile
LAUGH, SMILE   笑い声 WARAIGOE   laughter
10 strokes   笑顔 EGAO*   smiling face

Of confused etymology. ⺮ is **bamboo** 170, though this is a longstanding miscopying of **plant** ⩗ 9. 夭 is **person with bowed head** 279. 㗛 / 笑 originally referred to a type of **thistle** (presumably associated with a drooping head). It then became further confused with **smile/ laugh** 㗛 / 咲 1303 q.v., in which 笑 / 关 acts phonetically to express **crease** and also lends its own connotations of **thin** (from the stem of the thistle), combining with **mouth** 口 20 to give **thin creases around the mouth**, i.e. **smile** and hence **laugh**. Suggest taking 夭 literally as **big person** 大 53 with **head bent** ノ, and following the common but incorrect explanation that the character shows a person bent over (like bamboo bends) laughing.

Mnemonic: **BIG PERSON BENT OVER LIKE BAMBOO, LAUGHING**

901

SHŌ, kizu, ita*mi/mu/meru* 死傷者 SHISHŌSHA casualties
WOUND, INJURY   傷害 SHŌGAI   injury
13 strokes   傷付ける KIZUTSUKERU wound

亻 is **person** 39. 㥯 is to all intents and purposes a variant of **rising sun** 昜 144, technically showing a **person** ㇏ 39 watching the sun rise (see also 637). Here 㥯 acts phonetically to express **wound**, and may also lend connotations of (becoming) **intense** from its idea of rising. Thus a **(badly?) wounded person**, now **wound** in a broad sense.

Mnemonic: **WOUNDED PERSONS LEFT EXPOSED TO RISING SUN**

902

SHŌ, saw*aru*   障害 SHŌGAI   impediment
HINDER, BLOCK   障子 SHŌJI   shoji screen
14 strokes   差し障る SASHISAWARU hinder

阝 is **hill** 229, while 章 is **badge** 318 q.v. The latter acts phonetically to express **barrier**, but any semantic role is unclear. However, since it can also symbolise **slave** it is remotely possible that it also lends connotations of **impeded/ impediment** (i.e. not free). Thus **hill(s) forming barrier**, leading to **block** and **hinder**.

Mnemonic: **GET BADGE FOR OVERCOMING HINDERING HILL**

903

JŌ, shiro
CASTLE
9 strokes

城下町 JŌKAMACHI castle town
姫路城 HIMEJIJŌ Himeji Castle
城跡 SHIROATO castle ruins

土 is **earth** 60. 成 is **become/ consist/ make** 515 q.v., here acting phonetically to express **pile up** and also lending its connotations of **being properly finished**. 903 originally referred to **properly (i.e. soundly) constructed earthen ramparts**, then came by extension to mean **castle**.

Mnemonic: **CASTLE CONSISTS OF EARTHEN RAMPARTS**

904

JŌ, mu*su/reru*
STEAM
13 strokes

蒸気 JŌKI steam
蒸留 JŌRYŪ distillation
蒸し暑い MUSHIATSUI humid

Once written 𤑔, showing **plants/ grass** 艸/艹 9, **two fires** 炏/火 8, **two hands** 𦥑, and **smoke/ heat rising** 冫. This was a depiction of **hands throwing brushwood on a fire**, and the original meaning was **brushwood** (still found in Chinese). However, it was then used instead of the simpler 烝, a CO character meaning **heat rising from a fire** (i.e. 904 minus the plants/ brushwood 艹, with hands 𦥑/𠆢 retained in error or else in the sense of hands being warmed at a fire). For some unclear reason 904 later came to be used particularly of (rising) **steam**, though it has no element connected with water. It is possible however that 氶 became confused with **water** 氺 40. Suggest taking 氶 as a combination of **water** and **baby/ child** 子 25, with 一 as a **hotplate**.

Mnemonic: **GRASS COVERED WATERBABY STEAMS ON FIERY HOTPLATE**

905

SHIN, hari
NEEDLE, POINTER
10 strokes

方針 HŌSHIN policy, line
針路 SHINRO course
針金 HARIGANE wire

金 is **metal** 14. 十 is **ten** 33 q.v., here in its literal meaning of **needle**. Thus **metal needle**.

Mnemonic: **TEN METAL NEEDLES**

906	JIN, NI BENEVOLENT, HUMANITY 4 strokes	仁愛 JINAI	benevolence
		仁者 JINSHA	humanitarian
		仁王 NIŌ	Deva king

Popularly explained as an ideographic combination of **two** ニ 61 and **person** イ 39 to indicate the **relationship between two people**, which ideally should be one of **humanity** and **benevolence**. A useful mnemonic, but possibly incorrect since early forms such as ㇁ニ show a <u>bending</u> person. Some scholars feel that ニ acts phonetically to express **burden**, to give a meaning of **person bent under a burden**. This is then felt to have come by extension to a **person bearing someone else's burden** (possibly under the influence of two ニ , suggesting two [persons'] burdens), leading eventually to the present meanings.

Mnemonic: **TWO PEOPLE SHOW BENEVOLENT RELATIONSHIP**

907 垂	SUI, ta*reru*/*rasu* SUSPEND, HANG DOWN 8 strokes	垂直 SUICHOKU	verticality
		雨垂れ AMADARE	raindrops
		垂れ飾り TAREKAZARI	pendant

Once written 坙 , showing a combination of **ground** 土 60 and 朱, a **plant with drooping leaves**. Thus **plant with leaves hanging down to the ground**, now **hang** in a broader sense. Suggest remembering by association with **ride** 乗 320, from which distinguish.

Mnemonic: **LOOK LIKE RIDING HANGING DOWN TO GROUND!**

908 推	SUI, o*su* INFER, PUSH AHEAD 11 strokes	推理 SUIRI	reasoning
		推薦者 SUISENSHA	referee
		推進機 SUISHINKI	propeller

扌 is **hand** 32. 隹 is **bird** 216, here acting phonetically to express **thrust/ push** and almost certainly also lending an idea of **forward motion** (birds being unable to go backwards). Thus to **push forward with the hand**, now also used in the figurative sense of **promote**. **Infer** is a borrowed meaning.

Mnemonic: **PUSH BIRD AHEAD WITH HAND**

909 寸	SUN MEASURE, INCH 3 strokes	寸法 SUNPŌ	size, plan
		一寸 ISSUN	tiny bit, one inch
		寸分 SUNBUN	a little

Originally written 겨, though some later forms such as 겨 replace the **dot** · with **one** ― 1. 겨 is a **hand**. 909 originally referred to the **pulse**, as loosely indicated by the position of the dot relative to the hand. This was conveniently taken to be one SUN from the base of the palm, a SUN being the rough equivalent of the width of a finger (commonly taken as **one inch**, but now specifically standardised as 3.03 cms, which is a somewhat thick finger). Now also used to refer to **measure** in a broad sense, as well as **small amount**. In compounds sometimes confused with a simple hand, but often combining the ideas of both hand and measure to lend a meaning equivalent to **measured/ careful use of the hand.**

Mnemonic: **PULSE MEASURED AS ONE INCH FROM HAND**

910 是	ZE, kore PROPER, THIS 9 strokes	是正 ZESEI	correction
		是ら KORERA	these
		是非 ZEHI	right and wrong, at any cost

Of confused etymology. Very early forms such as 𤾕 show a **spoon/ ladle** 𤾕 and a **triple hook** ⩔ , which was used for hanging appliances on. The original meaning was thus **spoon kept on (proper) hook**. From an early stage hook ⩔ became confused with **foot/ stop** ⻊ / 止 129, with stop being taken transitively to mean **keep in place**, and the character became reinterpreted but without significant change of meaning as **spoon kept in proper place**. Spoon itself is now conveyed by the NGU character 匙ヒ, which adds ヒ (itself a CO character pictographically depicting a scoop/ ladle), while 910 came to convey the idea of **being in the proper place**, and hence **proper** in a broad sense. (However, some scholars maintain that proper is technically a borrowed meaning, not an extended one.) The modern form erroneously uses **correct/ proper** 疋 / 正 41, while spoon 𤾕 has become abbreviated to a form equivalent to **sun/ day** 日 62. **This** is a borrowed meaning.

Mnemonic: **SUN IS CORRECT -- THIS IS ONLY PROPER**

911

SEI, hijiri
SAINT, SAGE, SACRED
13 strokes

聖書 SEISHO   bible
聖人 SEIJIN   saint
神聖 SHINSEI   sanctity

Formerly 聖 . 耳 is **ear** 29, 口 is **opening/ hole** 20, and 壬 is **person standing still** 1610, here acting phonetically to express **clear** and possibly also lending a suggestion of **standing alertly**. 911 originally referred to a **person whose hearing** (literally **ear-hole) was excellent (clear)**, and who could hear things not heard by other people. This was in turn a reference to a **holy man**, who could hear the words of the gods. Thus **saint** and **sage**, with **sacred** being an extended meaning. 911 is also sometimes used as a term of respect to a ruler, which may have influenced the graphic evolution of 壬 into a form equivalent to **king** 王 5.

Mnemonic: **SAINTLY KING'S EARHOLE IS SACRED**

912

SEI, makoto
SINCERITY
13 strokes

誠意 SEII   sincerity
誠実 SEIJITSU   honesty
誠に MAKOTO ni   truly

言 is **words** 274. 成 is **consist/ become/ make** 515 q.v., here acting phonetically to express **pile up** and by extension **duplicate** and also lending its connotations of being **properly formed**. Though confusingly 912 contains no element specifically indicating **heart/ feelings** (e.g. 心 147), it originally referred to **words which properly duplicated one's heart/ feelings**, i.e. which contained **sincerity**. It now means sincerity in general.

Mnemonic: **WORDS BECOME SINCERE**

913

SEN
PROMULGATE, STATE
9 strokes

宣伝 SENDEN   propaganda
宣告 SENKOKU   verdict
宣教師 SENKYŌSHI missionary

宀 is **roof/ building** 28. 亘 is an NGU character now used to express request, but it was originally written 回 , showing a **vortex** @ 86 within **two boundaries** 二 , and meant **go around** in a broad sense (still found in Chinese). Thus **that which goes around a building**, namely a **fence/ wall**. (Some scholars feel that 亘 also acts phonetically to express **fence/ wall**.) A building with a wall around it was an **important building**, and this was the original meaning of 913 (not unlike institute 院 229 q.v.). Its present meanings result from borrowing. Suggest taking 亘 as **two** 二 61 **days** 日 62.

Mnemonic: **STATE THAT ROOF WILL BE FINISHED IN TWO DAYS**

288

914

SEN, moppara
EXCLUSIVE, SOLE
9 strokes

専門 SENMON　　specialty
専用 SENYŌ　　exclusive use
専制 SENSEI　　despotism

Somewhat obscure. Formerly 專 and earlier 叀, showing a **hand** 又 and a **round weighted device used in spinning** 叀 . The latter is taken by some scholars to have been largely used as a **child's toy.** Hand 又 was later replaced by **hand/ measure** 寸 909 q.v., which with its connotations of **careful use of the hands** tends to contradict the toy theory. However, adherents of the theory feel that 寸 simply meant hand, and that the character originally referred to a **child holding the toy.** Since a child is generally reluctant to release a toy it then came to symbolise **keeping possession for oneself,** leading to the present meanings. Other scholars feel that the character originally depicted a hand **dedicatedly performing the task of spinning,** with **dedication** leading to **exclusive devotion** and hence by extension the present meanings. The third and possibly most likely theory is that, not unlike a modern gyroscope, the spinning weight tended through its inertia to remain **fixed in place,** symbolising **unswerving devotion/ dedication** and hence the present meanings. Suggest taking 中 as **ten** 十 33 **fields** 田 59.

Mnemonic: **EXCLUSIVE POSSESSION OF TEN MEASURED FIELDS**

915

SEN, izumi
SPRING
9 strokes

温泉場 ONSENJŌ　　spa resort
泉水 SENSUI　　fountain
飛泉 HISEN　　waterfall

From a pictograph of **water emerging from a hole in a rock/ hillside** 泉 . Suggest taking 水 as **water** 40 and 白 as **white** 65. In fact, the modern form may have deliberately used 白, since it has connotations of **purity.**

Mnemonic: **SPRING PRODUCES WHITE WATER**

916

SEN, arau
WASH, INVESTIGATE
9 strokes

洗礼 SENREI　　baptism
洗濯 SENTAKU　(the) washing
手洗い TEARAI　　washroom

氵 is **water.** 先 is precede/ **tip** 49 q.v., here acting phonetically to express **feet** and almost certainly lending a similar meaning through its elements of **person** 儿 39 and **foot** 止 / 止 129. 916 originally referred to a **person washing their feet,** and then came to mean **wash** in general. The minor meaning of **investigate** is a figurative extension, from the idea of making something clean.

Mnemonic: **WASH TIP IN WATER**

917 染 **SEN, so*maru*/*meru*, shi*miru*** 染色 SENSHOKU dyeing
DYE, SOAK, PERMEATE 染め物 SOMEMONO dyed goods
9 strokes 染み込む SHIMIKOMU soak into

Once written , showing that 九 is not **nine** 九 12, though it may be useful to remember it as such, but a **person bending** 乁 39. 木 **is tree** 69, here meaning **shrub/plant.** 氺/氵 is **water** 40. 917 thus depicts a **person bending to soak a plant in water**, a reference to **dyeing** using the indigo plant or similar. Thus **dye** and **soak**, with **permeate** being an extended meaning.

Mnemonic: **SOAK NINE SHRUBS IN WATER TO MAKE DYE**

918 奏 **SŌ, kana*deru*** 伴奏 BANSŌ accompaniment
PLAY, REPORT 奏楽堂 SŌGAKUDŌ concert hall
9 strokes 奏上 SŌJŌ report to emperor

Somewhat obscure, largely since its old forms vary considerably. An old form  shows **hands offering**  what appears to be a **plant** Ψ (thus making it very similar to offer 奉 1793 q.v.), though some scholars interpret Ψ as a variant of **cow** 牛 97.  has been interpreted as **ten** 十 33 (indicating **many**) and **(big) person** 大 53, to give a meaning of **many persons offering things up** (to a ruler). However, those who take Ψ to be cow take  to be a highly stylised version of **sheep** 𦍌 / 羊 986 q.v., a view supported by another old form , and conclude that the character originally referred to **offering animal sacrifices** (to the gods). In any event, **offer to a high authority** came in time to mean **report to a ruler**, though it is not clear why that which was offered became narrowed to information. **Play an instrument** is felt by some scholars to be a borrowed meaning, by others to derive from the idea of a musical presentation for the benefit of a ruler, and by still others to be an associated meaning, from the fact that the offering of tribute was generally accompanied by a fanfare of musical instruments. Suggest taking 天 as **heaven** 58 and 夫 as **two** 二 61 **big men** 大 53.

Mnemonic: **TWO BIG MEN PLAY HEAVENLY MUSIC**

919 窓 **SŌ, mado** 窓口 MADOGUCHI window
WINDOW 出窓 DEMADO bow window
11 strokes 同窓会 DŌSŌKAI alumni association

Somewhat obscure. Formerly 窻. 囱 derives from a pictograph of a **window with grille** 囱 (the short upper stroke ノ being felt to be a stylistic embellishment), and **hole** 穴 849 was added later for emphasis. At a still later stage **heart/ feeling** 心 147 was added, giving 窻 (also 窗), though its role is unclear. (Some scholars interpret it as 'window of the heart', enforcing the idea of opening up.) Suggest taking 厶 as **nose** 134.

Mnemonic: **NOSE MAKES HOLE IN WINDOW, LEFT FEELING DOWN**

920 SŌ, haji*meru*　　　　　　創造 SŌZŌ　　　　creation
START, WOUND　　　　創立者 SŌRITSUSHA　　founder
12 strokes　　　　　　創い SŌI　　　　　　wound

刂 is **sword/ cut** 181. 倉 is **warehouse** 531 q.v., acting phonetically to express **wound**. It is not clear if 倉 also lends any meaning. (It is unlikely to lend its lesser meaning of **sudden**, since this is a later borrowed meaning, but by association with store-house 蔵 923 q.v. [note shared reading of kura] it may possibly lend loose connotations of **wounded person requiring harboring**.) Thus **wounded with a sword. Start** is a borrowed meaning.

Mnemonic: **FOR A START, PUT SWORD IN WAREHOUSE**

921 SŌ　　　　　　　　下層 KASŌ　　　　lower classes
STRATUM, LAYER　　　　層雲 SŌUN　　　　stratus cloud
14 strokes　　　　　　高層ビル KŌSŌBIRU　skyscraper

Formerly 層 . 尸 is technically **corpse** 236, but acts here as a simplification of **building** 屋 236 (see also 262). 曾/曽 is **build up** 741. Thus **built up building**, indicating a **building of more than one story**. It then came by association to mean **story, layer, stratum,** and so forth. Suggest taking 曽 as **eight** ヽ′ 66, **field** 田 59, and **day** 日 62.

Mnemonic: **LAYERS OF CORPSES BUILD UP IN FIELD OVER EIGHT DAYS**

922 SŌ, misao, ayatsu*ru*　　操縦士 SŌJŪSHI　　　　pilot
HANDLE, CHASTITY　　節操 SESSŌ　　　　integrity
16 strokes　　　　　　操り人形 AYATSURININGYŌ

　　　　　　　　　　　　　　　　　　　　　　　　　puppet

扌 is **hand** 32. 喿 is a CO character meaning **birds chirping**, and shows **three mouths** 口 20 in a **tree** 木 69. Here 喿 acts phonetically to express **take**, and may possibly also lend a loose suggestion of **intensity**. Thus to **take with the hand (firmly?)**. Just like the English term **handle**, this also came to mean **manage/ operate/ control**. **Chastity** is an associated meaning with control, from the idea of restraint. Suggest taking 品 as **three boxes**, and 木 in its meaning of **wooden**.

Mnemonic: **THREE WOODEN BOXES TAKE SOME HANDLING**

291

923

ZŌ, kura
STORE(HOUSE), HARBOR
15 strokes

蔵書 ZŌSHO   one's library
蔵匿 ZŌTOKU   harboring
酒蔵 SAKAGURA   wine cellar

Formerly 藏 . ⺾ is **grass** 9. 疒 is a variant of **sickness** 𡆢 / 疒 381, here indicating **incapacitated**. 臣 is **eye/ guard** 512, here in an extended sense of **protect**, and 戈 is **halberd/ weapon**, here symbolising **wound**. 923 originally referred to **concealing a wounded and incapacitated person with grass**, thereby **protecting** them (from their pursuers). This later extended to mean **put away and look after** in a broad sense, and hence **store** and **harbor**. Suggest taking 厂 as **cliff** 45.

Mnemonic: **STORE AND GUARD HALBERDS UNDER GRASSY CLIFF**

924

ZŌ, harawata
ENTRAILS, VISCERA
19 strokes

臓器 ZŌKI   intestines
内臓 NAIZŌ   viscera
心臓学 SHINZŌGAKU

          cardiology

Flesh/ of the body 月 365 and **store/ harbor** 蔵 923, giving **that stored/ harbored in the body**, i.e. the **viscera/ entrails**.

Mnemonic: **ENTRAILS ARE HARBORED IN BODY**

---

925 俗

ZOKU
WORLDLY, VULGAR,
CUSTOM
9 strokes

俗語 ZOKUGO   slang
俗化 ZOKKA   vulgarisation
風俗 FŪZOKU   customs

亻 is **person** 39. 谷 is **valley** 122 q.v., here acting phonetically to express **transmit (orally)** and possibly also lending connotations of **out of mouths** from its literal elements of a doubling of **out of** 八 66 and **mouth/ opening** 口 20. Thus **that transmitted orally from person to person**, a reference to **common rumors**. This led on the one hand to **worldly** and **vulgar**, and on the other by association to **custom** (i.e. that which is common).

Mnemonic: **VALLEY PEOPLE HAVE VULGAR CUSTOMS**

292

926		SON, ZON	生存 SEIZON	existence
		EXIST, KNOW, THINK 存じ寄り ZONJIYORI		opinion
		6 strokes	存在者 SONZAISHA	a being

Very similar in meaning and etymology to **dam firmly in place/ exist** 在 684 q.v. ← is the same variant of **dam** ォ 126, with **child** 子 25 acting phonetically to express **pile up** to give **piled up dam**, i.e. a dam **firmly in place** and hence the extended meaning of **exist**. Whereas 684 developed connotations of existence in a location 926 came to mean exist in a broader sense. It is not clear how in Japanese it also came to mean **know/ think**.

Mnemonic: **CHILD KNOWS OF EXISTENCE OF FUNNY DAM**

927		SON, tattoi/bu, tōtoi	尊重 SONCHŌ	respect
尊		VALUE, ESTEEM, YOUR 尊王家 SONNŌKA*		royalist
		12 strokes	尊慮 SONRYO	your will

Formerly 尊 and earlier 尊, clearly showing **hands** ᵧᵪ **offering up** (indicating doing something **for a superior**) a **wine jar** 酉 /酉 302. **Out of** ヽ′ 66 was added later to convey the idea of **pouring**, and hands ᵧᵪ were replaced by **hand/ measure** 寸 909 q.v., to lend an idea of careful use of the hands. (According to some scholars, 寸 also acts phonetically to express offer.) Thus to **offer and pour wine (for a superior)**. Some scholars feel that the present meanings are borrowed, but it seems more likely that they are all extended or associated meanings (i.e. pouring wine being a symbol of **respect**, with the use of the character as a **second person honorific** being an associated idea). Note that in Chinese 927 still retains a minor meaning of wine vessel, while in Japanese the addition of wood 木 69 gives the NGU character barrel 樽. Note also that 酋 exists as an NGU character meaning superior or chief, while in Chinese it means fermented liquor.

Mnemonic: **POUR OUT MEASURE OF WINE FOR ESTEEMED GUEST**

928		TAKU	自宅 JITAKU one's own house
		HOUSE, HOME	宅地 TAKUCHI housing land
		6 strokes	お宅 OTAKU you, your home

Once written 宅. ∩/宀 is **roof/ house/ building** 28. 乇 / 乇 is a depiction of a plant whose head and roots are both growing, indicating that it has **taken root**. Some scholars take these elements to act ideographically to express the **building in which one takes root/ settles**, i.e. one's **house/ home**, while others take 乇 to act essentially phonetically to express **open up** (also possibly lending similar connotations from a seed opening up into a growing plant), giving **open up a house**, which was a reference to digging out a hole that was then roofed to provide a primitive troglodytic dwelling (see 15). Suggest taking 乇 as **seven** 七 30 and a **top** ′.

Mnemonic: **SEVEN ROOMED HOUSE WITH ROOF ON TOP**

929

TAN, katsu*gu*, nina*u* 担当 TANTŌ responsibility
CARRY, BEAR 担い商人 NINAIAKINDO* peddler
8 strokes 学習負担 GAKUSHŪFUTAN
study load

Of somewhat confused and obscure etymology. Formerly 擔 and earlier 儋. Both of these now exist as CO characters with similar meanings of **carry a burden**, though 儋 is also used to express a small jar. 儋 is the older character. 扌 is **hand** 32 and 亻 is **person** 39. 詹 is a CO character with a confusing range of meanings, such as verbosity, reach, oversee, suffice, and excellent, and it is also used with some frequency in compounds, though it lends no obvious or consistent meaning. It is of unclear etymology, but an old form 詹 reveals words 㕣/言 274, bending person 𠂈/𠂉 39, and an unknown element 厃/㡿. Here it is known to act phonetically to express **bear/ carry**, thus giving 儋 a meaning of **person carrying something** and 擔 a meaning of **carry something in the hand** (suggesting a smaller load). The modern Japanese form uses the NGU character **dawn** 旦 (literally **sun** 日 62 over the **horizon** 一) as a simple phonetic substitute for 詹, but it should be noted that in Chinese 擔 is still used to mean bear, and that 担 exists as a separate character meaning to dust off (etymology unclear). Suggest taking 日 in its meaning of **day** and 一 as **one** 1.

Mnemonic: **CARRY BURDEN IN HAND FOR ONE WHOLE DAY**

930 探

TAN, sagu*ru*, saga*su* 探知 TANCHI detection
SEARCH, PROBE 探究者 TANKYŪSHA researcher
11 strokes 探り出す SAGURIDASU
search out

Hand 扌 32 and **hand reaching into a hole** 罙 325 q.v., ideographically expressing the idea of **groping about** for something. Hence **search/ probe**. Suggest taking 木 as **tree** 69 and 冖 as a variant of hole 穴 849.

Mnemonic: **HAND PROBES HOLE IN TREE**

931

DAN
STEP, GRADE
9 strokes

段階 DANKAI　　step, grade
段々 DANDAN　　gradually
回り階段 MAWARIKAIDAN
　　　　　　　　spiral stairs

Of disputed etymology. 殳 is **strike with weapon/tool** 153. As a result of an old form 段, 𠬝 is interpreted by some scholars as deriving from a variant 𠂋 of **cliff** 厂 45 that shows **steps** or terracing ⹀ (see also 625), but as a result of a later form 段 it is interpreted by others as deriving from a variant 𠂤 of the prototype 耑 of **bushy plant** 耑 1567 q.v., which is itself of somewhat unclear etymology. Adherents of the cliff theory see 931 as an ideograph meaning to **cut steps in a cliff/ hillside** and hence **step/ grade**. Adherents of the bushy plant theory take 𠂤 to act phonetically to express **beat** as well as lending a meaning of **grain plant**, to give **beat/ thresh grain**. The present meaning of **grade/ step** is then seen as a borrowing. The cliff theory seems the more likely.

Mnemonic: **CUT STEPS BY STRIKING CLIFF**

932

DAN, atatakai/maru/meru
WARM
13 strokes

暖房 DANBŌ　　　　　heater
暖流 DANRYŪ　warm current
暖冬 DANTŌ　　mild winter

日 is **sun** 62. 爰 is an NGU character now meaning **at this point**, but it originally meant **draw up/ draw to oneself**. It comprises **hand reaching down** 爫 303, **hand reaching up** 又, and a **knotted rope** 𠂆 (once 丨), and indicated one person **hauling up** another by means of the knotted rope. Here 爰 acts phonetically to express **warmth**, and almost certainly also lends its meaning of **drawing to oneself**. Thus **(to draw) the warmth of the sun (to oneself)**, later **warm** in a broader sense but usually of ambient temperature rather than warm to the touch. 932 is in fact a later version of the NGU character warm 煖, which uses **fire** 火 8 rather than sun. Suggest taking 𠂆 as a variant of another **hand** 手 32.

Mnemonic: **THREE HANDS WARMING IN THE SUN**

933

CHI, atai, ne
PRICE, VALUE
10 strokes

価値観 KACHIKAN　　values
値段 NEDAN　　　　　price
値引き NEBIKI　　discount

亻 is **person** 39. 直 is **fix/ direct** 349, which acts phonetically to express **equivalent** and probably also lends its meaning of **direct**. Thus a **person (directly?) equivalent (to another)**, conveying the idea that a person is **worth** as much as any other person, and hence **value** and **price**.

Mnemonic: **PERSON HAS FIXED PRICE**

295

934	CHŪ, naka RELATIONSHIP 6 strokes	仲裁 CHŪSAI mediation 仲人 NAKŌDO* go-between 仲良く NAKAYOKU cordially

Person イ 39 and **middle** 中 55, giving **person in the middle** and by extension a **relationship** (involving those parties on either side).

Mnemonic: **PERSON IN MIDDLE MAKES FOR GOOD RELATIONSHIP**

935	CHŪ SPACE, SKY 8 strokes	宇宙船 UCHŪSEN spaceship 宙返り CHŪGAERI somersault 宙乗り CHŪNORI aerial stunt

宀 is **roof** 28. 由 is **reason** 399 q.v., here used in its literal sense of **basket** and by extension conveying the idea of **contain**. Thus **that contained under a roof**, namely the **eaves** and the **space** directly under them. Like eaves/ heaven 宇 811, this came to be applied figuratively to the **firmament/ heaven** and by extension **space/ sky**, but unlike 811 it is now no longer used in its original sense.

Mnemonic: **REASON FOR SPACE UNDER ROOF IS TO LET IN SKY**

936	CHŪ LOYALTY, DEVOTION 8 strokes	忠実 CHŪJITSU na loyal 忠誠 CHŪSEI fidelity 忠告 CHŪKOKU advice

Heart/ feelings 心 147 and **middle/ center** 中 55. Some scholars take these elements to be used ideographically to convey the idea of **that which should be at the center/ core of one's heart**, namely **loyalty/ devotion**. Others take 中 to be used purely phonetically to express **void**, to convey the idea of **making one's heart a void**, i.e. **becoming selfless**, leading by extension to concerning oneself only with others and hence **devotion/ loyalty**. Suggest following the former theory.

Mnemonic: **LOYALTY AND DEVOTION AT CENTER OF ONE'S HEART**

937 CHO, ichijiru*shii*, arawa*su*   著者 CHOSHA   author
NOTABLE, WRITE BOOK   著名 CHOMEI   eminence
11 strokes   名著 MEICHO   masterpiece

Of disputed etymology. Formerly 著 . 艹 is **plants 9**, while 者/者 is **person 298** q.v., here with its connotations of **many and various**. Some scholars feel that 937 is a miscopying of the NGU character chopsticks 箸 , with plants/ grass 艹 being used instead of the latter's bamboo 竹 170. 者 is felt to be used phonetically to express **pluck**, as well as lending its literal connotations of **bits of wood**, to give **bits of bamboo used for plucking**. All the present meanings (including **wear** and **arrive** -- see below) are then seen as borrowings. Other scholars feel that 937 meant from the outset **variety of plants** and hence **profusion of flowers**, and that this in turn gave rise to a range of extended and associated meanings. To **reach a peak of growth** came to mean just **reach**, while **flowers in full bloom** came to mean **bedecked with color** and hence by association **adorn/ put on/ wear**. **Reach** and **wear** are now conveyed by 着 343 q.v., which is a variant of 937. Other meanings included **colorful** and **showy**, giving **prominent** and **notable**. Some scholars take **write a book** to be a borrowed meaning resulting from confusion with SHO **write** 書 142 and/or SHO **sign** 署 897 (the latter itself possibly being a borrowed meaning). However, in Chinese 937 can also mean **show/ display/ manifest**, and it should be noted that in Japanese arawasu (write a book) can mean show/ display/ manifest if a different character is used (379). Thus it seems likely that **write a book** is an extended meaning of **display**, i.e. displaying one's talent and/or views.

Mnemonic: **PERSON WRITES NOTABLE BOOK ABOUT PLANTS**

938 CHŌ   官庁 KANCHŌ   authorities
GOVERNMENT OFFICE,   庁令 CHŌREI   ordinance
AGENCY   環境庁 KANKYŌ CHŌ
5 strokes   Environment Agency

Formerly 廳 . 广 is **(large) building** 114, while 聽 is the old form of **listen carefully/ inquire** 聽 1598. Thus **large building associated with careful inquiry**, i.e. a **government office**. The modern form uses **exact** 丁 346.

Mnemonic: **GOVERNMENT OFFICE IS BUILDING OF EXACTITUDE**

| 939 | | CHŌ, kiza*shi/su*
 SIGN, OMEN, TRILLION
 6 strokes | 兆候 CHŌKŌ
 前兆 ZENCHŌ
 億兆 OKUCHŌ | sign <br> omen <br> zillion |

Once written 汌, showing the **cracks** 汋 appearing on a heated **turtle shell** (, the cracks being **signs** used in divination (see 91). Some scholars take (to be a sign of **separating/ analysing** rather than the shell itself. The shell/ sign of separation (was later doubled to 儿, though this appears unconnected with eight/ away 八 / ハ 66. **Trillion** is a borrowed meaning.

Mnemonic: **TWO CRACKED TURTLE SHELLS SHOW TRILLION SIGNS**

| 940 | 頂 | CHŌ, itadaki, itada*ku*
 RECEIVE, CROWN, TOP
 11 strokes | 頂点 CHŌTEN
 頂上 CHŌJŌ
 頂だい CHŌDAI | apex <br> summit <br> receiving, please |

頁 is **head** 93. 丁 is **exact/ nail** 346 q.v., here acting phonetically to express **top** and possibly also lending similar connotations through its depiction of a **nail** with a prominent **head/ top**. 940 originally referred to the **top/ crown of the head**, then came to mean **top/ peak** in general. The verb itadaku originally meant to **be crowned** with something, with **receive** being an extended meaning.

Mnemonic: **RECEIVE NAIL EXACTLY THROUGH TOP OF HEAD**

| 941 | | CHŌ, shio
 TIDE, SEAWATER
 15 strokes | 潮流 CHŌRYŪ
 潮水 SHIOMIZU
 潮時 SHIODOKI | tide, current <br> seawater <br> good chance |

朝 is **morning** 175 q.v., used in its literal sense of **rising waters**. Water 氵 40 was added after 175 lost its original meaning. 175 technically referred to a rising river, whereas 941 is generally applied to **tide** and by association **seawater**.

Mnemonic: **SEAWATER RISES WITH MORNING TIDE**

| 942 | | CHIN
 WAGES, FEE
 13 strokes | 賃金 CHINGIN
 運賃 UNCHIN
 家賃 YACHIN | wages <br> fare, freight <br> house rent |

貝 is **shell/ money** 90. 任 is **entrust** 764 q.v., here used in its literal sense of **person carrying a load**. 942 originally meant **money paid to person for carrying load**, i.e. porterage, and then came to mean **fee/ wages** in a general sense.

Mnemonic: **ENTRUST WITH WAGES MONEY**

298

---

943 TSŪ, ita*i/mu/meru* | 頭痛 ZUTSŪ headache
PAIN, PAINFUL | 痛手 ITADE bad wound
12 strokes | 痛切 TSŪSETSU na poignant

疒 is **sickness** 381, here indicating **affliction**. 甬 is **burst through** 176, acting phonetically to express **penetrate/ pass through** and also lending similar connotations of **pierce**. Thus a **piercing pain that afflicts one, passing through (the body)**. Now **pain** in general. Suggest remembering 甬 by association with **pass through** 通 176.

Mnemonic: **PAIN PASSES THROUGH SICK BODY**

---

944 **TEN** | 発展 HATTEN development
EXPAND, SPREAD, | 展覧会 TENRANKAI exhibition
DISPLAY | 展望 TENBŌ outlook
10 strokes

Once written 𡱕, showing **slumped figure/ buttocks** ⼹/尸 236, here indicating **sitting, clothes** 𠆢/衣 420, here meaning **cloth**, and **four tiles/ bricks** 𨑒, here indicating **weight(s)**. 944 originally referred to **sitting heavily on a piece of cloth as it is being spread out**, and later came to mean **spread** and **display** in a broad sense. Suggest taking ⼗⼗ as **grass** 9 and 𧘇 as a **'short'** version of **clothes** 衣, i.e. **shorts**.

Mnemonic: **SLUMPED FIGURE IN SHORTS SPREAD OUT ON GRASS**

---

945 TŌ, *utsu* | 討議 TŌGI debate
ATTACK, (TO) DEFEAT 討ち入る UCHIIRU raid
10 strokes | 討伐軍 TŌBATSUGUN
| punitive force

言 is **words** 274. 寸 is **hand/ measure** 909 q.v., here acting phonetically to express **censure** and probably also lending connotations of **acting carefully**. 945 originally meant to **make a (careful?) verbal attack** on someone, and then came to mean **attack** in general, usually with connotations of **defeating**.

Mnemonic: **ATTACK AND DEFEAT WITH MEASURED WORDS**

299

946 TŌ 　　　　　政党 SEITŌ 　　political party
PARTY, FACTION 　　労働党 RŌDŌTŌ 　Labor Party
10 strokes 　　　　　　党派 TŌHA 　　　faction

Formerly 黨. 黑 is the early form of **black** 黒 124 q.v., probably used here in its literal sense of **blackened window**. 尚 is furthermore 1392 q.v., here acting phonetically to express **cover** and probably also lending an idea of **window in a building** from its element 向. Thus to **cover something with blackness** (literally **building with blackened windows?**), a reference to **doing things in a clandestine fashion**. **Faction/ party** is an associated meaning. Suggest taking 党 as **elder brother** 兄 267 and **fancy roof** ⺌ (see 28 and 10).

Mnemonic: **ELDER BROTHER'S FACTION MEETS UNDER FANCY ROOF**

---

947 TŌ 　　　　　砂糖 SATŌ 　　　　sugar
SUGAR 　　　　　糖衣 TŌI 　　　sugar coating
16 strokes 　　　　　糖分 TŌBUN 　sugar content

米 is **rice** 201. 唐 is **Tang China** 1645 q.v., here acting phonetically to express **dry/ heat** and probably also lending its literal connotations of **pound**. Thus **heated (and pounded?) rice**, a reference to a form of **sweet confectionery**. It later came to be used of **sugar**.

Mnemonic: **RICE FROM TANG CHINA LOOKS LIKE SUGAR**

---

948 届 todo*ku/keru* 　　　　届け書 TODOKESHO 　　report
DELIVER, REPORT 　　届け出る TODOKEDERU 　notify
8 strokes 　　　　　　行き届く YUKITODOKU
　　　　　　　　　　　　　　　　　　　　be attentive

Formerly 屆. 尸 is **slumped person/ corpse** 236, here indicating a **sick/ injured person**. 凷 is formed from **earth** 土 (variant 圡 60, and not samurai 士 494) in a **container** 凵, indicating a **dead and inert weight**. 凷 also acts phonetically to express **move slowly**. 948 originally referred to a **sick/ injured person moving along slowly**. Some scholars take its present meanings to be borrowed, others see them as deriving from move slowly, namely move slowly but surely and eventually **reach**, with **deliver** being a transitive form of reach and **report** being an associated meaning. Suggest taking 由 as **reason** 399.

Mnemonic: **DELIVER CORPSE AND REPORT REASON**

949 難	NAN, muzukashii, katai	難民 NANMIN	refugees
	DIFFICULT, TROUBLE	難儀 NANGI	trouble
	18 strokes	見難い MIGATAI	hard to see

Obscure. Formerly 難. 隹 is **bird** 216. 堇/菫 is the obscure element seen in 漢 442 q.v., and has been interpreted variously as a variant of 董, which is itself an obscure element that has been interpreted by some scholars as a **beast being roasted** (see 勤 842), and as a variant of **yellow/ flaming arrow** 堇/黄 120. In view of the fact that in Chinese 949 is still listed as having a meaning of **bird with golden plumage**, which is known to have been its original meaning (though the exact name of the bird is unclear), the latter interpretation seems more likely. It is also not clear how it came to mean **difficult/ trouble**, but these are assumed to be borrowed meanings. Suggest remembering by association with a **'waterless' Han China** 漢 442 (氵 being water 40).

Mnemonic: **BIRD IN TROUBLE IN WATERLESS HAN CHINA**

950 弐	NI	弐万円 NIMANEN	20,000 yen
	TWO	弐拾 NIJŪ	twenty
	6 strokes	弐千 NISEN	two thousand

Formerly also 貳, though this is technically a separate character. 弐 derives from 弍, showing an ideographic combination of **two** 二 61 and **stake** 弋 177 q.v., the latter being used as a simplification of **halberd** 戈 493, to give **two stakes/ halberds** and hence just **two**. 貳 adds shell/ money 貝 90 as a phonetic element to express **double**, thereby reinforcing the concept of **two**. Note in passing that an early form of 貳, 𢎜, shows broad-bladed halberd 㦰/戉 515 and clearly illustrates the overlap between stake and the various forms of halberd.

Mnemonic: **TWO STAKE-LIKE HALBERDS**

951 乳	NYŪ, chichi, chi	牛乳 GYŪNYŪ	(cow's) milk
	BREASTS, MILK	乳酸 NYŪSAN	lactic acid
	8 strokes	乳房 NYŪBŌ/ CHIBUSA	
			breasts

Popularly explained as a **child** 子 25 **reaching** 𤓰 303 for a **breast** し. A useful mnemonic, but incorrect. While 𤓰 is indeed **reaching hand**, 孔 is **hole** 1241 q.v., here in its literal sense of **child-producing hole/ vagina**. 951 originally meant **manually assist in removing a child from the vagina**. Its present meanings are felt by some scholars to be borrowed, but it seems more likely that they derive from a core concept of **looking after an infant**, and it is possible that the semantic evolution was also influenced by a longstanding misinterpretation of し as a pictograph of a breast (giving the popular interpretation outlined above).

Mnemonic: **CHILD REACHES FOR BREAST SWOLLEN WITH MILK**

952

NIN, mito*meru*
RECOGNISE, APPRECIATE
14 strokes

認識 NINSHIKI   cognition
認可 NINKA   approval
認め印 MITOMEIN   signet

Formerly 認 . 言 is **words** 274. 忍/忍 is **endure** 1677. To **endure someone's words** leads by extension to the idea of **recognition** and **appreciation** of what they are saying. Some scholars feel that 忍 also acts phonetically to express **approve**. Suggest taking 忍 literally as **blade** 刃 1446 and **heart** 心 147.

Mnemonic: **WORDS OF APPRECIATION AS BLADE REACHES HEART!?**

953

納

NŌ, NA, NATSU, TŌ, osa*meru*
OBTAIN, STORE, SUPPLY
10 strokes

納税 NŌZEI   tax payment
納屋 NAYA   shed, barn
出納簿 SUITŌBO*   account book

Formerly 納 . 糸 is **thread** 27, here meaning **cloth**. 内/内 is **inside** 364 q.v., here in its literal sense of **enter a building**. A **building which cloth enters** was a reference to a **store(house)**, with **obtain** and **supply** being associated meanings. See also 703. There is an alternative theory to the effect that 内 acts purely phonetically to express **wet**, giving **wet threads**, with the present meanings being borrowed. This does not seem especially convincing.

Mnemonic: **STORE OBTAINED THREADS INSIDE, READY TO RESUPPLY**

954

脳

NŌ
BRAIN
11 strokes

頭脳 ZUNŌ   brain
主脳 SHUNŌ   leader
脳障害 NŌSHŌGAI   brain injury

Formerly 腦 and earlier 惱. 甾 is **brain** 131. 巛 is **hair**, combining with 甾 to give a meaning to 甾 of **head**. ヒ is **spoon/ scoop** 910. Some scholars feel that this acts phonetically to express **flesh/ fat**, to give **fleshy/ fatty part of the head** and thus **brain** (with the later **flesh/ of the body** 月 365 then being taken as **flesh**). However, it is by no means convincing that fleshy/ fatty part of the head connotes brain, and it seems far more likely that ヒ acts literally to give **that part of the head which is scooped out**, i.e. the **brain(s)**. Brains have long been a delicacy in China, and were traditionally eaten 'in situ', i.e. by being scooped out from a skull at the table. The later 月 would then act in its meaning of **of the body**, to focus on the brain within the body as opposed to as a food dish. Suggest taking ｀ as **hair**, ✕ as a **cross**, and 凵 as a **box** (cf. English slang brain-box).

Mnemonic: **BODY'S BRAIN-BOX MARKED BY CROSS AND HAIRS**

955 HA
FACTION, SEND
9 strokes

派遣 HAKEN   despatch
立派 RIPPA na   splendid
田中派 TANAKAHA

Tanaka faction

Tributary 𣲖 589 reinforced by **water/ river** 氵 40. Though tributaries flow <u>into</u> a larger body, the idea of convergence merged with that of divergence, leading to the idea of **branching/ splitting** and thus **faction. Send** is an associated meaning.

Mnemonic: **FACTION IS LIKE TRIBUTARY RELATIVE TO RIVER**

---

956 拝 HAI, oga*mu*
WORSHIP, RESPECTFUL
8 strokes

礼拝 REIHAI   worship
拝見 HAIKEN   looking
拝具 HAIGU   Yours faithfully

Somewhat obscure. Early forms such as 𥫗 show **hand** 屮 / 扌 32 and what appears to be a **thickly growing rice plant/ grain plant** 釆 (variant 米 / 禾 81). Thus a **hand offering a token from the harvest** (as part of a **religious act**), with **worship** and **respectful** being derived meanings. Some scholars interpret 釆 as intestines 𢆶 hanging from a tree 木 69, though this also was part of a religious ceremony and thus results in the same semantic evolution. There is also a theory that 釆 is used phonetically to express **line up**, giving **line up hands**, which is taken as a reference to **praying**. The first theory seems the most helpful. Suggest remembering 羊 as an **eight-leaved plant**.

Mnemonic: **HAND OFFERS EIGHT-LEAVED PLANT IN WORSHIP**

---

957 HAI, se, sei, somu*ku*/*keru*
BACK, STATURE, DEFY
9 strokes

背後 HAIGO   background
背中 SENAKA   back
背信 HAISHIN   betrayal

Meat/ of the body 月 365 and **north** 北 205, the latter acting in its literal sense of persons sitting **back to back**. Thus **back of the body**. Now also used of **stature**, and in the sense of **turn one's back/ defy**.

Mnemonic: **TURN BACK DEFIANTLY ON MEAT FROM THE NORTH**

958 肺

HAI
LUNG(S)
9 or 8 strokes

肺病 HAIBYŌ　lung disease
肺炎 HAIEN　pneumonia
肺臓 HAIZŌ　lungs

Once written 㸽. 夕/月 is flesh/ of the body 365. 朿 depicts a growing plant (to all intents and purposes a 'droopy-leaved' variant of growing plant 屮/生 42), and acts here phonetically to express expel as well as lending its own connotations of emerge. Thus that which is expelled from the body, a reference to breath. By association it later came to refer to that part of the body from which breath is expelled, i.e. the lungs. Suggest taking 市 as city 130.

Mnemonic: **BODIES IN CITIES HAVE BAD LUNGS**

959 俳

HAI
AMUSEMENT, ACTOR
10 strokes

俳優 HAIYŪ　actor
俳句 HAIKU　haiku poetry
俳人 HAIJIN　haiku poet

Person 亻 39 and not/ spread wings 非 773 q.v. Numerous theories exist as to the interpretation of these elements, of which two related theories seem particularly plausible. The first is that 959 originally meant 'non-person'/ outcast (note that when used as individual characters the same elements give HININ non-person 非人), and that, as in Europe (until recently), outcasts were associated with acting and other forms of entertainment/ amusement. The second agrees that the original meaning was non-person, but takes this rather in the sense of deformed person, largely because 非 is also felt to act phonetically to express ugly. As in medieval Europe, deformed persons were often employed as jesters, leading to both amusement and actor.

Mnemonic: **NON-PERSON IS AN AMUSING ACTOR**

960 班

HAN
SQUAD, GROUP, ALLOT
10 strokes

班長 HANCHŌ　group leader
救護班 KYŪGOHAN relief squad
班田 HANDEN
farmland allotment

玨 is a doubling of jewel 102, thus indicating many/ various jewels. 刂 is sword/ cut 181, here in the sense of divide. 960 originally referred to a ruler dividing up jewels (tribute) and allotting them to various nobles. This came to mean allot on the one hand and division on the other, with section/ group being an associated meaning.

Mnemonic: **SQUAD RECEIVES A CUT OF THE JEWELS**

304

961
BAN
EVENING, LATE
12 strokes

晩飯 BANMESHI evening meal
晩夏 BANKA late summer
今晩 KONBAN this evening

日 is **sun/ day** 62, here in an extended sense of **light**. 免 is **escape** 1849 q.v., here acting phonetically to express **obscure(d)** and also lending connotations of **striving with difficulty** to do something (from its literal meaning of a woman striving to give birth). Thus **striving with difficulty (to see) when the sun/ light is obscure**, a reference to **evening**. **Late** is an associated meaning.

Mnemonic: **SUN ESCAPES EVERY EVENING**

962
HI, ina, ina*mu*
NO, DECLINE, DENY
7 strokes

否認 HININ denial
否定語 HITEIGO negative
否めない INAMENAI undeniable

口 is **mouth/say** 20. 不 is **not** 572 q.v., which also lends its sound **FU** (the original reading of 962) as a sound of **denial/ negation**. Thus to **say the negative sound FU**.

Mnemonic: **DENY, SAYING NOT SO**

963
HI
CRITICISE,STRIKE,PASS
7 strokes

批判 HIHAN criticism
批評 HIHYŌ commentary
批准 HIJUN ratification

扌 is **hand** 32. 比 is **compare** 771 q.v., acting phonetically to express **strike** and possibly also lending an idea of **both together**. Thus to **strike with (both?) hand(s)**. This is now a very minor meaning in Japanese, though somewhat more common in Chinese. Strike came to mean **attack**, leading by figurative extension to **criticise**. **Pass/ endorse** (a very minor meaning in Japanese, but reasonably major in Chinese) is seen as a further extension, from the idea of critically examining something.

Mnemonic: **CRITICISM CAN INVOLVE A HANDY COMPARISON**

964
HI, hi*meru*
(KEEP) SECRET
10 strokes

秘密 HIMITSU secret
極秘 GOKUHI top secret
秘書 HISHO secretary

Formerly 祕. 示 is **altar/ of the gods** 695. 必 is **necessarily** 568 q.v., here acting phonetically to express **hide** and probably lending similar connotations of **concealment** from its literal meaning of encased halberd. Thus **hidden things of the gods**, i.e. **mystical secrets**, and now **secret** in a broad sense. The modern use of **rice plant** 禾 81 is almost certainly the result of miscopying.

Mnemonic: **RICE PLANT NECESSARILY KEPT SECRET**

965 腹 FUKU, hara
BELLY, GUTS
13 strokes

腹部 FUKUBU   abdomen
腹立ち HARADACHI   anger
中腹 CHŪFUKU   mid-slope

月 is flesh/ of the body 365. 复 is go back/ reverse 782 q.v., here used phonetically to express **bulge** and also felt by some scholars to lend connotations of a **central container with limbs either side** (from its literal meaning of reversible food container of that shape). Thus the **bulging central container of the body**, i.e. the **belly**. As with the English slang term **guts**, it is also used to indicate courage and resolve. Suggest taking 复 as **person** ⼏ 39, **sun** 日 62, and **sitting crosslegged** 夂.

Mnemonic: **PERSON SITS CROSSLEGGED, FLESHY BELLY IN SUN**

966 奮 FUN, furu*u*
BE EXCITED, STIR
16 strokes

奮起 FUNKI   stirring
奮闘 FUNTŌ   hard fight
奮い立つ FURUITATSU   be stirred

田 is **field** 59. 奞 is a CO character meaning **big stride**, but technically **big** 大 53 is a miscopying of **clothing** 衣 420. This combined with **bird** 隹 216 to give a meaning of **clothing flapping like a bird in flight**, hence a person walking quickly. Here, however, it lends an idea rather of **birds flapping in flight**, and also acts phonetically to express **fly**. 966 originally referred to **birds taking off from a field with much flapping**, indicating that they have been frightened/ **roused**, and hence the present meanings.

Mnemonic: **BIG BIRD STIRS, FLYING EXCITEDLY FROM FIELD**

967 陛 HEI
MAJESTY, THRONE
10 strokes

陛下 HEIKA   Majesty
陛見 HEIKEN   audience
天皇陛下 TENNŌ HEIKA *
    His Majesty the Emperor

阝 is **terraced hill** 229, here indicating **steps**. 坒 is a CO character now meaning **compare**, but it originally referred to a succession of hillocks/ terraces, comprising **compare/ in a row** 比 771 and **earth/ ground** 土 60. Here it lends a meaning of **in a row**, giving a **row of terraces/ steps**. By association this was applied to the **steps leading to a throne**, and by extension to the **throne** and its **encumbent**, i.e. the **emperor** and hence **majesty**. Note in passing that the seemingly inappropriate use of below/ bottom 下 7 in the term HEIKA/ majesty stems from the fact that most persons granted an audience with the emperor did not in fact speak directly with the emperor but with his advisers, who were positioned at the foot of the steps to the throne. Thus heika literally means those at the foot of the steps, but eventually came to represent the emperor himself.

Mnemonic: **HIS MAJESTY'S THRONE COMPARES TO EARTHEN HILL**

968

HEI, to*jiru*, shi*maru/meru* 閉店 HEITEN   closing store
CLOSE, SHUT 閉口 HEIKŌ   dumbfounded
11 strokes 閉め出す SHIMEDASU   shut out

門 is **door/ gate** 211. 才 is **talent** 126 q.v.; here used in its literal sense of **dam** and by extension **barrier**. Thus **barred gate**, leading to **shut** and **close**. Suggest taking 才 as a **cross** 十 with **prop** ✓ .

Mnemonic: **CLOSE GATE WITH PROPPED CROSS**

969

HEN, kata 断片 DANPEN   fragment
ONE SIDE, PIECE 片手 KATATE   one hand
4 strokes 片付ける KATAZUKERU   tidy up

A pictograph of a **tree** 出 / 木 69 **cut in half**, giving **one side** and also **(cut) piece**. See also 1389.

Mnemonic: **ONE SIDE OF A TREE IS SOME PIECE!**

970

HO, ogina*u* 補助 HOJO   support
MAKE GOOD, STOPGAP 補充 HOJŪ   supplementation
12 strokes 補強 HOKYŌ   reinforcement

衤 is **clothing** 420. 甫 is an NGU character meaning **begin**. It was originally written 𤰇, showing **use** 𤰇 / 用 215 and a **hand holding a tool** 又 (actually known to be an ax, though in practice to all intents and purposes a variant of hand holding stick 又101/197), and meant **start to use an ax** and later **start work** and just **start/ begin**. In compounds it often lends connotations of **hasty work** and by extension **temporary work**. Here it lends such connotations as well as lending its sound to express **patch**. 970 originally referred to the hasty repairing of clothing by **patching**, and then came to mean **stopgap** and **make good** in a broader sense (particularly supplement and compensate). Suggest taking 十 as **needle** 十 33 and **point** ヽ .

Mnemonic: **USE NEEDLE POINT TO MAKE GOOD TORN CLOTHES**

---

971 宝

HŌ, takara 宝石 HŌSEKI   jewel
TREASURE 財宝 ZAIHŌ   riches
8 strokes 子宝 KODAKARA   children

Formerly 寶 . 宀 is **roof/ house/ building** 28. 王/玉 is **jewel** 102. 貝 is **shell/ money/ precious item** 90. 缶 is **can** 1095 q.v., here lending its literal idea of **(securely) contain**. Thus **building securely containing jewels and other precious items**. Eventually building faded, leaving just **treasure**.

Mnemonic: **TREASURE HOUSE CONTAINS JEWELS**

972 訪	HŌ, otozu*reru*, tazu*neru* VISIT, INQUIRE 11 strokes	訪問 HŌMON 来訪者 RAIHŌSHA 探訪 TANBŌ	visit visitor inquiry

言 is words/ speak 274. 方 is side/ direction 204, here acting phonetically to express ask widely and possibly also lending an idea of line. 972 originally referred to asking widely in order to follow a line of inquiry. This involved visiting many people. Visit has come to prevail as the major meaning, while tazuneru in the sense of inquire is now usually (but not always) expressed by 1451.

Mnemonic: **VISIT SOMEONE TO HAVE WORDS ON THE SIDE**

973 亡	BŌ, MŌ, nai/*kunaru* DIE, ESCAPE, LOSE 3 strokes	死亡 SHIBŌ 亡者 MŌJA 亡命 BŌMEI	death deceased exile

Once written and 亡, showing person 人 / 人 / 人 39 and a corner ∟ 349, here indicating concealment. It originally meant a person no longer able to be seen, and referred to escaping. It later also came to mean lose and die, from the idea of no longer being visible/ actively present.

Mnemonic: **DEAD PERSON LOST IN CORNER**

974 忘	BŌ, wasu*reru* FORGET, LEAVE BEHIND 7 strokes	忘却 BŌKYAKU forgetfulness 忘恩 BŌON ingratitude 忘れ勝ち WASUREGACHI forgetful

心 is heart 147. 亡 is die 973 q.v., here used in a sense of no longer actively present. Thus that which is no longer actively present in the heart, i.e. something forgotten.

Mnemonic: **"DEAD IN ONE'S HEART" MEANS FORGOTTEN**

975 棒	BŌ POLE, BAR, CLUB 12 strokes	心棒 SHINBŌ 棒グラフ BŌGURAFU 棒紅 BŌBENI	axle, shaft bar graph lipstick

木 is tree/ wood 69. 奉 is offer up 1793 q.v., here acting phonetically to express staff as well as lending its literal meaning of hold something in both hands. Thus wooden staff held in both hands, i.e. a large pole or club. Suggest taking 夫 as big 大 53 plus two 二 61, and 丰 as a club with nails through it.

Mnemonic: **TWO BIG WOODEN CLUBS WITH NAILS THROUGH**

976

MAI	一 枚 ICHIMAI	one sheet
SHEET COUNTER	二 枚 舌 NIMAIJITA	duplicity
8 strokes	二 枚 貝 NIMAIGAI	bivalve

攵 is **hand holding stick** 101, with attention drawn to the stick itself by the addition of **wood** 木 69. The original meaning was **wooden stick**, and it was also used for **counting wooden sticks** (still very occasionally found in this meaning). It is not fully clear how it later came to be used as a **counter for thin flat objects**, but some scholars feel that it may stem from the fact that 976 was particularly used to refer to a special thin flat stick used for goading horses.

Mnemonic: **HAND HOLDS THIN FLAT WOODEN STICK FOR COUNTING**

977

MAKU, BAKU	天 幕 TENMAKU	curtain, tent
CURTAIN, TENT, ACT	開 幕 KAIMAKU	opening scene
13 strokes	幕 府 BAKUFU	Shogunate

巾 is **threads/ cloth** 778. 莫 is sun sinking among plants 788 q.v., here lending its meaning of **conceal**. Some scholars feel that 莫 also acts phonetically to express **conceal**. Thus **cloth which conceals**, a reference to a **curtain**. **Tent** is an associated meaning. **Act** is also an associated meaning, from the curtain long associated with the theater. Note that since 'tent government' was a reference to the **Shogunate**, 977 itself is sometimes used to refer to the Shogunate. Suggest taking 莫 as **grass** 艹 9, **sun** 日 62, and **big** 大 (variant 大 53).

Mnemonic: **BIG CURTAIN OF THREADED GRASS SHADES OUT SUN**

978

MITSU, hiso*ka*	密 度 MITSUDO	density
DENSE, SECRET	密 輸 MITSUYU	smuggling
11 strokes	綿 密 MENMITSU na	detailed

山 is **mountain** 24. 宓 is a CO character meaning both **quiet** and **stop**. It comprises **building** 宀 28, here meaning **temple**, and **necessarily** 必 568 q.v., here acting phonetically to express **comb** and also lending an idea of being **tightly packed** from its literal meaning of packed and bound halberd. Thus 宓 originally referred to **temples tightly 'packed' together in a cluster like teeth in a comb**. This presented an effective barrier to the outside world (hence stop), and was a place associated with **otherworldliness** and **quietness**. When combined with mountain 山 the meaning became one of **mountains clustered tightly/ densely together**, forming a mysterious and impenetrable (i.e. **secretive**) domain. Hence the present meanings of **dense** and **secret**. It also has connotations of **hushed**.

Mnemonic: **BUILDING IN DENSE MOUNTAINS NECESSARILY SECRET**

979	盟	MEI ALLIANCE, PLEDGE 13 strokes	連盟 RENMEI	federation
			同盟 DŌMEI	alliance
			加盟 KAMEI	affiliation

Once written and , showing that **blood** 皿 / 血 270 and **dish/ bowl** 皿/血 1307 have long been interchanged. The present form uses bowl though in fact blood is the more appropriate. The old forms show that 日 derives from ⊘, an element felt to show a **mouth and teeth** and indicating **taking in through the mouth** (possibly a variant of mortar ⊟ 648). 979 originally meant to **sup blood from a bowl**, which was a symbol of **making a pledge** and by association **forming an alliance**. It seems likely that the later addition ⼣ was originally intended to show **meat** ⼣ / 月 365, to emphasise the idea of blood, but it appears to have become confused with **moon** ⼣ / 月 16, almost certainly under the influence of **bright** 明 208. (The latter properly has an old form ⊙⼣, being an ideograph combining sun ⊙ / 日 62 with moon ⼣ / 月 , though some scholars feel that a character ⊘⼣ existed as a virtual variant, with ⊘ acting phonetically to express shine brightly to give brightly shining moon.) Suggest taking 明 as **bright**.

Mnemonic: **BRIGHT ALLIANCE PLEDGED OVER BOWL OF BLOOD**

980	模	MO, BO COPY, MODEL, MOLD 14 strokes	模型 MOKEI	model, mold
			模写 MOSHA	copy, copying
			規模 KIBO	scale

木 is **tree/ wood** 69. 莫 is sun sinking among plants (variant 莫 788 q.v.), here acting phonetically to express **standard** and possibly also lending an idea of envelop / **enclose**. 980 originally referred to a **wooden mold/ frame that ensured standardisation** (of those items that it **enclosed**?). **Model** and **copy** are associated meanings. Suggest taking 莫 as **plant** 艹 9, **sun** 日 62, and **big** 大 53.

Mnemonic: **PLANT COPIES MODEL TREE AND GROWS BIG IN SUN**

981	矢	ya, SHI ARROW 5 strokes	矢先 YASAKI	arrowhead, point
			矢印 YAJIRUSHI	arrow mark
			一矢 ISSHI	return shot, riposte

From a pictograph of an **arrow**. There was a range of such pictographs, such as , and the highly stylised and somewhat confusing 夨. Some appear to show exaggerated tailfeathers, some material bound to the shaft, and others material bound to the tip. The modern form probably derives from the stylised 夨. Suggest remembering by association with **big** 大 53, taking ├ as a **broken tip** (𐐣).

Mnemonic: **BIG ARROW WITH BROKEN TIP**

982		YAKU, wake	翻訳 HONYAKU	translation
		TRANSLATION,MEANING	通訳 TSŪYAKU	interpreting
		11 strokes	言い訳 IIWAKE	excuse

Formerly 譯. 言 is **words** 274. 睪 is eye watching prisoners 233 q.v., here acting phonetically to express **change** and probably also lending an idea of **link/ succession**. Thus to **change words (in a linked succession?)**, i.e. to **translate**. **Meaning** is an associated idea. Suggest taking the modern form 尺 as **person** 人 39 with a **pack/ load** on their back フ.

Mnemonic: **PERSON TRANSLATING CARRIES A LOAD OF WORDS**

983		YŪ	郵便 YŪBIN	mail
		MAIL, RELAY STATION	郵送 YŪSŌ	mailing
		11 strokes	郵亭 YŪTEI	relay station

阝 is **village** 355. 垂 is **dangle/ hang down** 907, acting phonetically to express **billowing flag** and possibly also lending connotations of **hanging**. 983 originally referred to a **relay station** on a messenger route, such a place being indicated by a flag (that was hung there and billowed). Messages were often written on the flag. It then came to mean **communication** in a general sense, and **mail** in modern times.

Mnemonic: **MAIL IN VILLAGE LEFT DANGLING**

984		YŪ, yasashii, sugureru	優秀 YŪSHŪ	excellence
		SUPERIOR, GENTLE,	優先 YŪSEN	priority
		ACTOR	女優 JOYŪ	actress
		17 strokes		

亻 is **person** 39. 憂 is **grief** 1871 q.v., here acting phonetically to express **dance with gestures** and also lending its own connotations of **moving slowly**. 984 originally referred to a **dancer performing a slow ritual dance**, then came to mean **actor**. Some scholars take **superior** and **gentle** to be borrowed meanings, but it seems more likely that they derive from the idea of a masterful performance of a slow and dignified ritual dance.

Mnemonic: **GENTLE ACTOR'S SUPERIOR DISPLAY OF PERSON'S GRIEF**

985		YŌ, osana*i* INFANCY 5 strokes	幼児 YŌJI 幼時 YŌJI 幼子 OSANAGO	infant infancy infant

幺 is **short thread** 111, here meaning **tiny/ little/ limited**. 力 is **strength** 74. Of **little strength** was a reference to a **young child/ infant**.

Mnemonic: **INFANT SHORT ON STRENGTH, LIKE TINY THREAD**

986		YŌ, hitsuji SHEEP 6 strokes	羊皮 YŌHI 羊水 YŌSUI 羊飼い HITSUJIKAI	sheepskin amniotic fluid shepherd

Stylised derivative of a pictograph of a **sheep's head and horns** 芊 (later 羊). In compounds usually found as 芏. Often lends connotations of **fine/ praiseworthy**, since a sheep was a prized animal. Suggest remembering in particular the **three cross-strokes** 三, taking them as **stripes**.

Mnemonic: **SHEEP WITH FINE HORNS MARKED WITH THREE STRIPES**

987		YOKU, ho*shii* GREED, DESIRE 11 strokes	欲望 YOKUBŌ 食欲 SHOKUYOKU 物欲しげ MONOHOSHIGE	desire appetite wistful

欠 is **lack** 471 q.v., here in its literal sense of **person with gaping mouth**. 谷 is **valley** 122 q.v., acting phonetically to express **continuous** and almost certainly also lending connotations of **big receptacle** and thereby reinforcing 欠. Thus **person with continuously gaping mouth**, symbolising a **person constantly desiring food** and hence **greedy**, with **desire** being an associated meaning. Some scholars feel that 谷 actually serves a double phonetic role in that it also expresses **cereal**, symbolising **food** and thus clarifying the meaning of gaping mouth.

Mnemonic: **GREEDY PERSON LACKS VALLEY SO DESIRES ONE**

988		YOKU NEXT (OF TIME) 11 strokes	翌日 YOKUJITSU 翌朝 YOKUCHŌ 翌翌年 YOKUYOKUNEN	next day next morning two years later

羽 is **wings** 812. 立 is **stand/ rise/ leave** 73, here acting phonetically to express **fly** and also lending an idea of **rise and leave**. 988 originally referred to a **bird flying off**. Its present meaning is borrowed, though it may be helpful to think of it as a figurative reference to the **wings of time** (not unlike the Japanese 'version' of day 曜 216, q.v.).

Mnemonic: **WINGS OF TIME LEAVE, TILL THE NEXT TIME**

312

989 **RAN, mida*reru/su***
DISORDER, RIOT
7 strokes

乱暴 RANBŌ   violence
反乱 HANRAN   rebellion
乱れ足 MIDAREASHI out of step

Formerly 亂. 矞 is **hands untying tangled threads** 500, symbolising **putting in order/ bringing under control.** ∟ is **person kneeling** 413, symbolising a **person being made to submit.** 989 originally referred to **bringing rebellious persons to submission** and thus **bringing a disturbance under control.** For some reason, however, the idea of **disturbance** and **disorder** prevailed, and in Japanese has now entirely replaced the idea of bringing under control. Somewhat confusingly, both meanings co-exist in Chinese, with 989 able to mean both bring about order and bring about disorder, but the latter is overwhelmingly the major meaning. Suggest taking 舌 as **tongue** 732.

Mnemonic: **KNEELING FIGURE PUTS TONGUE OUT -- LEADS TO RIOT**

---

990 **RAN, tamago**
EGG, ROE
7 strokes

卵黄 RANŌ   yolk
産卵 SANRAN   spawning
生卵 NAMATAMAGO raw egg

Somewhat obscure. For many centuries an early form 卯卩 has been interpreted as a stylised depiction of either **fish eggs** or **frogspawn.** However, some scholars now believe this to be a variant of **treadle** 卯 444, along with another early form 卯卩. **Egg/ roe** is then taken to be a purely borrowed meaning.

Mnemonic: **ANGULAR BACK-TO-BACK FISH EGGS?!**

---

991 **RAN**
SEE, LOOK
17 strokes

御覧 GORAN   look, try
回覧 KAIRAN   circulation
観覧 KANRAN   inspection

Formerly 覽. 臨 is **watch over** 1111, here meaning just **look/ watch,** and 見 is **look/ see** 18. Thus **look and see.** It is not clear why such an apparently unnecessary character should have evolved, especially in view of the complexity of its strokes. Suggest taking 臣 as **staring eye** 512, and ⺊ as **person** ⼃ 39 and **one** — 1.

Mnemonic: **PERSON WITH ONE STARING EYE SEES ALL**

313

992		**RI, ura**	裏面	RIMEN	inside, back
		REVERSE SIDE, REAR,	裏毛	URAKE	fleece lining
		INSIDE, LINING	裏付ける	URAZUKERU	back up
		13 strokes			

Formerly also 裡. ネ/ 衤/衣 is **clothing** 420. 里 is **village** 219, used purely phonetically to express **inside/ reverse side**. 992 originally referred to the **inside/ reverse side of clothing**, i.e. **lining**, but is now also used in a general sense.

Mnemonic: **CLOTHING MADE AT REAR OF VILLAGE HAS GOOD LINING**

993		**RITSU, RICHI**	法律	HŌRITSU	law
		LAW, CONTROL	規律	KIRITSU	discipline
		9 strokes	律義	RICHIGI	integrity

彳 is **road/ move** 118, here acting in the figurative sense of **path**. 聿 is a variant of **brush in hand** 聿 142, and here indicates **writing** and by extension **prescribing**, as well as lending its sound to express **one**. Thus **the one (and only) prescribed path** (to follow), i.e. **the law**. **Control** is an associated meaning.

Mnemonic: **MOVING HAND WRITES DOWN THE LAW**

994	臨	**RIN, nozomu**	臨時	RINJI	temporary
		FACE, VERGE ON,	臨海	RINKAI	seaside
		ATTEND, COMMAND	臨席	RINSEKI	attendance
		18 strokes			

臥 is a variant of 臥, an NGU character meaning **bend down/ be prostrate** (literally **staring eye** 臣 512 and **person** ト /人 39, indicating a person bending down to stare). 品 is **goods/ group of people** 382, acting phonetically to express **cliff** and possibly also lending a meaning of **group of people**. 994 originally meant **(a group of people?) crouched on a cliff top looking down**. This has given rise to a range of associated and extended meanings, such as **verge, face, command** (a view), **be in a certain place** and hence **attend**, and **be in a high position** (including figuratively of rank).

Mnemonic: **PERSON FACES GOODS AND STARES**

995

RŌ, hoga*raka*
CLEAR, FINE, CHEERFUL
10 strokes

明朗 MEIRŌ na   bright, clean
朗報 RŌHŌ   good news
朗読法 RŌDOKUHŌ   elocution

月 is **moon** 16. 良 is **good** (variant 良 598). A **good moon** is a **clear** one (in fact, some scholars feel 良 also acts phonetically to express **clear**), with **bright** and **cheerful** being associated meanings.

Mnemonic: **GOOD MOON IS CLEAR AND BRIGHT**

996

RON
ARGUMENT, OPINION
15 strokes

論文 RONBUN   thesis
理論 RIRON   theory
論理 RONRI   logic

言 is **words/ speak** 274. 侖 is **arrange neatly** 601 q.v., which according to some scholars also acts phonetically to express **sequence/ order**. Thus to **speak while arranging one's words neatly in order**, a reference to the presentation of an **argument**. Suggest taking 侖 literally as **capped** 亼 121 and **aligned/** stacked (bamboo tablets) 冊 874.

Mnemonic: **ARGUMENT OF NEATLY CAPPED AND ALIGNED WORDS**

END OF SIXTH GRADE

315

THE 949 GENERAL USE CHARACTERS

997 亜　A
NEXT, SUB-, ASIA
7 strokes

亜熱帯	ANETTAI	subtropics
欧亜	ŌA	Eurasia
亜流	ARYŪ	follower

Formerly 亞. Popularly thought to derive from some assumed pictograph of (hatted) **hunchbacks** facing each other, such as 㕣. 997 did indeed mean hunchback at one stage, leading to associated ideas such as **ugly** and **inferior** and hence **secondary/ next** and **sub-**. However, very old forms such as and 十 depict a particular type of underground dwelling with a central chamber and various passages and/or smaller chambers on each side. This came to acquire associated meanings such as **angular/ not straight/ crooked**, and was eventually applied to **hunchbacks**, leading to the evolution of meaning outlined above. Somewhat surprisingly, despite its negative associations it is also borrowed phonetically to express the first syllable of **Asia**. Suggest remembering by association with **two** 二 61 and **center** 中 55. See also 222.

Mnemonic: TWO ASIAN SUB-CENTERS NEXT TO EACH OTHER

998 哀　AI, aware/remu
SORROW, PITY
9 strokes

悲哀	HIAI	sadness
哀歌	AIKA	dirge, elegy
物の哀れ	MONONOAWARE	pathos

Mouth/ say 口 20 and **clothing** 衣 420. The latter is used primarily for its sound, which is now **I** but was once somewhere between **I** and **AI**, to express the sound of **wailing** and **lamenting**. It may also be felt to lend an extended figurative idea of **covering** (cf. English cloaked/clothed in sorrow). Thus to **say the sorrowful sound I/ AI**, symbolising **sorrow** and **pity**.

Mnemonic: MOUTH WAILS, CLOTHED IN SORROW

999 握　AKU, nigiru
GRASP, GRIP
12 strokes

握手	AKUSHU	handshake
握り屋	NIGIRIYA	miser
握り飯	NIGIRIMESHI	rice-ball

扌 is **hand** 32. 屋 is **store(keeper)** 236 q.v., here acting phonetically to express **seize** and possibly also lending some suggestion of **reaching** through its element 至 (reach 875). Thus to **(reach out and?) seize by the hand**. Though now also sometimes used in a broader sense, 999 still generally retains connotations of seizing with the hand.

Mnemonic: GRASP STOREKEEPER BY THE HAND

316

| 1000 | | atsuka*u*, ko*ku*
TREAT, HANDLE,
THRESH
6 strokes | 取り扱い TORIATSUKAI handling
扱き使う KOKITSUKAU keep busy
客扱い KYAKUATSUKAI
hospitality |

扌 is **hand** 32. 及 is **reach** 1148, here acting phonetically to express **control** and almost certainly also lending an idea of reach/ **attain**. Thus **attain something by controlling with the hand**, i.e. **handle**. As with the English term, this is also used figuratively in the sense of **treat/ deal with**. **Thresh** is a minor associated meaning.

Mnemonic: **REACH WITH HAND, THEN HANDLE CAREFULLY**

| 1001 | | I, E, yor*u*
DEPEND, AS IS
8 strokes | 依頼 IRAI request
依然 IZEN as before
依こ地 EKOJI spite |

Person 亻 39 and **clothing** 衣 420. The latter acts phonetically to express **deformity**, though any semantic role is unclear. Thus a **deformed person**. Such a person was **dependent** on others, leading to **depend** in general. (Some scholars feel rather that the deformed person **leaned** on a physical support/ crutch, with **depend** being a figurative extension of lean.) It is not clear how the lesser meaning of **as is** was acquired, though it is possibly an associated meaning from the idea of lack of movement.

Mnemonic: **PERSON DEPENDS ON CLOTHING**

| 1002 | | I, odos*u*
AUTHORITY, THREATEN
9 strokes | 威力 IRYOKU authority
威厳 IGEN dignity
威し文句 ODOSHIMONKU threat |

Once written 𢧌, showing **woman** 厶 / 女 35 and broad bladed **halberd** 㦰/戌 515/ 246. The latter acts phonetically to express **fearsome**, as well as lending similar connotations of its own. Thus **fearsome woman** (cf. English slang battle ax), originally used as a term of address by a new bride towards her mother-in-law (and still very occasionally found in this sense in Chinese). **Authority** and **threaten** are associated meanings.

Mnemonic: **AUTHORITATIVE WOMAN THREATENS WITH HALBERD**

317

1003

為

I, su*ru*, na*su*, tame
DO, PURPOSE
9 strokes

行為 KŌI — action, act
為筋 TAMESUJI — patron
為過ぎる SHISUGIRU — overdo

Formerly 爲 and earlier ⿱. 爫 is hand reaching down 303, here meaning just **hand** (and depicted as such in the older form, as ⿱), while 𧰨 is the prototype of **elephant** 象 533 q.v. That is, 爲 is a variant of 象. Some scholars have interpreted the character as referring to a controlling hand **training an elephant**, which involves **doing** the same **action** over and over again and thus by association gives the present meanings. However, other scholars take 爲/象 to be used in its sense of **form/ image/ resemble**, to express the idea of a hand making a shape which resembles something. This came to mean **imitate someone's gestures**, which involved **doing** the gestures **over and over again/ practice**, with **purpose/ benefit** being an associated idea. The fact that the addition of person 亻 39 gives imitate (literally imitating person) 偽 1135 suggests that the latter theory is correct. Suggest remembering 為 by association with **bird** 鳥 174.

Mnemonic: **DO PRACTICE FOR PURPOSE OF IMITATING FUNNY BIRD**

1004

尉

I
MILITARY RANK
11 strokes

大尉 TAII — captain
小尉 SHŌI — ensign
尉官 IKAN — company officer

Once written ⿱. 彐 is a hand, later replaced with measure/ **hand** 寸 909 q.v. to emphasise careful use of the hand. 火 is fire 8, here meaning **heat**. 亻 is a variant of benevolent 仁 906 q.v., here acting phonetically to express **press down** and probably also lending its own idea of pressing down through its assumed early meaning of a person bent down under a double load. 1004 originally meant **press down with something hot**, a reference to **ironing**. This meaning is now conveyed by the NGU character 熨, which adds an extra fire 火. Just as with the English term iron out, by figurative extension 1004 came to mean **smooth out creases/ put into shape**, and was eventually applied to a **lower ranking officer** given the task of 'knocking' new recruits into shape. Suggest taking 尸 as **corpse** 尸 236 and **show** 示 695.

Mnemonic: **HAND SHOWS CORPSE TO BE SOLDIER OF RANK**

318

1005 偉	I, era*i* GREAT, GRAND 12 strokes	偉大 IDAI	grandeur
		偉人 IJIN	hero, prodigy
		偉物 ERABUTSU	great person

イ is **person** 39. 韋 is opposed feet 422 q.v., here acting phonetically to express **differ** and also lending similar connotations of **going against the norm**. Thus a **person different from normal persons**, a reference to an **outstanding/ great person**. Suggest remembering 韋 by association with **differ** 違 1006 q.v.

Mnemonic: **GREAT PERSON DIFFERS FROM OTHERS**

1006 違	I, chiga*u* DIFFER 13 strokes	相違 SŌI	difference
		違反 IHAN	infringement
		言い違い IICHIGAI	misstatement

辶 is **movement** 129. 韋 is opposed feet 422 q.v., here acting phonetically to express **part from** and also lending its own connotations of **moving away**. Thus to **move away from something**, leading by extension to **differ**. Suggest taking 口 as **opening** 20, with a play on the word opening, 卄 as 'almost' five 五 19, and 卄 as 'almost' year 年 64.

Mnemonic: **AFTER ALMOST FIVE YEARS, OPENING MOVE DIFFERS**

1007 維	I FASTEN, ROPE, SUPPORT 14 strokes	維持 IJI	upkeep
		維新 ISHIN	restoration
		繊維 SENI	fiber

糸 is **thread** 27, here meaning **cord**. 隹 is **bird** 216, here acting phonetically to express **pull** and also lending connotations of **forward movement**. 1007 originally referred to a **rope fastened to something in order to pull it forward**. Thus **rope** and **fasten**, while **support** is an associated meaning, from the idea of helping along.

Mnemonic: **ROPE THREADED THROUGH BIRD HELPS SUPPORT IT**

1008 I, nagusa*mi/mu/meru*   慰問 IMON   condolence
COMFORT, CONSOLE,   慰安 IAN   solace, amusement
AMUSEMENT   慰み物 NAGUSAMIMONO
15 strokes   plaything

Heart/ **feelings** 心 147 and soldier of rank 尉 1004 q.v. Some scholars take the latter to have been used from the outset in its sense of **smooth out**, to give **smooth out someone's feelings**, i.e. **comfort/ console** them. Others take it to have originally been used phonetically to express **resentment**, as well as lending its literal connotations of **burning pressure**, to give **feelings of smoldering resentment**. It is then felt to have acquired its present meanings as a result of the popular reinterpretation of its elements as discussed above (i.e. smooth out someone's feelings). As with 1004, suggest taking 尉 as **corpse** 尸 236, **show** 示 695, and **hand**/ measure 寸 909.

Mnemonic: **SHOWN CORPSE'S HAND TO CONSOLE FEELINGS?!**

1009 I   緯度 IDO   latitude
HORIZONTAL, WEFT   経緯儀 KEIIGI   theodolite
16 strokes   緯糸 NUKIITO *   weft

糸 is **thread** 27. 韋 is opposed feet 422 q.v., here acting in a dual phonetic role to express both **cover** and **differ** and in a dual semantic role to lend supporting connotations both of **surrounding** (and hence **covering**) and **going in a different direction**. Thus **thread that covers by going in a different direction**, a reference to the **weft** relative to the warp. Suggest remembering 韋 by association with **differ** 違 1006.

Mnemonic: **HORIZONTAL WEFT THREADS DIFFER FROM WARP**

1010 ITSU, so*reru/rasu*   逸品 IPPIN   fine article
ESCAPE, GO ASTRAY,   逸れ矢 SOREYA   stray arrow
FAST, EXCEL   逸出 ISSHUTSU
11 strokes   escape, excellence

Formerly 逸, showing that 免 is not **escape** 1849 q.v. but a simplification of the NGU character **hare** 兔, which derives from a pictograph 兔 (though the simplification was almost certainly influenced by confusion with escape 免). This was combined with **movement** 辶 129 to express the idea of a **hare's movement**, which is **fast** and associated with **escaping**. **Go astray** is derived from escape, while **excel** is derived from fast. Suggest remembering by association with **escape** 免.

Mnemonic: **MOVE FAST AND ESCAPE**

1011 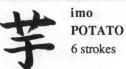	imo POTATO 6 strokes	里芋 SATOIMO	taro
		芋貝 IMOGAI	cone shell
		焼き芋 YAKIIMO	baked potato

艹 is **plant** 9. 于 is **emerge** 811, here also acting phonetically to express **big**. Thus **big (leaved) plant which emerges (from the ground)**, a somewhat vague reference to the **potato**. As with 811, suggest taking 于 as a **'stiff'** (i.e. dead) version of **child** 子 25.

Mnemonic: **CHILD IN RIGOR MORTIS AFTER EATING POTATO PLANT**

1012	IN MARRIAGE 9 strokes	婚姻 KONIN	marriage
		姻せき INSEKI	in-laws
		姻族閥 INZOKUBATSU	
			nepotism

女 is **woman** 35. 因 is **depend on** 614 q.v., here probably lending its assumed specific meaning of **become dependent on a person in whose house one stays**. Thus **woman becoming dependent** (on her new family), a reference to **marriage**. Suggest taking 因 as **big man** 大 53 in **confinement** 口 (see 123).

Mnemonic: **BIG MAN CONFINED BY WOMAN AFTER MARRIAGE**

1013	IN, kage SHADOW, SECRET, NEGATIVE 11 strokes	陰気 INKI	gloom, sadness
		陰部 INBU	private parts
		陰口 KAGEGUCHI	backbiting

阝 is **hill** 229. 侌 is a now defunct character meaning **obscure/ secret/ shadow**. It comprises now 今 125 q.v., used in its literal sense of **cover**, and say 云 78 q.v., used in its literal sense of **vapors**. Thus something **covered in vapors/ mist**. When combined with hill 阝 the meaning became **misty/ shaded side of a hill**, as opposed to the sunny side of the hill seen in 陽 406 q.v. It also retained its connotations of **secret**. Whereas 406 connotes the positive (yang), 1013 connotes the **negative (yin)**. Note that kage/ shade is also expressed by the NGU character 蔭, that adds plant 艹 9 and technically means shaded plants. Suggest remembering 侌 as a combination of **now** 今 and **meet** 会 87.

Mnemonic: **NOW MEET IN SECRET IN SHADOW OF HILL**

321

1014

IN, kaku*reru*/*su*
HIDE
14 strokes

隠居 INKYO   retirement
隠者 INJA   hermit
隠れ家 KAKUREGA   refuge

Formerly 隱. 阝 is **hill** 229. 㥥 is a CO character meaning **compassion/ care**. Its exact etymology is unclear but it comprises **heart/ feelings** 心 147, **reaching hand** 爫 303, a further **hand** ⼹ , and what appears to be tile/ weight/ **press down** 工 944. Thus presumably hands pressing down on heart, indicating compassion. In the case of 1014 㥥 acts phonetically to express **cover**, and possibly lends similar connotations from the idea of hands covering the heart. Thus **covered by a hill**, i.e. obscured from view and hence **hidden/ hide**.

Mnemonic: **HILL CAN'T HIDE FEELINGS -- NEED HANDS OVER HEART**

1015

IN
RHYME, TONE
19 strokes

韻文 INBUN   poetry
韻律 INRITSU   rhythm
音韻 ONIN   phoneme

音 is **sound** 6. 員 is **member** 228 q.v., here acting phonetically to express **round** and also lending its literal meaning of **round object** but in a figurative sense. Thus **rounded sound**, i.e. **rhyme/ rhythm**.

Mnemonic: **MEMBER'S RHYME DISPLAYS ROUNDED SOUNDS**

1016

EI, yom*u*
POEM, RECITE,
COMPOSE
12 strokes

詠歌 EIKA   composition
詠草 EISŌ   draft of poem
詠史 EISHI   epic

Formerly also 咏. **Words/ speak** 言 274 (or **mouth/ say** 口 20) and **long** 永 615, to convey the idea of **drawing out a verbal statement** (in the dramatic sense). Thus **recitation**, with **poem** and **compose** being associated meanings.

Mnemonic: **RECITED POEM CONTAINS LONG WORDS**

1017

EI, kage
SHADOW, LIGHT,
IMAGE
15 strokes

影響 EIKYŌ　　　　influence
影像 EIZŌ　　　shadow, image
影武者 KAGEMUSHA
　　　　　　　general's double

景 is scene/ **bright** 469 q.v., here in its early sense of **open to the sunlight.** 彡 is **delicate hairs** 93 q.v., here in an extended sense of **delicate pattern.** (Some scholars see 彡 as **rays of sunlight,** as in 144/618, and it is indeed highly likely that there was some confusion between hairs and sunrays, or even a deliberate merging of the two.) Thus the **delicate pattern formed by sunlight,** i.e. **dappling** or **shading.** This led to both **shadow** and **light,** though the former is by far the commoner meaning, while the idea of the pattern/ shape of the shadowing led to **form** and **image.** Suggest taking 景 literally as **sun(light)** 日 62 and **capital** 京 99, with 彡 as **streaming sunlight.**

Mnemonic: **SUN STREAMS DOWN ON CAPITAL, FORMING SHADOWS**

1018

EI, surudo*i*
SHARP, KEEN
15 strokes

鋭利 EIRI na　　　sharp, keen
鋭角 EIKAKU　　　acute angle
精鋭 SEIEI　　　elite, 'crack'

金 is **metal** 14. 兌 is **exchange** 524 q.v., which acts phonetically to express **small.** According to some scholars 兌 also lends an extended idea of reduction and hence **taper** from its connotations of dispersing. This does not seem particularly convincing, however, and it may be felt more likely that it lends a loose idea of **penetrativeness** from its literal meaning of a person dispersing words by way of explaining, instructing, or preaching. Thus **small (tapered?/ penetrating?) piece of metal,** namely a **tip,** symbolising something **sharp.** This is also used figuratively, i.e. **keen.** Suggest taking 兌 as **elder brother** 兄 267 and **out** ハ 66.

Mnemonic: **ELDER BROTHER IS SHARP WHEN MONEY GIVEN OUT**

1019

EKI, YAKU
EPIDEMIC
9 strokes

防疫 BŌEKI　　　disinfection
悪疫 AKUEKI　　　plague
疫病 EKIBYŌ/ YAKUBYŌ
　　　　　　　epidemic

Illness 疒 381 and **strike** 殳 153, to give **illness that strikes.** Some scholars feel that 殳 also acts phonetically to express **succession,** giving **illness that strikes people in succession.**

Mnemonic: **EPIDEMIC IS ILLNESS THAT STRIKES**

1020 悦 ETSU
JOY
10 strokes

喜悦 KIETSU — joy
悦楽 ETSURAKU — enjoyment
満悦 MANETSU — delight

忄 is heart/ **feelings** 147. 兑 is exchange 524 q.v., here acting phonetically to express **burst forth** and also lending an idea of **proclaim** from its literal meaning of person dispersing words. Thus **feelings which burst forth and are proclaimed**, namely **joy**. Suggest taking 兑 as **elder brother** 兄 267 and **out** 丷 66.

Mnemonic: **ELDER BROTHER GIVES OUT FEELINGS OF JOY**

1021 ETSU, ko*eru*/*su*
CROSS, EXCEED, EXCEL
12 strokes

優越 YŪETSU — superiority
越境 EKKYŌ — border violation
追い越す OIKOSU — overtake

走 is **run** 161. 戉 is **halberd**/ battle ax 515, which acts phonetically to express fleet/ **swift** and probably also lends an idea of **aggression**. Thus to **run swiftly** (like warriors attacking?). The idea of running swiftly led to the idea of **exceeding** (not unlike 629 q.v.) and thus **crossing**, as well as **excelling**. Scholars who emphasise the ideographic role of the elements feel that the present meanings stem from warriors **crossing** into other territory, with **excel** stemming from the idea of triumph. This theory is a useful mnemonic.

Mnemonic: **RUN WITH HALBERD AND CROSS BORDER**

1022 謁 ETSU
AUDIENCE (WITH RULER)
15 strokes

拝謁 HAIETSU — audience
謁見 EKKEN — audience
謁見室 EKKENSHITSU — audience chamber

Formerly 謁. 言 is **words**/ **speak** 274. 曷 is a CO character now used to indicate a range of **interrogatives**, and in compounds it often lends an idea of **ask** and/or **threaten**. It comprises **say** 日 /曰 688, **encircle**/ **surround** 勹 655, and **person** 人 39 **in a corner** ∟ 349 (see also 973). Its etymology is unclear, but it appears to indicate a person (possibly an escapee) trapped in a corner surrounded by interrogators, which would account for its connotations both of threaten and of the interrogative. However, it is also possible that person in a corner 𠤎 is used in its sense of dead person (973), particularly in view of the fact that the modern form uses fallen person ヒ 238, to give talking persons surrounding a dead person. In such case it is not clear how it came to acquire its various connotations. (Note that 匂 exists as a 'made in Japan' NGU character meaning smell, but this is also of unclear etymology.) In the case of 1022 曷 acts phonetically to express **state clearly**, and is also believed to lend connotations of **demand**, combining with words 言 to give **make a clear verbal demand**. This led by association to **audience**. Suggest taking 日 as **sun** 62, with 勹 as **cover** and ヒ as **sitting person/ man**.

Mnemonic: **MAN SITS COVERED IN SUNSHINE AFTER WORDY AUDIENCE**

1023 ETSU   閲兵 EPPEI   troop review
INSPECTION   検閲 KENETSU   censorship
15 strokes   閲覧室 ETSURANSHITSU
                                     reading room

門 is **gate** 211, here in an extended sense of **emerge in succession** (i.e. from a gate). 兑 is exchange 524 q.v., here acting phonetically to express **count** and possibly also lending its idea of speaking person. Thus to **count things emerging in succession** (i.e. troops who answer when called?), leading to **inspection**. Suggest taking 兑 as **elder brother** 兄 267 and **out** ⌣ 66.

Mnemonic: **INSPECT ELDER BROTHER WHEN HE COMES OUT OF GATE**

1024 EN, honō   火炎 KAEN   flame, blaze
FLAME   脳炎 NŌEN   encephalitis
8 strokes   炎天 ENTEN scorching weather

Fire/ flame 火 8 doubled for emphasis. It often has connotations of **excessive fire/ heat**.

Mnemonic: **TWO FIRES CAN MEAN TOO MUCH FLAME**

1025 EN, utage   宴会 ENKAI   banquet
BANQUET   宴楽 ENRAKU   revelry
10 strokes   酒宴 SHUEN   drinking bout

宀 is **house/ building** 28. 㬎 is a now defunct character meaning **attractive woman**. The latter comprises **woman** 女 35 and **sun/ bright** 日 62, and literally means **dazzling woman**. This was often used as a euphemistic reference to **prostitutes** and what might be termed professional party-goers. (Note that woman 女 combined with bright 昌 508 [double sun 日] gives the NGU character prostitute 娼 .) Thus, depending on one's level of interpretation, **house of prostitutes/ brothel** or **house of beauties**. By association this led to **revelry** and **banquet**.

Mnemonic: **BANQUET HOSTED BY WOMAN IN SUNNY HOUSE**

1026		EN	援助 ENJO	assistance
		HELP	応援 ŌEN	backing, aid
		12 strokes	声援 SEIEN	vocal support

爰 is draw to oneself 932 q.v., here in its literal sense of one person **helping** another by means of a rope. **Hand** 扌 32 draws emphasis to the 'helping hand', giving **help**. As with 932, suggest taking 爰 as **three hands** (hand 爫 303, hand 又, and 'hand' 二 [taken as variant hand 手 32]), thus giving **four hands** in total.

Mnemonic: **FOUR HANDS PROVIDE HELP**

1027	煙	EN, kemuri, kemui/tai	煙突 ENTOTSU	chimney
		SMOKE, FEEL AWKWARD	禁煙 KINEN	'no smoking'
		13 strokes	煙草 TABAKO*	tobacco

火 is **burn/ fire** 8. 垔 is a CO character meaning embankment/ **block**. It comprises **ground/ earth** 土 60 and **west** 西 152, the latter being used phonetically to express **block** to give **earth that blocks**. Thus 1027 means literally **fire that blocks**. **Smoke** is felt to be an associated meaning, from the idea of blocking vision and breathing. 1027 is now also sometimes used to refer to **mist** or **haze** in a broad sense. It is not fully clear how in Japanese it also came to mean **feel awkward/ shy**, but it seems likely that this is an associated figurative meaning, from the idea of not being able to see properly and hence not knowing which way to turn or how to proceed. Note that there is an occasionally encountered variant form 烟, which uses depend on/ cause 因 614. The latter acts phonetically to express block and also lends its meaning of cause. Thus that which is caused by fire and blocks.

Mnemonic: **SMOKE FROM BURNING GROUND IN WEST**

1028		EN, saru	類人猿 RUIJINEN	anthropoid
		MONKEY, APE	野猿 YAEN	wild monkey
		13 strokes	猿真似屋 SARUMANEYA	copycat

Formerly 猨 , which is the correct form. 犭 is dog 17, here meaning **animal**. 爰 is **pull up by hand** 932. Thus **animal which pulls itself up by hand**, a reference to the **monkey** and its tree-climbing agility. The later use of long robe 袁 79 is almost certainly the result of miscopying, but since it has the same pronunciation as 爰 it may be considered a phonetic substitution for the latter. Suggest remembering 袁 by association with **distant** 遠 79.

Mnemonic: **ANIMAL IN DISTANCE IS MONKEY**

1029	EN, namari	亜鉛 AEN	zinc
	LEAD	黒鉛 KOKUEN	graphite
	13 strokes	鉛筆入れ ENPITSUIRE	pencil case

金 is **metal** 14. 㕣 is hollowed out 158, here acting phonetically to express **white** and possibly also lending an idea of **extraction** from its literal elements **source/ opening** 口 20 and **out of** ハ 66. Thus **(extracted?) white metal**, a reference to **lead**. White metal is also the description of silver 銀 263 q.v., but it should be noted that the latter is specifically white metal that is <u>scrutinised</u> (to distinguish it from similar metals, such as lead). Some scholars feel that white is in fact a reference not to the color per se but to **cosmetics** (white and cosmetics conceptually overlapping and in Japanese sharing the same word shiro), since it is known that in ancient times many cosmetics were lead based. Thus the interpretation of 1029 then becomes **metal associated with cosmetics**. A combination of both theories is not impossible, i.e. **white metal associated with cosmetics**. Suggest taking 口 as **hole**.

Mnemonic: **METAL POURING OUT OF HOLES IS LEAD**

1030	EN, fuchi	縁側 ENGAWA	veranda
	RELATION(S), TIES,	縁縫い FUCHINUI	hemming
	FATE, EDGE	縁談 ENDAN offer of marriage	
	15 strokes		

Formerly 緣 . 糸 is **thread** 27. 豖 is a CO character meaning **running pig/ hedgehog**, and is to all intents and purposes a variant of **pig** 豕 1670. Here it acts phonetically to express **edge**, to give **threads used for edging/ hemming**. Why such a character should have been chosen as a phonetic is not clear, but it may possibly have been confused with and/or likened to streamers 勿 387, i.e. to suggest tassels. Edging came to mean **edge** in general. **Relation(s)**, **ties**, and **fate** are taken by some scholars to be the result of borrowing, but it seems more likely that the combination of threads and edge suggested **bringing things into contact**, and that they are therefore extended/ associated meanings. Fate is certainly a meaning figuratively associated with ties. Suggest taking 豖 as **pig with tusks**.

Mnemonic: **TUSKED PIG TIED WITH THREAD SUFFERS SAD FATE**

327

1031

O, kega*reru/su/rawashii*,
yogo*reru/su*, kitanai
DIRT, DISHONOR
6 strokes

汚染 OSEN — pollution
汚職 OSHOKU — bribery
汚れ物 YOGOREMONO — laundry

Also written 汙. 氵is **water** 40. 于/亐 is emerge 811 q.v., acting phonetically to express **dip/ hollow** and possibly also lending its own idea of **emerge** (though it may be felt that the **waterweed** element 亐 [see also 281] is the dominant connotation). 1031 originally referred to **water which collected in a hollow**, possibly having seeped (i.e. emerged) from the ground and/or becoming covered with waterweed. Unlike the pure connotations of spring 泉 915, it acquired connotations of **stagnancy** (still found as a meaning in Chinese) and hence **impurity** and eventually **dirt** and the figurative **dishonor**. As with 811, suggest taking 于 as a 'stiff' (i.e. dead) version of **child** 子 25, with 亐 as **'almost' stiff/ dead child**.

Mnemonic: **CHILD ALMOST DEAD AFTER DRINKING DIRTY WATER**

1032

Ō, kubo, boko, heko*mu*
HOLLOW, CONCAVE,
DENT
5 strokes

凹面 ŌMEN — concave
凹地 KUBOCHI — hollow, pit
凹み HEKOMI — dent

A symbolic representation of **concavity**. Suggest remembering by association with a **box** 口.

Mnemonic: **HOLLOW BOX DENTED, NOW RATHER CONCAVE**

1033

Ō, os*u*
PUSH
8 strokes

押収 ŌSHŪ — confiscation
押し入れ OSHIIRE — closet
手押し車 TEOSHIGURUMA — barrow

扌 is **hand** 32. 甲 is **shell/ casing** 1243, here acting phonetically to express **press/ push** and probably also lending its own connotations of **thrust** and **force** from its literal meaning of a seed bursting forth from its casing. Thus **press/ push with hand**.

Mnemonic: **HAND PUSHES SHELL**

1034　**Ō**

EUROPE, EU-

8 strokes

欧州 ŌSHŪ　　Europe

欧米 ŌBEI　　the West

欧氏管 ŌSHIKAN

Eustachian tube

Formerly 歐. 欠 is **lack** 471 q.v., here in its literal sense of **gaping mouth**. 區/区 is ward/ **section** 465 q.v. Though the 品 of 區 probably referred initially to various enclosures/ sub-sections, because of the similarities with **mouth** 口 20 區 was often chosen as a phonetic in words relating to the mouth. Here it is used to express the sound Ō. (Though as an independent character 區 is now invariably read KU it is also listed as having a minor reading Ō, both readings appearing to stem from an original reading of YOKU/ EOKU/ EUKU or similar.) Thus to **make the sound Ō (EO/EU) with a gaping mouth**, a reference to **groaning while vomiting**. It can still be used to mean vomit in Chinese, while in Japanese this is expressed by the NGU character 嘔, which uses an ordinary mouth 口 instead of gaping mouth 欠. The character was also chosen as the phonetic for the EU of **Europe**, as well as Eustachian, Euclid, etc. Why a character with such emetic connotations should be chosen to represent Europe is a matter of some conjecture. While it is true that there are very few characters with a reading of this particular type of Ō (EU/EO, as opposed to OO, OU, etc.), it should be noted that there is a perfectly good NGU character 謳 (言 is words 274), which is read Ō/EU/EO and has a meaning of praise/ extol.

Mnemonic: **SECTION OF EUROPE LACKING**

1035　**Ō, nagu***ru*

HIT, BEAT, ASSAULT

8 strokes

殴打 ŌDA　　blow, assault

殴り込み NAGURIKOMI gang raid

殴り合う NAGURIAU trade blows

Formerly 毆. 殳 is **hand holding weapon/ strike** 153. 區/区 is **ward/** section 465, here acting phonetically to express **beat** and possibly also suggesting through its sound Ō the groans and wails of someone being beaten (see 1034). Thus **strike (with weapon) and beat**.

Mnemonic: **ASSAULT IN WARD INVOLVING WEAPON**

329

1036

桜

Ō, sakura

CHERRY (BLOSSOM)

10 strokes

桜桃 ŌTŌ   cherry fruit

桜色 SAKURAIRO   pink

桜肉 SAKURANIKU

horsemeat

Formerly 櫻 . 木 is **tree** 69. 嬰 is an NGU character meaning **baby (girl)**, comprising **woman** 女 35 and the CO character **string of shells/ pearls** 賏 (a doubling of **shell** 貝 90). In Chinese 嬰 also has connotations of **roundness**. That is, plump baby girls were likened to a string of pearls. In combination with tree 木 the meaning became **tree that produces a string/ cluster of baby round things**. The peach (see 1646) was one of the commonest fruits, and the **cherry** was considered 'baby' relative to this. In Chinese 1036 is hardly used, but it is a popular character in Japanese. It should be noted that, despite the fact that 1036 was first applied to the cherry <u>fruit</u>, fruiting cherries appear to have become rare (certainly in Japan), and in Japanese it is now used almost exclusively of the <u>flowering</u> cherry. The cherry fruit is now often referred to as the 'Western fruit-cherry' (Seiyōmizakura 西洋実桜). Suggest taking the ソ of the modern form as a **'half'** variant of **claw** ⺥ 303.

Mnemonic: **WOMAN HALF CLAWS WAY UP TREE TO GET CHERRY BLOSSOM**

1037

Ō, okina

OLD MAN, VENERABLE

10 strokes

老翁 RŌŌ   old man

村翁 SONŌ   village elder

げん翁 GENOKINA

Old Man Gen

羽 is **wings/ feathers** 812. 公 is **public** 277 q.v., acting phonetically to express **head**. 1037 originally referred to the (soft) **plumage on either side of a hawk's head**. In view of this rather specific meaning it is possible that 公 was chosen as the phonetic for its suggestion of a **nose** 厶 134 (though technically 277 derives from 㕣, 口 was from an early stage often abbreviated to 厶), with ハ then becoming symbols of **either side**. Some scholars feel that the present meaning of **old man** is purely the result of borrowing, while others feel that an early form 翁 of 1037 became graphically confused with an early form 老 of old man 老 609. However, it seems equally possible that 1037 was applied by association to whiskered old men and/or those who had gone bald on top of the head and had hair left only on the sides.

Mnemonic: **OLD MAN RUFFLES FEATHERS IN PUBLIC**

330

1038

Ō, oku
DEEP INSIDE
12 strokes

奥底 OKUSOKO　inner depths
奥様 OKUSAMA　wife
奥義 ŌGI/ OKUGI　mysteries

Formerly 𡏇 and earlier 𡏈. 釆 and 釆 show the same apparent confusion between **rice** 米 201and **rice plant** 禾 81 as seen in 196, though the modern form has opted for **rice** 米. 冂 is clearly a variant of roof/ **building** 宀 28. 大 is not **big** 大 53, though it may be useful to take it as such, but clearly a simplification of a pair of hands 𦥑, which here indicate **pushing**. 1038 originally referred to **rice stored** (literally pushed) **deep inside a building**, with the idea of **deep inside** eventually prevailing as the meaning. Note that the reading OKU is believed by many scholars to be an ON (i.e. Chinese) reading, of which Ō is taken to be an abbreviated form , but it is officially classified as a KUN (i.e. Japanese) reading, and probably has etymological connections with the verb oku meaning to put in place (see 545). Further evidence for the KUN classification includes the fact that when used in compounds 1038 never lends a reading OKU. It does, however, very occasionally have an ON reading IKU.

Mnemonic: **BIG AMOUNT OF RICE DEEP INSIDE BUILDING**

1039

OKU
THINK, REMEMBER
16 strokes

記憶 KIOKU　memory
追憶 TSUIOKU　reminiscence
憶測 OKUSOKU　speculation

Thought/ think 意 226 and **heart**/ feelings 忄 147, conveying the idea of a **thought kept in the heart**, such as a lingering **memory**. Nowadays often interchanged in practice with the NGU character 臆, which uses flesh/ of the body 月 365 instead of heart 忄, but technically 臆 has connotations of timidity and hesitation.

Mnemonic: **A THOUGHT IN THE HEART IS A THOUGHT REMEMBERED**

1040

osore, GU
FEAR, ANXIETY
13 strokes

憂虞 YŪGU　distress
不虞 FUGU　unexpected
虞美人草 GUBIJINSŌ　poppy

虍 is **tiger** 281. 呉 is **give** 1237 q.v., acting phonetically to express **contrast** (of color) and probably also lending connotations of **not proven fact** from its literal meaning of a person not telling the truth. 1040 originally referred to a **mythical tiger-like creature** with black spots against a white background. Its present meanings result from confusion with **concern** 慮 1904.

Mnemonic: **TIGER GIVES ONE FEAR AND ANXIETY**

331

1041	OTSU, ITSU	乙 種 OSSHU	B Class
	ODD, B, 2ND, STYLISH	乙 女 OTOME*	maiden
	1 stroke	乙 に OTSUNI	strangely

From a pictograph of a **double bladed sword** 乚 (held in the middle). This was an **unusual** weapon, leading to **odd**. **Stylish** is felt to be a loosely associated meaning, from the idea that something unusual is something outstanding, with stylish being an associated meaning with outstanding. **Second/ B** is a borrowed meaning (First/ A being 甲 1243 and Third/ C being 丙 1773).

Mnemonic: **ODD DOUBLE BLADED SWORD IS B-GRADE STYLE**

1042	orosu, oroshi	卸売 OROSHIURI	wholesale
	WHOLESALE, GRATE	卸商 ORISHISHŌ	wholesaler
	9 strokes	卸し大根 OROSHIDAIKON	
			grated radish

Of unusual etymology in that it is formed from a larger character, without reference to which 1042 cannot be understood. The character in question is **honorable** 御 1158 q.v., used in its meaning of **drive a cart**. This has had **road/ movement** 彳 118 removed from its **moving foot/ movement** element 彳 129 q.v., to leave just **foot** 止 129, which changed to its meaning of **stop**. In combination with the **'drive a cart'** element 卩 (which confusingly only became drive a cart in combination with movement, since there is no cart element proper) this produced a meaning of **stop** (**driving**) **a cart**. This came to mean **unload**, which is its main meaning in Chinese. In Japanese there is a semantic overlap between unloading a vehicle and **selling wholesale** (i.e. selling there and then at the roadside rather than through a retail outlet), with the verb orosu meaning both lower/ unload and sell wholesale depending on the character (generally 下 7 is used for lower/ unload). 1042 is also sometimes used to express a separate homophonic word orosu meaning to **grate** (vegetables), though this is normally expressed by 下 7. Suggest remembering by association with **honorable** 御 1158, minus its **movement** radical 彳.

Mnemonic: **WHOLESALE MARKET HONORABLE BUT LACKS MOVEMENT**

1043

ON, oda*yaka*
PEACE, MODERATION
16 strokes

穏和 ONWA — moderation
穏当 ONTŌ na — reasonable
平穏 HEION — calm

Formerly 穏. 禾 is **rice plant** 81, while 急 / 急 is **care/ compassion** 1014 q.v. The latter acts phonetically to express **soften** and probably also lends connotations of **pressing** from its assumed original meaning of hands pressed to heart. 1043 originally referred to **softening rice by pressing it.** Some scholars take its present meanings to result from borrowing, while others see them as extended meanings, feeling that **soften rice** came to mean **soften** in a broad sense, leading to **make amenable** and thus **advocate peace** and **moderation.** Suggest taking 急 literally as **hands** (hand 𠂇 303 and hand ヨ) clasped to **heart** 心 147.

Mnemonic: **HANDS HOLD RICE PLANT TO HEART AS TOKEN OF PEACE**

1044

KA
BEAUTIFUL, GOOD
8 strokes

佳人 KAJIN — a beauty, belle
絶佳 ZEKKA — superb
佳作 KASAKU — a fine work

亻 is **person** 39, here meaning **woman.** 圭 is **edge/ jewel** 819, here acting phonetically to express **beautiful** and possibly also lending its meaning of **jewel.** Thus a **beautiful (jewelled?/ jewel-like?) woman.** This later became **beautiful/ fine/ good** in a broad sense. Suggest taking 圭 literally as a **doubling** of **ground** 土 60.

Mnemonic: **GOOD PERSON COVERS TWICE AS MUCH GROUND**

1045

KA, ka*karu/keru*
BUILD, SPAN, FRAME
9 strokes

架道橋 KADŌKYŌ — overbridge
書架 SHOKA — bookshelf
架空 KAKŪ — aerial, fanciful

木 is **tree/ wood** 69, here meaning **timber.** 加 is **add** 431, here also acting phonetically to express **build up.** Thus to **build up by adding timber,** a reference to **constructing a frame/ support,** usually with connotations of height and **spanning** (as a bridge).

Mnemonic: **ADD WOOD TO BUILD UP SPAN OF FRAME**

333

1046

KA, GE, hana
FLOWER, SHOWY,
CHINA
10 strokes

華美 KABI   splendor, color
中華 CHŪKA-   Chinese-
華華しい HANABANASHII
             brilliant

Originally 𦾔 , showing a **richly leafed plant coming into bud** 㞦 with a reinforcing **plant** radical 㞢/艹 9. A later form 𦾷 shows the plant radical on top and a simplified leafy plant 㐮 , with the idea of coming into bud conveyed by **emerge** 丂 811. It is from this later form that the modern character derives. 1046 is now generally used in the figurative sense of **flowery/ showy**, with the physical flower being conveyed by 花 9. It is also used as a reference to **China**. Suggest taking 茟 as an **eight-leaved plant** 丰 with the number being confirmed by **eight** ＼ノ 66.

Mnemonic: **SHOWY CHINESE FLOWER IS PLANT WITH EIGHT LEAVES**

1047

KA
FRUIT, CAKE
11 strokes

菓子 KASHI   candy, cake
製菓 SEIKA   confectionery
水菓子 MIZUGASHI   fruit

Fruit 果 627 with **plant** 艹 9 added after the the meaning of 627 became vague. **Cake** is an associated meaning, from the idea of sweet refreshment. Suggest taking 果 as **tree** 木 69 and **field** 田 59.

Mnemonic: **TREE PLANTED IN FIELD PRODUCES FRUIT FOR CAKE**

1048

KA, uzu
WHIRLPOOL, EDDY
12 strokes

渦巻き UZUMAKI   eddy, vortex
渦線 UZUSEN   spiral line
渦中 KACHŪ   maelstrom

Formerly 渦 , comprising **water/ river** 氵 40 and **pass/ flexible movement** 咼 629. 1048 is used as a proper noun to refer to a certain river in China, and some scholars feel that **whirlpool** results either from borrowing or from the particular nature of the river in question. Others feel that whirlpool is the older meaning, from the idea of **flexibly moving water**, and that the river in question was so named because of this. **Movement** 辶 129 has disappeared in the present form, which may be a useful mnemonic.

Mnemonic: **WATER IN WHIRLPOOL PASSES WITH DISAPPEARING MOVEMENT**

334

1049

KA, yome, totsug*u*
MARRY, BRIDE
13 strokes

花嫁 HANAYOME — bride
嫁資 KASHI — dowry
転嫁 TENKA — buck passing

Woman 女 35 and house 家 83, indicating a **woman going to a (new) house**, i.e. as a **bride**. Some scholars feel that 家 also acts phonetically to express **make-up**, to refer specifically to a bride making herself up before going to her new home.

Mnemonic: **MARRIED WOMAN GOES TO NEW HOME**

1050

KA, hima
LEISURE, FREE TIME
13 strokes

休暇 KYŪKA — holiday
余暇 YOKA — leisure
暇取る HIMADORU — be tardy

日 is **day** 62. 叚 is **false** 625, known to act here phonetically to express **space** but of unknown semantic role. Thus **day of space**, meaning a day of **leisure**. Suggest taking 𠤬 as **doorsteps** (door 𠃌 [variant 戸 108] and steps 二), and 𝟛 as a variant of **hand holding tool**/ weapon 殳 153 (i.e. **repair**).

Mnemonic: **USE HANDY TOOL TO REPAIR DOORSTEPS ON FREE DAY**

1051

KA, wazawai
CALAMITY
13 strokes

禍福 KAFUKU — ups and downs
災禍 SAIKA — calamity
禍根 KAKON — root of evil

Formerly 禍. 示/礻 is **altar**/ **of the gods** 695. 咼 is the somewhat unclear 'backbone' element 629 q.v., which is known to act here phonetically to express **rebuke** but is of unknown semantic role. Thus **rebuke from the gods**, a reference to a **calamity**. Suggest remembering 咼 by association with **pass** 過 629, taking it to be **'almost' pass**.

Mnemonic: **ALMOST PASS ALTAR -- COULD HAVE BROUGHT CALAMITY**

1052

KA, kutsu
SHOE
13 strokes

製靴 SEIKA — shoemaking
靴下 KUTSUSHITA — sock
長靴 NAGAGUTSU — boot

Leather 革 821 and **change/convert** 化 238. Shoes are **'converted' from leather**. Leather footwear was in fact quite rare in ancient China, and was used primarily for riding. Thus 1052 originally meant riding boots before coming to mean **shoe** in general.

Mnemonic: **SHOES ARE CONVERTED LEATHER**

1053 **KA**　　　　　　　寡黙 KAMOKU　　　silence
FEW, MINIMUM, WIDOW　寡婦 KAFU/YAMOME widow
14 strokes　　　　　　　寡言 KAGEN　　　reticence

An old form 寰 shows a **house** 冂/宀 28, a **face** 臾/直/頁 93 (here meaning **person**), and **divide** '分/分 199 (here meaning **separate**), indicating a **person separated from others and alone in a house**. This was a reference to a **widow**, but also conveyed the idea of **minimum** since one person is a minimal 'family'. **Few** is an associated meaning.

Mnemonic: **FEW SMILES ON FACE OF WIDOW IN DIVIDED HOUSE**

1054 **KA, KO**　　　　　箇条書 KAJŌGAKI　itemisation
ITEM (COUNTER)　　箇所 KASHO　　place, point
14 strokes　　　　　一箇 IKKO　　　　one item

⺮ is **bamboo** 170. 固 is **hard** 476, here acting phonetically to express **straight** and almost certainly also lending an idea of solid physical presence (i.e. actual existence). 1054 was originally used as a **counter for straight bamboo slats**, but later came to be used of other items. It has long been confused with 個 669 q.v.

Mnemonic: **COUNT ITEMS OF HARD BAMBOO**

1055 **KA, kase**gu　　　　稼業 KAGYŌ　　　one's trade
WORK, EARN MONEY　稼ぎ手 KASEGITE breadwinner
15 strokes　　　　　共稼ぎ TOMOKASEGI
　　　　　　　　　　　　　　　　　　　dual income

禾 is **rice plant** 81, while 家 is **house/ home** 83. Popularly interpreted as **bringing home the rice**, which is seen as an assumed equivalent to the English term **breadwinner**. A useful mnemonic, but incorrect. 家 is used primarily phonetically, to express **very big**, and also lends an idea of a **safe building** and by extension **storehouse**. 1055 originally meant a **crop of rice big enough to fill a (store)house**. It then also came to mean by association **work hard enough to produce such a crop**. In Chinese it still means harvested crop or work on the land, but in Japanese the idea of **working in order to achieve wealth** has come to prevail.

Mnemonic: **WORK TO EARN MONEY AND 'BRING HOME THE RICE'**

| 1056 |  ka, BUN MOSQUITO 10 strokes | 蚊 針 KABARI 大 蚊 GAGANBO* 蚊 遣 り 火 KAYARIBI | flyhook crane fly smudge fire |

虫 is insect 56. 文 is text 68, here used purely for its sound **BUN**. Thus **insect that makes a BUN sound**, a reference to the whine/ hum of a **mosquito**.

Mnemonic: **TEXT DESCRIBES MOSQUITO AS INSECT THAT GOES 'BUN'**

| 1057 | GA ELEGANCE, 'TASTE' 13 strokes | 優 雅 YŪGA 雅 号 GAGŌ 雅 趣 GASHU | elegance pen name artistry |

隹 is **bird** 216. 牙 is **fang** 434, used for its sound **GA**, and according to some scholars also lending connotations of **ugly** and/or **unpleasant**. Thus **(unpleasant?) bird that makes a GA sound**, a reference to the cawing of a **crow**. 216 can still mean crow in Chinese, though generally this is expressed by a character 鴉 which uses bird 鳥 174 instead of bird 隹 and which is also found in Japanese as an NGU character. Somewhat surprisingly, 1057 was later borrowed phonetically to express **elegant/ tasteful**, though it is unclear why a character with such connotations should have been chosen.

Mnemonic: **FANGED BIRD IS AN ELEGANT CROW**

| 1058 | GA, u*eru* STARVE 15 strokes | 飢 餓 KIGA 餓 鬼 GAKI 餓 死 GASHI | starvation hungry imp, brat starving to death |

Somewhat obscure. 食 is **food/ eat** 146. 我 is **I/ self** 817, felt by some scholars to act purely phonetically to express **empty/ lacking**, to give **lacking food**. However, it seems more likely that 我 was originally used in error instead of entrust 委 423. 餧 is a CO character meaning both **feed** and **be hungry/ starve**, in which 委 acts phonetically to express empty/ lacking and may at the same time lend connotations either of **food** through its rice plant element 禾 (see 81) or **give** through its later meaning of entrust. There seems to have been a conceptual association between starving and feeding, through the basic concept of being hungry (i.e. depending on whether one intransitively suffers the hunger or transitively reacts to it). However, 1058 is used only in the sense of **starve**.

Mnemonic: **I'M STARVING AND NEED FOOD**

1059

KAI

MEDIATE, SHELL

4 strokes

介入 KAINYŪ   intervention

介殻 KAIKAKU   sea shell

自己紹介 JIKOSHŌKAI

       self-introduction

Originally 川, showing a **person** 人 39 **encased**)(, indicating a **person wearing armor** (front and back). This led on the one hand to the idea of **casing**, including eventually even **sea shell**, and on the other to the idea of **being between things**, giving by extension **mediate**. Suggest taking 介 as an **arrow**.

Mnemonic: **SHELL PROTECTS MEDIATOR FROM ARROW**

1060

KAI, imashi*meru*

COMMAND, ADMONISH

7 strokes

警戒 KEIKAI   caution

戒律 KAIRITSU commandment

戒行 KAIGYŌ   penance

Originally 𢦠, showing **two hands** 廾 holding a **halberd/ weapon** 戈 493. This indicated a **threat**, leading to the ideas of **commanding** someone to do something and of **rebuking/ punishing** them. Suggest taking 廾 as two **tens** 十 33.

Mnemonic: **TWENTY HALBERDS ENFORCE COMMAND**

1061

KAI, KE, aya*shii/shimu*

WEIRD, SUSPICIOUS

8 strokes

怪談 KAIDAN   ghost story

怪物 KAIBUTSU   monster

怪しげ AYASHIGE questionable

忄 is **feelings** 147. 圣 is not the usual simplification of warp threads 巠/圣 269. It was formerly written 圣, showing a **hand** ⺈ over **earth/ ground** 土 60, and exists as a CO character meaning **work on the land**. However, it has long been used in Chinese as a simplification of **sacred** 聖 911, and consequently in the case of 1061 almost certainly lends 'borrowed' connotations of **otherworldliness** and **mysteriousness**. It also lends its sound to express **unusual**. 1061 originally meant **one's feelings when encountering something strange**, but, like the English term **suspicious**, it also came to be applied to the object itself.

Mnemonic: **WEIRD HAND ON GROUND GIVES SUSPICIOUS FEELING**

338

1062

KAI   拐帯者 KAITAISHA   absconder
DECEIVE, KIDNAP, BEND 誘拐 YŪKAI   abduction
8 strokes   拐じょう KAIJŌ   crooked staff

Formerly also written 拐 or, correctly, 拐. 扌 is **hand** 32, here meaning **arm**. 另 is the same variant of bone 冎 867 seen in split 列 579. Here it acts phonetically to express **bend**, and may also lend loose connotations of **flexibility** through its associations with the backbone (see also 629). 1062 originally meant to **bend one's arm around something and thus acquire it**. This usually meant to acquire in a furtive and/or illegal manner, leading to **deceive** and **kidnap**, while the minor meaning of **bend** derives from bent arm. Some scholars feel that bent arm in itself may also have symbolically suggested furtive or deviant behavior (cf. English crooked). Suggest taking 另 as **mouth** 口 20 and **cut** 刀 181.

Mnemonic: **RECEIVE CUTS TO HAND AND MOUTH IN KIDNAP**

1063

KAI, kuyamu, kuyashii, kuiru 後悔 KŌKAI   regret
REGRET, REPENT,   悔しさ KUYASHISA   vexation
VEXED   悔やみ状 KUYAMIJŌ
9 strokes   letter of condolence

忄 is **feelings** 147. 每 is **every** 206, here acting phonetically to express **resent** but of unknown semantic role. Thus **feelings of resentment**. For some reason this came in particular to mean **resentment against oneself**, leading to **remorse** and hence **repent/ regret**. Like the English term regret, it is now also used in a broad sense of **feel sorry**.

Mnemonic: **EVERY PERSON HAS FEELINGS OF REGRET**

1064

KAI, min[n]a   皆済 KAISAI   full payment
ALL, EVERYONE, FULL   皆無 KAIMU   none at all
9 strokes   皆様 MINASAMA   everyone

Once written 皆 and earlier 皆, showing **compare/ people lined up** 比 771 and **speak/ say** 㠯 / 曰 (old form and variant respectively of 曰 688: see also 307). 1064 originally meant **people in a row talking**, but gradually the idea of **all the people** came to prevail, leading to the present meanings. Note that 1064 is also used of **all** in the general sense of **full** or **complete**, and is not necessarily restricted to people. The use of **white** 白 65 in the present form appears to result from miscopying.

Mnemonic: **EVERYONE LINED UP, ALL IN WHITE**

1065

塊

KAI, katamari
LUMP, CLOD, MASS
13 strokes

金塊 KINKAI   gold bullion
塊鋼 KAIKŌ   steel ingot
山塊 SANKAI   massif

Somewhat obscure. Once written simply as 坴, namely **mass of earth in a container** 948, leading to **mass/ lump** in a broad sense. For reasons that are not clear the simple container 凵 (which technically existed as an independent character with a reading KI) was replaced by **devil** 鬼 1128 (also read KI), used apparently as a purely phonetic replacement. **Earth** 土 60 was then placed alongside the new element.

Mnemonic: **DEVILISH LUMP OF EARTH**

1066

壊

KAI, kowa*reru/su*
BREAK, DESTROY, RUIN
16 strokes

破壊 HAKAI   destruction
壊滅 KAIMETSU   destruction
壊血病 KAIKETSUBYŌ   scurvy

Formerly 壞 and earlier 𡍩. 土 is **earth**, here meaning **earthen rampart**. 襃/裹 is a CO character meaning wrap/ conceal/ carry in the sleeve. Its etymology is unclear, but it comprises **clothing** 衣/衤 420 and an element 罒 that includes eye 罒/目 72 and is possibly a variant of multitude 眾/衆 705 q.v. (thus giving many things enveloped by one's clothing?). In the case of 1066 裹 acts phonetically to express **destroy**, but any semantic role is unclear. Thus to **destroy/ break down an earthen rampart**, now **destroy/ break** in a broad sense. Suggest taking 𠂤 as **ten** 十 33 and **four** 罒 (variant 四 26), i.e. **fourteen**.

Mnemonic: **RUIN CLOTHES DESTROYING FOURTEEN EARTHEN WALLS**

1067

懐

KAI, futokoro, natsu*kashii*
BOSOM, YEARN, FOND
16 strokes

懐中 KAICHŪ-   pocket-
懐手 FUTOKORODE   idleness
述懐 JUKKAI   reminiscence

Formerly 懷. 忄 is **heart/ feeling** 147. 襃/裹 is the somewhat unclear character **carry in the sleeve** 1066 q.v. It should be noted that both in Chinese and Japanese there is a conceptual overlap between sleeve (or in the case of western clothes pocket) and **bosom**, both loosely meaning that part of the person which carries things. Thus 1067 came to mean the **feeling carried in one's bosom**, a reference to **yearning**. **Fond** is an associated meaning. 1067 is also used to refer to **bosom/ pocket**. There is an alternative but less likely theory that 裹 means simply carry, to give that carried in the heart. Suggest taking 裹 as **clothes** 衣 420, **ten** 十 33, and **four** 罒 (variant 四 26).

Mnemonic: **YEARNING FEELING FOR FOURTEEN SETS OF CLOTHES**

1068 **GAI** 弾劾者 DANGAISHA denunciator

INVESTIGATE (WRONG) 弾劾 DANGAI impeachment

8 strokes 劾奏 GAISŌ

reporting offense to ruler

力 is strength/ **effort** 74. 亥 is pig 865, here used phonetically to express **examine thoroughly**. Thus **examine thoroughly and with great effort**. This came to acquire particular connotations of **investigating wrongdoing**. Suggest taking 亥 as a **'broken'** variant of **(short) thread** 幺 111.

Mnemonic: **MAKE EFFORT TO INVESTIGATE BREAKING OF THREAD**

1069 **GAI** 生涯 SHŌGAI life

SHORE, EDGE 際涯 SAIGAI limits

11 strokes 天涯 TENGAI horizon

氵 is **water** 40. 厓 is an NGU character meaning **(tall) cliff**, comprising **cliff** 厂 45 and **raised earth** 圭 819 (literally a doubling of **earth** 土 60). Thus **waterside cliff**, a reference to the **shoreline** and by association **edge** of the land/ water. Now also used of **edge** in a general sense. Note that cliff is now usually conveyed by an NGU character 崖, which adds **hill/ mountain** 山 24.

Mnemonic: **CLIFF OF RAISED EARTH STANDS AT WATER'S EDGE**

1070 **GAI** 慨嘆 GAITAN lamentation

LAMENT, DEPLORE 感慨 KANGAI deep emotion

13 strokes 慨然 GAIZEN to indignantly

Formerly 慨. 忄 is **heart/ feelings** 147. 既/旣 is **already** 1126 q.v., acting phonetically to express **anger / detestation** and possibly also lending connotations of **something ceasing to be**. Thus **feelings of anger (at something ceasing to be?)**, a reference to **lamenting/ deploring**.

Mnemonic: **ALREADY HAVE FEELINGS OF LAMENT**

341

1071 **GAI**   該当 GAITŌ   relevance

RELEVANCE, THE SAID-   当該 TŌGAI-   the relevant-

13 strokes   該博 GAIHAKU   profundity

言 is **words** 274. 亥 is pig 865, here acting phonetically to express **binding**. 1071 originally referred to a **binding agreement,** then as a result of a reinterpretation of its elements (some scholars see it as a pure borrowing) came to mean **words that are bound to something,** i.e. that are **relevant.** Suggest taking 亥 as a **'broken'** variant of **(short) thread** 幺 111.

Mnemonic: **THREAD BINDING SAID WORDS HAS BEEN BROKEN**

1072 **GAI, ōmu***ne*   概念 GAINEN   general idea

ROUGHLY, IN GENERAL   概略 GAIRYAKU   outline

14 strokes   大概 TAIGAI   in general

Formerly 槩. 木 is **tree/ wood** 69. 旡/既 is **already** 1126 q.v., acting phonetically to express **rub across** and possibly also lending a loose idea of finished/ **complete.** 1072 originally referred to a **strickle,** which is a piece of wood passed across the top of a filled open container (usually of grain) in order to ensure an approximately full (i.e. complete) measure. It still retains this meaning in Chinese. **Rough measure** came to mean **rough/ roughly** and by association **in general.**

Mnemonic: **ALREADY ROUGHLY MEASURED WITH PIECE OF WOOD**

1073 **kaki**   垣根 KAKINE   fence, hedge

FENCE, HEDGE   生け垣 IKEGAKI   hedge

9 strokes   垣間見る KAIMAMIRU*   peep

Ground/ earth 土 60 and **go around** 亘 913, to give **earth that goes around** (a building), namely a **wall** and later, by association, a **hedge.** Suggest taking 亘 as **sun** 日 62 and **two** 二 61.

Mnemonic: **SUNNY GROUND BETWEEN TWO FENCES**

1074

核

KAKU
CORE, NUCLEUS,
NUCLEAR
10 strokes

核心 KAKUSHIN core, kernel
結核 KEKKAKU tuberculosis
核兵器 KAKUHEIKI
nuclear weapon

木 is **tree/ wood** 69. 亥 is **pig** 865, here acting phonetically to express **(hard) casing**. 1074 originally referred to an item with a **hard wooden casing**, i.e. a **box**, then as a result of a reinterpretation of its elements (some scholars see it as a pure borrowing) it came to mean **that with a hard casing found on a tree**, a reference to the stone/ **kernel** of some fruits. This also came to mean **nucleus** and in modern times **nuclear**. Suggest taking 亥 as a **'snapped'** variant of (**short**) **thread** 幺 111.

Mnemonic: **TREES SNAPPED LIKE THREADS IN NUCLEAR BLAST**

1075

殻

KAKU, kara
SHELL, HUSK, CRUST
11 strokes

貝殻 KAIGARA sea shell
甲殻 KŌKAKU shell
地殻 CHIKAKU earth's crust

Formerly 殼 and in ancient times 肵殳, showing a **hand** 又 holding a **gong/striker** ⼃ and striking a **large hanging bell** 肓. 殳 later became graphically confused with **striking hand holding weapon/ tool** 攴 / 攵 153, while the bell and its supporting ropes became stylised to 肖, 壱, then finally 壱. Bell gave rise to the idea of **hard cover**, leading to the present meanings. Suggest taking 士 as **samurai** 494, 冖 as **cover**, and 几 as **desk** 832, with 殳 as **strike a blow**.

Mnemonic: **SAMURAI COVERS DESK AGAINST BLOWS, SAVES SHELL**

1076

郭

KAKU
QUARTER, ENCLOSURE
11 strokes

輪郭 RINKAKU outlines
城郭 JŌKAKU citadel
遊郭 YŪKAKU gay quarter

阝 is **village** 355, here meaning **settlement**. 享 is **receive** 1162 q.v., here in its original meaning of **well guarded castle**. 1076 originally referred to a **settlement within a castle** (or under its protection), such as a citadel. It later came to mean **enclosed area** or **quarter** in a broader sense, though it is still occasionally used in the sense of fortification and can mean castle walls in Chinese. Suggest taking 享 as lid/ **cover** 亠 , **child** 子 25, and **entrance** 口 20.

Mnemonic: **CHILD COVERS ENTRANCE TO VILLAGE ENCLOSURE**

343

1077	KAKU, KŌ COMPARISON 13 strokes	比較 HIKAKU	comparison
		較量 KŌRYŌ	comparison
		大較 TAIKŌ	approximation

Once written 較 , showing that 交 is not crossed legs/ exchange 交 115 but a derivative of (or confusion with) **crossed sticks** 爻 10 q.v., which in itself contains the idea of **matching** and thus by association **comparing**. 車 is **carriage/ vehicle** 31. 1077 originally referred to small **cross-spars built out from the shaft of a dignitary's carriage,** used for boarding and alighting. Symmetrical spars were a sign of good workmanship, and were thus the object of scrutiny and **comparison.** Some scholars see comparison as resulting from confusion with check 校 21 q.v., but it seems more likely to be an extended meaning from matching cross-spars. Note that in Chinese 1077 still retains a minor meaning of state carriage. Suggest taking 交 as **exchange** 115.

Mnemonic: **EXCHANGE VEHICLES FOR COMPARISON**

1078	KAKU, heda*taru/teru* SEPARATE, INTERPOSE 13 strokes	隔離 KAKURI	quarantine
		間隔 KANKAKU	spacing
		隔週 KAKUSHŪ	fortnightly

Formerly 隔 , and earlier 𨻶 and 𨻶. 阝/阝 is **hill** 229. 鬲 is a CO character meaning **large pot/ cauldron,** comprising the large **pot** itself 口 /占 and a **stand** 丙 (stand 丅 , as in altar 示 695 q.v., and frame 冂 with cross- supports 八). Here 鬲 acts phonetically to express **block,** and probably also lends connotations of **obstacle** (being a bulky item that would occupy considerable space in a house). Thus **hills that block,** leading to **screen/ separate/ interpose.** Suggest remembering by association with **one/ single** 一 1 and **round** 口 (see also 228).

Mnemonic: **SEPARATED BY SINGLE HILL LIKE ROUND POT ON STAND**

1079	KAKU, *eru* OBTAIN, GAIN, SEIZE 16 strokes	獲得 KAKUTOKU	acquisition
		漁獲 GYOKAKU	fishing
		獲物 EMONO	prey

犭 is **dog** 17, while 蒦 is **seize** (crested) **bird** (in hand) 670. Thus a **dog seizing a bird,** leading to **seize/ obtain** in a broad sense but still also occasionally found with specific hunting connotations. Suggest taking 蒦 as **grass** 艹 9, **bird** 隹 216, and **paws** (literally hand) 又 .

Mnemonic: **DOG SEIZES BIRD IN GRASS WITH PAWS**

1080 嚇 KAKU, odosu/kasu 威嚇 IKAKU threat
THREATEN, MENACE 嚇怒 KAKUDO fury
17 strokes 威嚇的 IKAKUTEKI threatening

口 is mouth/ say 20. 赫 is an NGU character meaning **bright/ intense/ sudden** and comprises a doubling of **red** 赤 46, used in its literal sense of big fire (cf. English flare up). Here 赫 acts phonetically to express **round on/ retort**, and also lends connotations of **sudden** and **intense**. Thus to **round suddenly and intensely on someone verbally**, and by extension **speak angrily** (again cf. English flare up). It came to acquire particular associations with **threatening**.

Mnemonic: **THREATENING WORDS MAKE ONE SEE RED TWICE OVER**

1081 穫 KAKU 収穫 SHŪKAKU harvest
HARVEST 多穫 TAKAKU good crop
18 strokes 収穫高 SHŪKAKUDAKA yield

禾 is **rice plant** 81. 蒦 is **seize a crested bird in hand** 670, here meaning simply **take/ obtain**. Thus **obtained rice plants**, namely the **harvest**. Suggest taking 蒦 as **plants** 艹 9, **bird** 隹 216, and **hand** 又.

Mnemonic: **HARVEST OF RICE PLANTS BETTER THAN BIRD IN HAND**

1082 GAKU, take 山岳 SANGAKU mountains
PEAK, IMPOSING 岳父 GAKUFU father-in-law
8 strokes 雲ぜん岳 UNZENDAKE
Mount Unzen

Formerly also written 嶽, though technically they are separate characters. 岳 comprises **mountain** 山 24 and **hill** 丘 1149, the latter probably being used in its early sense of **hills in the plural**. Thus **many hills and mountains**, a reference to an **imposing mountain range** and hence the present meanings of **peak** and **imposing**. 嶽 comprises **mountain** 山 and **prison** 獄 1274 q.v., here acting phonetically to express **tower up** and almost certainly also lending connotations of **fearsome** and/or **daunting** from its early meanings of fight and litigation. Thus **(fearsome/ daunting?) towering mountain(s)**.

Mnemonic: **IMPOSING PEAK OF HILL TOWERS OVER MOUNTAIN!**

1083

kakari, ka*karu*/keru 掛かり人 KAKARIBITO hanger-on
BE CONNECTED, APPLY, 見掛け MIKAKE appearance
HANG, DEPEND, COST 腰掛ける KOSHIKAKERU sit
11 strokes

扌 is **hand** 32. 卦 is an NGU character meaning **divination point**, comprising **divination** ト 91 q.v. and **angle/ edge** 圭 819. 1083 originally referred to divination by hanging various bamboo strips from the hand and interpreting the groupings formed as they hung. Thus **hang (together)**, leading by figurative extension to a range of associated and extended meanings as listed above. Suggest taking ト literally as **crack** and 圭 literally as a **doubling** of **earth/ soil** 土 60.

Mnemonic: **CRACK IN HAND CONNECTED WITH DOUBLE LOAD OF SOIL**

1084

kata, SEKI 干潟 HIGATA tidal flat
BEACH, LAGOON 潟湖 SEKIKO lagoon
15 strokes 新潟市 NIIGATASHI Niigata City

氵 is **water** 40. 舄 is the somewhat obscure **bird** element seen in 寫 297 q.v. It acts here phonetically to express **salt**, and may also lend an idea of **take**. 1084 originally referred to **salty water** as in a **saltmarsh**, i.e. water which has taken in salt. Its meaning has now broadened to include **lagoon** and **beach**, and it is also sometimes used of **creek** and **flats**. Suggest taking 舄 as **bird** 勹 (simplified variant 鳥 174) and **talons** 臼.

Mnemonic: **LAGOON TRAPS WATER LIKE BIRD TRAPS WITH TALONS**

1085

KATSU, kuku*ru* 一括 IKKATSU (en) bloc
BIND, WRAP, FASTEN 括弧 KAKKO parentheses
9 strokes 包括的 HŌKATSUTEKI blanket-

扌 is **hand** 32. 舌 is not tongue 舌 732 but, as an old form 甛 shows, the same corruption of hollowed out space 㗊 seen in 活 244 q.v. Here 舌 acts phonetically to express **bind**, but any semantic role is unclear. Thus to **bind the hands** (some scholars feel rather bind <u>with</u> the hand, i.e. with hand 扌 playing a purely clarifying role), later **bind/ fasten/ wrap** in a broader sense. Suggest taking 舌 as **tongue**.

Mnemonic: **HAND BINDS AND WRAPS TONGUE**

1086 喝 KATSU
SHOUT, SCOLD
11 strokes

喝さい KASSAI — applause
恐喝 KYŌKATSU — threat
一喝 IKKATSU — yell, roar

Somewhat obscure. Formerly 喝 . 口 is **mouth/ say**. 昌/昌 is the somewhat obscure interrogative element seen in 謁 1022 q.v. Some scholars feel that 昌 is used purely phonetically to express **dry up** (as in 1087), to give **dried up voice/ hoarse**, and take **shout/ scold** to be a borrowing. However, if it is indeed the case that 1086 originally meant hoarse, it might be felt that shout/ scold is an associated meaning, as in shouting oneself hoarse. Others scholars take 昌 to act semantically in its assumed early meaning of **interrogate/ threaten**, with **shout/ scold** thus being an extended meaning. The latter theory seems the more likely. Suggest taking 昌 as **person/ man sitting** ヒ 238 **covered** 冖 in **sunshine** 日 62.

Mnemonic: MAN SITS COVERED IN SUNSHINE, SHOUTS OPEN MOUTHED

1087 渇 KATSU, kawa*ku*
THIRST, PARCHED
11 strokes

渇水 KASSUI — water shortage
渇望 KATSUBŌ — craving
渇き KAWAKI — thirst

Formerly 渇 . 氵 is **water** 40. 昌/昌 is the somewhat obscure interrogative element seen in 謁 1022 q.v., here acting phonetically to express **dry up** and possibly also lending its assumed connotations of **threaten/** menace. Thus a **(threatening?) drought**, now used of **dry up** and **parched** in a broader sense, including **thirst**. Suggest taking 昌 as **person/ man sitting** ヒ 238 **covered** 冖 in **sunshine** 日 62.

Mnemonic: MAN SITS COVERED IN SUNSHINE, THIRSTING FOR WATER

1088 KATSU, sube*ru*, name*raka*
SLIP, SLIDE, SMOOTH
13 strokes

円滑 ENKATSU — smoothness
滑走路 KASSŌRO — runway
滑り易い SUBERIYASUI — slippery

氵 is **water** 40. 骨 is **bone** 867 q.v., here acting phonetically to express **emerge** and possibly also lending some idea of flexibility and hence **smoothness** from its association with the backbone (see also 1048). Thus **water emerging (smoothly?)**, i.e. **flowing**. The flowing of water suggested by association a smooth **sliding/ gliding** movement and by further association the idea of **slip** and **slippery**.

Mnemonic: WATER ON BONES MAKES THEM SMOOTH AND SLIPPERY

347

1089 KATSU   褐色 KASSHOKU   brown
      BROWN, COARSE CLOTH   褐炭 KATTAN   lignite
      13 strokes   褐夫 KAPPU   ragged beggar

Formerly 褐 . 衤 is **clothing/ cloth** 420. 曷/曷 is the somewhat obscure interrogative element seen in 謁 1022 q.v., here used as a simple form of 葛 . The latter is an
NGU character meaning arrowroot/ strong vine/ **strong fiber**. It comprises plant 艹 9
and 曷 , which is here used phonetically to express bind but is of unknown semantic role.
Thus binding plant. In the case of 1089 曷 itself thus means **strong fiber**, giving **cloth
of strong (coarse) fiber**. This was a reference to a popular type of **brown cloth**, and
hence the acquisition of the meaning **brown**. Suggest taking 曷 as **person/ man sitting** ヒ 238 **covered** 勹 in **sunshine** 日 62.

Mnemonic: **MAN IN COARSE BROWN CLOTHING SITS COVERED IN
SUNSHINE**

1090 KATSU   所轄 SHOKATSU   jurisdiction
      CONTROL, LINCHPIN   管轄 KANKATSU   jurisdiction
      17 strokes   統轄 TŌKATSU   control

車 is **vehicle** 31. 害 is **harm** 437 q.v., here acting phonetically to express **lock** and almost certainly also lending connotations of **cover/ cap** (firmly). 1090 originally referred
to a wedge-shaped **linchpin** inserted in the end of an axle to lock the wheel in place. Just
like the English term linchpin, it came to mean **vital element** and hence by extension controlling element and eventually **control**.

Mnemonic: **VEHICLE HARMED -- CONTROLLING LINCHPIN REMOVED**

1091 且 ka*tsu*, SHO, SO   且つ又 KATSUMATA   moreover
      FURTHERMORE, BESIDES 且つ KATSU   besides
      5 strokes   こう且 KŌSHO   for a while

From a pictograph of a **cairn** 皂 , the piled up stones of which came to mean **one thing
on top of others** and hence **in addition/ furthermore**. Suggest remembering as **three
layers and a base**.

Mnemonic: **FURTHERMORE, CAIRN HAS THREE LAYERS AND A BASE**

1092	*karu* **REAP, CUT, SHEAR** 4 strokes	刈り入れ KARIIRE	harvesting
		刈り込む KARIKOMU	crop, trim
		草刈り機 KUSAKARIKI	mower

Originally 丱 and later 刈殳. 丱 (now 乂) depicts a pair of **shears**, with **cut** 刀/刂 181 added later for clarity. Thus **cut with shears**.

Mnemonic: **CUT WITH CROSSED SHEARS**

1093	KAN, *amai/eru/yakasu* **SWEET, PRESUME UPON** 5 strokes	甘酒 AMAZAKE	sweet sake
		甘言 KANGEN	sweet words
		甘え AMAE	presumption

Originally 甘, showing a **mouth** 口/口 20 with **something held in it** ‑. (Note that the same combination of elements can confusingly indicate a tongue in a mouth and mean speak or vocalise, as in 6/688 etc.) Something held in the mouth suggests something **savored**, i.e. something **sweet**. Suggest taking 甘 as an **'exaggerated'** mouth 口.

Mnemonic: **MOUTH EXAGGERATEDLY SAVORS SWEET THING**

1094	KAN, *ase,* **ase**bamu **SWEAT** 6 strokes	発汗 HAKKAN	sweating
		汗顔 KANGAN	shame
		一汗水 ASEMIZU	heavy sweat

氵 is **water** 40, here meaning **watery liquid**. 干 is **dry** 825 q.v., here acting phonetically to express **scatter**. 1094 thus means literally **scattered watery liquid**, a somewhat vague reference to **sweat** (which is scattered by/over the body).

Mnemonic: **WATERY SWEAT DRIES**

1095	KAN, *kama* **CAN, BOILER** 6 strokes	缶詰 KANZUME	canned goods
		缶切り KANKIRI	can opener
		汽缶 KIKAN	steam boiler

Formerly also written 罐, though technically they are separate characters. 缶 derives from 缶, a pictograph of a **vessel** 凵 with a **double lid** 午, the double lid indicating security (see also 258). 雚 is heron 445, acting phonetically to express **pour** and possibly also lending loose connotations of accommodate/ take in (from a heron's ability to consume large quantities of fish). Thus 罐 means a **secure vessel for pouring liquid into**. It is not clear how it later developed particular associations with **metal** containers, but it is possible that 缶 became confused with **metal** 金 14. Suggest taking 缶 as a combination of **noon** 午 110 and mountain 山 24.

Mnemonic: **OPEN CAN FOR NOON PICNIC ON MOUNTAINTOP**

1096   KAN, kimo   肝臓 KANZŌ   liver
               LIVER, COURAGE   肝心 KANJIN   vital
               7 strokes   肝っ玉 KIMOTTAMA guts, pluck

月 is **meat/of the body** 365. 干 is **dry** 825, acting phonetically to express **vital**. Thus **that which is vital to the body**, a somewhat vague reference to the **liver**. Also used figuratively to refer to **courage** (cf. English slang guts).

Mnemonic: **DRIED MEAT PROVES TO BE LIVER**

1097   KAN, kanmuri   王冠 ŌKAN   royal crown
               CROWN   栄冠 EIKAN   laurels
               9 strokes   冠毛 KANMŌ   crest, plume

冖 is **cover**, here meaning **on top of**. 寸 is **hand/ measure** 909 q.v., here meaning **careful use of the hand**. 元 is **origin** 106 q.v., here in its literal sense of **head**. Thus **something placed carefully on a head**, a reference to a **crown**.

Mnemonic: **MEASURE ORIGINAL CROWN TO ENSURE COVERS HEAD**

1098   KAN, ochiiru   陥没 KANBOTSU   cave-in
               COLLAPSE   欠陥 KEKKAN   defect
               10 strokes   陥落 KANRAKU   surrender

Formerly 陷 . 阝 is **hill** 229, here meaning **high place**. 臽 is a CO character meaning **hole**, comprising **stumbling person** 勹 / 𠂊 39 and mortar 臼 648, the latter indicating a **hollow/ hole**. 臽 acts here phonetically to express **fall**, and also lends an idea of **low place**. Thus **to fall from a high place to a low place**, i.e. **collapse**. Suggest taking 旧 as **old** 648.

Mnemonic: **OLD PERSON STUMBLES AND COLLAPSES ON HILL**

1099   KAN, kawaku   乾電地 KANDENCHI dry battery
               DRY   乾燥器 KANSŌKI   drier
               11 strokes   乾いた KAWAITA   dry, dried

乙 is **odd** 1041q.v., here in its sense of **twisted**. 𠦝 is **rising sun** 637 q.v., here acting phonetically to express **straighten** and probably also lending similar connotations of straight/ undeviating by association with the course of the rising sun. Thus 1099 originally meant to **straighten something twisted**. **Dry** is generally seen as a borrowing, but may stem from the idea of becoming hot and drying out associated with the rising sun, with 乙 (at one stage written 乀) possibly being taken to be vapors/ steam (see 11). Suggest taking 𠦝 as **sun** 日 62 rising through **plants** ＋＋ 9, with 乚 as **person** 39.

Mnemonic: **ODD PERSON DRIED BY SUN RISING THROUGH PLANTS**

1100

KAN
ENDURE, CONSIDER,
INVESTIGATE, SENSE
11 strokes

勘弁 KANBEN   pardon
勘定 KANJŌ   bill, account
勘違い KANCHIGAI
             misjudgment

力 is strength/ **effort** 74. 甚 is **great/ exceedingly** 1449 q.v., acting phonetically to express **endure/ tolerate** and probably also lending connotations of great emotion. Thus **make an effort to endure something** (very emotional?), leading to the idea of **great tolerance** and **perseverance** and in turn to such ideas as **strive to understand**.

Mnemonic: **MAKE EXCEEDINGLY GREAT EFFORT TO INVESTIGATE**

1101

KAN, wazura*u*
DISEASE, BE ILL
11 strokes

患者 KANJA   patient, victim
患部 KANBU   diseased part
長患い NAGAWAZURAI
             long illness

心 is **heart/ feelings** 147. 串 is an NGU character meaning **skewer/ pierce** (often taken to comprise two items 呂 pierced |, which is a useful mnemonic, but an old form suggests rather that it derives from hands thrusting a stake ( ). Thus **pierced heart**, meaning to **grieve** (still a meaning in Chinese). This came to mean **be afflicted** in a broad sense (also a meaning in Chinese) before coming to acquire particular associations with **being afflicted by an illness/ disease** (despite the absence of the sickness radical 疒 381).

Mnemonic: **FALL ILL AFTER SKEWER PIERCES HEART**

1102

KAN, tsuranu*ku*
PIERCE
11 strokes

貫通 KANTSŪ   penetration
縦貫 JŪKAN   traversing
貫流 KANRYŪ
            flowing through

Originally 𫐄 , showing **two shells/ units of money** 臼/貝 90 **threaded/pierced** |. 1102 originally referred to **money threaded on a string or stick**, but then came to mean **thread/ pierce** in general. Suggest taking 毌 as a variant of **mother** 母 203.

Mnemonic: **MOTHER PIERCED BY SHARP SHELL**

1103

KAN, wame*ku*
SHOUT, YELL
12 strokes

喚問 KANMON   summons
叫喚 KYŌKAN   cry, scream
喚き声 WAMEKIGOE shout, yell

口 is **mouth/ say** 20. 奐 is a CO character meaning lively and excellent, originally written 㝮. 冎 / 冎 is a **woman's genitals** (bending person ㇄ 39 and spread thighs 冂 317 [see also 1849 and 1105]), while ㅆ is a **pair of hands**. The original meaning appears to have been **spread a woman's thighs with the hands**, with connotations both of **intercourse** and **childbirth**. In the case of 1103 奐 acts phonetically to express **cry out**, reinforced by mouth/ say 口, but it is not clear whether it connotes a woman crying out during childbirth or during intercourse. It now means **shout** or **cry out** in a broad sense. Suggest taking 奐 as **big** 大 53, **hole** 宀 (variant 穴 849), and **stumbling person/man** 冂 (see also 1098), with 口 in its sense of **opening/open**.

Mnemonic: **MAN SHOUTS AS HE STUMBLES INTO BIG OPEN HOLE**

1104

KAN, TAN, ta*eru*
ENDURE, WITHSTAND
12 strokes

堪忍 KANNIN   patience
堪能 TANNŌ   skill
堪え難い TAEGATAI unendurable

土 is **earth** 60. 甚 is **great/ exceedingly** 1449, here acting phonetically to express **thrust (up)** and probably also lending an idea of **great**. Thus a **great upthrusting of earth**, a reference to **raised ground**. Its present meaning of **endure/ withstand** stems from confusion with **endure** 勘 1100 q.v.

Mnemonic: **EXCEEDINGLY LARGE EARTHEN MOUND WILL ENDURE**

1105

KAN, ka*eru*
EXCHANGE
12 strokes

換気 KANKI   ventilation
換え着 KAEGI   spare clothes
交換学生 KŌKANGAKUSEI
                 exchange student

扌 is **hand** 32. 奐 is **woman with spread legs** 1103 q.v. The latter acts phonetically to express **exchange**, and is also felt by some scholars to lend an idea of **careful handling** from an assumed meaning of assisting in the delivery of a child. Thus to **exchange something (carefully?) by hand**, later **exchange** in a broad sense. Suggest taking 奐 as **big** 大 53, **hole** 宀 (variant 穴 849), and **falling person/man** 冂 (see 1103).

Mnemonic:**MAN FALLS INTO BIG HOLE DURING EXCHANGE OF HANDS**

1106 敢 **KAN, ae*te*, ae*nai***
DARING, TRAGIC
12 strokes

勇敢 YŪKAN bravery, valor
敢然 KANZEN bravely
敢なく AENAKU tragically

Of very distorted graphic evolution. Originally 𢼸, showing **two hands** 又 **pulling** (symbolised by ノ) **something** 一 out of a **container** 凵. The original meaning was to **pull out with both hands**. This came to mean **make a great effort**, leading to the idea of a **make-or-break effort** and hence **do something daring**. **Tragic** is a negatively associated meaning. The present form results from a stylised intermediate form 敢, amongst other things showing confusion with **strike** 殳 153 (now **strike** 攵 101). Suggest remembering 耳 by association with **ear** 耳 29, taking it as **top of the ear.**

Mnemonic: **DARING STRIKE TO TOP OF EAR -- TRAGIC RESULTS**

1107 棺 **KAN, hitsugi**
COFFIN
12 strokes

棺おけ KANOKE coffin, casket
石棺 SEKKAN sarcophagus
棺台 HITSUGIDAI bier

木 is tree/ **wood** 69. 官 is **official** 441 q.v., here acting phonetically to express **coffin** and possibly also lending a loose suggestion of **that which covers a corpse** through its elements roof/ building 宀 28 (which can mean cover) and buttocks 𠂤 350 (which can mean corpse [see 236]). Thus **wooden coffin**, now **coffin** in a general sense.

Mnemonic: **OFFICIAL RESTS IN WOODEN COFFIN**

1108 款 **KAN**
FRIENDSHIP, CLAUSE,
ENGRAVE
12 strokes

借款 SHAKKAN loan, credit
落款 RAKKAN signature
款待 KANTAI hospitality

Somewhat obscure. Formerly also written 欵. 示 is **altar/ of the gods** 695. 欠 is **lack** 471 q.v., here used to mean **open** from its literal meaning of **gaping mouth**. Old forms such as 𣢟 and 𣢟 show that 木 / 士 derives from a **thickly growing plant** 𣎳 or 𡳿. 𣎳 is believed to have been a variant of **rice plant** 禾 / 禾 81, but has the same form as tree 木 / 木 69. 𡳿 is an old form of **growing plant** 生 42, but has long been confused with emerge 出 34 q.v. Note that it has this 'emerge' form in the NGU character 祟, which has evolved from 祟 and now means curse. It literally depicts **plants placed on an altar** and originally meant **make an offering to the gods by way of supplication** to them, possibly acquiring its modern meaning in similar fashion to the English term oath, which can either mean sincere statement or curse depending on the circumstances. In the case of 1108 it appears in the form 𡗜 and lends a meaning of **sincere wish**, as well as acting phonetically to express **open** and thus reinforcing 欠. 1108 originally meant an **open and sincere statement of a wish**, with open having the same connotations of **sincerity** and **earnestness** as in English, and it can still mean earnest wish in Chinese. Some scholars see its present meaning of **friendship** as an association/ extension of earnest/ open statement, i.e. a situation in which there is no duplicity and only goodwill, while others see it as a borrowing. **Engrave** is likewise seen as a borrowing by some scholars, and by others as an alternative line of semantic evolution from the emphasised idea of open, leading to open up a hole and thus by association engrave (i.e. make a groove). While the latter theory seems somewhat unlikely it should be noted that in Chinese 1108 can also mean empty/ hollow. **Clause** is felt to be an associated meaning with engrave, from the idea of a piece of writing that is endowed with permanence. Suggest taking 士 as **samurai** 494, with 示 in its other meaning of **show**. It should also be noted that 1108 is occasionally encountered written as 欵, resulting from graphic confusion between 素 and the 'lost person' element of doubt 矣 835.

Mnemonic: **SAMURAI SHOWS LACK OF FRIENDSHIP**

1109	閑	**KAN** **LEISURE, QUIET** 12 strokes	閑静 KANSEI	tranquility
			閑散 KANSAN	leisure, quiet
			閑人 KANJIN	idle person

木 is tree/ **wood** 69, while 門 is **gate** 211. 1109 originally referred to a **piece of wood used to bar a gate**, and meant **block/ obstruct/ defend** (meanings still found in Chinese). **Leisure** results from confusion with **space** 閒 / 間 92, which once had an associated meaning of **free time**, while **quietude/ quiet** is in turn an associated meaning with leisure.

Mnemonic: **BUILD WOODEN GATE IN A QUIET MOMENT OF LEISURE**

1110	寛	**KAN, kutsuro***gu* **MAGNANIMOUS, RELAX** 13 strokes	寛大 KANDAI	liberality
			寛容 KANYŌ	tolerance
			寛衣 KANI	loose clothes

Somewhat obscure. Formerly 寬 . 宀 is **house/ roof** 28. 莧 is found as a CO character with the unhelpful meaning of vegetables, but it is not certain that this is the same character as the 莧/萈 element of 1110. (If it is, then its present meaning is presumably borrowed.) The latter was once written , showing that 艹 is not grass/ plant 艹 9 but apparently a derivative of a **crest** of some sort 艹. 兒 is the old form 見 of (**bend down to**) **look** 見 18, with 丶/ · possibly some form of **support**. Its meaning is unclear, though in the case of 1110 it is known to have acted phonetically to express **big**, thus giving a meaning of **big house**. By association this came to mean a place where one could **relax**, i.e. where one was not cramped, and it also developed associated figurative connotations of '**easy going**'/ **largesse**/ **magnanimity**. Suggest taking 見 as **see** and 艹 as **grass**, with 宀 as **cover**.

Mnemonic: **SEE GRASS COVERED SPOT AND RELAX THERE**

1111 KAN   監 視 KANSHI   observation
SUPERVISE, WATCH   総 監 SŌKAN   superintendent
15 strokes   監 禁 KANKIN   imprisonment

Once written 監, showing a **person** ㇆/㇄ 39 bending over to **stare** 臣 /臣 512 q.v. at the **surface of water** ─ in a **bowl** 皿 /皿 1307. The person was **staring at his reflection**, which was the original meaning of 1111, but this then came to mean **look carefully** and hence **supervise/ watch**. Suggest taking 臣 literally as **staring eye**, and ─ as **one** 1. See also 991.

Mnemonic: **PERSON WITH ONE STARING EYE WATCHES BOWL**

1112 KAN, yurui/*mu*/*meru*/*yaka*   緩 和 KANWA   mitigation
LOOSE, EASY, SLACK   緩 流 KANRYŪ   gentle current
15 strokes   緩 緩 YURUYURU   leisurely

糸 is **thread** 27, here meaning **cord**. 爰 is draw to oneself 932 q.v., here acting phonetically to express **loose(ly)** and also lending an idea of **pulling on a rope/ cord** and hence **bind**. Thus to **bind something loosely with cord**. **Slack** is now also used figuratively, in the sense of **easy**. Suggest taking 爰 as **three hands** (i.e. reaching hand ⺥ 303, hand 又 , and hand 𠂇 [variant 手 32]).

Mnemonic: **THREE HANDS RESULT IN LOOSELY TIED THREAD**

1113 憾 KAN, ura*mu*   遺 憾 IKAN na   regrettable
REGRET   憾 恨 KANKON   grudge
16 strokes   憾 み URAMI   regret

Heart/ **feeling** 忄 147 and **(intense) feeling** 感 246, to give **doubly intense feeling**. An intense feeling is one that lingers in the heart, a somewhat vague reference to **regret**. (Some scholars feel that 感 also acts phonetically to express **regret**, thus clarifying the meaning.) See also 1277, and note the overlap between resent and regret.

Mnemonic: **REGRET IS DOUBLY STRONG FEELING**

355

1114 還 **KAN** **RETURN** 16 strokes

還元 KANGEN restoration
生還者 SEIKANSHA survivor
返還 HENKAN restitution

辶 is **movement** 129, here meaning **go**. 睘 is a CO character meaning **gaze in terror**. Its etymology is not fully clear but it appears to comprise **eye** 罒/目 72, here presumably meaning **look**, and a variant 袁 of **sorrow** 衷 998, and presumably originally meant **look of sorrow**. Here it acts phonetically to express **turn back**, and may possibly also have originally lent connotations of **alarm** and/or **despair**. Thus to **go back/ return (in alarm/ despair?)**, now **return** in a broad sense.

Mnemonic: **RETURN, MOVING WITH SORROWFUL LOOK**

1115 環 **KAN, wa** **RING, CIRCLE** 17 strokes

指環 YUBIWA finger ring
環状線 KANJŌSEN loop line
環境 KANKYŌ environment

Jewel 王 102 and **gaze in terror** 睘 1114 q.v. The latter acts phonetically to express **fit**, and may possibly also lend an idea of **looking in awe** (i.e. at something **wondrous**). 1115 originally referred to a **jeweled ring or bracelet (of wondrous quality?) that fitted perfectly,** and later came to mean **ring** or **circle** in a broad sense. Suggest taking 睘 in its assumed literal meaning of **sorrowful** 袁 (variant sorrow 衷 998) **look** 罒 (variant eye 目 72).

Mnemonic: **JEWELED RING EVOKES SORROWFUL LOOK**

1116 艦 **KAN** **WARSHIP** 21 strokes

軍艦 GUNKAN warship
艦隊 KANTAI fleet
艦種 KANSHU warship class

舟 is **boat/ ship** 1354. 監 is **watch (over)** 1111, here acting phonetically to express **protected** (by cladding) and possibly also lending its own idea of **watch over**. Thus a **ship which is protected (and which watches over other ships?)**, i.e. a **warship**.

Mnemonic: **SHIP THAT WATCHES OVER OTHERS IS A WARSHIP**

1117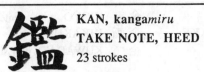

KAN, kanga*miru*
TAKE NOTE, HEED
23 strokes

年鑑 NENKAN　　yearbook
鑑賞 KANSHŌ　appreciation
鑑みて KANGAMITE in view of

金 is **metal** 14. 監 is **watch** 1111 q.v., here with its literal meaning of **stare at one's reflection**. Thus to **stare at one's reflection in a metal mirror** (metal mirror still being listed as a meaning in Chinese). This came to mean **scrutinise** and hence **take note of/ heed**. Note that the verb kangamiru derives from kagami (mirror) and miru (look).

Mnemonic: **WATCH SELF IN METAL MIRROR, HEEDING REFLECTION**

1118

GAN, fuku*mu/meru*
INCLUDE, CONTAIN
7 strokes

包含 HŌGAN　　　inclusion
含有量 GANYŪRYŌ　content
含めて FUKUMETE　including

口 is **mouth** 20. 今 is **now** 125 q.v., here in its literal sense of **cover**. Thus **covered by the mouth**, i.e. **contained in the mouth**, leading to **contain** and by association **include**. See also 1182.

Mnemonic: **NOW CONTAINED IN THE MOUTH**

1119

GAN
STUBBORN
13 strokes

頑固 GANKO　　stubbornness
頑健 GANKEN　robust health
頑張る GANBARU　persevere

頁 is **head** 93. 元 is **origin** 106 q.v., here rather unusually acting in three roles. First, it lends its literal meaning of **head**, and by extension **brain** and **thought**. 106 also often has connotations of **roundness**, partly because of the round shape of the head and partly because its sound (GAN) is the same as the sound for round (GAN 丸 830), and its second role in the case of 1119 is to lend such connotations (and/or it may be taken to act phonetically to express round). Third, it lends its later meaning of **origin**. 1119 could literally mean a **person with a round head**, but it was also used to refer to a person whose **thinking went round in circles** (i.e. back to the origin), i.e. a **stubborn** person.

Mnemonic: **STUBBORN HEAD GOES ROUND AND BACK TO ORIGIN**

1120

KI, kuwada*teru*
PLAN, UNDERTAKE
6 strokes

企業 KIGYŌ　　　enterprise
企画 KIKAKU　　　　　plan
企て KUWADATE plot, scheme

人 is a variant of **person** 人 39. 止 is **foot** 129, here also acting phonetically to express **precarious**. 1120 originally meant **person of precarious footing**, a reference to a person **standing on tiptoe** (still a meaning in Chinese). Stand on tiptoe led to a wide range of associated/ extended meanings, such as stand erect, look out, and be alarmed (all still found in Chinese), while in Japanese the idea of **standing up in some alarm** led to **take action**, which in turn led to **undertake** and by association **plan**. Suggest taking 止 in its commoner meaning of **stop**.

Mnemonic: **PERSON STOPS AND PLANS UNDERTAKING**

1121

岐

KI
FORK
7 strokes

岐路 KIRO　　　　forked road
分岐 BUNKI　　　　divergence
多岐 TAKI　　many directions

山 is **mountain** 24. 支 is **branch** 691, here acting phonetically to express **fork** and probably also lending an idea of **branching/ bifurcation**. 1121 originally referred to a specific mountain in ancient China noted for its **twin peaks**, then came to mean **forked mountain** in general and eventually just **fork**.

Mnemonic: **BRANCHED MOUNTAIN IS FORKED**

1122

KI, i*mu*/*mawashii*
MOURN, ABHOR,
ODIOUS
7 strokes

忌中 KICHŪ　　　mourning
禁忌 KINKI　　　　taboo
忌み嫌う IMIKIRAU　　detest

心 is **heart**/feeling 147. 己 is **self** 855 q.v., here acting phonetically to express **abhor** and possibly also lending an idea of **thoroughly** from its literal meaning of thread from end to end. Thus **feeling of (total?) abhorrence**. **Odious** is an associated meaning. **Mourn** is also seen as an associated meaning, since something abhorred was usually something shunned, which came to mean something taboo. Taboos were frequently associated with conventions observed during mourning. Note that there is an occasionally encountered form 忌, which appears to have mistaken 己 for bending body/ serpent 己 (see 250) and used a variant form 巳 of this (also 250).

Mnemonic: **ABHOR ONESELF IN ONE'S HEART**

1123		KI **STRANGE, ODD** 8 strokes	奇数 KISŪ	odd number
			新奇 SHINKI	novelty
			奇形 KIKEI	deformity

Somewhat obscure, though its elements are clearly **big** 大 53 q.v. and **can** 可 816 q.v. Some scholars take the latter to act phonetically to express **one-legged** and take 大 to mean literally **standing person**, thus giving **person standing on one leg**, which is something **strange**. Note that there is a CO character 踦 which means one-legged, combining 1123 with the foot/leg radical 足 51. It is possible that in the latter case 奇 itself acts phonetically to express one-legged (as well as lending a meaning of strange), or else that leg 足 was simply added to 奇 (assuming for argument's sake that this does mean one-legged) for clarity. However, it seems unlikely that a spoken word meaning one-legged existed, and more likely that 可 lent its connotations of **twisted** (and possibly also acted in some unclear phonetic role), giving either a **person standing in a twisted fashion** or else something **greatly twisted**. In view of the association between **twisted** and **odd** (see 1041), the 'greatly twisted' theory seems the most likely. (踦 would then mean greatly twisted leg, leading to cripple and presumably later also amputee.)

Mnemonic: **SOMETHING BIG CAN BE SOMETHING STRANGE**

1124		KI, ino*ru* **PRAY, HOPE** 8 strokes	祈念 KINEN	prayer
			祈とう KITŌ	prayer
			祈り合う INORIAU	pray together

Formerly 祈. 示/礻 is **altar/of the gods** 695. 斤 is **ax** 1176, acting phonetically to express **desire/wish**. Thus **desire something of the gods**, i.e. **pray** or **hope**.

Mnemonic: **AX AT ALTAR ENFORCES PRAYER**

1125		KI **TRACK, RUT, WAY** 9 strokes	軌道 KIDŌ	track, orbit
			無軌道 MUKIDŌ no	wayward
			常軌 JŌKI	normal way

車 is **vehicle** 31. 九 is **nine** 12, acting phonetically to express **parallel**. Thus **that which is parallel and associated with a vehicle**, a somewhat vague reference to its **tracks/ruts**. Later **track/path** in a broad sense.

Mnemonic: **TRACK RUTTED AFTER NINE VEHICLES PASS**

1126 KI, sude ALREADY, FINISHED 10 strokes

既製 KISEI — ready-made
既婚 KIKON — married
既定 KITEI — established

Formerly 旣. 皀/皀 are variants of **food/ eat** 食 146. 旡 is **without** 688 q.v. Thus **without food**, indicating that one has **already finished** it. Suggest taking 旡 literally as **long haired kneeling man**.

Mnemonic: **HAIRY KNEELING MAN HAS ALREADY FINISHED EATING**

1127 KI, u*eru* STARVE, HUNGER 10 strokes

飢寒 KIKAN — hunger and cold
飢え死に UEJINI death from hunger
飢餓行進 KIGAKŌSHIN
hunger march

食 is **food/ eat** 146. 几 is **table** 832, acting phonetically to express **few/ little** and probably also lending its meaning of **table**. Thus **little food (on the table?)**, indicating **hunger** and **starvation**.

Mnemonic: **FOOD ON THE TABLE, BUT STILL STARVING**

1128 KI, oni DEVIL, DEMON, GHOST 10 strokes

鬼界 KIKAI — nether world
鬼籍 KISEKI — the dead
鬼ごっこ ONIGOKKO tag (game)

From a pictograph 鬼, showing a **person crouching** 儿/儿 39 wearing a **mask** ⊕/ 甶 807. This was actually a **death-mask**, worn in a religious ritual in which contact was made with **spirits of the dead**. Thus the masked figure came to represent **spirits/ ghosts**, which for some reason came to acquire frequently malicious connotations. The later addition 厶 is seen by some scholars as a graphic derivative of the kneeling figure's lower leg, but by others as nose/self 134 used phonetically to express **dead/ death** and thus clarify the nature of the mask. Suggest remembering by association with think/ **thought** 思 131 q.v., taking 儿厶 as a **'distorted' heart** 心 (147).

Mnemonic: **DISTORTED HEART PRODUCES DEVILISH THOUGHT**

| 1129 幾 | KI, iku-
HOW MANY, HOW MUCH
12 strokes | 幾何学 KIKAGAKU
幾つ IKUTSU
幾ら IKURA | geometry
how many?
how much? |

絲 is a doubling of **(short) thread** 111, the doubling indicating many. 戎 is a variant of **broad bladed halberd** 515/ 246 q.v., here used in its sense of **trim/ put into shape** and also lending its sound to express **control**. Thus **that which controls threads and puts them into shape**, i.e. a **loom**. This is now conveyed by 機 453, which adds wood 木 69, while 1129 itself has undergone a convoluted change of meaning. Controlling threads on a loom came to represent **predictable movement**, which by association came to mean **predictable quantity** and hence **how many/ how much**.

Mnemonic: **HOW MANY SHORT THREADS CAN A HALBERD TRIM?**

| 1130 棋 | KI
(ORIENTAL) CHESS
12 strokes | 棋士 KISHI
将棋 SHŌGI
棋敵 KITEKI | go/shogi player
Japanese chess
chess opponent |

Formerly also 棊 . 木 is **wood** 69. 其 is **winnowing device** 251, here acting phonetically to express **little** and possibly also lending loose connotations of **selecting**. Thus **little wooden pieces (which are selected?)**, a reference to **chess pieces** and hence **chess** itself. See also 1240.

Mnemonic: **PLAY WITH WOODEN CHESS PIECES WHILE WINNOWING**

| 1131 棄 | KI, su*teru*
ABANDON, RENOUNCE
13 strokes | 放棄 HŌKI
棄権 KIKEN
棄児 KIJI | abandonment
abstention
abandoned child |

Once written , showing **newborn child** 古 / 去 227 (literally inverted child 孕 / 子 25) and **hands** 艸. The hands are actually **throwing away** the child, though since this is not especially clear later forms such as 棄 (the prototype of the modern form) added a **broom** 帚, which symbolised **clearing away/ disposing**. To **abandon a child** came to mean **abandon** in general. Suggest remembering by association with **leaf** 葉 405, from which distinguish.

Mnemonic: **ABANDON CHILD, TOSSING AWAY LIKE A LEAF**

1132 輝

KI, kagaya*ku/kashii*
SPARKLE, SHINE
15 strokes

光輝 KŌKI   luster, splendor
輝石 KISEKI   pyroxene
輝き KAGAYAKI   light

Correctly written 煇 , though in practice **fire** 火 8 was some time ago replaced by **light** 光 116. 軍 is **army** 466, acting phonetically to express **light** but of unknown semantic role. Thus **firelight**, now **shine/ sparkle** in a broad sense.

Mnemonic: **ARMY PROVIDES SHINING LIGHT**

1133 騎

KI
RIDER
18 strokes

騎士 KISHI   rider, knight
騎兵 KIHEI   cavalry
一騎打ち IKKIUCHI single combat

馬 is **horse** 191. 奇 is **strange** 1123, acting phonetically to express **straddle** but of unknown semantic role. Thus to **straddle a horse**, i.e. **ride**, though now usually found in the sense of **rider**.

Mnemonic: **RIDER ON STRANGE HORSE**

1134 宜

GI, yoro*shii*
GOOD, RIGHT
8 strokes

適宜 TEKIGI   suitability
便宜 BENGI   convenience
宜しく YOROSHIKU

well, best regards

Though long written as **roof/ building** 宀 28 and **furthermore/ cairn/ pile up** 且 1091, very old forms such as show (a bird's eye view of) **meat** 夕 / 月 / 肉 365 (doubled to indicate considerable quantity) on the **sacrificial slab** 目 of an altar (= presumably being **grooves** to let blood drain). 1134 is to all intents and purposes a variant of the NGU character 俎 , which also means sacrificial altar (and in modern times chopping board) and shows a similar miscopying resulting in pile up 且 , with 仌 being additional meat (technically the grains 仌 of meat seen in 肉). **Good/ right** is an associated meaning, i.e. offering meat in a sacrifice being **proper** behavior.

Mnemonic:**FURTHERMORE,GOOD BUILDING IS RIGHT FOR SACRIFICE**

1135

GI, nise, itsuwar*u*
FALSE, LIE
11 strokes

偽物 NISEMONO — forgery
偽善 GIZEN — sacrifice
偽り者 ITSUWARIMONO — liar

Formerly 僞 . 亻 is **person** 39. 爲 /為 is **do/ purpose** 1003 q.v., here acting phonetically to express **change** and almost certainly also lending connotations of **imitate**. 1135 originally referred to a **person changing his appearance in order to imitate** someone, and thus came to mean **deception** and **falsehood**.

Mnemonic: **PERSON LIES TO SUIT OWN PURPOSES**

1136

GI, azamu*ku*
CHEAT, DECEIVE
12 strokes

詐欺 SAGI — fraud
欺まん GIMAN — deception
欺き取る AZAMUKITORU defraud

欠 is **lack** 471 q.v., here in its literal sense of **gaping mouth/ yawn**. 其 is **winnowing device** 251, here acting phonetically to express **exhaustion** but of unclear semantic role. Thus to **yawn with exhaustion**. **Cheat/ deceive** is a borowed meaning.

Mnemonic: **LACK WINNOWING DEVICE SO RESORT TO CHEATING**

1137

GI
CEREMONY, RULE, CASE
15 strokes

儀式 GISHIKI — ceremony
儀典 GITEN — rite, ritual
礼儀 REIGI — etiquette

Person 亻 39 and **righteousness** 義 645, to give a **righteous person**. The meaning gradually changed to refer to the **way in which a person becomes righteous**, i.e. **rules, norms,** and **conventions. Ceremony** is an associated meaning.

Mnemonic: **RIGHTEOUS PERSON OBEYS RULES IN CEREMONY**

1138

GI, tawamu*reru*
PLAY, FROLIC, JOKE
15 strokes

遊戯的 YŪGITEKI — playful
戯画 GIGA — caricature
戯言 TAWAGOTO* — gibberish

Formerly also written 戲 . 戈 is **halberd** 493. 虗 is **empty/ hollow** 1156 q.v., here acting phonetically to express **play** and almost certainly also lending figurative connotations of **not in earnest** (虍 fulfils the same phonetic role and probably the same semantic role, with vessel 豆 1640 replacing hollow crowned tall hill 屮 1149). Thus **halberd used in play/ sport** (and not in earnest), leading to **play/ frolic** in general.

Mnemonic: **EMPTY THREATS WITH HALBERD -- JUST A JOKE**

1139		**GI**	模 擬	MOGI	imitation
		IMITATE, MODEL	擬 勢	GISEI	bluff
		17 strokes	擬 声	GISEI	onomatopoeia

扌 is **hand** 32. 疑 is **doubt** 835 q.v., here acting phonetically to express **confusion** and also lending similar connotations of its own. Thus to **cause confusion with the hands**, meaning to **make something resembling something else**, i.e. **imitate/ model**.

Mnemonic: **MAKE DOUBTFUL IMITATION BY HAND**

1140		**GI**	犠 牲	GISEI	sacrifice
		SACRIFICE	犠 打	GIDA baseball sacrifice hit
		17 strokes	犠 牲 制 度	GISEISEIDO
					sacrificial system

Formerly also 犠. 牛 is **cow/ bull** 97. 義 is a CO character now meaning breath. Its etymology is somewhat obscure, but its elements are sheep/ excellent 羊 986 q.v., hal- berd/ cut 戈 493, rice plant 禾 81, and seek exit 丂 281 (possibly here meaning grow), and it may originally have meant cut excellently grown rice, i.e. **a fine crop**. Breath may be a borrowed meaning, or else an associated meaning from the idea of life-giving. Here it acts phonetically to express **good**, and probably also lends similar connotations. The later form uses **righteousness** 義 645, which likewise acts phonetically to express **good** and also lends similar connotations. Thus **good bull**, a reference to a bull of outstanding quality which was chosen as a **sacrifice** (see also 760).

Mnemonic: **RIGHTEOUS BULL IS JUST RIGHT FOR SACRIFICE**

1141		**KIKU**	野 菊	NOGIKU	aster
		CHRYSANTHEMUM	菊 花	KIKKA	chrysanthemum
		11 strokes	菊 判	KIKUBAN	small octavo

Plant 艹 9, **encircle** 勹 655 (here meaning **circle**), and **rice grains/ head of rice** 米 201 (here meaning **head of plant**). Thus **plant with a circular head**, a reference to the **chrysanthemum**.

Mnemonic: **CHRYSANTHEMUM PLANT ENCIRCLED BY RICE**

1142 KICHI, KITSU   吉日 KICHINICHI   lucky day
GOOD LUCK, JOY   吉報 KIPPŌ   good news
6 strokes   不吉 FUKITSU   ill omen

Of confused etymology. Once written 击, showing a **double-lidded** ‡ **container** ⼝. Such a container potentially symbolised **plenty** and hence **good fortune** and **contentment**. In the case of go/ leave 去 258 q.v. it confusingly suggests the opposite, but in the case of 1142 the auspicious connotations appear to have been reinforced by confusion with an ancient character 㕭, in which ⼝ is **mouth** 20 and ⼚ is a variant of the early form 义 of **dam** ‡ 126 q.v., here meaning **block** and thus giving **blocked mouth**. This is potentially confusing in itself but is known to have been a reference to **full mouth**, and hence also symbolised contentment and good fortune. Another ancient character 㕭 seems to have confused block ⼚ with a lid or stopper 合, and it is not clear whether it means full mouth or lidded container. However, it clearly shows the overlap between **full mouth**, **lidded container**, and **good fortune/ contentment**. **Joy** is an extension of contentment. Suggest taking ⼝ as **open mouth** and 士 as **samurai** 494. See also 1159.

Mnemonic: **SAMURAI OPEN MOUTHED WITH JOY AFTER GOOD LUCK**

1143 喫 KITSU   喫煙 KITSUEN   smoking
INGEST, RECEIVE   喫茶店 KISSATEN   cafe
12 strokes   喫水線 KISSUISEN   waterline

⼝ is **mouth** 20. 契 is **pledge** 1195 q.v., here acting phonetically to express **chew** and probably also lending reinforcing connotations of **bringing jagged edges together**. Thus to **chew in the mouth**, later just **take in/ ingest through the mouth** and also by extension **take in/ receive** in a broader sense.

Mnemonic: **MOUTH PLEDGED TO INGEST**

1144 詰 KITSU, tsu*mu/maru/meru*   詰問 KITSUMON   grilling
PACK, PACKED, FULL 詰まり TSUMARI   in short
13 strokes   詰め込む TSUMEKOMU   cram

言 is **words** 274. 吉 is **good luck/ joy** 1142 q.v., here in its meaning of **full mouth/ container** and also acting phonetically to express **extremely**. Thus a **mouth extremely full of words**, which was originally a reference to **grilling/ 'bombarding' with questions** but later came to mean just **full to bursting** in general.

Mnemonic: **WORDS PACKED WITH JOY**

1145

KYAKU, kae*tte*
(ON THE) CONTRARY
7 strokes

却下 KYAKKA   rejection
退却 TAIKYAKU   retreat
却説 SATE*   well now

去 is go/ leave 258. ㄗ is **bending person** 425, here meaning **person on their knees.** Thus to **leave on one's knees,** meaning to leave the presence of a superior. Some scholars take **contrary** to be a borrowing, others an associated meaning from the idea of **withdrawing** and thus **going away from.** The latter seems more likely.

Mnemonic: **LEAVE ON BENDED KNEES, JUST TO BE CONTRARY**

1146

KYAKU, KYA, ashi
LEG, FOOT
11 strokes

脚下 KYAKKA   at one's feet
脚立 KYATATSU   stepladder
脚荷 ASHINI   ballast

却 is **on the contrary** 1145 q.v., here in its literal sense of **leave on one's knees.** 月 is flesh/ **of the body** 365, serving to draw attention to the part of the body involved. Thus the **knee** and by association **leg,** especially the **lower leg** and thus sometimes **foot.**

Mnemonic: **LEG CAN BE CONTRARY TO BODY**

1147

GYAKU, shiita*geru*
CRUELTY, OPPRESS
9 strokes

虐殺 GYAKUSATSU massacre
虐待 GYAKUTAI maltreatment
残虐 ZANGYAKU   cruelty

Once written 㿝, showing a **tiger** 㿟/ 虍 281 **clawing** ㅌ/ ㅌ a **person** 人 39. This came to represent **cruelty,** with **oppress** being an associated meaning. Person has disappeared in the modern form.

Mnemonic: **TIGER'S CLAWS SYMBOLISE CRUELTY**

1148 及

KYŪ, oyo*bu/bosu/bi*
REACH, EXTEND, AND
3 strokes

及第点 KYŪDAITEN   pass mark
追及 TSUIKYŪ   catch up
及び腰 OYOBIGOSHI bent back

Originally 乃又, showing a **person** 乃 39 and a **hand** 又 **reaching** out to seize them. Later forms such as 乃又 show a stylised <u>bent</u> person, the bending being felt to emphasise the idea of the person's attempt to escape. Reach out for an escaping person came to mean **reach** in general, with **extend** being an associated meaning. **And** is also an associated meaning, from the idea of a range of items extending to include an additional one. Note that very occasionally 1148 still appears to retain connotations of bending. Suggest remembering partly by association with **movement** 廴 129.

Mnemonic: **HAND REACHES OUT FOR BENT PERSON MOVING OFF**

1149

KYŪ, oka
HILL
5 strokes

砂丘 SAKYŪ   sand dune
丘しん KYŪSHIN   pimple
丘辺 OKABE   near a hill

Originally **ᗰᗰ**, depicting two **hills**. Later greatly stylised to **ᗡ** and eventually miscopied as two **persons back to back** 北 / 北 (イ being person 39), from which the present shape derives. Suggest taking **斤** as **ax** 1176 and **一** as **ground level**.

Mnemonic: **REDUCE HILL TO GROUND LEVEL WITH AX!**

1150

KYŪ, kuchiru
DECAY, ROT
6 strokes

老朽 RŌKYŪ   decrepitude
不朽 FUKYŪ   imperishability
朽ち葉 KUCHIBA   dead leaves

木 is **tree/ wood** 69. 丂 is **seek an exit / twisting waterweed** 281 q.v., acting phonetically to express **rot** and possibly also lending an idea of **twisting**. Thus **rotting (twisted?) wood**, now **rot** in general.

Mnemonic: **TWISTING WEED ON ROTTING TREE**

1151

KYŪ
ENTWINE, EXAMINE
9 strokes

紛糾 FUNKYŪ   complication
糾弾 KYŪDAN   impeachment
糾明 KYŪMEI   examination

糸 is **thread** 27. 丩 is **intertwined threads** 703. Thus **many intertwined threads**, indicating a **tangle** or **complication**. **Examine** is felt by some scholars to be a borrowing, and by others to be an associated meaning. Suggest taking 丩 as a **pitchfork**.

Mnemonic: **EXAMINE ENTWINED THREADS WITH PITCHFORK**

1152

KYŪ, kiwamaru/meru
EXTREME, SUFFER
15 strokes

窮極 KYŪKYOKU   ultimate
窮境 KYŪKYŌ   predicament
窮屈 KYŪKUTSU   constraint

Formerly 竆. 躬/躬 is an NGU character meaning **body**. 躬 comprises **body** (of a pregnant woman) 身 323 and **backbone** 呂 256, and originally referred to a pregnant woman's body **pulling** against the backbone. 弓 is **bow** 836, here used to convey the same idea of **pulling/distorting**. In the case of 1152 躬/躬 acts phonetically to express **extreme** and also lends similar connotations (i.e. from extremely pregnant), as well as lending connotations of **discomfort**. It combines with **hole** 穴 849 q.v., here in its literal sense of **primitive dwelling**, to refer to **uncomfortable** quarters in the **extreme** innermost part of such a dwelling. It later came to mean **be in an extreme situation**, including the idea of **suffering/ constraint**, and can also mean **extreme** in general.

Mnemonic: **BODY BOWED IN HOLE -- EXTREME SUFFERING**

367

1153 巨 KYO
HUGE, GIANT
5 strokes

巨人 KYOJIN　　　　giant
巨大 KYODAI na　　massive
巨費 KYOHI　　great cost

Once written 𠃊. Some authoritative Japanese scholars take this to be a hole in the base of an ax head into which the handle was inserted, and take **huge** to be a borrowed meaning. Others take it to be a tool similar to a **carpenter's square** 工 113, characterised by its **large** size. Since 1153 has a minor meaning of carpenter's square in Chinese, and since it often lends relevant connotations in compounds (e.g. measuring square 矩 342), the latter theory seems the more likely. The present form appears to have used only half of the character (as 969 etc.), but the reason for this is not clear. Suggest remembering by association with **staring eye** 臣 512, from which distinguish.

Mnemonic: **GIANT CHARACTERISED BY HUGE STARING EYE**

1154 拒 KYO, koba*mu*
REFUSE, RESIST
8 strokes

拒絶 KYOZETSU　　refusal
拒否 KYOHI　　　　denial
拒止 KYOSHI　　　refusal

扌 is **hand** 32. 巨 is **huge** 1153 q.v., here acting phonetically to express **block/ prevent** and possibly also lending loose connotations of **impediment** from its assumed depiction of a huge and presumably cumbersome tool (see also 1078). 1154 originally meant to **hold in check with the hand,** but then came to mean **refrain/ restrain** and hence **refuse** and **resist**.

Mnemonic: **REFUSAL ENFORCED BY HUGE HAND**

1155 拠 KYO, KO, yo*ru*
BASE, BASIS
8 strokes

根拠 KONKYO　　base, basis
証拠 SHŌKO　　　　proof
拠り所 YORIDOKORO　grounds

Formerly 擴 and 據. 扌 is **hand** 32. 處 /処 is **place/ deal with** 896 q.v., here acting phonetically to express **take hold of/ use as a support** and almost certainly also lending its literal meaning of **resting/ leaning upon**. 豦 is tiger attacking pig 848, which acts in a similar phonetic role and also lends connotations of taking hold of. Thus **that which one takes hold of with the hand by way of support**, i.e. a **prop**, with **base/ basis** being an extended meaning.

Mnemonic: **HANDS IN PLACE, GIVING FIRM BASE**

1156

KYO, KO, uro

EMPTY, HOLLOW, DIP

11 strokes

虚偽 KYOGI   falsehood

虚空 KOKŪ   empty space

虚無主義 KYOMUSHUGI nihilism

Formerly 虛 and earlier 𡆎. ⼋/业 are early forms of **hill** 丘 1149 q.v. 𠂆/虍 is **tiger** 281, here acting phonetically to express **big** and possibly also lending connotations of **awesome**. 1156 originally meant **large and imposing hill**. The shape of ⼋ suggested a hill with a **hollow crown**, such as an extinct volcano, and this came to mean **empty/ hollow** in a broad sense. Note that 1156 can mean specifically a **hollow/ dip in the ground**. Note also that this is read **uro**, and distinguish both this reading and the character itself from the similar NGU character uso 嘘, which combines empty with mouth/ say 口 20 and means a lie. Suggest remembering 业 by association with row/ line up 並 1775.

Mnemonic: **EMPTY TIGERS LINED UP IN HOLLOW**

1157

KYO

DISTANCE, COCKSPUR

12 strokes

距離 KYORI   distance

距骨 KYOKOTSU anklebone

測距儀 SOKKYOGI range finder

⾜ is **leg/ foot** 51. 巨 is **huge** 1153, here acting phonetically to express **spear/ lance** and also lending a meaning of **big**. Thus **big spear on the foot**, a reference to a **cockspur**. It still retains this as a lesser meaning in Chinese, and it is also found very occasionally in related meanings in Japanese (e.g. see anklebone above). Cockspur came to mean by association **repel**, which in turn came to mean **keep at a distance** and hence **distance** in a broader sense.

Mnemonic: **HUGE FOOT COVERS GREAT DISTANCE**

1158 御

GYO, GO, o[n]-, mi-

HANDLE, DRIVE,

HONORABLE, YOUR

12 or 11 strokes

御者 GYOSHA   driver

御用 GOYŌ   your business

御中 ONCHŪ   Messrs

A combination of **movement (along a road)** 彳 118/129 q.v. and 卸. The latter is a now defunct character meaning **pound/ soften**, comprising **bending person** 卩 425 and **pestle** 午 110. Pound/ soften came by figurative extension to mean **make tractable/ manageable**, and thus **handle/ control**. In combination with movement along a road 彳 it came to mean **drive a team of horses/ vehicle**, either being confused with or deliberately merged with 馭, the prototype of a character 馭. This shows **horse** 馬

/馬 191 and **striking hand** 攴 (technically 攴 101, but now simply hand 又). In Chinese 馭 is interchangeable with 1158, but in Japanese it exists as a separate NGU character meaning **drive horses**. 1158 itself can still mean specifically **drive a cart/ carriage**, especially with connotations of tradesman's cart, and also retains connotations of **handling** and **controlling** in a more general sense. It later came to acquire a meaning of **imperial** as a result of its being used instead of the more complex 禦 , an NGU character meaning prevent/ bar. This comprises **drive a cart** 御 and 示 , which is not show 示 695 but a simplification of **prohibit** 禁 654, and its original meaning was equivalent to the modern expression **"tradesmen's vehicles prohibited"**. This was originally a reference to the **grounds of the imperial palace**, but the character later became used as a reference to **imperial** in a broad sense. In Chinese it still has a strong meaning of imperial, but in Japanese has come by extension to be used as a general **honorific prefix**. See also 1042.

Mnemonic: **BENDING PERSON HANDLES HONORABLE PESTLE WITH UNUSUAL MOVEMENT**

1159 凶	**KYŌ** **BAD LUCK, DISASTER** 4 strokes	凶悪 KYŌAKU na	atrocious
		凶作 KYŌSAKU	bad harvest
		吉凶 KIKKYŌ	one's fortune

凵 is a **container** (some scholars see it as a variant of **mouth** 口 20), while メ is a symbol **drawing attention**, in this case to the inside of the container/ mouth. This was a potentially confusing reference to the fact that the container/ mouth was **empty** (some scholars feel that メ also acted phonetically to express empty, thereby clarifying the meaning). By contrast with full container/ mouth 吉 1142, which indicated good fortune, the **empty container/ mouth** of 1159 indicated **ill fortune**.

Mnemonic: **X INDICATES BOX IS EMPTY -- WHAT BAD LUCK**

1160 叫	**KYŌ, sakebu** **SHOUT, YELL** 6 strokes	絶叫 ZEKKYŌ	scream
		叫び声 SAKEBIGOE	shout, yell
		叫び出す SAKEBIDASU	cry out

口 is **mouth/ say** 20. 丩 is **entwined threads** 703, here acting phonetically to express **sudden** and possibly also lending connotations of complication/ **difficulty**. Thus to **make a sudden sound with the mouth**, i.e. **cry out (in difficulty?)**. Suggest taking 丩 as a **pitchfork**.

Mnemonic: **PITCHFORK IN MOUTH EVOKES YELL**

1161 KYŌ, kuru*u*
LUNATIC, MAD
7 strokes

狂人 KYŌJIN — lunatic
狂言 KYŌGEN — farce
狂った KURUTTA — crazy

Once written 㹰. 犭/ 方 is **dog** 17. 㞷 is a variant of the prototype 㞷 of emperor 皇 861 q.v., which literally shows a crown 㞷 on a **king** 王 5, and in the modern form only king 王 has been retained. 㞷 / 王 acts here phonetically to express **convulsion**, but any semantic role is unclear. 1161 originally referred to a **convulsing dog**, i.e. a **mad dog**, and later came to mean **mad** in general.

Mnemonic: **THE KING IS A MAD DOG**

1162 KYŌ
RECEIVE, HAVE
8 strokes

享受者 KYŌJUSHA — recipient
享有 KYŌYŪ — possession
享楽 KYŌRAKU — enjoyment

From an ideograph 㡰 (later 㡰 and hence the modern form), showing a **castle watchtower** 㡰 extending in two directions to indicate **on both sides/ on all sides**. This was a representation of a **well guarded castle**, which was the original meaning. The present meaning is a borrowing. Suggest taking ⊥ as a **lid**, 口 as **mouth** 20, and 子 as **child** 25.

Mnemonic: **CHILD RECEIVES LID OVER MOUTH**

1163 況 KYŌ, ma*shite*
MORE SO, SITUATION
8 strokes

状況 JŌKYŌ — situation
実況 JIKKYŌ — real situation
況んや IWANYA* — still more

Formerly also written 况 , i.e. with ice 冫 378 instead of **water** 氵 40. 兄 is **elder brother** 267, here acting phonetically to express **very cold** and possibly also lending connotations of big. 1163 originally referred to (a big expanse of?) **icy cold water**. Its present meanings are borrowed, though in the case of **more so** it technically appears to have been used as a simplification of two talking persons 吅 475 q.v., which could be used to represent the idea of plurality and addition and hence moreover/ more so.

Mnemonic: **WET SITUATION -- FOR ELDER BROTHER EVEN MORE SO**

1164

KYŌ
RAVINE, GORGE
9 strokes

峡谷 KYŌKOKU ravine, gorge
地峡 CHIKYŌ   isthmus
海峡 KAIKYŌ   strait(s)

Formerly 峽. 山 is **mountain** 24. 夾 is an NGU character meaning **insert**, deriving from a (big) **person** 大 53 **squeezed between two other persons** 人 39. Thus **that which is squeezed between mountains**, i.e. a **ravine/ gorge**. Suggest taking 夾 as **man** 夫 573 and **out of** ＼／ 66.

Mnemonic: **MAN TRIES TO GET OUT OF MOUNTAIN GORGE**

1165

KYŌ, hasa*maru*/*mu*
INSERT, PINCH,
SQUEEZE BETWEEN
9 strokes

挟撃 KYŌGEKI   pincer attack
板挟み ITABASAMI   dilemma
挟み虫 HASAMIMUSHI   earwig

Formerly 挾. 扌 is **hand** 32. 夾 is **insert/ squeeze between** 1164 q.v. Thus to **squeeze by hand**, now **squeeze in/ squeeze between** in general. Note that the addition of metal 金 14 to 夾 gives the NGU character hasami/ scissors 鋏. Suggest taking 夾 as **man** 夫 573 and **away** ＼／ 66.

Mnemonic: **MAN SQUEEZED BY HAND CAN'T GET AWAY**

1166

KYŌ, sema*i*
NARROW, SMALL
9 strokes

狭義 KYŌGI   narrow sense
広狭 KŌKYŌ   extent, area
狭苦しい SEMAKURUSHII
                            cramped

Formerly 狹 and earlier 㚒, showing that **dog** 犭 17 is a miscopying of **hill** 阝/阝 229. 夾 is **insert/ squeeze** 1164 q.v. Thus the original meaning of 1166 was **that squeezed between hills**. Although 'that squeezed between mountains' referred to a gorge (see 1164), this was a reference to a **narrow strip of (arable) land**. It now means **narrow** in a general sense. Suggest taking 夾 as **man** 夫 573 and **away** ＼／ 66.

Mnemonic: **MAN TRIES TO GET AWAY FROM DOG IN NARROW LANE**

1167

KYŌ, oso*reru*/*roshii*
FEAR, AWE
10 strokes

恐怖 KYŌFU   fear
恐英病 KYŌEIBYŌ Anglophobia
恐れ入る OSOREIRU be awed, sorry

心 is **heart/ feelings** 147. 巩 is **hand striking instrument** 751, here acting phonetically to express **fear** and possibly also lending a meaning of **strike**. Thus **(struck by?) feelings of fear**. Awe is an associated meaning. Suggest taking 巩 as **work/ worker** 工 113 and **mediocre** 凡 1827.

Mnemonic: **STRIKE FEAR INTO HEART OF MEDIOCRE WORKER**

1168

KYŌ, uyauya*shii*
RESPECTFUL
10 strokes

恭順 KYŌJUN　　obedience
恭敬 KYŌKEI　　respect
恭謙 KYŌKEN　　deference

小 is a variant of **heart/ feelings** 心 147. 共 is **together** 460 q.v., here in its literal sense of **hands offering up a precious object**. The **feelings of the giver** symbolise **respectfulness**.

Mnemonic: **RESPECTFUL FEELINGS GO TOGETHER WITH GIVING**

1169 脅

KYŌ, odo*[ka]su*, obiya*kasu*
THREATEN, COERCE
10 strokes

脅迫 KYŌHAKU　　threat
脅威 KYŌI　　threat, menace
脅かして ODOKASHITE by threats

 is **strong arm/ strength** 力 74 trebled for emphasis, indicating **great force/ pressure**. 月 is flesh/ **of the body**. Thus **(put) great pressure upon the body**, now used figuratively as **threaten/ coerce**.

Mnemonic: **THREE STRONG ARMS THREATEN ONE'S BODY**

1170 矯

KYŌ, ta*meru*
STRAIGHTEN, FALSIFY
17 strokes

矯正的 KYŌSEITEKI corrective
奇矯 KIKYŌ　　eccentricity
矯め直す TAMENAOSU　correct

矢 is **arrow** 981. 喬 is tall structure bent at the tip 259, here meaning simply **bent at the tip**. 1170 originally referred to a **bent arrow**, which symbolised something **not straight** and thus by figurative extension **false** and by association **falsify**. Confusingly, it also came to mean an **arrow in need of straightening** and thus eventually by association to **straighten/ correct**. Rather like disturbance 乱 989, which in Chinese can mean both disorder and (bring) order (to chaos), both meanings are still prominent in Chinese despite the fact that they are opposites. In Japanese **straighten/ correct** is by far the major meaning. Suggest remembering 喬 by association with **(arched) bridge** 橋 259.

Mnemonic: **STRAIGHTEN ARROW BENT LIKE ARCHED BRIDGE**

373

| 1171 | KYŌ, hibik*u* RESOUND, ECHO, EFFECT 20 strokes | 響き渡る HIBIKIWATARU resound 悪影響 AKUEIKYŌ bad influence 交響曲 KŌKYŌKYOKU symphony |

Formerly 響. 音 is **sound** 6. 鄉 / 郷 is **village** 841 q.v., here in its sense of **village feast**. Thus the **sound of a village feast**, i.e. the noise and hubbub of a crowd of people. This was a **far-reaching noise**, giving **resound** and **echo**, with **effect/ repercussion** being a figurative extension of this.

Mnemonic: **SOUND OF VILLAGE FEAST ECHOES AFAR**

| 1172 | KYŌ, odorok*u*/kas*u* SURPRISE 22 strokes | 驚異 KYŌI miracle, wonder 驚がく KYŌGAKU shock 驚くべき ODOROKUBEKI startling |

馬 is **horse** 191. 敬 is **respect/ respectful** 846 q.v., here acting phonetically to express **startle** and possibly also lending connotations of **timidity/ nervousness** or of **forcing obedience**. Thus a **startled horse** (which is **nervous?/ which one attempts to control?**), leading to **startle/ surprise** in general.

Mnemonic: **SURPRISINGLY RESPECTFUL HORSE**

| 1173 | GYŌ, KŌ, aog*u*, ōse LOOK UP, STATE, RESPECT 6 strokes | 仰天 GYŌTEN amazement 信仰 SHINKŌ faith, creed 仰せ出す ŌSEDASU proclaim |

卬 is a CO character meaning **raise**. It was once written 卬, showing **bending person** 145 (now **bending person** 卩 425) **looking up respectfully** at another **person** 人 39. A further **person** イ 39 was added later, though its role tends to confuse and **look** 見 18 or **eye** 目 72 would have seemed a more logical choice (giving 䀰 or 䀩). **State** is an associated meaning, from the idea of being granted an audience with one's lord.

Mnemonic: **BENDING PERSON LOOKS UP RESPECTFULLY AT OTHERS**

1174	暁	GYŌ, akatsuki DAWN, LIGHT, EVENT 12 strokes	暁天 GYŌTEN dawn 通暁 TSŪGYŌ conversancy 暁星 GYŌSEI Venus, rarity

Formerly 曉 . 日 is sun/ day 62. 堯 is high 509, here acting phonetically to express **clear** and almost certainly also lending a meaning of **rise**. Thus **when the sun rises and the day becomes clear**, i.e. **dawn**. Also used figuratively in the sense of **enlightenment**. **Event** is a minor associated meaning. Suggest remembering 堯 by association with **burn** 焼 509.

Mnemonic: **BURNING SUN RISES AT DAWN**

1175		GYŌ, koru/rasu STIFF, ENGROSSED, ELABORATE 16 strokes	凝視 GYŌSHI stare 凝り性 KORISHŌ fastidiousness 凝った KOTTA elaborate

冫 is **ice** 378. 疑 is **doubt** 835 q.v., here acting phonetically to express **stiff/ immobile** and also lending connotations of **not moving** (from its literal meaning of not knowing how to proceed). Thus **firmly frozen ice**. Ice has now faded as a semantic element, leaving just **stiff** and **immobile**. Like the English term stick/ stickler, it also has connotations of **fastidiousness** (i.e. not budging), and by further figurative extension **elaborate** (i.e. from attention to detail). **Engrossed** is an associated meaning, from the idea of not moving from something.

Mnemonic: **DOUBT IF ICE IS STIFF ENOUGH**

1176		KIN AX, WEIGHT 4 strokes	斤量 KINRYŌ weight 斤目 KINME weight ふ斤 FUKIN ax

From a pictograph of an **ax with a shaped handle** ⟨. Ax is nowadays usually conveyed by an NGU character 斧, which adds striking hand 父 197. 1176 was borrowed to express the **kin weight** (600 grams). Suggest taking it as resembling a **hacksaw** ₲.

Mnemonic: **HACKSAW-LIKE AX**

375

1177	KIN FUNGUS, BACTERIA 11 strokes	細菌 SAIKIN	bacteria
		菌類 KINRUI	fungi
		保菌者 HOKINSHA	germ carrier

艹 is **plant** 9. 囷 is a CO character meaning granary, comprising **rice plant** 禾 81 q.v. and **enclosure** 口 123. It acts here phonetically to express **shade** and also lends connotations of a **plant with prominent head** (the literal meaning of 禾) growing in a delineated (i.e. given/ certain) area. Thus a **plant with prominent head growing in a certain shaded area**, a reference to the **mushroom** and other **fungi. Bacterium/ bacillus** is an associated meaning.

Mnemonic: **RICE PLANT IN ENCLOSURE DEVELOPS FUNGUS**

1178	KIN, koto KOTO (HARP) 12 strokes	手風琴 TEFŪKIN	accordion
		琴線 KINSEN	heartstrings
		琴づめ KOTOZUME	plectrum

Somewhat obscure. Once written 珡, taken by some scholars to be a pictograph of an instrument with **strings with bridges** 王王 and a **shaped base** ⊊, though the positioning of these elements is a little baffling. There is also a theory that the present form 琴 shows the **strings** 王王 and KIN/ now 今 125, the latter acting phonetically to express **closed over** and possibly also lending similar connotations from its original meaning of covered, thus giving **(instrument with) strings and closed over (wooden box)**, the latter being a reference to the base. Another old form 珡 shows a different arrangement of strings 𣏾 and an early form 金 of KIN/ gold 金 14, used in a similar phonetic role but of unclear semantic role. The existence of this second form suggests that the 'strings plus phonetic' theory is correct, but in such case the meaning of ⊊ is unclear.

Mnemonic: **KOTO HARP NOW HAS STRINGS**

1179	KIN TIGHT, COMPACT 15 strokes	緊張 KINCHŌ	tension
		緊急 KINKYŪ	crisis
		緊密 KINMITSU	compactness

糸 is **thread** 27. 臤 is an NGU character meaning both **hard** and **wise**, though how it acquired these meanings is not clear. It comprises staring eye 臣 512 and hand 又, and may possibly have originally meant a hand pressed hard against an eye, while wise might result from its being used as a simplification of wise 賢 1221. In any event, it acts here phonetically to express **entwine** and almost certainly also lends a meaning of **hard/ compact**. 1179 thus referred to **threads tangled in a tight knot**, leading to **tight/ compact** in a broad sense. It is also used figuratively in similar fashion to the English term knotted up, i.e. to refer to a highly strung state of nerves or similar.

Mnemonic: **EYE STARES AT HAND BINDING THREAD TIGHT**

1180

KIN, tsutsushi*mu*
CIRCUMSPECT
17 strokes

謹厳 KINGEN   seriousness
謹啓 KINKEI   Dear Sirs
謹んで TSUTSUSHINDE
           respectfully

言 is **words** 274. 茣 is the obscure element violet/ **few**/ season 842 q.v., here acting phonetically to express **few** and almost certainly lending similar connotations of its own. Thus **few words**, a reference to **circumspect** behavior. Suggest remembering 茣 by association with **work** 勤 842.

Mnemonic: **BE CIRCUMSPECT AT WORK, USING FEW WORDS**

1181

KIN, eri
COLLAR, NECK, HEART
18 strokes

胸襟 KYŌKIN   bosom
襟度 KINDO   magnanimity
襟首 ERIKUBI   nape of neck

衤 is **clothing** 420. 禁 is **forbid**/ **ban** 654, here acting phonetically to express **closed** and almost certainly also lending similar connotations of **not open**. Thus **that part of the clothing which is closed**, a somewhat vague reference to the **collar**. Later **neck area** in a more general sense, including a figurative meaning of **bosom/ heart**.

Mnemonic: **COLLARS ARE BANNED ITEMS OF CLOTHING**

1182

GIN
RECITE
7 strokes

吟詠 GINEI   recital
吟味 GINMI   scrutiny
吟遊詩人 GINYŪSHIJIN   minstrel

口 is **mouth**/ **say** 20. 今 is **now** 125 q.v., here acting phonetically to express **howl** and possibly also lending loose connotations of **suppress**/ **stifle** from its literal meaning of cover. 1182 originally referred to a **howl of pain (which one has tried to suppress?)**, and later came to mean **drawn out vocal emission** in a broader sense but with particular associations with **recitation**. Note that the same elements of mouth 口 and now 今 are found in include 含 1118 q.v.

Mnemonic: **MOUTH NOW USED FOR RECITING**

377

1183

KU, ka*keru*, ka*ru*
GALLOP, SPUR ON
14 strokes

先駆者 SENKUSHA   pioneer
駆り出す KARIDASU   flush out
駆け落ち KAKEOCHI   elopement

Formerly 驅 . 馬 is **horse** 191. 區 /区 is **ward**/ section 465/1034 q.v. here acting phonetically to express **strike/ beat** and almost certainly also lending its sound (once **EO/ Ō**)
to refer to the cries of exhortation of a rider urging on his horse (now OI/ Ō in Chinese,
though confusingly the similar sounding English whoa is intended to have the opposite effect). Thus **beating a horse (and crying Ō)**, i.e. **spurring it on** at the **gallop**.

Mnemonic: **SPURRED ON HORSE GALLOPS THROUGH THE WARD**

1184

GU, oroka
FOOLISH
13 strokes

愚人 GUJIN   fool
愚図る GUZURU   grumble
愚行 GUKŌ   foolish act

心 is **heart/ feelings** 147. 禺 is a CO character now meaning begin, though in compounds it often seems to lend a meaning of **not clear** or **not open**. Its etymology is somewhat obscure, but an old form 禺 shows what appears to be a 'clawless' version of
scorpion with twisting tail 禼 392 (the prototype of ten thousand 萬 392), and it
is possible that the idea of **twisting** came to symbolise something **convoluted** and hence
obscure/ not clear. In the case of 1184 it acts phonetically to express **unclear** and almost certainly lends similar connotations of its own. Thus **unclear feelings**. This came
to mean **incomprehensible feelings**, and hence by association **irrational** and then
foolish feelings. Now **foolish** in general. Suggest taking 禺 as a combination of **insect** 虫 56 and **field** 田 59, with 冂 as **long legs**.

Mnemonic: **LONG-LEGGED INSECT IN FIELD GIVES FOOLISH FEELING**

1185

GŪ
**BY CHANCE, SPOUSE,
DOLL**
11 strokes

偶然 GŪZEN   by chance
偶像 GŪZŌ   idol, image
配偶者 HAIGŪSHA   spouse

亻 is **person** 39. 禺 is the somewhat obscure begin 1184 q.v., here acting phonetically
to express **meet (by chance)** and possibly also lending connotations of **not predictable**
(i.e. not planned). Thus **persons meeting by chance**. On the one hand this led to **by
chance** in a general sense, and on the other to **companion**. Companion in turn led to
spouse. **Doll/ effigy** is believed to stem from the ancient practice of burying effigies
with dead persons of rank as companions for them in the after-life. That is, it is taken to be
an associated meaning with companion. Suggest taking 禺 as a combination of **insect** 虫
56 and **field** 田 59, with 冂 as **long legs**.

Mnemonic: **BY CHANCE, PERSON FINDS LONG-LEGGED FIELD INSECT**

1186 **GŪ**
MEET, RECEIVE, TREAT
12 strokes

奇遇 KIGŪ   chance meeting
待遇 TAIGŪ   reception
不遇 FUGŪ   misfortune

As 偶 1185 q.v., but with person 亻 39 replaced by **movement (along a road)** 辶 129. Thus to **meet (by chance) while moving along a road**. Whereas 1185 developed associations with chance and companionship, 1186 developed associations rather with the **act of meeting**. Eventually the by chance connotation largely disappeared, and ironically 1186 even came instead to have not infrequent connotations of a planned meeting/ reception, leading to **receive/ treat**. As with 1185 and 1184, suggest taking 禺 as a combination of **insect** 虫 56 and **field** 田 59, with 冂 as **long legs**.

Mnemonic: **MEET LONG-LEGGED INSECT MOVING ALONG IN FIELD**

1187 **GŪ, sumi**
CORNER, NOOK
12 strokes

一隅 ICHIGŪ   corner, nook
隅石 SUMIISHI   cornerstone
片隅 KATASUMI corner, nook

阝 is **terraced hill** 229. 禺 is the somewhat obscure begin 1184 q.v, here acting phonetically to express **fold/ recess** and almost certainly also lending connotations both of **twisting/ undulating** and **not clear/ not visible**. 1187 originally referred to a **hidden recess/ hollow in a terraced/ undulating hillside**, then came to mean **nook** and by association **corner**. As with 1184/5/6, suggest taking 禺 as a combination of **insect** 虫 56 and **field** 田 59, with 冂 as **long legs**.

Mnemonic: **LONG-LEGGED INSECT IN CORNER OF HILLSIDE FIELD**

1188 **KUTSU**
SUBMIT, CROUCH
8 strokes

屈服 KUPPUKU   surrender
不屈 FUKUTSU   unyielding
屈折 KUSSETSU   refraction

Usually explained simply as **buttocks** 尸 236 and **put out** 出 34, to give **thrust out the buttocks** and thereby **crouch**, with crouch leading by association to **adopt a position of humility/ submit**. A useful mnemonic, but incorrect. Old forms such as 屈 show that, while 出 is indeed put out 出 (屮 being its old form), 尸 is in fact a simplification of **tail** 尾 1734 q.v. This was not infrequently used as a reference to the genitals, especially the **testicles**, and here it has such a meaning. 出 acts phonetically to express **remove**, as well as lending its meaning of **put out** (but in the sense of put out an eye), to give **put out/ remove the testicles**, i.e. **castrate**. This was a form of **punishment**, and thus **submit** is seen as an associated meaning (i.e. submit to punishment). **Crouch** is in turn taken to be an associated meaning, since crouching was a gesture of submission.

Mnemonic: **PUT OUT BUTTOCKS IN SUBMISSIVE CROUCH**

1189

掘

KUTSU, ho*ru*
DIG
11 strokes

発掘 HAKKUTSU excavation
掘り出す HORIDASU unearth
採掘 SAIKUTSU mining

扌 is **hand** 32. 屈 is **crouch** 1188 q.v., here acting phonetically to express **dig** and also lending its connotations of **remove** (and possibly also of **crouch**). Thus to (**crouch down to?**) **dig by hand and remove soil**, i.e. **dig a hole**.

Mnemonic: **CROUCH AND DIG BY HAND**

1190

繰

kuru
REEL, TURN
19 strokes

繰り糸 KURIITO silk reeling
繰り越す KURIKOSU transfer
繰り返す KURIKAESU repeat

Of disputed etymology. Formerly also written 繰, though according to some scholars this is a separate character. 糸 is **thread** 27. 巢/巣 is **nest** 1521, here symbolising **gathering of birds** and by extension **gathering** in general. 喿 is **birds in a tree** 922, felt by some scholars similarly to symbolise **gathering** (conceptually as 309) but by others to act phonetically to express **dark blue**. 繰 is thus an ideograph meaning to **gather threads**, and by association **reel/turn**. Some scholars feel that from the outset 繰 was a variant ideograph of similar meaning. Others feel that 繰 originally meant **dark blue threads** before becoming confused with 繰. The variant ideograph theory seems the more convincing. Suggest taking 木 as **wood** 69 and 品 as **three boxes**.

Mnemonic: **PUT REELED THREADS INTO THREE WOODEN BOXES**

1191

勲

KUN
MERIT
15 strokes

勲章 KUNSHŌ medal
殊勲 SHUKUN great merit
勲位 KUNI order of merit

Formerly 勳, and in ancient times 𠠄. 𠠄/力 is **strength/effort** 74. 熏 is an NGU character meaning **smoke**, comprising black 㬎/黑/黒 124 q.v., here with its original connotations of burning, and 屮, a variant of growing plant 生 42 but here with a meaning of emerge (as a plant emerges from the ground). That which emerges during burning is smoke. (Note also the more common NGU character for smoke, 燻, which adds a further fire 火 8.) 熏 often has connotations of **pleasant-smelling smoke** (see 1192), being a controlled fire usually associated with cooking. In the case of 1191 熏 acts phonetically to express **many**, and possibly also lends loose associated connotations of **desirable/good**. Thus **many (good?) efforts**, i.e. **meritorious service**. The graphic evolution of the present form has almost certainly been influenced by **heavy/pile up** 重 311, suggesting piled up/accumulated efforts. Suggest using this as a mnemonic, with ⺍ literally as fire/**burn** 8.

Mnemonic: **BURN SELF OUT WITH HEAVY EFFORT -- GREAT MERIT**

1192 KUN, kao*ri*　　　　薫香 KUNKŌ　　　incense

AROMA, FRAGRANCE,　　薫育 KUNIKU　　education

AURA　　　　　　　　薫風 KUNPŪ　　balmy breeze

16 strokes

Formerly 薫 . 艹 is **plants** 9. 熏 / 熏 is **(pleasant-smelling) smoke** 1191 q.v., here acting phonetically to express **fragrant** and also lending similar connotations. Thus the **fragrant smell of plants** (possibly originally the **fragrant smell of burning plants**), later **fragrance/ aroma** in a broader sense. **Aura** is a minor associated meaning. Suggest taking 重 as **heavy** 311, with 灬 as fire/ **burn** 8.

Mnemonic: **BURNING PLANTS PRODUCE HEAVY FRAGRANCE**

1193 刑 KEI　　　　　　　　処刑 SHOKEI　　　punishment

PUNISH　　　　　　　死刑 SHIKEI　　　death penalty

6 strokes　　　　　　　刑事 KEIJI penal case, detective

刂 is **sword/ cut** 181. 开 derives from 井 , which is not **well** 井 1470 but **grille/ lattice window** 104. Here 井 /开 acts phonetically to express **injure**, and may also suggest **shackles** or similar instruments of punishment. Thus to **injure someone with a sword,** which came to refer to cutting with a sword by way of **punishment** and eventually **punish** in a general sense. Suggest taking 开 as a **well-frame.**

Mnemonic: **CUT UP WHILE IN WELL-FRAME -- WHAT A PUNISHMENT!**

1194 KEI, kuki　　　　　球茎 KYŪKEI　　　　bulb

STALK, STEM　　　地下茎 CHIKAKEI　　root stock

8 strokes　　　　　　歯茎 HAGUKI　　　the gums

Formerly 莖 . 艹 is **plant** 9. 巠/圣 is **warp threads** 269 q.v., here acting phonetically to express **straight** and also lending its own connotations of **straight** and possibly also of **bare**. Thus the **straight (and bare?) part of a plant,** i.e. its **stalk/ stem.** Suggest taking 圣 as **hand** 又 and **earth** 土 60.

Mnemonic: **HAND PLUCKS PLANT STEM FROM THE EARTH**

1195 KEI, chigi*ru*
PLEDGE, JOIN
9 strokes

契約 KEIYAKU   contract
契機 KEIKI   opportunity
契印 KEIIN   joint seal

切 is **serrated tally** 659 q.v. Joining the tallies indicated the conclusion of an **arrangement** or pledge. **Big** 大 53 suggests an **important** arrangement/ pledge. 1195 also has connotations of **joining**. Suggest taking 切 literally as **serrated/ notched wood** 圭 and **cut** 刀 181.

Mnemonic: **JOINING CUT NOTCHED WOOD HONORS BIG PLEDGE**

1196 KEI, E, megu*mu*
BLESSING, KINDNESS
10 strokes

恵与 KEIYO   bestowal
知恵 CHIE   wisdom
恵み深い MEGUMIBUKAI merciful

Formerly 惠 , with a variant 恵. 心 is **heart/ feeling** 147. 叀 is the same spinning weight seen in 専/專 914 q.v., here acting phonetically to express **give** and possibly also lending an idea of **all around**. Thus **heart which gives (all around?)**, i.e. a **generous** and **kind** heart. **Blessing** is an associated meaning. Suggest taking 叀 as **ten** 十 33 and **field** 田 59.

Mnemonic: **KIND HEARTED PERSON BLESSED WITH TEN FIELDS**

1197 啓 KEI
ENLIGHTEN, STATE
11 strokes

啓発 KEIHATSU enlightenment
啓示 KEIJI   revelation
拝啓 HAIKEI Dear.. (in letters)

Formerly 啟 . 启 is to all intents a variant of **door** 戸 531 q.v. (comprising **door** 戸 / 戸 / 戸 108 and **open/ opening** 口 20), here acting phonetically to express **open** and also lending connotations of **open a door**. 攵 is **force/ coerce** 101, here acting as a causative element. Thus to **force someone to open a door**, later just **open up** in a broad sense and eventually in particular in the figurative sense of **enlighten**. **State** is felt to be an associated meaning, from the idea of explain/ inform.

Mnemonic: **FORCE OPEN DOOR AND SHED LIGHT**

1198

KEI, kaka*geru*
DISPLAY, HOIST, PRINT
11 strokes

掲示板 KEIJIBAN notice board
前掲 ZENKEI aforementioned
掲揚 KEIYŌ hoisting

Formerly 揭 . 扌 is **hand** 32. 曷/曷 is the somewhat obscure interrogative seen in 1022 q.v, here acting phonetically to express **hoist/ hold aloft** and possibly also lending connotations of aggression and hence defiance. Thus to (defiantly?) **hold something aloft in the hand**, now **hoist** in general. **Display** and **print** are associated meanings. Suggest taking 曷 as **sun** 日 62, **cover** 勹 , and **sitting person/man** 匕 238.

Mnemonic: **MAN SITS COVERED IN SUNSHINE, DISPLAYING HAND**

1199

KEI
VALLEY, GORGE
11 strokes

溪谷 KEIKOKU valley, gorge
雪溪 SEKKEI snowy valley
溪流 KEIRYŪ mountain stream

Formerly 溪 , and correctly 谿 . 谷 is **valley** 122. 奚 is a CO character now used as an interrogative expressing doubt. Its etymology is not clear, but it comprises **hand reaching down** 爫 303, and either **short thread** 幺 111 plus **big** 大 53 or a variant 糸 of **thread** 糸 27, and may originally have had a meaning of **twisting threads** (short threads together to make bigger thread?). Certainly it often appears to lend a meaning of **twisting** in compounds. Here it acts phonetically to express **blocked**, and may also lend connotations of **twisting**. Thus **(twisting?) valley that is blocked**, i.e. a **blind ravine** and later **gorge/ valley** in a general sense. (Note that the use of **mountain** 山 24 gives a CO character 嵠, which also means mountain gorge [literally that which twists through the mountains?].) The character 溪 , which adds **water/ river** 氵 40 and appears to mean literally a **twisting stream/ river**, exists in Chinese as a separate character with that very meaning, but in Japanese it has been used as a simpler substitute for 谿. Suggest taking 奚 as **hand/ claw** 爫 303 and **man** 夫 573.

Mnemonic: **MAN CLAWS WAY ALONG WATERY GORGE**

1200

KEI, hotaru
FIREFLY
11 strokes

螢光 KEIKŌ fluorescence
螢雪 KEISETSU studying
螢狩り HOTARUGARI
catching fireflies

Formerly 螢 . 炏 is **covered in fire/ light** 427 (fire 火 8 and cover 冖), while 虫 is **insect** 56. Thus **insect covered in fire/ light**, i.e. a **firefly**. Suggest taking 炏 as an **ornate cover**.

Mnemonic: **FIREFLY IS INSECT ORNATELY COVERED IN FIRE**

1201 傾	KEI, katamuku/keru **INCLINE, DEDICATE** 13 strokes	傾向 KEIKŌ 傾倒 KEITŌ 傾斜度 KEISHADO	tendency devotion gradient

頃 is an NGU character now used to mean **about** (of time), but is in fact the prototype of 1201. It comprises **head** 頁 93 and **fallen/slumped person** 匕 238, to indicate **slumped head** and by extension a **person slumped** or **fallen to one side. Person** 亻 39 was added for emphasis at this stage. However, despite this addition the person element presently faded from the meaning, leaving just **fall to one side** and hence **incline. Dedicate** is an associated meaning, from the idea of bias/ concentration. Suggest remembering by partial association with **change** 化 238.

Mnemonic: **FALLEN PERSON CHANGES INCLINATION OF HEAD**

1202 携	KEI, tazusawaru/eru **CARRY, PARTICIPATE** 13 strokes	携帯 KEITAI- 提携 TEIKEI 必携 HIKKEI	portable cooperation indispensable, handbook

Formerly 攜 and 攜. 扌 is **hand** 32. 雟/巂 is obscure, though 巂 (and a variant form 雟, of which 凹 is almost certainly a variant of 冏 [old forms such as 巂 show 冏 to be the earlier]) exists as a CO character meaning **fatty/ fleshy/ fine**. 崔 appears to be a **crested bird** (not unlike crested bird 萑/雚 634), i.e. a variant of **bird** 隹 216, rather than bird 隹 plus mountain 山 24 (but see 1293). It would seem likely that 冏 is vagina 317 q.v., here used for its **fleshy thighs** element 冂 (i.e. with hole/ opening 口 20 redundant), to give **plump thighed bird** and thereby fatty/ fleshy/ fine. The later 乃 may thus be a variant of **(plump) buttocks** 巴 350 q.v. In any event, in the case of 1202 巂 is used phonetically to express **carry**, to give **carry in the hand**, though originally it almost certainly would have also lent its assumed meaning of plump bird to give carry a plump bird in the hand. **Participate** is a minor associated figurative meaning, from the idea of involvement (i.e. having something [business] in one's hands). Suggest remembering 乃 as **plump buttocks**.

Mnemonic: **CARRY PLUMP-BUTTOCKED BIRD IN HAND**

1203 **KEI, tsu*gu*, mama-** 継続 KEIZOKU continuation
INHERIT, FOLLOW, 継子 MAMAKO stepchild
JOIN, STEP-, PATCH 継ぎ足し TSUGITASHI extension
13 strokes

Formerly 繼. 糸 is **thread** 27. 㡭/迷 is **cut threads** 750. Though the combination of these elements is somewhat vague, 1203 is an ideograph referring to the **splicing** of small cut threads into a larger whole thread. Its core meaning is thus to **join threads**, leading on the one hand to the idea of physically mending and **patching** and on the other to figurative associated meanings such as **inheriting** and **following**. Suggest taking 迷 as **rice** 米 201 in a **corner** ∟ 349.

Mnemonic: **FOLLOW THREAD TO INHERIT RICE PILED IN CORNER**

1204 **KEI** 慶祝 KEISHUKU celebration
JOY 慶事 KEIJI happy event
15 strokes 慶賀 KEIGA congratulation

Of convoluted and disputed etymology. 严 is a simplification of 鹿, an NGU character meaning **deer** which derives with much stylisation from a pictograph 鹿. 严 was combined with 与, to all intents and purposes a simplification of **horse** 馬 191, to give 麃, a CO character referring to a fabulous beast which was a cross between a horse and a deer and which represented **goodness** (see also 1499). Some scholars feel that 麃 was simplified back to 严, i.e. the same form as the simplification for deer but this time indicating the beast of goodness and by extension goodness itself, and that it was combined with a simplification of **love** 愛 417, namely 㣺, to give the present character 慶. The core meaning of this is thus taken to be **love and goodness**, with **joy** being an associated meaning. However, other scholars feel that old forms such as 㥯 suggest strongly that 㣺 is not a variant of love 愛, but that 严 is a variant of 麃, and that this combines with **heart/ feeling** 心/忄 147 to give **goodness in the heart**. Such a core meaning might logically suggest virtue but appears to have evolved rather into **joy**, with some scholars attributing this to the fact that 麃 had the same pronunciation as the word for **feasting** (again see 1499) and thus suggested by association **happiness** and **contentment**. Suggest taking 严 as a combination of **building** 广 114 and 'funny' **west** 西 152, with 㣺 as a variant of **love** 愛.

Mnemonic: **LOVE AND JOY IN FUNNY WESTERN BUILDING**

1205

憩

KEI, ikou
REST
16 strokes

休憩　KYŪKEI　rest, recess
少憩　SHŌKEI　brief rest
憩い　IKOI　rest, spell

A combination of **breath/ rest** 息 332 q.v. and **hollowed space** 舌 244. The latter acts phonetically to express **stop and rest**, and may also lend an associated idea of not being busy/ having free time (see 1109). Thus **stop and rest/ stop and 'take a breather'**. Suggest taking 舌 as **tongue** 732, and 息 literally as **heart** 心 147 and **nose** 自 134.

Mnemonic: **TONGUE, NOSE, AND HEART ALL TAKE A REST**

1206

鶏

KEI, niwatori
CHICKEN, HEN, COCK
19 strokes

鶏卵　KEIRAN　hen's egg
鶏舎　KEISHA　henhouse
鶏鳴　KEIMEI　cockcrow

Formerly 鷄. 鳥 is **bird** 174. 奚/奚 is the obscure element seen in valley 渓 1199 q.v., here used as a phonetic substitute for a more complex character meaning **cockscomb**. It is not clear why a still simpler character was not chosen as the phonetic, and it may be the case that 奚 also lent reinforcing connotations of twisting and by association undulating, or else, from an earlier form 奚, graphically suggested a cock and comb. In any event, **bird with cockscomb** refers to a **cock/ hen/ chicken**. There is also an occasionally encountered variant form 雞, which uses bird 隹 216. Suggest taking 爫 as **talons** (see 303), and 大 as **man** 573.

Mnemonic: **BIRD SEIZING MAN IN TALONS IS A CHICKEN!?**

1207

迎

GEI, mukaeru
**GREET, WELCOME,
MEET**
7 strokes

歓迎会　KANGEIKAI　reception
迎合　GEIGŌ　ingratiation
迎え酒　MUKAEZAKE　'hair of dog'

辶 is **movement** 129. 卬 is **raise** 1173 q.v., here acting phonetically to express **greet** and also lending similar connotations from its literal meaning of one person being respectful in an encounter with another. 1207 originally meant to **move (out of one's house) to greet someone**, and now means **meet/ greet** in a broad sense. Suggest taking 卬 literally as **person** L 39 (originally ㇐) and **bending person** ㇆ 425.

Mnemonic: **BENDING PERSON MOVES TO GREET ANOTHER**

1208 **GEI, kujira** 鯨油 GEIYU whale oil
WHALE 捕鯨 HOGEI whaling
19 strokes 座頭鯨 ZATŌKUJIRA
humpback whale

魚 is **fish** (or more exactly fishlike creature) 98. 京 is **capital** 99, here acting phonetically to express **big** and also lending an idea of **chief/ principal**. Thus **principal big 'fish'**, i.e. **whale**.

Mnemonic: **THE WHALE IS A CAPITAL 'FISH'**

1209 **GEKI, u***tsu* 狙撃 SOGEKI sniping
STRIKE, ATTACK, FIRE 攻撃 KŌGEKI attack
15 strokes 早撃ち HAYAUCHI rapid firing

Formerly 擊, and earlier 撃. 殳 is **strike** 153. 軎 depicts a **vehicle** 車 31 with attention drawn to its **axle/ hub** 〇. 轂 referred to a **vehicle striking its own axle**, i.e. (constantly) rubbing or chafing. **Hand** 手 32 was added to give the idea of **(persistently) striking with the hand**, leading by association to **attack**. For some reason it has also developed particular associations with **discharging a firearm**.

Mnemonic: **ATTACK VEHICLE BY STRIKING WITH HAND**

1210 **GEKI, hage***shii* 感激 KANGEKI deep emotion
AGITATED, INTENSE 激化 GEKKA intensification
16 strokes 激しさ HAGESHISA intensity

氵 is **water** 40. 敫 is a CO character meaning **strike/ beat**. It comprises **release**放 391q.v., here with its literal connotations of **strike** (a person), and **white** 白 65, which acts phonetically to express **beat** (as in 1695). 1210 originally referred to **water striking** against something (and according to some scholars, who interpret 敫 as also acting phonetically to express **leap**, sending spray leaping into the air). This indicated **agitated water**, i.e. **'fierce' water**, and hence 1210 came to mean **agitated** as well as **fierce/ intense**.

Mnemonic: **FIERCELY AGITATED WATER RELEASES WHITE SPRAY**

1211 傑 **KETSU**
OUTSTANDING
13 strokes

傑士 KESSHI hero
傑出 KESSHUTSU excelling
傑作 KESSAKU masterpiece, blunder

亻 is **person** 39. 桀 is a CO character meaning **bird's roost**, **cruel**, and **heroic**. It was once written 桀, showing the same combination of **opposed feet** 舛/夕ヰ 422 (夕 being a variant of 㐄) and **tree** 木/木 69 as seen in climb 乗/乘 320 q.v., and similarly meant **person in treetop**. Bird's roost derives from the idea of treetop, while heroic comes from the associated idea of **outstanding** (i.e. a person higher than others). Cruel is a misleading meaning derived from association with a particular tyrant in ancient China, noted both for his outstanding prowess as a warrior and for his cruelty. In the case of 1211 桀 lends only its meaning of **outstanding**, combining with **person** 亻 to give **outstanding person** and eventually **outstanding/ excellent** in a broad sense. Suggest taking 夕 as **evening** 44 and ヰ as a variant of **well(-frame)** 井 1470, with 木 in its sense of **wooden**.

Mnemonic: **OUTSTANDING PERSON BUILDS WOODEN WELL NIGHTLY**

1212 肩 **KEN, kata**
SHOULDER
8 strokes

肩章 KENSHŌ epaulette
比肩 HIKEN comparison
肩書き KATAGAKI title of rank

Flesh/ of the body 月 365 and **door** 戸 108. Though the oldest forms of 1212 found to date do show door, it is believed to be a miscopying of some earlier pictograph of a **shoulder**, such as ⺁. Thus the **shoulder part of the body**.

Mnemonic: **USE FLESHY SHOULDER AGAINST DOOR**

1213 倹 **KEN**
THRIFTY, FRUGAL
10 strokes

倹約 KENYAKU frugality
節倹 SEKKEN frugality
勤倹 KINKEN thrift

Formerly 儉. 亻 is **person** 39. 僉/㑒 is **combine**/ judge 475 q.v., here acting phonetically to express **few** and possibly also lending associated connotations of avoidance of duplication (i.e. from the idea of combining things). 1213 referred to a **person of few possessions**, which came to symbolise **thrift** and **frugality**. Suggest taking 㑒 as a combined variant of **elder brother** 兄 267 and cover/ **cap** 亼 87/121.

Mnemonic: **ELDER BROTHER WEARS ONLY A CAP -- THRIFTY PERSON**

1214

KEN, tsurugi
SWORD, BAYONET
10 strokes

剣道 KENDŌ   kendo
剣舞 KENBU   sword dance
短剣 TANKEN   dagger, dirk

Formerly 劍. 刂 is **sword** 181, while 僉/僉 is **combine/** judge 475 q.v. The latter acts phonetically to express **taper(ed)**. Any semantic role is not clear, but it is possible that it lends an idea of combining the function both of a sword and a dagger. Thus **tapered sword**, i.e. **a short stabbing sword**, though it is occasionally used in a wider sense. Suggest taking 僉 as a combined variant of **elder brother** 兄 267 and **cover** 亼 87.

Mnemonic: **ELDER BROTHER PUTS COVER ON SWORD**

1215

KEN, noki
EAVES, HOUSE COUNTER
10 strokes

一軒 IKKEN   one house
軒灯 KENTŌ   eaves lantern
軒先 NOKISAKI   frontage

Carriage/ vehicle 車 31 and **dry/ forked weapon** 干 825 q.v. The latter acts phonetically to express **high/ raised** and probably also lends its idea of forking to refer to the forked support of a **canopy over a carriage**. 1215 originally referred to such a **raised canopy**, and can still be used in this sense in Chinese, where it can also mean raised/ high in a broader sense. In Japanese it was applied by association to the **canopy of a house**, i.e. the **roof**, and eventually came by further association to mean **eaves**. It is also used for counting houses.

Mnemonic: **VEHICLE KEPT DRY UNDER EAVES**

1216

KEN
RANGE, SPHERE, ZONE
12 strokes

成層圏 SEISŌKEN   stratosphere
圏外 KENGAI   outside bounds
共産圏 KYŌSANKEN
                   Communist Bloc

Formerly 圈. 囗 is **enclosure** 123. 卷/巻 is **roll (up)** 826 q.v., here acting phonetically to express **block** and also lending its own idea of **containment**. Thus **that contained by a blocking enclosure**, i.e. **zone, range**, etc.

Mnemonic: **ENCLOSURE IS ROLLED AROUND ZONE**

389

1217 堅	KEN, katai	堅実 KENJITSU	reliable
	FIRM, SOLID, HARD	堅固 KENGO	firm, steady
	12 strokes	中堅 CHŪKEN	mainstay

Earth/ ground 土 60 and hard 臤 1179. Originally firm ground, later firm/ hard/ solid in a broad sense, including reliable. Suggest taking 臤 literally as staring eye 臣 512 and hand 又.

Mnemonic: HAND THROWS HARD EARTH AT STARING EYE

1218 嫌	KEN, GEN, kirau/i, iya	嫌悪 KENO	loathing
	DISLIKE(D)	機嫌 KIGEN	mood
	13 strokes	嫌嫌 IYAIYA	reluctantly

女 is woman 35. 兼 is combine/ do two things at once 850, here acting phonetically to express dissatisfaction and almost certainly also lending its own idea of two at once. 1218 originally referred to a woman's feelings of dissatisfaction, and, to judge from the fact that in Chinese it can also mean suspicion and jealousy, almost certainly referred specifically to her feelings at sharing her husband's affections with another woman. Now dislike/ disliked in a general sense.

Mnemonic: WOMAN DISLIKES BEING COMBINED WITH ANOTHER

1219 献	KEN, KON	献上 KENJŌ	presentation
	DEDICATE, PRESENT	献立 KONDATE	menu, plan
	13 strokes	献身 KENSHIN	dedication

Formerly 獻. 鬳 is a now defunct character referring to a particular type of dog used in sacrifices, a dog presumably considered to have tiger-like attributes (虍 is tiger 281) and eaten after the sacrifice (鬲 is cooking pot on stand 1078). Dog 犬 17 was added later for clarity. Sacrificial dog came to symbolise sacrifice and the idea of dedicating/ presenting in general. The modern form uses south 南 190 as a simplification of 鬳.

Mnemonic: SOUTHERN DOG IS VERY DEDICATED

1220

KEN, tsuka*u*, ya*ru*
SEND, USE, DO
13 strokes

派遣 HAKEN   dispatch
小遣い KOZUKAI pocket money
遣り直す YARINAOSU   redo

追 is a variant of **pursue** 追 350 q.v., here used in the sense of **follow**. 虫 is **gather 834**. 1220 originally referred to a **gathering of followers**, i.e. a retinue, then came to be used of **retainer/ servant**. Probably because of the presence of the movement radical 辶 129, it became particularly associated with a **messenger**, i.e. someone sent on errands, and thus came to mean **send**. In Japanese it also developed connotations of **use**, which later broadened to **act/ do** in general, whereas in Chinese send came to mean send off/ banish and thus acquired the connotations which 追 350 itself later acquired in Japanese. Suggest taking 虫 as **middle/ midst** 中 55 and **one** 一 1. See also 331.

Mnemonic: **USE ONE FROM AMIDST FOLLOWERS TO SEND IN PURSUIT**

1221

KEN, kashiko*i*
WISE
16 strokes

賢者 KENJA   sage
賢明 KENMEI   wisdom
賢立て KASHIKODATE
            pretence of wisdom

貝 is shell/ **money** 90, here meaning **assets/ wealth**. 臤 is **hard/ wise** 1179 q.v., here acting phonetically to express **bountiful** but of unclear semantic role due to its somewhat obscure nature. 1221 originally referred to **great wealth** in terms of tangible assets, but was later applied figuratively to a person endowed with a **wealth of wisdom**. Suggest taking 臤 literally as **staring eye** 臣 512 and **hand** 又.

Mnemonic: **WISE PERSON STARES HARD AT MONEY IN HAND**

1222

KEN, herikuda*ru*
HUMBLE, MODEST
17 strokes

謙そん KENSON   humility
謙虚 KENKYO   modesty
謙譲 KENJŌ   humility

言 is words/ **speak** 274. 兼 is combine/ **be unable** 850, here acting phonetically to express **awe** as well as lending its meaning of **be unable**. Thus to **be awed and unable to speak**, as in the presence of a great superior. This later came to mean **be respectfully reserved**, leading to **humble** and **modest**.

Mnemonic: **MODEST PERSON UNABLE TO SPEAK**

1223

KEN, mayu
COCOON
18 strokes

繭ちゅう KENCHŪ　　　pongee
大繭　OMAYU　　double cocoon
空繭　KARAMAYU

waste cocoon

Formerly 𦃨. 糸 is **thread** 27, while 虫 is **insect** 56. 芇 derives from an ideograph 芇, which combines a **cocoon** ∩ with 丷, a simplification of a ram's horns (see 986) used to symbolise **symmetry/ equal on both sides**. 1223 thus literally means **symmetrical cocoon of thread-making insect**. Suggest taking 芇 as **grass** 艹 9 and a **double chambered cocoon** 冂.

Mnemonic: **INSECT THREADS DOUBLE COCOON UNDER GRASS**

1224

KEN, arawa*reru*
MANIFEST, VISIBLE
18 strokes

顕著　KENCHO　　noticeable
顕要　KENYŌ　　prominence
顕微鏡 KENBIKYŌ microscope

Formerly 顯. 頁 is **head** 93, though old forms of 1224 such as 㬎兒 reveal that this is a miscopying of **look/ see** 見 18. 㬎 is a CO character meaning **motes** (small particles of dust) and by association **minute**. It comprises **sun(-light)** 日 62 and 絲, which is a simplified doubling of thread 糸 27 and here means **small things**. Thus **small things (showing up) in sunlight**, i.e. motes. In the case of 1224 㬎 acts phonetically to express **clear/ visible** and almost certainly also lends a similar meaning of being visible (if small). Thus something **(small but) visible upon looking**, leading to **visible** in general and hence also **manifest**. Suggest taking 业 as a variant of **line up** 並 1775.

Mnemonic: **ODD LINE UP OF HEADS VISIBLE IN SUN**

1225

KEN, KE, ka*karu*/*keru*
ATTACH, HANG, APPLY
20 strokes

懸命　KENMEI　　eagerness
懸念　KENEN　　anxiety
命懸け INOCHIGAKE perilous

縣 is the old form of **prefecture** 県 273 q.v., here in its early sense of **attach/ hang**. 心 is **heart** 147. Thus **that which hangs on the heart**, i.e. a **worry/ anxiety**. It can still have this meaning in Chinese, but in Japanese it has mostly lost its heart connotations to leave just **hang** in a broad sense, being virtually interchangeable with 掛 1083.

Mnemonic: **HEART STILL ATTACHED TO OLD PREFECTURE**

1226	GEN, maboroshi ILLUSION, MAGIC 4 strokes	幻想 GENSŌ 幻像 GENZŌ 幻術 GENJUTSU	illusion phantom magic

Originally written 甶, being an inversion of **weaving shuttle** 甲 403 q.v. and having a similar meaning. Its highly stylised present form clearly shows confusion with **short thread** 幺 111. Its present meanings result from borrowing, to an extent involving confusion with occult 玄 1227 q.v. Suggest taking ㄱ as a **hook**.

Mnemonic:**SHORT THREAD BECOMES HOOK!? -- A MAGICAL ILLUSION**

1227	GEN OCCULT, BLACK 5 strokes	玄妙 GENMYŌ 玄関 GENKAN 玄人 KURŌTO*	mystery porch expert

Of very extended semantic evolution. 幺 is **short thread** 111. ㅗ is the same **twisting device** seen in 率 803 q.v. (for twisting bits of thread into rope). Thus 1227 originally meant **short thread suitable for twisting**. It then came to mean something **very small** and by association something **hard to see**, leading to **obscure** both in the physical sense of **dark/ black** and in the figurative sense of **mysterious**, including **occult**.

Mnemonic: **TWISTED BLACK THREAD SYMBOLISES OCCULT**

1228	GEN, tsuru (BOW)STRING 8 strokes	正弦 SEIGEN sine (of angle) 弓弦 YUMIZURU bowstring 弦楽器 GENGAKKI stringed instrument

弓 is **bow** 836. 玄 is **occult/ black** 1227 q.v., here in its sense of **twisted thread** and by association **cord twisted taut**, and also acting phonetically to express **attach**. Thus **cord attached to bow and twisted taut**, i.e. **bowstring**. Now also **string** in a broader sense.

Mnemonic: **BOW HAS STRING OF TWISTED BLACK THREAD**

1229	KO ORPHAN, LONELY 9 strokes	孤児院 KOJIIN 孤独 KODOKU 孤立 KORITSU	orphanage loneliness isolation

子 is **child** 25. 瓜 is an NGU character meaning **melon** (once written 𤓰, thought to be a pictograph of a melon hanging from a frame). The latter acts phonetically to express **alone**, and may possibly also lend similar connotations from its depiction of a single melon. Thus **child alone**, i.e. an **orphan**. Also **alone/ lonely** in a wider sense.

Mnemonic: **LONELY ORPHAN CHILD GIVEN MELON**

1230		KO ARC, ARCH, BOW 9 strokes	弧形 KOKEI 弧状 KOJŌ 弧灯 KOTŌ	arc arcuate arc light

弓 is **bow** 836. 瓜 is **melon** 1229, here acting phonetically to express **rounded** and also lending similar connotations of its own from the shape of the melon. 1230 originally referred to a particularly **curved type of bow**, but later, like the English term **bow**, came to mean **arc/ arch** in a general sense.

Mnemonic: **BOW ARCHED AS ROUND AS A MELON**

1231		KO, kareru/rasu WITHER, DECAY 9 strokes	枯死 KOSHI withering away 冬枯れ FUYUGARE winter decay 枯れ葉 KAREHA dead leaf

木 is **tree** 69. 古 is **old** 109 q.v., acting phonetically to express **bone** (and by extension **skeleton**) and almost certainly also lending similar connotations from its assumed literal meaning of ancient skull. Thus a **tree reduced to a skeleton**, symbolising **decaying** and **withering**.

Mnemonic: **WITHERED OLD TREE**

1232		KO, yatou EMPLOY, HIRE 12 strokes	雇用 KOYŌ employment 雇い人 YATOININ employee 解雇 KAIKO dismissal

Bird 隹 216 and **door** 戸 108. 1232 originally referred to a bird whose wings flapped like the leaves of a door, i.e. in a somewhat stiff and ungainly fashion, specifically a type of **quail** (still retained in Chinese). **Employ/ hire** is generally assumed to be a purely borrowed meaning, but it is possible that it was used by association of an apprentice ungainly in his work.

Mnemonic: **PUT BIRD UNDER DOOR TO GAIN EMPLOYMENT**

1233	誇	KO, hokoru PROUD, BOAST 13 strokes	誇大 KODAI exaggeration 誇示 KOJI ostentation 誇り顔 HOKORIGAO proud look

夸 is a CO character meaning **brag/ boast** (big 大 53 and **emerge** 亐 811), here reinforced by **words**/ speak 言 274. Thus **boastful words**, with **proud** being an associated meaning.

Mnemonic: **BIG WORDS EMERGE IN PROUD BOAST**

1234 KO, tsuzumi   鼓動 KODŌ   beating
DRUM   大鼓 TAIKO   big drum
13 strokes   小鼓 KOTSUZUMI hand drum

支 is **branch** 691q.v., here meaning literally **hand holding bamboo stick**. 壴 is edible plants in a food vessel 450 q.v. The latter was used for its sound (generally believed to have been **CHŪ** at the time in question [or **SHOKU** by some scholars], though **KO** might seem more appropriate), and almost certainly also for its elements, with **food vessel on a stand** 豆 1640 q.v. being likened to a drum on a stand, and plant ± / 业 (variant 生 42) probably being reinterpreted as **emerge** (an occasional connotation of plant 生 , which emerges from the ground). Thus 1234 literally means **instrument resembling a food vessel on a stand from which the sound CHŪ (SHOKU? KO?) emerges when struck with a bamboo stick**, i.e. a **drum**. Suggest taking 士 as **samurai 494**.

Mnemonic: **SAMURAI WIELDS BRANCH, USING FOOD POT AS DRUM**

1235 KO, kaeri*miru*   顧慮 KORYO   concern
LOOK BACK   回顧 KAIKO   retrospection
21 strokes   顧問 KOMON   adviser

頁 is **head** 93. 雇 is **employ**/ quail 1232 q.v., here acting phonetically to express **turn around** and possibly also lending connotations of ungainly movement (as in a panic or similar). Thus to **turn the head around** (in a panic?), now **look back** in a broad sense including the figurative.

Mnemonic: **EMPLOY HEAD TO LOOK BACK**

1236 互 GO, taga*i*   相互 SŌGO-   mutual
MUTUAL   互助 GOJO   mutual aid
4 strokes   互い違い TAGAICHIGAI alternately

From a pictograph 㸦 , showing a **special spool used for evenly crosswinding** thread. It thus came to symbolise **balance** and **symmetry**, and hence by association **equality, mutuality, reciprocity**, etc. Note the similarity of shape to reel/ **five** 五 19, which may be useful as a mnemonic.

Mnemonic: **MUTUALITY AWKWARD FROM FIVE**

1237

GO, ku*reru*
GIVE, WU CHINA
7 strokes

呉服　GOFUKU　　　　drapery
呉呉も　KUREGUREMO earnestly
呉れ手　KURETE　　　　donor

Formerly 吳 and in ancient times 𠀝. ㅂ/口 is **mouth/ say** 20, deliberately tilted in the original form to reinforce 夭, which shows a **man** 大 53 with his **head tilted at an angle** ⌒. This expressed the idea of **deviating from the truth**, as in **bragging**, and was also used to express putting the head back and bawling (still found in Chinese). For reasons that are not clear it was later used to refer to a **district in China**, and in Japanese was also borrowed to express **give** (to an inferior). Suggest taking 矢 as a combination of **corner** ㇄ 349 and **six** 六 76, with 口 as a **box**.

Mnemonic: **GIVEN A CHINESE BOX WITH SIX CORNERS**

1238

娯

GO
PLEASURE, AMUSEMENT
10 strokes

娯楽　GORAKU　　　　pleasure
歓娯　KANGO　　　　　pleasure
娯楽品　GORAKUHIN　plaything

女 is **woman** 35. 呉 is **give** 1237 q.v., here acting phonetically to express **talk** and possibly also lending its literal meaning of **brag**. Thus to **talk with (brag to?) a woman**, which came to symbolise **pleasure** and **amusement**.

Mnemonic: **WOMAN GIVES PLEASURE AND AMUSEMENT**

1239

悟

GO, sato*ru*
PERCEIVE, DISCERN
10 strokes

悟性　GOSEI　　　　　wisdom
覚悟　KAKUGO　mental resolve
悟り　SATORI　　enlightenment

忄 is **heart/ feelings** 147. 吾 is **I/me** 112 q.v., here acting phonetically to express **enlightenment** and possibly also lending connotations of balance and by extension proper proportion. Thus **enlightenment in the heart** (seeing things in proper proportion?), leading to **perceive** and **discern**. Suggest taking 吾 as **five** 五 19 and **mouth** 口 20.

Mnemonic: **I LISTEN TO FIVE MOUTHS AND PERCEIVE FEELINGS**

1240

碁

GO
(THE GAME OF) GO
13 strokes

碁石　GOISHI　　　　go stone
碁盤　GOBAN　checkerboard
碁打ち　GOUCHI　　go player

As **chess** 棋 1130 q.v., but with **wood** 木 69 replaced by **stone** 石 45.

Mnemonic: **'GO' IS A TYPE OF CHESS PLAYED WITH STONES**

1241 孔 KŌ, ana
HOLE, CONFUCIUS
4 strokes

鼻孔 BIKŌ — nostril
気孔 KIKŌ — pore
孔子 KŌSHI — Confucius

Once written 𢎀, showing **child** 𢎀 / 子 25 and a semi-abstract depiction of a **cavity** 𢎀, later confusingly stylised to ㇄ and retaining the convex rather than concave element. 1241 originally meant the **cavity/ hole through which children emerge**, i.e. the **vagina**, but then came to mean **hole** in general. It was also borrowed phonetically to express the first syllable of **Confucius**. Suggest taking ㇄ as a **hook**, for an irreverent mnemonic.

Mnemonic: CONFUCIUS SAY CHILD WHO PLAY WITH HOOK GET HOLE

1242 KŌ, takumi
SKILL
5 strokes

技巧 GIKŌ — skill
巧言 KŌGEN — flattery
精巧 SEIKŌ — elaborateness

工 is **work/ carpenter's square** 113, here meaning **accurate carpentry**. 丂 is **twisting waterweed** 281, here with its meaning of **flat/ level** (see 388). 1242 originally referred to a carpenter **planing a piece of wood till it was exactly flat/ level**, and this eventually came to symbolise **skilled work** and **skill** in general.

Mnemonic: WORK WITH WATERWEED CALLS FOR SKILL

1243 甲 KŌ, KAN, kōra
SHELL, ARMOR,
HIGH, 1ST, A
5 strokes

甲虫 KŌCHŪ — beetle
甲種 KŌSHU — Grade A
甲高い KANDAKAI — shrill

Once written ⊕ or simply ✛, indicating a **hard-shelled seed** ○ with a **split** ✛ (see 162) in its case. ｜, which represents a sprout, was added later to clarify the meaning, giving 甲. Though the original emphasis was on sprouting, in time 1243 came to refer rather to the **case** of the seed, giving **shell** and **armor**. **1st/ A** and **high** are borrowed meanings. Suggest taking 甲 as a combination of **field** 田 59 and the **figure 1**.

Mnemonic: AN 'A 1' FIELD

1244 KŌ, e
INLET, RIVER
6 strokes

入り江 IRIE — creek, inlet
江湖 KŌKO — world, public
江戸 EDO — Edo, old Tokyo

氵 is **water** 40, here meaning **river**. 工 is **carpenter's square** 113, here acting phonetically to express **huge** and possibly also indirectly lending similar connotations of its own (see 1153). Thus **huge river**, which was also applied to an **arm of the sea/ inlet**.

Mnemonic: FIND CARPENTER'S SQUARE IN WATERS OF INLET

| 1245 坑 | KŌ
MINE, PIT, HOLE
7 strokes | 炭坑 TANKŌ
坑夫 KŌFU
坑道 KŌDŌ | coal mine
miner
mine shaft |

Of confusing semantic evolution. Originally written 阬, showing **hill** 阝/β 229 and **high/ straight** 介/亢 479. The latter also acted phonetically to express **high**, thus giving **steep high hill**. This came to mean **sheer** and **precipitous**, which by a confusing process of assocation came in turn to mean a **precipitous drop**, and hence eventually **deep hole** and the present meanings. **Ground/ earth** 土 60 was later used as an alternative to hill 阝, eventually prevailing in Japanese though in Chinese 阬 and 坑 are interchangeable. Suggest taking 亠 as a **top** and 几 as **desk** 832, with 土 as **soil/ dirt**.

Mnemonic: **HOLE IN DESKTOP FULL OF DIRT**

| 1246 抗 | KŌ
RESIST, OPPOSE
7 strokes | 対抗 TAIKŌ
抗議 KŌGI
抗争 KŌSŌ | opposition
protest
dispute |

扌 is **hand** 32. 亢 is **high/ straight** 479, here acting phonetically to express **block** and also lending loose connotations of obstacle/ **obstruct** from its idea of rising sheer. Thus to **block with the hand**, leading to **resist** and by association **protest**. Suggest taking 亠 as a **top** and 几 as **desk** 832.

Mnemonic: **HAND THUMPED ON DESKTOP SHOWS OPPOSITION**

| 1247 攻 | KŌ, semeru
ATTACK
7 strokes | 攻撃者 KŌGEKISHA
専攻 SENKŌ
攻め入る SEMEIRU | aggressor
specialty
invade |

攵 is **strike** 101. 工 is **carpenter's square** 113, here acting phonetically to express **strike/ beat** and possibly also lending connotations of an implement resembling a weapon. Thus to **strike and beat**, leading to **attack**.

Mnemonic: **ATTACK, STRIKING WITH CARPENTER'S SQUARE**

1248 KŌ, sara, fu*keru*/*kasu*
ANEW, CHANGE,
AGAIN, GROW LATE
7 strokes

更新 KŌSHIN　　　　renewal
今更 IMASARA now, belatedly
夜更け YOFUKE　　late at night

Formerly 霅 . 攴 is **striking hand/ coerce** 101, here meaning **(en)force**. 丙 is third rate 1773 q.v., here acting phonetically to express **change** and also, from its literal meaning of sturdy altar, lending an idea of being **firmly planted**, which was a reference to a **guard**. 1248 originally referred to an **enforced change of guard**, then came to refer to **unavoidable duty rosters**. The **night watch** (still a meaning in Chinese) was one such duty, leading to **stay up late** and **grow late**. On the other hand, change of guard led to **change** in general, including **renew/ anew** and by association **(yet) again**. Suggest taking 日 as **day** 62 and 丈 as a variant of **force** 攵 101.

Mnemonic: **DAY GROWS LATE, FORCING CHANGE**

1249 KŌ, kakawa*ru*
SEIZE, ADHERE TO
8 strokes

拘束 KŌSOKU　　　restriction
拘引 KŌIN　　arrest, custody
拘らず KAKAWARAZU
　　　　　　　regardless

扌 is **hand** 32, here meaning **arm**. 句 is **phrase** 655 q.v., here acting phonetically to express **stop** and also lending connotations of **encircle** through its element 勹. Thus to **stop with the arms by encircling**, i.e. **seize/ cling**, now also in a figurative sense.

Mnemonic: **SEIZE ONTO A HANDY PHRASE**

1250 KŌ
CONSENT, AGREE, VITAL
8 strokes

首肯 SHUKŌ　consent, assent
肯定 KŌTEI　　　affirmation
肯けい KŌKEI　　　the point

Once written 肎. 夕/ 月 is **meat/** of the body 365. 冂 is an abbreviation of **bone** 骨 867 q.v. Thus to all intents and purposes 1250 is a variant of **bone** 骨 867. Its present major meaning of **consent/ agree** is a borrowing, felt to stem from confusion with 叮/ 可 816 q.v. Its early meaning of bone is still seen indirectly in some compounds, as in the CO character gnaw 啃 , which adds **mouth** 口 20, and in the minor meaning of **vital part/ substance**. The reason for the later use of **stop** 止 129 is not clear. Some scholars feel it refers to meat stopping on the bone, but it is more likely to have been used in some now unclear phonetic role.

Mnemonic: **CONSENT TO MEAT STOPPAGE**

1251 KŌ, tsune
ALWAYS, CONSTANT
9 strokes

恆常 KŌJŌ   constancy
恆久 KŌKYŪ   perpetuity
恆例 KŌREI   common usage

Formerly 恆 . 忄 is **heart/ feelings** 147. 亘 is a CO character meaning **limit**, showing a **moon** 夕 / 月 16 between **two boundaries** 二 (see 913). The boundaries symbolised limits and fixed course, and 亘 originally referred to the **fixed trajectory of the moon**. In combination with heart 忄 it expressed the idea of **fidelity/ constancy**, now **constant** in a general sense. The later use of around 亘 913 q.v. almost certainly results from a misinterpretation of 日 as **sun** 62 (though it is actually a derivative of vortex ℮), to give an alternative idea of fixed trajectory of the sun (sun and moon often being interchanged, as in 閒 / 閒 92 etc.). Suggest taking 日 as **day** 62, with 二 as **two** 61.

Mnemonic: **FEELINGS CONSTANT OVER TWO DAYS**

1252 KŌ
FLOOD, VAST
9 strokes

洪水 KŌZUI/ ŌMIZU*   flood
洪積層 KŌSEKISŌ   diluvium
洪大 KŌDAI na   vast

氵 is **water** 40. 共 is **together** 460 q.v., here acting phonetically to express **big** and probably also lending an idea of coming together. Thus a **big body/ volume of water** (coming together from various sources?), leading to **flood** and occasionally **vast** in a general sense.

Mnemonic: **WATERS COME TOGETHER IN VAST FLOOD**

1253 KŌ, arai, *areru/rasu*
ROUGH, WILD, WASTE
9 strokes

荒天 KŌTEN   stormy weather
荒れ地 ARECHI   wasteland
荒波 ARANAMI   rough sea

艹 is **grass** 9. 㠩 is a CO character meaning **(vast) watery waste**, comprising **river** 巛/川 48 and **death** 亡 973, which acts phonetically to express **vast** as well as lending connotations of death and by association **destruction**. In combination with grass 艹 it meant **grassy waste**, i.e. a place once inhabited but now **ruined** and **overgrown with grass**. Thus **uncared for, rough, wild**, etc.

Mnemonic: **RIVER AND DEAD GRASS IN WILD WASTELAND**

1254 KŌ
SUBURBS
9 strokes

郊外 KŌGAI — suburbs
近郊 KINKŌ — suburbs
郊野 KŌYA — suburban field

阝 is **village/ settlement** 355, while 交 is **mix/ cross/ exchange** 115. Thus **settlement at crossing** (i.e. crossroads). Whereas the similar 街 819 q.v. came to mean town, 1254 came rather to mean community <u>outside</u> a town, giving **suburbs**.

Mnemonic: **VILLAGE MIXED WITH SUBURBS**

1255 KŌ, ka, kaoru/ri
FRAGRANCE, INCENSE
9 strokes

香水 KŌSUI — perfume
香気 KŌKI — fragrance, aroma
色香 IROKA — woman's charms

日 is a simplification of **sweet** 甘 1093, while 禾 is **rice plant/ grain plant** 81. 1255 originally referred to a certain type of **aromatic millet,** and then came to mean delicate flavor and eventually **fragrance** and **incense**. Suggest taking 日 as **sun** 62.

Mnemonic: **SUN BRINGS OUT FRAGRANCE OF GRAIN PLANT**

1256 KŌ
MARQUIS, LORD
9 strokes

侯爵 KŌSHAKU — marquis
太田侯 ŌTAKŌ — Marquis Ota
王侯 ŌKŌ — royalty

Somewhat obscure, having become etymologically confused with **sign/ ask** 候 478 q.v. It appears to be a variant of **meet/ greet** (humbly) 矦 (also 478), with 丿 becoming **person** 亻 39, but from an early stage meant **archery** or **target range** (still in fact a lesser meaning in Chinese), apparently having become confused with target range 厌 (also 478). It was borrowed phonetically to express **marquis**. Unfortunately there is no easy mnemonic for the character, but suggest remembering by partial association with **arrow** 矢 981, taking 矦 as a **'fancy' arrow**.

Mnemonic: **PERSON WITH FANCY ARROW IS MARQUIS**

1257 貢 KŌ, KU, mitsugu
TRIBUTE
10 strokes

貢献 KŌKEN — contribution
年貢 NENGU — tax, dues
貢ぎ物 MITSUGIMONO — tribute

貝 is **shell/ money** 90, here meaning **assets**. 工 is **work** 113, here also acting phonetically to express **offer up**. Thus **offer up assets and work** (i.e. corvee), namely the **tribute** paid to one's lord.

Mnemonic: **BOTH WORK AND MONEY OFFERED AS TRIBUTE**

| 1258 | | KŌ, hikae*ru*
 REFRAIN, WRITE DOWN,
 HAVE NEAR, WAIT
 11 strokes | 控え所 HIKAEJO waiting room
 控訴 KŌSO legal appeal
 控え書き HIKAEGAKI memo, note |

Of broad and somewhat unclear semantic evolution. 扌 is **hand** 32. 空 is **sky** 15, here acting phonetically to express **pull back** and possibly also lending an idea of space (i.e. distance). Thus to **pull back with the hand** (over a distance?). This originally meant to pull back a bow or to pull on reins (both meanings still found in Chinese). However, just like the English pull back, it also came to mean **refrain**, **wait**, and **be patient**. **Have near** is taken to be an associated meaning, from the idea of pulling something towards one-self. **Write down** is felt to derive from the idea of keeping something (i.e. as a record), which in turn derives from association with holding back.

Mnemonic: **REFRAIN, HANDS REACHING FOR THE SKY**

| 1259 | | KŌ, awa*teru*/tadashii
 BE FLUSTERED
 12 strokes | 恐慌 KYŌKŌ panic, scare
 大慌て ŌAWATE big fluster
 慌て者 AWATEMONO blunderer |

忄 is heart/ **feelings** 147. 荒 is **wild** 1253, here acting phonetically to express **unclear/ incomprehensible** and almost certainly also lending an idea of wild. Thus **wild incomprehensible feelings**, a reference to a state of being **panicked** or **flustered**.

Mnemonic: **WILD FEELINGS SHOW ONE IS FLUSTERED**

| 1260 | | KŌ, katai
 HARD
 12 strokes | 硬化 KŌKA hardening
 硬貨 KŌKA coin
 硬水 KŌSUI hard water |

石 is **rock/ stone** 45. 更 is **change** 1248 q.v., here acting phonetically to express **solid** and possibly also lending an idea of change to suggest petrification. Thus (become?) **solid as a rock**, i.e. **hard**.

Mnemonic: **CHANGE TO STONE AND BECOME HARD**

| 1261 | | KŌ, shi*boru*, shi*meru*
STRANGLE, WRING
12 strokes | 絞首台 KŌSHUDAI gallows
絞め殺す SHIMEKOROSU strangle
絞り出す SHIBORIDASU
squeeze out |

糸 is **thread** 27, here essentially meaning **cloth**. 交 is **mix/ cross/** exchange 115 q.v., here acting phonetically to express **twist** and also lending an idea of **criss cross**. Thus to **put cloth over something in a criss cross fashion and twist** (in order to squeeze out the contents), giving **wring** and later **strangle**.

Mnemonic: **STRANGLED WITH MIXED THREADS**

| 1262 | | KŌ, unaji
CLAUSE, ITEM, NAPE
12 strokes | 項目 KŌMOKU clause, item
事項 JIKŌ matters
条項 JŌKŌ articles |

頁 is **head** 93. 工 is **work** 113, here acting phonetically to express **rear/ back**. Thus the **back of the head**, and by extension **back of the neck** (i.e. **nape**). Rather like the English term **heading**, it also came to be used figuratively of an **item** or **clause**.

Mnemonic: **WORK HEADINGS INCLUDE SUNDRY ITEMS**

| 1263 | | KŌ, mizo, dobu
DITCH, CHANNEL
13 strokes | 下水溝 GESUIKŌ drain
溝切り MIZOKIRI grooving
溝ねずみ DOBUNEZUMI sewer rat |

氵 is **water** 40. 冓 is **build up/ accumulation** 675 q.v., here acting phonetically to express **criss cross** and probably also lending an idea of accumulation/ plurality. 1263 originally referred to (a number of?) **crisscrossing irrigation channels**, giving the present meanings. Suggest taking 冓 literally as **pile of baskets**.

Mnemonic: **BUILD WATER CHANNEL WITH PILE OF BASKETS?!**

| 1264 | 綱 | KŌ, tsuna
CABLE,LINE,PRINCIPLE
14 strokes | 要綱 YŌKŌ gist
大綱 TAIKŌ main principles
綱引き TSUNABIKI tug-of-war |

糸 is **thread** 27, here meaning **cord**. 岡 is **(towering) hill** 864 q.v., here acting phonetically to express **strong** and probably also lending an idea of **formidable**. Thus **strong (and formidable?) cord**, i.e. a **rope** or **cable**. **Line** is an associated meaning, with **principle** being a figurative associated meaning with line/ thread (cf. English thread of argument etc.).

Mnemonic: **CABLE THREADS WAY UP HILLSIDE**

403

1265

酵

KŌ

FERMENT, YEAST

14 strokes

酵母 KŌBO　　　　yeast
酵素 KŌSO　　　　enzyme
発酵 HAKKŌ　　　fermentation

酉 is **wine jar** 302, here meaning **alcohol**. 孝 is **filial piety** 860 q.v., here acting phonetically to express **yeast** and probably also suggesting the process of **aging** through its elements of young (i.e. child 子 25) and old (i.e. old man 耂 117). (Aging) yeast is involved in the process of **fermentation** in the production of alcohol.

Mnemonic: **FILIAL PIETY IS A JAR OF FERMENTED ALCOHOL**

1266

稿

KŌ

MANUSCRIPT, STRAW

15 strokes

原稿 GENKŌ　　　manuscript
投稿 TŌKŌ　　　　contribution
草稿 SŌKŌ　　　　rough draft

Formerly also 稾. 禾 is **rice plant / grain plant** 81, while 高 is **tall** 119. The tall part of a grain plant is its **stem**, which was the original meaning of 1266, with **straw** being an associated meaning. Nowadays straw is usually conveyed by the NGU character 藁, which adds plant 艹 9. **Manuscript** is a borrowed meaning.

Mnemonic: **MANUSCRIPT ABOUT TALL RICE PLANTS**

1267

衡

KŌ, kubiki

SCALES, YOKE

16 strokes

均衡 KINKŌ　　　balance
平衡 HEIKŌ　　　equilibrium
衡器 KŌKI　　　　scales

大 is **big man** 53, here meaning simply **man**. 甶 is a simplification of **horn** 角 243. 行 is **go** 118 q.v., here acting phonetically to express **crosswise** and also lending similar connotations from its literal meaning of crossroads. 1267 originally referred to a **piece of wood fixed across a cow's horns** to prevent them from goring the herdsman. It was later also used to refer to a **yoke**, though technically this is a different device. **Balance/scales** is felt by some scholars to be a borrowed meaning, and by others to derive from the fact that the piece of wood was fixed horizontally and thus suggested a set of scales. Suggest remembering 甶 as a **'stumpy' horn**, with 大 in its commoner sense of **big**.

Mnemonic: **BIG STUMPY HORN GOES ON TO THE SCALES**

1268	購	KŌ	購入 KŌNYŪ	purchase
		BUY	購買 KŌBAI	buying
		17 strokes	購読 KŌDOKU	subscription

貝 is shell/ money 90. 冓 is build up/ piled up baskets 675 q.v., here acting phonetically to express desire and almost certainly also lending connotations of pile/ large amount. 1268 originally referred to desiring something to the extent of paying out (a large amount of?) money for it, and eventually came to mean buy in a broad sense.

Mnemonic: USE SHELL-MONEY TO BUY PILE OF BASKETS

1269	拷	GŌ	拷問 GŌMON	torture
		TORTURE, HIT	拷責 GŌSEKI	torture
		9 strokes	拷問台 GŌMONDAI	the rack

扌 is hand 32. 考 is consider 117 q.v., here acting phonetically to express beat/ hit and possibly also lending its connotations of bent figure. Thus to beat someone with the hand (causing them to double up?), which also came to mean hurt and later, by association, torture.

Mnemonic: CONSIDER HOW TO USE HAND TO TORTURE

1270	剛	GŌ	剛健 GŌKEN	fortitude
		STRENGTH	剛毛 GŌMŌ	bristle
		10 strokes	剛直 GŌCHOKU	integrity

刂 is sword/ cut 181. 岡 is (towering) hill 864 q.v., here acting phonetically to express strong and almost certainly also lending connotations of formidable. Thus a strong (and formidable?) sword, which later came to symbolise strength and power in general.

Mnemonic: CUTTING DOWN A HILL TAKES STRENGTH

1271		**GŌ**	豪雨 GŌU	heavy rain
		STRENGTH, SPLENDOR,	豪壮 GŌSŌ	splendor
		AUSTRALIA, BRUSH	豪州 GŌSHŪ	Australia
		14 strokes		

Of confusing semantic evolution. A modified combination of **pig/ pig-like creature** 豕 1670 and **tall** 高 119. The latter acts phonetically to express **fearsome sword-like weapon** (in effect being a phonetic substitute for strong sword 岡刂 1270) and almost certainly also originally lent its meaning of tall. Thus **pig-like creature with (tall?) fearsome sword-like weapons**. This was technically a reference to the **porcupine** (a meaning still found in Chinese and very occasionally in Japanese), but was apparently also used to refer to the **wild boar,** thus leading to **strength** (and in Chinese prowess) and the occasionally encountered associated meanings of **mane** and **bristle** (including **writing brush**) and by further confusing association **down** and **plumage. Splendor** is felt to be an associated meaning with plumage. Of late 1271 has also been used instead of the NGU character moat 濠 (i.e. water 氵 40 plus 豪 in its sense of formidable) to refer to **Australia.** Suggest taking 豪 as a combination of **tall** 高 and **house** 家 83.

Mnemonic: **AUSTRALIA BOASTS SPLENDID STRONG TALL HOUSES**

1272		**KOKU**	克服 KOKUFUKU subjugation	
		CONQUER, OVERCOME	克己 KOKKI	self-denial
		7 strokes	克明 KOKUMEI	diligence

Somewhat obscure. 儿 is **bending person** 39. 古 is **old** 109 q.v., here in its assumed literal meaning of **skull-like mask.** 1272 originally appeared to refer to a person bending under the weight of a heavy ceremonial mask, then came by association to mean **withstand** (i.e. the weight of the mask) and eventually **overcome/ conquer.**

Mnemonic: **OVERCOME BENT OLD PERSON**

1273		**KOKU**	酷使 KOKUSHI	exploitation
		SEVERE, INTENSE,	残酷 ZANKOKU	cruelty
		CRUEL, HARSH	酷暑 KOKUSHO	intense heat
		14 strokes		

酉 is wine jar/ **alcohol** 302. 告 is **proclaim** 481 q.v., here acting phonetically to express **strong** and possibly also lending connotations of reeking from its idea of emerging from the mouth. Thus **strong alcohol,** leading to **strong/ intense/ astringent** in a general sense, with **cruel/ harsh** being an associated meaning.

Mnemonic: **CRUEL PROCLAMATION ABOUT ALCOHOL**

1274

GOKU

PRISON, LITIGATION

14 strokes

獄門 GOKUMON — prison gate
地獄 JIGOKU — hell
疑獄 GIGOKU — criminal case

Two **dogs** 犭/犬 opposed to each other, indicating a **fight**, with **words/ speak** 言 274. 1274 originally referred to a **dispute**, then came to mean **litigation** (still a strong meaning in Chinese). This gradually broadened to mean **going through the legal process**, leading to **imprisonment** and **prison**.

Mnemonic: **WORDS IN DOG FIGHT LEAD TO LITIGATION AND PRISON**

1275

ko*mu/meru*

PUT IN, BE CROWDED

5 strokes

見込み MIKOMI — prospect
人込み HITOGOMI — crowd
込め物 KOMEMONO — stuffing

Movement 辶 129 and **enter/ put in** 入 63, giving **move into/ put into** and by association **be crowded**. A 'made in Japan' character.

Mnemonic: **IT BECOMES CROWDED AS PEOPLE MOVE TO ENTER**

1276

KON

MULTITUDE, INSECT, DESCENDANTS

8 strokes

昆虫 KONCHŪ — insect
昆布 KONBU — kelp
後昆 KŌKON — descendants

A long-misinterpreted character. Usually taken to comprise **sun/ day** 日 62, in the sense of **time**, and compare 比 771 q.v., in its literal sense of **line of people**, to give **line of people over time**, i.e. **descendants**, with **multitude** being an associated meaning and **insect** taken to be an associated meaning in turn from the idea of swarm. However, very old forms such as 𦎡 show that 1276 is in fact a pictograph of an **insect** with **legs** 𠈌/ 比 and **carapace** ㅁ/日. Thus insect is the original meaning. However, since early times it was miscopied as day 日 and people 比, thus giving descendants and multitude as per the interpretation cited above, but somewhat incongruously the original meaning of insect was retained.

Mnemonic: **DESCENDANTS LINE UP OVER MANY DAYS, LIKE INSECTS**

1277 恨 KON, ura*mu*
RESENT, REGRET
9 strokes

悔恨 KAIKON remorse
遺恨 IKON grudge
恨み言 URAMIGOTO grievance

忄 is heart/ feelings 147. 艮 is **stop and stare/ turn round and stare** 263, here acting phonetically to express **contrary** and also lending similar connotations of **turning against**. 1277 originally meant to have **contrary feelings/ be opposed**. Possibly because of the idea of staring contained in 艮 (as opposed to voicing), it came to acquire particular (but not exclusive) connotations of opposition kept in the heart rather than openly expressed, giving **resentment** and by association **regret**.

Mnemonic: **STOP AND STARE WITH RESENTFUL FEELINGS**

1278 KON
MARRIAGE
11 strokes

婚約 KONYAKU engagement
結婚式 KEKKONSHIKI wedding
新婚夫婦 SHINKONFŪFU
newly weds

Somewhat obscure. 女 is **woman** 35. 昏 is an NGU character meaning **dim/ sunset**. It comprises **sun** 日 62 and **scoop** 氏 495 q.v., though the role of the latter element is unclear (some scholars take it to be an abbreviation of bottom 氐 548, giving sun at the bottom [of its trajectory] and hence sunset). Woman 女 and sunset 昏 are popularly interpreted as being used ideographically to refer to some supposed practice of **wedding ceremonies being held at sunset**, but there is no historical foundation for this. Some authoritative Japanese scholars take 昏 to be used purely phonetically to express **root** (KON 根 282), which was a euphemism for **male organ**, and thus take 婚 to refer to the **penetration of a woman**. As in Western societies, this was a symbol of the **consummation of marriage**. Suggest taking 氏 in its meaning of **Mr**. (It is remotely possible, but chronologically unlikely, that 昏 was deliberately chosen as a phonetic with 氏 in its later sense of Mr, to give a balance between man and woman.)

Mnemonic: **WOMAN MARRIES MISTER, WITH SUN SINKING BELOW**

1279 紺 KON
DARK BLUE, DYE
11 strokes

紺色 KONIRO dark blue
紺屋 KONYA dyer
濃紺 NŌKON dark blue

糸 is **thread** 27. 甘 is **sweet** 1093, here acting phonetically to express **dark blue**. Thus **threads (dyed) dark blue**, later **dark blue** in general, with **dye** a minor meaning.

Mnemonic: **THREADS DYED A SWEET DARK BLUE**

1280 KON, tama, tamashii   霊魂 REIKON   soul
                   SOUL, SPIRIT   商魂 SHŌKON   salesmanship
                   14 strokes   魂消る TAMAGERU* be shocked

鬼 is **ghost**/ demon 1128 q.v., here meaning **spirit of a dead person**. 云 is **say**/ speak 78 q.v., here acting phonetically to express **move**/ **swirl** and also lending its literal meaning of **vapors**. Thus **swirling vapors which are the spirit of a dead person**, later **spirit** and **soul** in a broader sense. Suggest taking 云 as **two** 二 61 **noses** 厶 134.

Mnemonic: **GHOST WITH TWO NOSES IS A FUNNY SPIRIT**

1281 KON   開墾 KAIKON   reclamation
                   CULTIVATE, RECLAIM   墾田 KONDEN   new fields
                   16 strokes   未開墾地 MIKAIKONCHI
                                                        virgin land

Somewhat obscure. Formerly 墾, and in earlier times 𡐦. 艮 is **stop and stare** 263. 堇 is the obscure element seen in 漢 442 q.v., and is taken by some scholars to have originally meant **beast** . In this case it does indeed appear to have been interchangeable with beast 豸 (see below). In combination with stop and stare 艮 it gives the NGU character **difficult** 艱, though it is not clear how these elements are used. 堇 was later replaced by **pig** 豕 1670, presumably meaning simply beast, and later still by 豸. This is a CO character used of a range of mythical beasts. It shows **claws** ⺥ 303 and **dog/ beast** 犭 17, and is generally known as the **clawed beast** (affectionately Claude Beast) or **clawed dog** radical. In the case of 1281 艱/豭/豤 acts phonetically to express **difficult** and also lends a similar meaning, combining with **earth/ ground** 土 60 to give **earth that is difficult (to till/ cultivate)**. This was a reference to **virgin land**, leading by association to **reclaim** and **cultivate**.

Mnemonic: **STOP AND STARE AT CLAWED BEAST ON RECLAIMED GROUND**

409

1282

KON, nengoro
COURTESY, CORDIALITY,
EARNEST WISH
17 strokes

懇談 KONDAN　　　　chat
懇願 KONGAN　　　　entreaty
懇意 KONI kindness, friendship

心 is **heart/ feelings** 147. 銀 is the somewhat obscure element seen in 墾 1281 q.v., here acting phonetically to express **wish/ request** and possibly also lending connotations of difficulty. Thus a **wish/ request from the heart** (which is difficult to make?). In Chinese earnest wish/ beseech is a major meaning, but in Japanese the idea of **earnestness/ sincerity** gave rise to the associated meanings of **cordiality** and hence **courtesy**, which are now the major meanings. Suggest taking 銀 literally as **clawed beast** (claws ⺥ 303 and beast 豸 17) and **stop and stare** 艮 263.

Mnemonic: **STOP AND STARE AT CLAWED BEAST, CORDIALITY IN HEART**

1283

SA
ASSIST, ASSISTANT
7 strokes

補佐 HOSA　　　　assistance
佐官 SAKAN　　　field officer
大佐 TAISA　　　　colonel

Left 左 22 q.v., here with its original meaning of **assist**, with **person** 亻 39. Originally **assistant**, but now also **assist/ assistance**.

Mnemonic: **ASSISTED BY PERSON ON ONE'S LEFT**

1284

SA, sosonokasu, sosoru
ENTICE, INCITE
10 strokes

示唆 SHISA　　　　suggestion
教唆 KYŌSA　　　incitement
教唆者 KYŌSASHA　　abettor

口 is **mouth/ say** 20. 㚍 is **linger** 689, here acting phonetically to express **coerce/ exhort** but of unclear semantic role. Thus to **urge someone to do something**, often with connotations of wrongdoing. Suggest taking 口 in its extended sense of **words**.

Mnemonic: **LINGERING WORDS OF ENTICEMENT**

1285

SA
LIE, DECEIVE
12 strokes

詐欺師 SAGISHI　　　swindler
詐取 SASHU　　　　　fraud
詐称 SASHŌ misrepresentation

Words/ speak 言 274 and **make/ make up** 乍 127 q.v., which also lends its later connotations of **deceit**. Thus **made up deceitful words**, i.e. a **lie** or similar.

Mnemonic: **MAKE UP WORDS IN DECEITFUL LIE**

1286 SA, kusari 鎖国 SAKOKU closed country
CHAIN, LINK 連鎖 RENSA chain, series
18 strokes 鎖止め KUSARIDOME sprocket

金 is **metal** 14. 貟 is an element meaning **chain/ link**, comprising **shell** 貝 90 and **small** ⺌ /小 36 (small shells being strung together in a chain). Some scholars feel that 貟 also acts phonetically to express **connect**. Thus **metal chain** (of small connected links). 1286 was also formerly written 鏁 , though this is technically a separate character of similar meaning using nest 巢 1521, the latter acting in a similar phonetic role to 貟 and possibly also lending connotations of round and hollow. Suggest taking 金 in its meaning of **gold**.

Mnemonic: **CHAIN OF SMALL GOLD SHELLS**

1287 SAI, kuda*ku/keru* 砕氷船 SAIHYŌSEN icebreaker
BREAK, SMASH 砕片 SAIHEN fragment
9 strokes 砕けた KUDAKETA informal

Formerly 碎 . 石 is **stone/ rock** 45. 卒 is **soldier** 537, here acting phonetically to express **smash/ break up** but of unknown semantic role. Thus **smash rock**, later **smash/ break up** in a broader sense. Suggest taking 卆 as **nine** 九 12 and **ten** 十 33.

Mnemonic: **SMASH ROCK INTO NINETEEN FRAGMENTS**

1288 SAI 主宰者 SHUSAISHA leader
ADMINISTER 宰領 SAIRYŌ management
10 strokes 宰相 SAISHŌ prime minister

宀 is **house/ building** 28. 辛 is **needle** 1432 q.v., but is known to have symbolised **prisoner** and thus derives from the variant 𦍋 /宰 that appears to have been an instrument of torture. Thus **prisoners in a building**. This was actually a reference to prisoners being <u>made to work</u> in a building (at one stage strike 攴 153 was added to act as a causative particle, giving 𡜦, which is still found in Chinese as a variant of 1288). In Chinese 1288 can also mean to slaughter animals, which appears to be a reference to one of the tasks usually assigned to prisoners. In general , however, the idea of prisoners at work led by association to the idea of **supervising** such work, giving supervisor/ ruler in Chinese and **administer** in Japanese. Suggest taking 辛 in its sense of **sharp**.

Mnemonic: **BUILDING HOUSES SHARP ADMINISTRATION**

1289		SAI PLANTING 10 strokes	栽培 SAIBAI 盆栽 BONSAI 前栽 SENZAI*	cultivation bonsai garden

木 is **tree** 69. 𢦏 is **cut/ fancy halberd** 872, here acting phonetically to express **plant** and possibly also loosely lending similar connotations from the occasional practice of thrusting a halberd/ lance into the ground as a crude marker (see 698). Thus **to plant trees**, later **plant/ planting** in a broader sense.

Mnemonic: **PLANT TREES USING FANCY HALBERD!?**

1290		SAI, *irodoru* COLOR 11 strokes	色彩 SHIKISAI 淡彩 TANSAI 彩雲 SAIUN	color(ing) light coloring glowing clouds

彡 is **delicate hairs** 93, here meaning **attractive adornment**. 釆 is **hand plucking from tree** 483 (literally hand 爫 303 and tree 木 69), here acting phonetically to express **variety** and possibly also lending similar connotations (釆 does in fact have a lesser meaning of variety of color, but it is not clear whether this is a meaning acquired in its own right, such as by extension from a bouquet of picked blossoms or similar, or whether it results from its use as a simplification of color 彩 1290). Thus **attractive and varied adornment**, which later came to mean in particular an **attractive variety of color** and finally just **coloration/ color**. Suggest taking 彡 as the **hairs of a brush**.

Mnemonic: **BRUSH PAINTS COLORS OF BLOSSOMS TAKEN FROM TREE**

1291		SAI PURIFICATION, ABSTAIN, WORSHIP, A STUDY 11 strokes	斎戒 SAIKAI 書斎 SHOSAI 潔斎 KESSAI	purification a study abstinence, purification

Formerly 齋. 示 is a variant of **altar/ of the gods** 示 695. 㐫 is a variant of similar 齊 1473 q.v., here acting phonetically to express **pure/ purified** and also lending similar connotations from its literal meaning of **food arranged for offering**. Thus **purified food for offering to the gods**, leading to **purification** and **worship**. By association it also came to mean **abstain**, from the fact that priests ate only purified foods and abstained from others. **Study** derives from 1291's use as a simplification of a now defunct character 齋, which added building 广 114 to give place of worship. This came to mean (room in a) temple, which was a place of contemplation/ study. Suggest taking the modern form 斎 as **altar** 示, **text** 文 68, and a **frame** 丨丨.

Mnemonic: **TEXT ON PURIFICATION USING FRAMED ALTAR**

1292		SAI	債務 SAIMU	liabilities
		DEBT, LOAN	債券 SAIKEN	debenture
		13 strokes	債権者 SAIKENSHA	creditor

Liability 責 728 q.v., here in its literal meaning of **money which can be demanded**, and **person** イ 39, here referring to the person doing the demanding. Thus **money demanded by a person**, namely a **debt/ loan**.

Mnemonic: **DEBT IS A PERSON'S LIABILITY**

1293		SAI, moyō*su*	主催 SHUSAI	sponsorship
		ORGANISE, MUSTER	催促 SAISOKU	urging
		13 strokes	催眠 SAIMIN	hypnosis

Obscure. イ is **person** 39. 崔 is a CO character meaning **high mountain**, thus suggesting that the character comprises two distinct elements of **mountain** 山 24 and **bird** 隹 216 and is not one of the graphically similar crested bird characters (see 1202). The etymology of 崔 is not clear, but 隹 presumably suggests height (either from a bird soaring or a high place where birds gather) and probably also plays some unclear phonetic role. In the case of 1293 the role of 崔 is also unclear. Some scholars feel that it originally acted phonetically to express **forge** (metal), giving **person who forges metal**, i.e. **swordsmith**, and that it was later borrowed to express **organise/ muster**. However, the evidence for this is not entirely convincing. An alternative hypothesis might be that 崔 acts phonetically to express **administer/ supervise** (see 1288), in a sense of **control**, and also lends connotations of **gathering** (birds occasionally symbolising this), thus giving a **controlled gathering of persons** and hence both **organise** and **muster**.

Mnemonic: **PERSON MUSTERS AND ORGANISES BIRDS ON MOUNTAIN**

1294	歳	SAI, SEI	二歳 NISAI	two years old
		YEAR	歳費 SAIHI	annual expenses
		13 strokes	歳暮 SEIBO	year-end gift

Old forms such as 歲 show 步, the old form of **walk** 歩 202 q.v., and **halberd/ trimming tool** 戌 246 (now halberd/ trimming tool 戉 515). The latter acts phonetically to express **circuit** and may also lend supporting figurative connotations of cut/ cut off (cutting often being associated with halberds -- see 493), as in the English term cut-off point. 1294 originally referred to **walking one lap/ circuit**, but was then applied to the **completion of a cycle of time**, specifically a **year**. Suggest taking 止 as **foot** 129, 示 as a variant of **altar** 示 695, and 戊 as **halberd**.

Mnemonic: **EVERY YEAR HALBERDS PLACED AT FOOT OF ALTAR**

1295		SAI, noru/seru LOAD, CARRY 13 strokes	積載 SEKISAI	loading
			掲載 KEISAI	publication
			記載 KISAI	mention

車 is **vehicle** 31. 戈 is **fancy halberd/ cut** 872 q.v., here acting phonetically to express **load** and almost certainly also lending connotations of **trim/ adjust**. Thus **that which is loaded onto a vehicle (and adjusted?)**, i.e. **load/ cargo**, now **load/ carry**.

Mnemonic: **VEHICLE CARRIES LOAD OF FANCY HALBERDS**

1296		ZAI MEDICINE, DRUG 10 strokes	薬剤師 YAKUZAISHI pharmacist	
			薬剤 YAKUZAI	drug
			緩下剤 KANGEZAI	laxative

Formerly 劑. 刂 is **sword/ cut** 181, here meaning **trim**. 齊/斉 is **similar** 1473 q.v., here acting phonetically to express **put in order** and also lending its own connotations of **arrange and make similar**. 1296 originally referred to **fine trimming something until all aspects were similar**, and thus came to mean **adjust/ regulate/ make just right**. This was later applied to **medicines/ drugs**, which regulate the body (some scholars feel rather that the adjustment was carried out on the drugs themselves, to ensure the optimal mix). Suggest remembering **similar** 斉 by partial association with **text** 文 68.

Mnemonic:**TEXT SAYS DRUGS CAN BE SIMILAR IN EFFECT TO SWORD**

1297		saki, KI CAPE, STEEP 11 strokes	長崎 NAGASAKI	Nagasaki
			島崎 SHIMAZAKI	a surname
			崎く KIKU	steep road

Mountain 山 24 and **strange** 奇 1123. The latter acts phonetically to express **dangerous** and almost certainly also lends connotations of **unusual/ exceptional**. Thus **(exceptionally?) dangerous mountain**, i.e. one that is very **steep**. In Japanese it has come to mean **promontory/ cape**, being a reference to a steep mountain rising from the sea.

Mnemonic: **CAPE FORMED BY STRANGE STEEP MOUNTAIN**

1298
SAKU, kezuru
PARE, REDUCE
9 strokes

削除 SAKUJO　　deletion
削減 SAKUGEN　　reduction
削り取る KEZURITORU　shave off

Of disputed etymology. 刂 is **sword/ cut** 181, while 肖 is **be like** 1391 q.v. Some scholars feel that the latter acts phonetically to express **put in**, giving **that into which one puts a sword**, i.e. a **scabbard**, and take **pare/ reduce** to be a borrowing. (In such case 肖 might also be felt to lend an idea of similarity [of shape], i.e. the scabbard matching the sword.) There is some evidence to support this theory in that the use of leather 革 821 instead of sword 刂 gives the CO character scabbard/ sheath 鞘. However, other scholars take 肖 to lend connotations of **reduce** from its original meaning of miniature version, as well as possibly acting phonetically to express **few/ little** (see 消 316), to give **reduce by cutting**. It is possible that both theories are correct, in that 1298 may originally have meant scabbard, but that pare/ reduce results from a reinterpretation of its elements (in similar fashion to the reinterpretation of 1276) rather than a simple borrowing. Suggest taking 肖 literally as **small** 丷 / 小 36 and **flesh** 月 365.

Mnemonic: **TO CUT AWAY SMALL BITS OF FLESH IS TO PARE**

1299
SAKU
ROPE, SEARCH
10 strokes

索引 SAKUIN　　index
思索 SHISAKU　　speculation
鉄索 TESSAKU　　cable

Old forms such as 𣺈 show **hands** 𦥑 and **thread** 叀 / 糸 27. The hands are in fact **plaiting** the thread into **rope**. **Search** is a borrowed meaning. Suggest taking 宀 as a roof with a cross, i.e. a **church roof**.

Mnemonic: **SEARCH FOR ROPE: FIND THREAD UNDER CHURCH ROOF**

1300
SAKU, su, suppai
VINEGAR, SOUR
12 strokes

酢酸 SAKUSAN　　acetic acid
酢の物 SUNOMONO　　pickles
酢づけ SUZUKE　　pickling

酉 is **wine jar/ alcohol** 302, here meaning **wine**. 乍 is **make** 127, here also acting phonetically to express **passage of time**. Thus **that which is made from wine with the passage of time**, i.e. **vinegar**.

Mnemonic: **VINEGAR IS MADE FROM WINE**

415

1301 　　SAKU, shibo*ru*　　　搾取 SAKUSHU　　exploitation
　　　　　　　　　　WRING, PRESS　　　　圧搾 ASSAKU　　　　　pressure
　　　　　　　　　　13 strokes　　　　　　搾り取る SHIBORITORU　extract

A 'made in Japan' character comprising **hand** 扌 32 and 窄, an NGU character meaning
squeeze/ make narrow (from **hole** 穴 849 and **make** 乍 127) which also acts here phonetically to express **press**. Thus **press and squeeze with the hand**, now **press**/
wring in a broader sense.

Mnemonic: **MAKE HOLE BY PRESSING WITH HAND**

1302 　　SAKU　　　　　　　　錯誤 SAKUGO　　　　mistake
　　　　　　　　　　MIX UP, CONFUSE　　　錯覚 SAKKAKU　　　　illusion
　　　　　　　　　　16 strokes　　　　　　倒錯 TŌSAKU　　　　perversion

金 is **metal** 14. 昔 is **olden times** 1481 q.v., here acting phonetically to express **cover**
and almost certainly also lending its connotations of **duplicate**. Thus to **cover with metal**
(thereby making a second surface?), i.e. to **plate** and by association **inlay** (still a minor
meaning in Chinese). Some scholars take **mix up**/ **confuse** to be a borrowed meaning,
while others take it to be an associated meaning from the idea of mixing elements involved
in inlaying/ plating.

Mnemonic: **IN OLDEN TIMES METALS WERE OFTEN MIXED UP**

1303 咲　　saku　　　　　　　　四季咲き SHIKIZAKI　　perennial
　　　　　　　　BLOOM, BLOSSOM　　　遅咲き OSOZAKI　late blooming
　　　　　　　　9 strokes　　　　　　　咲き残る SAKINOKORU
　　　　　　　　　　　　　　　　　　　　　　　　　　　stay in bloom

Formerly 咲. 口 is **mouth**/ **say** 20. 关/关 is not **raise repeatedly** 关 1603 but a variant or miscopying of (drooping?) **thistle** 実 900 q.v., as is clear from an old form ᄇ关.
実/ 关/关 acts phonetically to express **crease** and almost certainly also lends connotations of **thin** (from the stem of the thistle), to give (thin) **creases around the mouth**.
This was a reference to **smiling** and **laughing**, the original meanings of 1303 (and still its
only meanings in Chinese). In Japanese the idea of laughing led by association to the idea
of a **plant opening its mouth**, giving **blossom**/ **bloom**, while smile/ laugh has disappeared. Suggest taking 关 as **heaven** 天 58 and out of/ **forth** ⸼ 66, with 口 in its
literal sense of **open mouth**.

Mnemonic: **HEAVENLY FLOWERS OPEN MOUTHS TO BLOSSOM FORTH**

1304	**SATSU, fuda** **TAG, BILL, NOTE** 5 strokes	札入れ	SATSUIRE	billfold
		名札	NAFUDA	nameplate, tag
		千円札	SENENSATSU	1000 yen note

木 is **tree/ wood** 69. し is not **praying figure** し 413, though it may be helpful to remember it as such, but a variant of **odd** 乙 1041, here used purely phonetically to express **slice/ shave thinly**. Thus **thinly shaved piece of wood**, i.e. a **tag**, which was later also applied to **money bills/ notes**.

Mnemonic: **PERSON PRAYS AT TREE FOR MONEY BILLS**

1305	**SATSU, to***ru*, **tsuma***mu* **PLUCK, TAKE** 15 strokes	撮影	SATSUEI	photography
		撮り直す	TORINAOSU	retake
		撮み食い	TSUMAMIGUI	'graft'

扌 is **hand** 32. 最 is **most** 484 q.v., here in its literal sense of **take by force**. Thus **take by force with the hand**, i.e. **snatch/ pluck**, often with connotations of theft or improper possession. It is also used of **taking photographs**, probably from the idea of quick action.

Mnemonic: **TAKE MOSTLY BY HAND**

1306	**SATSU, su***ru/reru*, **kosu***ru* **RUB, CHAFE, BRUSH** 17 strokes	擦過傷	SAKKASHŌ	abrasion
		擦れ違う	SURECHIGAU	brush past
		擦り込む	SURIKOMU	rub in

扌 is **hand** 32. 察 is **realise** 489 q.v., here acting phonetically to express **rub** and possibly also lending an idea of scouring from its assumed early connotations of purify. Thus to **rub with the hand**, now **rub** in a broader sense.

Mnemonic: **REALISE HAND IS CHAFED**

1307	**sara** **DISH, BOWL, PLATE** 5 strokes	灰皿	HAIZARA	ashtray
		大皿	ŌZARA	large dish
		皿洗い	SARAARAI	dishwashing

Stylised derivative of a stemmed **bowl** with exaggerated lip 𝓨. Suggest taking ‖ as **fluting**, with ⊥ as a **dish on a plate**.

Mnemonic: **FLUTED DISH ON PLATE**

417

1308		SAN SPAR, BEAM, FRAME 10 strokes	桟橋 SANBASHI	jetty
			桟敷 SAJIKI*	stand, box
			桟道 SANDŌ	
				walkway made of planks

Formerly 棧. 木 is tree/ wood 69. 戔 is lances/ halberds 493, here acting phonetically to express **interweave** and probably also lending an idea of pole. Thus **interwoven pieces of wood**, a reference to a **frame** and the **spars/ beams** forming it. Suggest taking 戔 as **two** 二 61 **lances** 戈 493.

Mnemonic: **FRAME MADE USING TWO WOODEN LANCES AS SPARS**

1309		SAN, ZAN, mugo*i*, miji*me* CRUEL, MISERABLE 11 strokes	惨劇 SANGEKI	tragedy
			惨殺 ZANSATSU	massacre
			悲惨 HISAN	misery

忄 is **heart/ feelings** 147. 參 is **attend/ go** 490 q.v., here acting phonetically *to* express **needle/ pierce** and probably also lending reinforcing connotations of needle/ pin from its original meaning of woman with ostentatious hairpins. Thus to **pierce the heart** (figuratively with a needle), i.e. **torment**, symbolising **cruelty** from one point of view and **misery** from another.

Mnemonic: **CRUELTY ATTENDED BY FEELINGS OF MISERY**

1310		SAN, kasa UMBRELLA, PARASOL 12 strokes	傘下 SANKA-	affiliated
			雨傘 AMAGASA	umbrella
			日傘 HIGASA	parasol

A pictograph of an **umbrella/ parasol** showing its **frame** 十, **hood** 𠆢, and **supports** 㐅㐅. Suggest taking 𠆢 as a **cover** (see 87), 㐅㐅 as **four persons** 人 39, and 十 as **ten** 33.

Mnemonic: **UMBRELLA COVERS FOURTEEN PERSONS!**

1311

ZAN, shibara*ku*
A WHILE, BRIEFLY
15 strokes

暫定的 ZANTEITEKI　　tentative
暫時 ZANJI　　short time
暫くして SHIBARAKUSHITE
　　after a while

日 is **sun/ day** 62, here meaning **time**. 斬 is an NGU character meaning **behead/ kill**. Its exact etymology is unclear, but it comprises **vehicle** 車 31 and **ax/ cut** 斤 1176, and may possibly have originally referred to cutting someone down in their carriage/ palanquin. Here it acts phonetically to express **brief/ quick**, and presumably also lends similar connotations from the swiftness associated with beheading. Thus **brief time**. Confusingly, but in exactly the same way as the English term **a while**, in practice it can also mean a **considerable time**.

Mnemonic: **AX TAKES A WHILE -- A DAY -- TO CHOP UP VEHICLE**

1312

SHI, mune, uma*i*
TASTY, GOOD, GIST
6 strokes

要旨 YŌSHI　　gist
趣旨 SHUSHI　　spirit
旨旨 UMAUMA　　nicely

日 is a simplification of **sweet** 甘 1093 q.v., here also with its connotations of **lingering in the mouth**. ヒ is **spoon** 910. Thus **something sweet which is spooned into the mouth and (whose taste) lingers**. This came to mean **tasty**, and **good** in a broad sense. **Gist** is a borrowed meaning, resulting from 1312's being used instead of 惛, a CO character meaning gist which combines 旨 with **heart/ feelings** 忄 147 and presumably means literally that which (is good and?) lingers in the heart. Suggest taking 日 as **sun** 62 and ヒ as **sitting person** 238.

Mnemonic: **GIST IS THAT PERSON THINKS IT'S GOOD TO SIT IN SUN**

1313

SHI, ukaga*u*
VISIT, SEEK, ASK,
HEAR
7 strokes

伺い事 UKAGAIGOTO　　inquiry
伺候 SHIKŌ　　courtesy call
伺い探る UKAGAISAGURU
　　spy out

亻 is **person** 39. 司 is **administer/ official** 497 q.v., here acting phonetically to express **observe**. Since 1313 is a character of relatively recent origin it is probable that 司 also lends its later meaning of **official** (as opposed to its original meaning of **anus**). Thus **(an official?) person who observes**, actually a reference to an **investigator**. The present meanings are all derived from the idea of investigating.

Mnemonic: **OFFICIAL PERSON VISITS AND ASKS**

419

1314

SHI, sa*su*/*saru*, toge
PIERCE, STAB, THORN
8 strokes

名刺 MEISHI   name card
刺身 SASHIMI   sashimi
刺抜き TOGENUKI   tweezers

刂 is **sword/ cut** 181. 朿 is **thorn** 873 q.v., here also used in a general sense to indicate something **sharp** and **piercing**. 1314 originally meant **stab with a sword** before coming to mean **pierce/ stab** in general, and it is also occasionally found as **cut** in a broader sense (e.g. sashimi [sliced fish]). As with 873, suggest taking 朿 as a **tree** 木 69 with **droopy branches** 冖.

Mnemonic: **CUT PIERCING THORNS FROM DROOPY BRANCHED TREE**

1315

SHI, eda
BRANCH
8 strokes

枝隊 SHITAI troop detachment
枝角 EDAZUNO   antlers
枯れ枝 KAREEDA   dead branch

Branch 支 691 q.v. with **tree** 木 69. Whereas 691 is now used largely in a figurative sense 1315 is largely (but not exclusively) used literally.

Mnemonic: **TREE BRANCH**

1316

SHI
WELL-BEING,
HAPPINESS
8 strokes

祉福 SHIFUKU   well-being
福祉 FUKUSHI   welfare
福祉国家 FUKUSHIKOKKA
       welfare state

Formerly 祉. 示/礻 is **altar/ of the gods** 695, while 止 is **foot/ stop** 129. The latter acts phonetically to express **bestow** but any semantic role is unclear. Thus **that bestowed by the gods**, a reference to **happiness/ well-being**.

Mnemonic: **FIND HAPPINESS AT FOOT OF ALTAR**

1317

SHI
LIMB, PART
8 strokes

肢体 SHITAI   the limbs
下肢 KASHI   lower limbs
選択肢 SENTAKUSHI   option

Flesh/ of the body 月 365 and **branch** 支 691. The **branches of the body** are the **limbs**.

Mnemonic: **LIMBS ARE BRANCHES OF THE BODY**

1318	**SHI, SE, hodoko**su **PERFORM, CHARITY** 9 strokes	施設 SHISETSU facilities 実施 JISSHI implementation 施薬 SEYAKU free medicine

方 is **fluttering flag** 333. 也 is **twisting creature** 167, here acting phonetically to express **wave/ billow** and almost certainly also lending its own similar connotations of undulating. Thus **billowing flag**. **Perform** and **charity** (which both derive from the same core concept of doing an action for someone) result from borrowing. Suggest taking 方 as **side** 方 204 and **person** 亻 39.

Mnemonic: **PERSON SHOWS CHARITY TO TWISTING CREATURE AT SIDE**

1319	**SHI, abura, yani** **FAT, GREASE, RESIN** 10 strokes	脂肪 SHIBŌ fat 脂気 ABURAKE greasiness 脂目 YANIME gummy eyes

Meat/ of the body 月 365 and **tasty** 旨 1312. **Fat** was often considered tastier than lean meat.

Mnemonic: **FAT IS TASTY MEAT**

1320	**SHI, murasaki** **PURPLE, VIOLET** 12 strokes	紫煙 SHIEN tobacco smoke 紫色 MURASAKIIRO purple 紫外線 SHIGAISEN ultraviolet rays

糸 is **thread** 27. 此 is an NGU character meaning **this/ here**, and comprises **foot/ stop** 止 129 and **sitting person** ヒ 238 (both presumably indicating not moving from a given point). 此 acts here phonetically to express **purple**, but any semantic role is unclear. Thus **purple threads**, now simply **purple**.

Mnemonic: **PERSON SITS AND TIES PURPLE THREAD ON FOOT**

1321		SHI, tsug*u* **HEIR, SUCCEED TO** 13 strokes	嗣子 SHISHI	heir
			後嗣 KŌSHI	heir
			皇嗣 KŌSHI	crown prince

Of somewhat confused and obscure evolution. Originally written 㖸, showing **bound bamboo writing-tablets** 卌/用/冊 874 and the component parts of **administer/ official/ anus** 司 497 q.v., namely (reversed) **buttocks** ㇆ and hole/ **opening** 口 20. The reason for the dislocation of these elements is not clear. When an opening 口 was later put under buttocks ㇆ , giving the proper form 司 , the original opening 口 was also left over the bound tablets element 用 , giving the present form 嗣 . It is not clear whether this was simply an error or whether it was left there deliberately to serve some special and presumably different purpose, such as perhaps suggesting encircling (with binding). 司 is known to have acted phonetically to express **control**, and probably (at least at the stage at which ㇆ became written as 司) also lent similar connotations of its own (though since administer is a later meaning, it is possible that at the time of the earliest form 㖸 it still meant anus, in which case any semantic role is unclear). Thus to **control bound tablets**, a reference to **binding them together particularly securely**. This came to mean **bind/ join** in general, with **inherit** and **succeed (to)** being associated meanings (as tsugu 継 1203). These associated meanings have now prevailed over bind/ join. Suggest taking 司 in its sense of **official**, and 口 as **circular/ round** (see 228).

Mnemonic: **OFFICIAL HEIR TO BOUND CIRCULAR TABLETS**

1322		SHI, ka*u* **REAR ANIMALS** 13 strokes	飼育 SHIIKU	breeding
			飼い主 KAINUSHI	owner
			飼い犬 KAIINU	pet dog

食 is **food**/ eat 146. 司 is **administer**/ official 497, here acting phonetically to express **give** and almost certainly also lending its meaning of administer/ supervise. Thus to **give food to people** (under one's supervision?). In Chinese it still has this meaning, and is interchangeable with a CO character 飤 (food/ eat 食 and person 人 39), but in Japanese it came to refer rather to **feeding animals**, and thus by extension to **rearing** them.

Mnemonic: **REAR ANIMALS BY ADMINISTERING FOOD TO THEM**

1323	雌	SHI, mesu, me **FEMALE** 14 strokes	雌雄 SHIYŪ	gender, outcome
			雌牛 MEUSHI	cow, heifer
			雌犬 MEINU	bitch

隹 is **bird** 216. 此 is **this**/ here 1320, here acting phonetically to express **small** but of unclear semantic role. The smaller bird of a pair is generally the **female**. Suggest taking 此 literally as **stop** 止 129 and **sitting person** ヒ 238.

Mnemonic: **FEMALE PERSON STOPS AND SITS ON BIRD**

1324

SHI, tamawa*ru*
BESTOW
15 strokes

賜暇 SHIKA   furlough
恩賜 ONSHI   imperial gift
賜物 TAMAMONO* gift, boon

貝 is shell/ **money** 90, here meaning **valuable item**. 易 is **easy**/ divination 618 q.v, here acting phonetically to express **great volume** and possibly also lending an idea of dazzling from its literal meaning of iridescent. 1324 originally referred to a **voluminous and valuable** (and dazzling?) **reward bestowed by a ruler**, leading to **bestowal**. It still retains occasional connotations of an imperial bestowal.

Mnemonic: **BESTOWAL IS EASY MONEY**

1325

SHI, haka*ru*
CONSULT, INQUIRE
16 strokes

諮じゅん SHIJUN   consultation
諮問 SHIMON   inquiry
諮問機関 SHIMONKIKAN
                 advisory body

咨 is an NGU character meaning **investigate/ inquire**. It comprises **mouth/ say** 口 20 and **next** 次 292 q.v., here acting phonetically to express **consult/ inquire** and almost certainly also lending connotations of sequence. Thus to **inquire verbally** (and in sequence, i.e. systematically?). 1325 adds **words/ speak** 言 274 for emphasis. Nevertheless, the verbal aspect has now faded, leaving just **inquire/ consult**.

Mnemonic: **IN INQUIRY, ONE MOUTH SPEAKS, THEN THE NEXT**

1326

JI, samurai, habe*ru*
ATTEND (UPON)
8 strokes

侍従 JIJŪ   chamberlain
侍女 JIJO   lady-in-waiting
侍僧 JISŌ   acolyte

亻 is **person** 39. 寺 is **temple** 133, here acting phonetically to express **serve** and also lending its connotations of **clerical work**. Thus **person serving in a clerical capacity**, later **servant/ attendant** in general, including **samurai**.

Mnemonic: **PERSON IN ATTENDANCE AT TEMPLE IS SAMURAI**

423

1327 **JI**
LUXURIANT, RICH,
STRENGTHEN, ENLIVEN
12 strokes

滋養 JIYŌ — nourishment
滋味 JIMI — savoriness
滋雨 JIU — welcome rain

Somewhat obscure. Formerly 滋玄. 氵 is **water/ river** 40, while 玆/ 兹 is the some-what obscure double twisted thread element seen in 磁 881 q.v. Its role is unclear. Some scholars feel that it originally acted phonetically to express the name of a certain river, and take the present meanings to have derived from the life-giving nature of the river in ques-tion. However, it may be felt to have acted phonetically to express **rear/ grow** (as in 1328), as well as possibly lending connotations of mysteriousness and/or draw (see 881), to give **water/ river that brings growth** (and draws forth the mysterious power of life?), with any use as a proper noun stemming from this. Suggest remembering 兹 by as-sociation with **double** (short) **thread** 幺 111.

Mnemonic: **DOUBLE THREAD OF RIVER BRINGS LUXURIANT GROWTH**

1328 **JI, itsuku**shimu
LOVE, PITY, AFFECTION
13 strokes

慈悲 JIHI — mercy
慈善 JIZEN — charity
慈愛 JIAI — benevolence

Formerly 慈. 心 is **heart/ feelings** 147. 玆 / 兹 is the somewhat obscure double twist-ed thread element seen in 磁 881 q.v., here acting phonetically to express **rear/ raise** and probably also lending connotations of **small** and hence **child** (from the early meaning of very small of 玄 [see 1227]). 1328 originally referred to the **tender feelings** involved in **caring for a small child** (and in Chinese still retains connotations of motherhood), and then came to mean **(show) affection** in a general sense, including **love** and **pity**. Sug-gest remembering 兹 by association with **double** (short) **thread** 幺 111.

Mnemonic: **DOUBLE THREADS OF LOVE AND PITY IN HEART**

1329 **JI**
IMPERIAL SEAL
19 strokes

御璽 GYOJI — imperial seal
国璽 KOKUJI — seal of state
印璽 INJI — imperial seal

Once written 璽. 爾 is an NGU character now borrowed to express **you** and **so**, but it originally pictographically depicted a **device used in spinning** 爾. Here it acts phoneti-cally to express **press**, combining with **earth** 土 60 (here in the sense of **clay**) to express **that pressed into clay**, a reference to a **seal**. It is not clear why such a complex charac-ter was chosen as a phonetic, but it is possible that its complexity suggested the intricacy of a seal of a person of high rank. Earth 土 was later replaced by **jewel/ jade** 玉 102, sym-bolising **nobility** (particularly the **imperial house**). Unfortunately there is no easy mne-monic for 爾, but suggest remembering it by partial association with **four crosses** 爻.

Mnemonic: **JEWELED IMPERIAL SEAL INCLUDES FOUR CROSSES**

1330

軸　JIKU
AXLE, SHAFT, SCROLL
12 strokes

車軸　SHAJIKU　　　axle
地軸　CHIJIKU　　earth's axis
軸物　JIKUMONO scroll picture

車 is **vehicle** 31. 由 is **reason** 399, here acting phonetically to express **support** but of unclear semantic role. Thus **that which supports a vehicle**, a reference to its **axle(s)**. This later gave **spindle/ shaft** in a broad sense and, by association (of shape), **scroll**.

Mnemonic: **AXLE IS REASON VEHICLE MOVES**

1331

疾　SHITSU
ILLNESS, SWIFTLY
10 strokes

疾患　SHIKKAN　　　disease
疾走　SHISSŌ　　　scamper
疾つく　TOKKU ni*　long since

Once written 𤶤 , showing a **person** 大 (see 53) hit by an **arrow** ⟋ 981 and indicating a **sudden strike/ affliction**. The present form uses **arrow** 矢 981 and the **sickness radical** 疒 381. It can also be used of **swiftness** unrelated to illness.

Mnemonic: **ILLNESS STRIKES SWIFTLY AS AN ARROW**

1332

執　SHITSU, SHŪ, toru
TAKE, GRASP
11 strokes

執筆　SHIPPITSU　　writing
執念　SHŪNEN　　　tenacity
執り成す　TORINASU　mediate

Very old forms such as 𡘲 clearly show **shackles** 㚔/幸 233 and **kneeling person with outstretched arms** 㔔 / 丸 470. Thus **to shackle a prisoner**, leading to **seize/ grasp** and **take**. Note that the addition of thread/ cord 糸 27 gives the CO character fetter 縶 . Suggest taking 幸 as **happiness** 279 and 丸 as **round** 830.

Mnemonic: **HAPPINESS ROUNDED OFF BY TAKING A PRISONER**

1333

湿　SHITSU, shimeru/su
DAMP, MOIST, HUMID
12 strokes

湿度　SHITSUDO　　humidity
湿地　SHITCHI　　marshland
湿っぽい　SHIMEPPOI damp, dismal

Formerly 濕 . 氵 is **water/ river** 40. is **motes/ small particles** 1224 q.v., here acting phonetically to express **wet** and also lending its connotations of **small bits of thread**. 1333 originally referred to a **river broken up into pools** (i.e. not flowing in a continuous thread), giving **wetland/ marshland** and later **damp** in a broad sense. Note that very old forms such as 㬎 show that 㬎 is either a miscopying of or deliberate substitution for cut threads 絲 750 (㬎 being an old form of this), but both elements clearly play a similar role. Suggest taking 日 as **sun** 62 and 业 as a variant of **row** 並 1775.

Mnemonic: **SUN ON ROW OF WATERY DROPS MAKES IT HUMID**

425

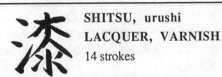

1334 漆

SHITSU, urushi
LACQUER, VARNISH
14 strokes

漆器 SHIKKI   lacquerware
漆黒 SHIKKOKU   jet black
漆塗り URUSHINURI lacquering

Formerly 桼 and earlier 𣠽 , showing a **tree** 朮 / 木 69 with **droplets of moisture** ⺊⺊ to indicate **resin/ sap**. This was a reference to **lacquer** (the sap of the lacquer-tree), with **varnish** being an associated meaning. **Water** 氵 40 was added to emphasise the liquid. Suggest taking 氺 as a variant of **water** 水 40, with 八 as **extra branches**.

Mnemonic: **EXTRA WATERY LACQUER FROM EXTRA BRANCHED TREE**

1335 芝

shiba
TURF, LAWN
6 or 5 strokes

芝生 SHIBAFU*   lawn
芝居 SHIBAI   drama, show
芝刈り機 SHIBAKARIKI
                lawnmower

艹 is **plant/ grass** 9. 之 is an NGU character now borrowed to mean **this**, but it is in fact a highly stylised derivative of the variant 止 / 屮 of **plant** 生 42 q.v., and at one stage meant **emerge** (as a plant emerges from the ground) and by association **from**. In the case of 1335 it is used literally to mean (emerging) **plant**, with plant/ grass 艹 acting as a reinforcing element. In Japanese it has come to mean specifically **grass** (especially in the sense of **turf/ lawn**), but note that in Chinese it means lily. Suggest taking 之 as a **zig-zag path**.

Mnemonic: **ZIGZAG PATH CROSSES GRASSY LAWN**

1336 赦

SHA
FORGIVENESS
11 strokes

容赦 YŌSHA   forgiveness
赦免 SHAMEN   clemency
恩赦 ONSHA   amnesty

攵 is **strike with stick/ beat** 101. 赤 is **red** 46 q.v., which acts phonetically to express **abandon/ stop** and may possibly also lend connotations of **raging** (from its literal meaning of large fire). Thus to **beat someone (in a rage?) and then stop**, with the act of stopping coming to symbolise **forgiveness**.

Mnemonic: **BEAT TILL RED, THEN SHOW FORGIVENESS**

1337		SHA, nana*me*	斜面 SHAMEN	slope

SHA, nana*me*
SLANTING, DIAGONAL   斜方形 SHAHŌKEI   rhombus
11 strokes   斜め継ぎ NANAMETSUGI

斜面 SHAMEN   slope

miter joint

斗 is **measure/ ladle** 1633. 余 is **ample/** excess 800, here acting phonetically to express **scoop out** and also lending its meaning of **ample**. Thus to **scoop out an ample measure**. **Slanting/ diagonal** is essentially a borrowed meaning, with 1337 being used instead of a more complex character with that meaning, but it may be that the borrowing process was influenced by the slope of the cross stroke in 斗 and the idea of ample contained in 余 (a diagonal giving the amplest measure across a square).

Mnemonic: **DIAGONAL GIVES AMPLEST MEASURE**

1338   **SHA, niru/eru/yasu**
BOIL, COOK
12 strokes

煮沸 SHAFUTSU   boiling
生煮え NAMANIE   undercooked
煮立てる NITATERU   bring to boil

Formerly 煮. ⺍ is **fire** 8. 者/者 is **person** 298 q.v., here acting phonetically to express **boil** and also lending its early meaning of **various things**. Thus **boil various things over a fire**.

Mnemonic: **PERSON BOILS THINGS OVER FIRE**

1339   **SHA, saegi*ru***
OBSTRUCT,
INTERRUPT
14 strokes

遮二無二 SHANIMUNI   recklessly
遮光幕 SHAKŌMAKU   a shade
遮断器 SHADANKI   circuit-
breaker, crossing-gate

辶 is **movement** 129. 庶 is **various** 1381 q.v., here acting phonetically to express **put** and also lending similar connotations from its early meaning of **put things on a fire**. Thus to **put something in the way of movement**, i.e. **obstruct**, with **interrupt** being an associated meaning.

Mnemonic: **VARIOUS THINGS CAN OBSTRUCT MOVEMENT**

1340	JA WICKEDNESS 8 strokes	邪悪 JAAKU	wickedness
		無邪気 MUJAKI	innocence
		風邪 FŪJA/ KAZE	a cold

Somewhat obscure. β is **village** 355, while 牙 is **fang** 434. The role of the latter is not clear, since 1340 was originally used as a proper noun referring to a specific village in ancient China. It is also not clear whether the present meaning of **wickedness** derives from association with the village in question (cf. etymology of terms such as sodomy), or whether it is a borrowed meaning.

Mnemonic: **FANGS ARE BARED IN VILLAGE OF WICKEDNESS**

1341	JA, DA, hebi SNAKE, SERPENT 11 strokes	蛇管 JAKAN	hose
		蛇行 DAKŌ	meandering
		蛇皮 HEBIKAWA	snakeskin

虫 is **insect** 56 q.v., here in its original meaning of **large headed (or hooded) snake**. 它 is a CO character now borrowed for a confusing range of meanings such as hang down and impute, but it derives from a pictograph of a **large headed snake** 𨑃 and is to all intents and purposes a variant of 虫 56. Suggest taking 它 as **house/ roof** 宀 28 and **sitting person/ man** 匕 238.

Mnemonic: **MAN IN HOUSE SITS ON 'INSECT' -- REALLY A SNAKE!**

1342	SHAKU LADLE, MEASURE 3 strokes	一勺 ISSHAKU	one shaku
		三勺 SANSHAKU	three shaku
		十勺 JISSHAKU	ten shaku

Also written 勺. From a pictograph of a **ladle/ scoop** 勺 (also 勺), with 丶/ー indicating the **contents**. It is now used almost exclusively to mean **scoopful** (specifically a **measure** of 0.02 liters), while ladle/ scoop is conveyed by the NGU character 杓, which adds **wood** 木 69.

Mnemonic: **TILTED LADLE STILL KEEPS MEASURE OF CONTENTS**

428

1343 **酌** **SHAKU, ku*mu***
SERVE WINE, LADLE, SCOOP, DRINK
10 strokes

酌婦 SHAKUFU waitress
晩酌 BANSHAKU 'nightcap'
酌量 SHAKURYŌ consideration

Ladle/ measure 勺 1342 and **wine** (jar) 酉 302. A **ladleful of wine** represented both **serving** and **drinking**. 1343 is also occasionally used to mean **scoop up**, including in the figurative sense of taking all circumstances into account, but this is generally conveyed by the NGU character 汲 (water/ liquid 氵 40 and reach 及 1148).

Mnemonic: **DRINK WINE SERVED BY LADLEFUL**

1344 **爵** **SHAKU**
PEERAGE
17 strokes

爵位 SHAKUI peerage
授爵 JUSHAKU ennoblement
男爵 DANSHAKU baron

Somewhat obscure, and of confused graphic evolution. Originally written , showing an ornate **vessel used for pouring wine** (apparently with three legs, two handles, and a spout, and, according to some scholars, shaped like a bird with spread wings). Note that in Chinese 1344 still retains a minor meaning of wine vessel. Its evolution became confused with the addition and deletion of sundry sometimes obscure elements. The present form is best taken as an ideograph comprising **hand** 爫 303 (though in fact this is a miscopying of wood 木 69), dish/ **bowl** 罒 (variant 皿 1307), here meaning **vessel**, **food**/ eat 艮 146, here meaning **ingest**, and measure/ **hand** 寸 909 q.v. (apparently a miscopying of an ordinary hand , though it is possible that it is a deliberate substitution to suggest careful use of the hand). Thus a **vessel whose contents are ingested and which is lifted with two hands**. It is not clear how 1344 came to mean **peerage**. It does not appear to be a borrowing, and it is possible that the particular wine vessel was a symbol of high rank and hence nobility.

Mnemonic: **PEER'S HANDS CLUTCH FOOD BOWL**

1345 **寂** **JAKU, SEKI, sabi, sabi*shii***
QUIET, LONELY
11 strokes

静寂 SEIJAKU silence
寂ばく SEKIBAKU no desolate
寂しさ SABISHISA loneliness

宀 is roof/ **building** 28. 叔 is **uncle** 1367, here acting phonetically to express **quiet** but of unclear semantic role. Thus **quiet building**, now **quiet/ lonely** in a broader but usually melancholy sense.

Mnemonic: **UNCLE LONELY IN QUIET BUILDING**

1346	朱	SHU	朱色 SHUIRO	vermilion
		VERMILION, RED	朱肉 SHUNIKU	red ink pad
		6 strokes	朱筆 SHUHITSU	
				red pen, correction

Once written 朱 and later 朱, showing **tree** 朱 / 朱 / 木 69 and a symbol ○ / ⌐ indicating **center** (here in the sense of **inside**). The **inside of a tree(trunk)** is often **red**, and hence 1346 came to acquire this meaning. Somewhat surprisingly it came to acquire particular connotations of bright orange-red/ **vermilion**, though a pinkish red might have seemed more appropriate. Distinguish from immature/ treetop 未 794. Suggest in fact taking 1346 as a **treetop** (tree 木 69 with extra branches ⌐), with ✓ as a **ribbon**.

Mnemonic: **BRIGHT RED RIBBON IN TREETOP**

1347	狩	SHU, ka*ru*/*ri*	狩猟 SHURYŌ	hunting
		HUNT	狩犬 KARIINU	hunting dog
		9 strokes	狩り込み KARIKOMI	round-up

犭 is **dog** 17. 守 is **protect** 300 q.v., here acting phonetically to express **on all sides** and also lending a meaning of **be attentive and protective**. Thus a **dog which protects (its master) and is attentive on all sides**, i.e. a **hunting dog** (still a meaning in Chinese). Hunting dog came to symbolise **hunt** in general.

Mnemonic: **DOG PROTECTS MASTER WHEN OUT HUNTING**

1348	殊	SHU, koto	特殊 TOKUSHU	special
		ESPECIALLY	殊勝 SHUSHŌ na	laudable
		10 strokes	殊更 KOTOSARA	especially

歹 is **bare bones/ death** 286. 朱 is **red** 1346 q.v., here acting phonetically to express **cut down/ attack** and almost certainly also lending its own connotations of inside the body/ trunk. 1348 originally meant to **cut someone to the very bone** (i.e. inside the body) and **kill them** (still a meaning in Chinese). This symbolised an **extreme attack**, giving **extremely** and hence **especially**.

Mnemonic: **RED BARE BONES ARE ESPECIALLY RARE**

1349		SHU JEWEL, PEARL 10 strokes	珠玉 SHUGYOKU jewel, gem 真珠 SHINJU pearl 数珠 JUZU* rosary

王 is **jewel** 102. 朱 is **red** 1346 q.v., here acting phonetically to express **round** and almost certainly also lending its connotations of inside. Thus **round jewel/ pearl** (a pearl being a jewel inside a shell).

Mnemonic: **PEARL IS A RED JEWEL!?**

1350		SHU, omomuki GIST, TENDENCY 15 strokes	趣味 SHUMI hobby 趣意 SHUI gist, view 趣向 SHUKŌ scheme, plan

Run 走 161 and **take/ grasp** 取 301, to give a meaning of **run after something to take hold of it**. This came to mean **hurry after something** (still a meaning in Chinese), and then by association **go in a certain direction**. In the physical sense this is now usually conveyed by omomuku 赴 1751, whereas 1350 has come to be used rather in the abstract sense of **incline towards** and hence **tend/ tendency**. In Japanese it has also come to mean by association the **'drift'** or **gist** of an argument.

Mnemonic: **TENDENCY TO HAVE TO RUN FAST TO GRASP GIST**

1351		JU, kotobuki LONG LIFE, CONGRATULATION 7 strokes	寿命 JUMYŌ life span 長寿 CHŌJU longevity 米寿 BEIJU 88th birthday

Somewhat obscure. Formerly written 壽 . 耂 is a simplification of **old man** 耂 117 (now usually ⺹). 吾 is a simplification of 𠤏 . This is an unclear element that was once written 𠄎 , indicating perhaps continuity/ flow (possibly a symbol of flowing 乙 and mouths/ openings 口 20, though to judge from another form 𠄏 , showing speak 曰 688, the bottom one of the mouths was originally a separate element meaning speak). 吾 is known to have acted phonetically to express **long time,** though any semantic role is unclear, with **hand/** measure 寸 909 (a relatively late addition) playing a similar phonetic role for reinforcement. Thus an **old man who has lived a long time.** A **long life** is cause for **congratulation.** Note that eighty-eight is considered a particularly felicitous age, owing to the fact that the character for rice (a symbol of bounty and the life-force), 米 201, can be graphically interpreted as ten 十 33, times eight ⺌ 66, with a further eight 八 66. Suggest taking 龶 as a variant of **hand** 手 32, and 寸 also in its sense of **hand**.

Mnemonic: **PUT HANDS TOGETHER TO CONGRATULATE LONG LIFE**

1352		JU CONFUCIANISM 16 strokes	儒教 JUKYŌ	Confucianism
			儒者 JUSHA	Confucianist
			儒学 JUGAKU	Confucianism

イ is **person** 39. 需 is **demand** 887 q.v., here acting phonetically to express **gentle** and possibly also lending similar connotations of soft through its original meaning of wet beard. Thus **gentle person**, later applied to **followers of Confucius** and hence **Confucianism** itself.

Mnemonic: **CONFUCIANIST IS PERSON IN DEMAND**

1353		SHŪ PRISONER 5 strokes	囚人 SHŪJIN	prisoner
			囚役 SHŪEKI	prison labor
			死刑囚 SHIKEISHŪ	
				condemned prisoner

A **person** 人 39 inside an **enclosure** 囗 123, indicating an **imprisoned person**.

Mnemonic: **PERSON CONTAINED WITHIN ENCLOSURE IS PRISONER**

1354		SHŪ, fune, funa- BOAT, SHIP 6 strokes	舟航 SHŪKŌ	navigation
			舟遊び FUNAASOBI	boating
			小舟 KOBUNE	little boat

Once written 𣥂, pictographically depicting a **boat with raised stern and raised pointed prow**. Often found in early compounds as 𣥂 or 𣥂, and occasionally lends a meaning of **convey(ance)**. Popularly likened to a **sternless rowing boat** 𠈓 viewed from above, with **two people** ゛ sitting in it, an **oar** — laid across it, and a **mooring rope** ノ.

Mnemonic: **MOORED STERNLESS BOAT WITH TWO ROWERS AND OAR**

1355		SHŪ, hii*deru* EXCEL, EXCELLENT 7 strokes	秀才 SHŪSAI	able student
			秀逸 SHŪITSU	excellence
			秀美 SHŪBI	great beauty

禾 is **rice plant** 81 (literally plant with head of grain). 乃 derives from a **bending person** 乃 (normally simplified to ル 39, but in this case deliberately exaggerated to emphasise **bending**, and possibly showing some graphic influence from reach 及 1148). Thus **rice plant bent** (under exceptionally heavy head), indicating an **excellent plant/ crop** and thus **excel/ excellent** in general.

Mnemonic: **GREATLY BENT RICE PLANT MEANS EXCELLENT CROP**

1356

SH Ū, kusa*i*
SMELL, SMACK
9 strokes

臭気 SHŪKI   bad odor
俗臭 ZOKUSHŪ   vulgarity
臭味 KUSAMI   smell, smack

Formerly 臭 , showing **dog** 犬 17 and **nose** 自 134. 1356 originally referred to a dog using its nose to follow a scent when hunting, but now means **smell** in a broader but frequently unpleasant sense. Also used figuratively as **smack (of)**. Suggest taking 犬 as **big** 53.

Mnemonic: **BIG NOSE GOOD FOR SMELLS**

1357

SH Ū, urei/*eru*
GRIEF, SADNESS
13 strokes

愁傷 SHŪSHŌ   grief
哀愁 AISHŪ   sorrow
愁い顔 UREIGAO   sad face

心 is **heart/ feelings** 147. 秋 is **autumn** 140, here acting phonetically to express **grief** and possibly also lending its own connotations of melancholy. Thus **feelings of grief/ sadness**.

Mnemonic: **AUTUMNAL FEELINGS OF SADNESS**

1358

SHŪ
REWARD, TOAST, REPLY
13 strokes

報酬 HŌSHŪ   reward
応酬 ŌSHŪ   response
献酬 KENSHŪ
         exchange of sake cups

酉 is **wine jar/ alcohol** 302. 州 is **province/** sandbank 304, here acting phonetically to express **toast/ exchange drinking cups** and possibly also lending loose connotations of **flowing** from its **river** element 川 (see 48). 1358 originally referred to a **toast** (involving an exchange of cups), then came by extension to mean **recognise something worthy of toasting**, leading eventually to **reward**. **Reply/ response** is an associated meaning.

Mnemonic: **GAIN REWARD OF PROVINCIAL ALCOHOL**

433

1359	SHŪ, minikui UGLY, SHAMEFUL 17 strokes	醜悪 SHŪAKU 醜聞 SHŪBUN 醜さ MINIKUSA	foulness scandal ugliness

Somewhat obscure. 酉 is **wine jar/ alcohol** 302. 鬼 is **devil** 1128 q.v. Some scholars take the latter to act literally to mean **crouching person wearing a death-mask**, and by extension simply **crouching/ bending person**, and take 酉 to act phonetically to express **bent**. Thus **doubly bent person**, a reference to a **hunchback** and by extension **ugly** (see 997). However, although both the earliest and the latest forms of 1359 do show a wine jar it seems possible that these present meanings result rather from confusion at some point with **hunchback/ ugly** 亞 997 q.v., which at one stage had a stylised form 𠅫 that closely resembled a (wine) jar. The original meaning may have been **person wearing a death mask offering wine (to the ancestor-gods)**, i.e. in some religious ceremony (see also 386). **Shameful** is an associated meaning with ugly.

Mnemonic: **UGLY DEVIL WITH ALCOHOL**

1360	SHŪ, osou ATTACK, INHERIT 22 strokes	襲来 SHŪRAI 空襲 KŪSHŪ 世襲 SESHŪ	invasion air raid heredity

衣 is **clothing** 420. 龍 is **dragon** 1899, here used phonetically to express **fold**. 1360 originally referred to a type of **burial garment with the collar folded over (in a special way)**, the folding having a certain religious significance. It still retains this meaning in Chinese, and in Japanese is very occasionally used in the associated sense of wearing double layers of clothing. It is not clear why such a complex character was chosen as a phonetic. The idea of **religious ritual** led to ritual and **convention** in a broad sense, and eventually to the associated idea of **inheriting** (something from the past). **Attack** stems from confusion with a now defunct character 褺 , which combines clothing 衣 with grasp 靮 1332 and originally meant **grapple/ scuffle**.

Mnemonic: **DRAGON ATTACKS INHERITED CLOTHES**

1361 汁	JŪ, shiru JUICE, SOUP, LIQUID 5 strokes	果汁 KAJŪ 墨汁 BOKUJŪ 味そ汁 MISOSHIRU	fruit juice India ink miso soup

氵 is **water** 40, here meaning **liquid**. 十 is **ten** 33, here acting phonetically to express **liquid** and thus reinforcing 氵. Now used for a range of liquids (but not water).

Mnemonic: **JUICE MIXED WITH TEN PARTS OF WATER**

1362 JŪ, a*teru*, mi*tasu*   充分 JŪBUN   enough
FULL, FILL, PROVIDE   充実 JŪJITSU   fullness
6 strokes   充てがう ATEGAU   allot, apply

Once written 㐬. 古/㒸 is **new born child** 227 (literally inverted child 𠫓 / 子 25). ル is crouching person/ **bent legs** 39, here acting phonetically to express **grow** and possibly also lending its own connotations of **big** (see 267). Thus a **new born babe growing (big?)**, which later came to refer by association to something **becoming full. Allot/ provide** is an associated meaning with fill.

Mnemonic: **NEWBORN BABE HAS FULL SET OF LEGS, IF BENT**

1363 JŪ, NYŪ, yawa*rakai*   柔道 JŪDŌ   judo
SOFT, GENTLE, WEAK   柔弱 NYŪJAKU   weakness
9 strokes   柔らか物 YAWARAKAMONO

silks

矛 is halberd/ **lance** 1843, while 木 is **tree/ wood** 69. Usually explained to the effect that a **wooden lance** is weak (relative to a metal one), and that weak led by association to **soft** and **gentle**. A useful mnemonic, but almost certainly incorrect. It seems more likely that 木 acts in its sense of **tree**, and that 矛 acts phonetically to express **newborn** as well as lending connotations of **thrust**. Thus **newborn growth that thrusts forth from a tree**, a reference to **new shoots**. Such shoots symbolised **softness** and **weakness**, with **gentle** being an associated meaning.

Mnemonic: **WOODEN LANCE IS WEAK, INDEED SOFT**

1364 渋 JŪ, shibu*i/ru*   渋滞 JŪTAI   delay
HESITATE, ASTRINGENT   渋味 SHIBUMI   astringency
11 strokes   渋渋 SHIBUSHIBU grudgingly

Formerly 澁, showing **water/ liquid** 氵 40 and an emphatic trebling of **stop** 止 129. The original meaning was **not flow smoothly**, which came to mean by association **be tardy** and hence **delay/ hesitate. Astringent** is felt by some scholars to be a borrowing, and by others to stem from the idea of preventing the juices flowing. Suggest taking 氵 as (four) **drops.**

Mnemonic:**ASTRINGENCY MAKES WATER DROPS HESITATE AND STOP**

435

1365 銃	JŪ	小銃 SHŌJŪ	rifle
	GUN	銃剣 JŪKEN	bayonet
	14 strokes	銃火 JŪKA	gunfire

金 is **metal** 14. 充 is **fill** 1362, here acting phonetically to express **hole** and also lending its meaning of **fill**. 1365 originally referred to the **hole in a metal ax head** (which is filled by the handle). It was later applied to **firearms**, by association with the hole in the barrel (which is filled by the ammunition).

Mnemonic: **GUN IS FILLED WITH METAL**

1366 獣	JŪ, ke[da]mono	獣医 JŪI	veterinarian
	BEAST	獣的 JŪTEKI	bestial
	16 strokes	鳥獣 CHŌJŪ	wildlife

Somewhat obscure. Formerly 獸, and earlier 嘼犬 and 嘼犬. 犮/犬 is **dog** 17. As shown by the early forms, 単 is an abbreviation of **simple** 單/单 542 q.v., here used phonetically to express **guard/ protect** and probably also lending similar connotations from its original meaning of forked weapon. Thus **dog that protects** (see also 1347), i.e. **guard dog**. The role of the later addition **mouth/ say** 口 20 is not clear. Some scholars take 嘼 to be a now defunct character meaning **beast**, though the evolution of such a meaning is not clear. Moreover, if 嘼 did exist as an independent character with a meaning of beast, then it may well be a derivative of beast 獸犬 1366 (see below). It should be noted that a different arrangement of the same elements gives the CO character **snort** 口單 (with 單 presumably acting in some unclear phonetic role), and thus it is possible that 嘼 replaced 呻 to give a meaning of **snorting/ snarling dog**, thereby emphasising its fearsomeness and efficacy as a guard dog. It is not clear how (snarling?) guard dog came to mean **beast**. Dog and beast have long overlapped conceptually (see 17), and it may just be an extension of this, particularly if the dog were indeed seen as snarling and fierce. Suggest taking 単 as 'seeming like' **simple** 単, with 口 as **say** (i.e. **bark**).

Mnemonic: **DOG'S BARK MAKES IT SEEM A SIMPLE BEAST**

436

1367 **叔** **SHUKU**
UNCLE, YOUNG BROTHER
8 strokes

叔父 OJI* uncle
叔母 OBA* aunt
伯叔 HAKUSHUKU uncles

Once written 尗又, showing a **hand** 又 pulling up a **potato** 尗 (plant 上 [variant 㞢/之/生 42] with tuber 丨 and side roots 八). Note that in Chinese it can still mean gather vegetables. Some scholars see the present meanings as borrowings, but others feel that the task of pulling up potatoes came to symbolise following a row, leading by association to (line of) **younger brothers** (see 177), with **uncle(s)** being one's parents' younger brothers. Younger brother is now rare. Suggest taking 尗 as 'almost' **walk** 歩 202.

Mnemonic: **WITH HELPING HAND, UNCLE CAN ALMOST WALK**

1368 **淑** **SHUKU**
PURE, GRACEFUL
11 strokes

貞淑 TEISHUKU chastity
淑女 SHUKUJO lady
私淑 SHISHUKU admiration

氵 is **water** 40. 叔 is **uncle** 1367, here acting phonetically to express **pure** but of unclear semantic role. Thus **pure water**, later **pure** in the figurative sense of **virtuous** (especially of women). **Graceful** is an associated meaning.

Mnemonic: **UNCLE DRINKS PURE WATER**

1369 **粛** **SHUKU**
SOLEMN, QUIET
11 strokes

粛然 SHUKUZEN to solemnly
自粛 JISHUKU self-control
厳粛 GENSHUKU solemnity

Formerly 肅. 聿 is a variant of **hand holding brush** 聿 142. It acts here phonetically to express **dark**, but is of unclear semantic role. 𣶒 represents a **deep pool** (now usually conveyed by an NGU character 淵, which adds water 氵 40), of unclear etymology but apparently comprising inner chamber 非 (variant 卯 997) and confines 丨丨, with old forms such as 𣶒 also showing water 丶丶. 1369 originally referred to a **dark deep pool**, which came to symbolise something **hushed** and rather **foreboding**, with **solemn** being an associated meaning. Suggest taking 米 as **rice** 201, 丨丨 as an **open container**, and 聿 as a **hand holding a stick** (to pound).

Mnemonic: **HAND SOLEMNLY POUNDS RICE IN OPEN CONTAINER**

1370	**JUKU** **JUKU, PRIVATE SCHOOL** 14 strokes	塾生 JUKUSEI 塾則 JUKUSOKU	juku student juku rules
		私塾 SHIJUKU	home-based juku

Though 孰 has now acquired the same form and sound as boil 孰 894 q.v., old forms such as 𡒌 show that it is in fact **castle** 亯 / 㐭 / 享 1162 q.v. plus **person bending with outstretched arms** 𤰇 / 𠃌 / 丸 470 q.v. The person is in fact **building the castle walls**, with **earth** 土 60 being the material used. Thus **castle walls built of earth**. 1370 originally referred to a **walled settlement**, then later came to mean **walled compound** and eventually, by association, **school**. In Japanese it has come in particular to refer to a **private after-hours 'cramming' school** (known as a **juku**). Suggest taking 享 as **child** 子 25, **top hat** 亠, and **mouth** 口 20, with 丸 as **round** 830.

Mnemonic: **EARTHY PRIVATE SCHOOL FOR ROUND-MOUTHED TOP-HATTED CHILDREN**

1371 俊	**SHUN** **EXCELLENCE, GENIUS** 9 strokes	俊才 SHUNSAI 俊傑 SHUNKETSU 俊童 SHUNDŌ	genius hero prodigy

亻 is **person** 39. 夋 is **linger** 689. The latter acts phonetically to express **stand apart from**, thus giving **person who stands apart from others**, but its meaning would confusingly appear to connote someone who stood apart from others in the sense of being behind rather than leading. There is a similarly confusing NGU character 駿, which uses horse 馬 191 instead of person 亻, and means fast horse rather than tardy/ slow horse. Thus it would appear that in both these cases linger 夋 has connotations of **giving others a start but still being able to outstrip them**. Note that in most other cases 夋 means linger in a less confusing sense, such as the NGU character fall back 逡 (which uses movement 辶 129), the CO character fall back/ stop/ hop 蹲 (which uses foot 足 51), and the CO character remains of a meal 餕 (which uses food/eat 食 146).

Mnemonic: **GENIUS IS PERSON WHO EXCELS DESPITE LINGERING**

438

1372

SHUN, matata*ku*
FLASH, TWINKLE,
BLINK
18 strokes

一瞬 ISSHUN　　　　an instant
瞬間 SHUNKAN　　　　instant
瞬く間 MATATAKUMA ni
　　　　in the twinkling of an eye

Once written 眹 (still found as a variant in Chinese), showing **eye** 目 72 and **arrow** 矢 981. The latter indicates **rapidity**, to give an ideograph referring to the rapid movement of the eye, i.e. **blinking**, with **twinkle** and **flash** being associated meanings. Arrow 矢 was later replaced by straighten an arrow 寅 621, which was used phonetically to express blink and also retained connotations of arrow, and this was in turn replaced by 舜 . The latter is a CO character meaning wise and is also used of a legendary ruler. Its etymology is unclear, though its elements appear to be **hand reaching down to convey** 爫 303 and **opposed feet** 舛 1211. It appears to have been used phonetically to express **blink**, but any semantic role is unclear. It is also unclear why the seemingly straightforward ideograph 眹 was modified with increasing complexity. Suggest taking 爫 as **hand reaching down**, 冖 as **cover**, and 舛 as **splayed feet**.

Mnemonic: **IN BLINK OF AN EYE HAND REACHES DOWN TO COVER SPLAYED FEET**

1373

JUN
TEN DAY PERIOD
6 strokes

上旬 JŌJUN first part of month
中旬 CHŪJUN middle of month
下旬 GEJUN last part of month

日 is **sun/ day** 62. 勹 is **encircle** 655, here acting phonetically to express cycle and almost certainly also lending similar reinforcing connotations of **circle**. Thus **cycle of days**, a rather vague reference to a **ten day cycle** which was a standard unit of time in ancient China.

Mnemonic: **TEN DAY CYCLE OF CIRCLING SUN**

1374

JUN, megu*ru*
GO AROUND
6 strokes

巡回 JUNKAI　　　tour, patrol
巡査 JUNSA　　　policeman
一巡り HITOMEGURI one round

辶 is **movement** 129. 巛 is **river** (variant 川 48: see also 680), here acting phonetically to express **see** and also lending its own connotations of movement. Thus to **move and see**, a reference to an **inspection**, leading to **go around**. Suggest remembering 巛 as a **river with sharp bends**.

Mnemonic: **MOVING RIVER GOES AROUND SHARP BENDS**

1375

JUN, tate
SHIELD, PRETEXT
9 strokes

矛盾 MUJUN   contradiction
後盾 USHIRODATE   backing
盾突く TATETSUKU   oppose

目 is **eye** 72, here meaning **look**. 厂 is a **shield**. Thus 盾 means **shield from be-hind which one looks out**. The meaning of ┼ is unclear. Since no very early forms of this character have been discovered it is possible that it derives from some earlier depic-tion of a **hand** holding the shield ㄓ, but it is also possible that it lends the same idea of **piercing** as in 直 349 q.v. (i.e. look piercingly/ intently out from behind a shield). Sug-gest taking it as **ten** ┼ 33. Note that the physical shield is now usually conveyed by an NGU character 楯, which adds **wood** 木 69, whereas 1375 is usually used in a figurative sense.

Mnemonic: **TEN EYES LOOK OUT FROM BEHIND SHIELD**

1376

JUN
QUASI-, CONFORM,
PERMIT
10 strokes

准尉 JUNI   warrant officer
批准 HIJUN   ratification
准許 JUNKYO   approval

Technically the same character as quasi/ conform 準/準 709 q.v., of which it is a simpli-fied form. However, for reasons that are not clear, 1376 also came to acquire connotations of **permission**, presumably from some association with conforming. Its elements are **ice/ freeze** 冫 378 and **bird** 隹 216.

Mnemonic: **FREEZE BIRD IN CONFORMITY WITH STANDARDS**

1377 殉

JUN
DUTIFUL DEATH
10 strokes

殉死 JUNSHI   dutiful death
殉教者 JUNKYŌSHA   martyr
殉職 JUNSHOKU

death at one's post

歹 is **bare bones/ death** 286. 旬 is **ten day period** 1373, here acting phonetically to express **conform/ follow** and probably also lending loose connotations of **being fixed/ inexorable**. Thus to **follow (inexorably?) in death**, a reference to the suicide of a retainer upon the death of his lord.

Mnemonic: **DUTIFUL DEATH, BUT BARE BONES AFTER TEN DAYS**

1378	JUN FOLLOW 12 strokes	因循 INJUN 循環 JUNKAN 悪循環 AKUJUNKAN	indecision cycle, circle vicious circle

亻 is **movement** 118. 盾 is **shield** 1375, here acting phonetically to express **follow** and probably also lending similar connotations (from the idea of moving forward behind a shield).

Mnemonic: **FOLLOW, MOVING BEHIND SHIELD**

1379 潤	JUN, uruou/su MOISTEN, ENRICH 15 strokes	潤滑 JUNKATSU 利潤 RIJUN 潤沢 JUNTAKU	lubrication profit moisture, profit, plenty, gloss

氵 is **water** 40. 閏 is an NGU character meaning **intercalation/ insert(ed) between**. It comprises **gate/ doorway** 門 211 and **king** 王 5 (though some old forms show **standing person** 壬 1610). Thus **king/person between doorposts**, a reference to **someone/ something coming between things**. (Note that 閏 can have the specific meaning of illegitimate reign, i.e. an unlawful 'king' coming between two lawful reigns.) In the case of 1379 閏 acts phonetically to express **wet** and probably also lends connotations of **coming between** (as water seeping through cracks etc.). Thus **make wet (with water)**, i.e. **moisten**, with **enrich** being an associated meaning.

Mnemonic: **KING AT GATE MOISTENED WITH ENRICHING WATER**

1380	JUN FOLLOW, OBEY 15 strokes	遵守 JUNSHU 遵奉 JUNPŌ 遵法 JUNPŌ	observance observance law abiding

辶 is **movement (along a road/path)** 129. 尊 is **respect/ esteem** 927, here acting phonetically to express **follow** and possibly also lending an idea of respected. Thus **follow a path** (possibly follow after someone respected or follow a respected path), with **obey** being an associated meaning.

Mnemonic: **WHEN MOVING, OBEDIENTLY FOLLOW RESPECTED PATH**

1381

SHO
MULTITUDE, VARIOUS
ILLEGITIMATE
11 strokes

庶民 SHOMIN the masses
庶務 SHOMU general affairs
庶子 SHOSHI illegitimate child

Of somewhat unclear etymology. Once written 庶. 火 /… is **fire** 8, but it is not clear whether 庶 /庶 is a stylised variant of **stone** 石 45, used phonetically to express **put (on)**, or whether it is a combination of **building** (in the sense of **house**) 广 114 and an **object** 廿/口 . The former theory seems more likely. In any event, the early meaning is known to have been **put things on a fire** (in a house?). It then appears to have become confused with **boil various things over a fire** 煮 1338 q.v., and to have come to mean **various things**. **Various** came to mean sundry and hence common, leading to commoners/ the masses/ **multitude**. 1381 was also borrowed to express concubine (still a minor meaning in Chinese), leading by association to **illegitimate**. Suggest taking 广 as building/ **house**, and 廿 as an **object**.

Mnemonic: **VARIOUS OBJECTS BURN IN HOUSE FIRE**

1382

緒

SHO, CHO, o
BEGINNING, CORD,
CLUE, CONNECTION
14 strokes

一緒 ISSHO together
端緒 TANSHO beginning
鼻緒 HANAO clog thong

Formerly 緒 . 糸 is **thread** 27. 者/者 is **person** 298 q.v., here acting phonetically to express **end/ beginning** (conceptually the same in the case of a thread) and almost certainly also lending its early connotations of **various** (things). Thus the **start/ end of a thread** (sticking out from amongst various threads?). This gave rise to a range of meanings, such as **thread/ cord** and **beginning**, and also to the idea of starting to unravel a tangle, giving **clue** and **connection**.

Mnemonic: **PERSON FOLLOWS THREAD FROM BEGINNING**

1383

如

JO, NYO, gotoku
SIMILAR, EQUAL
6 strokes

如上 JOJŌ no aforesaid
如実 NYOJITSU realism
如何 IKAGA* how?

口 is **mouth/ say** 20, here meaning **tell** (someone to do something). 女 is **woman** 35, here acting phonetically to express **comply** and also lending connotations of compliance and submissiveness. Thus to **comply with what one is told**. The idea of doing (the same) as one is requested to do led to the associated ideas of **similar** and **equal** (cf. English slang do <u>like</u> one is told).

Mnemonic: **WOMEN'S MOUTHS ARE SIMILAR**

1384 JO 叙術 JOJUTSU description
DESCRIBE, CONFER 叙情的 JOJŌTEKI lyrical
9 strokes 叙勲 JOKUN

conferment of decoration

Formerly also written 敍 and 敘, i.e. with **striking hand** 攵/攴 101 (here indicating **coercion**) instead of a simple **hand** 又. 余 is **ample/ excess** 800, here acting phonetically to express **sequence/ order** but of unclear semantic role. Thus to **make someone put things in order**, i.e. **arrange** (still a meaning in Chinese). This was applied by association to the idea of relating a series of events in their proper order, giving **describe**. It is not fully clear how the meaning of **confer** evolved, but it may relate to conferring things in a set order.

Mnemonic: **AMPLE DESCRIPTION OF HAND**

1385 JO, omomu*ro* 徐行 JOKŌ going slowly
SLOWLY, GRADUALLY 徐徐 JOJO ni slowly
10 strokes 徐歩 JOHO walking slowly

彳 is **movement** 118. 余 is **ample/ excess** 800, here acting phonetically to express **slowly** and probably also lending a meaning of **excessive/ very**. Thus **move (excessively?) slowly**, with **gradually** being an associated meaning.

Mnemonic: **MOVE EXCESSIVELY SLOWLY**

1386 SHŌ, masu 升目 MASUME measure
LIQUID MEASURE 二升 NISHŌ two shō
4 strokes 一升びん ISSHŌBIN one shō bottle

Once written 𠦚, showing a **scoop/ ladle** 斗 with **contents** -. Now a standardised **liquid measure** of 1.8 liters, particularly associated with sake. Suggest taking 𠆢 as **person** 39 and 𠂇 as a variant of **ten** 十 33.

Mnemonic: **LIQUID MEASURE ENOUGH FOR TEN PEOPLE**

1387

SHŌ, mes*u*
**SUMMON, PARTAKE,
WEAR**
5 strokes

召集 SHŌSHŪ summons, call
召喚 SHŌKAN summons
召し使い MESHITSUKAI servant

Of disputed etymology. An old form 𠮦 is interpreted by some scholars as an ideograph combining **mouth/ say** ㅂ /ㅁ 20 and **bending person** ㇟ 39, to give a **person/ servant bending** (a symbol of humility) **as they answer their master's summons.** **Sword/ cut** 刀 181 is thus taken to be a miscopying. Other scholars feel that 𠃌 is simply a variant of the old form 𠃌 of 刀, and take this to be used purely phonetically to express **summon.** Thus **summon verbally** (i.e. with the mouth). The former theory seems more likely. In either case, **partake** and **wear** are associated meanings, relating to actions for which a master might summon a servant.

Mnemonic: **CUT MOUTH AND SUMMON HELP**

1388

SHŌ
CRAFTSMAN, PLAN
6 strokes

師匠 SHISHŌ master
巨匠 KYOSHŌ great master
意匠 ISHŌ idea, design

匸 is a **container** (see 225), here meaning **box.** 斤 is **ax** 1176, here indicating **tool.** Thus **tool box**, a symbol of an **artisan** and by extension **craftsman.** **Plan** is felt to be an associated meaning, from the way in which a craftsman sets about his work.

Mnemonic: **CRAFTSMAN KEEPS AX IN BOX**

1389

SHŌ, toko, yuka
BED, FLOOR, ALCOVE
7 strokes

病床 BYŌSHŌ sickbed
床張り YUKABARI flooring
床の間 TOKONOMA
ornamental alcove

Formerly 牀 and 牀. 爿 / 爿 is a **plank of wood**, being a mirror image of **piece of wood** 片 969 q.v. (literally one side of a tree 𣏌 / 木 69), and came by association to mean **bed** (originally sickbed [see 381] but later bed in general). In Japanese it also refers to **flooring/ floor** and an **alcove**, the latter now used for ornamental purposes but originally a place where a bed was placed. The reason for the later use of **building/ house** 广 114 is unclear. It is taken by some scholars to be a miscopying of (or simplification of) 爿, by others to be a miscopying of the sickness radical 疒 381, and by still others to be a deliberate attempt to indicate being indoors.

Mnemonic: **BUILDING HAS WOODEN FLOOR AND BED IN ALCOVE**

1390		SHŌ	抄本	SHŌHON	extract
		EXCERPT, EXTRACT	詩抄	SHISHŌ	selected poems
		7 strokes	抄訳	SHŌYAKU	
					abridged translation

A later variant of the similar meaning NGU character 鈔. 金 is **metal** 14. 少 is **few/ little** 143, here acting phonetically to express **take** and also lending its meaning of **little**. 1390 originally referred to **extracting a little of something by removing it with a metal tool** (felt by some scholars to be specifically a pair of scissors). Metal 金 was later replaced by **hand** 扌 32, giving **take away a little by hand**. Now **extract/ excerpt** in a broad sense.

Mnemonic: **EXTRACT A LITTLE BY HAND**

1391		SHŌ, ayaka*ru*	肖像	SHŌZŌ	portrait
		BE LIKE, BE LUCKY	不肖	FUSHŌ	unlike, I/me
		7 strokes	肖り者	AYAKARIMONO	
					lucky person

月 is **flesh/ of the body** 365. ⺌ is a variant of **little/ small** 小 36, which also lends its sound to express **resemble**. 1391 originally referred to **offspring resembling their parents** (i.e. being little versions of their body), but later came to mean **be like** in a broader sense. For some reason it also acquired connotations of **being** (as) **lucky** (as anyone else).

Mnemonic: **LITTLE ONE IS LIKE PARENTS IN BODY AND IN LUCK**

1392	尚	SHŌ, nao, tatto*bu*	尚早	SHŌSŌ	prematurity
		FURTHERMORE, ESTEEM	高尚	KŌSHŌ	loftiness
		8 strokes	尚尚	NAONAO	still more

Of broad semantic evolution. Formerly 尙 and earlier 尙, showing a combination of **out of/ away** ハ/ ソ 66 and **face** (towards) 向/ 向 (here 向) 278 q.v., the latter being used in its literal sense of **house with window**. 1392 originally referred to **smoke rising out of the window of a house**, and thus came to symbolise **height** and **rising/ raising to a height**. **Esteem** is an extension of the latter. **Furthermore** is seen as an associated meaning, from the idea of rising ever higher (i.e. giving one thing on top of all others: see also 1091).

Mnemonic: **FURTHERMORE, FACING AWAY IS A SIGN OF ESTEEM!**

1393

SHŌ, nobor*u*
RISE, ASCENT
8 strokes

昇進 SHŌSHIN   promotion
上昇 JŌSHŌ   ascent
昇降機 SHŌKŌKI   elevator

日 is **sun** 62. 卅 is (liquid) **measure** 1386, here acting phonetically to express **rise** and possibly also lending a loose idea of **measurably**, i.e. **noticeably**. Thus **sun rising (noticeably?) high**, later **rise/ ascend** in a broad sense. Sugest taking 卅 as **person** イ 39 and **ten** 十 (variant 十 33).

Mnemonic: **SUN RISES, MEASURED BY TEN PERSONS**

1394

SHŌ, matsu
PINE
8 strokes

松葉 MATSUBA   pine needle
松原 MATSUBARA pine grove
松竹梅 SHŌCHIKUBAI

pine-bamboo-plum

木 is **tree** 69. 公 is **public** 277, here acting phonetically to express **needle** and probably also lending connotations of **common**. Thus **(common?) tree bearing needles**, a reference to the **pine**.

Mnemonic: **PINE IS A PUBLIC TREE**

1395

SHŌ, numa
SWAMP, MARSH
8 strokes

沼気 SHŌKI   methane
沼沢 SHŌTAKU swamp, marsh
沼地 NUMACHI   marshland

氵 is **water** 40, here meaning **body of water**. 召 is **summon** 1387 q.v., here acting phonetically to express **little**. Thus **little body of water** (i.e. a small volume of water relative to a lake or river), a reference to a **swamp/ marsh**. Since there is no obvious reason why the simpler SHŌ little 小 36 or SHŌ little 少 143 were not used, 召 presumably also lent some meaning, but this is not clear. It may perhaps suggest **gathering**, i.e. a **place where water gathers/** collects (though still smaller in volume than a river).

Mnemonic: **SUMMON WATERS OF SWAMP**

1396 宵	SHŌ, yoi	徹宵 TESSHŌ all night
	EVENING	宵月 YOIZUKI evening moon
	10 strokes	宵越し YOIGOSHI overnight

Somewhat obscure. Formerly 宵 . 宀 is **roof/ house** 28, here meaning **indoors**. 肖/ 肖 has for many centuries been interpreted as **be like** 1391 q.v., which is assumed to act phonetically to express **vanish** to give **vanishing (light) indoors**, i.e. **evening**. Indeed, there is a very old form 宵, clearly showing **meat** 夕 / 月 365 and **little** 小 36, the component elements of 1391. However, since there is no element specifically meaning light this has never been a fully convincing explanation. In fact, the very oldest form of all, 宵, shows clearly that meat 夕 / 月 is a longstanding miscopying of **moon** 夕 / 月 16, which presumably indicated **light** (though sun 日 62 may have been more appropriate). Thus it seems most likely that 1396 was originally an ideograph meaning **little light indoors**, rather than vanishing light, though both result in **evening**.

Mnemonic: **SMALL MOON SEEN UNDER ROOF AS EVENING ARRIVES**

1397 症	SHŌ	症状 SHŌJŌ symptoms
	SYMPTOM, ILLNESS	炎症 ENSHŌ inflammation
	10 strokes	恐怖症 KYŌFUSHŌ phobia

疒 is **sickness/ illness** 381. 正 is **correct/ proper** 41, here acting phonetically to express **sign** and probably also lending its meaning of **proper** and by extension **authentic**. Thus the **(authentic?) signs of an illness**, i.e. the **symptoms**, as well as the **illness** itself.

Mnemonic: **PROPER SYMPTOMS OF ILLNESS**

1398 祥	SHŌ	発祥地 HASSHŌCHI birthplace
	GOOD FORTUNE, OMEN	吉祥 KISSHŌ good omen
	10 strokes	不祥事 FUSHŌJI
		bad omen, scandal

Formerly 祥 . 示/礻 is **altar/ of the gods** 695. 羊 is **sheep** 986 q.v., here acting phonetically to express **auspicious (sign)** and possibly also lending its own connotations either of **fine** or of **sacrifice**. **Auspicious sign from the gods** was a good **omen**, symbolising **good fortune**.

Mnemonic: **SHEEP SACRIFICED ON ALTAR TO BRING GOOD FORTUNE**

447

1399		SHŌ **CROSS OVER, LIAISE** 11 strokes	交渉 KŌSHŌ negotiations 干渉 KANSHŌ interference 渉外 SHŌGAI public relations

Formerly also written 涉. 氵 is **water** 40, here meaning **river**, while 歩/步 is **walk** 202. To **walk across a river**, i.e. ford it, came to mean **cross carefully from one side to another** in a broader sense, including that of **liaise**.

Mnemonic: **LIAISON CAN INVOLVE WALKING ON WATER**

1400		SHŌ **INTRODUCE, INHERIT** 11 strokes	紹介 SHŌKAI introduction 紹介者 SHŌKAISHA introducer 紹介状 SHŌKAIJŌ letter of introduction

糸 is **thread** 27. 召 is **summon** 1387, here acting phonetically to express **join** and possibly also lending supporting connotations of **gather/ muster** and thus **bring together**. 1400 originally meant to **join threads**, and was later used by association to mean **put people together**, i.e. to **introduce** them. **Inherit** is an associated meaning, from the idea of joining threads in a figurative sense.

Mnemonic: **THREAD ONE'S WAY TO INTRODUCTION AFTER SUMMONS**

1401		SHŌ **ACCUSE, SUE** 11 strokes	訴訟 SOSHŌ litigation 訴訟人 SOSHŌNIN plaintiff 訴訟費用 SOSHŌHIYŌ court costs

言 is **words/ speak** 274. 公 is **public** 277, here acting phonetically to express **dispute** and probably also lending its meaning of **public**. Thus **words spoken in a (public?) dispute**, with **accuse** being an associated meaning and **sue** being a further association.

Mnemonic: **PUBLIC WORDS OF ACCUSATION LEAD ONE TO SUE**

1402	掌	SHŌ, tanagokoro **CONTROL, PALM (HAND)** 12 strokes	掌中 SHŌCHŪ in one's hand 車掌 SHASHŌ conductor 職掌 SHOKUSHŌ duties

手 is **hand** 32. 尚 is **furthermore** 1392, here acting phonetically to express **hold** but of unclear semantic role. Thus **that part of the hand which holds**, a somewhat vague reference to the **palm** rather than the fingers. **Control** is an associated meaning, from the idea of handling/ manipulating.

Mnemonic: **FURTHERMORE, PALM OF HAND CONTROLS**

1403	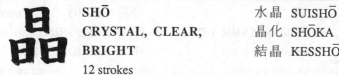	SHŌ	水晶	SUISHŌ	crystal, quartz
		CRYSTAL, CLEAR,	晶化	SHŌKA	crystallisation
		BRIGHT	結晶	KESSHŌ	crystallisation
		12 strokes			

A trebling of **sun/ light** 日 62, to mean **many points of light** (and at one stage applied to stars: see 154). This came to mean **bright** and then by association **clear**, and was eventually used to refer to **crystals**.

Mnemonic: **THREE SUNS MAKE IT BRIGHT AND CRYSTAL CLEAR**

1404		SHŌ, ko*geru*/*gasu*, a*seru*, *jireru*	焦土	SHŌDO	scorched earth
		SCORCH, FRET	焦心	SHŌSHIN	impatience
		12 strokes	黒焦げ	KUROKOGE	charring

An ideograph showing a **bird** 隹 216 **roasting** over a **fire** 灬 8. This came to acquire associated connotations of **scorching** and **charring**, and was also applied figuratively to the idea of **fretting**. There is an alternative theory that 隹 acts purely phonetically to express blacken, to give blacken with fire, but this is not convincing.

Mnemonic: **BIRD FRETS WHEN SCORCHED OVER FIRE**

1405		SHŌ	硝酸	SHŌSAN	nitric acid
		NITER, GUNPOWDER	硝薬	SHŌYAKU	gunpowder
		12 strokes	硝子	GARASU*	glass

石 is **rock** 45. 肖 is **be like** 1391 q.v., here acting phonetically to express **digest** and possibly also lending connotations of **growing from** as an extension of its literal meaning of small version of a (bigger) body. Thus **that associated with rock and digestion** (which grows out from rock?), a reference to **niter**. Niter is found as an incrustation on rock (cf. English term saltpeter, meaning literally salt of rock), and is also used medicinally to aid digestion as well as in the making of gunpowder.

Mnemonic: **NITER IS LIKE A ROCK**

449

1406　SHŌ
ADORN, MAKE UP
12 strokes

化粧　KESHŌ　make-up
化粧品　KESHŌHIN　cosmetics
化粧室　KESHŌSHITSU
powder room

A character of relatively recent origin, with a history of only six hundred years or so. Nevertheless, its etymology is somewhat confused. 米 is **rice** 201, here symbolising **white** and by association **face powder** (see 1029). 庄 is an NGU character meaning manor/cottage, popularly believed to comprise **building** 广 114 and **ground/ earth** 土 60 but in fact a variant/ miscopying of manor/ villa 荘 1515 q.v. (though its graphic evolution may well have been influenced by 广 and 土). Here it acts phonetically to express **adorn**, giving **adorn oneself with face powder**. Note that in Chinese 荘 1515 can also be interchanged with 1406 to mean adorn/ make up. Note also that 荘 is often interchanged with its principal component manly 壮 1514 q.v., which has an assumed literal meaning of erect male organ in bed (male organ 士 494 and bed 丬 1389) and thus strong sexual connotations. 壮 is itself the 'male equivalent' of 牀, a CO character literally meaning woman in bed (woman 女 35 and bed 丬 / 爿 1389) which is also interchangeable in Chinese with 1406. Thus originally 1406 clearly had strong connotations of making oneself up with a specific view to increasing sexual allure, though nowadays it is usually used in a general esthetic sense. Suggest taking 庄 as **building** 广 and **earth** 土.

Mnemonic: **ADORN EARTHEN FLOOR OF BUILDING WITH RICE**

1407　SHŌ, mikotonori
IMPERIAL EDICT
12 strokes

詔書　SHŌSHO　imperial edict
詔令　SHŌREI　imperial edict
大詔　TAISHŌ　imperial edict

言 is **word/ speak** 274. 召 is **summon** 1387 q.v., here especially with its connotations of a high ranking person summoning a lower ranking person. 1407 became particularly associated with an **emperor's summons/ edict**.

Mnemonic: **SUMMONED TO HEAR WORDS OF IMPERIAL EDICT**

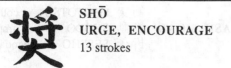

1408	SHŌ	奨励	SHŌREI	encouragement
	URGE, ENCOURAGE	推奨	SUISHŌ	recommendation
	13 strokes	奨学金	SHŌGAKUKIN	
				scholarship

Of somewhat confused evolution. Formerly 將, showing **command** 將/将 899 q.v. and **big** 大 53. However, older forms such as 將 and 將 show clearly that the modern forms stem from a miscopying of the elements **bed** 爿/爿/丬 1389, **meat** 丹/月/月 365, and **dog** 犬/大 17. There is a theory that 將 was from an early stage a simplification of command 將, giving **command a dog** and hence **order** and by association **urge/encourage**, but it seems equally if not more likely that 爿 acts phonetically to express **offer** (as in 899 itself), and that 1408 thus originally meant **offer meat to a dog**, thereby leading to **encourage** and by association **urge**. Suggest taking 奨 as **command(er)** 将 and big/ **great** 大.

Mnemonic: **URGED ON BY GREAT COMMANDER**

1409	SHŌ, kuwa*shii*	詳細	SHŌSAI	details
	DETAILED	未詳	MISHŌ	unclear
	13 strokes	詳しく	KUWASHIKU	in detail

言 is **word** 274, here meaning **talk/ discuss**. 羊 is **sheep** 986, here acting phonetically to express **examine thoroughly** and possibly also loosely lending similar connotations (a sheep being a prized object that would necessarily be examined carefully prior to purchase). Thus to **discuss with a view to examining thoroughly**, with thorough examination/discussion leading by association to **detailed**.

Mnemonic: **DETAILED TALK ABOUT SHEEP**

1410	SHŌ	表彰	HYŌSHŌ	commendation
	MANIFEST,	顕彰	KENSHŌ	manifestation
	OPENLY ACKNOWLEDGE	彰徳	SHŌTOKU	public praise
	14 strokes			

彡 is **delicate hairs** 93 q.v., here in its sense of **attractive decoration**. 章 is **badge** 318 q.v., here in its sense of **attractive pattern**. 1410 originally referred to an **attractive decorative pattern**, and in Chinese still retains lesser meanings of beautiful and ornamental. By association it also came to mean **display something attractive**, with the idea of display leading by further association to **manifest** and **make something clear to the world at large**, i.e. **openly acknowledge** (often in the sense of praise).

Mnemonic: **OPENLY ACKNOWLEDGE BADGE HAS THREE HAIRS ON IT**

451

1411 衝 SHŌ

COLLIDE, CLASH, ROAD

15 strokes

衝突 SHŌTOTSU　collision
衝動 SHŌDŌ　impulse
折衝 SESSHŌ　negotiations

Somewhat obscure. Once written 衛. 行 is **move/ go** 118 q.v, here with its literal meaning of **road(s)**. 童 is **child/ slave** 363 q.v., here acting phonetically to express **pass**. Thus **road that (people) pass along**. It is not clear whether 童 also plays any semantic role, though its complexity would suggest that it does. It may possibly lend its literal connotations of slaves bearing loads, i.e. porters, and thereby suggest a file of people moving along, or it may simply suggest people from the outset. It is also possible that it lends figurative associations of heavy usage (cf. English term heavy traffic), though this is unlikely. The modern form uses the simpler **heavy** 重 311 q.v., which at one stage had the same pronunciation as 童 (then SHŌ) and thus plays a similar phonetic role, as well as having the same (possibly relevant) literal connotations of persons bearing loads. **Road** is now a minor meaning. **Collide/ clash** is taken by some scholars to be a purely borrowed meaning, but it may stem from a reinterpretation of the elements 童/重 and 行 as **heavy** and **move** respectively, suggesting **heavy objects coming together**.

Mnemonic: **COLLISION OF HEAVY OBJECTS MOVING ON ROAD**

1412 償 SHŌ, tsugunau

RECOMPENSE, REDEEM

17 strokes

償金 SHŌKIN　reparation
償却 SHŌKYAKU　redemption
弁償 BENSHŌ　compensation

亻 is **person** 39. 賞 is **prize** 511 q.v., here acting phonetically to express **return/ back** and also lending its connotations of **bestowing money**. 1412 originally referred to **buying back a person**, i.e. **redeeming** a slave by **recompensing** the owner. It now means **redeem** and **recompense** in a broader sense.

Mnemonic: **PERSON RECOMPENSED WITH PRIZE**

1413 礁 SHŌ

(HIDDEN) REEF

17 strokes

岩礁 GANSHŌ　reef
暗礁 ANSHŌ hidden reef, snag
さんご礁 SANGOSHŌ　coral reef

Of relatively recent origin. 石 is **rock** 45. 焦 is **scorch/ fret** 1404, here acting phonetically to express **tapered** and almost certainly also lending a meaning of **fret/ worry**. Thus **tapered rock (that causes worry?)**, a somewhat vague reference to a **submerged rock/ reef** of which only the tip is visible above the water. It is not clear why water 氵/水 40 was not added for clarity, to give 濊 or similar.

Mnemonic: **FRET OVER ROCKY REEF**

1414 SHŌ, kane
BELL
20 strokes

警鐘 KEISHŌ　　　alarm bell
釣鐘堂 TSURIGANEDŌ　belfry
鐘乳石 SHŌNYŪSEKI　stalactite

Of disputed etymology, though its elements are clearly **metal** 金 14 and **child/ slave** 童 363 q.v. Some scholars take the latter to lend its connotations of **heavy**, to give **heavy metal object**, a rather vague reference to a **large hanging bell**. Others take 童 (once pronounced SHŌ) to be used essentially phonetically to express **handle** (with any semantic role unclear), to give **metal object with a handle**, a similarly vague reference to a **hand bell**. Though confusingly 1414 does nowadays usually refer to a large and unwieldy type of bell, the latter theory seems the more likely. Evidence for this includes the fact that 1414 is interchangeable with an NGU character 鉦, which uses SHŌ correct 正 41 in an apparently similar phonetic role, and the fact that there exists a CO character 鍾, which uses heavy 重 311 (also once pronounced SHŌ and sometimes interchanged with 童 [see 1411]) in a similar role, though it actually means large goblet rather than bell (i.e. handle becoming interpreted as stem). Suggest taking 童 as **stand** 立 73 and **village** 里 219.

Mnemonic: **METAL BELLS STANDS IN VILLAGE**

1415 JŌ, take
LENGTH, STATURE,
MEASURE
3 strokes

丈夫 JŌBU　　　sturdy, robust
背丈 SETAKE　　　height
方丈 HŌJŌ　abbot's chamber,
　　　　abbot, ten feet square

Once written 𠬛, showing **hand** 又 and **ten** 十 33. A hand represented the **span of one hand**, namely **one shaku** (30.3 cms) 尺 884 q.v. Thus **ten shaku/ one jō**, namely a **measure** of approximately **ten feet**. It is now also used of **length** and **height** in a more general sense, including a person's **stature** (clearly initially with some degree of exaggeration). Suggest taking 丈 as a **hand** 乂 holding a **stick** ‾.

Mnemonic: **HAND HOLDS STICK TEN FEET IN LENGTH**

1416 JŌ
SUPERFLUOUS
4 strokes

冗談 JŌDAN　　　joke
冗長 JŌCHŌ　　　verbosity
冗語 JŌGO　redundant word

Formerly also written 冗, and earlier 冗. ∩/冖 is **house** (variant 宀 28), while 儿/ 几 / 几 is **crouching person** 39 (probably a **hunchback**). **Person (/hunchback?) at home** was a reference to a **person with no work**, presumably as a result of incapacity, which came to mean **superfluous person** and eventually **superfluous** in a broad sense. Note that in Chinese it can by extension mean tramp/ vagrant, and also mean potter about and do various things, leading by association to a somewhat confusing and paradoxical meaning of various duties/ business. Suggest taking 几 as **table** 832 and 冖 as **cover**.

Mnemonic: **COVER UP SUPERFLUOUS TABLE**

1417　浄　JŌ

PURE, CLEAN

9 strokes

浄化 JŌKA　　purification
不浄 FUJŌ　　filth
浄水 JŌSUI　　clean water

Formerly 淨 . ⺡ is **water** 40. 爭/争 is **vie/ conflict** 529, here acting phonetically to express **pure** and possibly also lending connotations of something that is vied for and hence desirable. Thus (desirable?) **pure water**.

Mnemonic: **VIE FOR PURE, CLEAN WATER**

1418　剰　JŌ, amatsusae

SURPLUS, BESIDES

11 strokes

剰余 JŌYO　　surplus
余剰 YOJŌ　　surplus
過剰 KAJŌ　　surplus, excess

Formerly 剩 . Obscure, though its elements are clearly **sword/ cut** ⺉ 181 and **ride/ mount** 乗/乘 320. Some authoritative Japanese scholars believe it to be a later simplification/ miscopying of the CO character **surplus** 賸, with which it is indeed interchangeable in Chinese. This comprises shell/ money/ valuable item 貝 90 and royal we 朕/朕 1603 q.v., here acting phonetically to express **give** and also lending its own supporting connotations of **raise/ offer (up)**. Thus to give valuables. Some scholars take surplus to be a borrowed meaning, while others see it as an extended meaning, either from the idea of giving away surplus items or the idea of giving items away with excessive generosity. In any event, the theory that 剰 is a simplification/ miscopying of 賸 is by no means convincing. The forms are too distinct for a miscopying or deliberate variation to be likely, and 剰 is too complex to be used as a simplification. It seems more likely that 剰 did exist as a primitive character in its own right, but that no primitive forms have yet been discovered. A possible explanation of its etymology might be that ⺉ meant **cut (away)**, with 乗 acting phonetically to express **surplus/ superfluous** (see 1416) and possibly also lending supporting connotations of **extremity** (from its original connotations of treetop). Thus a **superfluous part (such as an extremity?) which is cut away**, leading eventually to **surplus**.

Mnemonic: **RIDE WITH SURPLUS SWORD**

1419

JŌ, tatami, tata*mu*
TATAMI MAT, SIZE,
FOLD, PILE, REPEAT
12 strokes

畳句 JŌKU repeated phrase
二畳 NIJŌ two-mat (size)
畳み込む TATAMIKOMU fold up

Formerly 疊 and 疉. 宜 is a variant of good/ **meat piled on altar** 宜 1134 q.v., here meaning **pile up** in a broad sense. 畾 is a CO character meaning divided fields, being a trebling of **field** 田 59, while 晶 is bright 1403, being a trebling of sun 日 62. Both 畾 and 晶 are used for their trebled composition simply to indicate **quantity** and **repetition**, thus reinforcing 宜. 1419 originally meant to **pile something up layer upon layer**, giving by association **fold** and **repeat**. In Japanese it also came to be applied to **matting** (which can be folded and stored), especially the **tatami mat**, and is also used as a **unit of size** based upon the tatami (approximately six feet by three feet). Suggest taking 宜 as **cover** 冖 and **besides/ cairn/ pile** 且 1091.

Mnemonic: **BESIDES, PILE OF FOLDED MATS IN FIELD IS COVERED**

1420

JŌ, nawa
ROPE, CORD
15 strokes

沖縄 OKINAWA Okinawa
縄張り NAWABARI cordon, area
自縄自縛 JIJŌJIBAKU

falling in one's own trap

Formerly 繩. 糸 is **thread** 27. 黽 derives from a pictograph 黽 of a type of **fly** with bulging eyes, double wings, and tail/ sting. (Note that fly in a general sense is now conveyed by the NGU character 蠅/蝿, which adds insect 虫 56.) 黽 acts here phonetically to express **twist (together)**. It is not clear why it was chosen as a phonetic, but it may possibly also lend loosely associated connotations of **many** (from the swarming associated with flies). Thus **(many?) threads twisted together**, giving **rope/ cord**. Suggest taking 黽 as **two days** 日 62 and a **(long) rope** し.

Mnemonic: **THREADING ROPE TAKES LONGER THAN TWO DAYS**

1421 壊	JŌ	土壌 DOJŌ	earth, soil
	EARTH, SOIL	壌土 JŌDO	earth, soil
	16 strokes	天壌 TENJŌ	heaven and earth

Somewhat obscure. Formerly 壞. 土 is **earth/ ground/ soil** 60. 襄 is a CO character with a confusing range of meanings, such as disrobe, assist, high, yoke, and change position. Its exact etymology is unclear, but its earliest form was 𦳊. This is known to have comprised a trebling of **mouth/ say** ㅂ / 口 20 and a symbol of **reciprocity/ mutuality** ㄨ, and to have meant **people accusing one another** (see also 1424). 𦳊 later became 㗊, with plural mouths ㅂㅂ, symbols of reciprocity 𠬛, and 乩. 乩 is known to be a simplification of 㕚, the obscure element seen in 1351 q.v. which appears to mean (here) **flowing from one mouth to another**. Thus 㗊 also appears to have meant **mutual accusations**. At some later point **clothing** 衣 / 衤 420 was added and 乩 became abbreviated to 𡈼, thus giving the semi-modern form 襄. Unfortunately the role of clothing 衣 is not clear, though it obviously relates to the meaning disrobe and also appears to have lent connotations of softness and pliancy, since these sometimes seem associated with 襄 in compounds. In the case of 1421 襄/襄 acts phonetically to express **soft**, and may also lend similar connotations of its own. Thus **soft earth**, i.e. **rich earth**, though now it is used of **earth/ soil** in a broader sense. Suggest taking 六 as **six** 76, 井 as a variant of **well** 井 1470, and 衣 as a variant of **clothing/ clothe** 衣.

Mnemonic: **GROUND AROUND SIX WELLS CLOTHED IN RICH SOIL**

1422 嬢	JŌ	令嬢 REIJŌ	young lady
	YOUNG LADY,	愛嬢 AIJŌ	beloved daughter
	DAUGHTER	お嬢さん OJŌSAN	
	16 strokes		young lady, daughter

Formerly 孃. 女 is **woman** 35. 襄/襄 is the somewhat obscure element seen in 1421 q.v., here acting phonetically to express **control** according to some scholars and **upper** according to others (though both have the same result). It may possibly also lend its own connotations of **high** and thus reinforce upper. 1422 originally referred to the **upper woman in a house**, i.e. the **lady in control/ principal lady** of the house. Initially this was used as a polite reference to a **mother**, but later, not unlike the English term Mistress, it was applied to women in general, and came to acquire particular associations with **young ladies** (**daughter** being an associated meaning). As with 1421, suggest taking 襄 as **six** 六 76, **well** 井 (variant 井 1470), and **clothes** 衣 (variant 衤 420).

Mnemonic: **YOUNG LADY HAS ENOUGH CLOTHES TO FILL SIX WELLS**

1423	錠	JŌ LOCK, TABLET 16 strokes	錠前 JŌMAE	lock
			手錠 TEJŌ	handcuffs
			錠剤 JŌZAI	pill, tablet

Somewhat obscure. 金 is **metal** 14. 定 is **fix/ establish** 351 q.v. Often explained as **metal that fixes in place**, i.e. a **lock**. This is a useful mnemonic but possibly an over-simplification, since it does not have a meaning of lock in Chinese (though it can mean anchor, which can be interpreted as a metal object that fixes in place [but see below]). It seems more likely that it originally referred to a **slab of metal forming the foundation/ base** of something, thus using the similar connotations of framework/ starting-point of 定, and in Chinese it does indeed have a principal meaning of slab or ingot (with anchor presumably an associated meaning from the idea of heavy metal). Some scholars feel that the 正 element of 定, namely correct/ lower leg 41, lent particular connotations of base, and also feel that 1423 was initially used specifically to refer to a metal goblet/ dish with a broad base. Its Japanese meanings of **lock** and **tablet** are taken by some scholars to be borrowings, but it seems more likely that lock results either from a reinterpretation of the elements as outlined above (i.e. metal that fixes in place) or from the associated idea of a heavy metal base/ slab keeping something firmly in place. Tablet may similarly result from an association (of shape) with ingot.

Mnemonic: **LOCK IS METAL OBJECT THAT FIXES IN PLACE**

1424	譲	JŌ, yuzuru HAND OVER, YIELD 20 strokes	譲歩 JŌHO	concession
			譲渡 JŌTO	transfer
			親譲り OYAYUZURI	patrimony

Formerly 讓, and originally simply 㐀. The latter is the prototype of the somewhat obscure element 裏/ 裏 (see 1421), and is here used in its original meaning of **people accusing each other**. After the meaning of 裏 became vague **words/ speak** 言 274 was added to stress the idea of **dispute/ argument**. **Yield** is felt by some scholars to be a borrowing, and by others to be an associated meaning, from the idea of yielding in an argument. **Hand over** is an associated meaning in turn with yield. Suggest taking 襄 as **six** 六 76, **well** 井 (variant 丼 1470), and **clothes** 衣 (variant 衣 420).

Mnemonic: **YIELD TO WORDS -- HAND OVER CLOTHES AND SIX WELLS**

1425 JŌ, kamo*su*
BREW, CAUSE
20 strokes

醸造 JŌZŌ brewing
醸成 JŌSEI brew, cause
醸し出す KAMOSHIDASU cause

Formerly 釀 . 酉 is **alcohol** 302. 襄/襄 is the somewhat obscure element seen in 1421 q.v., here acting phonetically to express **brew** and possibly also lending loose connotations of **change** or of **soften/ break down**. Thus **brew alcohol**, with **cause** being an associated meaning (cf. English brew up trouble etc.). Suggest taking 襄 as **six** 六 76, **well** 井 (variant 井 1470), and **clothes** 衣 ('ruined' variant 衣 420).

Mnemonic: **BREW ALCOHOL IN SIX WELLS AND RUIN CLOTHES**

1426 SHOKU, fu*eru/yasu*
INCREASE, ENRICH
12 strokes

生殖 SEISHOKU procreation
利殖 RISHOKU money making
殖え高 FUEDAKA increment

歹 is **bare bones/ death** 286. 直 is **direct** 349, here acting phonetically to express **soft/ pulpy** but of unclear semantic role. 1426 originally referred to a **corpse putrefying**, and in Chinese still retains occasional connotations of bones. **Enrich** is a borrowed meaning, with **increase** being an associated meaning with enrich.

Mnemonic: **INCREASED BARE BONES DIRECTLY ENRICH GROUND**

1427 SHOKU, kazar*u*
DECORATE
13 strokes

装飾 SŌSHOKU decoration
首飾り KUBIKAZARI necklace
飾り物 KAZARIMONO
decoration

巾 is **cloth** 778. 飠 is a variant of **feed** 食 1322, here acting phonetically to express **rub** but of unclear semantic role. Thus to **rub with a cloth**, meaning to **polish/ make clean** and by extension to **beautify/ decorate**. Suggest taking 飠 literally as food/ **eat** 食 146 and **person** 人 39.

Mnemonic: **PERSON USES DECORATIVE CLOTH WHEN EATING**

1428

SHOKU, fu*reru*, sawa*ru*
TOUCH, FEEL, CONTACT
13 strokes

触手 SHOKUSHU   feeler
接触 SESSHOKU   contact
触れ合う FUREAU   contact

Formerly 觸 . 角 is **horn** 243. 蜀 is **caterpillar** 744 q.v., here acting phonetically to express **make contact** and also lending its own similar connotations. 1428 originally referred to **horns making contact** with something/ someone, i.e. **goring**. It still has this meaning in Chinese, including derived figurative meanings such as insult, arouse, etc. In Japanese also it can occasionally have connotations of conflict (in similar fashion to brush in the English term brush with the law etc.), but in general it has come to mean **make contact** in a much broader sense, including **feel** and **touch**. The modern form uses **insect** 虫 56 instead of caterpillar 蜀 .

Mnemonic: **TOUCHED HORNED INSECT -- UNFORGETTABLE FEEL!**

1429

SHOKU
REQUEST, ENTRUST
15 strokes

委嘱 ISHOKU   commission
嘱望 SHOKUBŌ   expectation
嘱託 SHOKUTAKU

                 commission

Formerly 囑 . 口 is **mouth**/ **say** 20. 屬/属 is **belong** 744 q.v., here acting phonetically to express **bring into contact**/ **join** and probably also lending its own connotations of **join**. Thus **verbally enjoin**, leading to **request, charge, entrust**, etc.

Mnemonic: **ENTRUSTED TO SAY WHAT BELONGS**

1430 辱

JOKU, hazuka*shimeru*
INSULT, HUMILIATE
10 strokes

侮辱 BUJOKU   insult
屈辱 KUTSUJOKU humiliation
雪辱 SETSUJOKU vindication

Clam(shell) 辰 366 q.v., here in its sense of **cutting tool**, and **hand**/ **measure** 寸 909 q.v., here meaning **careful use of the hand**. Thus **careful use of a cutting tool**, a reference to **using a scythe**/ **sickle**. Some scholars take **insult**/ **humiliate** to be a borrowing, but it seems equally if not more likely to be a figurative extension (cf. English cutting remark etc.).

Mnemonic: **HAND OUT INSULTS AS CUTTING AS CLAMSHELL**

1431

SHIN, no*biru/basu*
STRETCH, EXTEND
7 strokes

伸縮 SHINSHUKU elasticity
追伸 TSUISHIN postscript
背伸び SENOBI stretch on tiptoe

イ is **person** 39. 申 is **say** 322 q.v., here used phonetically to express **stretch**. 申 may also lend its own suggestion of stretching/ straightening through its early form 𦥑, which is actually a stylisation of a jagged bolt of lightning but looks very similar to hands 𦥑 straightening a stick ｜ (see hands straightening an arrow 寅 621, and see also 1439). Thus a **person stretching**, now **stretch/ extend** in a broad sense.

Mnemonic: **PERSON STRETCHES OUT WHAT HE HAS TO SAY**

1432

辛

SHIN, kara*i*, tsura*i*
SHARP, BITTER
7 strokes

辛苦 SHINKU hardship
辛味 KARAMI sharp taste
辛うじて KARŌJITE barely

Also written 𨐌, and earlier 𨐌 or 𨐌, and depicting a **tattooist's needle**. ∨ is an exaggeration of a barb, generally felt to be used symbolically to emphasise the idea of **piercing** but it should be noted that there appears to have been a type of needle used as an instrument of torture. This is usually found as a variant form 𨑒 or 𨑒 (e.g. see 1288). Both this variant form and the conventional tattooist's needle could symbolise **prisoners** and **slaves**, who were variously tortured and tattooed (e.g. see 318/ 340). 1432 also symbolised **sharpness** and by figurative association **bitterness**, both in the sense of taste and of hardship. Suggest taking 辛 as **stand** 立 73 and **ten/ needle** 十 33.

Mnemonic: **STAND ON TEN SHARP NEEDLES -- BITTER EXPERIENCE**

1433

SHIN, okas*u*
INVADE, VIOLATE
9 strokes

侵入 SHINNYŪ invasion
侵害 SHINGAI violation
侵略 SHINRYAKU aggression

Once written 𠈱, showing that 彐 is a simplification of **hand holding broom** 帚 96. 𠆢/イ is **person** 39. ⺕ is a further **hand**, presumably indicating sweeping with both hands though in reality redundant. Thus a **person sweeping**. **Invade/ violate** is taken by some scholars to be a borrowing, but it seems equally likely that the idea of sweeping led to that of moving gradually forward, which in turn led to **encroach** (still a strong meaning in Chinese) and hence **invade/ violate**. Suggest taking 彐 as **hand**, ⺕ as another **hand**, and ⺍ as **cover**.

Mnemonic: **INVADED BY PERSON WITH COVERED HANDS**

1434

SHIN, tsu
HARBOR, CROSSING
9 strokes

津津 SHINSHIN　　brimful
津波 TSUNAMI　　tidal wave
津津浦浦 TSUTSUURAURA
　　　　　　throughout the land

氵 is **water** 40, here meaning **river** or **body of water**. 聿 is **brush in hand** 993/ 142, here acting phonetically to express **advance** and possibly also lending its own similar connotations (from the movement of a hand when writing). Thus to **advance across water**, leading to **cross** and **crossing (place)**. In Japanese crossing also led by association to **harbor/ port**, from the idea of a safe stretch of water.

Mnemonic: **CROSS WATERS OF HARBOR, BRUSH IN HAND**

1435

SHIN, kuchibiru
LIP(S)
10 strokes

唇音 SHINON　　labial sound
口唇 KŌSHIN　　lips
紅唇 KŌSHIN　　red lips

Somewhat obscure, though its elements are clearly **mouth/ say** 口 20 and **clam** 辰 366. Some scholars feel that the latter acts phonetically to express **tremble** and also lends its own connotations of **closing**, thus giving **that part of the mouth which trembles and closes**, i.e. the **lips**. Other scholars feel that 1435 originally referred ideographically to the mouth of a clam, i.e. the edges of its shells and thus by association lips. The former theory is supported by the existence of the NGU character lip 脣 (to all intents and purposes interchangeable with 1435), which uses **meat/ of the body** 月 365. It is unlikely that this could mean mouth of a clam (though meat of a clam is a possibility), and it would seem to be the case that 辰 again acts phonetically to express **tremble** and also lends its own connotations of closing, to give that part of the body which trembles and closes.

Mnemonic: **LIPS SHUT MOUTH LIKE A CLAM**

1436

SHIN
PREGNANCY
10 strokes

妊娠 NINSHIN　　pregnancy
妊娠可能 NINSHINKANŌ　fertile
妊娠検査 NINSHINKENSA
　　　　　　pregnancy test

女 is **woman** 35. 辰 is **clam(shell)** 366, here acting phonetically to express **duplicate** and probably also lending its own connotations of a living thing contained within a casing. Thus **woman duplicating**, a reference to **pregnancy**.

Mnemonic: **PREGNANT WOMAN IS LIKE CLAM**

461

1437

SHIN, furi/ru/ruu
WAVE, SWING,
AIR, MANNER, AFTER
10 strokes

振動 SHINDŌ   swing
振り切る FURIKIRU   shake off
二年振り NINENBURI
             after two years

Of broad semantic evolution. 扌 is **hand** 32. 辰 is **clam/ cutting tool** 366 q.v., here acting phonetically to express **shake/ wave** and possibly also lending its own connotations of **swing** from the action of using a scythe. Thus to **shake/ swing/ wave the hands**, with the hand element later fading. **Air/ manner** (often in the sense of **pretense**) is felt to be an extended figurative meaning, from the idea of brandish (i.e. show off/ put on airs and graces). It is not clear how 1437 came to acquire the meaning of **after** (in the sense of something happening after a period of not happening), but this may possibly be an associated figurative meaning from the idea of rousing/ bringing about action after inertia.

Mnemonic: **WAVE CLAM IN HAND IN STRANGE MANNER**

1438

SHIN, hitasu/ru
SOAK, IMMERSE
10 strokes

浸食 SHINSHOKU   erosion
浸水 SHINSUI   inundation
水浸し MIZUBITASHI   flooding

氵 is **water** 40. 㑒 is the simplified **hands holding broom** seen in 1433 q.v., here acting phonetically to express **advance** and probably also lending similar connotations of its own. Thus **water advancing**, a reference to **flooding** and hence the associated meanings of **soak** and **immerse**. Suggest taking ヨ as **hand**, 又 as another **hand**, and 冖 as **cover**.

Mnemonic: **SOAK HANDS, COVERING THEM WITH WATER**

1439

紳

SHIN
GENTLEMAN, BELT
11 strokes

紳士 SHINSHI   gentleman
紳商 SHINSHŌ   rich merchant
紳士録 SHINSHIROKU
               Who's Who

糸 is **thread** 27, here meaning **cloth**. 申 is **say** 322, here acting phonetically to express **pull/stretch** and possibly also lending a similar suggestion through its early form 㑒 (see 1431). Thus **cloth which is pulled/ stretched**, a reference to a **waistband/ belt**. It later came to acquire associations with a **gentleman**.

Mnemonic: **FINE THREADS ON BELT SAY HE'S A GENTLEMAN**

1440 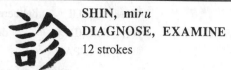 SHIN, mi*ru*
DIAGNOSE, EXAMINE
12 strokes

診断 SHINDAN   diagnosis
診察 SHINSATSU examination
往診 ŌSHIN   house call

言 is **words/ speak/ state** 274. 㐱 is a CO character meaning **hair**, being to all intents and purposes **hair** 彡 93 plus **person** 人 39. Here 㐱 acts phonetically to express **examine**, and may also lend loose suggestions of delicate and hence in (fine) detail (see 93). It is not clear whether 1440 originally meant to **examine someone's words** or, more likely, to **examine and then make a pronouncement** (i.e. diagnosis), but from a very early stage it became associated with a **medical examination**.

Mnemonic: **PERSON EXAMINED: DIAGNOSIS STATES TOO HAIRY**

1441 SHIN, ne*ru*/*kasu*
SLEEP, LIE DOWN
13 strokes

寝室 SHINSHITSU   bedroom
寝入る NEIRU   fall asleep
寝かし物 NEKASHIMONO
       unsold stock

宀 is **roof/ building** 28. 爿 is **(sick)bed** 1389, here indicating someone being 'laid up' with sickness (see also 381). 寻 is the simplified **hands holding broom** seen in 1433 q.v., here acting phonetically to express **cleanse** and also lending similar connotations of sweep away/ remove impurities. 1441 originally referred to a type of temple outbuilding where sick persons were laid to be cleansed of the evil spirit believed to be causing their sickness. It later came to mean **rest** or **lie down** in a broad sense, and is now also often used of **sleep**. Suggest taking 寻 as **hand** ヨ, another **hand** 又, and **cover** 冖.

Mnemonic: **SLEEP IN BUILDING, HANDS OUT OF BED-COVER**

1442 SHIN, tsutsushi*mu*
BE DISCREET, REFRAIN
13 strokes

慎重 SHINCHŌ   prudence
勤慎 KINSHIN   good conduct
慎み深い TSUTSUSHIMIBUKAI
       discreet

Formerly 愼. 忄 is **heart/ feelings** 147. 眞/真 is **true** 514 q.v., here acting phonetically to express **constrain/ restrain** and possibly also lending connotations of **proper** (or, less likely, **true**). Thus to (**act properly and?**) **restrain one's (true?) feelings**, i.e. **refrain**, with **be discreet** being an associated meaning.

Mnemonic: **DISCREETLY REFRAIN, MASKING TRUE FEELINGS**

1443

SHIN
JUDGE, INVESTIGATE
15 strokes

審議 SHINGI   deliberation
不議 FUSHIN   doubt
審判 SHINPAN
                judging, refereeing

宀 is roof/ **building** 28. 番 is **number** 196 q.v., here acting phonetically to express **know (thoroughly)** and possibly also lending connotations of **systematic/ in order**. Unlikely as it may seem, 1443 originally referred to having a **thorough (and systematic?) knowledge of a building**, later coming to mean **have a thorough knowledge** in general. **Judge** and **investigate** are associated meanings.

Mnemonic: **INVESTIGATE HOUSE NUMBERS PRIOR TO JUDGING**

1444

SHIN, furu*u/eru*
SHAKE, TREMBLE
15 strokes

地震 JISHIN   earthquake
身震い MIBURUI   trembling
震え声 FURUEGOE
                trembling voice

雨 is **rain** 3, here meaning **storm**. 辰 is **clam/ cutting tool** 366 q.v., here acting phonetically to express **shake/ wave/ tremble** and possibly also lending its own connotations of (swinging) movement from the action of using a scythe. 1444 originally referred to a **violent storm causing things to shake and sway**, then later came to mean **shake/ tremble/ sway** in a general sense.

Mnemonic: **RAIN MAKES CLAM SHAKE AND TREMBLE?!**

1445

SHIN, takigi, maki
FIREWOOD, KINDLING
16 strokes

薪炭 SHINTAN   fuel
薪小屋 TAKIGIGOYA woodshed
薪割り MAKIWARI
                woodchopping

新 is **new** 148 q.v., here in its original meaning of **chop down a tree/ chop wood**, with **plant** 艹 9 added to draw attention to the wood itself. It came to acquire connotations of small pieces of wood, i.e. **firewood/ kindling**, rather than timber/ lumber.

Mnemonic: **USE NEWLY CHOPPED PLANTS AS KINDLING**

1446

JIN, ha, yaiba
BLADE, SWORD
3 strokes

白 刃 HAKUJIN　drawn sword
刃 物 HAMONO　bladed object
両 刃 RYŌBA　　double blade

Sword 刀 181 with a **mark** ﹨ to indicate the **blade**. Note that the blade is on the <u>inside</u> edge of the sword, unlike the now famed katana which is also expressed by 181.

Mnemonic: **SWORD WITH MARKED BLADE**

1447

JIN, tsu*kiru*/*kusu*
USE UP, EXHAUST
6 strokes

尽 力 JINRYOKU　　　effort(s)
尽 未 来 JINMIRAI　　　forever
心 尽 く し KOKOROZUKUSHI care

Formerly 盡 and originally 盡. ⊿/皿 is **dish** 1307. 叓/聿 is **hand holding brush** (old form/ variant 聿 142), here acting phonetically to express **empty** and almost certainly also lending connotations of **soaking up**. **Fire** ⺗ 8 was added later, presumably to lend a supporting idea of **dry**. 1447 originally meant **dry and empty bowl**, with **use up/ exhaust** being an associated meaning. Suggest taking 尺 of the modern form as **person** 人 39 with **back-pack** ⊃, and ⫶ as a variant of **two** 二 61, with a play on the word **exhaust**.

Mnemonic: **PERSON EXHAUSTED BY CARRYING TWO BACK-PACKS**

1448

JIN, haya*i*
FAST, INTENSE
6 strokes

迅 速 JINSOKU　　rapidity
迅 雷 JINRAI　　thunderclap
奮 迅 FUNJIN　　great rage

辶 is **movement** 129. 卂 is an obscure element, once written 卂 and apparently comprising **bending person** ⺅ 39 and **needle/ ten** 十 33 but of unclear meaning. It is however known to act here phonetically to express **fast**, giving **fast movement**. **Intense** is an associated meaning. Suggest taking ㇈ as a **sprinter kneeling (at the blocks)**.

Mnemonic: **TEN KNEELING SPRINTERS, READY TO MOVE FAST**

1449 甚

JIN, hanaha*da[shii]*
GREAT(LY), EXTREME
9 strokes

甚 大 JINDAI na　　immense
甚 六 JINROKU　　dunce
幸 甚 KŌJIN　　very glad

A combination of **sweet** 甘 1093 (here 廿) and **match/ matched pair** 匹 1736. Unlikely as it may seem, **sweet matched pair** was a reference to a **pair of lovers**, and symbolised **great happiness**. Eventually **great** came to prevail over happiness.

Mnemonic: **SWEET MATCHED PAIR GREATLY IN LOVE**

1450 **JIN**
POSITION, CAMP
10 strokes

陣頭 JINTŌ　　　van of army
陣地 JINCHI　　　position
陣痛 JINTSŪ　　　labor pains

Hill 阝 229 and **vehicle** 車 31. **Vehicles drawn up around a hill** indicated an **army encampment** (see 466 and 540). Now also **position** in a broader sense.

Mnemonic: **VEHICLES POSITIONED AROUND HILL SHOW ARMY CAMP**

1451 尋 **JIN, tazu**neru, **hiro**
INQUIRE, NEXT,
USUAL, A FATHOM
12 strokes

尋問 JINMON　　　questioning
尋常 JINJŌ　　　normal
尋ね出す TAZUNEDASU seek out

Once written 𤔲. 㕛 is **right hand** 2. 彐 is a derivative of 𠂇, an old form of **left hand** 左 22. 㣽/寸 is **hand/ measure** 909, here also acting phonetically to express **stretch**. 1451 originally referred to the **span between two outstretched arms/ hands**, to give a measure of **one fathom** (six feet or 1.82 m. in Japan [as England] but an exaggerated eight feet in China: note the similar etymology of the English term fathom, which in Old English literally means the span of the arms). Outstretched arms also came to symbolise **making an appeal**, leading to **inquire/ ask**. **Usual** is felt to stem from the usual/ standard span of the arms (though ironically the Japanese and Chinese interpretations have been seen to differ). It is not clear how **next** evolved. Suggest taking 彐 as **hand**, 寸 as another **hand**, 口 as **opening** 20, and 工 as **work** 113.

Mnemonic: **INQUIRE ABOUT OPENING FOR WORKING HANDS**

1452 **SUI, fuk**u
BLOW, BREATHE OUT
7 strokes

鼓吹 KOSUI　　　advocacy
吹雪 FUBUKI*　　　snowstorm
吹き倒す FUKITAOSU blow down

口 is **mouth** 20 while 欠 is **lack** 471 q.v., here in its literal meaning of **gaping mouth**. 1452 is a somewhat vague ideograph indicating a **person letting out a big breath**, with **blow** being an associated meaning.

Mnemonic: **LACK MOUTH, BUT BREATHE AND BLOW NONETHELESS?**

466

1453 	SUI, taku COOK, BOIL 8 strokes	炊事 SUIJI	cooking
		飯炊き MESHITAKI	cook, maid
		自炊 JISUI	cooking for self

火 is **fire** 8. 欠 is **lack/ gaping mouth** 471 q.v., here acting phonetically to express **blow** (i.e. to all intents and purposes a simplification of blow 吹 1452 q.v.). 1453 referred to **blowing on a fire to make it flare up prior to cooking,** and thus by extension symbolised **cooking/ boiling.**

Mnemonic: **LACK FIRE, BUT COOK NONETHELESS?**

1454	SUI COMMANDER 9 strokes	統帥 TŌSUI supreme command
		元帥 GENSUI field marshal
		将帥 SHŌSUI commander

𠂤 has long been confused with **hill** 𠂤 (see 師 693, from which distinguish), but in fact old forms of 1454 such as  show it to be a **pair of hands** 𠂤 and a **stick** |. 巾 is **cloth** 778. 1454 originally referred to a **person waving a stick with a piece of cloth attached,** i.e. a **banner-waver** and by association **leader.** Suggest taking 𠂤 as **hill.**

Mnemonic: **COMMANDER CARRIES CLOTH BANNER UP HILL**

1455	SUI, iki PURE, ESSENCE, 'STYLE' 10 strokes	粋美 SUIBI	true beauty
		粋事 IKIGOTO	romance
		粋人 SUIJIN	man of taste,
			man about town

Formerly 粹. 米 is **rice** 201. 卒 is **soldier** 537, here acting phonetically to express **pure** but of unclear semantic role. Thus **pure rice,** later **pure/ quintessential** in a broader sense. From association with **essence** it also came to acquire connotations of knowing just the right thing to do, in particular in the sense of being worldlywise, and thus also came to mean **style** (as in the English to have style). Suggest taking 卆 as **nine** 九 12 and **ten** 十 33.

Mnemonic: **NINETEEN GRAINS OF PURE RICE**

467

1456　SUI, otoro*eru*　　衰弱 SUIJAKU　　debility
　　　WEAKEN, WANE　老衰 RŌSUI　　senility
　　　10 strokes　　　盛衰 SEISUI　　vicissitudes

Once written 衮, showing **clothing** 衣 / 衣 / 衣 420 and 朮. The latter shows two **plants** ⺀ (inverted variant 屮 9 or 生 42), here indicating **straw**, joined together ∩. Rather like thatching a roof, (inverted) straw was fashioned into a topcoat for keeping out rain and cold, and 1456 originally meant **straw raincoat**. This meaning is now conveyed by the NGU character 蓑, which adds plant 艹 9. Its present meaning of **weaken/ wane** results from borrowing. Suggest taking 口 as a **pierced** 一 **hole**/ opening 口 20.

Mnemonic: **CLOTHING WEAKENED AFTER HOLE PIERCED**

1457　SUI, *you*　　　麻酔 MASUI　　anesthesia
　　　DRUNK, DIZZY　酔払い YOPPARAI　drunkard
　　　11 strokes　　　船酔い FUNAYOI　seasickness

Formerly 醉, showing **wine jar**/ alcohol 酉 302 and soldier/ **end** 卒 537. The latter acts phonetically to express **finish** and probably lends its own similar connotations. Thus to **finish off a wine jar**, meaning to **become drunk**. In Japanese also **become dizzy** in a broader sense. Suggest taking 卆 as **nine** 九 12 and **ten** 十 33.

Mnemonic: **DRUNK AND DIZZY AFTER NINETEEN WINE JARS**

1458　SUI, tog*eru*, tsui　遂行 SUIKŌ　　attainment
　　　ATTAIN, FINALLY　未遂 MISUI no　attempted
　　　12 strokes　　　仕遂げる SHITOGERU accomplish

家 is an element meaning **(group of) pigs moving**. It comprises **pig** 豕 1670 and **away**/ **out of** ⼌ 66, to refer to the action of pigs when moving out of an enclosure, and often has connotations of pushing and jostling. Here the idea of movement is reinforced by **movement** ⻌ 129. Pigs moving in a group came to refer to **group movement** in general, especially in the sense of **attaining a goal through the brute force of the group** (not unlike the English term bulldoze one's way). Now **attain** in a general sense, with **finally** being an associated meaning. Suggest taking ⼌ in its meaning of **eight**.

Mnemonic: **EIGHT MOVING PIGS FINALLY ATTAIN GOAL**

1459　SUI, nemu*ru*　　睡眠 SUIMIN　　sleep
　　　SLEEP　　　熟睡 JUKUSUI　sound sleep
　　　13 strokes　　　午睡 GOSUI　nap, siesta

Eye 目 72 and **droop** 垂 907. **Droopy eyes** indicate **sleepiness** and hence **sleep**.

Mnemonic: **DROOPY EYES LEAD TO SLEEP**

1460		SUI, ho	穂状 SUIJŌ	spear shape
		EAR/ SPEAR (OF GRAIN)	稲穂 INAHO	ear of rice
		15 strokes	穂先 HOSAKI	spear

Formerly 穗. 禾 is **rice plant/ grain plant** 81. 心 is **heart** 147, here meaning **main part.** 叀 /甴 is spinning weight 914 q.v., here acting phonetically to express **hang** and also lending its own connotations of **hanging weight**. Thus **that which hangs heavily down from a grain plant and is its main part,** namely the **head/ ear/ spear**. Suggest taking 甴 as **ten** 十 33 and **field** 田 59.

Mnemonic: **HEARTENED BY EARS ON GRAIN PLANTS IN TEN FIELDS**

1461		SUI, tsumu, omori	紡錘 BŌSUI	spindle
		SPINDLE, SINKER	錘状 SUIJŌ	spindle shape
		16 strokes	丸錘 MARUOMORI	ball sinker

Metal 金 14 and **hang down** 垂 907, giving **metal object that hangs down,** i.e. **plumb-bob**, **spindle**, **sinker**, etc.

Mnemonic: **SINKER IS METAL OBJECT THAT HANGS DOWN**

1462	随	ZUI	随筆 ZUIHITSU	random notes
		FOLLOW, RANDOM	随行員 ZUIKŌIN	attendant
		12 strokes	随分 ZUIBUN	considerably

Formerly 隨. 辶 is **movement** 129. 隋 is a CO character now meaning both **fall** and **scraps of meat**. It comprises **hill** 阝 229 and an element meaning **falling scraps of meat** 肖 (meat 月 365 and [left] hand 左 22, to indicate scraps of meat falling from the hand). The combination of hill 阝 and falling scraps of meat 肴 indicates a hillside falling/ crumbling, i.e. a **landslide**, but clearly this meaning was eventually replaced by the meanings properly belonging to 肖 itself (i.e. with hill 阝 becoming redundant). Note that the addition of earth 土 60 gives fall/ landslide 墮 /堕 1539. In the case of 1462 隋 acts phonetically to express **follow**, and almost certainly also lends connotations of **unstoppable movement** from its literal meaning of landslide. Thus **move and follow (in unstoppable fashion).** On the one hand this has led to connotations of great momentum and inexorability, and on the other to doing what one wishes regardless, somewhat paradoxically often with its own connotations of acting in a capricious or desultory manner (thus giving **random**). Suggest taking 有 as **exist** 401.

Mnemonic: **MOVEMENT EXISTS TO FOLLOW HILLS AT RANDOM**

1463 **ZUI**
MARROW
19 strokes

骨 髄 KOTSUZUI bone marrow
脳 髄 NŌZUI   brain
真 髄 SHINZUI   essence

Of confused and somewhat obscure etymology. Formerly 髓, and in ancient times 骨隋 with an occasionally encountered variant 骨隋. 冎/骨 is **bone** 867. 阝/阝 is **hill** 229. 差 is a doubling of **left hand** 22. As an element 差 is obscure, but it seems most likely that 隋 is a variant or miscopying of **landslide/ fall/ scraps of meat** 隋 1462 q.v. In the case of 1463 隋/隋 acts phonetically to express **fat**, here meaning **fatty meat**, and almost certainly also lends connotations of **bits of meat**. Thus **fatty meat within the bones**, i.e. **marrow**. The modern form replaces **hill** 阝 with **movement** 辶 129, probably a miscopying under the influence of 随 1462. Suggest taking 有 as **exist** 401.

Mnemonic: **MARROW EXISTS IN MOVING BONES**

1464 **SŪ, toboso**
PIVOT, DOOR
8 strokes

枢 軸 SŪJIKU   axis
枢 要 SŪYŌ   importance
中 枢 CHŪSŪ   center, pivot

Formerly 樞. 木 is **tree/ wood** 69. 區/区 is **ward/ section** 465 q.v., here acting phonetically to express **important** and almost certainly also lending connotations of **hole** and **container** (since the elements of 區 can be reinterpreted as **opening/ hole** 口 20 and container 匚 225). 1464 originally referred to a **hole containing/seating an important shaft**, namely the **pivot** on which a certain type of **door** swung. It thus came to be used of the **pivot** itself, and occasionally also of **door**. As in the English term pivot, it has connotations of importance.

Mnemonic: **PIVOT IS IMPORTANT SECTION OF WOODEN DOOR**

1465 **SŪ, aga*meru***
LOFTY, NOBLE, REVERE
11 strokes

崇 拝 SŪHAI   worship
崇 高 SŪKŌna   sublime
崇 敬 SŪKEI   reverence

山 is **mountain** 24. 宗 is **religion** 889, here acting phonetically to express **duplicate/ layer** and also lending its connotations of **respect/ awe**. 1465 originally referred to a **tall mountain towering over others** (i.e. forming another layer of mountain). It is still occasionally found in this sense of **lofty peak**, but is usually found in a figurative sense of **something lofty and noble which inspires respect and awe**.

Mnemonic: **RELIGIOUSLY REVERE LOFTY MOUNTAIN**

1466

sueru/waru
SET, PLACE, SIT
11 strokes

据え置く SUEOKU   leave as is
据え物 SUEMONO   ornament
据え付け SUETSUKE   installation

扌 is **hand** 32. 居 is **be**/ reside 649 q.v., here with its literal meaning of **be fixed in a place**. Thus to **fix something in a place by hand**, i.e. **set**/ **place**, with **sit** being an associated meaning that overlooks the presence of hand 扌 (note that in English also set and sit are etymologically related).

Mnemonic: **SET SOMETHING DOWN WHERE HAND IS**

1467

sugi
CRYPTOMERIA, CEDAR
7 strokes

杉あや SUGIAYA   herringbone
杉垣 SUGIGAKI   cedar hedge
杉並木 SUGINAMIKI

               avenue of cedars

木 is **tree**/ wood 69. 彡 is (delicate) **hairs** 93, here acting phonetically to express **enduring** and also lending its shape to suggest **hair-like leaves**. Thus **enduring tree with hair-like leaves**, a reference to the **cedar**/ **cryptomeria**.

Mnemonic: **CEDAR IS TREE WITH HAIR-LIKE LEAVES**

1468 畝

se, une
RIDGE,
SQUARE MEASURE
10 strokes

畝立て UNEDATE   furrowing
二畝 NISE   two se
畝織り UNEORI   ribbed fabric

Formerly 畞, showing **field** 田 59, **lasting** 久 647, and what appears to be ten 十 33. 久 acts phonetically to express **ridge**, and may also lend connotations of permanence. The role of 十 is not clear, but it may possibly lend its shape to suggest intersecting paths. 1468 originally referred to the **ridges running through/ separating fields**. It later also came to be used of a **square measure** (presumably the area between ridges), specifically a standard 99.3 sq.m. in Japanese but of variable size in Chinese. Suggest taking 亠 as a symbol of **top**.

Mnemonic: **MEASURED FIELDS TOPPED BY LASTING RIDGES**

1469

se
SHALLOWS, RAPIDS
19 strokes

浅 瀬 ASASE   shoal, shallows
瀬 戸 SETO   strait, channel
瀬 戸 物 SETOMONO   porcelain

Formerly 瀨 . 氵 is **water/ river** 40. 賴/頼 is **rely/ request** 1889 q.v., here acting phonetically to express **fast** and probably also lending its connotations of **dividing**. Thus **where a river (divides and?) flows fast**, a reference to **shallows/ rapids**.

Mnemonic: **RELY ON WATER HAVING SHALLOWS**

1470

井

SEI, SHŌ, i
WELL
4 strokes

油 井 YUSEI   oil well
天 井 TENJŌ   ceiling
井 戸 IDO   well

From a pictograph of a **well crib/ well frame** 井. Once also written 丼, with ・ indicating water within the well, but 丼 is now a separate character meaning receptacle/ bowl (see 43).

Mnemonic: **WELL WITH FRAME**

1471

SEI, SHŌ
SURNAME
8 strokes

姓 名 SEIMEI   surname
改 姓 KAISEI   name change
百 姓 HYAKUSHŌ   farmer

Woman 女 35 and **birth** 生 42. Often interpreted as children being given (at birth) the family name of their mother rather than father, this practice being connected with an attempt to preserve the mother's lineage in a polygamous situation. There may have been some truth to this at some stage, but it seems more likely that 女 indicates **female children** rather than mother, since in ancient China it was generally only women who used a family name. Thus **that given a female child at birth**, i.e. a **family name**.

Mnemonic: **WOMAN GIVEN SURNAME AT BIRTH**

1472

SEI
SUBJUGATE, TRAVEL
8 strokes

征 服 SEIFUKU   subjugation
遠 征 ENSEI   expedition
征 衣 SEII   traveling clothes,
    military clothes

彳 is **movement (along a road)** 118. 正 is **proper** 41 q.v., here in its literal meaning of lower leg/ **foot**. Thus to **set foot on a road/ move off**. This can mean **travel** in a general sense, but has particular connotations of **setting forth on a military campaign**, with **subjugate** being an associated meaning.

Mnemonic: **MOVE OFF PROPERLY TO SUBJUGATE**

| 1473 | | SEI, hito*shii*
EQUAL, SIMILAR
8 strokes | 一斉 ISSEI all together
斉一 SEIITSU equality
斉唱 SEISHŌ singing in unison |

Formerly 齊 . The earliest form ᎒ᎶᎶ shows **similar heads of grain** (arranged for religious offering). The idea of similarity and belonging to the same category was reinforced by the addition of a symbol ニ , giving 𣪠 , which was later stylised to 𪗉 and eventually became 齊 . **Similarity/ equality** came to prevail over the original meaning of religious offering of grain. Suggest taking 文 as **text** 68 and 冎 as a 'partially eclipsed' **moon** 月 16.

Mnemonic: **TEXTS ABOUT LUNAR ECLIPSE ALL VERY SIMILAR**

| 1474 | | SEI
SACRIFICE
9 strokes | 犠牲者 GISEISHA victim
犠牲 IKENIE* live sacrifice
犠牲的 GISEITEKI self-sacrificing |

牛 is **cow/ bull** 97. 生 is **live** 42, here also acting phonetically to express **purify**. A **purified cow** was offered as a **live sacrifice**. Now **sacrifice** in a general sense. See also 1140.

Mnemonic: **SACRIFICE OF LIVE COW**

| 1475 | | SEI, yu*ku*
DIE, PASS ON, DEATH
10 strokes | 逝去 SEIKYO death
急逝 KYŪSEI sudden death
長逝 CHŌSEI death |

辶 is **movement** 129. 折 is **bend/ break** 522 q.v., here acting phonetically to express **sever** and also lending similar connotations of its own from its literal meaning of chop down. Thus a **movement that severs**, a reference to **passing on/ death**.

Mnemonic: **MOVEMENT BREAKS DOWN THROUGH DEATH**

| 1476 | | SEI, JŌ, m*oru*, saka*ru/n*
PROSPER,HEAP,SERVE
11 strokes | 全盛期 ZENSEIKI golden age
大盛り ŌMORI large helping
燃え盛る MOESAKARU flare up |

皿 is **dish** 1307. 成 is **become** 515 q.v., here acting phonetically to express **pile up** and probably also lending connotations of completion and by extension fullness. Thus a **piled up dish**, leading to **heap** and **serve** and by figurative association **grow/ prosper**.

Mnemonic: **SERVE HEAPED DISHES WHEN ONE BECOMES PROSPEROUS**

1477

SEI, muko
SON-IN-LAW
12 strokes

女婿 JOSEI　　　son-in-law
花婿 HANAMUKO bridegroom
婿入り MUKOIRI
　　　　　marrying heiress

Formerly also written 壻, i.e. with **male** 土/士 494 instead of **woman** 女 35. 胥 is a CO character with a range of confusing meanings, such as together, assist, wait, examine, distant, clerk, store, and minced crabs. Its etymology is unclear, though its elements are **meat**/ of the body 月 365 and **proper**/ lower leg 足 / 疋 41 (though technically the variant 疋 has become a separate NGU character now used as a cloth measure and animal counter). Here 胥 acts phonetically to express **partner**, but any semantic role is unclear. Thus 壻 means a **male who is a partner (for a woman)**, while 婿 means a **partner for a woman**, both being references to a **husband**. In particular it has come to mean husband viewed from the standpoint of the woman's parents, i.e. an adopted husband/ **son-in-law**.

Mnemonic: **MEATY SON-IN-LAW IS PROPER PARTNER FOR WOMAN**

1478

SEI, chika*u*
PLEDGE, VOW, OATH
14 strokes

誓約 SEIYAKU　　　pledge
宣誓 SENSEI　　　　oath
誓い言 CHIKAIGOTO　pledge

言 is **word** 274. 折 is bend/ **break** 522 q.v., here acting phonetically to express **cut/ sever** and also lending similar connotations of its own from its literal meaning of chop down. A **broken/ severed word** rather confusingly suggests the very opposite of a **pledge**, but in fact the character refers to the practice of **cutting a piece of wood in two as tallies** to be joined again upon completion of a (verbal) arrangement or similar (see 1195), and thus symbolises a **pledge**.

Mnemonic: **BROKEN WORD IS ACTUALLY A PLEDGE!**

1479

請

SEI, SHIN, k*ou*, u*keru*
REQUEST, UNDERTAKE
15 strokes

請求 SEIKYŪ　　　request
普請 FUSHIN　　construction
請負人 UKEOININ　contractor

言 is **word/ speak** 274. 青 is green/ **blue** 43, here acting phonetically to express **audience** but of unclear semantic role. 1479 originally referred to a **person requesting an audience**, and later came to mean **request** in a broader sense. **Undertake** is an associated meaning (cf. connotations of English tender [a bid etc.]).

Mnemonic: **EXPRESS REQUEST IN BLUE WORDS**

| 1480 | | **SEKI**, shirizo*keru* **REPEL, REJECT** 5 strokes | 排斥 HAISEKI boycott
斥候 SEKKŌ scout, patrol
斥力 SEKIRYOKU repulsive force |

Once written 庐 . 广 is **building** 114. 中 is **reverse** 646 q.v., here acting phonetically to express **empty** and probably also lending its connotations of opposite to normal. 1480 originally referred to an **empty building** (i.e. one normally occupied), and **repel/ reject** is a borrowed meaning. Suggest taking the modern form 斥 as **ax** 斤 1176 plus a down stroke ＼ indicating **coming down** (see 下 7).

Mnemonic: **REPELLED BY AX COMING DOWN**

| 1481 | | **SEKI, SHAKU, mukashi** **OLDEN TIMES, PAST** 8 strokes | 昔日 SEKIJITSU old days
昔風 MUKASHIFŪ oldstyle
今昔 KONJAKU past and present |

Once written 昔. ⊙/日 is **sun/ day** 62, while ≋ is an abstract symbol felt to express the idea of piling up/ **accumulating** (possibly originally some variant of mountains ⼭ 24). Thus **accumulation of days**, i.e. **history/ the past**. Suggest taking 昔 as a combination of **two tens** 十 33 and **one** — 1.

Mnemonic: **TWENTY-ONE DAYS AGO IS WELL IN THE PAST**

| 1482 | | **SEKI** **DIVIDE, ANALYSE** 8 strokes | 分析 BUNSEKI analysis
解析 KAISEKI analysis
析出 SEKISHUTSU eduction |

Tree/ wood 木 69 and **ax** 斤 1176, here with its connotations of **chop**. Thus to **chop up a tree/ wood**, leading to the idea of **reduce to small bits** and hence **divide** and by association **analyse**.

Mnemonic: **ANALYSE TREE BY CHOPPING AND DIVIDING WITH AX**

1483

SEKI
ONE OF A PAIR,
SHIP COUNTER
10 strokes

隻手 SEKISHU　　　　one arm
一隻 ISSEKI　　one ship/ boat
一隻眼 ISSEKIGAN discernment

Bird 隹 216 and **hand** 又. **A bird in the hand** indicated **one bird** (especially of a pair/ brace), as opposed to two birds in the hand/ pair 雙 / 双 1513 q.v., and 1483 has thus come to mean **one of a pair** in a broad sense. Also originally a counter for birds, though for some reason it has now become a **counter for ships/ boats** (possibly through a figurative reference to sails, which are frequently likened in poetry to wings).

Mnemonic: **ONLY ONE BIRD IN THE HAND**

1484

SEKI, o*shii*/*shimu*
REGRET, BE LOATH TO
11 strokes

痛惜 TSŪSEKI　　　deep regret
惜し気 OSHIGE　　　　　regret
骨惜しみ HONEOSHIMI
　　　　　　　　　sparing oneself

忄 is **heart/ feelings** 147. 昔 is **past** 1481, here acting phonetically to express **pierce** and possibly also lending connotations of the past. Thus **pierced heart** (over a matter in the past?), a somewhat vague reference to **feelings of regret**, with **reluctance/ being loath to** an associated meaning. Note that in the case of 1101 q.v. pierced heart means grieve/ be afflicted.

Mnemonic: **FEELINGS FOR THE PAST ARE FULL OF REGRET**

1485

SEKI, ato
TRACE, REMAINS
13 strokes

追跡 TSUISEKI　　　　pursuit
足跡 ASHIATO　　　footprint
遺跡 ISEKI　　　　　ruins

足 is **foot** 51, here meaning **footprint**. 亦 is again 212 q.v., here acting phonetically to express **accumulate** and probably also lending its own connotations of duplication. Thus **accumulation of footprints**, namely a trail, being the **traces/ remains** of someone's passing. Note that there is an NGU character 迹, i.e. using movement 辶 129 instead of foot 足, which is identical in pronunciation and meaning to 1485. Suggest taking 亦 as 'partly' red 赤 46.

Mnemonic: **THE ONLY REMAINS ARE A PARTLY RED FOOT**

1486  **SEKI** 書 籍 SHOSEKI publications
REGISTER 戸 籍 KOSEKI family register
20 strokes 国 籍 KOKUSEKI nationality

⺮ is **bamboo** 170. 耤 is a CO character meaning **rely on/ avail**. Its exact etymology is unclear, but it appears to comprise **past** 昔 1481 and serrated piece of wood/ tally/ **pledge** 耒 (tally 丰 659 and wood 木 69), and may mean literally a **pledge given in the past upon which one can rely**. (耒 may however be the variant of plow seen in 673, in which case its etymology is even less clear.) In the case of 1486 耤 acts phonetically to express **write**, and if taken to be pledge would almost certainly also lend connotations of a piece of wood on which something is written. Thus **bamboo for writing on**, a reference to **bamboo tablets used for keeping records,** with **register** being an extended meaning. Suggest taking 耒 as a **'heavily branched' tree** 木 69.

Mnemonic: **REGISTER OF BAMBOO AND BRANCHED TREES FROM PAST**

1487 **SETSU, tsutana***i*, **mazu***i* 拙 者 SESSHA I, me
CLUMSY, POOR 拙 劣 SETSURETSU na clumsy
8 strokes 拙 速 SESSOKU
rough-and-ready

扌 is **hand** 32. 出 is **put out** 34, here acting phonetically to express **clumsy** but of unclear semantic role. Thus **clumsy hand**, later **clumsy/ poor** in a broad sense.

Mnemonic: **PUT OUT A CLUMSY HAND**

1488 **SETSU, nusu***mu*, **hiso***ka* 窃 盗 SETTŌ theft
STEAL, STEALTHY 票 窃 HYŌSETSU plagiarism
9 strokes 窃 取 SESSHU theft

Formerly 竊 and in ancient times 竊 . 宀 / 穴 is **hole** 849, with ㅂ being an additional **hole/ opening** 20 to emphasise **depth** and by extension **secrecy**. 米 /釆 is **rice** 201/ 196. Thus 竊 indicates **rice (stored away) in a deep hole/ hidden place**. 禼/离 is a variant of **scorpion** 禼/萬 392, here acting phonetically to express **take** and almost certainly also lending connotations of **grasp/ clutch**. 1488 originally referred to **taking someone's stored rice**, then came to mean **steal** in general. **Stealthy** is an associated meaning (as in English). The modern form uses **cut** 切 156 as a simpler phonetic to express **take**, retaining **hole** 穴 .

Mnemonic: **STEALTHILY CUT HOLE TO STEAL CONTENTS**

477

| 1489 | SETSU
TAKE, ACT AS PROXY
13 strokes | 摂取 SESSHU intake
摂政 SESSHŌ regency, regent
摂生 SESSEI health care |

Formerly 攝. 扌 is **hand** 32. 聶 is a trebling of **ear** 耳 29, and forms an NGU character meaning whisper (i.e. something whispered to a succession of ears). Here 聶 acts phonetically to express **pull** but is of unclear semantic role. 1489 orginally referred to **pulling something out by hand**, later coming to mean **take out** and eventually just **take**. **Act as proxy** is an associated figurative meaning, from the idea of taking on a role/ duties. Though the use of the same elements of hand and ear as in **take** 取 301 is coincidental, this may be helpful in remembering 1489. Suggest taking ﹀ as **four marks**.

Mnemonic: **TAKE EAR IN HAND TO EARN FOUR MARKS**

| 1490 | SEN
HERMIT, WIZARD
5 strokes | 仙人 SENNIN hermit, wizard
酒仙 SHUSEN hard drinker
水仙 SUISEN narcissus |

A **person** 亻 39 who lives in the **mountains** 山 24, i.e. a **recluse/ hermit**, with **wizard** being an associated meaning.

Mnemonic: **HERMIT IS PERSON LIVING IN MOUNTAINS**

| 1491 | SEN, uranau, shimeru
DIVINE, OCCUPY
5 strokes | 独占 DOKUSEN monopoly
占い者 URANAISHA diviner
占めた SHIMETA Good! |

卜 is a variant of **divination (cracks)** 卜 91 q.v., while 口 is mouth/ **say** 20. Thus **that which is said by a diviner**, namely a prediction, symbolising **divining**. **Occupy** is a borrowed meaning.

Mnemonic: **TO DIVINE IS TO SAY WHAT CRACKS MEAN**

| 1492 扇 | SEN, ōgi, aogu
FAN
10 strokes | 扇子 SENSU (folding) fan
扇風機 SENPŪKI electric fan
扇形 ŌGIGATA/ SENKEI
fan shape |

Door 戸 108 and **wings** 羽 812. Thus the **wings of a door**, i.e. very similar etymologically to door/ gate 門 211 or (wings of a) door 扉 1730, but in this case used by association to refer to **flapping action** and **fan**.

Mnemonic: **WINGS OF DOOR ACT AS FAN**

1493 SEN   栓抜き SENNUKI   corkscrew
STOPPER, PLUG, TAP   給水栓 KYŪSUISEN   water tap
10 strokes   消火栓 SHŌKASEN   fire hydrant

木 is **wood** 69. 全 is **complete** 330, here also acting phonetically to express **insert**. Thus **wooden item inserted (into a hole), completely (filling it)**, i.e. a **bung/ stopper**. Now used of a range of stopping devices.

Mnemonic: **WOODEN STOPPER DOES JOB COMPLETELY**

1494 SEN   旋回 SENKAI   rotation
ROTATE, TURN   旋盤 SENBAN   lathe
11 strokes   周旋 SHŪSEN   mediation

疋 is the variant of **proper** 正 41 seen in 1477, here meaning **set foot (on a road)/ travel** from its literal meaning of lower leg (see also 1472). 㫃 is fluttering flag 333, here (unusually) acting phonetically to express **return** and possibly also lending a loose idea of **following**, from its associations with rallying under a banner. 1494 originally referred to **returning along a road** (still a meaning in Chinese), with **return** later coming to mean **turn** in a broad sense, including **rotate**. Suggest taking 㫃 as **person** ⺊ 39 and **side** 方 204.

Mnemonic: **PERSON TURNS PROPERLY ON SIDE**

1495 SEN, fumu   実践 JISSEN   practice
STEP, ACT   実践的 JISSENTEKI   practical
13 strokes   実践主義 JISSENSHUGI   activism

Formerly 踐 . 足 is **foot/ leg** 51. 戔 is a doubling of **halberd** 戈 493, here acting phonetically to express **tread** and possibly also lending an idea of **decisiveness** from its connotations of cutting (see also 750). Thus to **tread/ step (with the foot) (decisively?)**, later also to **take action** in a broader sense. Suggest taking 戔 as **halberd** 戈 and **two** 二 61.

Mnemonic: **FOOT STEPS ON TWO HALBERDS, LEADING TO ACTION**

1496	SEN, zuku PIG IRON 14 strokes	銑鉄 SENTETSU pig iron 銑鋼 SENKŌ pig iron 溶銑 YŌSEN molten iron

金 is metal 14. 先 is precede/ tip 49, here acting phonetically to express **dull gleam** and almost certainly also lending connotations of **prior** (i.e. prior to refining). Thus **metal with dull gleam (prior to refining?)**, a reference to **pig iron**.

Mnemonic: **METAL TIP OF PIG IRON**

1497	SEN, hisomu, moguru DIVE, LURK, HIDE 15 strokes	潜在 SENZAI latency 潜水 SENSUI diving 潜り込む MOGURIKOMU 'hole up'

Formerly 潛 . 氵 is **water** 40. 替 is **if/ supposing** 688, here acting phonetically to express **sink** and probably also lending connotations of **uncertainty**. Thus to **sink in water** (and thus become of uncertain whereabouts?). The meaning has now broadened to include the idea of **lurking/hiding**. Suggest taking 替 as **sun(light)** 日 62 and two **men** 夫 573.

Mnemonic: **TWO MEN DIVE INTO SUNLIT WATERS**

1498	SEN, utsuru SHIFT, MOVE, CHANGE 15 strokes	遷延 SENEN procrastination 変遷 HENSEN changes 遷化 SENGE death of dignitary

Once written 遷變. 墨 (also 褒) is a CO character meaning **soar on high/ go to heaven/ die**. 甶由/西 is the somewhat obscure element seen in 票 570 q.v., and as in 570 seems to lend a meaning of upper part and by extension **raised/ high**. 艸/大 is hands offering up, an element often used to indicate **raising** and by extension **height**. 乙/己 is **bending person** (see 45), with a variant form 褒 using curling person 己 768. It is not clear whether 己 / 己 depicts a **person offering** (from a position of humility) or, more likely, a **slumped person** (symbolising a **dead person**). Thus 墨 /褒 means to **raise/ rise to a height**, a reference to **dying and moving to heaven** (of dignitaries). 1498 emphasises the idea of **moving** by adding **movement** 辶/辶 129. Moving to heaven later came to mean **move to a high place/ climb** and eventually **move/ shift/ change** in a broader sense, though 1498 occasionally still reveals connotations of **dying**. Suggest taking 西 as **west** 152, 大 as a variant of **big** 大 53, and 己 as **self** 855.

Mnemonic: **MOVE ONESELF IN BIG SHIFT TO WEST**

1499		SEN, susu*meru*, komo **RECOMMEND, MAT** 16 strokes	推薦 SUISEN recommendation 薦骨 SENKOTSU sacrum 自薦 JISEN self-recommendation

艹 is **grass** 9. 鷹 is **fabulous beast between horse and deer** 1204, here acting as a rather elegant reference simply to **grazing beasts** and also lending its sound to express both **fresh** and **feast/ eat**. 1499 originally meant **fresh grass such as eaten (first) by grazing beasts**, and in Chinese still retains choice grazing grass as a minor meaning. Good/ selected grass led on the one hand to **grass mat** (now a minor meaning) and on the other to the idea of **selecting the best** in a broad sense, leading in turn to **recommend**. Suggest taking 庿 as a modified combination of **building** 广 114 and **west** 西 152, with .馬 as a 'short' variant of **horse** 馬 191.

Mnemonic: **SHORT HORSE RECOMMENDS GRASS MATS IN WESTERN BUILDING**

1500		SEN **FINE, SLENDER** 17 strokes	繊維 SENI fiber 繊細 SENSAI fine, delicate 繊毛 SENMŌ cilia, fine hair

Formerly 纖 . 糸 is **thread** 27. 韱 is a CO character meaning **wild onion/ leek**. 雀 is to all intents and purposes a variant of 韭 (also found simply as 韭), an NGU character similarly meaning **leek** (韭 deriving from a pictograph of a leafy leek and 艹 being **grass/ plant** 9). 戈 is **halberd/ lance** 493, here almost certainly lending connotations of **thrusting** and presumably also acting in some unclear phonetic role. Thus **leek that thrusts up** (from the ground). In the case of 1500 韱 acts phonetically to express **fine/ slender** and almost certainly lends similar connotations from the shape of the leek. Thus **fine, slender thread**, now **fine/ slender** in a general sense. Suggest taking the modern form as a combination of **red** 亦 (variant 赤 46), **one** 一 1, and **halberd** 戈 493.

Mnemonic: **CUT ONE SLENDER RED THREAD WITH HALBERD**

1501		SEN, aza*yaka* **FRESH, VIVID, CLEAR** 17 strokes	鮮魚 SENGYO fresh fish 鮮明 SENMEI na clear, vivid 朝鮮 CHŌSEN Korea

魚 is **fish** 98. 羊 is **sheep** 986, here lending its connotations of **fine**. Thus **fine fish**, a reference to **fresh fish** and hence **fresh** in general. **Clear/ vivid** is a borrowing.

Mnemonic: **SHEEP LIKES FISH TO BE FRESH**

1502 **ZEN**
ZEN, MEDITATION
13 strokes

座禅 ZAZEN　　meditation
禅宗 ZENSHŪ　　zen sect
禅寺 ZENDERA　　zen temple

Formerly 禪. 示/ネ is **altar/ of the gods** 695. 單/単 is **simple** 542 q.v., here acting phonetically to express **clear land** and possibly also lending a meaning of **simple**. 1502 originally referred to **clearing land in order to build a (simple?) altar**, and still retains this as a minor meaning in Chinese. The present meanings are felt by some scholars to be borrowed, but may in fact result from a reinterpretation of the character as an ideograph meaning **simple religion**, i.e. **zen** based on **meditation**.

Mnemonic: **ZEN ENTAILS SIMPLE MEDITATION AT ALTAR**

1503 漸 **ZEN**
GRADUAL ADVANCE
14 strokes

漸次 ZENJI　　gradually
漸進的 ZENSHINTEKI　gradual
東漸 TŌZEN eastwards advance

氵 is **water** 40, here meaning **river**. 斬 is behead 1311 q.v., which acts phonetically to express **advance** and presumably originally lent connotations of **rapidity** and/or **force**. 1503 was originally used as a proper noun to refer to a river in ancient China, probably one associated with flowing swiftly and powerfully. In time the assumed connotations of **rapid advance** became **gradual advance**, though the reasons for such a change are not clear. Suggest taking 斬 literally as **vehicle** 車 31 and **ax/ chop/ cleave** 斤 1176.

Mnemonic: **VEHICLE GRADUALLY ADVANCES, CLEAVING THROUGH WATER**

1504 **ZEN, tsukuro*u***
REPAIR, MEND
18 strokes

修繕 SHŪZEN　　repair(s)
修繕工 SHŪZENKŌ　repairman
繕い飾る TSUKUROIKAZARU
　　cover up, conceal error

糸 is **thread** 27, here meaning **clothes**. 善 is **good** 735, here also acting phonetically to express **repair**. Thus to **repair clothes and make them good (again)**, now **mend/ repair** in general.

Mnemonic: **MEND WITH GOOD THREAD**

482

1505

SO, haba*mu*
OBSTRUCT, HINDER
8 strokes

阻止 SOSHI — hindrance
阻外 SOGAI — obstruction
険阻 KENSO na — steep

阝 is **hill** 229. 且 is **furthermore** 1091 q.v., here with its literal meaning of **pile (up)**. Thus **piled up hills**, indicating a **hindrance/ obstruction** to travelers.

Mnemonic: **FURTHERMORE, HILL CAN BE A HINDRANCE**

1506

SO
LEVY, TITHE
10 strokes

租税 SOZEI — taxes, rates
租借 SOSHAKU — lease
租借権 SOSHAKKEN — leasehold

禾 is **rice plant** 81, here indicating **harvested rice**. 且 is **furthermore** 1091 q.v., here acting phonetically to express **pay** and almost certainly also lending its connotations of accumulate and hence **burden**. 1506 originally referred to **rice paid as a tithe**, and now means **levy/ tithe** in general.

Mnemonic: **FURTHERMORE, THERE IS A LEVY ON RICE**

1507

SO
PLACE, DISPOSE
11 strokes

措置 SOCHI — step, action
措辞 SOJI — phraseology
挙措 KYOSO — behavior

扌 is **hand** 32. 昔 is **past** 1481, here acting phonetically to express **dispose** but of unclear semantic role. Thus to **dispose of something with the hand**, meaning both physically **place** and figuratively **handle/ manage** (cf. English dispose).

Mnemonic: **HAND FROM PAST PLACED AT ONE'S DISPOSAL**

1508

粗

SO, ara*i*
COARSE, ROUGH
11 strokes

粗末 SOMATSU — coarseness
粗糖 SOTŌ — raw sugar
粗筋 ARASUJI — rough outline

米 is **rice** 201. 且 is **furthermore** 1091 q.v. here acting phonetically to express **neglect** and almost certainly also lending its connotations of accumulate. 1508 originally referred to (spilled) **rice left neglected** (in a corner of a storehouse), and later came to mean **poor quality/ coarse/ rough** in a broad sense.

Mnemonic: **FURTHERMORE, RICE IS COARSE**

1509

疎

SO, utoi/mu
DISTANT, SHUN,
COARSE
12 strokes

疎隔 SOKAKU   alienation
疎開者 SOKAISHA   evacuee
疎疎しい UTOUTOSHII unfriendly

Correctly written , as seen from an earlier form 疏, though 疏 is now technically a separate NGU character with identical readings and meanings. 足/正 is **foot** 51/41/ 1477, here (unusually) acting phonetically to express **emerge** and possibly also lending its connotations of movement. 㐬/流 is **child being born** 409. 1509 originally referred to a **child emerging from its mother**, indicating the moment of **parturition**. This later came to mean **(become) separate** in a broader sense, and for unclear reasons also came to acquire negative connotations such as **shunning**. **Coarse** is a borrowed meaning. The modern form uses **bundle** 束 1535.

Mnemonic: **SHUN COARSE BUNDLE AT ONE'S FEET**

1510

訴

SO, uttaeru
SUE, APPEAL
12 strokes

訴訟事件 SOSHŌJIKEN   lawsuit
告訴 KOKUSO   legal action
哀訴 AISO   appeal

言 is **word/ speak** 274. 斥 is **reject** 1480, here acting phonetically to express **appeal** (to a higher authority) and possibly also lending an idea of rejection. Thus to **appeal verbally** (following a rejection? / only to be rejected?), leading by association to **take legal action** in a general sense.

Mnemonic: **WORDS OF REJECTION LEAD ONE TO APPEAL AND SUE**

1511

塑

SO
MODEL, FIGURINE
13 strokes

塑像 SOZŌ   figure, figurine
彫塑 CHŌSO   plastic arts
可塑性 KASOSEI   plasticity

土 is **earth** 60, here meaning **clay**. 朔 is an NGU character meaning **new moon/ north**, comprising **moon** 月 16 and **inversion/ reversal** 屰 646 q.v.(here indicating change of form) to give **change of moon**. Here 朔 acts phonetically to express **model/ copy** and probably also lends connotations of change of form/ shape. Thus **clay model**, now **model** in a wider sense. Suggest remembering 屰 as a sign of **inversion**.

Mnemonic: **EARTHEN MODEL OF INVERTED MOON**

1512 SO, ishizue   礎石 SOSEKI foundation stone
FOUNDATION STONE   基礎 KISO   basis
18 strokes   基礎的 KISOTEKI   elementary

石 is **stone** 45. 楚 is an NGU character now meaning cane/ rod. It comprises **foot** 疋
51/ 41/ 1477 and a doubling of **tree** 木 69, and originally referred to the **foot of a tree**
(i.e. the lower part without branches, hence cane/ rod). Here it acts phonetically to express
place/ lay, and also lends a meaning of **foot of a wooden pillar**. Thus **stone laid at
the foot of a wooden pillar,** now **foundation stone** in general.

Mnemonic: **FOUNDATION STONE LAID AT FOOT OF TWO TREES**

1513  SŌ, futa-   双方 SŌHŌ   both sides
PAIR, BOTH   無双 MUSŌno   matchless
4 strokes   双子 FUTAGO   twins

Formerly 雙, showing **two birds** 隹 216 in a **hand** 又 (as opposed to one bird in a
hand 隻 1483). This came to represent **pair/ both** in a broad sense. The modern form
uses **two hands** 又.

Mnemonic: **PAIR OF HANDS MEANS BOTH HANDS**

1514 SŌ   壮大 SŌDAI   grandeur
MANLY, STRONG,   強壮 KYŌSŌ   robustness
GRAND, FERTILE   壮者 SŌSHA   man in prime
6 strokes

Formerly 壯. 爿/丬 is **bed** 1389, while 士 is **samurai/ male/ erect male organ**
494. Some scholars take 丬 to act phonetically to express **big**, and take 士 in its sense
of **male**, thus giving **big male** and hence **manly/ strong** etc. This is not convincing, especially in view of the existence of the CO character woman in bed 妝 (see 1406). While
丬 may express **big**, it almost certainly also lends its meaning of **bed**, and 士 almost certainly acts in its literal meaning of **erect male organ**. Thus **(big?) erect male organ
in bed,** a reference to copulation and by extension **virility/ fertility/ manliness** etc.
That is, it is a 'male equivalent' to woman in bed 妝.

Mnemonic: **MANLY SAMURAI IN BED**

1515 SŌ, SHŌ   荘厳 SŌGON   majesty
VILLA, MANOR,   荘園 SHŌEN   manor
SOLEMN, MAJESTIC   別荘 BESSŌ   country villa
9 strokes

Formerly 莊. 艹 is **grass** 9. 壮/壯 is manly/**fertile** 1514, here acting phonetically to express **keep in order** and also lending its connotations of **fertile**. Thus **place where grass is fertile but kept in order**, a reference to a **country estate/ manor**. It is not clear how 1515 also acquired the meanings of **majestic** and **solemn**, but it is possible that majestic was applied to a grand estate, with solemn then being a later associated meaning with majestic. Note that 1515 is occasionally interchanged with manly/ fertile 壮 1514, and in Chinese is also interchanged with make up/ adorn 粧 1406. Suggest taking 壯 literally as **samurai** 士 494 and **bed** 丬 1389.

Mnemonic: **SAMURAI BEDS DOWN IN MAJESTIC GRASSY MANOR**

1516   SŌ, sagas*u*   捜査 SŌSA   investigation
SEARCH   捜索 SŌSAKU   search
10 strokes   捜し出す SAGASHIDASU seek out

Formerly 搜. 叟 is an NGU character now borrowed to express old man, but it original-ly meant **search**. It derives from 叜, showing a **hand** 又 holding up a **torch/ fire** 火 8 inside a **building** 冖, and meant literally to **search for something by torchlight in a building**. **Hand** 扌 32 was added to emphasise holding the torch. Suggest taking 申 as **field** 田 59 and **stick** |.

Mnemonic: **SEARCHING HANDS PROBE FIELD WITH STICK**

1517   SŌ, sas*u*   挿入 SŌNYŪ   insertion
INSERT   挿話 SŌWA   episode
10 strokes   挿し絵 SASHIE   illustration

Formerly 插. 臿 is a CO character meaning **grind**, comprising **mortar** 臼 648 and **pestle** 千 (variant 午110). **Hand** 扌 32 was added to emphasise the idea of **thrust**-ing the pestle into the mortar, leading to **insert** in a general sense. Suggest taking 舌 as a combination of **thousand** 千 47 and sun/ **day** 日 62.

Mnemonic: **HAND INSERTS A THOUSAND ITEMS PER DAY**

1518 SŌ, kuwa
MULBERRY
10 strokes

桑園 SŌEN   mulberry farm
桑色 KUWAIRO   light yellow
桑畑 KUWABATA
             mulberry field

A stylised derivative of , a pictograph of a **mulberry bush**. Suggest taking 木 as **tree** 69 and 叒 as **three hands** 又.

Mnemonic: **THREE HANDS TEND MULBERRY TREE**

1519 SŌ, ha*ku*
SWEEP
11 strokes

掃除機 SŌJIKI   vacuum cleaner
一掃 ISSŌ   sweeping away
掃き出す HAKIDASU   sweep out

Hand holding broom 帚 96, with **hand** 扌 32 added to emphasise the action of **sweeping**.

Mnemonic: **HOLD BROOM IN TWO HANDS TO SWEEP**

1520 曹 SŌ, ZŌ
OFFICIAL, COMPANION
11 strokes

法曹 HŌSŌ   lawyer
軍曹 GUNSŌ   sergeant
曹司 ZŌSHI   cadet

Once written 朁. 日 is **say** 688. 棘 is a doubling of **east**/ **sack** 184 q.v., here acting phonetically to express **equal**/ **match** and also graphically lending an idea of **two**. 1520 originally referred to **two well matched people**/ **parties on opposed sides in a debate**, and thus became used of **lawyers**/ **legal officials** and later **official** in a broader sense. **Companion** is felt to be an associated meaning, from the idea of one's legal representative/ ally, but it probably also reflects the influence of the two sacks side by side 棘. Suggest taking 曹 as **two suns** 日 62 and a **'long'** version 廾 of **grass** 艹 9.

Mnemonic: **OFFICIAL SAYS DOUBLE SUN MAKES GRASS GROW LONG**

1521 SŌ, su
NEST
11 strokes

帰巣 KISŌ   homing
巣箱 SUBAKO   nesting box
巣立つ SUDATSU   leave nest

Formerly 巢. 木 is **tree** 69. 甾 derives from 甶, namely the old form of **basket** 由 399. Some scholars feel that 甾 also acts phonetically to express **gather**. Thus **basket in a tree (where [birds] gather?)**, namely a **nest**. Suggest taking 果 as **fruit (tree)** 627 and ⼩ as **three sticks**.

Mnemonic: **THREE STICKS ATOP FRUIT TREE FORM NEST**

487

1522 SŌ, mo
MOURN, LOSS, DEATH
12 strokes

喪失 SŌSHITSU   loss
喪服 MOFUKU mourning dress
喪中 MOCHŪ   in mourning

Somewhat obscure. Old forms such as 器 clearly show **die** ヒ / 亡 973 and **vessel** 哭/器 452 q.v. The latter is itself somewhat obscure, but is believed to show a **dog wheeling around open mouthed (i.e. barking) to face all quarters**. Thus 1522 appears to be an ideograph indicating a **dog acting frantically upon the death of its master**, later coming to mean **mourn** on the one hand and **loss/ death** on the other. Suggest taking 吅 as **ten** 十 33 and **two mouths** 口 20 (i.e. **twelve mouths**), and 𧘇 as a **'missing'** variant of **clothes** 衣 420.

Mnemonic: **TWELVE MOUTHS MOURN MISSING CLOTHES**

1523 SŌ, hōmuru
BURY
12 strokes

葬式 SŌSHIKI   funeral
葬儀屋 SŌGIYA   undertaker
葬歌 SŌKA   dirge

死 is **death** 286 q.v., here meaning **dead person**. 艹 is **grass** 9, while 廾 (formerly 𠦹) is also **grass**. Thus **surround/ cover a dead person with grass**, i.e. **bury** (originally a reference to covering the corpse with grass rather than interment in the ground, but now bury in a broad sense).

Mnemonic: **DEATH FOLLOWED BY BURIAL SURROUNDED BY GRASS**

1524 SŌ, SHŌ, yosōu
WEAR, CLOTHING, GEAR
12 strokes

装置 SŌCHI   device
衣装 ISHŌ   clothing
変装 HENSŌ   disguise

Formerly 裝. 衣 is **clothing** 420. 壯/壮 is **manly/ grand** 1514, here acting phonetically to express **wrap** and almost certainly also lending its meaning of **grand**. Thus **wrap (oneself) in (grand?) clothing**, i.e. **wear**. (Wear) clothing came by extension to mean **gear/ equipment** in a broad sense, including even mechanical devices. Suggest taking 壮 literally as **samurai** 士 494 and **bed** 丬 1389.

Mnemonic: **SAMURAI WEARS CLOTHES IN BED**

488

1525  SŌ

PRIEST

13 strokes

僧院 SŌIN monastery, temple

高僧 KŌSŌ high priest

僧職 SŌSHOKU priesthood

Formerly 僧. 亻 is **person** 39. 曾/曾 is **formerly**/ build up 741, here acting phonetically to express the first syllable of sangha, a Sanskrit word for **priest**. Since 1525 is of relatively recent origin 曾 may possibly also lend its later meaning of **formerly**. Thus **person who is a priest** (possibly priest-person who was formerly a lay person). Suggest taking 曾 as **away** ∨ 66, **field** 田 59, and **day** 日 62.

Mnemonic: **PERSON TAKEN AWAY DAILY FROM FIELD IS PRIEST**

1526 SŌ, a*u*

ENCOUNTER, MEET

14 strokes

遭遇 SŌGŪ encounter

遭難 SŌNAN accident

遭難信号 SŌNANSHINGŌ SOS

辶 is **movement** 129. 曹 is official/ **companion** 1520, here acting phonetically to express **meet**/ **encounter** and possibly also lending connotations of **falling in with**. Thus to **encounter while moving**, later **encounter**/ **meet** in a broader sense. Suggest remembering companion 曹 by association with **grass** 丗 (variant 艹 9) and (double) **sun** 日 62.

Mnemonic: **ENCOUNTER COMPANION MOVING ON SUNNY GRASS**

1527 SŌ

TANK, TUB, VAT

15 strokes

水槽 SUISŌ water tank

浴槽 YOKUSŌ bathtub

歯槽 SHISŌ tooth socket

木 is **wood** 69, here meaning **wooden item**. 曹 is official/ **companion** 1520 q.v., here acting phonetically to express **damaged grain** and possibly also lending loose connotations of **dumping** and/or **containing** from the double sack element 棘 in its early form 蕚. 1527 originally referred to a **wooden tub used for holding damaged grain**, but later came to mean **tub/ vat/ receptacle** in a broader sense. Suggest remembering companion 曹 by association with **grass** 丗 (variant 艹 9) and two **days** 日 62.

Mnemonic: **COMPANION SPENDS TWO DAYS IN WOODEN TUB ON GRASS**

489

1528		SŌ	乾燥 KANSŌ	dryness
		DRY, PARCH	焦燥 SHŌSŌ	impatience
		17 strokes	高燥地 KŌSŌKI	
				high and dry ground

火 is **fire** 8. 喿 is birds chirping in tree 922 q.v., here acting phonetically to express **dry** and possibly also lending loose connotations of intensity. Thus to **dry by fire**, later giving **dry/ parch** in a broad sense. Suggest taking 木 as **wood** 69 and 品 as **three boxes**.

Mnemonic: **DRY THREE WOODEN BOXES BY FIRE**

1529	霜	SŌ, shimo	霜害 SŌGAI	frost damage
		FROST	霜夜 SHIMOYO	frosty night
		17 strokes	霜降り肉 SHIMOFURINIKU	
				marbled beef

雨 is **rain** 3, here meaning loosely **moisture associated with weather**. 相 is **mutual** 530 q.v., here acting phonetically to express **freeze/ frozen** and possibly also lending a loose idea of appearance. Thus (the appearance of?) **frozen moisture**, i.e. **frost**.

Mnemonic: **MUTUAL RELATIONSHIP BETWEEN RAIN AND FROST?**

1530		SŌ, sawagu/gashii	騒音 SŌON	cacophony
		NOISE, DISTURBANCE	騒動 SŌDŌ	disturbance
		18 strokes	大騒ぎ ŌSAWAGI	uproar, chaos

Formerly 騷. 馬 is **horse** 191. 蚤 is an NGU character meaning **flea**, comprising **insect** 虫 56 and **hand** 又 (from 叉, and variant 又), and presumably meaning insect found on hand or insect squashed with hand/ fingers. In the case of 1530 蚤 acts phonetically to express **confusion** and also lends its connotations of **troublesome insect**. Thus **confusion caused by insect troubling horse**, now **noise/ disturbance** in general.

Mnemonic: **HAND SLAPS INSECT ON HORSE: DISTURBANCE FOLLOWS**

1531

SŌ, mo

WATERWEED, SEAWEED

19 strokes

藻抜け MONUKE　　cast off skin
海藻 KAISŌ　　　　seaweed
詞藻 SHISŌ rhetorical flourish

艹 is grass/ **plant 9.** 氵 is **water 40.** 喿 is birds chirping in tree 922, here acting phonetically to express **gather** and also lending similar connotations of its own. Thus **waterplant that gathers (in clusters)**, originally a reference to a particular type of **waterweed** but now also **waterweed/ seaweed** in a broader sense. Suggest taking 木 as **wood 69** and 品 as **three boxes.**

Mnemonic: **THREE WOODEN BOXES OF PLANTS ARE ALL WATERWEED**

1532

ZŌ, niku*mu*/*i*/*shimi*

HATE(FUL)

14 strokes

憎悪 ZŌO　　　　malice, hatred
憎らしい NIKURASHII　　hateful
憎み合う NIKUMIAU mutually hate

Formerly 憎. 忄 is **heart/ feelings 147.** 曾/曽 is formerly/ **build up 741** q.v., here acting phonetically to express **hatred** and almost certainly also lending its connotations of **accumulation.** Thus **(accumulated?) feelings of hatred.** Suggest taking 曽 as **away** 丷 **66, field** 田 **59, and day** 日 **62.**

Mnemonic: **FEEL HATE ON DAY FIELD TAKEN AWAY**

1533

ZŌ, SŌ, oku*ru*

PRESENT, GIVE

18 strokes

贈与 ZŌYO　　　　presentation
寄贈 KIZŌ/ KISŌ　　donation
贈り物 OKURIMONO　　present

Formerly 贈. 貝 is **shell/ money/ valuable item 90.** 曾/曽 is formerly/ **build up 741** q.v., here acting phonetically to express **send/ give** and almost certainly also lending its connotations of accumulation and hence **large volume.** Thus **send/ give (large volume of?) vaulable items,** later just **present/ give.** Suggest taking 曽 as **away** 丷 **66, field** 田 **59, and day** 日 **62.**

Mnemonic: **ONE DAY GIVE AWAY FIELD AND MONEY**

491

1534

SOKU, sunawa*chi*
IMMEDIATE, NAMELY,
ACCESSION
7 strokes

即位 SOKUI   enthronement
即刻 SOKKOKU   immediately
即席 SOKUSEKI   impromptu

Formerly 卽 and in ancient times 𠨐, showing **food** 豆 / 皀 / 良 / 食 146 and **kneeling/ bending person** 入 / 卩 39/ 425. 1534 originally referred to **taking one's place at the table**, later coming to mean take one's (rightful) place and thus **accede**. **Immediate** is felt to be an associated meaning from the idea of being prompt, while **namely** is felt to be an associated meaning from the idea of things being proper/ as they should be.

Mnemonic: **UPON ACCESSION PERSON IMMEDIATELY KNEELS BY FOOD**

1535

SOKU, taba*[neru]*, tsuka*[neru]*
BUNDLE, MANAGE
7 strokes

結束 KESSOKU   bond, union
花束 HANATABA   bouquet
束の間 TSUKANOMA   moment

An old form 朿 has led to the popular interpretation that 1535 originally depicted **trees** 木 / 木 69 being **bound together** ○. However, in view of the fact that only one tree is shown this is rather unconvincing. In fact, other old forms such as 㯂 suggest strongly that it is merely a variant of east/ **sack** 東 / 東 184 q.v. Putting things into a bundle led by figurative association to the idea of **handling/ managing**. Suggest taking 木 as **tree** and 口 as **box**.

Mnemonic: **MANAGE TO PUT BOX-LIKE BUNDLE IN TREE**

1536

SOKU, unaga*su*
URGE, PRESS
9 strokes

促進 SOKUSHIN   promotion
催促 SAISOKU   demand
促成 SOKUSEI
              growth, promotion

Of disputed etymology, though its elements are clearly **person** 亻 39 and **foot/ leg** 足 51. Some scholars feel that 足 acts phonetically to express **shorten/ compress** and also lends its meaning of **leg**, to give **person with short(ened) legs**. This later came to mean **be short/ make short** in general, with **press down** being an associated meaning that later led to **press** in a general sense. Opinion is then divided as to whether **urge** is a borrowed meaning or an associated figurative meaning with press. An alternative theory is that 足 is used in its associated sense of **set foot/ set off** (see 1494), giving **person setting off**, with **urge** and **press** being either associated or borrowed meanings.

Mnemonic: **PERSON URGED TO PRESS WITH FOOT**

492

1537  **ZOKU**
REBEL, PLUNDER,
INJURE
13 strokes

海賊 KAIZOKU — pirate
盗賊 TŌZOKU — thief
賊軍 ZOKUGUN — rebel army

Once written 賊, showing that 貝十 is a miscopying of rule 則 742 q.v., here acting phonetically to express **injure** and also lending its early connotations of **cutting**. 戈 is **halberd** 493, here meaning **cutting weapon**. Thus to **cut and injure with a weapon**, later also used to refer to a person associated with perpetrating such injuries, namely a **bandit** and by further association **rebel**. **Plunder** is another associated meaning. Suggest taking 貝 as shell/ **money** 90 and 十 as **ten** 33.

Mnemonic: **TEN REBELS WITH HALBERDS PLUNDER MONEY**

1538 **DA**
PEACE, SETTLED
7 strokes

妥当 DATŌ na — appropriate
妥協 DAKYŌ — compromise
妥結 DAKETSU — agreement

Of disputed etymology, though its elements are clearly **hand** (reaching down) 爫 303 and **woman** 女 35. Some scholars take 爫 to be a miscopying of **rice plant** 禾 81. That is, 1538 is taken to be a variant of entrust 委 423 q.v., whose literal meaning of **be soft and pliant** is felt to have led to the idea of **being peaceful and settled**. Other scholars take 爫 to act purely phonetically to express **soft and delicate**, giving **soft and delicate woman** and hence soft/ pliant and peaceful/ settled as above.

Mnemonic: **WOMAN'S HAND SYMBOLISES PEACE**

1539 **DA**
FALL(EN), DEGENERATE
12 strokes

堕落 DARAKU — depravity
堕胎 DATAI — abortion
堕落坊主 DARAKUBŌZU — apostate priest

Formerly 墮. 隋 is **fall/ landslide** 1462. **Earth** 土 60 was added after the original meaning of 隋 (i.e. landslide) became vague. However, landslide has now disappeared and 1539 has come to mean **fall/ slip** in a broad sense, but particularly in moral terms. Suggest taking 隋 as **hill** 阝 229 and **exist** 有 401.

Mnemonic: **EARTH FALLS BUT HILL STILL EXISTS**

1540	**DA** **LAZY, INERT** 12 strokes	惰力 DARYOKU inertia 怠惰 TAIDA laziness 惰気 DAKI indolence

忄 is heart/ **feelings** 147. 青 is fall 1462, here acting phonetically to express **listless** and probably also lending connotations of slumping and heaviness. Thus **listless feelings**, a reference to **laziness**, with **inertia** being an associated meaning. See also listless feelings/ laziness/ neglect 怠 1543. Suggest taking 青 as **left hand** 左 22 and **meat** 月 365.

Mnemonic: **FEEL LAZY AND EAT MEAT WITH LEFT HAND**

1541	**DA** **PACK-HORSE,** **POOR QUALITY** 14 strokes	駄物 DAMONO cheap goods 駄馬 DABA pack-horse 無駄 MUDA waste

Formerly also written 馱, which is technically the correct form. 馬 is **horse** 191, while 大 is **big** 53. The modern form uses **fat/ big** 太 164. **Big horse** was a reference to a **pack-horse**. Since this was not considered an especially valuable beast, 1541 also came to symbolise **poor quality/ cheap**.

Mnemonic: **FAT PACK-HORSE OF POOR QUALITY**

1542 耐	**TAI, ta**eru **ENDURE, BEAR** 9 strokes	耐久 TAIKYŪ endurance 耐火 TAIKA fireproof 耐え難い TAEGATAI unbearable

而 is **beard** 887. 寸 is **measure/ hand** 909 q.v., here meaning **careful use of the hand**. 1542 is a somewhat vague ideograph referring to **shaving off a beard**. This was a minor official punishment (the next grade being to shave the hair), and thus symbolised something **not too bad** and **bearable**. Suggest taking 而 as a **rake**.

Mnemonic: **CAN ONE BEAR TO PUT HAND ON RAKE?**

1543	**TAI, okota**ru, **nama**keru **BE LAZY, NEGLECT** 9 strokes	怠業 TAIGYŌ go-slow 怠け者 NAMAKEMONO idler 怠り勝ち OKOTARIGACHI neglectful

心 is heart/ **feelings** 147. 台 is **stand** 166, here acting phonetically to express **listless** but of unclear semantic role. Thus **listless feelings**, giving **laziness** and by association **neglect** (as opposed to listless feelings/ laziness/ inertia in the case of 惰 1540 q.v.).

Mnemonic: **FEEL TOO LAZY TO MOUNT THE STAND**

494

1544 胎	TAI WOMB 9 strokes	胎児 TAIJI	fetus
		受胎 JUTAI	conception
		胎盤 TAIBAN	placenta

月 is **flesh/ of the body** 365. 台 is **stand/ platform** 166, here acting phonetically to express **pregnancy** but of unclear semantic role. Thus **that part of the body associated with pregnancy**, i.e. the **womb**.

Mnemonic: **WOMB IS A SORT OF FLESHY PLATFORM**

1545 泰	TAI CALM, SERENE, BIG, THAI 10 strokes	泰然 TAIZEN	composure
		安泰 ANTAI	peace
		泰西 TAISEI	Occident

Obscure. Once written 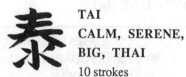, showing **big** 大 / 大 53, **hands** 𦥑, and **water** 氺 / 水 (old form/ variant 水 40). Some scholars believe that 大 acts phonetically to express **slip/ lose**, and that 1545 originally referred to **losing something while washing it** (i.e. have it slip from the hands). **Calm/ serene** and **big** are assumed to be borrowed meanings (though the presence of big 大 53 raises the possibility of some now unclear association), and the character has also been borrowed to refer to **Thailand**. In Chinese it can also mean extravagant/ liberal, which is similarly assumed to be a borrowing. Suggest taking 夫 as a combination of **two** 二 61 and **big man** 大 53.

Mnemonic: **TWO BIG THAI MEN SIT CALMLY BY WATER**

1546	TAI, fukuro BAG, POUCH 11 strokes	郵袋 YŪTAI	mailbag
		有袋類 YŪTAIRUI	marsupial
		手袋 TEBUKURO	gloves

衣 is **clothing** 420, here meaning **cloth**. 代 is **replace** 338, here acting phonetically to express **container** but of unclear semantic role. Thus **cloth container**, i.e. **bag/ pouch**.

Mnemonic: **REPLACE ONE'S CLOTHES WITH A BAG!?**

1547	TAI CHASE, SEIZE 11 strokes	逮捕 TAIHO	arrest
		逮捕者 TAIHOSHA	captor
		逮夜 TAIYA	(eve of)
			anniversary of death

辶 is **movement** 129. 隶 is a CO character now meaning fox cub. It was once written 𡱖, showing a **hand** ⺕ **seizing/ holding a tail** 木 (**hair** ⺿/毛 210, but here representing tail 尾 1734), and thus 隶 originally meant **seize an animal by the tail**. The addition of movement 辶 gives 1547 a meaning of **chase** and **seize**.

Mnemonic: **MOVE IN CHASE AND SEIZE TAIL BY HAND**

1548	TAI, ka*eru*/wa*ru* EXCHANGE, SWAP 12 strokes	代替 DAITAI	substitution
		両替え RYŌGAE	money changing
		取り替え TORIKAE	swapping

Somewhat obscure. Originally written 𣅀, showing **two standing men** 竝 (see **stand** 立 73) and **say** 𠙵/曰/日 688. The modern form uses two **men** 夫 573. It is not clear how these elements are used. Some scholars feel that 曰 acts phonetically to express **lean/ fall**, to give **falling persons** and by extension **fall/ collapse** in a general sense, with **exchange** being a borrowed meaning. Other scholars feel that 1548 ideographically referred to **one person speaking for another**, i.e. **in place of another**, with **exchange** deriving from **in place of**. The latter theory seems the more helpful. Suggest taking 曰 as **day** 62.

Mnemonic: **ONE DAY, ONE MAN EXCHANGED FOR ANOTHER**

1549 滞	TAI, todokō*ru* STOP, STAGNATE 13 strokes	滞在 TAIZAI	sojourn, stay
		停滞 TEITAI	stagnation
		滞納 TAINŌ	non-payment

Formerly 滯. 氵 is **water** 40. 帶/帯 is **belt** 539, here acting phonetically to express **stop** and almost certainly also lending its own connotations of contain/ restrict. 1549 originally referred to **a flow of water stopping**, and now means **stop/ stagnate** in a general sense.

Mnemonic: **USE BELT TO STOP WATER**

1550 taki

CASCADE, WATERFALL

13 strokes

清滝 KIYOTAKI clear cascade
滝川 TAKIGAWA rapids
華厳滝 KEGONDAKI
Kegon Falls

Formerly also written 瀧. 氵 is **water/ river** 40. 龍/竜 is **dragon** 1899, here acting phonetically to express **fall** and probably also lending connotations of **fearsome** and/or **flying**. Thus **(fearsome?) falling water/ river (that flies through the air?)**, i.e. **waterfall/ cascade**.

Mnemonic: **WATER-DRAGON LIVES IN WATERFALL**

1551 **TAKU**, era*bu*, yo*ru*

CHOOSE, SELECT

7 strokes

採択 SAITAKU adoption
選択 SENTAKU choice
選択科目 SENTAKUKAMOKU
elective subject

Formerly 擇. 扌 is **hand** 32, here meaning by extension **take in the hand**. 睪 is **watch over (file of) prisoners** 233 q.v., here acting phonetically to express **arrange** and probably also lending supporting connotations of putting in sequence. 1551 originally referred to **taking things in the hand and putting them in order**, then later came by association to mean **pick out by hand** and then **select** in a broad sense. Suggest taking 尺 as **person** 人 39 with **back-pack** コ.

Mnemonic: **PERSON CARRIES HANDY BACK-PACK**

1552 **TAKU**, sawa

MARSH, MOISTEN, MUCH, MANY, BENEFIT, GLISTEN

7 strokes

光沢 KŌTAKU luster
沢山 TAKUSAN much, many
沢地 SAWACHI marshland

Formerly 澤. 氵 is **water** 40. 睪 is **watch over (file of) prisoners** 233 q.v., here acting phonetically to express **confusion** and probably also lending an idea of stretching out in a line. 1552 originally referred to an **area where land and water became confused** (though the fact that it contains no element to indicate land is itself a source of confusion), i.e. **marshland** (where pools of water stretch out ahead? -- see 1333). Some scholars take **much/ many** to be a borrowed meaning, but in fact 1552 has long had connotations of much water/ many pools (especially in Japanese, where since classical times the word sawa has had a secondary meaning of many/ much). **Moisten** is an associated meaning, with **glisten** and **enrich/ benefit** being further associations (see also 1379). Suggest taking 尺 as **person** 人 39 with **back-pack** コ.

Mnemonic: **PERSON CARRIES PACK THROUGH WATER OF MARSH**

1553		**TAKU**	卓球 TAKKYŪ	table tennis
		TABLE, EXCEL, HIGH	卓越 TAKUETSU	excellent
		8 strokes	食卓 SHOKUTAKU	
				dining table

Obscure. The earliest form is 𣎼, but the meaning of this is unclear. Some scholars take 𠦝 to be **early** 早 50 q.v., and indeed it has been copied as such for many centuries, but the upward tilt of the lower cross-stroke(s) indicates that this is incorrect. It is more likely to be **sun** ⊙ / 日 62 and possibly **plant** 屮 (variant 屮 9), and may suggest the **sun rising high** (i.e. above the plants). Certainly 1553 has long had a core meaning of **high**, with **prominent/ excellent** being an associated meaning. The meaning of ﾄ / ト is unknown. At one stage it was written ⌂, suggesting a variant of slumped figure ヒ 238, and this has led to a theory that it indicated a lame person (reinforced by the fact that the pronunciation of 早 was the same as that of a word for cripple). Lame person is said to have symbolised leaning and unevenness, with the latter eventually leading by association to height. This does not seem at all convincing, though it is a theory favored by authoritative Japanese scholars. In any event, **table** is categorically a borrowed meaning. Specifically, 1553 was borrowed as a simpler version of the NGU character 棹. This combines high 卓 with wood 木 69 (here meaning wooden item) to give high wooden item, a reference to a table. Confusingly, while 棹 still means table in Chinese, in Japanese it now means oar/ pole. Suggest taking 早 as **early** and ト as a variant of **cracks** ト 91.

Mnemonic: **EXCELLENT TABLE CRACKED AT EARLY STAGE**

1554		**TAKU**	拓殖 TAKUSHOKU colonising
		RECLAIM, CLEAR, RUB	開拓 KAITAKU reclamation
		8 strokes	魚拓 GYOTAKU fish print

扌 is **hand** 32. 石 is **stone** 45, here also acting phonetically to express **remove**. Thus to **remove stones by hand**, i.e. **clear/ reclaim land**. From an early stage its elements were also interpreted as **remove by hand from stone**, a reference to **taking a rubbing from a stone inscription**, leading to **rub/ make a print** in a broader sense.

Mnemonic: **HAND PICKS UP STONES TO CLEAR LAND**

1555		**TAKU**	託宣 TAKUSEN	oracle
		ENTRUST, COMMIT	託送 TAKUSŌ	consignment
		10 strokes	委託 ITAKU	commission

言 is **words/ speak** 274. 乇 is plant taking root 928, here acting phonetically to express **commit/ entrust** and possibly also lending connotations of firmness. Thus (firmly?) **entrust verbally**, later **entrust/ commit** in a broad sense. Suggest taking 乇 as **seven** 七 30 and **top** ノ.

Mnemonic: **COMMIT SEVEN TOP WORDS TO MEMORY**

1556 **TAKU**
WASH, RINSE
17 strokes

洗濯 SENTAKU washing
洗濯機 SENTAKUKI washer
洗濯物 SENTAKUMONO laundry

氵 is **water** 40. 翟 is **bird's wings/ plumage** 216 (bird 隹 216 and wings 羽 812), here acting phonetically to express **beat** and probably also lending its own connotations of **beat/ flap**. Thus to **beat in water**, a reference to **washing** (clothes).

Mnemonic: **WASH BIRD'S WINGS IN WATER**

1557 **DAKU**
CONSENT, AGREE
15 strokes

受諾 JUDAKU acceptance
承諾 SHŌDAKU consent
快諾 KAIDAKU ready consent

若 is **young** 886 q.v., here in its original meaning of **compliant words/ agree**. **Words/ speak** 言 274 was added after 若 lost its original meaning.

Mnemonic: **AGREE WITH YOUNGSTER'S WORDS**

1558 **DAKU,** nigo*ru/su*
IMPURE, TURBID, VOICED
16 strokes

濁流 DAKURYŪ turbid stream
濁音 DAKUON voiced sound
濁り江 NIGORIE muddy creek

氵 is **water** 40. 蜀 is **caterpillar** 744, here acting phonetically to express **impure** and probably also lending connotations of **unpleasant**. Thus **(unpleasant?) impure water**. Also used of a **voiced** sound (cf. English thick). In Chinese it has much stronger connotations of unpleasantness, and its meanings include foul and corrupt.

Mnemonic: **TURBID WATER, FULL OF CATERPILLARS**

1559 但 tada*shi*, **TAN**
BUT, HOWEVER
7 strokes

但し書き TADASHIGAKI proviso
但し付き TADASHIZUKI condition
但島 TAJIMA* a place-name

Of convoluted etymology. 亻 is **person** 39. 旦 is **dawn** 929, here acting phonetically to express **naked** and probably also lending its own connotations of **expose**. Thus **naked man**, a reference to a person stripped of outward signs of rank and thus **merely a man**. **Merely** came to prevail as a meaning, leading eventually to merely in the sense of "the only thing is....", i.e. **but/ however** (cf. range of nuances of tada). Suggest taking 日 as **sun** 62 and 一 as **one** 1.

Mnemonic: **SUN SHINES ON ONE PERSON, BUT.... (HE'S NAKED!)**

499

1560 脱	**DATSU, nug*u*** **TAKE OFF, SHED, ESCAPE** 11 strokes	脱衣 DATSUI 脱皮 DAPPI 脱出 DASSHUTSU	undressing emergence escape

Formerly 脱. 月 is **flesh/ of the body** 365. 兌/兌 is exchange 524 q.v., here acting phonetically to express **lose** and probably also lending its own connotations of disperse. Thus to **lose flesh**. This was originally a reference to losing weight, but was also later applied by association to a range of **things leaving the body**, such as a child during parturition and clothes. **Escape** is also an associated meaning, from the extended idea of losing something in one's possession (i.e. expressed intransitively). Suggest taking 兌 as **elder brother** 兄 267 and away/ off ヽノ 66.

Mnemonic: **ELDER BROTHER TAKES CLOTHES OFF BODY AND ESCAPES**

1561	**DATSU, uba*u*** **SNATCH, CAPTIVATE** 14 strokes	奪取 DASSHU 奪回 DAKKAI 奪い去る UBAISARU	seizure recovery carry off

隹 is **bird** 216. 寸 is **hand/ measure** 909, here meaning **hand** (it is not clear why the simpler hand 又 was not used). 大 is **big** 53, here also acting phonetically to express **lose**. Thus to **lose a big (i.e. prized) bird from the hand**. This came to mean lose from the hand in general, and by association have something **snatched** from the hand. Now **snatch** in a broad sense, with **captivate** being an associated figurative meaning. Distinguish from 奮 966, and note the different etymology of 雀.

Mnemonic: **BIG BIRD IS SNATCHED FROM HAND**

1562	**tana** **SHELF, TRELLIS** 12 strokes	戸棚 TODANA 本棚 HONDANA ぶどう棚 BUDŌDANA	cupboard bookshelf grapevine trellis

Somewhat obscure. Formerly 棚 and earlier 棚. 米/木 is **wood/ tree** 69. 𢆡 is felt to show **strings of matching jewels** 丰 (see 102), the strings themselves also being attached to each other ろ, and to symbolise **matching**. (Note that 朋/朋 exists as an NGU character meaning match and by association companion.) In the case of 1562 𦰩/朋/朋 acts phonetically to express **join** and also lends its connotations of **matching**. Thus **matched and joined pieces of wood**, a reference to **trellis**. In Japanese it is also applied by association to **shelves**, whereas in Chinese it can mean a crude shed. The modern form uses two **moons** 月 16, almost certainly a miscopying but one that retains an idea of matching. Suggest taking 月 in its meaning of **month**.

Mnemonic: **TAKE TWO MONTHS TO PUT UP WOODEN SHELVES**

1563 丹 **TAN, ni**　　丹念 TANNEN　　diligence
RED, SINCERE　　丹精 TANSEI　　assiduity
4 strokes　　丹塗り NINURI　　painted red

Somewhat obscure. Originally 㲋, with a meaning of **red earth/ clay**, and believed to be a variant of **contents of well** 井 1470/ 43 q.v. but with the contents extended to clay rather than water. **Sincere** is a borrowed meaning. Suggest remembering 丹 by association with **boat** 舟 1354, taking it as 'half' a boat.

Mnemonic: **ONLY HALF THE BOAT IS RED**

1564 胆 **TAN, kimo**　　大胆 DAITAN　　bravery
LIVER, GALL, COURAGE　　胆石 TANSEKI　　gallstone
9 strokes　　落胆 RAKUTAN

discouragement

Formerly 膽. 月 is flesh/ **of the body** 365. 詹 is the obscure element seen in 擔/担 929 q.v., here acting phonetically to express **jar** but of unclear semantic role. Thus the **jar of the body**, a reference to the (jar shaped) **liver**. **Gall** is an associated meaning, while **courage** is a figurative association. As with 929, the modern form uses dawn 旦 (see 929) as a simple phonetic. Suggest taking this as **one** 一 1 **day** 日 62.

Mnemonic: **BODY NEEDS LIVER TO SURVIVE EVEN ONE DAY**

1565   **TAN, awai**　　淡水 TANSUI　　freshwater
PALE, LIGHT, FAINT　　淡色 TANSHOKU　　light color
11 strokes　　淡雪 AWAYUKI　　light snow

氵 is **water** 40. 炎 is **flame(s)** 1024 (literally a doubling of flame/ fire 火 8), here acting phonetically to express **plain** but of unclear semantic role. Thus **plain water**, i.e. water with nothing mixed in. While this may seem logically to suggest pure water, in fact it came rather to mean insipid and uninteresting (still meanings in Chinese), with **light/ faint/ pale** being associated meanings.

Mnemonic: **WATER ON FLAMES MAKES THEM FAINT AND PALE**

1566		TAN, nage*ku/kawashii* LAMENT, ADMIRE 13 strokes	嘆息 TANSOKU	sigh
			驚嘆 KYŌTAN	admiration
			嘆き叫ぶ NAGEKISAKEBU	wail

Formerly 嘆 . 口 is **mouth/ say** 20, here meaning **cry out**. 莫/𦰩 is the obscure element seen in 442 q.v., here acting phonetically to express **stifle** but of unclear semantic role. Thus **stifled cry**. This usually indicates a gasp of **despair** or **alarm**, but occasionally of **admiration**. Suggest taking 𦰩 as **man** 夫 573, **grass** ⺾ 9, and **hole** 口 20.

Mnemonic: **CRY OF LAMENT OVER MAN IN GRASSY HOLE**

1567		TAN, hashi, hata, ha EXTREMITY, EDGE, BIT, UPRIGHT 14 strokes	極端 KYOKUTAN	extreme
			端正 TANSEI	upright
			道端 MICHIBATA	roadside

立 is **stand** 73. 耑 is a CO character now borrowed to express **only**. Its etymology is unclear, but some scholars interpret an old form 耑 as a **bushy plant** growing vigorously, while others note the similarity of the lower half to beard 而/而 887, take 𠂉 to be flowing hair (see 173), and take 耑/耑 to mean **divided beard**. The bushy plant theory seems the more likely. In any event, in the case of 1567 耑 acts phonetically to express **upright** and may possibly also lend similar connotations of upright/ vertical (either from a plant growing upright or a beard hanging vertically). Thus **stand upright**, later **upright** in a broad sense including the moral one. The other meanings are borrowed. Suggest taking 山 as **mountain** 24 and 而 as a **rake**.

Mnemonic: **RAKE STANDS UPRIGHT ON EDGE OF MOUNTAIN**

1568		TAN BIRTH, DECEIVE 15 strokes	誕生日 TANJŌBI	birthday
			荒誕 KŌTAN	lie, nonsense
			降誕 KŌTAN	holy/royal birth

言 is **words** 274. 延 is **stretch/ extend** 814, here also acting phonetically to express **big**. Thus **big stretched words**, a reference to **bragging/ exaggeration** and hence **deception**. Its main modern meaning of **birth** is a borrowing, specifically being felt to derive from the term kōtan (see above). This originally meant to 'make a fuss'/ talk big about a holy/royal birth and thus established an association between 1568 and birth.

Mnemonic: **USE STRETCHED WORDS TO DECEIVE ABOUT BIRTH**

1569

TAN, kita*eru*
FORGE, TRAIN
17 strokes

鍛工所 TANKŌJO   smithy
鍛練 TANREN   forge, train
鍛金 TANKIN   beating gold

金 is **metal** 14. 段 is **step** 931 q.v., here acting phonetically to express **beat** and possibly also lending its own similar connotations. Thus to **beat metal**, i.e. **forge/ temper**, with **train** being an associated figurative meaning.

Mnemonic: **FORGING METAL IS A STEP IN ONE'S TRAINING**

1570

DAN, hi*ku*, hazu*mu*, **tama**
BULLET, SPRING, PLAY
12 strokes

弾薬 DANYAKU   ammunition
弾力 DANRYOKU   elasticity
弾き手 HIKITE   player

Formerly 彈 and in ancient times ଌ . ß /弓 is **bow** 836, here meaning by association **catapult**, while • shows a **small round object** used as a projectile. Later forms use **simple/ weapon** 單 / 単 542 q.v., here acting phonetically to express **small round object** and probably also lending its connotations of **weapon**. The action of **using a catapult** led to **spring** and by further association **pluck/ play** a stringed instrument, while **bullet** derives from projectile.

Mnemonic: **BULLET SPRINGS FORTH FROM SIMPLE BOW?!**

1571

DAN, TAN
STAGE, PLATFORM
16 strokes

花壇 KADAN   flower bed
壇場 DANJŌ   stage
土壇場 DOTANBA

         execution scaffold

土 is **earth/ ground** 60. 亶 is a CO character now meaning **indeed/ truly**, but its etymology is unclear. Its original meaning appears to have been **raised/ built up/ high**, and it is possibly a variant of **high/ watchtower** 髙 /高 119. Here it acts phonetically to express **high/ raised**, and possibly lends similar connotations of its own. Thus **raised earth/ ground**, leading to **stage** and **platform**. Suggest taking ⼇ as **top**, 回 as **rotate/ revolve** 86, 日 as **day** 62, and 一 as **one** 1.

Mnemonic: **EARTHY SHOW ONE DAY ATOP REVOLVING STAGE**

1572

恥

CHI, haji, ha*jiru/zukashii*
SHAME, ASHAMED
10 strokes

恥辱 CHIJOKU   disgrace
無恥 MUCHI   shamelessness
恥じ入る HAJIIRU   be ashamed

心 is **heart/ feelings** 147. 耳 is **ear** 29, here acting phonetically to express **shrink** but of unclear semantic role. Thus **shrinking heart**, a reference to **feeling ashamed** (cf. English feel small).

Mnemonic: **FEEL ASHAMED TO HAVE HEART NO BIGGER THAN EAR**

1573

致

CHI, ita*su*
DO, SEND, CAUSE
10 strokes

一致 ITCHI   unity, accord
致命的 CHIMEITEKI   fatal
致し方 ITASHIKATA   means

Once written 致, i.e. with **upturned foot** 夂 438 q.v. (here in its sense of **visit and stop**) rather than **striking hand/ coerce** 攵 101. 夂 is correct, as seen from an old form 𦥔 that shows person 人 39 and upturned foot 夂. 㐬/至 is **arrive/ reach** 875. 1573 originally referred to a **person reaching their destination and stopping**. However, the miscopying of 夂 as 攵 brought about causative connotations, giving **make someone visit** and hence **send**. As with send/ do 遣 1220 q.v., send broadened to **act/ do** in general. 1573 is also occasionally used to mean **cause**.

Mnemonic: **COERCIVELY SEND SOMEONE, WHO DOES ARRIVE**

1574

遅

CHI, oku*reru*, oso*i*
TARDY, SLOW, LATE
12 strokes

遅刻 CHIKOKU   lateness
遅遅 CHICHI   slowly
遅咲き OSOZAKI   late blooming

Formerly 遲. 辶 is **movement** 129. 犀 is an NGU character now used to mean rhinoceros. It comprises **tail** 尾 1734 and **cow** 牛 97, and originally referred to **bovine beasts** in general. Here it acts phonetically to express **slow**, and also lends similar connotations of its own (cf. English bovine). Thus **slow movement**. The modern form uses **sheep** 羊 986, primarily as a graphic simplification. Suggest taking 尸 as **corpse** 236.

Mnemonic: **MOVE LIKE A SHEEP'S CORPSE -- SLOWLY!**

504

1575

CHI
FOOLISH
13 strokes

白痴 HAKUCHI   idiot
愚痴 GUCHI   idle complaint
痴情 CHIJŌ   infatuation

Formerly 癡. 疒 is **illness** 381, here meaning affliction/ **impairment**. 疑 is **doubt** 835 q.v., here acting phonetically to express **slow(-witted)** and probably also lending its connotations of being in doubt/ dithering. Thus **impairment associated with slow-wittedness** (and dithering?), a reference to **stupidity/ foolishness**. The modern form uses **know** 知 169, giving **impaired knowledge**.

Mnemonic: **ILLNESS IMPAIRS KNOWLEDGE, LEAVES ONE FOOLISH**

1576

CHI
YOUNG, IMMATURE
13 strokes

稚魚 CHIGYO   fish fry
稚拙 CHISETSU   naivety
幼稚園 YŌCHIEN   kindergarten

禾 is **rice plant** 81. 隹 is **bird** 216, here acting phonetically to express **slow** but of unclear semantic role. 1576 originally referred to **rice that was slow to mature**, and later came to mean **immature** in general.

Mnemonic: **BIRD FINDS IMMATURE RICE**

1577

CHIKU
LIVESTOCK
10 strokes

家畜 KACHIKU   livestock
畜生 CHIKUSHŌ beast, Damn!
畜産 CHIKUSAN

                 stockbreeding

田 is **field** 59. 玄 is **occult** 1227 q.v., here acting phonetically to express **store/ accumulate** and possibly also lending connotations of mysterious (power). 1577 originally referred to **leaving a field fallow** in order for its fertility to be (mysteriously?) regenerated. Fallow fields were often used for **grazing**, and hence 1577 came to represent **livestock**. It still also retains connotations of accumulate/ regenerate, and is sometimes interchanged with accumulate 蓄 1579 q.v. Suggest remembering 玄 by association with **short thread** 幺 111.

Mnemonic: **LIVESTOCK TETHERED IN FIELD BY SHORT THREAD**

1578	**CHIKU,** *ou* **CHASE, PURSUE** 10 strokes	駆逐 KUCHIKU 逐一 CHIKUICHI 逐語的 CHIKUGOTEKI	driving off one by one literal

Move 辶 129 and **pig** 豕 1670, meaning to **pursue a pig** and later **pursue/ chase** in a broad sense. Distinguish 遂 1458, q.v.

Mnemonic: **MOVE IN PURSUIT OF PIG**

1579	**CHIKU,** *takuwaeru* **ACCUMULATE, STORE** 13 strokes	貯蓄 CHOCHIKU 蓄電 CHIKUDEN 蓄積 CHIKUSEKI	savings charging stockpiling, accumulation

蓄 is **livestock** 1577 q.v., here with its original connotations of **leaving a field fallow** in order to **regenerate**, with **grass/ plants** 艹 9 added to emphasise growth. The idea of regeneration gradually broadened, and 1579 came by association to mean **accumulate/ store** in general.

Mnemonic: **LIVESTOCK CONSUMES STORED GRASS**

1580	**CHITSU** **ORDER, STIPEND** 10 strokes	秩序 CHITSUJO 官秩 KANCHITSU 秩ろく CHITSUROKU	order, system official rank stipend

禾 is **rice plant** 81, here meaning harvested rice. 失 is **lose** 501, which acts here phonetically to express **arrange/ put in order** and probably originally also lent its meaning of lose. 1580 originally referred to **putting in order rice paid as a tithe** (i.e. rice 'lost' from the farmer's point of view), and eventually the idea of **putting in order** came to prevail. **Order/ rank** is now 1580's sole meaning in Chinese, but in Japanese it is also occasionally used in the sense of **stipend**, i.e. in effect reversing the assumed original viewpoint of donor to that of recipient.

Mnemonic: **LOSE RICE IN ORDERLY FASHION!?**

1581	**CHITSU** **BLOCK UP, PLUG** 11 strokes	窒死 CHISSHI 窒息 CHISSOKU 窒素 CHISSO	asphyxia suffocation nitrogen

穴 is **hole** 849. 至 is **reach** 875 q.v., here acting phonetically to express **block** and probably also lending connotations of cover a given area. Thus **block a hole**.

Mnemonic: **REACH INTO HOLE AND PLUG IT**

1582 **CHAKU**

LEGITIMATE HEIR

14 strokes

嫡子 CHAKUSHI legal heir

廃嫡 HAICHAKU disinherit

嫡妻 CHAKUSAI legal wife

女 is **woman** 35. 啇 is base/ starting point 755 q.v., here acting phonetically to express **dutiful** and probably also lending connotations of **appropriate**. An **(appropriately?) dutiful woman** refers to a **legitimate wife**, as opposed to a concubine. In Japanese 1582 has by extension now come mainly to mean **legitimate offspring**, and hence **heir**. Suggest taking 啇 as a combination of **emperor** 帝 1616 and **old** 古 109.

Mnemonic: **OLD EMPEROR'S WIFE PRODUCES LEGITIMATE HEIR**

1583 **CHŪ, oki**

OPEN SEA, SOAR

7 strokes

沖天 CHŪTEN ascendancy

沖合い OKIAI offshore

沖づり OKIZURI offshore fishing

氵 is **water** 40. 中 is **middle** 55, here acting phonetically to express **move/ be unsettled** and originally also lending a meaning of **middle**. 1583 originally referred to **unsettled waters in the middle** (of a channel). In Japanese it has now come to mean rather waters far from land, i.e. the **open sea**, whereas in Chinese the idea of moving/ distant waters has led to a range of extended and associated meanings such as seethe, be restless, wander, dash against, and **fly in the air/ soar** (from dash against). **Soar** is also occasionally found in Japanese.

Mnemonic: **WATER IN THE MIDDLE OF THE SEA IS OPEN WATER**

1584 **CHŪ**

PULL, DRAW OUT

8 strokes

抽出 CHŪSHUTSU extraction

抽象 CHŪSHŌ abstraction

抽せん CHŪSEN lottery

扌 is **hand** 32. 由 is **reason** 399 q.v., here acting phonetically to express **pull** and almost certainly also lending its early connotations of **from**. Thus **pull something by hand** (out from somewhere?), now **pull/ extract** in a broad sense.

Mnemonic: **THERE'S A REASON FOR PULLING BY HAND**

1585 CHŪ
INNER FEELINGS
9 strokes

折衷 SETCHŪ　　compromise
衷心 CHŪSHIN　　true feelings
苦衷 KUCHŪ　　anguish

Once written 裒, showing **clothing** 仌/衣/衣 420 and **middle/ inside** 中/中 55 (here 中). 1585 originally referred to **inner clothing**, i.e. **underwear**, and still retains this meaning in Chinese. However, it became confused with **loyalty/ inner feelings** 忠 936 q.v. (literally middle/ inner 中 and heart/ feelings 心 147), and came to acquire the meaning of **inner feelings** (but not necessarily loyalty).

Mnemonic: **INNER FEELINGS KEPT INSIDE ONE'S CLOTHES**

1586 CHŪ, *iru*
CAST, FOUND, MINT
15 strokes

鋳造 CHŪZŌ　　casting
鋳鉄 CHŪTETSU　　cast iron
鋳型 IGATA　　mold

Formerly 鑄. 金 is **metal** 14. 壽/寿 is **long life** 1351, though in fact 壽 is a longstanding miscopying of , which shows **hands** ㄓ彐 **inverting a vessel** 冂 and **pouring** 丸 (/ causing to flow: see also 1421) into another **vessel** 皿 1307. Thus to **pour out metal into a vessel**, i.e. **cast**.

Mnemonic: **CAST METAL HAS LONG LIFE**

1587 駐 CHŪ
STOP, STAY
15 strokes

駐車 CHŪSHA　　parking
駐在 CHŪZAI　　residence
駐日 CHŪNICHI
　　resident in Japan

馬 is **horse** 191. 主 is **master** 299 q.v., here acting phonetically to express **stop/ stay** and possibly also loosely lending similar connotations from its original depiction of a lamp which was generally fixed in one (central) place in a house. 1587 was originally a reference to a **horse stopping**, and later came to mean **stop/ stay** in a broader sense.

Mnemonic: **MASTER'S HORSE STOPS**

| 1588 |  | CHŌ, tomura*u*
MOURN
4 strokes | 敬弔 KEICHŌ condolence
弔問 CHŌMON sympathy call
弔い合戦 TOMURAIGASSEN
battle of revenge |

Obscure. The numerous early forms sometimes show a **snake coiled round a person**, as 夆 or 夆 (person 人 / 亻 39), and sometimes a **snake coiled round a stick**, as 弔 or 弔. It is not clear which is the very earliest form, and thus not clear if stick is a mis-copying of person or vice-versa. Some scholars have taken 1588 to be a variant of younger brother/ binding on a stake 東 /弟 177 q.v., but the 'binding' in the case of 1588 is cate-gorically a snake and thus any overlap between 1588 and 177 seems unlikely. Other schol-ars have assumed snake round person to be the older version, and take this to be an ideo-graph depicting a **person killed by a snake**, thus leading by association to **mourning**. Still others have similarly assumed snake round person to be the older form, but have taken the snake to indicate twisting, giving twisted person/ hunchback. Mourn is then assumed to be a borrowed meaning. The 'person/ man killed by snake' theory seems the most helpful.

Mnemonic: **MOURN MAN CRUSHED LIKE STICK BY TWISTING SNAKE**

| 1589 | | CHŌ, idom*u*
CHALLENGE, DEFY
9 strokes | 挑発 CHŌHATSU provocation
挑戦 CHŌSEN challenge
挑戦的 CHŌSENTEKI aggressive |

扌 is **hand** 32. 兆 is sign/ **trillion** 939, here acting phonetically to express **stir** but of un-clear semantic role. Thus **stir by hand**. Later stir in a figurative sense, i.e. **rouse**, with **challenge/ defy** being an associated meaning.

Mnemonic: **TRILLION HANDS RAISED IN DEFIANCE**

| 1590 | | CHŌ, hor*u*
CARVE, SCULPTURE
11 strokes | 彫刻 CHŌKOKU carving
彫像 CHŌZŌ sculpture
手彫り TEBORI hand carving |

彡 is **hairs** 93, q.v., here in its sense of delicate/ attractive and by extension **decorative/ patterned**. 周 is **around**/ circumference 504 q.v., here acting phonetically to express **cut/ carve** and possibly also lending connotations of all around. Thus **decorative/ pat-terned carving** (all around, i.e. three-dimensional?). Suggest taking 彡 as **three lines**.

Mnemonic: **THREE LINES CARVED AROUND SCULPTURE**

1591
CHŌ, naga*meru*
GAZE, LOOK
11 strokes

眺望 CHŌBŌ　　view, outlook
眺め NAGAME　　view
眺望絶景 CHŌBŌZEKKEI
　　　　　　fine view

目 is **eye** 72, here meaning **look**. 兆 is **sign/ trillion** 939, here acting phonetically to express **distance** but of unclear semantic role. Thus to **look into the distance**, i.e. **gaze**.

Mnemonic: **TRILLION EYES GAZING**

1592
CHŌ, tsu*ru/ri*
FISH, LURE, CHANGE
11 strokes

釣り場 TSURIBA　　fishing spot
釣魚 CHŌGYO　　fishing
釣り銭 TSURISEN　change, coin

金 is **metal** 14. 勺 is **ladle/ measure** 1342, here acting phonetically to express **catch/ snare** and almost certainly also lending its shape to suggest a **hook**. Thus to **catch with metal (hook)**, i.e. **fish**. Now also used to mean **lure/ trap** in a broad sense. It is not clear how it also came in later times to mean **change/ coin**.

Mnemonic: **FISH WITH LADLE-LIKE METAL HOOK**

1593
CHŌ, fuku*ramu/reru*
SWELL, BULGE
12 strokes

膨脹 BŌCHŌ　　expansion
脹れ面 FUKUREZURA　　pout
脹らし粉 FUKURASHIKO*
　　　　　　baking powder

月 is **flesh/ of the body** 365. 長 is **long** 173, here acting phonetically to express **swell** and probably also lending connotations of **stretch**. Thus **swollen (and stretched?) body**. This was originally a reference to a certain type of illness (and at one stage was written 痕, i.e. with the sickness radical 疒 381, which in Chinese is still interchangeable with 脹), but it later came to mean **swollen** in a broader sense.

Mnemonic: **BODY SWELLS A LONG WAY**

1594
CHŌ, koe*ru/su*
EXCEED, CROSS, SUPER-
12 strokes

超人 CHŌJIN　　superman
超過 CHŌKA　excess, surplus
入超 NYŪCHŌ imports excess

走 is **run** 161. 召 is **summon** 1387, here acting phonetically to express **leap high (in a dance)** and possibly also lending connotations of being requested (to dance). To **run and leap high** came by association to mean **go beyond a normal level** in a broad sense, including in the sense of **exceed** and of the prefix **super-**.

Mnemonic: **SUPERFAST RUNNER SUMMONED FOR EXCEEDING LIMIT**

1595

CHŌ, ha*neru*, to*bu*   跳躍 CHŌYAKU   spring, jump
SPRING, JUMP, LEAP   跳び板 TOBIITA   springboard
13 strokes   跳ね返る HANEKAERU   rebound

足 is foot/ leg 51. 兆 is sign/ **trillion** 939, here acting phonetically to express **leap high** but of unclear semantic role. Thus to **leap using the legs**, now **leap/ spring** in a broad sense.

Mnemonic: **TRILLION LEGS LEAPING**

1596

CHŌ, shirushi   象徴 SHŌCHŌ   symbol
SIGN, SUMMON, LEVY   徴収 CHŌSHŪ   levy
14 strokes   特徴 TOKUCHŌ   characteristic

Somewhat obscure. Formerly 徵 and earlier 徵 徵 is the early form of small/ **secretive** 㣲/ 微 1735 q.v., while 土 is a simplification of the early form 呈 of **person standing** (attentively) 壬 1610. The latter is believed to have also been used phonetically to express **reveal**, thus giving 1596 a meaning of **reveal something to a person in a secretive manner**, as by a **sign**. **Summon** is felt to derive from the associated idea of searching for a sign, which came to mean search/ seek in general and eventually by extension summon. **Levy** is then taken to be an associated meaning with summon. Suggest taking 彳 as **go** 118, 山 as **mountain** 24, 王 as **king** 5, and 攵 as coerce/ **force** 101.

Mnemonic: **SIGN FORCES KING TO GO TO MOUNTAIN**

1597

CHŌ, su*mu*/*masu*   清澄 SEICHŌ na   clear
CLEAR, SETTLE   澄み切る SUMIKIRU   be clear
15 strokes   澄まし顔 SUMASHIGAO

                                              smug look

氵 is **water/ river** 40. 登 is **climb** 360, here acting phonetically to express transparent/ **clear** and possibly also loosely lending a suggestion of upstream/ headwaters. Thus **clear water** (at head of river?), later **clear** in a broad sense. **Settled** is an associated meaning with clear.

Mnemonic: **WATER CLEARS AS ONE CLIMBS UP RIVER**

511

1598 聴 CHŌ, ki*ku*
LISTEN (CAREFULLY)
17 strokes

聴講 CHŌKŌ attending lecture
盗聴 TŌCHŌ wiretapping
聴心器 CHŌSHINKI stethoscope

Formerly 聽 . 耳 is **ear** 29, here meaning **listen**. 王 is **person standing still** (variant 壬 1610). Thus 聽 means **person standing still listening** (see also 911). 悳 /惪 is **virtue** 762. Thus **stand listening virtuously**, i.e. attentively, now **listen carefully** in a broader sense. Suggest taking 十 as **ten** 33, 罒 as **eye** 72, and 心 as **heart** 147.

Mnemonic: **EAR IS WORTH TEN EYES WHEN LISTENING TO HEART**

1599 CHŌ, ko*riru*/*rasu*
CHASTISE, LEARN
18 strokes

懲罰 CHŌBATSU punishment
懲戒 CHŌKAI reprimand
懲り懲り KORIKORI to one's cost

心 is **heart**/ feelings 147. 徵 is **sign** 1596, here acting phonetically to express **reform** and possibly also lending an idea of sign/ visible evidence. Thus to **reform in one's heart**, i.e. mend one's ways (publicly?). This suggested by association reforming after learning the error of one's old ways, and hence 1599 came to mean **learn** by some unfortunate experience. Probably because of the presence of the causative element 攵 (see 101), 1599 also came to mean cause to reform, i.e. **chastise**.

Mnemonic: **SIGN THAT CHASTISED HEART HAS LEARNED LESSON**

1600 勅 CHOKU
IMPERIAL EDICT
9 strokes

勅語 CHOKUGO imperial edict
勅旨 CHOKUSHI imperial will
勅任 CHOKUNIN
imperial appointment

Formerly 敕 , i.e. with strike/ **force**/ **cause** 攵 101 instead of strength/ **power** 力 74. 束 is **bundle**/ **manage** 1535, here acting phonetically to express **correct** as well as lending its meaning of **manage**. Thus to **manage a situation by making someone act correctly**. All **imperial pronouncements** were considered to be of this nature, i.e. of setting people on the right course.

Mnemonic: **IMPERIAL EDICTS COME IN POWERFUL BUNDLE**

1601

CHIN, shizumu/meru
SINK
7 strokes

沈没 CHINBOTSU sinking
沈滞 CHINTAI stagnation
沈下 CHINKA subsidence

氵 is **water** 40. 冗 is a CO character now meaning **move in**, but its original meaning was **hang down** (etymology unclear, but originally written 冘, suggesting a bending person 几 39 and what is possibly a symbol of drooping/ hanging 冂). Thus to **hang down in the water**, i.e. to **sink**. Suggest taking 冗 as **big man** 大 53 with **broken arms** 冖 and **broken leg** 乚.

Mnemonic: **BIG MAN WITH BROKEN ARMS AND LEG SINKS IN WATER**

1602

CHIN, mezurashii
RARE, CURIOUS
9 strokes

珍奇 CHINKI na novel, rare
珍品 CHINPIN rarity, curio
珍本 CHINPON rare book

王 is **jewel** 102. 㐱 is **person and hair** 1440 (person 人 39 and delicate hairs 彡 93 q.v.), here acting phonetically to express pure/ **unblemished** and probably also lending connotations of **attractive** from its delicate hairs element 彡. Thus an **(attractive?) unblemished jewel**, which was a relatively **rare** item. Now **rare/ curious** in general.

Mnemonic: **PERSON HAS RARE JEWEL WITH CURIOUS HAIR-LIKE PATTERN**

1603

CHIN
(ROYAL) WE
10 strokes

朕 CHIN We
朕の CHIN no Our
朕徳 CHINTOKU Our virtue

Formerly 朕. The oldest form 月朕 shows that 月 is derived from **boat** 月/舟 1354 and that 关 is derived from **two hands** 廾 **holding up an item** ｜. The latter is believed by some scholars to be a spigot or tool, and by others to be a pestle, but in any event 廾 is known to have had a core meaning of **work with the hands** and strong connotations both of **raising** and **repetitiveness**/ continuity. The original meaning of 1603 was to **repair a boat**, but it was later borrowed as a **first person pronoun**, and in practice is now almost exclusively used as a **royal 'we'**. Suggest taking 月 as **flesh/ (of the) body** 365 and 关 as **from/ out of** ⺲ 66 **heaven** 天 58.

Mnemonic: **OUR ROYAL BODY DESCENDS FROM HEAVEN**

1604		**CHIN** **STATE, SHOW, OLD** 11 strokes	陳情 CHINJŌ　　　　petition 陳列 CHINRETSU　exhibition 新陳代謝 SHINCHINTAISHA 　　　　renewal, metabolism

阝 is **hill** 229, here meaning **mound of earth**. 東 is **east** 184, here acting phonetically to express **encircling embankment** but of unclear semantic role. 1604 originally referred to the **raised earthen path around a field** (and still has a minor meaning of path in Chinese). **Raised** gradually led by association to **show/ expose**, with **express/ state** being a further association (though some scholars feel these meanings are borrowed). It is not clear how the meaning of **old/ of long standing** was acquired, but it may relate to an idea of permanence possibly attributed to such ridges (see 1468).

Mnemonic: **STATEMENT SHOWS EASTERN HILLS ARE OLD**

1605		**CHIN, shizu*maru/meru*** **CALM, SUPPRESS,** **WEIGHT** 18 strokes	鎮痛剤 CHINTSŪZAI　painkiller 鎮静 CHINSEI　　calm, quiet 文鎮 BUNCHIN　paperweight

Formerly 鎭. 金 is **metal** 14. 眞/真 is **true** 514 q.v., here acting phonetically to express **heavy** and almost certainly also lending its early meaning of **upside-down**. 1605 originally meant **(inverted?) heavy metal weight**, leading by association to **press down** and hence the figurative meanings of **suppress** and **quieten/ calm**.

Mnemonic: **SUPPRESS WITH TRULY HEAVY METAL WEIGHT**

1606		**TSUI** **FALL** 15 strokes	墜落 TSUIRAKU　　　　fall 撃墜 GEKITSUI shooting down 墜死 TSUISHI　falling to death

隊 is **corps/ unit** 540 q.v., here with its original meaning of **fall down a hill** reinforced by earth/ **ground** 土 60. Now **fall** in a broader sense.

Mnemonic: **CORPS FALLS TO GROUND**

1607		**tsuka, CHŌ** **MOUND, TUMULUS** 12 strokes	貝塚 KAIZUKA　shell mound 塚穴 TSUKAANA　　　　grave 宝塚 TAKARAZUKA 　　　　place-name

Formerly also 塚. 土 is **earth** 60. 冖 is roof/ **cover** (variant 冖 28), here meaning **cover**. 豕/家 is **pig** 1670, here acting phonetically to express **pile** but of unclear semantic role. Thus **pile of earth that covers**, i.e. a **tumulus**.

Mnemonic: **EARTHEN MOUND COVERS PIG**

1608		tsu*karu/keru*, SHI PICKLE, SOAK 14 strokes	漬け物 TSUKEMONO	pickles
			茶漬け CHAZUKE	tea on rice
			塩漬け SHIOZUKE	salting

氵 is **water/ liquid** 40. 責 is **blame** 728 q.v., here acting phonetically to express **build up** and possibly also lending similar connotations of **accumulate**. Thus to **build up in water/ liquid**, a reference to leaving layers of items to **soak/ pickle**.

Mnemonic: **TAKE BLAME FOR WATERY PICKLES**

1609		tsubo, HEI TSUBO, SQUARE MEASURE 8 strokes	建坪 TATETSUBO	floor space
			五坪 GOTSUBO	five tsubo
			坪数 TSUBOSŪ	area

Ground 土 60 and **flat/ level** 平 388, giving **level ground**. In Chinese this is 1609's only meaning, but in Japanese it has come to be used principally to refer to a **tsubo**, a **square measure** of 3.31 sq.m.

Mnemonic: **TSUBO IS MEASURED ON FLAT GROUND**

1610	廷	TEI COURT, GOVERNMENT OFFICE 7 strokes	宮廷 KYŪTEI	court
			法廷 HŌTEI	law court
			廷臣 TEISHIN	courtier

廴 is **movement** 129. 壬 is a CO character now borrowed for a range of meanings such as artful and great, but it derives from 𡈼, showing a **person** 人 39 **standing** (still) on the **ground** 土 60. Thus **move to (take up) a standing position on the ground**, a rather vague reference to people at **court** moving to take up their designated position as the emperor appeared. Suggest taking 壬 as a **hatted** ノ **samurai** 士 494.

Mnemonic: **HATTED SAMURAI MOVES TO COURT**

1611		TEI PRESENT, OFFER 7 strokes	呈上 TEIJŌ	presentation
			贈呈 ZŌTEI	donation
			進呈 SHINTEI	presentation

Formerly 呈. 口 is **mouth/ say** 20. 壬 is **person standing** (at court) 1610, here acting phonetically to express **reveal** and also lending connotations of a person in the presence of a dignitary. 1611 originally referred to a **person giving a revealing (i.e. detailed) verbal statement** to a dignitary, i.e. **presenting a report**, but now means **present/ offer** in a broad sense. Suggest taking 王 as **king** 5.

Mnemonic: **PRESENT ITEM FOR KING'S MOUTH**

1612	TEI **RESIST, MATCH** 8 strokes	抵抗 TEIKŌ	resistance
		抵当 TEITŌ	mortgage
		大抵 TAITEI	generally

扌 is **hand** 32. 氏 is **bottom of hill** 548, here acting phonetically to express **push back** (with equal force) but of unclear semantic role. Thus **to push back with the hand**, leading to **resist** and **match/ prove equal**. Suggest taking 氏 as **clan** 氏 495 and **one** 一 1.

Mnemonic: **RESIST CLAN WITH ONE HAND**

1613	TEI **MANSION, RESIDENCE** 8 strokes	邸宅 TEITAKU	mansion
		邸内 TEINAI	premises
		官邸 KANTEI	official residence

Of confusing etymology. 阝 is **village** 355, felt by some scholars to be used here in an extended sense of metropolis/capital (i.e. as an abbreviation of capital 都 355) and by others to indicate person from a village. 氏 is **bottom of hill** 548, here acting phonetically to express **reside** and also lending an idea of **house at the bottom of a hill** (see 548). Normally a house at the bottom of a hill was associated with a commoner, while a house on a hilltop was associated with a noble (see 99 and 548). Confusingly, however, some low ranking provincial nobles (i.e. those from villages) were unable to secure hilltop residences in the capital, and were thus obliged to live in houses at the bottom of hills. 1613 originally referred to such a residence, i.e.**'townhouse'** (at the foot of a hill) where a low ranking provincial noble resided when in the capital. In Chinese it can still mean **noble's townhouse in the capital**, while in Japanese it has come to mean **residence** in a broader sense, usually of a reasonably impressive nature such as a **mansion**. Suggest taking 氏 as **clan** 氏 495 and **one** 一 1.

Mnemonic: **CLAN LIVES IN ONE MANSION IN VILLAGE**

1614 亭	TEI **PAVILION, INN** 9 strokes	亭主 TEISHU	host, husband
		旅亭 RYOTEI	inn
		料亭 RYŌTEI	restaurant

亠 is a simplification of **tall** 高 119 q.v., here with its connotations of **tall edifice/ building**. 丁 is **exact/ nail** 346, here acting phonetically to express **stay/ stop**. Thus **tall (/large) building where people stay**, a reference to an **inn**. **Pavilion** is an associated meaning.

Mnemonic: **NAIL SUPPORTS TALL PAVILION**

516

1615 **TEI**

CHASTITY, VIRTUE

9 strokes

貞操 TEISŌ   chastity

貞節 TEISETSU   chastity

貞実 TEIJITSU   fidelity

Once written 鼑 . 卜 is a variant of **divination (crack)** 卜 91. 鼑 / 貝 is a simplified **round kettle** 鼎 228, here acting phonetically to express **request/ seek** but of unclear semantic role. 1615 originally referred to **seeking to learn the will of the gods by means of divination**, and can still have this meaning in Chinese. Some scholars feel that **chastity/ virtue** is a borrowed meaning, while others see it as an extended meaning, i.e. seeking to act in a manner approved by the gods (cf. English godly). It has now acquired particular connotations of **female virtue**. Suggest taking 貝 as **shell** 90, and 卜 in its literal meaning of **crack**.

Mnemonic: **CRACKED SHELL A SYMBOL OF CHASTITY?**

1616 帝 **TEI**

EMPEROR

9 strokes

帝国 TEIKOKU   empire

帝王 TEIŌ   emperor

帝王切開 TEIŌSEKKAI   caesarian

Formerly 帝 and earlier 帚, showing a large **two-tier table** 帀 supported by **cross-struts** × with an **item** － placed on top. The (firm) table was used in religious services and is to all intents and purposes an elaborate variant of **altar** 丁 / 示 695 q.v., with similar connotations of **relating to the gods**. **Ruler/ emperor** is taken by some scholars to be a borrowed meaning, but seems more likely to be an associated meaning with god. Suggest taking 帝 as a combination of **stand** 立 73 and **broom** 帚 96.

Mnemonic: **EMPEROR STANDS OVER BROOM**

1617 **TEI**

CORRECT, REVISE

9 strokes

訂正 TEISEI   correction

改訂 KAITEI   revision

改訂版 KAITEIBAN

revised edition

言 is **words/ speak** 274. 丁 is **exact** 346, here acting phonetically to express **fair/ just**. 1617 originally meant to **make a fair statement (and thereby settle an issue)**. In Chinese it still means settle, but in Japanese it has come rather to mean **amend/ revise/ correct**.

Mnemonic: **USE EXACT WORDS IN CORRECTION**

517

1618 TEI
RELAY, IN SEQUENCE
10 strokes

遞送 TEISŌ forwarding
遞信 TEISHIN communications
遞次 TEIJI in succession

Formerly 遞. 辶 is **movement (along a road)** 129. 虒 is a CO character referring to a **mythical beast** resembling a **tiger** 虎 281 with a large curved **horn** ⎞ (now ⎞), and was also used of a certain district in ancient China. Here it acts phonetically to express **change**, but its semantic role is unclear. Thus **change in those moving along a road**, a reference to a change of messengers and hence the present meanings of **relay** and **in sequence**. Suggest taking 帚 as a combination of **ten** 十 33 and **city** 市 130, with ⌐ as **building/ house** (variant 广 114).

Mnemonic: **MOVE TO RELAY IN SEQUENCE TO HOMES IN TEN CITIES**

1619 TEI
SPY, INVESTIGATE
11 strokes

探偵 TANTEI detection
内偵 NAITEI secret inquiry
偵察 TEISATSU reconnaissance

亻 is **person** 39. 貞 is **chastity** 1615 q.v., here in its literal sense of **seeking to know the will of the gods by divination**. Thus person who seeks to know by divination, i.e. a **diviner**. This later came to mean **investigator/ investigate** in a broader sense, but still retains connotations of acting in an esoteric and hence secretive manner (i.e. **spy**).

Mnemonic: **SPY ON PERSON'S CHASTITY**

1620 TEI, tsutsumi
EMBANKMENT
12 strokes

防波堤 BŌHATEI breakwater
堤防 TEIBŌ levee, dike
堤防伝い TEIBŌZUTAI along bank

土 is **earth** 60. 是 is **proper** 910, here acting phonetically to express **firm** but of unclear semantic role. **Firm earth** was a reference to an **embankment**.

Mnemonic: **USE PROPER EARTH FOR EMBANKMENT**

1621 TEI
BOAT
13 strokes

艦艇 KANTEI naval vessel
艇庫 TEIKO boathouse
救命艇 KYŪMEITEI lifeboat

舟 is **boat** 1354. 廷 is **court** 1610, here acting phonetically to express **small** but of unclear semantic role. Thus **small boat**, now **boat** in a broader sense.

Mnemonic: **COURT HAS ITS OWN BOAT**

1622		**TEI, shi**_maru/meru_	締め切り	SHIMEKIRI	deadline
		BIND, TIGHTEN, CLOSE	締約	TEIYAKU	treaty
		15 strokes	締め出し	SHIMEDASHI	shutout

糸 is **thread** 27, here meaning **cord**. 帝 is **emperor** 1616 q.v., here acting phonetically to express **bind** and possibly also lending loose connotations of **firmly** from its original meaning of firmly braced table. Thus to **bind (firmly?) with cord**, later also **tighten/ shut** and figuratively as **tie up/ conclude**.

Mnemonic: **BIND EMPEROR WITH THREAD**

1623		**DEI, doro, nazu**_mu_	泥土	DEIDO	mud, mire
		MUD, ADHERE TO	拘泥	KŌDEI	adherence
		8 strokes	泥足	DOROASHI	muddy feet

Somewhat obscure. 氵 is **water** 40, here meaning **river**. 尼 is **nun** 1674 q.v. Some scholars feel the latter is used purely phonetically to express the name of a certain river in ancient China, with **mud** being either an associated meaning or a borrowing. However, it seems equally if not more likely that 尼 acts phonetically to express **stop** (originally being pronounced SHI, as in stop SHI 止 129) and also lends its own early connotations of **stop**. Thus a **river which stops flowing**, i.e. leaving an expanse of **mud**. In either case, **adhere to** is an associated meaning with mud, from the idea of sticking.

Mnemonic: **NUN IN MUDDY WATER**

1624		**TEKI, fue**	汽笛	KITEKI	steam whistle
		FLUTE, WHISTLE	笛手	TEKISHU	flutist, flautist
		11 strokes	口笛	KUCHIBUE	whistle

⺮ is **bamboo** 170. 由 is **reason** 399 q.v., here acting phonetically to express **pure/ clear (sound)** and almost certainly also lending its connotations of **from**. Thus **bamboo from which pure/clear sound (emerges)**, i.e. a **flute**. Now also **whistle** in a broad sense.

Mnemonic: **THERE'S A REASON FOR MAKING FLUTE FROM BAMBOO**

| 1625 | 摘 | TEKI, tsu*mu*, tsuma*mu*
PLUCK, PICK, EXTRACT
14 strokes | 摘要 TEKIYŌ summary
摘発 TEKIHATSU exposure
摘み取る TSUMITORU pluck, pick |

扌 is **hand** 32. 商 is starting point 755 q.v., here acting phonetically to express **pick** and possibly also lending connotations of **appropriate**. Thus to **pick (something appropriate?) by hand**. It was originally used in a physical sense, as in picking/ plucking flowers or fruit, but is now often used in a figurative sense, such as **extracting** or **revealing**. Suggest taking 商 as a combination of **emperor** 帝 1616 and **old** 古 109.

Mnemonic: **PICKED BY OLD EMPEROR'S HAND**

| 1626 | 滴 | TEKI, shizuku, shitata*ru*
DROP, DRIP
14 strokes | 水滴 SUITEKI water drop
一滴 ITTEKI one drop
滴下 TEKIKA dripping |

氵 is **water** 40. 商 is **starting point** 755, here acting phonetically to express **tap**/ strike and possibly also lending its connotations of starting point. Thus **water which taps against something**, namely a **drip** (the starting point of a larger flow?). Suggest taking 商 as a combination of **emperor** 帝 1616 and **old** 古 109.

Mnemonic: **WATER DRIPS ONTO OLD EMPEROR**

| 1627 | | TETSU
ALTERNATE, ROTATE
8 strokes | 更迭 KŌTETSU reshuffle
迭立 TETSURITSU alternating
迭起 TEKKI alternate occurrence |

辶 is **movement (along a road)** 129. 失 is **lose** 501, here acting phonetically to express **change** but of unclear semantic role. Like 逓 1618, 1627 originally referred to **changing those moving along a road**, i.e. messengers, and later came to mean **alternate/ rotate** in a broader sense.

Mnemonic: **ALTERNATING CAN INVOLVE LOSS OF MOVEMENT**

| 1628 | 哲 | TETSU
WISDOM
10 strokes | 哲学 TETSUGAKU philosophy
哲人 TETSUJIN sage
先哲 SENTETSU sage of old |

口 is **mouth/ say** 20, here meaning **words**. 折 is **break** 522 q.v., here acting phonetically to express **correct** and probably also lending connotations of **understanding** from its original meaning of chop and hence divide/ analyse (see also 199). Thus **correct words** (full of understanding?), a symbol of **wisdom**.

Mnemonic: **SPEECH BROKEN BUT STILL SHOWS WISDOM**

1629 徹	**TETSU** **GO THROUGH, CLEAR,** **REMOVE** 15 strokes	徹夜 TETSUYA 徹底的 TETTEITEKI 貫徹 KANTETSU	all night thorough fulfillment

Of confused evolution. Originally written 㽞, showing **hand** 又 and **pot on a stand** 鬲 (a very early form of 鬲 1078). It originally meant to **remove a pot from a stand**, and still retains connotations of **remove** (though remove is nowadays usually conveyed by 撤 1630, with which 1629 is sometimes interchanged). Remove came to mean **clear away**, and then by association **have a clear passage** (note that pot on a stand was almost certainly also a symbol of an impediment -- see 1078). Like 通 176, this then came to mean **pass clear through**, with **road/ go** 彳 118 being added for clarity. Thus **road that passes clear through/ go clear through**. Pot on stand 鬲 / 鬲 was later miscopied as child being born/ **educate** 育 227, and hand 又 miscopied as striking hand/ **force** 攵 101.

Mnemonic: **FORCED TO GO CLEAR THROUGH ONE'S EDUCATION**

1630 撤	**TETSU** **REMOVE, WITHDRAW** 15 strokes	撤収 TESSHŪ 撤去 TEKKYO 撤回 TEKKAI	removal removal withdrawal

Remove a pot 敵 1629 q.v. (correctly 㽞) with **hand** 扌 32 added after the meaning had become vague. Now **remove/ withdraw** in a broader sense. Suggest taking 育 as **educate (a child)** 227 and 攵 as **force** 101.

Mnemonic: **FORCE EDUCATED CHILD TO REMOVE HAND**

1631 添	**TEN**, sou/eru **ACCOMPANY, ADD** 11 strokes	添加 TENKA 添付 TENPU 添え木 SOEGI	addition appending splint, brace

氵 is **water** 40. 忝 is an NGU character meaning grateful/ embarrassed, though in Chinese it has stronger meanings of ashamed/ disgraced (literally the **feelings** 小 [variant 心 147] of a **person/ man with head bowed** 夭 279). Here 忝 acts phonetically to express **fill**, but any semantic role is unclear. Thus to **fill with water**. Add water later came to mean **add** in a broad sense, with the intransitive version coming to mean **join/ accompany** (not unlike 431). Since no early forms of 添 have been found some scholars conclude that it is in fact a later variant of 沾 , an NGU character meaning moisten/ add water which uses divine/ occupy 占 1491 in a similar phonetic role to 忝, but this is not especially convincing.

Mnemonic: **MAN WITH BOWED HEAD FEELS NEED FOR ADDED WATER**

1632 殿 DEN, TEN
PALACE, LORD, MR
13 strokes

宮殿 KYŪDEN   palace
御殿 GOTEN   palace
殿様 TONOSAMA   lord

Somewhat obscure. Once written 房殳. 殳 is **strike** 153, ⺆/尸 is **buttocks**/ slumped figure 236, while 冂 is obscure. However, 房 appears to have meant **buttocks**, and also to have lent its sound (known to have once been **TON**). Thus to **strike someone on the buttocks with a TON sound**. Note that in Chinese 1632 can still mean **rear**. **Palace** is a borrowed meaning, specifically resulting from 1632's being used in place of a now defunct character 壂 . This combines **earth/ ground** 土 60 with 殿, which is known to have acted phonetically to express **raised** (any semantic role being unclear), thus giving **raised earth/ ground**. This originally referred to **earthen ramparts**, which came to symbolise **castle**, with **palace** being an associated meaning. In Japanese 1632 is also used by further association to refer to the person living in a palace/ castle, namely a **lord**, and is also used as a general term of respect. Suggest taking 共 as **together** 460.

Mnemonic: **STRIKE BUTTOCKS TOGETHER AT LORD'S PALACE**

1633 斗 TO
DIPPER, MEASURE
4 strokes

北斗星 HOKUTOSEI Big Dipper
斗酒 TOSHU   gallons of sake
泰斗 TAITO   an authority

To all intents and purposes a variant of **ladle** 升 1386 q.v., being a derivative of a highly stylised variant 斗 of 1386's early form 斗 (a pictograph of a ladle) but technically without the contents ⌐ . Confusingly, however, while 1386 has become a standard measure of 1.8 liters, 1633 is a **measure** ten times that amount, namely 18 liters.

Mnemonic: **BIG DIPPER HAS SLOPING CROSS AND TWO DOTS?!**

1634 吐 TO, ha*ku*
DISGORGE, VOMIT
6 strokes

吐剤 TOZAI   emetic
吐き気 HAKIKE   nausea
吐息 TOIKI   gasp, sigh

口 is **mouth** 20. 土 is **soil/ ground** 60, here acting phonetically to express **pour forth** and possibly also lending extended connotations of **filth**. Thus to **pour forth (filth?) from the mouth**, i.e. **vomit/ disgorge**.

Mnemonic: **DISGORGE VOMIT FROM MOUTH TO GROUND**

1635		TO ROAD, WAY 10 strokes	途中 TOCHŪ	on the way
			途端 TOTAN	verge, point
			前途 ZENTO	future

辶 is movement (along a road) 129. 余 is ample 800, here also acting phonetically to express road/ way. Thus ample road (permitting) (easy) movement, now road/ way in a general sense including the figurative.

Mnemonic: **ROAD PERMITTING AMPLE MOVEMENT**

1636		TO, wataru/su CROSS, HAND OVER 12 strokes	渡航 TOKŌ	passage, crossing
			渡世 TOSEI	livelihood
			言い渡す IIWATASU	sentence

氵 is water 40, here meaning **river**. 度 is **degree** 356 q.v., here acting phonetically to express **span** and possibly also loosely lending similar connotations from its literal meaning of measure with the hand. Thus to **span a river**, later **cross (over)** in a general sense. **Hand over** is the transitive version.

Mnemonic: **CROSS WATER BY DEGREES**

1637		TO, nuru PLASTER, COAT, PAINT 13 strokes	塗り物 NURIMONO	lacquerware
			塗装 TOSŌ	painting
			塗り薬 NURIGUSURI	ointment

Once written simply as 涂 , which still exists in Chinese as a variant of 塗 . 氵 is **water** 40, here meaning **river**. 余 is **ample/ excess** 800. Thus **ample/ excessive river**, a reference to a **large river prone to flood**. This came by association to mean **leave a coating of mud**, with **earth** 土 60 being added for clarity. Now to **coat** in a general sense, but note that in Chinese 1637 can still mean mud.

Mnemonic: **EXCESS RIVER-WATER LEAVES COATING OF EARTHY MUD**

1638		DO, yatsu, yakko, -me SLAVE, SERVANT, GUY 5 strokes	奴隷 DOREI	slave
			奴等 YATSURA	those guys
			奴様 YAKKOSAN *	that guy

Somewhat obscure, though its elements are clearly **hand** 又 and **woman** 女 35. Some scholars feel that woman 女 symbolises **compliance** and hand 又 symbolises **work**, to give a meaning of **work compliantly** and by association **be a slave/ servant**. Other scholars take woman 女 to be used literally and hand 又 to indicate **control**, to give **woman under one's control**, a reference to a **slave-girl**. The former theory seems the more likely. 1638 is also used as a pejorative suffix and slang reference to a **person**.

Mnemonic: **HAND-MAIDEN IS A SLAVE**

1639

DO, ikaru, okoru
ANGER, RAGE
9 strokes

怒気 DOKI   anger
怒鳴る DONARU   shout, bawl
怒り狂う IKARIKURUU rage madly

心 is heart/ **feelings** 147. 奴 is **slave** 1638, here acting phonetically to express **anger** and possibly also suggesting feelings associated with being a slave or (more likely) directed towards a slave. Thus **feelings of anger** (directed towards a slave?). Now **anger/ rage** in a broad sense.

Mnemonic: SLAVE'S FEELINGS ARE OF ANGER

1640

TŌ, ZU, mame
BEANS, MINIATURE
7 strokes

豆腐 TŌFU   beancurd
大豆 DAIZU   soybean
豆本 MAMEHON

miniature book

Once written 豆 , showing a **monopedal table-cum-food vessel** (known as takatsuki in Japanese) 豆 with **contents** ‾ . Some scholars take **bean** to be a borrowing, while others see it as an associated meaning with food in general, which was in turn associated with food vessel 豆 (see also 146). In compounds 1640 is often used to indicate both food and vessel/ container in a broader sense. Confusingly, depending on one's point of view the takatsuki could be considered quite tall (i.e. relative to a normal dish), and occasionally it seems to lend such connotations (as in 360), but in general it was considered short (i.e. relative to a table) and usually lends these connotations (see 342). **Miniature** is an associated meaning with short. It also occasionally appears to lend connotations of fixed height/ dimensions (again see 342). Suggest taking ‾ as **one** 1, 口 as a **box**, and 丷 as a variant of **stand** 立 73.

Mnemonic: ONE MINIATURE BOX ON STAND, FULL OF BEANS

1641

TŌ, itaru
GO, REACH, ARRIVE
8 strokes

到来 TŌRAI   arrival, advent
到達 TŌTATSU   arrival
到底 TŌTEI   absolutely

Once written 到, showing that **sword/ cut** ⺉ 181 is actually a miscopying of **person** 刀 / 亻 39. 至 /至 is **arrive/ reach** 875 q.v., here in its literal sense of arrow falling upside-down and thus indicating being **upside-down**. 1641 originally referred to a **person being upside-down**, i.e. **falling**. This meaning is now conveyed by 倒 1643 q.v., which adds a further person 亻 . The meaning of 1641 itself evolved in similar fashion to that of 至 875, i.e. to give **reach/ arrive**.

Mnemonic: REACH SWORD

524

1642 TŌ, ni*geru*/*gasu*, noga*reru*/*su*　逃亡者 TŌBŌSHA　　fugitive
ESCAPE, EVADE, MISS　見逃す MINOGASU　　overlook
9 strokes　　　　　　　　　　　逃げ道 NIGEMICHI　escape route

辶 is **movement** 129. 兆 is sign/ **trillion** 939 q.v., here acting phonetically to express
escape and possibly also lending supporting connotations of separation. Thus to **move
and escape**.

Mnemonic: **ESCAPE THROUGH A TRILLION MOVES**

1643 TŌ, tao*reru*/*su*　　倒産 TŌSAN　　bankruptcy
FALL, TOPPLE, INVERT　面倒 MENDŌ　　trouble
10 strokes　　　　　　　　　　倒置 TŌCHI　　inversion

Reach 到 1641 q.v., here in its literal sense of **person fallen over/ upside-down**,
with **person** 亻 39 added for clarity. Suggest remembering reach 到 by association
with **reach** 至 875 and **sword** 刂 181.

Mnemonic: **REACH FALLEN PERSON WITH SWORD**

1644 TŌ, kō*ru*, kogo*eru*　　冷凍剤 REITŌZAI　　refrigerant
FREEZE　　　　　　　　　　凍結 TŌKETSU　　freezing
10 strokes　　　　　　　　　　凍り付く KŌRITSUKU　freeze to

冫 is **ice** 378. 東 is **east** 184 q.v., here acting phonetically to express **hard** and possibly
also lending loose connotations of mass from its early meaning of heavy sack. **Hard ice**
symbolises **freezing**.

Mnemonic: **ICE FREEZES OVER EAST**

1645 TŌ, kara　　　　　　　　唐本 TŌHON　　Chinese book
(T'ANG) CHINA　　　　　毛唐人 KETŌJIN　　foreigner
10 strokes　　　　　　　　　　唐手 KARATE　　karate

Formerly 唐 and earlier 啻, showing **mouth/ say** 口 20 and hands holding a pestle 庚
480. The latter acts phonetically to express **brag/ boast** but is of unclear semantic role.
Thus to **speak boastfully** (still a meaning in Chinese). It was later borrowed to refer to
T'ang and by extension **China** in general (and from a Japanese perspective can also mean
foreign), but the reason for the borrowing is not clear. Suggest taking 广 as **building**
114 and 丰 as a **hand** ヨ holding a **stick** l, with 口 in its sense of opening/ **entrance**.

Mnemonic: **HAND HOLDS STICK AT ENTRANCE TO CHINESE BUILDING**

1646

桃

TŌ, momo
PEACH
10 strokes

白桃　HAKUTŌ　white peach
桃色　MOMOIRO　pink
桃原境　TŌGENKYŌ　Shangri-La

木 is **tree** 69. 兆 is **sign/ trillion** 939 q.v., here in its meaning of **sign**. In the ancient Orient the peach was a **symbol of fertility/ pregnancy**, partly for the similarity of its appearance to female genitalia (cf. the Japanese legend of Momotarō, the Peach Boy) and partly for the fact that, along with the plum (see 1689), it was a favorite fruit of pregnant women. Thus the **peach tree** was literally a **'pregnancy-sign tree'**. Note that in Chinese 1646 can also mean marriage, clearly showing its procreative associations.

Mnemonic: **TREE BEARING A TRILLION PEACHES**

1647

透

TŌ, suku/kasu/keru
CLEAR, TRANSPARENT
10 strokes

透明　TŌMEI　transparency
透写　TŌSHA　tracing
透き通る　SUKITŌRU　be clear

辶 is **movement** 129. 秀 is **excel** 1355, here acting phonetically to express **lead** and also lending similar associated connotations of its own. 1647 originally referred to a **person leading another** in a physical sense. Some scholars feel its present meanings are borrowed, while others feel that **lead the way** came by association to mean **clear the way** and eventually **clear** in a broad sense (not unlike 1629). **Transparent** is an associated meaning. Note that 1647 can still be used in the sense of **clear/ unobstructed**, though it is usually used in the sense of **clear/ transparent**.

Mnemonic: **EXCELLENT MOVEMENT CLEARS WAY**

1648

悼

TŌ, itamu
GRIEVE, MOURN
11 strokes

哀悼　AITŌ　mourning
追悼　TSUITŌ　mourning
悼むべき　ITAMUBEKI　lamentable

忄 is **heart/ feelings** 147. 卓 is **excel/ table** 1553, here acting phonetically to express **sway/ move** but of unclear semantic role. Thus to **have one's heart swayed**, a somewhat vague reference to **mourning/ grieving**.

Mnemonic: **GRIEVE WITH HEART ON THE TABLE**

1649

TŌ, nusum*u*
STEAL
11 strokes

盗用 TŌYŌ — appropriation
強盗 GŌTŌ — robbery
盗人 NUSUBITO * — thief

Formerly 盜 , showing that 次 is not **next** 次 292 -- though it may be useful to remember it as such -- but a miscopying/ simplification of 次. The latter is a CO character meaning **saliva** (literally **water** 氵 40 and **gaping mouth** 欠 471). A **watering mouth** is a universal symbol of **desire for food**, here reinforced by **dish** 皿 1307. 1649 originally meant to **have a strong desire to eat**. The idea of having a strong desire for something came to prevail, leading to **desiring to acquire at any cost** and eventually to **appropriating/ stealing**.

Mnemonic: **STEAL DISH NEXT**

1650

TŌ
CERAMIC, HAPPY,
EDUCATE
11 strokes

陶器 TŌKI — ceramic ware
薫陶 KUNTŌ — education
陶然 TŌZEN — enraptured

Of confused etymology. Correctly written simply as 匋, which still exists in Chinese and is interchangeable with 陶. 匋 comprises **surround/ womb** 勹 655 and **can/ vessel** 缶 1095, and originally ideographically indicated an **outer covering protecting an inner vessel**. 缶 originally referred to a pottery vessel, and thus 匋 meant **protected pottery vessel**, eventually coming to mean **pottery/ ceramic** in a broad sense. The idea of protection also led by association to **care for/ rear/ educate**. In the case of 陶匋, **hill** 阝 229 combines with **pottery** 匋 , which also acts phonetically to express **successive**, to refer to a type of **kiln** build in successive stages up a hillside (a type still found in China and Japan). It can still mean kiln in Chinese, and also came to refer to a hill with terracing. Eventually, however, 陶 and 匋 became confused. It is not clear how the lesser meaning of **happy** was acquired.

Mnemonic: **HILL SURROUNDED BY CANS AND CERAMIC VESSELS**

1651

TŌ
TOWER, MONUMENT
12 strokes

石塔 SEKITŌ — tombstone
卒塔婆 SOTOBA * — stupa
五重の塔 GOJŪNOTŌ — five storied pagoda

土 is **earth** 60. 荅 is a CO character now used in a range of confusing meanings such as undertake and iron spike. Its etymology is obscure, though it appears to comprise **grass/ plants** 艹 9 and **join together/ fit** 合 121. Here it acts phonetically to express **build up**, to give **build up (a mound of) earth**. 1651 was then borrowed phonetically to express the 'tu' sound of **stupa** (see above), a Sanskrit term for **shrine** (presumably also being felt to be semantically appropriate). **Monument** and **tower** are associated meanings.

Mnemonic: **JOIN PLANTS AND EARTH TOGETHER TO MAKE MONUMENT**

1652 搭 **TŌ**
LOAD, BOARD
12 strokes

搭載 TŌSAI   loading
搭乗 TŌJŌ   boarding
搭乗券 TŌJŌKEN boarding pass

扌 is **hand** 32. 荅 is the obscure element seen in 塔 1651 q.v., here similarly acting phonetically to express **build up**. Thus **build up with the hands**, a reference to placing one thing on top of another and hence **load**. **Board** is the intransitive version of load. Suggest taking 荅 as **plants** 艹 9 and **join together** 合 121.

Mnemonic: **HANDS JOIN PLANTS TOGETHER FOR LOADING**

1653 棟 **TŌ, mune, muna-**
RIDGEPOLE, BUILDING
12 strokes

病棟 BYŌTŌ   ward
棟木 MUNAGI   ridgepole
別棟 BETSUMUNE outbuilding

木 is **tree/ wood** 69. 東 is **east** 184 q.v., here acting phonetically to express **center** and also lending its original connotations of **supporting pole**. Thus **central wooden supporting pole**, a reference to a **ridgepole**. Also used later to refer to a **building**.

Mnemonic: **WOOD FROM EAST BEST FOR BUILDING'S RIDGEPOLE**

1654 痘 **TŌ**
SMALLPOX
12 strokes

天然痘 TENNENTŌ smallpox
水痘 SUITŌ   chicken pox
種痘 SHUTŌ   vaccination

A character of relatively recent origin (approximately the fourth century A.D.). 疒 is **sickness** 381. 豆 is **food vessel/ beans** 1640, here unusually used in its later sense of **beans** to refer to **bean-like pustules**. Thus **sickness producing bean-like pustules**, a reference to **smallpox**.

Mnemonic: **SMALLPOX IS ILLNESS WITH BEAN-LIKE PUSTULES**

1655 筒 **TŌ, tsutsu**
TUBE, CYLINDER
12 strokes

円筒 ENTŌ   cylinder
筒抜け TSUTSUNUKE directly
筒形 TSUTSUGATA cylindrical

竹 is **bamboo** 170. 同 is **same** 187 q.v., here acting phonetically to express **pass (clear) through** and according to some scholars also lending connotations of having the same diameter at all points, i.e. being round. Thus (round?) **bamboo with a clear passage through it**, a reference to a **bamboo tube**. Later **tube/ cylinder** in general .

Mnemonic: **CYLINDER IS SAME SHAPE AS BAMBOO**

1656 稲	TŌ, ine, ina RICE (PLANT) 14 strokes	水稲 SUITŌ	paddy rice
		稲作 INASAKU	rice crop
		早稲田 WASEDA*	place-name

Formerly 稻 . 禾 is **rice plant** 81. 舀/臽 is a CO character now meaning **to bale**. It comprises **hand** 爪/⺥ 303 and **mortar** 臼/⺽ 648 and appears to have originally meant hand holding mortar/ bowl. Here it acts phonetically to express **soft** and may also lend similar connotations (from the idea of material being ground in a mortar). Thus **soft rice (plant)**. Since rice plant 禾 in itself has connotations of soft, 舀 is in effect redundant. Suggest taking 旧 as **old** 648.

Mnemonic: **HAND PICKS OLD RICE PLANT**

1657 踏	TŌ, fumu/maeru TREAD, STEP ON 15 strokes	踏破 TŌHA	tramping
		踏み込む FUMIKOMU	step into
		足踏み ASHIBUMI	step, standstill

足 is **foot** 51. 沓 is a CO character meaning **connect** (etymology unclear, but apparently comprising **water** 氵 40 and **sun** 日 62 and possibly referring ideographically to the connection between these elements in the scheme of the universe). Here 沓 acts phonetically to express **come into contact with**, and almost certainly also lends similar connotations of its own. Thus **foot coming into contact with (the ground)**, a reference to **treading/ stepping on**.

Mnemonic: **FOOT STEPS ON SUNLIT WATER**

1658 謄	TŌ COPY 17 strokes	謄本 TŌHON	manuscript
		謄写 TŌSHA	copy
		謄写機 TŌSHAKI	copier

言 is **words** 274. 朕 is **royal we** (variant 朕 1603 q.v.), here acting phonetically to express **write** and probably also lending its connotations of **repetition**. Thus to **write words (repetitively?)**, i.e. **copy**. Suggest taking 月 as **moon(light)** 16, and 关 as **two** 二 61 and **fire** 火 8.

Mnemonic: **COPY TWO FIERY WORDS BY MOONLIGHT**

1659 闘 TŌ, tataka*u* 闘志 TŌSHI fighting spirit
FIGHT 闘士 TŌSHI fighter
18 strokes 戦闘機 SENTŌKI fighter plane

Somewhat obscure. Formerly 鬥 and earlier 鬥, showing that 鬥 is not **door/ gate** 門 211 but a derivative of 鬥. This shows **two people facing each other** ⟨ ⟩ (variants **person** ⟨ / ⟩ 39) and **hands** ⟨ (variant ⟨ / 手 32), and in turn derives from a pictograph ⟨, the prototype of 1659 which clearly shows **two people hitting each other**. The later addition 斲 is a CO character meaning **carve/cut**, comprising **ax** 斤 1176 and an unclear element 畐. Here 斲 acts phonetically to express **hit** and almost certainly also lends connotations of **strike with a weapon**. 斲 was later replaced with 豆寸. It is not clear if this is intended as a combination, in which case it is possibly a variant of plant upright 尌 888 (lending an idea of standing erect/ **squaring up**), or whether the elements (**food vessel** 豆 1640 q.v. and measure/ **hand** 寸 909) are used individually, in which case both could act phonetically to express **fight**, 豆 could also lend connotations of standing erect/ **squaring up**, and 寸 could lend connotations of **hand to hand** (combat). In any event, 1659 clearly has its origins in the depiction of two persons fighting each other, but now means **fight** in a broad sense. Suggest taking 鬥 as **doorway**.

Mnemonic: **FIGHT IN DOORWAY OVER HANDY FOOD VESSEL**

1660 騰 TŌ 騰貴 TŌKI (price-) rise
RISE, LEAP 騰落 TŌRAKU fluctuations
20 strokes 暴騰 BŌTŌ sharp rise

馬 is **horse** 191. 朕 is royal we (variant 朕 1603 q.v), here acting phonetically to express **leap** and almost certainly also lending its own connotations of raise/ rise. 1660 originally referred to a **horse leaping**. It is now used of rise/ leap in a broader sense, but especially of price rises. Suggest taking 月 as **moon** 16 and 关 as **two** 二 61 **fires** 火 8.

Mnemonic: **HORSE LEAPS TWO FIRES AS MOON RISES**

1661 洞 DŌ, hora 洞察 DŌSATSU insight
CAVE, PENETRATE 空洞 KŪDŌ cavern, cavity
9 strokes 洞くつ DŌKUTSU cave

氵 is **water** 40, here meaning **river/ stream**. 同 is **same** 187 q.v., here acting phonetically to express **pass clear through** and according to some scholars also lending loose connotations of **round**. Thus **that** (round thing?) **which a stream passes clear through**, a somewhat vague reference to a **cave**, with **penetrate** being an associated meaning. It is not clear why cliff 厂 45 or hole 穴 849 was not added for clarity, giving 㖌 or 窬 or similar.

Mnemonic: **SAME WATER PENETRATES CAVE**

530

1662	DŌ **BODY, TRUNK, TORSO** 10 strokes	胴体 DŌTAI 双胴船 SŌDŌSEN 胴回り DŌMAWARI	body, trunk catamaran girth

月 is **flesh/ of the body** 365. 同 is **same** 187 q.v., here acting phonetically to express **big** and according to some scholars also lending loose connotations of round. The **big (round?) part of the body** is the **trunk/ torso**.

Mnemonic: **TORSO IS OF SAME FLESH AS BODY**

1663	tōge **PASS, CREST, CRISIS** 9 strokes	峠道 TŌGEMICHI う水峠 USUITŌGE 四十の峠 YONJŪNOTŌGE	pass Usui Pass mid-life crisis

A 'made in Japan' character combining **mountain** 山 24 with **up** 上 37 and **down** 下 7, to refer to **that which goes up and down a mountain**, i.e. a **pass**. **Crest** and **crisis** are associated meanings.

Mnemonic: **PASS GOES UP AND DOWN MOUNTAIN**

1664	TOKU **CONCEAL** 10 strokes	匿名 TOKUMEI 隠匿 INTOKU 秘匿 HITOKU	pseudonym concealment concealment

匸 is **box/ container** 225. 若 is **young** 886 q.v., here acting phonetically to express **put** and possibly also lending connotations of bend from its early meaning of pliant. Thus to **put something in a container** (by bending it?), which came to indicate **concealing**.

Mnemonic: **YOUNG PERSON CONCEALED IN BOX**

1665 督	TOKU **SUPERVISE, URGE** 13 strokes	監督 KANTOKU 督励 TOKUREI 督促 TOKUSOKU	supervision encouragement urging

目 is **eye** 72. 叔 is **uncle** 1367 q.v., here acting phonetically to express **fix (on)** and probably also lending an idea of uncle or similar senior person. Thus (uncle?) **fixing an eye** (on someone), meaning to **supervise**. **Encourage/ urge** is an associated meaning.

Mnemonic: **UNCLE'S EYE SUPERVISES**

| 1666 | | **TOKU**
SINCERE, SERIOUS
16 strokes | 篤志 TOKUSHI
危篤 KITOKU
篤と TOKUTO | benevolence
seriously ill
seriously |

馬 is **horse** 191. 竹 is **bamboo** 170, here unusually acting as a phonetic to express **step** and possibly also lending connotations of strong but supple. 1666 originally referred to a **horse stepping surefootedly** (with suppleness and strength?). **Sincere** and **serious** are borrowed meanings.

Mnemonic: **SINCERE HORSE SERIOUS ABOUT BAMBOO**

| 1667 | | **TOTSU, deko**
CONVEX, PROTRUSION
5 strokes | 凸面 TOTSUMEN
凸凹 DEKOBOKO
凹凸 ŌTOTSU | convexity
unevenness
unevenness |

A symbolic representation of **convexity**, being the opposite of concavity 凹 1032.

Mnemonic: **BOX HAS BIT PROTRUDING, MAKING IT CONVEX**

| 1668 | | **TOTSU, tsuku**
THRUST, LUNGE,
PROTRUDE
8 strokes | 突然 TOTSUZEN
突入 TOTSUNYŪ
突っ込む TSUKKOMU | suddenly
plunge
thrust in |

Of disputed etymology. Formerly 突 , showing **dog** 犬 17 and **hole** 穴 849. For many centuries taken to be an ideograph indicating a **dog bolting from a hole**, with the present meanings thus being seen as extended and/or associated meanings. However, some authoritative Japanese scholars take dog 犬 to be used purely phonetically to express **protrude**, to give a paradoxical **hole that protrudes**. This is seen as a reference to an ancient style of **chimney**, which instead of emerging from the roof **protruded** from the side of a dwelling. Thus **thrust out/ protrude** are seen as ancient meanings, with **lunge** being an associated meaning. The ideographic theory seems the more helpful . However, in the case of the modern form suggest taking 大 as **big** 53.

Mnemonic: **THRUST INTO BIG HOLE**

532

1669	TON	屯営 TONEI	barracks
	BARRACKS, CAMP, POST	駐屯 CHŪTON	posting
	4 strokes	駐屯地 CHŪTONCHI	post

Of somewhat obscure evolution, though it clearly derives from a pictograph 乇, showing a **sprouting plant** 屮 928 with a **bud** •. In Chinese it can still mean sprout/ shoot. Confusingly, though in compounds it sometimes lends an idea of **fresh** from its depiction of a budding plant (e.g. 895), it also seems at times to refer to a **bud that fails to open** (e.g. 1671). Some scholars believe that the latter is in fact its principal meaning, and that this led to the idea of **failing to progress** and hence **being stationary**, giving by association such meanings as **camp/ barracks/ post**. Others see the present meanings as borrowings, which seems more likely. Suggest remembering by association with **hair** 毛 210.

Mnemonic: **HAIR-LIKE SPROUTING PLANT FOUND IN CAMP**

1670	TON, buta	豚毛 TONMŌ	pig bristle
	PIG, PORK	豚肉 BUTANIKU	pork
	11 strokes	豚カツ TONKATSU	pork cutlet

豕 is an NGU character meaning **pig**, deriving from a rather confusingly stylised pictograph 豕. The addition of **meat/ of the body** 月 365 suggests that 1670 originally meant **pig meat/ pork**, but it is now also used of **pig** in general instead of the simpler 豕.

Mnemonic: **PIG MEAT IS PORK**

1671	DON, nibui/ru	鈍感 DONKAN	insensitivity
	BLUNT, DULL	鈍才 DONSAI	stupidity
	12 strokes	鈍色 NIBUIRO	dull gray

金 is **metal** 14, here meaning **metal implement**. 屯 is camp/ **sprout** 1669 q.v., here acting phonetically to express **blunt** and almost certainly also lending connotations of **failing to do what is expected** (from a bud that fails to blossom). Thus **blunt (and ineffective?) metal implement**, i.e. a **dull blade**. Also used of **dull** in an extended sense, as of wits and colors. Suggest remembering 屯 by association with **hair** 毛 210.

Mnemonic: **METAL BLADE TOO BLUNT TO CUT HAIR-LIKE SPROUT**

1672	DON, kumo*ru* TO CLOUD, DIM, MAR 16 strokes	曇天 DONTEN cloudy sky 曇り勝ち KUMORIGACHI cloudy 花曇り HANAGUMORI hazy spring sky

Sun 日 62 and cloud 雲 78, to give **sun obscured by cloud**. As in English, to **cloud** is also used in extended senses such as **dim** and **mar**.

Mnemonic: **SUN IS DIMMED BY CLOUD**

1673	NAN, yawa*rakai* SOFT 11 strokes	軟化 NANKA softening 軟水 NANSUI soft water 軟弱 NANJAKU weakness

Formerly 輭. 車 is **vehicle** 31, while 耎 is a CO character meaning **soft** (comprising big 大 53 and beard 而 887, a beard being a symbol of softness). 1673 originally referred to the practice of **wrapping reeds around the wheels of a vehicle to soften the ride**, and now means **soft** in a general sense. The modern form uses **lack** 欠 471, apparently as a graphic simplification.

Mnemonic: **VEHICLE LACKS SOFTNESS**

1674 尼	NI, ama NUN, PRIESTESS 5 strokes	尼僧 NISŌ priestess, nun 尼寺 AMADERA convent 比丘尼 BIKUNI * Buddhist priestess

尸 is **corpse/ slumped figure** 236, here meaning **injured/ maimed person**. ヒ is similarly a **slumped figure** 238, here also acting phonetically to express **stop**. 1674 originally referred to a **person too badly injured/ maimed to move**, and later came to mean **not move/ stop** in a broad sense (still a minor meaning in Chinese). It was borrowed phonetically to express the **'ni'** of **bikuni**, a Sanskrit term for **priestess** (see above), and may possibly also have been considered to lend suitable extended connotations of unswerving/ dedicated.

Mnemonic: **SLUMPED CORPSE OF NUN**

1675	NYŌ URINE 7 strokes	糖尿病 TŌNYŌBYŌ diabetes 尿素 NYŌSO urea 尿意 NYŌI nature's call

Once written 屎. 屎 is **tail** 尾 1734 q.v., here in its extended sense of **genitals**. 水 is **water** 40. Thus **water from genitals**, i.e. **urine**. The modern form uses **buttocks** 尸 236 as a simplification.

Mnemonic: **'BUTTOCK WATER' REFERS TO URINE**

1676

NIN, hara*mu*
PREGNANT, SWOLLEN
7 strokes

妊婦 NINPU   pregnant woman
不妊症 FUNINSHŌ   infertility
妊娠調節 NINSHINCHŌSETSU
birth control

女 is **woman** 35. 壬 is spindle 764 q.v., here acting phonetically to express **swell** and possibly also lending its connotations of **bearing/ carrying**. Thus **swollen (carrying?) woman**, i.e. a **pregnant woman**. Suggest taking 壬 as a **hatted** ノ **samurai** 士 494.

Mnemonic: **WOMAN MADE PREGNANT BY HATTED SAMURAI**

1677

NIN, shinob*u*
ENDURE, STEALTH
7 strokes

忍耐 NINTAI   patience
忍者 NINJA   ninja (spy)
忍び込む SHINOBIKOMU
sneak into

心 is **heart/ feelings** 147. 刃 is **blade** 1446, here acting phonetically to express **bear** and also lending connotations of something **sharp and painful**. Thus to **bear something painful in the heart**, i.e. **endure**. Concealing one's pain led to the idea of being secretive and hence by association **being stealthy**.

Mnemonic: **ENDURE PAIN OF BLADE IN THE HEART**

1678

NEI, mushi*ro*
PEACE, PREFERABLY
14 strokes

安寧 ANNEI   public peace
丁寧 TEINEI   civility, care
寧日 NEIJITSU   quiet day

Once written 寧. 宀 is **roof/ house** 28. 寍 is a now defunct character meaning **peace**. Its etymology is unclear, but it comprises **heart/ feelings** 心 147, **dish** 皿 / 罒 1307, and twisting waterweed/ seek an exit 丂 281, and may have originally referred to **feelings of contentment when one has food** (with 丂 in some unclear phonetic role). Thus 1678 means **peace at home**. **Preferably/ rather** is an associated meaning, i.e. peace being a preferred situation. Suggest taking 丁 as **nail** 346 and 罒 as **eye** 72.

Mnemonic: **FEEL PEACEFUL HOME PREFERABLE TO NAIL IN EYE**

1679

粘

NEN, neba*ru*
STICKY, GLUTINOUS
11 strokes

粘土 NENDO   clay
粘着 NENCHAKU   adhesion
粘り強い NEBARIZUYOI tenacious

Formerly 黏 . 黍 is an NGU character meaning **(glutinous) millet**, once written 黍 and comprising **grain plant** 禾 / 条 (variant 禾 81) and **water/ liquid** 氺 / 水 (old form/ variant 水 40). (Distinguish 黍 from lacquer 桼 / 漆 1334, and note the different etymology.) 占 is occupy/ **divine** 1491, here acting phonetically to express **adhere/ stick** but of unclear semantic role. Thus **glutinous millet that sticks**, now **sticky/ glutinous** in general. The modern form uses **rice** 米 201.

Mnemonic: **DIVINE USING STICKY RICE?**

1680

悩

NŌ, naya*mu/masu/mashii*
WORRY, DISTRESS,
TEASE
10 strokes

苦悩 KUNŌ   distress
悩殺 NŌSATSU   captivation
おう悩 ŌNŌ   torment

Formerly 惱 and earlier 㛖 . 女 is **woman** 35. 甾 / 凶 is head 954 q.v., here meaning **brain/ mind** and also acting phonetically to express **torment**. According to some scholars 㛖 originally referred to the torment on a woman's mind, but in view of the connotations of nayamashii, nōsatsu (see above) bonnō (see 1717) etc., which refer to a **woman teasing/ tormenting a man**, it is far more likely that it referred from the outset to a **man being tormented by having a woman on his mind**. Though it still retains strong connotations of sexual torment it can also mean **torment/ distress** in a broader sense. The modern form uses **heart/ feelings** 忄 147. Suggest remembering 凶 as **brain** (i.e. a simplification of brain 脳 954).

Mnemonic: **WORRY AFFECTS BOTH HEART AND BRAIN**

1681

濃

NŌ, ko*i*
THICK, DEEP, RICH
16 strokes

濃化 NŌKA   thickening
濃厚 NŌKŌ no   rich, intense
脂濃い ABURAKOI   fatty

氵 is **water** 40. 農 is **farming** 366, here also acting phonetically to express **abundant**. Thus **abundant water for farming**, which came to indicate **fertile land** and then **rich** in general. **Thick** and **deep** are associated meanings.

Mnemonic: **RICH WATER AIDS FARMING**

1682 把 HA, to*ru*, -wa 把握 HAAKU — grasp
TAKE, GRASP, BUNDLE 把住 HAJŪ — retention
7 strokes 把手 TOTTE — handle

扌 is **hand** 32. 巴 is **crouching figure** 145, here acting phonetically to express **grasp** and possibly also lending connotations of bending down . Thus (bend down and?) **grasp in the hand**, later **grasp** in a broad sense including the figurative. It is also used to count **armfuls/ bundles**.

Mnemonic: **CROUCHING FIGURE GRASPS BUNDLE IN HAND**

1683 覇 HA 覇権 HAKEN — domination
DOMINATION, RULE 覇気 HAKI — ambition
19 strokes 制覇 SEIHA — supremacy

Formerly 霸 , comprising **moon** 月 16 and 䍃 . The latter is a now defunct character meaning bleach and by extension **white**. It shows **leather/ hide** 革 821 being exposed to the weather -- symbolised by **rain** 雨 3 -- and refers to a carcass being reduced to bleached white bones. Thus 霸 originally meant **white moonlight**. It acquired the meaning of **domination/ rule** as a result of its being borrowed as an elegant substitute for count/ principal person 伯 1694 q.v. (literally person 亻 39 and white 白 65, though technically white 白 is used to mean principal). Principal person came to mean ruler/ dominant person, and thus symbolised rule/ domination. The modern form uses **west** 西 152 as a simplification of rain/ weather 雨 . Suggest taking 月 as meat/ (of the) **body** 365.

Mnemonic: **BODIES IN WESTERNS DOMINATED BY LEATHER**

1684   BA, baba 老婆 RŌBA — old woman
OLD WOMAN 産婆 SANBA — midwife
11 strokes 鬼婆 ONIBABA — witch, hag

女 is **woman** 35. 波 is **wave** 367, here acting phonetically to express **white** and also lending connotations of **white and billowing**. 1684 originally referred to an **old woman with billowing white hair**. Now **old woman** in general.

Mnemonic: **WOMAN SINKING UNDER WAVES IS OLD WOMAN**

537

| 1685 | | HAI, sakazuki
WINECUP, CUP(FUL)
8 strokes | 玉杯 GYOKUHAI jade cup
一杯 IPPAI cup, full, all
杯事 SAKAZUKIGOTO
exchange of cups |

木 is **wood** 69, here meaning **wooden item**. 不 is calyx/ **not** 572 q.v., here acting phonetically to express **hold**. Thus **wooden item for holding**, i.e. a **wooden vessel**. From the outset this was associated with a **wooden winecup/ goblet**, suggesting that 不 may also have been chosen for its shape, since its early form 呆 may be felt to be similar to a goblet or to the early form 呈 of dish/ vessel 皿 1307. Note that both 盃 and 桮 are found as variants of 杯. 1685 is now also used to refer to **cup(ful)** in a broad sense.

Mnemonic: **WINECUP NOT NECESSARILY OF WOOD**

| 1686 | | HAI
REJECT, EXPEL,
PUSH, ANTI-
11 strokes | 排除 HAIJO removal
排水 HAISUI drainage
排気ガス HAIKIGASU exhaust gas |

扌 is **hand** 32. 非 is **not/ spreading wings** 773 q.v., here acting phonetically to express **open** and also lending its own connotations of **spread apart/ open up**. Thus to **push apart with the hands and open up**, as of doors etc. (see 1730). Later used in a range of extended/ associated meanings, such as **push aside**, **reject**, **expel**, and **anti-**.

Mnemonic: **REJECTED, BUT NOT NECESSARILY WITH THE HANDS**

| 1687 | 廃 | HAI, sutaru/reru
ABANDON(ED),
OBSOLETE
12 strokes | 廃止 HAISHI abolition
廃寺 HAIJI ruined temple
廃り物 SUTARIMONO
obsolete thing |

Formerly 廢. 广 is **building** 114. 發/発 is discharge/ **leave** 370 q.v., here acting phonetically to express **abandon(ed)** and also lending similar connotations of **leave**. Thus an **abandoned building**, now **abandoned/ obsolete** in general.

Mnemonic: **LEAVE BUILDING TO BE ABANDONED**

538

1688 **HAI**
FELLOW, COMPANION,
LINE
15 strokes

我輩 WAGAHAI I, me
先輩 SENPAI one's senior
輩出 HAISHUTSU
  successive appearance

車 is **vehicle** 31. 非 is **not/ spreading wings** 773 q.v., here acting phonetically to express **line up** and also lending its own connotations of **spread out**. 1688 originally referred to a **procession of vehicles**, and came to mean **line/ file** on the one hand and **co-traveler/ companion** on the other. It is also used to refer to **person(s)** in general.

Mnemonic: **COMPANIONS IN A LINE, IF NOT IN VEHICLES**

1689 **BAI, ume**
PLUM
10 strokes

梅花 BAIKA plum blossom
梅酒 UMESHU plum wine
梅雨 BAIU/ TSUYU*
  summer rain

Formerly 梅. 木 is **tree** 69. 每/毎 is **every/** each 206 q.v., here in its early sense of **fertile growth**. Like the **peach** 桃 1646 q.v., the plum was a favorite fruit of pregnant women and was thus associated with pregnancy and hence procreation/ fertility. 1689 means literally **tree of fertility**, i.e. **plum tree**. There is a theory that 毎 is used purely phonetically to express big, giving big tree, and that plum is a pure borrowing, but this is far from convincing.

Mnemonic: **EVERY TREE SHOULD BE A PLUM TREE**

1690 **BAI, tsuchika*u***
CULTIVATE, GROW
11 strokes

培養 BAIYŌ cultivation
栽培者 SAIBAISHA grower
培地 BAICHI culture (medium)

土 is **soil/ ground** 60. 咅 is the obscure element spit 384, here acting phonetically to express **build up** but of unclear semantic role. 1690 originally referred to **building up soil (to ensure fertility)**, and later came to mean **cultivate/ grow** in a broad sense. Suggest taking 立 as **stand** 73 and 口 as **opening/ hole** 20.

Mnemonic: **STAND IN HOLE TO CULTIVATE GROUND**

1691

BAI
ATTEND, ACCOMPANY
11 strokes

陪席者 BAISEKISHA　attendant
陪審 BAISHIN　jury
陪音 BAION　harmonics

阝 is **hill** 229. 音 is the obscure element spit 384, here acting phonetically to express **build up** but of unclear semantic role. 1691 originally referred to **one hill 'built on' another**, i.e. a **range of hills**. By association it was later applied to **groups of things** in general, especially people, and thus came to mean **one person added to others in a group**, i.e. an **attendant/ accompanying person**. Suggest taking 立 as **stand** 73 and 口 as opening/ **hole** 20.

Mnemonic:**ACCOMPANYING ATTENDANT STANDS IN HOLE IN HILLSIDE**

1692 媒

BAI
INTERMEDIARY
12 strokes

媒介 BAIKAI　mediation
触媒 SHOKUBAI　catalyst
媒体 BAITAI　medium

女 is **woman** 35. 某 is **a certain** 1811 q.v., here acting phonetically to express **seek/ inquire** and also lending its connotations of **liaison** and **matchmaking**. 1692 originally referred to making an **inquiry about a (pregnant?) woman's suitability as a prospective marriage partner** (some scholars feel rather inquiry about a woman's feelings towards marriage). From this it came to mean (be an) **intermediary** in a broad sense. See also 1818.

Mnemonic: **ACT AS INTERMEDIARY REGARDING A CERTAIN WOMAN**

1693

BAI
COMPENSATE
15 strokes

賠償 BAISHŌ　compensation
賠償金 BAISHŌKIN　damages
損害賠償 SONGAIBAISHŌ
indemnity

貝 is shell/ **money** 90. 音 is the obscure element spit 384, here acting phonetically to express **compensate** but of unclear semantic role. Thus to **compensate with money**. Suggest taking 立 as **stand** 73 and 口 as opening/ **hole** 20.

Mnemonic: **COMPENSATED WITH MONEY FOR STANDING IN HOLE**

1694

HAKU 伯爵 HAKUSHAKU count, earl
COUNT, SENIOR FIGURE 伯父 OJI* uncle
7 strokes 画伯 GAHAKU master artist

亻 is **person** 39. 白 is **white** 65 q.v., here in its literal sense of **thumb(nail)**. Since a thumb was the principal finger it often symbolised **principal/ leading**, as here. Thus **principal person**, a reference to a leader. It is now applied to a range of 'leading persons'/ **senior figures** such as elder brother, uncle, chief official etc., but is used in particular of **count/ earl**.

Mnemonic: **COUNT IS A WHITE PERSON**

1695

HAKU, HYŌ 拍手 HAKUSHU hand clapping
BEAT, TAP, CLAP 拍子 HYŌSHI beat, rhythm
8 strokes 拍車 HAKUSHA spur

扌 is **hand** 32. 白 is **white** 65 q.v., here acting phonetically to express **beat/ tap**. It is not clear whether 白 also plays any semantic role, but it may possibly suggest either **leading** or **fingernail** (from its original meaning of thumbnail: see also 1694). Thus to **tap with the hand** (fingernail?), a reference to tapping out a beat/ tune (thereby leading a rhythm?). Now **beat/ tap** in a broader sense, as well as **clap**.

Mnemonic: **CLAP TILL HANDS GO WHITE**

1696

HAKU, tomaru/meru 宿泊 SHUKUHAKU lodging
STAY, LODGE 泊まり番 TOMARIBAN night duty
8 strokes 一泊 IPPAKU overnight,
one night's stay

氵 is **water** 40. 白 is **white** 65, here acting phonetically to express **shallow**. It is possible that originally 白 also lent its meaning of white, since white water is generally associated with shallows. However, from an early stage 1696 became associated with shallow water suitable for an **anchorage**, then came to mean **stopping place** and eventually **stop/ stay** in general.

Mnemonic: **STAY IN WHITE WATER?!**

1697

HAKU, sema*ru*
PRESS, DRAW NEAR
8 strokes

迫害 HAKUGAI　　oppression
迫力 HAKURYOKU　　force
切迫 SEPPAKU　　pressure

辶 is **movement** 129. 白 is **white** 65, here acting phonetically to express **draw near** but of unclear semantic role. Thus **move and draw near**, later also used figuratively in the sense of **press/ be imminent/ be compelling**.

Mnemonic: **PRESSING MOVEMENT TURNS ONE WHITE**

1698

HAKU
SHIP, SHIPPING
11strokes

船舶 SENPAKU　　shipping
舶来 HAKURAI　　importation
舶用 HAKUYŌ　　marine-

舟 is **boat** 1354. 白 is **white** 65, here acting phonetically to express **large** and possibly also lending a suggestion of principal/ chief (see 1694). Thus **large boat** (principal of fleet?), i.e. a **ship**, with **shipping** being an associated meaning.

Mnemonic: **WHITE BOAT USED FOR SHIPPING**

1699

HAKU, usu*i/maru/meru*
THIN, WEAK,
SHALLOW, LIGHT
16 strokes

薄着 USUGI　　light clothes
軽薄 KEIHAKU　　frivolity
薄皮 USUKAWA　　thin skin

Formerly 薄. 艹 is **plants** 9. 溥/溥 is a CO character meaning **extensive/** pervasive, comprising **water** 氵 40 and **spread** 尃/専 564 and presumably originally meaning extensive body of water. 1699 originally meant **extensive vegetation**, i.e. **luxuriant/ dense growth**, and still retains this as a minor meaning in Chinese. Its present core meaning of **sparse/ insubstantial**, which confusingly is the opposite of its real meaning, results from borrowing. It is unclear why such a seemingly inappropriate character was borrowed.

Mnemonic: **THIN PLANT COVERING SPREAD OVER SHALLOW WATER**

1700

BAKU
VAGUE, VAST, DESERT
13 strokes

漠然 BAKUZEN   vague
漠漠 BAKUBAKU vast, vague
砂漠 SABAKU   desert

氵 is **water** 40. 莫 is sun sinking in grass 788 q.v., here acting phonetically to express **smothered/ covered** and also lending its own similar connotations of **hidden**. A place where the **water is hidden/** covered (i.e. inaccessible) is a **desert**. **Vast** is an associated meaning, with **vague/ undelineated** being a further association. Suggest taking 艹 as **plant** 9, 日 as **sun** 62, and 大 as **big** 53.

Mnemonic: **IN VAST DESERT, BIG PLANTS NEED SUN AND WATER**

1701

BAKU, shiba*ru*
BIND
16 strokes

束縛 SOKUBAKU   restraint
捕縛 HOBAKU   capture
縛り首 SHIBARIKUBI hanging

Formerly also 縛. 糸 is **thread** 27, here meaning **cord**. 尃/専 is **spread** 564 q.v., here acting phonetically to express **bind** and probably also lending connotations of **extensive**. Thus to **bind (extensively?) with cord**, now **bind** in a broad sense.

Mnemonic: **BIND WITH SPREAD THREADS**

1702

BAKU
BURST, EXPLODE
19 strokes

爆発 BAKUHATSU explosion
爆弾 BAKUDAN   bomb
原爆 GENBAKU atom bomb

火 is **fire** 8. 暴 is **violence/ expose** 793 q.v., here acting phonetically to express **burn** and possibly also lending connotations of **heat** and/or **violent action**. 暴 also lends its sound **BAKU** in an onomatopoeic sense. 1702 originally referred to something **burning in a fire and bursting/ exploding (violently?) with a BAKU sound**. Now **burst/ explode** in general.

Mnemonic: **VIOLENT FIRE CAUSES EXPLOSION**

1703 箱

hako, SŌ
BOX
15 strokes

小箱 KOBAKO   little box
箱舟 HAKOBUNE   ark
箱入り HAKOIRI   boxed

竹 is **bamboo** 170. 相 is **mutual** 530, here acting phonetically to express **both sides** and also lending similar connotations. 1703 originally referred to bamboo frames put on either side of a cart, then came to mean **container/ box** in a broad sense.

Mnemonic: **BAMBOO SIDES MUTUALLY OPPOSED IN BOX**

1704	hada, KI SKIN, TEXTURE, GRAIN 6 strokes	肌色 HADAIRO flesh color 素肌 SUHADA bare skin 肌理 KIME * texture, grain

月 is **meat/ of the body** 365. 几 is **table/ desk** 832, here acting phonetically to express **cover** and possibly also lending a similar suggestion through its shape (cover often being represented by ⌐). **That which covers the meat/ body** is the **skin**. **Texture** and **grain** are associated meanings.

Mnemonic: **BODY AT DESK COVERED IN SKIN**

1705	HACHI, HATSU BOWL, POT, SKULL 13 strokes	植木鉢 UEKIBACHI plant pot 鉢巻き HACHIMAKI headband 衣鉢 IHATSU master's mantle

A relatively recent character, but of obscure and disputed etymology due to a dearth of earlier forms. 金 is **metal** 14. 本 is taken by some scholars to be **root/ source** 70, here in a sense of **base**. Thus **item with metal base**, a rather vague reference to a **bowl**. Other scholars believe that 本 derives from 朩, an element felt to show a **thickly growing plant**, and that it acts here phonetically to express **big** as well as possibly lending connotations of **edible plant**. Thus **big metal item (for vegetables?)**, a similarly vague reference to a **bowl**. Neither of these theories seems especially convincing. It is equally likely that 本 is root 70 (usually pronounced HON) acting phonetically to express **basket**, specifically the NGU character HON basket 畚 (etymology unclear, but 由 is basket 399). Thus **metal basket**, i.e. **metal bowl**. The pronunciation may have changed to HATSU/ HACHI under the influence of a now defunct character with those readings 盋 , which also meant (big) bowl (vessel 皿 1307 and the obscure element 犮 [see 1706], the latter acting phonetically to express big). 1705 clearly originally referred to a metal vessel, but is now used of a range of vessels, including the **skull**.

Mnemonic: **ROOTED IN METAL BOWL**

1706 髪	HATSU, kami HAIR 14 strokes	頭髪 TŌHATSU the hair 散髪 SANPATSU haircut 髪型 KAMIGATA hairstyle

Formerly 髮 . 髟 is a CO character meaning **hair**, comprising **hairs** 彡 93 and **long** 長 (variant 镸 173). 犮 is an obscure element, though an early form 犮 appears very similar to an early form 犮 of dog 犬 17. Here 犮 acts phonetically to express **grow**, while any semantic role is unclear. Thus **growing hair**, now simply **hair**. Suggest taking 友 as **friend** 214, and 彡 as **three strands**.

Mnemonic: **FRIEND'S HAIR INCLUDES THREE LONG STRANDS**

1707 BATSU, HATSU   伐採 BASSAI   felling
ATTACK, CUT DOWN   征伐 SEIBATSU   punishment
6 strokes   殺伐 SATSUBATSU na brutal

Person 亻 39 and **halberd** 戈 493, meaning to **cut down a person with a halberd** and hence **attack**. Now also **cut down** in a broad sense. The Japanese reading BATSU/ HATSU (originally FUA, and in Chinese now FA) is onomatopoeic, expressing the sound of a sword/ halberd cutting a person down. It is also related to the adverb bassari, used of cutting people down.

Mnemonic: **PERSON ATTACKED AND CUT DOWN WITH HALBERD**

1708 BATSU, nu*ku*/*karu*/*keru*/*kasu*   抜群 BATSUGUN preeminence
PLUCK, EXTRACT,   抜け穴 NUKEANA   loophole
MISS   手抜かり TENUKARI   omission
7 strokes

Formerly 拔. 扌 is **hand** 32. 犮 is the obscure element seen in 1706, here acting phonetically to express **extract** but of unclear semantic role. Thus to **extract with the hand**, now **extract/ pluck** in a broad sense. **Miss (out)** is an associated meaning. Suggest taking 友 as **friend** 214.

Mnemonic: **PLUCK FRIEND AWAY BY THE HAND**

1709 罰 BATSU, BACHI   罰金 BAKKIN   fine
PUNISHMENT   処罰 SHOBATSU punishment
14 strokes   罰当り BACHIATARI no damned

刂 is **sword**/ **cut** 181. 詈 is an NGU character meaning ridicule/ **criticise**, comprising **net** 罒 193 (here meaning **trap**/ **ensnare**) and **words** 言 274. Here 詈 acts phonetically to express **threaten** and also lends its meaning of **criticise**. Thus to **threaten someone with sword and critical words**, meaning to **rebuke**. This later came to mean **punish**.

Mnemonic: **NETTED, THEN PUNISHED WITH WORDS AND SWORD**

| 1710 | | **BATSU** **FACTION, CLAN,** **LINEAGE** 14 strokes | 門閥 MONBATSU 閥族 BATSUZOKU 財閥 ZAIBATSU | lineage clan zaibatsu |

門 is door/ **gate** 211, here symbolising **house** in a broad sense. 伐 is **cut down** 1707 q.v., here acting phonetically to express **emerge** but of unclear semantic role. The **house from which one emerges** indicates one's **clan** and by extension **lineage**, with **faction** being an associated meaning. It is not clear why a character with such sinister overtones as 伐 should be chosen as a phonetic. Though its reading BATSU is perfectly valid, it seems possible that it was confused with the graphically and phonetically similar BATSU 犮 1706, which unfortunately is an element of unclear meaning.

Mnemonic: **CLAN MEMBER CUT DOWN AT GATE**

| 1711 | | **HAN, ho** **SAIL** 6 strokes | 帆船 HANSEN 帆柱 HOBASHIRA 帆掛ける HOKAKERU | sailboat mast set sail |

巾 is **cloth** 778. 凡 is **common/ mediocre** 1827, here acting as a simplification of **wind** 風 198 q.v. and almost certainly also used for its shape (which may be felt to suggest a sail). Thus **'wind cloth'**, i.e. **sail**.

Mnemonic: **MEDIOCRE CLOTH USED FOR SAIL**

| 1712 | | **HAN, BAN, tomona**u **ACCOMPANY** 7 strokes | 同伴者 DŌHANSHA companion 伴奏者 BANSŌSHA accompanist 相伴う AITOMONAU accompany |

Of disputed etymology, though its elements are clearly **person** 亻 39 and **half** 半 195 q.v. Some scholars believe that 半 originally acted phonetically to express **fat** (as well as lending similar connotations from its literal meaning of half a cow?), and that 1712 originally meant **fat person** before being borrowed to express **accompany**. Other scholars feel that 半 acts phonetically to express **accompany** and also lends a suggestion of **less than whole**, i.e. to the effect that **one person alone is less than whole** and thus needs **company**. The latter theory seems the more helpful.

Mnemonic: **PERSON ONLY HALF COMPLETE UNLESS ACCOMPANIED**

1713

HAN, aze
RIDGE, EDGE
10 strokes

池畔　CHIHAN　　　edge of pond
湖畔　KOHAN　　　　lakeside
湖畔詩人　KOHANSHIJIN

Lake Poet

田 is **(paddy) field** 59. 半 is **half** 195 q.v., here in its literal meaning of **divide**. Thus **that which divides a (paddy) field**, i.e. **ridge/** raised path. **Edge** is an associated meaning.

Mnemonic: **RIDGE DIVIDES FIELD IN HALF, FROM EDGE TO EDGE**

1714

HAN
GENERAL, TIME, CARRY
10 strokes

一般　IPPAN　　　　general
全般　ZENPAN　　　the whole
過般　KAHAN　　　　recently

舟 is **boat** 1354 q.v. 殳 is **striking hand** 153, here acting as a causative element. 1714 originally meant to **cause a boat (to move)**, i.e. **to sail**. Since boats were also associated with **conveying** it also came to mean **convey/ carry** (a meaning now largely assumed by 搬 1716, which adds hand 扌 32). The present main meaning of **general** and the lesser meaning of **time** are both borrowed. Suggest remembering by a play on the words **hand** (as in worker) and **strike** (as in go on strike).

Mnemonic: **HAND ON BOAT GOES ON GENERAL STRIKE**

1715

HAN
SELL, TRADE
11 strokes

販売　HANBAI　　　selling
市販　SHIHAN　　　marketing
販路　HANRO　　　　market

貝 is **shell/ money** 90. 反 is **oppose** 371 q.v., here acting phonetically to express **accumulate** and also lending connotations of **exchange** from its literal meaning of turning over the hand (cf. English term turn-over). Thus to **accumulate money by exchanging** (goods for money), i.e. **sell/ trade**.

Mnemonic: **OPPOSED TO USE OF MONEY IN SELLING?!**

1716

HAN
CARRY, TRANSPORT
13 strokes

運搬　UNPAN　　　transportation
搬送　HANSŌ　　　conveyance
搬送帯　HANSŌTAI conveyor belt

General/ carry 般 1714 q.v., here in its original meaning of **carry**, with the addition of hand 扌 32. Thus to **carry by hand**, now **carry** in a broad sense.

Mnemonic: **GENERAL TRANSPORT CAN INCLUDE CARRYING BY HAND**

547

1717

HAN, BON, wazura*u/washii*
TROUBLE, PAIN,
TORMENT
13 strokes

煩雑 HANZATSU complication
煩悩 BONNŌ   carnal desire
煩労 HANRŌ   trouble, worry

Fire 火 8 in the **head** 頁 93, indicating **fever** and by association **torment** and **pain**. **Trouble** is a further associated meaning.

Mnemonic: **FIRE IN HEAD CAUSES TORMENT AND PAIN**

1718

HAN
DISTRIBUTE, DIVIDE
13 strokes

頒布 HANPU   distribution
頒行 HANKŌ   distribution
頒白 HANPAKU graying hair

頁 is **head** 93, here meaning **mind**. 分 is **divide** 199. Thus a **divided mind**, later **divide** in general. **Distribute** is an associated meaning. Some scholars believe that 分 acts phonetically to express big and that 1718 originally meant big head (in a physical sense), with divide and distribute being borrowed meanings. This is not convincing.

Mnemonic: **DIVIDED HEAD DISTRIBUTES THOUGHTS**

1719 範

HAN
MODEL, NORM, LIMITS
15 strokes

模範 MOHAN   model
規範 KIHAN   standard, norm
範囲内 HANINAI   within limits

Obscure. 竹 is **bamboo** 170, 車 is **vehicle** 31, and 㔾 is **slumped person** 768. The original meaning is believed to have been **purify a vehicle** (as part of a religious ceremony), thus indicating that 車 acts semantically. It is not clear whether the phonetic element (expressing **purify**) is 范 or 㔾 alone. There does not appear to have been any character 范, though it is possible that it is a variant of the CO character 笆, which means bamboo fence (巴 being bending figure 145, thus giving bending bamboo, and possibly also playing some unclear phonetic role). In any event, **model** is a borrowed meaning, with **norm** being an associated meaning with model. **Limit(s)** is felt to be a further association in turn with norm (i.e. from the idea of guidelines).

Mnemonic: **PERSON SLUMPED BESIDE BAMBOO MODEL OF VEHICLE**

| 1720 | | **HAN, shige*ru*** **PROFUSE, RICH,** **COMPLEX** 16 strokes | 繁盛 HANJŌ prosperity 繁雑 HANZATSU complexity 繁殖 HANSHOKU propagation |

Somewhat obscure. Formerly 緐糸. 糸 is **thread** 27. 每 is **every** 206 q.v., here acting phonetically to express **intertwine** and also lending connotations of **profusion** from its original meaning of fertile growth. 1720 originally referred to **strong cord made by intertwining numerous threads**. The reason for the later addition of **striking hand/ cause** 攵 101 is unclear, but it is believed to draw attention to the <u>making up</u> of such cord. Some scholars see the present meanings as borrowings, but it seems equally likely that the **profusion of threads** associated with 每 gave rise to the idea of **profusion** in general, with **rich** and **complex** being further associated meanings.

Mnemonic: **HAND STRIKES EVERY THREAD IN PROFUSELY COMPLEX TANGLE**

| 1721 | | **HAN** **FIEF, CLAN, FENCE** 18 strokes | 藩主 HANSHU feudal lord 藩べい HANBEI fence 加賀藩 KAGAHAN Kaga Clan/Fief |

艹 is **grass/** plants 9, here meaning **brushwood** (as 904). 潘 is a CO character used to refer to a tributary of the Han River. It comprises **water/ river** 氵 40 and **turn/** number 番 196 q.v., the latter being used as the phonetic HAN but almost certainly also being used for its literal elements of **rice** 釆 (variant 米 201) and **field** 田 59, thus combining with water/ river 氵 to give a strong and appropriate suggestion of **fertile area**. In the case of 1721 潘 acts phonetically to express **fence** and almost certainly also lends a suggestion of fertile area. Thus **brushwood fence** (around fertile area?). It is still occasionally used in this meaning, but is generally used in the associated meaning of **fief** (i.e. the [fertile?] area enclosed by a fence) or the further associated meaning of **clan**.

Mnemonic: **CLAN TAKES TURNS TO USE GRASS AND WATER OF FIEF**

1722	蛮	BAN BARBARIAN 12 strokes	蛮人	BANJIN	barbarian
			蛮行	BANKŌ	barbarism
			野蛮	YABAN	barbarism

Formerly 蠻. 虫 is **snake/ insect** 56 q.v., while 絲 is **tied together/ complicated** 581. 絲 was also used to refer to a **certain region in southern China** (largely for phonetic reasons, but it presumably also lent connotations of troublesome), a region considered **barbarous/** uncivilised, and thus it is technically the correct prototype of 1722. **Snake** 虫 was added to refer to a snake associated with the region in question (still retained as a minor meaning of 1722 in Chinese), but in time 蠻 came like 絲 to refer to the region itself and hence to symbolise **barbarity/ barbarism**. Suggest remembering 亦 by association with **red** 赤 46, taking it as **reddish**.

Mnemonic: **'REDDISH INSECT' REFERS TO BARBARIAN**

1723	盤	BAN TRAY, BOARD, BOWL, PLATE 15 strokes	円盤	ENBAN	disc, discus
			基盤	KIBAN	base
			水盤	SUIBAN	bowl

General/ carry 般 1714 q.v., here in its original meaning of **carry**, with **dish/ bowl/ plate** 皿 1307 added. Thus **dish/ bowl/ plate for carrying things**. Later also **board/ plate** in a broader sense.

Mnemonic: **DISH IS GENERALLY CARRIED ON TRAY**

1724	妃	HI QUEEN, PRINCESS 6 strokes	王妃	ŌHI	queen, empress
			妃殿下	HIDENKA	Her Highness
			皇太子妃	KŌTAISHIHI	crown princess

女 is **woman/ women** 35. 己 is **self/ thread** 855, here acting phonetically to express **line** and also lending similar connotations of **thread/ sequence**. Thus **women in a line**, a reference to **imperial consorts** and by association **queen/ princess**.

Mnemonic: **WOMAN THINKS HERSELF A PRINCESS**

1725

HI, kare, kano, are, *ano*
HE, THAT,
DISTANT GOAL
8 strokes

彼氏 KARESHI he, boyfriend
彼女 KANOJO she, girlfriend
彼岸 HIGAN equinox,
other shore, goal

彳 is **movement** (along a road) 118. 皮 is **skin** 374 q.v., here acting phonetically to express **distance** and probably also lending connotations of part (from its literal meaning of parting the skin from the flesh). Thus to **move into the distance** (thus parting?), a reference to **heading for a distant destination/ goal**. It also came to mean **yonder**, and hence **that** (over there). Its use as a **third person pronoun** results from the associated idea of **that person**.

Mnemonic: HE HAS MOVING SKIN, DOES THAT PERSON!

1726

HI
OPEN, DISCLOSE
8 strokes

披見 HIKEN perusal
披歴 HIREKI disclosure
披露 HIRŌ announcement

扌 is **hand** 32. 皮 is **skin** 374 q.v., here acting phonetically to express **open** and almost certainly also lending connotations of **pull off cover** (from its literal meaning of pulling the skin off an animal). Thus **(pull?) open by hand**, now **open/ disclose** in a broad sense.

Mnemonic: SKIN ON HAND OPENED UP

1727

HI, iya*shii/shimu*
LOWLY, MEAN, DESPISE
9 strokes

卑下 HIGE humility
卑屈 HIKUTSU baseness
卑近 HIKIN na common

Once written 𤰞 , showing a **hand** 又 holding a **wine-pressing basket** 甶 (variant 甶 / 由 399) upside-down, in order to extract the last drops. This was considered **mean** and **petty**, leading to **mean/ lowly** in a general sense. **Despise** is an associated meaning. Suggest taking 田 as **field** 59, 十 as a variant of **ten** 十 33, and 丿 as **bits**.

Mnemonic: MEAN AND LOWLY PERSON PICKS BITS FROM TEN FIELDS

1728

HI, tsuka*reru*
TIRE, EXHAUSTION
10 strokes

疲労 HIRŌ   fatigue
疲れ目 TSUKAREME   eyestrain
疲れ切る TSUKAREKIRU
           be worn out

疒 is **sickness** 381, here indicating **being unwell/ lacking vitality**. 皮 is **skin** 374 q.v., here indicating **break down/ collapse** and probably also lending supporting connotations of a body breaking into pieces (from its literal meaning of skin being separated from the meat). Thus to **collapse and lack vitality**, a rather vague reference to **exhaustion**.

Mnemonic: **SKIN SICKNESS CAN BE TIRESOME**

1729

HI, kō*muru*, ō *u*
SUSTAIN, COVER, WEAR
10 strokes

被害者 HIGAISHA   victim
被服 HIFUKU   clothing
被告人 HIKOKUNIN   defendant

衤 is **clothing** 420. 皮 is **skin** 374, here acting phonetically to express **cover** and almost certainly lending similar connotations of its own. Thus **cover (oneself) with clothes**, i.e. **wear**. Now also used in a range of associated and extended meanings, such as **don**, **take on**, **sustain**, **suffer** etc.

Mnemonic: **SUSTAINED BY CLOTHES COVERING SKIN**

1730

HI, tobira
DOOR, FRONT PAGE
12 strokes

開扉 KAIHI   opening of door
門扉 MONPI   doors of gate
扉絵 TOBIRAE   frontispiece

戸 is **door** 108. 非 is **not/ spreading wings** 773, here meaning literally **spreading wings/ flaps**. 1730 technically refers to the **flaps/ wings of a door**, but is generally used to refer to the **door** in its entirety, and is also used by association of **pages** (especially the **front page**).

Mnemonic: **A DOOR IS NOT A DOOR!? MUST MAKE THE FRONT PAGE!**

1731

HI
TOMBSTONE, MONUMENT
14 strokes

碑銘 HIMEI   epitaph
石碑 SEKIHI   tombstone
記念碑 KINENHI   monument

石 is **stone/ rock** 45. 卑 is **lowly** 1727, here acting phonetically to express **upright** but of unclear semantic role. 1731 originally referred to a **rock/ stone placed upright in the ground as a primitive sundial**, and then came to mean **upright stone** in a broader sense, eventually coming to mean in particular **tombstone** and **monument**.

Mnemonic: **TOMBSTONE IS A LOWLY STONE**

1732 **HI, maka***ru*	罷業 HIGYŌ	strike
CEASE, LEAVE, GO	罷免 HIMEN	dismissal
15 strokes	罷り通る MAKARITŌRU	pass

罒 is **net** 193. 能 is **ability/ bear** 766 q.v., here acting phonetically to express **set/ leave** and possibly also lending its early meaning of **bear**. Thus to **set/ leave a net (for a bear?)**, a very similar meaning to that of put 置 545. However, in the case of 1732 the idea of leaving something broadened to give a range of extended and associated meanings, such as **leave a place** and thus **go**, and also **abandon** and thus **cease** (doing something). Suggest taking 能 in its sense of **bear**.

Mnemonic: **CEASE WORK, LEAVING BEAR IN NET**

1733 **HI, sa***keru*	回避 KAIHI	avoidance
AVOID	不可避 FUKAHI	unavoidable
16 strokes	避妊 HININ	contraception

辟 is an NGU character with a wide range of meanings, such as false, punish, crime, law, and ruler, while in Chinese (even after discounting the obvious borrowings) it can also mean punish, castrate, execute, wail, perverse, specious, flattery, decadent, remove, twist, open, develop, summon, and appoint. It comprises **buttocks** 尸 236, **opening/ hole** 口 20, and **needle/ sharp** 辛 1432 q.v. Buttocks 尸 and hole 口 clearly combine to give **anus**, as in 后 858 q.v. Needle 辛 is used in its sense of **pierce/ penetrate**, to give **anal penetration** (see also vaginal penetration 商 317). This core meaning gave rise on the one hand to a range of meanings associated with **torture/ punishment**, which also symbolised **law** and **authority**, and on the other to meanings associated with **sodomy**, which when used in relation to a male partner was also a symbol of **flattery**. (Note that when combined with woman 女 35 it gives an NGU character 嬖, which in Chinese means sexual partner/ lecherous/ depraved [though in Japanese it is listed with the euphemistic meaning of agreeable person]. When 嬖 is itself combined with child 童 363 it gives in Chinese a compound term meaning catamite.) In the case of 1733 辟 acts phonetically to express **evade**, though its semantic role is a matter of conjecture, and combines with **movement** 辶 129 to give **evasive movement**.

Mnemonic: **MOVE TO AVOID NEEDLE IN ANUS**

1734 **BI, o**
TAIL
7 strokes

尾骨 BIKOTSU coccyx
交尾 KŌBI copulation
しっ尾 SHIPPO* tail

Buttocks ア 236 and **hair** 毛 210, a reference to a **tail**. Also sometimes used to refer to **genitals** (especially male). In compounds often found as 尸 (or, early on, simply 木).

Mnemonic: **TAIL IS HAIR BELOW BUTTOCKS**

1735 **BI**
TINY, OBSCURE,
FAINT, SECRETIVE
13 strokes

微細 BISAI minuteness
微光 BIKŌ faint light
微行 BIKŌ traveling incognito

Once written 徴, showing **movement (along a road)** 彳 118, hand holding stick/ **force** 攵/攴 101, and **bent old man** 长 (variant 耂 117/173, and here meaning simply **crouched**). Thus to **make someone move (along a road) in a crouched fashion**, i.e. so as to avoid detection and hence **secretively**. The causative aspect presently faded, leaving just **move secretively**. Though this meaning is still occasionally encountered (see bikō above), 1735 is usually used in the associated meanings of **obscure, faint,** and **tiny** (i.e. from the idea of being hard to see -- see also 1227). Suggest taking 山 as **mountain** 24 and 几 as a variant of **table** 几 832.

Mnemonic: **FORCED TO MOVE TINY TABLE UP MOUNTAIN IN SECRET**

1736 匹 **HITSU, hiki**
MATCH,COMMON,CLOTH
ANIMAL COUNTER
4 strokes

匹敵 HITTEKI match
匹夫 HIPPU common man
一匹 IPPIKI one animal

Once written ᶕᶘ, showing that ⊏ is not container ⊏ 225 but a stylised miscopying of 厂. This is itself a simplification of oppose/ **(roll of) cloth** 反 371 q.v., here in its sense of **roll of cloth**. ᶘ shows **two rolls of cloth of equal length**. It is in effect a doubling of 厂, and in fact can refer to a specific quantity of cloth twice the length of 反 (i.e. approximately 20 m.), but is generally used in the extended sense of **equal/ match**. **Common** is an associated meaning with equal, i.e. one item much the same as any other. It is not clear how 1736 also came to be used as a **counter for animals**. Note that hiki is a Japanese (i.e. kun) reading, and not a Chinese (i.e. on) reading as popularly believed. Suggest remembering 匹 by association with **four** 四 26.

Mnemonic: **COUNT MATCHING ANIMALS -- NOT QUITE FOUR?!**

1737

HITSU, HI
FLOW, SECRETE
8 strokes

分泌 BUNPITSU　　　secretion
泌尿 HINYŌ　　　urination
泌尿器科 HINYŌKIKA　　urology

氵 is **water** 40. 必 is **necessarily** 568, here acting phonetically to express **unceasingly** and possibly also lending supporting connotations of **inexorably**. Thus **unceasingly (flowing) water**. In Chinese **steady flow** is 1737's only meaning, but in Japanese it has also come by association to mean **secrete/ ooze**.

Mnemonic: WATER NECESSARILY SECRETED

1738

hime, KI
PRINCESS, LADY,
LITTLE, PRETTY
10 strokes

姫宮 HIMEMIYA　　　princess
姫垣 HIMEGAKI　　low fence
洋子姫 YŌKOHIME
　　　　　Princess Yōko

Somewhat obscure. Formerly 女臣 and earlier 𠨰, showing **woman** 𠂇 / 女 35 and also showing that **staring eye/ retainer/ guard** 𦣞 / 臣 512 q.v. is a miscopying of 𦣞 / 匝. Unfortunately the latter element is of obscure origin, but is known to have acted phonetically to express the name of a certain river (the **River Chi**), near which the legendary emperor **Huangti** (third millenium B.C.) is believed to have been born. 𦣞 / 匝 thus came to symbolise **Huangti**. 1738 originally meant **woman of the Huangti imperial family/ line**, and later came by extension to mean **princess/ noble lady** in general. **Pretty** and **little** are associated meanings. The miscopying of 匝 (intermediate form 匝) as 臣 may well have been influenced by an assumption that 1738 was intended to indicate ideographically a woman who is guarded/ protected or a woman with retainers.

Mnemonic: EYE STARES AT PRETTY LITTLE WOMAN -- A PRINCESS

1739

HYŌ, tadayou
FLOAT, DRIFT, BOB
14 strokes

漂白 HYŌHAKU　　　bleaching
漂着 HYŌCHAKU　drift ashore
漂流者 HYŌRYŪSHA　castaway

氵 is **water** 40. 票 is **sign/ vote** 570 q.v., here acting phonetically to express **float/ bob** and possibly also lending loose connotations of **bobbing/ dancing** from its original meaning of leaping flames. Thus **float/ bob on water**.

Mnemonic: FLOATING VOTE DRIFTING ON WATER?!

1740 苗 BYŌ, MYŌ, nae, nawa   種苗 SHUBYŌ   seedlings
SEEDLING, OFFSPRING   苗字 MYŌJI   family name
8 strokes   苗木 NAEGI   sapling

Plants 艹 9 still in the **field** 田 59, i.e. not yet ready for cropping. **Young plants/ seedlings** also came by association to refer to human **offspring**.

Mnemonic: **PLANTS IN FIELD ARE SEEDLINGS**

1741 描 BYŌ, egaku   描写 BYŌSHA   depiction
DEPICT, DRAW, WRITE   点描 TENBYŌ   sketch
11 strokes   描き出す EGAKIDASU   delineate

扌 is **hand** 32. 苗 is **seedling** 1740, here acting phonetically to express **copy** and possibly also originally lending a suggestion of incomplete. Thus **copy by (free-)hand** (roughly?), now **draw/ depict** in a broader sense including the figurative.

Mnemonic: **DRAW SEEDLINGS FREEHAND**

1742 BYŌ, MYŌ, neko   愛貓 AIBYŌ   pet cat
CAT   貓背 NEKOZE   a stoop
11 strokes   シャム貓 SHAMUNEKO
    Siamese cat

Formerly 貓 , i.e. with **clawed beast** 豸 1281 rather than dog/ **beast** 犭 17. 苗 is **seedling** 1740, here acting phonetically (MYŌ in Japanese, **MIAO** in Chinese) to express the **sound of a cat's call/ miaow** and possibly also lending connotations of little. Thus (little?) **clawed beast that cries MIAO**, i.e. **cat**.

Mnemonic: **BEAST AMONGST SEEDLINGS IS CAT**

1743 HIN, hama   海浜 KAIHIN   seashore
BEACH, SHORE   浜辺 HAMABE   beach, shore
10 strokes   浜跳び虫 HAMATOBIMUSHI
    sand-hopper

Formerly 濱 . 氵 is **water** 40. 賓 is **guest** 1744 q.v., here acting phonetically to express **edge** and almost certainly also lending its early meaning of **display of shells**. Thus **edge of water (where shells are to be seen?)**, i.e. **beach/ shore**. The modern form uses **soldier** 兵 578.

Mnemonic: **SOLDIERS COME BY WATER AND MAKE BEACH LANDING**

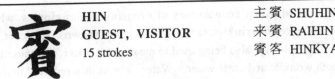

1744

HIN
GUEST, VISITOR
15 strokes

主賓 SHUHIN　guest of honor
来賓 RAIHIN　guest, visitor
賓客 HINKYAKU
　　　　　guest of honor

Somewhat obscure, and of confused etymology. Formerly 賓. 貝 is **shell/ money/ valuable item** 90. (One early form 賓 shows kettle 晟 / 鼎 / 貝 228, but this appears to be a one-off miscopying: still earlier and later forms all show shell.) 宀/宀 is a now defunct character meaning **guest**. 宀 is **roof/ house** 28, but otherwise the etymology of 宀/宀 is rather obscure. It appears to use different elements at different stages. The earliest forms such as 宀 show 丂, which is believed to be a variant of **twisting weed** 丁 / 丂 281 q.v. and may have acted symbolically to indicate **reaching and stopping** (from its characteristic of reaching the surface and then stopping -- see the parallel with inverted foot below). Later forms such as 宀 show what appears to be a stylised version of **foot** 止 /正 129 q.v./ 41, possibly in its meaning of **stopping** and thus being similar to stopping/ inverted foot 夂 438 q.v. and giving a similar character to guest/ visitor 客 252 q.v. Note however that there is a CO character 㐫 meaning **curtain/ hidden/ protected** (of unclear etymology, but possibly itself a version of foot 止 /正 -- see also 1805), and it is possible that 丆 /丆 derives from this, to give a literal meaning to 宀/宀 such as **person protected under a roof**. In any event, in the case of 1744 宀/宀 is known to have acted phonetically to express **display**, and probably also originally lent connotations of visitor. 1744 originally referred to **displaying shells/ valuable items** (believed to have been literally shells at first, as these were primitive symbols of wealth and ostentation, but later valuable items in general), probably on the occasion of a visit to one's home. It later came to mean **display** in a broader sense, but at a still later stage became confused with **guest/ visitor** 宀 /宀 and eventually replaced this (despite being the more complex of the two). Suggest taking 丆 as a combination of **one** 一 1 and **few** 少 143.

Mnemonic: **JUST ONE OR A FEW SHELLS TO SHOW VISITOR TO HOME**

1745

HIN, shikiri
FREQUENTLY, FROWN
17 strokes

頻繁 HINPAN ni　frequently
頻発 HINPATSU　frequency
頻度 HINDO　frequency

Of confused evolution. At one early stage the same character as the NGU character 瀕, which now means **verge/ shore**. The key elements are **head** 頁 93 and **cross water** 渉 1399 q.v. (**water** 氵 40 and **walk** 歩 202). 渉 originally acted phonetically to express **wave/ ripple** and also lent connotations of **crossing**. Thus **ripples which cross the head**, a reference to **wrinkles** (and by association **frown**). However, the strong presence of 涉 led to 瀬 also being used to mean **cross water**, and thus at one stage 瀬 meant both wrinkles and cross water. Water 氵 was then removed to distinguish between the meanings, with the 'waterless' 頻 being used to represent wrinkles while 瀬 developed its acquired meaning of cross water, eventually coming by association to mean **shore/ verge**. It is not fully clear how 頻 then came to mean **frequently**. Some scholars feel it is a borrowed meaning, but it seems equally likely to be an associated meaning with wrinkle through a linking concept of many/ numerous. Confusingly, 頻 is still very occasionally interchanged with 瀬 to mean shore. It is now used only rarely to mean wrinkles/ frown, this meaning having been largely assumed by an NGU character 顰 which adds lowly 卑 1727 (the role of the latter unclear).

Mnemonic: **FREQUENTLY WALK ON ONE'S HEAD**

1746 敏	BIN **AGILE, ALERT, QUICK** 10 strokes	敏速 BINSOKU	alacrity
		鋭敏 EIBIN	sharpness
		機敏 KIBIN	smartness

攵 is **hand holding stick/ striking hand** 101, here used to indicate a **moving hand.** 毎 is **every** 206 q.v., here acting phonetically to express **quick** and possibly also loosely lending an associated idea of rapidity from its connotations of rapid/ fertile growth. 1746 originally referred to **deftness in performing manual tasks**, then came to mean **deft/ quick/ agile** in a broader sense, including the mental.

Mnemonic: **EVERY HAND THAT STRIKES SHOULD BE AGILE**

1747 瓶	BIN, kame **BOTTLE, JUG, JAR** 10 strokes	瓶詰め BINZUME	bottling
		花瓶 KABIN	flower vase
		釣瓶 TSURUBE*	well-bucket

Formerly 絣瓦. 幷/并 is **put together/ pair** 1774. 瓦 is an NGU character meaning **tile** in Japanese but also **earthenware/ vessel** in Chinese (deriving from 𤓰, felt by some scholars to show interlocking tiles but by others to show two outer items 乙乙 interlocking to contain an inner item 丶). 1747 originally referred to **well-buckets**, which were often earthenware and used in tandem, but now refers to a range of vessels (particularly **jar** and **bottle**). Suggest taking 丷 as **out of** 66 and 井 as a variant of **well** 井 1470.

Mnemonic: **TILES, BOTTLES AND JARS TAKEN OUT OF WELL**

1748		FU **HELP, SUPPORT** 7 strokes	扶助 FUJO	aid
			扶養 FUYŌ	support
			扶育 FUIKU	raising children

扌 is **hand** 32. 夫 is **man/ adult male** 573, here acting phonetically to express **help** and probably also lending its meaning. Thus **helping hand (of an adult male?)**, now generally **help/ support** in a less physical sense.

Mnemonic: **MAN GIVES HELPING HAND**

1749		FU, kowa*i* **FEAR, AFRAID** 8 strokes	恐怖症 KYŌFUSHŌ	phobia
			い怖 IFU	dread, awe
			恐怖小説 KYŌFUSHŌSETSU	
				horror story

忄 is **heart/ feelings** 147. 布 is **cloth** 778, here acting phonetically to express **fear** and possibly also lending an associated suggestion of wrapping/ **enveloping**. Thus **feelings of fear** (which envelop the heart?).

Mnemonic: **FEAR WRAPS HEART LIKE CLOTH**

1750	附	FU **ATTACH** 8 strokes	附属 FUZOKU-	affiliated
			寄附 KIFU	contribution
			附近 FUKIN	vicinity

阝 is **hill** 229. 付 is **attach** 574, here acting phonetically to express **swelling** and also lending its meaning of **attach**. 1750 originally referred to a **swelling/ hillock on the side of a larger hill** (i.e. attached to it), but has now become confused with 付 itself. That is, hill 阝 has become redundant.

Mnemonic: **ATTACHED TO HILL**

1751		FU, omomu*ku* **PROCEED, GO** 9 strokes	赴援 FUEN	going to rescue
			赴任 FUNIN	taking up post
			赴任地 FUNINCHI	post, posting

走 is **run** 161, here meaning **rush**. 卜 is **divination** 91, here acting phonetically to express **announce** and also lending similar extended connotations of its own. Thus to **rush to announce** something (still a minor meaning in Chinese), later **rush to do** something in a broad sense and hence **proceed (quickly)/ go**. It has become particularly associated with proceeding to a new posting.

Mnemonic: **DIVINATION PROMPTS ONE TO PROCEED AT RUN**

1752 FU, u*ku*/*kabu*/*kaberu*/*kareru*　浮力 FURYOKU　buoyancy
FLOAT, FLEETING, GAY　浮気 UWAKI*　inconstancy
10 strokes　浮き世 UKIYO　fleeting world

氵 is **water**/ **liquid** 40. 孚 is a CO character now meaning hatch/ brood (over eggs). It comprises **reaching hand** 爫 303 and **child** 子 25, and is clearly related to hand reaching for child to remove it from the vagina 乳 951 q.v. It presumably has a core meaning of **assist at birth** (with hatch/ brood an associated meaning). Here 孚 acts phonetically to express **float**, and almost certainly also originally lent a meaning of **reach for a child at birth**. That is, it is almost certain that water 氵 represented **amniotic fluid** (see 409 and 227), and that 1752 originally meant **reach for a child at birth to help it 'float' forth**, before later coming to mean **float** in a general sense. **Fleeting** is an associated meaning with floating (note that in English fleet and float are etymologically the same word), with **gay** felt to be a further association with fleeting (from fleeting pleasures).

Mnemonic: **HAND PLUCKS FLOATING CHILD FROM WATER**

1753 FU　切符 KIPPU　ticket
TALLY, SIGN　符号 FUGŌ　symbol, code
11 strokes　符合 FUGŌ　agreement

竹 is **bamboo** 170, here indicating a **bamboo tally** cut in two and then joined upon fulfillment of an agreement (see 1195). 付 is **attach** 574, here meaning **join**. Thus 1753 originally meant **join tallies**, but later came to refer rather to the **tally** itself. **Sign** is an associated meaning.

Mnemonic: **ATTACH BAMBOO TALLIES TOGETHER**

1754 FU, amane*ku*　普通 FUTSŪ　ordinary
WIDELY, GENERALLY　普遍 FUHEN　universality
12 strokes　普及 FUKYŪ　diffusion

日 is **sun(light)** 62. 並 is **line**/ **row** 1775, here acting phonetically to express **weak** and almost certainly also lending connotations of **spread out**. Thus **(spread out?) weak sunlight**. Some scholars see **widely**/ **generally** as a borrowed meaning, others as an extended meaning from the idea of diffuse. Suggest taking 日 in its meaning of **day**.

Mnemonic: **GENERALLY, ONE DAY FOLLOWS ANOTHER IN A ROW**

560

1755		FU, kusa*ru/reru* ROT, DECAY, BAD 14 strokes	腐心 FUSHIN	pains, trouble
			腐敗 FUHAI	decay, rot
			腐れ KUSARE-	worthless

肉 is meat 365. 府 is government center 575 q.v., here acting phonetically to express rot and possibly also lending its original meaning of storehouse. Thus **meat rotting** (in a storehouse?), now **rot/ decay** in a broad sense. Like the English term rotten, it is also used figuratively to mean **worthless**.

Mnemonic: **MEAT IN GOVERNMENT CENTER IS ROTTEN**

1756		FU, shi*ku* SPREAD, LAY 15 strokes	敷設 FUSETSU	laying
			敷き物 SHIKIMONO	rug
			屋敷 YASHIKI	residence

Formerly 旉攵. 攵 is **striking hand/ force** 101, here meaning **apply the hand**. 尃 is **spread** 564, here also acting phonetically to express **cloth**. 1756 originally meant to **spread a cloth and apply the hand to smooth it**, later **spread/ lay** in a broader sense. Suggest taking 尃 as **beside** 方 204, **field** 田 59, **ten** 十 33, and a **bit** 丶.

Mnemonic: **FORCED TO SPREAD OUT BESIDE TEN AND A BIT FIELDS**

1757		FU, hada SKIN 15 strokes	皮膚炎 HIFUEN	dermatitis
			完膚 KANPU	utterly
			膚着 HADAGI	underwear

Popularly believed to comprise **belly/ stomach** 胃 424 q.v. and **tiger** 虍 281, the latter being assumed to be a miscopying of **skin** 皮 374, thus giving **skin over belly** and later **skin** in general. A useful mnemonic, but incorrect (apart from the link with the belly). Old forms such as 𧆧 show that 田 derives from **basket** 甘 399 (now usually 由) and not belly 田 424. 膚 is in fact a simplified variant of a CO character 臚, which shows **(of the) body** 月 365 and **container** 盧 1934 q.v. (the latter comprising **basket** 田, **vessel** 皿 1307, and **tiger** 𠂉/虍, the role of which is unclear) and means both **belly** (literally **body's container**) and **skin**. That is, 1757 is 臚 minus vessel 皿 and with **(of the) body** 月 in a different position. The relationship between belly and skin is not fully clear. Some scholars believe it is a natural association (the belly showing an expanse of skin), while others feel that because 膚 had the same pronunciation as a word for **cover**, 膚 could also be interpreted as that **which covers the body**.

Mnemonic: **SKIN FROM A TIGER'S BELLY**

1758		FU LEVY, TRIBUTE, ODE 15 strokes	賦課 FUKA	levy, tax
			賦詩 FUSHI	writing poetry
			月賦 GEPPU	monthly payment

貝 is **shell/ money** 90, here meaning **valuable item(s)**. 武 is **warrior** 781, here acting phonetically to express **divide** and probably also originally lending its connotations of soldier. Thus to **divide valuable assets**, probably originally a reference to soldiers sharing the spoils of a campaign. Giving out valuable items led by association to **paying tribute**, both in the form of a **levy** and in the eulogistic form of an **ode**.

Mnemonic: **WARRIOR PAYS TRIBUTE IN SHELL-MONEY**

1759		FU NOTATION, GENEALOGY 19 strokes	楽譜 GAKUFU	musical score
			系譜 KEIFU	genealogy
			年譜 NENPU	chronological record

言 is **words/ speak** 274, here meaning **express/ state**. 普 is **widely** 1754 q.v., here acting phonetically to express **in sequence** and possibly also lending its own similar connotations of **in a line** from its row/ line element 並 (1775). Thus to **state/ express in sequence**, leading to **chronology/ genealogy** on the one hand and **(musical) notation** on the other.

Mnemonic: **GENEALOGY WIDELY SPOKEN OF**

1760		BU, anado*ru* SCORN, DESPISE 8 strokes	侮辱的 BUJOKUTEKI	insulting
			軽侮 KEIBU	contempt
			侮慢 BUMAN	offense, insult

イ is **person** 39. 毎 is **every** 206 q.v., here acting phonetically to express **ridicule/ insult** and possibly also lending connotations of **profusely**. Thus to **insult a person** (profusely?), with **scorn/ despise** being an associated meaning.

Mnemonic: **DESPISE EVERY PERSON**

1761		BU, ma*u* DANCE, FLIT 15 strokes	舞台 BUTAI	stage
			舞子 MAIKO	dancing girl
			振舞い FURUMAI	behavior

Dancing person 無 796 and **opposed feet** 舛 1211, the latter indicating **footwork** and thus reinforcing 無. Suggest taking 無 as a **wheatsheaf**, 夕 as **night** 44, and 廾 as a variant of **well** 井 1470.

Mnemonic: **DANCE NIGHTLY AMONGST WHEATSHEAFS BESIDE WELL**

1762 封 FŪ, HŌ

CLOSE OFF, FIEF

9 strokes

封筒 FŪTŌ — envelope
封鎖 FŪSA — blockade
封建 HŌKEN — feudalism

Once written 𡊫 and originally 𡊫, showing that 圭 is not doubled/piled **earth 土** 60 (see also 819) -- though this would be semantically appropriate -- but a derivative of a **bushy branched** (and originally thick trunked) **tree** 𡳃 / 𡳃 (tree normally written 朩 / 木 69). The tree was used to **block a road**, thus giving **close off** and by extension **closed off area**, with **fief** being an associated meaning. **Hand**/ measure 寸 909 q.v. was added later to show **deliberate action** (with the hand). Suggest taking 圭 as **double earth**.

Mnemonic: **HAND DOUBLES UP EARTH TO CLOSE OFF FIEF**

1763 伏 FUKU, fu*su/seru*

CROUCH, HIDE, AMBUSH

6 strokes

起伏 KIFUKU — undulations
潜伏 SENPUKU hiding, lurking
伏して FUSHITE — humbly

Obscure, though its elements are (and have been since its ancient origin) **person** 亻 39 and **dog** 犬 17. Its oldest known meaning is **crouch**, and some authoritative Japanese scholars believe it is an ideograph intended to indicate a **dog crouching low when barking at a person**. However, as an ideograph it clearly has a vast range of potential meanings, and one such specific interpretation seems a little forced. It seems equally likely that 犬 once acted phonetically to express **crouch**, thus giving **crouching person** (possibly one crouching like a dog). In any event, **hide** is an associated meaning with crouch, and **ambush** is a further association.

Mnemonic: **DOG CROUCHES TO AMBUSH PERSON**

1764 幅 FUKU, haba

WIDTH, SCROLL

12 strokes

振幅 SHINPUKU — amplitude
画幅 GAFUKU — picture scroll
横幅 YOKOHABA — breadth

巾 is **cloth** 778. 畐 is **full** 386, here also acting phonetically to express **width**. Thus the **full width of** (a roll of) cloth, later **width** in general. **Scroll** is an associated meaning with roll of cloth. Suggest taking 畐 as **field** 田 59, opening/ **entrance** 口 20, and **one** 一 1.

Mnemonic: **ONE CLOTH SPANS WIDTH OF ENTRANCE TO FIELD**

1765 FUKU, ōu, kutsugaeru/su   転覆 TENPUKU   overturn
OVERTURN, COVER   覆面 FUKUMEN   mask
18 strokes   覆水 FUKUSUI   spilt water

Correctly written 覆 , showing 西 rather than **west** 西 152. 西 derives from a pictograph of an **upturned dish** 冖. 復 is **again/ return** 782 q.v., here acting phonetically to express **invert/ overturn** and also lending its own connotations of reverse. Thus to **turn a dish over,** giving both **overturn** and **cover.** Overturn is now also used in a figurative sense.

Mnemonic: **WEST OVERTURNED AGAIN**

1766 FUTSU, harau   払い戻す HARAIMODOSU refund
PAY, SWEEP AWAY, RID   払底 FUTTEI   shortage
5 strokes   払い出す HARAIDASU   drive out

Formerly 拂 . 扌 is **hand** 32. 弗 is **unwind/ disperse** 567, here acting phonetically to express **sweep** and also lending similar connotations of **remove.** 1766 originally referred to **sweeping something away with the hand,** and was later also used to mean **rid** in a broad sense. It is particularly used of ridding oneself of a debt, i.e. by means of **paying.** Suggest taking 厶 as **nose** 134.

Mnemonic: **HAND GIVES SWEEPING BLOW TO NOSE TO GET PAYMENT**

1767 FUTSU, waku/kasu   沸点 FUTTEN   boiling point
BOIL, GUSH   沸き立つ WAKITATSU   seethe
8 strokes   沸き出る WAKIDERU   gush forth

氵 is **water** 40. 弗 is **unwind/disperse** 567, here acting phonetically to express **emerge** and also lending its own connotations of **away/ out.** 1767 originally referred to **water gushing out (of the ground),** but is now more commonly found in the associated meaning of **boil** (from the idea of bubbling up).

Mnemonic: **WATER 'UNWINDS' WHEN IT BOILS**

1768	**FUN, mag**ireru/rasu/rawashii	紛失	FUNSHITSU	loss
	CONFUSION, STRAY	紛争	FUNSŌ	dispute
	10 strokes	紛紛	FUNPUN	in confusion

糸 is **thread** 27. 分 is **divide** 199 q.v., here acting phonetically to express **sort/ arrange** and probably also lending similar connotations of **bringing about order by separation**. Thus to **(separate and?) sort threads**. The present meaning of **stray/ be confused** is a borrowing.

Mnemonic: **DIVIDED THREADS GO ASTRAY, CAUSING CONFUSION**

1769	**FUN**	雰囲気	FUNIKI	atmosphere
	ATMOSPHERE, AIR	霧雰	MUFUN	misty air
	12 strokes	霜雰	SŌFUN	frosty air

雨 is **rain** 3, here indicating **weather conditions** in a broad sense and by extension **atmosphere**. 分 is **divide** 199, here acting phonetically to express **powder** (namely 粉 577, of which it can in effect be considered a simplification). 1769 refers to **conditions in which the atmosphere becomes 'powdery'**, such as when it snows, sleets, drizzles, is misty, etc. It is also used of **unclear air**, and of **atmosphere** in a figurative sense. Note that in Chinese 1769 has now been largely replaced by 氛, a CO character (of long standing) which uses vapors 气 11 instead of rain/ weather/ atmosphere 雨.

Mnemonic: **RAIN DIVIDES THE ATMOSPHERE**

1770	**FUN, fu**ku	噴火	FUNKA	eruption
	EMIT, SPOUT, GUSH	噴水	FUNSUI	fountain
	15 strokes	噴き出す	FUKIDASU	spurt out

Somewhat obscure due to the obscure nature of 賁 This is an NGU character with a meaning of decorate/ ornament, but in Chinese it can also mean large, strenuous, bright, honor, and defeated. Its early form 賁 shows **shell/ money** 貝 90 and what appears to be **three plants** 芔 (plant 屮 9: note that 芔/卉 is an NGU character meaning grass/ plants). Its core meaning is not clear, but in compounds it often seems to be associated with **swelling/ rising/ building up**, suggesting that either the plants symbolised growth and by extension growing big/ swelling or else they became reinterpreted as hands 屮 raising/ offering something up. In any event, in the case of 1770 賁 is known to have lent its sound (originally **PON**) onomatopoeically, combining with **mouth/ say** 口 20 to give **make a PON sound with the mouth**, i.e. **snort** or **puff** (i.e. a sound building up within the mouth and then bursting forth?). Snort and puff are still retained as minor meanings in Chinese. By extension this came to mean **vent/ emit** in a broad sense, including **spout/ gush**. Suggest taking 卉 as a trebling of ten 十 33 and 口 in its sense of **opening**.

Mnemonic: **THIRTY SHELLS GUSH FROM OPENING**

1771

FUN
(BURIAL-) MOUND
15 strokes

古墳 KOFUN   tumulus
墳墓 FUNBO   tomb
墳墓の地 FUNBONOCHI
           birthplace

土 is **earth/ ground** 60. 賁 is the obscure element seen in 1770 q.v., here acting phonetically to express **swelling** but of unclear semantic role (though it may possibly lend its own connotations of swelling). Thus a **swelling of earth**, i.e. **mound**. It is now used especially of **burial mounds**. Suggest taking 卉 as a trebling of **ten** 十 33 and 貝 as **shell** 90.

Mnemonic: **THIRTY SHELLS FOUND IN EARTH OF BURIAL MOUND**

1772

FUN, ikidōru
INDIGNANT, ANGRY
15 strokes

憤慨 FUNGAI   indignation
憤怒 FUNDO   rage
義憤 GIFUN
        righteous indignation

忄 is **heart/ feelings** 147. 賁 is the obscure element seen in 1770 q.v., here acting phonetically to express **overflow/ burst forth** but of unclear semantic role (though it may possibly lend its own connotations of building up). Thus **feelings bursting forth**, indicating **indignation**. Suggest taking 卉 as a trebling of **ten** 十 33 and 貝 as **shell** 90.

Mnemonic: **THIRTY SHELLS CAUSE INDIGNANT FEELINGS**

1773

丙

HEI
C, 3RD
5 strokes

丙種 HEISHU   C class
甲乙丙 KŌOTSUHEI   ABC/ 123
丙 HINOE* third calendar sign

In ancient times written as 冈 or 夬, showing a **(large) altar with sturdy legs**. Later forms such as 内 show an **item** 一 placed on the altar (as altar 丁 / 示 695 q.v.). 1773 was later borrowed to express **third** in a sequence. Suggest taking it as **inside** 内 364 and **one** 一 1, with a play on 'one'.

Mnemonic: **THIRD ONE INSIDE IS RATED C**

1774		HEI, awa*seru* UNITE, JOIN 8 strokes	合併 GAPPEI	merger
			併用 HEIYŌ	joint use
			併発 HEIHATSU	complication

Formerly 倂 or 併. 亻 is person 39. 幵/开 is an NGU character meaning **put to-gether**. Some scholars take its earliest form 幵幵 to show **two** stylised **persons** 𠂉𠂉 (variant 𠂉 39) **linked** by the symbol **two** 二 61, here doubled for emphasis. However, since 千 could mean two thousand (see 47) it is unlikely that it would be used in a totally different sense here, and it seems more likely that 幵幵 shows **two persons** 人人 and **matching stakes** 幵/开 272 (especially in view of the existence of fence 屏 1777 q.v.), thus giving the idea of **matching persons** and hence **going together**. In any event, the original meaning was clearly **two persons together**, with the later person 亻 presumably merely for emphasis. This came to symbolise **uniting** in a broad sense. Sug-gest taking ゝ丿 as **out of** 66 and 开 as a variant of **well** 井 1470.

Mnemonic: **UNITE TO GET PERSON OUT OF WELL**

1775		HEI, nami, nara*bu/beru/bi* ROW, LINE, RANK WITH, ORDINARY 8 strokes	並行 HEIKŌ	parallelism
			並木 NAMIKI	line of trees
			月並 TSUKINAMI	
				commonplace

Formerly 竝, showing a doubling of **standing person** 立 73. 1775 originally meant **line of standing people**, and now means **row/ line** in a broad sense. It also came to mean **rank alongside** and by association **be ordinary** (cf. English term rank and file). Suggest taking 𝕀𝕀 as a Roman **two** and ゝ and 丶 丿 as **eight** 66 (i.e. two eights).

Mnemonic: **LINE UP IN TWO ROWS OF EIGHT**

1776	柄	HEI, gara, e HANDLE, PATTERN, POWER, NATURE 9 strokes	横柄 ŌHEI	arrogance
			家柄 IEGARA	pedigree
			大柄 ŌGARA	big frame/ pattern

木 is **wood** 69. 丙 is **third** 1773 q.v., here acting phonetically to express **grasp** and probably also lending connotations of **sturdy** from its literal meaning of sturdy altar. Thus (sturdy?) **wooden part that is grasped**, a reference to a **handle**. It is not clear how it acquired its other meanings, but they are assumed to be borrowings (though **power** may result from the idea of a lever).

Mnemonic: **WOOD OF THIRD RATE NATURE USED FOR HANDLE**

1777 **HEI** 板塀 ITABEI board fence
FENCE, WALL 土塀 DOBEI earthen wall
12 strokes 塀越し HEIGOSHI over fence

Formerly 堺屏. A 'made in Japan' character formed by adding **earth** 土 60 to the NGU character **fence/ wall/ screen** 屏/屏 . The latter comprises **corpse** 尸 236, here acting as a simplification of **building** 屋 236, and put together 幷/并 1774 q.v., here acting phonetically to express **block/ screen** and probably also lending connotations of **matching stakes** from its 幵/开 element (see also 272). Thus 屏 literally means **that (matching stakes?) screening a building**, i.e. a **fence**, later **wall/ screen** in a broader sense. Despite the addition of **earth** 土 in the case of 塀 1777, presumably originally intended to give wall but not fence, 1777 can now also be used of fence. Suggest taking ∨/ as **out of** 66 and 开 as a variant of **well** 井 1470.

Mnemonic: **CORPSE TAKEN OUT OF WELL BEHIND EARTHEN WALL**

1778 **HEI** 紙幣 SHIHEI paper money
OFFERING, MONEY 貨幣 KAHEI coin, money
15 strokes 御幣 GOHEI paper strips
in Shinto shrine

Of confused evolution. Formerly also written 㡀攵. 攵 is striking hand 101, here meaning simply **use of the hand** (though it is not clear why hand/ careful use of the hand 寸 909 q.v. was not used). Opinion is divided as to whether 敝 is **cloth** 巾 778 plus four (small) **bits** ⺮ or a slightly modified combination of cloth 巾, two bits ハ, and **small** 小/⺌ 36 (the latter seeming the more likely). 敝 referred to the practise of **cutting up (i.e. by hand) small bits of cloth (later paper) as symbolic offerings to the gods**, now associated with Shintoism but also once found in ancient China. It also came to mean **my/ humble,** by association with the idea of making a humble offering (note that 敝 does in fact exist independently in Chinese with a main meaning of my/ humble, whereas in Japanese this is now conveyed by 弊 1779 q.v.). A further cloth 巾 was added at some stage, presumably to draw attention to the offering itself. Cloth/ paper offering was later applied by association to **paper money**, and eventually was used of **money** in a broad sense including coin. The idea of making an offering to the gods also came to symbolise repentance over a wrongdoing, and later confusingly to symbolise **wrongdoing** itself, but this meaning is now conveyed by 弊 1779 q.v. Suggest taking 攵 in its sense of **force**.

Mnemonic: **FORCED TO MAKE OFFERING OF MONEY AND BITS OF CLOTH**

1779	弊	HEI MY (HUMBLE), EVIL, EXHAUSTION 15 strokes	弊社 HEISHA	our company
			疲弊 HIHEI	exhaustion
			弊害 HEIGAI	evil, abuse

Formerly 獘, with **dog** 犬 17 (at one stage miscopied as big 大 53) and **hand cutting cloth/ paper strips** 敝 1778 q.v. The latter acts phonetically to express **collapse** and may also lend connotations of breaking into pieces (see 1728). 1779 originally referred to **collapsing like a dog**, i.e. with **exhaustion** (cf. English dog tired). It is still occasionally used in this sense, but became confused with 幣 1778 q.v. and adopted the latter's one-time meanings of **my/ humble** and **wrongdoing/ evil**, which are now its main meanings. Suggest taking 卄 as a stylised combination of two **tens** 十 33 (i.e. **twenty**), and 米 as **cloth** 巾 778, **bits** 八, and **force** 攵 101.

Mnemonic: **EVILLY FORCED TO CUT MY CLOTH INTO TWENTY STRIPS**

1780	壁	HEKI, kabe WALL 16 strokes	壁画 HEKIGA	mural
			岩壁 GANPEKI	rock face
			壁紙 KABEGAMI	wallpaper

土 is **earth** 60, here meaning **earthen embankment**. 辟 is anal penetration 1733 q.v., here acting phonetically to express **surround** but of unclear semantic role (though it may possibly lend its later connotations of turn). Thus **earthen embankment that surrounds (a building)**, a reference to a **wall** (now in a broad sense). Suggest taking 辟 literally as **anus** 尸 (**buttocks** 尸 236 and **opening/ hole** 口 20) and **needle** 辛 1432.

Mnemonic: **SITTING ON EARTHEN WALL CAN BE LIKE NEEDLE IN ANUS**

1781	癖	HEKI, kuse HABIT, KINK 18 strokes	盗癖 TŌHEKI	kleptomania
			習癖 SHŪHEKI	habit
			癖毛 KUSEGE	kinky hair

An indelicate character. 疒 is **sickness** 381. 辟 is **anal penetration/ sodomy** 1733 q.v., here acting phonetically to express **build up** and also lending an idea of **blocked anus**. 1781 originally referred to **constipation**, and can still mean this in Chinese. It later acquired a meaning of (pathologically?) **deviant habits** as a result of the strong presence of **sodomy** 辟 and of confusion with female sexual partner 嬖 1733 (literally sodomy 辟 with a woman 女 35) and its male equivalent 僻, an NGU character now meaning **prejudice/ bias** but in Chinese still having connotations of dissolute behavior (combining **person** 亻 39 [here meaning man] and **sodomy** 辟). **Deviant habits** then led on the one hand to **habits** in general and on the other to **kink**, i.e. something not straight/ normal (which like the English term is used both physically and figuratively). Suggest taking 辟 literally as **anus** 尸 (**buttocks** 尸 236 and **opening/ hole** 口 20) and **needle** 辛 1432.

Mnemonic: **SICK AND KINKY HABIT OF NEEDLE IN ANUS**

1782

HEN, katayo*ru*
INCLINE, BIAS
11 strokes

偏向 HENKŌ　　inclination
偏見 HENKEN　　prejudice
偏屈 HENKUTSU　　bigotry

亻 is **person** 39. 扁 is **doorplate** 785 q.v. (literally **door** 戸 108 and **writing tablets** 冊 874), here acting phonetically to express **incline/ lean** and possibly also lending its own connotations of **to one side**. 1782 originally referred to a **person who leans to one side/ limps**, i.e. a **cripple**, but later came to mean **lean/ incline** in a broader sense, including **bias**. Cripple/ limp is now conveyed by the NGU character 蹁, which uses foot/ leg 足 51.

Mnemonic: **PERSON INCLINED TO LEAVE WRITING TABLETS AT DOOR**

1783

HEN, amane*ku*
WIDELY, EVERYWHERE
12 strokes

普遍性 FUHENSEI　universality
遍在 HENZAI　　ubiquity
一遍 IPPEN　　(all at) once

辶 is **movement** 129. 扁 is **doorplate** 785 q.v. (literally **door** 戸 108 and **writing tablets** 冊 874), here acting phonetically to express **roundabout/ indirect** and possibly also lending its own connotations of **to one side** (and thus not straight). Thus **move in a roundabout fashion**, leading by association to **widely** and **everywhere**. Note that 1783 can be interchanged with an NGU character 徧, which uses movement 彳 118 instead of movement 辶.

Mnemonic: **MOVE WIDELY, LEAVING WRITING TABLETS AT DOORS**

1784

HO, to*ru/raeru*,
tsuka*maru/maeru*
SEIZE, CAPTURE
10 strokes

捕獲 HOKAKU　　seizure
捕らえ所 TORAEDOKORO　point
捕まえ所 TSUKAMAEDOKORO
　　　　hold

扌 is **hand** 32. 甫 is **begin** 970 q.v., here acting phonetically to express **envelop** but of unclear semantic role. Thus to **envelop with the hand**, i.e. **seize/ capture**. Suggest taking 甫 as **use** 用 215, **needle** 十 33, and **point** 丶.

Mnemonic: **HAND SEIZES NEEDLE TO USE POINT**

1785 浦	HO, ura COAST, INLET, BAY 10 strokes	浦波 URANAMI	breaker
		浦風 URAKAZE	bay breeze
		浦里 URAZATO	coastal village

氵 is water 40. 甫 is begin 970 q.v., here acting phonetically to express **edge** but of unclear semantic role (though it may possibly lend loose connotations of beginning/ edge). Thus the **water's edge**. In Chinese usually associated with the bank of a river, but in Japanese with the shore of the sea. Suggest taking 甫 as **use** 用 215, **needle** 十 33, and **point** 丶.

Mnemonic: **USE COMPASS NEEDLE POINT TO FIND INLET AND WATER**

1786 舖	HO SHOP, LAY, PAVE 15 strokes	店舗 TENPO	shop, store
		舗装 HOSŌ	paving
		舗装道路 HOSŌDŌRO	sealed road

Of confused and somewhat obscure evolution. Once written 鋪, showing **metal** 金 14 and begin 甫 970 q.v. The latter is felt by some scholars to have been used phonetically to express **turn** (with any semantic role unclear), to give **metal item that turns**, a reference to a type of **lock**. This is then assumed to have been borrowed to express **lay/ spread**. However, there is little evidence to support this, and it seems equally likely that 甫 is used as a simplification of **spread** 尃 564 q.v., and that 1786 originally meant **spread metal** (i.e. gild, plate, or similar) before coming to mean **spread/ lay** in a broader sense. In any event, in Japanese spread/ lay came in particular to have associations with **paving**. **Shop** is a later borrowing, and as a result of this new meaning metal 金 14 was replaced by the semantically more appropriate **quarters/ building** 舎 700. Note that in Chinese 鋪 still exists and is used to mean spread/ lay, while 舖 is used to mean shop. Suggest taking 甫 as **use** 用 215, **needle** 十 33, and **point** 丶.

Mnemonic: **USE NEEDLE POINT TO PAVE SHOP QUARTERS?!**

1787	BO, tsunoru GATHER, RAISE, ENLIST GROW INTENSE 12 strokes	募集 BOSHŪ	recruitment
		募金 BOKIN	fund raising
		応募 ŌBO	response to call

力 is strength/ **effort** 74. 莫 is sun sinking among plants 788 q.v., here acting phonetically to express **seize/ take** and probably also lending its connotations of **cover/ enfold**. 1787 originally meant to **make efforts to bring someone into one's fold**, and thus came to mean **raise/ enlist/ gather**. Like the English term **gather** in expressions such as a gathering storm, it also came to mean **grow intense/ strong**. Suggest taking 莫 as **grass** 艹 9, **sun** 日 62, and **big** 大 (variant 大 53).

Mnemonic: **BIG EFFORT TO GATHER GRASS WHILE SUN SHINES**

1788 BO, shita*u*
YEARN, ADORE, DEAR
14 strokes

慕情 BOJŌ — longing
敬慕 KEIBO — admiration
慕心 BOSHIN — yearning

小 is **heart/ feelings** (variant 心 147). 莫 is sun sinking among plants 788 q.v., here acting phonetically to express **seek** and possibly also lending its connotations of **envelop**. Thus to **seek something with the heart** (something which envelops the heart?), a reference to **yearning/ longing**. **Dear** and **adore** are associated meanings. Suggest taking 莫 as **grass** 艹 9, **sun** 日 62, and **big** 大 (variant 大 53).

Mnemonic: **BIG YEARNING IN HEART TO LIE ON SUNNY GRASS**

1789 BO, kure*ru*/rasu
LIVE, SUNSET, END
14 strokes

暮春 BOSHUN — late spring
夕暮れ YŪGURE — evening
暮らし方 KURASHIKATA — lifestyle

Sun setting among plants 莫 788 q.v. with an extra **sun** 日 62 added after the original meaning became vague. Thus **sunset**, with **end** being an associated meaning. **Live** is also felt to be an associated meaning, from the idea of surviving/ seeing out another day (it still generally has connotations of making a living/ getting by). Suggest taking 莫 as **plants** 艹 9, **sun** 日, and **big** 大 (variant 大 53), with the extra 日 in its sense of **day**.

Mnemonic: **LIVE TO SEE SUN SET AMONG BIG PLANTS AT END OF DAY**

1790 BO, HAKU
REGISTER, RECORD(S)
19 strokes

名簿 MEIBO — (name) register
簿記 BOKI — bookkeeping
帳簿 CHŌBO — register, lease

Formerly 簿 . 竹 is **bamboo** 170, here indicating **bamboo tablets used for keeping records**. 溥 / 溥 is **extensive** 1699, here acting phonetically to express **bind** and probably also lending its meaning of **extensive**. 1790 originally referred to an **(extensive?) collection of bamboo tablets bound together**, i.e. a **register/ set of records**. Suggest taking 溥 literally as **water** 氵 40 and **spread** 尃 564.

Mnemonic: **WATER SPREADS OVER BAMBOO REGISTER**

1791 芳   HŌ, kanba*shii*   芳香 HŌKŌ   fragrance
FRAGRANT, GOOD, YOUR   芳志 HŌSHI   your kindness
7 strokes   芳紀 HŌKI   girl's age

艹 is **plant 9**. 方 is **side/ direction 204**, here acting phonetically to express **fragrant** and possibly also lending its meaning of direction. Thus **fragrant plant** (fragrance from direction of plant?), now **fragrant** in a broad sense. Also used of **good** in a broad sense, and as a polite reference to the **second person/ you**.

Mnemonic: **FRAGRANT SMELL FROM DIRECTION OF PLANT**

1792 邦   HŌ   邦画 HŌGA   Japanese picture
COUNTRY, JAPAN   連邦 RENPŌ   federation
7 strokes   本邦 HONPŌ   our country

丰 is a variant of **bushy tree used as barrier** 丰 / 丯 / 㞢 **1762** q.v., while β is **village 355**. Thus **village of barred access**, indicating a **guarded area**. This later broadened to mean **region** or **country**. In Japanese only it has also acquired associations with **one's own country**, i.e. **Japan**. Suggest taking 丰 as a **(bent) telegraph pole**.

Mnemonic: **JAPAN A COUNTRY WHERE VILLAGES HAVE BENT TELEGRAPH POLES**

1793 奉   HŌ, BU, tatematsu*ru*   奉仕 HŌSHI   service
OFFER, RESPECTFUL   奉納 HŌNŌ   offering
8 strokes   信奉 SHINPŌ   faith, belief

Once written , showing **two hands** 𦥑 **offering** up a **thickly growing plant** 丰 (variant 㞢 **42**), either as tribute to a lord or in a religious ritual. Later forms such as 𡗗 show an additional **hand** 又 **32** (now 手). This came to mean **offer** in general and by association **show respect**. Note that there is an NGU character 捧, which adds yet another **hand** 扌 **32** and is to all intents and purposes interchangeable with 1793. Suggest taking 夫 as **two** 二 **61** and **big** 大 **53**, and 丰 as a **club with nails through it**.

Mnemonic: **RESPECTFULLY OFFER CLUB WITH TWO BIG NAILS**

1794 抱   HŌ, [i]da*ku*, kaka*eru*   抱き付く DAKITSUKU   hug
EMBRACE, HUG, HOLD   抱懐 HŌKAI   cherishing
8 strokes   抱え込む KAKAEKOMU   hold

扌 is **hand 32**, here meaning **arm(s)**. 包 is **wrap/ envelop 583**. Thus to **wrap/ envelop with the arms**, i.e. **hug/ embrace**. Also used figuratively.

Mnemonic: **TO EMBRACE IS TO ENVELOP WITH THE ARMS**

| 1795 | | HŌ, awa FROTH, BUBBLE, FOAM 8 strokes | 気泡 KIHŌ 発泡 HAPPŌ 泡立つ AWADATSU | air bubble foaming bubble, froth |

氵 is water 40. 包 is wrap/ envelop 583. In Chinese 1795 can mean either to **envelop with water**, i.e. **immerse**, or **that which envelops water**, i.e. **froth/ foam**, but in Japanese almost always has the latter meaning.

Mnemonic: **WATER WRAPPED IN FROTHY BUBBLES**

| 1796 | | HŌ PLACENTA, WOMB 9 strokes | 胞子 HŌSHI 胞衣 HŌI/ ENA* 細胞 SAIBŌ | spore placenta cell |

Flesh/ **of the body** 月 365 and wrap/ **envelop** 包 583. **That part of the body which envelops** is the **womb**, with **placenta** being an associated meaning.

Mnemonic: **WOMB IS PART OF THE BODY THAT ENVELOPS**

| 1797 | | HŌ SALARY, PAY 10 strokes | 俸給 HŌKYŪ 年俸 NENPŌ 俸ろく米 HŌROKUMAI | salary, pay annual salary rice allowance |

Offer 奉 1793 with **person** 亻 39 added to indicate the **person offering**. The meaning has now changed rather to **that which is offered a person**, a reference to **salary/ pay**. Suggest taking 夫 as **two** 二 61 and **big** 大 53, and ‡ as a **club with nails**.

Mnemonic: **PERSON USES CLUB WITH TWO BIG NAILS TO GET PAY**

| 1798 | 倣 | HŌ, narau IMITATE, FOLLOW 10 strokes | 模倣 MOHŌ 模倣者 MOHŌSHA 倣い削り NARAIKEZURI | imitation imitator profiling |

Not **person** 亻 39 and **release** 放 391, though this may be useful as a mnemonic, but **strike/ force** 攵 101 plus the NGU character 仿 . The latter comprises **person** 亻 and **side** 方 204, which is used phonetically to express **resemble** (semantic role unclear), and originally meant **resemble a person**. The causative element 攵 thus gave 倣 a meaning of **make to resemble a person**, i.e. **imitate/ follow**. 仿 itself then became confused with 倣 and also came to mean imitate/ follow, and in Chinese is now interchangeable with 1798. 仿 is listed in some Japanese dictionaries (but without illustration) as having meanings of wander and stand still, but the reason for this listing is not clear.

Mnemonic: **RELEASED PERSON MUST IMITATE OTHERS**

1799	峰	HŌ, mine PEAK, TOP 10 strokes	主峰 SHUHŌ	main peak
			連峰 RENPŌ	mountain range
			峰打ち MINEUCHI	striking with back of sword

Formerly 峯. 山 is **mountain** 24. 夆 is a CO character meaning butt/ **gore**. It was once written 夅, showing a stylised upturned foot 夂 (early form 又 438 q.v.) -- here meaning **go back** -- and cow's horns 半 (variant 半 / 牛 97), and thus literally means person sent back by cow's horns. In compounds 夆 can lend connotations both of **go back** and/or of **tapered/ sharp**. In the case of 1799 it means **sharp**, thus giving **sharp part of mountain**, i.e. **peak**. It can also mean **top** in a wider sense, somewhat confusingly including the back of a sword (which is the opposite of the sharp part). Suggest taking 夂 as **sitting crosslegged** and 丰 as a **telegraph pole**.

Mnemonic: **SIT CROSSLEGGED ON TELEGRAPH POLE ON MOUNTAIN PEAK**

1800	砲	HŌ GUN, CANNON 10 strokes	砲丸 HŌGAN	cannonball
			鉄砲 TEPPŌ	firearms
			大砲 TAIHŌ	gun, cannon

石 is **rock/ stone** 45. 包 is **wrap/ envelop** 583, here acting phonetically to express **release/ discharge** and probably also lending a meaning of **encircling/ encasing**. 1800 originally referred to a primitive type of **cannon which fired small rocks through a tube**, said to be in use from as early as the fifth century B.C.

Mnemonic: **ENVELOPED IN ROCKS DISCHARGED FROM CANNON**

1801	崩	HŌ, kuzureru/su CRUMBLE, COLLAPSE 11 strokes	崩壊 HŌKAI	collapse
			雪崩 NADARE*	avalanche
			山崩れ YAMAKUZURE	landslide

Formerly 崩 and in ancient times 阝甮, showing that 朋 derives from the somewhat obscure **matching jewels** 甮 /朋 1562. Here it acts phonetically to express **collapse**, combining with **mountain** 山 24 (or in the ancient form **hill** 阝 /阝 229) to give **collapsing mountainside** (/hillside). Now **collapse/ crumble** in a broader sense. Suggest taking 月 as **month** 16.

Mnemonic: **MOUNTAIN CRUMBLES AWAY IN JUST TWO MONTHS**

1802

HŌ, *aku/kiru/kasu*
TIRE, SATIATE
13 strokes

飽和 HŌWA saturation
飽食 HŌSHOKU satiation
飽き性 AKISHŌ fickleness

食 is **food/ eat** 146. 包 is **wrap/ envelop** 583, here acting phonetically to express **full** and possibly also lending supporting connotations of smothered. Thus **satiated with food**, now **satiated/ tired** in a broader sense.

Mnemonic: **TIRED OF WRAPPED FOOD**

1803

HŌ, *homeru*
PRAISE, REWARD
15 strokes

褒章 HŌSHŌ medal
褒美 HŌBI praise, reward
褒め言葉 HOMEKOTOBA praise

衣 is **clothing** (variant 衣 420). 保 is **preserve** 787, here acting phonetically to express **long** but of unclear semantic role. 1803 originally referred to a special **long robe** presented by the emperor to deserving officials, and hence symbolises **praise** and **reward**. 褒 is an occasionally encountered variant form.

Mnemonic: **PRAISED AND REWARDED FOR PRESERVING CLOTHES**

1804

HŌ, *nuu*
SEW, STITCH
16 strokes

縫合 HŌGO stitching
縫い物 NUIMONO needlework
縫い目 NUIME seam, stitch

糸 is **thread** 27. 逢 is an NGU character now meaning **meet**, but in Chinese it also means **penetrate**. It comprises **movement** 辶 129 and **gore** 夆 1799 q.v., the latter lending its connotations of **sharpness**, and literally means **penetrative movement** (in order to attain something). Here 逢 acts phonetically to express **join** and also lends its connotations of **penetration**. Thus to **join by penetrating with thread**, i.e. **sew/ stitch**. Suggest taking 夂 as **sit crosslegged** and 丰 as a **telegraph pole**.

Mnemonic: **SIT CROSSLEGGED ON MOVING TELEGRAPH POLE, SEWING WITH THREAD**

1805		BŌ, tobo*shii* SCARCE, DESTITUTE 4 strokes	欠乏 KETSUBŌ	dearth
			貧乏 BINBŌ	poverty
			耐乏 TAIBŌ	austerity

Obscure. Felt by some scholars to derive from an ancient character 丂, though it is not fully clear that this is in fact the prototype of 1805. 丂 is said to be a mirror image of **hidden/ curtain/ protected** 丏 1744, which is itself obscure and may or may not be a variant of **foot** 㫃/ 止 /正 129/ 41 (the mirror image possibly being intended to emphasise reversal of movement , a view supported by the fact that the curtain in question is believed to have been used to ward off [i.e. send back] arrows in an archery range -- see also 478). **Scarce/ destitute** is then taken to be a borrowing, specifically resulting from 1805's being used in place of the NGU character 貶. This now means look down upon/ belittle, but originally referred to **lacking money/ destitute** (shell/ **money** 貝 90 and 乏, the latter acting phonetically to express **lack** and possibly also lending similar connotations of **not existing** from its assumed meaning of **hidden**: see also the similar link between hidden and not existing in the case of 莫 788). Other scholars believe that 1805 is a variant of **this/ emerging plant** 之 1335, though agree that the present meanings are borrowings involving 貶. Suggest taking 之 as a **zigzag path** and ノ as a variant of **one** 一 1.

Mnemonic: LIFE OF A DESTITUTE LIKENED TO ONE ZIGZAG PATH

1806		BŌ, isoga*shii* BUSY 6 strokes	多忙 TABŌ na	very busy
			繁忙 HANBŌ	pressure of work
			忙殺 BŌSATSU	
				being worked to death

忄 is **heart/ feelings** 147. 亡 is **die** 973, here acting phonetically to express **be busy** and possibly also lending a figurative meaning of die. 1806 originally referred to **one's heart being busy** (to the point where it 'dies'/ can take no more?), a reference to being **flustered/ pressured**. Now **busy** in a broader sense, with particular connotations of work (as opposed to traffic etc.).

Mnemonic: HEART DEATH THROUGH BEING TOO BUSY

1807	坊	BŌ PRIEST, BOY, TOWN 7 strokes	坊主 BŌZU*	priest
			坊や BŌYA	boy
			坊間 BŌKAN	around town

Earth/ ground 土 60 and **side** 方 204. 1807 originally referred to the **(raised) earth at the side of a river**, i.e. an **embankment**, and by association later came to mean **town** (towns often being built on riverbanks). It was later borrowed to refer to an **acolyte**, thus giving both **boy** and **priest** (and very occasionally [by association] **temple**).

Mnemonic: BOY-PRIEST FOUND AT SIDE OF EARTHEN BANK IN TOWN

1808

BŌ, samata*geru*
HAMPER, OBSTRUCT
7 strokes

妨害 BŌGAI   obstruction
防止 BŌSHI   prevention
妨げなし SAMATAGENASHI

                      without hindrance

女 is **woman** 35. 方 is **side** 204, here acting phonetically to express **vilify** and possibly also originally meaning **beside**. 1808 originally referred to a **woman** (possibly initially a woman at a lord's side) **vilifying** someone and thereby **hampering** the progress/ request of that person. Now **hamper/ obstruct** in general.

Mnemonic: **WOMAN AT SIDE CAUSES OBSTRUCTION**

1809

BŌ, fusa
ROOM, WIFE, TUFT
8 strokes

房室 BŌSHITSU   chamber
房房 FUSAFUSA   fleecy
世話女房 SEWANYŌBŌ

                      devoted wife

戸 is **door** 108, here meaning **partition**, and 方 is **side** 204. 1809 originally referred to a **little room partitioned off at the side of a larger room**. On the one hand this led to **room** in general, and on the other to a range of extended and associated meanings based on ideas such as **being appended** (giving concubines and **wives**) and **sticking out** (giving **tuft**).

Mnemonic: **DOOR TO ONE SIDE LEADS TO WIFE'S ROOM**

1810

肪

BŌ
FAT
8 strokes

脂肪 SHIBŌSŌ   fat layer
脂肪過多 SHIBŌKATA   obesity
脂肪組織 SHIBŌSOSHIKI

                      fatty tissue

月 is **meat** 365, here meaning **lean meat**, while 方 is **side** 204. That found at the side of lean meat is fat.

Mnemonic: **FAT IS FOUND AT SIDE OF MEAT**

| 1811 | | BŌ, BAI, nanigashi
A CERTAIN-, SOME-
9 strokes | 某氏 BŌSHI a certain man
某所 BŌSHO a certain place
太田某 ŌTANANIGASHI*
a certain Mr Ōta |

木 is **tree** 69. 甘 is **sweet** 1093, here meaning literally **something tasty** (and therefore **favorite**) kept in the mouth. 1811 originally referred to the **favored produce of certain trees**, specifically the plums and peaches favored by **pregnant women** (see 1646 and 1689). It thus became a symbol of **pregnancy**. This led to its becoming associated with **rumor** (and matchmaking -- see 1692), and thus it came to acquire its present meaning of **a certain somebody**. Also used as a general prefix meaning **a certain-**.

Mnemonic: **SOMEBODY IS SWEET ON FRUIT OF A CERTAIN TREE**

| 1812 | | BŌ, okasu
DEFY, RISK, ATTACK
9 strokes | 冒険 BŌKEN adventure
感冒 KANBŌ a cold
冒して OKASHITE at the risk of |

Formerly 冒 and earlier 冃, with the original form being 冃. 冂/冂/冃/日 is a **protective helmet**, while 目/目 is **eye** 72. Thus **protective helmet worn over the eyes**, a symbol of a **fighting man**. By association this came to mean **attack**, with **risk** and **defy** being further associations. Suggest taking 日 as **sun** 62.

Mnemonic: **RISK SUN ATTACKING EYES**

| 1813 | | BŌ
DIVIDE, CUT UP
10 strokes | 解剖 KAIBŌ dissection
解剖学 KAIBŌGAKU anatomy
生体解剖 SEITAIKAIBŌ vivisection |

刂 is **sword/ cut** 181. 咅 is the obscure element **spit** 384, here acting phonetically to express **open up** but of unclear semantic role. Thus **cut open**, with **cut up** and **divide** associated meanings. Suggest taking 立 as **stand** 73 and 口 as opening/ **entrance** 20.

Mnemonic: **STAND AT ENTRANCE AND GET CUT UP BY SWORD**

| 1814 | | BŌ, tsumugu
SPIN (YARN)
10 strokes | 紡機 BŌKI spinning machine
紡毛 BŌMŌ carded wool
紡績業 BŌSEKIGYŌ
spinning industry |

糸 is **thread** 27. 方 is **side/ direction** 204, here acting phonetically to express **twist together** and possibly also lending loose connotations of **in a given way**. Thus to **twist threads together** (in a given way?), a reference to **spinning**.

Mnemonic: **SPIN THREADS ON THE SIDE**

1815 傍 BŌ, katawara
SIDE, BESIDE(S)
12 strokes

傍聴 BŌCHŌ — attendance
傍観 BŌKAN — looking on
傍注 BŌCHŪ — margin notes

Somewhat obscure, and of confused evolution. Once written 亻㐼, showing **person** 丿 / 亻 39 and 㐼 /旁. The latter is an NGU character meaning **side**, felt to show two **boats** 方 / 㐅 (taken to be a simplification of boat 舟 1354: see also 204) tethered **side by side** but confusingly depicted as one overlaid by the other in highly stylised mirror image fashion. (The reason for this stylisation is not clear.) Thus 旁 had a core meaning of **boats side by side**. As an independent character it eventually came to mean simply **side**, but in the case of 1815 lent a meaning rather of **at the side of boats**, to give **person at the side of boats/ boatman**. In time, however, 傍 became confused with 旁, and eventually took on the latter's later meaning of **side/ beside**. As is the case in English, **beside** also came to be used in the sense of **in addition to**, i.e. **besides**. Suggest taking 旁 as **side** 方 204 and **stand** 亠 (variant 立 73).

Mnemonic: **PERSON STANDING AT SIDE**

1816 帽 BŌ
CAP, HEADGEAR
12 strokes

帽子 BŌSHI — hat
帽章 BŌSHŌ — cap badge
学帽 GAKUBŌ — school cap

冒 is **attack** 1812 q.v., here in its literal sense of **helmet/ cap** (but without its connotations of battle helmet). **Cloth** 巾 778 -- here in the sense of **apparel** -- was added after 冒 underwent a change of meaning. Suggest taking 日 as **sun** 62 and 目 as **eye** 72.

Mnemonic: **WEAR CLOTH CAP TO SHADE EYES FROM SUN**

1817 膨 BŌ, fuku*ramu/reru*
SWELL, EXPAND
16 strokes

膨大 BŌDAI — swelling
膨満 BŌMAN — inflation
膨脹弁 BŌCHŌBEN — expansion valve

月 is **flesh/ of the body** 365. 彭 is an NGU character meaning **swell/ drumbeat/ strong**. It is believed to comprise **emerge from a drum/ vessel** 壴 1234 and **delicate (hairs)** 彡 93, the latter meaning **delicate** and also serving graphically to indicate **regular repetition**. 彭 thus indicates a **drumbeat starting delicately and rising steadily to a crescendo**, i.e. **swelling in intensity**. In the case of 1817 it lends its meaning of **swell**, to give **swelling body**, used initially of pregnancy but now **swell/ expand** in a broad sense. Suggest taking 壴 as **samurai** 士 494 and **beans** 豆 (variant 豆 1640).

Mnemonic: **SAMURAI'S BODY SWELLS AFTER EATING HAIRY BEANS**

1818 謀	BŌ, MU, hakaru, hakarigoto	陰謀 INBŌ	plot, intrigue
	PLOT, STRATAGEM	謀反 MUHON*	insurrection
	16 strokes	謀略 BŌRYAKU	stratagem

言 is **word/ speak** 274. 某 is **a certain** 1811 q.v., here acting phonetically to express **seek** and also lending connotations of a **secret relationship**. 1818 originally meant to **seek a confidential discussion with someone**, and came by association to mean **plot/ conspire**. **Stratagem** is also an associated meaning.

Mnemonic: **PLOT HINGES ON A CERTAIN WORD**

1819 朴	BOKU, hō	純朴 JUNBOKU	simplicity
	SIMPLE, MAGNOLIA	素朴 SOBOKU	artlessness
	6 strokes	朴の木 HŌNOKI	magnolia

木 is **tree/ wood** 69. 卜 is **divination crack** 91, here acting phonetically to express **tear** and probably also lending connotations of **split**. 1819 originally referred to **tree-bark**, i.e. **that which is torn from a tree**. It became particularly associated with a type of **magnolia** (hypoleuca), presumably because its bark was used for some now un-clear purpose. **Simple** is a borrowing.

Mnemonic: **MAGNOLIA WOOD SIMPLY CRACKS**

1820 僕	BOKU, shimobe	公僕 KŌBOKU	public servant
	(MAN)SERVANT, I	奴僕 DOBOKU	manservant
	14 strokes	僕ら BOKURA	we/ us

Once written 𦰩, clearly showing a **slave** 𦰩 (person 𠃌, with tail/ **testicles** 𠂆 1734 q.v. to indicate a **male** and **tattooist's needle** 辛 1432 q.v. to indicate **slave status**) carrying a **container** ⊠ with **bits** ∴ in it . 𦰩 is taken by some authoritative Japanese scholars to be specifically a **chamber-pot and turds**, but in any event the pictograph clearly depicts a slave performing a (menial) task. **Slave/ manservant** then came to mean **servant** in general (though is still used largely of males), and was also used as a **humble reference to oneself** (though now considered rather colloquial). **Person** 亻 39 was added at a later stage for clarity. The modern form 業 derives from a simplified 𦰩, showing **hands** 丷丷, **needle/ slave** 辛 , and **basket/ container** 甘 (see 399). In com-pounds 業 often lends an idea of **rough/ crude**, but note that it is listed as a CO character with the rather confusing meaning of **thicket**. This is presumably either a borrowing or an associated meaning with **rough** (i.e. rough area). Suggest remembering 業 by association with **profession** 業 260, taking it as an **'odd'** variant of this.

Mnemonic: **I'M A PERSON WITH ODD PROFESSION -- MANSERVANT**

1821

BOKU, sumi
INK, INKSTICK
14 strokes

筆墨 HITSUBOKU   stationery
白墨 HAKUBOKU   chalk
墨絵 SUMIE   ink drawing

Formerly 墨 . 土 is **earth** 60. 黑/黒 is **black** 124 q.v., here with its literal meaning of **soot**. 1821 originally referred to a type of **ink** formed by mixing **soot** with a certain kind of **earth** (plus water -- it is not clear why water 氵 40 was not added to the character). Now **ink/ writing wherewithal** in a broader sense.

Mnemonic: **BLACK EARTH MAKES INK**

1822

BOKU
STRIKE, BEAT
15 strokes

打撲 DABOKU   strike, blow
相撲 SUMŌ*   sumo
撲殺 BOKUSATSU
           beating to death

扌 is **hand** 32. 業 is **servant** 1820, here acting phonetically to express **beat** and almost certainly also originally lending its meaning of **servant**. Thus to beat (a servant?) **with the hand**, now simply **beat/ strike**. Suggest taking 業 as a 'sort of' variant of **profession** 業 260.

Mnemonic: **BEATING WITH HAND IS A SORT OF PROFESSION**

1823

BOTSU
SINK, DISAPPEAR,
DIE, LACK, NOT
7 strokes

没収 BOSSHŪ   forfeiture
日没 NICHIBOTSU   sunset
没後 BOTSUGO   after death

Formerly 沒 and earlier 沝⊚. 氺/氵 is **water/ river** 40, 又 is a **hand**, and ⊚ is a **vortex/ whirlpool** 86. 1823 originally referred to a **whirlpool where the hand can find no hold**, and thus came to mean **disappear and die by sinking into a whirlpool**. Disappear/ die led by association to **not (be present)/ be lacking**. Suggest taking 殳 as **strike** 153.

Mnemonic: **STRIKE WATER AND SINK, DISAPPEAR, AND DIE**

1824 hori, KUTSU
MOAT, DITCH, CANAL
11 strokes

外堀 SOTOBORI　outer moat
つり堀 TSURIBORI fishing pond
堀川 HORIKAWA　canal

土 is **earth** 60. 屈 is **crouch**/ submit 1188 q.v., here acting phonetically to express **dig** and probably also lending its meaning of crouch (and possibly also connotations of remove). Thus (crouch down and?) **dig earth** (thereby removing it?), i.e. **dig a hole/ ditch**. At one stage 1824 was interchangeable with dig 掘 1189, but eventually it came to indicate the noun (i.e. **that which is dug**) rather than the verb (dig). Now **moat/ ditch** rather than just any shape of hole.

Mnemonic: **CROUCH IN EARTHEN MOAT**

1825 HON
RUN, BUSTLE
8 strokes

奔走 HONSŌ　bustle
奔放 HONPŌ na　uninhibited
出奔 SHUPPON　absconding

Once written 𡔖, showing a **man running** 大 161 and **three footprints** 止 129, thus indicating a **man running and leaving a trail of footprints** (suggesting distance). However, as a result of the confusing similarity of growing plant 虫 42 q.v., from an early stage the three footprints 𣥂 became confused with **three plants** 𡴋/屮屮/卉 1770 q.v., giving **man running over plants/ grass** (see also plants/ grass 屮 9). However, the core meaning of **run** remained unchanged. **Bustle** is an associated meaning. Suggest taking 大 as **big man** 53 and 卉 as a combined **trebling** of ten 十 33.

Mnemonic: **THIRTY BIG MEN RUNNING AND BUSTLING**

1826 HON, hirugaeru/su
FLAP, CHANGE
18 strokes

翻訳家 HONYAKUKA translator
翻意 HONI　changing mind
翻って HIRUGAETTE
　　　　on second thought

Formerly 飜, i.e. with **fly/ spread wings** 飛 566 q.v. instead of **wings** 羽 812. 番 is number/ turn 196 q.v., here acting phonetically to express **reverse/ change** and also lending connotations of **in turn/ sequence**. Thus to **change the wings in turn** (in flight), i.e. **flap**. Now **flap/ flutter/ change** in a broad sense.

Mnemonic: **WINGS FLAP, CHANGING IN TURN**

1827 凡	BON, HAN, oyo*so* MEDIOCRE, COMMON, ROUGHLY, IN GENERAL 3 strokes	平凡 HEIBON mediocrity 凡戦 BONSEN dull game 凡例 HANREI explanatory notes

Formerly also 凢 and originally 囗 . 囗 indicates a **shallow tray**. – /丶 is taken by some scholars to indicate contents, but it is far more likely to be the displaced bottom stroke of 囗 . The present core meaning of **commonplace** (with **mediocre** and **[in] general** being associated meanings, and **roughly** being a further association in turn of in general) is felt by some scholars to be a borrowing, while others feel that the simple tray in itself symbolised something commonplace. Suggest taking 几 as **table** 832 and 丶 as a **mark**.

Mnemonic: **IT'S COMMON FOR MEDIOCRE TABLES TO BE MARKED**

1828	BON TRAY, BON FESTIVAL 9 strokes	盆地 BONCHI land basin 盆踊り BONODORI Bon Dance 盆景 BONKEI tray landscape

Formerly also 盆 . 皿 is **dish** 1307. 分 /分 is **divide/ understand** 199 q.v., here acting phonetically to express **big/ wide** and probably also lending its own connotations of **opened up/ out**. Thus **wide dish** (opened out?), i.e. **tray**. In Japan it was also borrowed to refer to the **Bon Festival**, a lantern festival held in summer to welcome the spirits of the dead (from the Sanskrit Ura*bon*).

Mnemonic: **UNDERSTAND DISH TO BE TRAY USED IN BON FESTIVAL**

1829	MA, asa HEMP, FLAX, NUMB 11 strokes	麻布 MAFU/ ASANUNO linen 麻薬 MAYAKU narcotic 麻綱 ASAZUNA hemp rope

Formerly also 麻, and in ancient times 麻. 厂 is a simplification of **oppose** 反 371 q.v., here in its meaning of **cloth**, while 林 indicates **plants/ bushes** (variant **tree/ bush** 朩 /木 69). 'Cloth plant' was a reference to **hemp** or **flax**. The later use of **building** 广 114 instead of cloth 厂 is felt by some scholars to be an error and by others to be an attempt to indicate the storing of hemp cloth indoors. As a result of the narcotic potential of hemp 1829 is also used to refer to **narcotics** and **numbness**. Suggest taking 林 as **forest** 75.

Mnemonic: **FOREST OF HEMP AND FLAX GROWN IN BUILDING**

| 1830 | | MA, su*ru*
RUB, GRAZE, SCRAPE
15 strokes | 摩天楼 MATENRŌ skyscraper
摩擦 MASATSU friction
摩擦音 MASATSUON fricative |

Hand 手 32 and **hemp/ flax** 麻 1829. 1830 originally referred to **rubbing hemp/ flax by hand** in order to separate the fibers, and now means **rub** in a broad sense. Often interchanged with rub 磨 1831.

Mnemonic: **HAND RUBS HEMP**

| 1831 | | MA, miga*ku*
POLISH, SCOUR, RUB
16 strokes | 研磨 KENMA grinding
磨滅 MAMETSU wear and tear
靴磨き KUTSUMIGAKI
shoeshine |

A simplification of 礦. 石 is **stone** 45. 靡 is an NGU character now used in a wide range of confusing meanings such as wave and yield, but in Chinese it can mean **separate** and clearly relates to the act of **separating** 非 773 q.v. the fibers of **hemp/ flax** 麻 1829. It thus originally had a meaning very similar to that of **separate fibers/ rub** 摩 1830 q.v., with the addition of stone 石 giving 1831 a meaning of **rub hemp/ flax with a stone** (as opposed to by hand in the case of 1830, though the two are often interchanged). Now **grind/ scour/ rub** in a broad sense, with **polish** being an associated meaning.

Mnemonic: **RUB HEMP WITH A STONE, TO POLISH IT!?**

| 1832 | | MA
DEMON, DEVIL
21 strokes | 悪魔 AKUMA devil
魔法 MAHŌ magic, sorcery
魔羅 MARA demon, penis |

鬼 is **devil/ demon** 1128. 麻 is **hemp/ flax** 1829, here used phonetically to express **mara**, a Sanskrit term for a particularly evil **demon** (see above). In Japanese mara is also used to refer to the penis (but note that it is an extremely vulgar term which should be avoided).

Mnemonic: **HEMP CAN BE A DEVIL**

585

1833		MAI, u[zu]*maru/meru/moreru*	埋葬 MAISŌ	burial
		BURY	埋め立て UMETATE	reclamation
		10 strokes	埋れ木 UMOREGI	fossil wood

土 is **earth** 60. 里 is **village** 219 q.v., here acting phonetically to express **cover** and possibly also lending loose connotations of **mound of earth** from its own original connotations of raised earthen path. Thus to **cover with earth**, i.e. **bury**. Now used in a broad sense.

Mnemonic: **VILLAGE BURIED IN EARTH**

1834		MAKU	鼓膜 KOMAKU	eardrum
		MEMBRANE	網膜 MŌMAKU	retina
		14 strokes	膜質 MAKUSHITSU	
				membranous

月 is **flesh/ meat** 365. 莫 is **sun sinking among plants** 788 q.v., here acting phonetically to express **wrap** and also lending its own connotations of **envelop**. Thus **that which wraps/ envelops flesh**, a reference to **membrane**. Suggest taking 艹 as **grass** 9, 日 as **sun** 62, and 大 as **big** 53.

Mnemonic: **BIG FLESHY MEMBRANE STRETCHED OVER SUNNY GRASS**

1835	又	mata	又は MATAWA	or
		AGAIN	又と無い MATATONAI	unique
		2 strokes	又貸し MATAGASHI	sublease

Formerly 又, deriving from a pictograph of a (right) hand 又. **Again** is a borrowed meaning.

Mnemonic: **HAND APPEARS AGAIN**

1836		MATSU	抹殺 MASSATSU	erasure
		ERASE, RUB, PAINT	抹茶 MATCHA	powdered tea
		8 strokes	一抹 ICHIMATSU	tinge

扌 is **hand** 32, here meaning **action with the hand**. 末 is **tip/ end** 587 q.v., here acting phonetically to express **paint over/ coat** but of unclear semantic role. Thus **paint over (using the hand)**, with **erase** and **rub out** being associated meanings. Rub out later broadened to mean **rub** in a general sense. Suggest taking 末 literally as **treetop** (tree 木 69 and top 一).

Mnemonic: **HAND TRIES TO ERASE TREETOP BY PAINTING OVER**

586

1837	慢	MAN LAZY, RUDE, BOASTFUL 14 strokes	怠慢 TAIMAN	neglect
			自慢 JIMAN	vanity
			慢性 MANSEI	chronic

忄 is heart/ **feelings** 147. 曼 is an NGU character now meaning full/ **expansive**. Its etymology is unclear, but old forms such as 曼 appear to show a variant 冒 of attack/ helmet (over eye) 冒 / 冒 1812 plus **hand** 又, and it may have originally meant either cover with the hand or (less likely) attack with the hand. In the case of 1837 曼 acts phonetically to express **loose** and may also lend similar connotations of spread (i.e. as opposed to constrained). **Loose feelings** indicated being **easy-going** and **unconcerned**, giving lazy and by association **rude** (cf. English term **sloppy**). It is not fully clear how it also acquired the meaning of **boastful**, but this may be an associated meaning with rude. Suggest taking 日 as **sun** 62, with 罒 literally as **eye** 72.

Mnemonic: FEEL LAZY AS HAND SHADES EYE FROM SUN

1838	漫	MAN, sozoro RANDOM, DIFFUSE, INVOLUNTARY 14 strokes	漫画 MANGA	cartoon, comic
			散漫 SANMAN na	diffuse
			漫ろ言 SOZOROGOTO	rambling

氵 is **water** 40. 曼 is **expansive** 1837, here acting phonetically to express **spread** and probably also lending an idea of **widely**. 1838 originally referred to **water spreading** (widely?), i.e. **flooding** (still a major meaning in Chinese). Since flooding water generally spreads **indiscriminately** and **inexorably** 1838 also came to acquire these connotations, the former leading to **diffuse/ random** and the latter to **involuntar(il)y**. Suggest taking 日 as **sun** 62, 罒 as **eye** 72, and 又 as **hand**.

Mnemonic: HAND INVOLUNTARILY SHADES EYE WATERING IN DIF-FUSE SUNLIGHT

1839	魅	MI BEWITCH, CHARM 15 strokes	魅力 MIRYOKU	charm, appeal
			魅惑 MIWAKU	fascination
			魅了 MIRYŌ	charm

鬼 is **devil/ demon** 1128. 未 is **immature** 794, here acting phonetically to express **beast**. Thus **beast-like demon**, a reference to a particular demon with human face but four legs (a meaning still listed for 1839 in some Chinese dictionaries). **Bewitch/ charm** is an associated meaning (demons being believed to possess the power of bewitching).

Mnemonic: BEWITCHED BY CHARMING IMMATURE DEVIL

1840

misaki, saki, KŌ
PROMONTORY, CAPE
8 strokes

岬角 KŌKAKU   point, spit
岬湾 KŌWAN   indentations
コッド岬 KODDOMISAKI

                 Cape Cod

Of disputed etymology, though its elements are clearly **mountain** 山 24 and **grade A/ high** 甲 1243. Some scholars believe that 甲 originally acted phonetically to express **insert/ be between** (as well as possibly lending connotations of **high**), and that 1840 originally referred to a **valley between (high?) mountains** before coming to mean simply **mountainous** and then by association **promontory**. Other scholars feel that 甲 lent its meaning of **high** and played no phonetic role (though its pronunciation necessarily became 1840's [on/ Chinese] reading), thus giving a meaning from the outset of **high mountain** and then by association **promontory**. The latter theory seems the more helpful.

Mnemonic: **PROMONTORY CONTAINS GRADE 'A' HIGH MOUNTAINS**

1841

MYŌ
EXQUISITE, ODD
7 strokes

妙案 MYŌAN   great idea
微妙 BIMYŌ   subtlety
奇妙 KIMYŌ na   odd

女 is **woman** 35. 少 is **few/ little** 143, here acting phonetically to express **delicate** and probably also lending similar connotations of not bulky. 1841 originally referred to an **exceptionally willowy and graceful woman**. On the one hand such beauty led to **exquisite**, and on the other hand its exceptional nature led to **unusual** and **odd**.

Mnemonic: **FEW WOMEN ARE AS EXQUISITE, OR AS ODD**

1842

MIN, nemuru/i
SLEEP, SLEEPY
10 strokes

不眠症 FUMINSHŌ   insomnia
眠気 NEMUKE   sleepiness
居眠り INEMURI   doze, nap

目 is **eye** 72. 民 is the somewhat obscure **people/ populace** 590 q.v., here acting phonetically to express **close**. Thus **close the eyes**, a reference to **sleeping**. It is not clear whether 民 also plays any semantic role. It may lend connotations of **not using the eyes** through a possible early meaning of **blind**, but since 1842 is a character of relatively late origin it is more likely that any connotations lent by 民 would relate to its later meaning of **populace**, such as perhaps **common to all**.

Mnemonic: **POPULACE CLOSES ITS EYES IN SLEEP**

1843 **MU, BŌ, hoko**
HALBERD, LANCE,
SPEAR
5 strokes

矛げき BŌGEKI　spear, halberd
矛先 HOKOSAKI　spearpoint
矛盾した MUJUNSHITA
contradictory

From a pictograph of a **barbed lance** 𠂤 (earlier simply a **spear** ↑). It is not clear whether the lower extra stroke ／ is an additional **barb** or, more likely, a **hand-guard**. Lance and halberd conceptually overlap (see also 493).

Mnemonic: **LANCE WITH TWO POINTS AND HAND-GUARD**

1844 **MU, yume**
DREAM
13 strokes

夢中 MUCHŪ　absorbed
悪夢 AKUMU　nightmare
夢見る YUMEMIRU fancy,dream

Somewhat obscure. Once written 夢, showing **evening** ▽／夕 44, encircle/ **cover** ⌐ ／冖 (see 655), **eye** ⌑／罒／目 72, and an obscure element 犭. Its earliest meaning is known to have been **dark night when one cannot see**, so presumably 夢 originally referred to the **eye when covered by the night** (or similar). **Dream** is taken by some scholars to be a borrowing, and by others to be an associated meaning (either from the idea of that 'seen' by the eye when it cannot really see or from the idea of covered eye, giving sleep and then dream). Suggest taking ⺿ as **grass** 9.

Mnemonic: **COVER EYES AT NIGHT AND DREAM OF GRASS**

1845 **MU, kiri**
MIST, FOG
19 strokes

霧笛 MUTEKI　foghorn
濃霧 NŌMU　thick fog
朝霧 ASAGIRI　morning mist

Once written 霧. 雨 is **rain** 3, here meaning **rain-like conditions**. 敄／務 is per-form/ **duty** 795, here acting phonetically to express **cover** but of unclear semantic role. Thus **rain-like conditions that cover**, a reference to **fog/ mist**.

Mnemonic: **PERFORM DUTIES IN RAIN, MIST, AND FOG**

589

1846

musume, JŌ
GIRL, DAUGHTER
10 strokes

小娘 KOMUSUME young girl
娘子軍 JŌSHIGUN amazons
娘盛り MUSUMEZAKARI
prime of womanhood

Of recent origin, combining **woman** 女 35 and **good** 良 598 to give **good woman**, meaning a (**young**) **woman in her prime**. **Daughter** is an associated meaning with **girl/ young woman**.

Mnemonic: **ONE'S DAUGHTER IS A GOOD WOMAN**

1847

MEI
INSCRIBE, SIGN
14 strokes

銘柄 MEIGARA brand
銘記 MEIKI remembering
銘銘 MEIMEI severally

Metal 金 14 and **name** 名 71. 1847 originally meant to **inscribe a name in metal** (at first a dead person's, later one's own), giving both **inscribe** and **sign**. It can also symbolise an **individual/ person**.

Mnemonic: **INSCRIBE ONE'S NAME IN METAL**

1848

METSU, horo*biru/bosu*
DESTROY
13 strokes

絶滅 ZETSUMETSU extinction
滅亡 METSUBŌ collapse
破滅 HAMETSU destruction

戌 is a CO character which is interchangeable (in Chinese) with 滅. It comprises **broad bladed halberd** 戌 246, here meaning **weapon/ attack**, and **fire** 火 8. It is not clear whether it originally meant attack with halberd and fire or attack with (the weapon of?) fire, but in any event it meant **attack and destroy**. In combination with **water** 氵 40 it technically meant **destroy water** (**-supply**), but has come to mean **destroy** in a general sense.

Mnemonic: **DESTROYED BY HALBERD, FIRE, AND WATER**

1849

免

MEN, manuka*reru*
ESCAPE, AVOID
8 strokes

免除 MENJO   exemption
免税 MENZEI   tax-exempt
放免 HŌMEN   acquittal

Formerly also written 免. 田 and 由 derive from 内, namely **woman's genitals/ spread legs** 1103, while ル is **bending/ crouching person** 39. 1849 originally referred to a **woman squatting with legs apart striving to give birth** (birth still being retained as a meaning in Chinese, but now usually conveyed by 娩 [which adds woman 女 35] or 挽 [which adds child 子 25] -- see 390). **Escape** is believed to be an associated meaning with parturition, i.e. the 'escaping' of the child from the woman, with **avoid** being a further association with escape. However, some scholars believe that it stems from confusion with the similar character **hare** 兎 1010 q.v., which symbolised fleetness and hence escaping. Suggest taking ク as **crouching person** 39/ 145, ル as **another crouching person** 39, and ロ as **boxes**.

Mnemonic: TWO PERSONS ESCAPE BY CROUCHING BEHIND BOXES

1850

茂

MO, shige*ru*
GROW THICKLY
8 strokes

繁茂 HANMO   thick growth
茂林 MORIN   dense forest
茂み SHIGEMI   thicket

艹 is **grass/ plants** 9. 戊 is **broad bladed halberd** 515, here acting phonetically to express **flourishing** and possibly also lending an idea of thrusting. Thus **flourishing plants** (thrusting forth?), indicating **thick growth**.

Mnemonic: PLANTS GROW THICKLY, THRUSTING LIKE HALBERDS

1851

妄

MŌ, BŌ, midari
IRRATIONAL, RASH
6 strokes

妄言 BŌGEN   harsh words
妄想 MŌSO   delusion
迷妄 MEIMŌ   fallacy

女 is **woman** 35. 亡 is **die** 973 q.v., here acting phonetically to express **blind** and almost certainly also lending its own connotations of **unable to see**. 1851 originally referred to a **man 'blinded' by his infatuation with a woman**, and hence came to symbolise **loss of reason** and **irrational/ rash** behavior.

Mnemonic: ACT IRRATIONALLY AFTER DEATH OF WOMAN

1852		MŌ, mekura BLIND 8 strokes	盲目 MŌMOKU	blindness
			文盲 MONMŌ	illiteracy
			盲判 MEKURABAN	
				'rubber stamp'

Eye 目 72 and **die/ cease to exist** 亡 973. Thus **no eyes/ blind.**

Mnemonic: DEAD EYES ARE BLIND

1853	耗	MŌ, KŌ WASTE, DECREASE 10 strokes	消耗 SHŌMŌ	consumption
			損耗 SONMŌ	wastage, loss
			心神耗弱 SHINSHINKŌJAKU	
				feeble minded

Correctly written 秏. 禾 is **rice plant/ grain plant** 81. 毛 is **hair** 210, here acting phonetically to express **not/ cease to be** and possibly also suggesting a wispy and insubstantial plant. 1853 originally referred to a **failed crop**, with **waste** and **decrease** being associated meanings. The modern form uses **plow** 耒 673 q.v. (which may itself once have depicted a plant), felt by some scholars to be a simple miscopying. Suggest taking 耒 as a **heavily branched** variant of **tree** 木 69.

Mnemonic: HEAVILY BRANCHED TREE WASTES AWAY TO HAIRS

1854	猛	MŌ FIERCE, RAGING, BRAVE 11 strokes	猛烈 MŌRETSU na	fierce
			猛獣 MŌJŪ	fierce animal
			猛者 MOSA*	a stalwart

犭 is **dog** 17. 孟 is an NGU character meaning **chief/ first**. Its etymology is unclear, but it combines **child** 子 25 and **dish** 皿 1307, and the fact that in Chinese it can also mean eldest, rude, and rush forward suggests that it may originally have been an ideograph depicting the eldest child rushing rudely to eat. Here it acts phonetically to express **spirited** and possibly also lends loose connotations of aggression, thus giving **spirited dog**. This came to mean **spirited** in a broader sense, eventually leading by association to **fierce**, **raging**, and **brave**.

Mnemonic: FIERCE DOG BEATS BRAVE CHILD TO DISH

| 1855 | | MŌ, ami
NET, NETWORK
14 strokes | 漁網 GYOMŌ fishing net
網戸 AMIDO screen door
通信網 TSŪSHINMŌ
news network |

Once written simply as 网 (now 网), a pictograph of a **net** with hauling ropes (see 193). **Die** 亡 973 was added for its sound, to express **interwoven**, but any semantic role is unclear. Finally **thread** 糸 27 (in a sense of **cord**) was also added for clarity. Now also used figuratively, as **network**. Suggest taking 冂 as **cover** and 丷 as **horns**.

Mnemonic: **DEAD HORNED CREATURE COVERED BY THREADED NET**

| 1856 | | MOKU, damaru
BE SILENT
15 strokes | 黙殺 MOKUSATSU ignoring
沈黙 CHINMOKU silence
黙り込む DAMARIKOMU fall silent |

Formerly 默. 犬 is **dog** 17. 黑/黒 is **black** 124 q.v., here acting phonetically to express **silence** but of unclear semantic role (though it may possibly lend some suggestion of being blocked, from its original meaning of soot forming on a grille/ window). 1856 originally referred to a **silent dog**, and now means **silence** in a broad sense.

Mnemonic: **BLACK DOG IS SILENT**

| 1857 | | MON
CREST, PATTERN
10 strokes | 紋章 MONSHŌ heraldic crest
指紋 SHIMON fingerprint
波紋 HAMON ripple |

Thread 糸 27 and **text/ writing** 文 68 q.v., here in its early meaning of **intricate pattern**. Thus **patterned threadwork**, a reference to a **crest**.

Mnemonic: **THREADS IN CREST FORM PATTERN LIKE WRITING**

| 1858 | | monme
MONME, WEIGHT, COIN
4 strokes | 二匁 NIMONME two monme
五匁 GOMONME five monme
三匁 SANMONME three monme |

A 'made in Japan' character formed on a phonetic basis from a stylised combination of MON 文 68 and the katakana ME メ, thus giving **MONME**. A monme was a **small weight** (3.75 grams) and a **small coin**. Suggest remembering 匁 by association with **thing** 物 387.

Mnemonic: **A MONME LOOKS LIKE AN AWKWARD THING**

1859 厄	YAKU	厄介 YAKKAI	trouble
	MISFORTUNE, DISASTER	厄日 YAKUBI	bad day
	4 strokes	災厄 SAIYAKU	calamity

Often felt to be associated with **dangerous** 厄 831 q.v., which is a useful mnemonic, but the overlap of elements is coincidental. 1859 was once written , showing **cliff** 厂 45 and **bending figure** 乚 145, and in similar fashion to 831 later had its bending figure 乚 changed to **slumped figure** 匕 768. However, it does not refer to a figure falling down a cliff. 厂 is used phonetically to express **thrust upwards**, and almost certainly lends similar connotations of its own, combining with bending figure 乚 to give **person bent (with back) thrust upwards**. This was applied to a **hunchback**. Some scholars feel that the present meanings are borrowed, but others see them as associated, since a hunchback was generally a symbol of something unpleasant (e.g. see 997).

Mnemonic: **NOT QUITE DANGEROUS, BUT STILL A MISFORTUNE**

1860 躍	YAKU, odoru	躍進 YAKUSHIN	rush, dash
	LEAP, DANCE, RUSH	飛躍 HIYAKU	leap
	21 strokes	躍り込む ODORIKOMU	rush into

足 is **foot/ leg** 51. 翟 is **bird's wings** 216 q.v. (**bird** 隹 216 and **wings** 羽 812), here acting phonetically to express **leap** and probably also lending its own connotations of soaring high. Thus to **leap (with the legs)**. **Dance** and **rush** are associated meanings.

Mnemonic: **LEAP WITH FEET FLYING LIKE BIRD'S WINGS**

1861 愉	YU	愉快 YUKAI	pleasure
	JOY, PLEASURE	愉悦 YUETSU	joy
	12 strokes	愉楽 YURAKU	pleasure

忄 is **heart/ feelings** 147. 俞 is **convey** 799, here acting phonetically to express **good** and possibly also lending its meaning of convey. Thus **good feelings** (conveyed to the heart?), i.e. **pleasure/ joy**. Suggest taking 俞 as **cut** 刂 181, **meat** 月 365, and **cover** 亼 121.

Mnemonic: **FEELINGS OF JOY ABOUT CUT MEAT BEING COVERED**

594

1862		YU, sato*su* INSTRUCT, ADMONISH 16 strokes	教諭 KYŌYU	instructor
			説諭 SETSUYU	admonition
			論旨 YUSHI	official advice

言 is **words/ speak** 274. 俞 is **convey** 799, here acting phonetically to express **clear/ clarify** and possibly also lending its meaning of **convey**. Thus **clarify verbally**, i.e. **instruct**, usually with connotations of **correcting** and/or **admonishing**. Suggest taking 俞 as **cut** 刂 181, **meat** 月 365, and **cover** 亼 121.

Mnemonic: ADMONISH VERBALLY AND INSTRUCT TO COVER CUT MEAT

1863		YU, iyasu CURE, HEAL, VENT 18 strokes	治癒 CHIYU	cure
			平癒 HEIYU	recovery
			癒合 YUGŌ	knitting (wound)

Formerly 瘉 . 疒 is **sickness** 381. 俞 is **convey** 799, here acting phonetically to express **remove** and possibly also lending an idea of transport/ move (away). Thus **remove sickness**, i.e. **heal/ cure**, with **vent** being a minor associated meaning. 俞 was later replaced by 愈, a CO character combining convey 俞 with **heart/ feelings** 心 147 and meaning **cure**. Its etymology is unclear, just as the reason for its replacing 俞, but it contains the same elements as joy 愉 1861 and was presumably originally a variant of same. Thus its use in 1863 may have been an attempt to indicate joyful feelings following a cure. 愈 would then have acquired by association 1863's meaning of cure (i.e. in effect as a simplification of it). Suggest taking 俞 as **cut** 刂 181, **meat** 月 365, and **cover** 亼 121.

Mnemonic: FEEL ILL OVER COVERED CUT MEAT -- NEED CURE

1864	唯	YUI, I, tada ONLY, PROMPT (ANSWER) 11 strokes	唯一 YUIITSU	sole, unique
			唯今 TADAIMA	now; I'm home
			唯唯諾諾 IIDAKUDAKU	readily

口 is **mouth/ say** 20. 隹 is **bird** 216, here lending its sound (once I) to express a vocalisation indicating a **prompt response** (now E in Japanese). It is not clear whether 隹 also plays any semantic role. Thus **prompt answer (saying I)**, which could also symbolise promptness in a wider sense. It is still very occasionally found with this meaning, but is usually used to mean **only**, which is a borrowing.

Mnemonic: BIRD HAS MOUTH, ONLY DON'T EXPECT PROMPT ANSWER

1865		YŪ, kasuka DARK, OBSCURE, FAINT, LONELY 9 strokes	幽境 YŪKYŌ 幽玄 YŪGEN 幽界 YŪKAI	lonely place mystery nether world

Once written 88/心. 心 is **fire** 8 (now 火), and not **mountain** 山/山 24. 88/幺 is a doubling of **short thread** 幺 111, here acting phonetically to express **black** and possibly also lending supporting connotations of obscure (see 1227). 1865 originally referred to **something blackened by flame** and thus of **unclear appearance**, and hence came to mean **obscure** and **dark**. **Faint** is an associated meaning. It can also be used to mean **lonely**, and, as with 玄 1227, can have connotations of mysteriousness/ otherworldliness. Suggest taking 山 as **mountain**.

Mnemonic: **FOLLOW FAINT THREAD THROUGH DARK AND LONELY MOUNTAINS**

1866		YŪ COMPOSED, DISTANT, LONG TIME, AMPLE 11 strokes	悠然 YŪZEN 悠長 YŪCHŌ na 悠久 YŪKYŪ	calmly leisurely eternity

Somewhat obscure. 心 is **heart/ feelings** 147. 攸 is **strike a person with a stick** 704 q.v. (person 亻 39, stick 丨, and **striking hand** 攵 101), here acting phonetically to express **afflict** and probably lending similar connotations of attack/ beset. Thus **that which afflicts the heart,** namely **grief/ worry** (still a meaning in Chinese). **Composed/ calm** is believed by some scholars to be a borrowing, and by others to be an associated meaning, from the idea of being worried but composed. **Distant** is definitely a borrowing, with **long time** and **ample** being associated meanings with distant. Note that 攸 does exist as an independent CO character with a wide range of confusing meanings, including distant (which appears to result from its being used as a simplification of 悠 after the latter had borrowed this meaning).

Mnemonic: **STRIKE PERSON WITH STICK, BUT FEELINGS COMPOSED**

1867

YŪ, nao
MOREOVER, STILL,
HESITATE, SIMILAR
12 strokes

猶子 YŪSHI adopted child
猶予 YŪYO postponement
猶予期間 YŪYOKIKAN
period of grace

犭 is dog/ **beast** 17, here indicating a **monkey** and thus to all intents and purposes a simplification of monkey 猿 1028. 酋 is chief/ liquor 927 q.v. (literally **out of** 丷 66 and **wine jar** 酉 302), here acting phonetically to express **hesitate** and presumably chosen as the phonetic partly for the association between a jar and a hesitant monkey (as in the method of using a jar as a trap). Thus **hesitant monkey**, later **hesitant/ hesitate** in general. **Delay** is an associated meaning. **Still** is also believed to be an associated meaning, from the idea of still not bringing oneself to do something (cf. mada), with **moreover** then being an associated meaning in turn from a generalised still. It is not clear how the minor meaning of **similar** came about. Note that there is an occasionally encountered miswritten variant 猶, which uses esteem 尊 927 instead of 酋 .

Mnemonic: **BEAST STILL HESITANT TO COME OUT OF WINE JAR**

1868

YŪ, yutaka
RICH, PLENTIFUL
12 strokes

裕福 YŪFUKU opulence
余裕 YOYŪ margin, surplus
富裕階級 FUYŪKAIKYŪ
wealthy classes

衤 is **clothing** 420. 谷 is **valley** 122, here acting phonetically to express **ample** and probably also lending connotations of big. Thus **ample clothes** (in the sense of loose fitting), later **ample** in general. **Rich** and **plentiful** are associated meanings, from the idea of not being constrained.

Mnemonic: **PLENTIFUL CLOTHES, ENOUGH TO FILL VALLEY**

1869

YŪ, osu, o-
MALE, POWERFUL
12 strokes

雄弁 YŪBEN eloquence
雄者 YŪSHA hero
雄牛 OUSHI bull

隹 is **bird** 216. 厷 is a CO character meaning **arm**. It was once written 厷 , showing an **arm** 又 and an **elbow** ㄥ (note that the addition of flesh/ of the body 月 365 gives the NGU character arm/ elbow 肱). Here 厷 acts phonetically to express **fine/ showy**, and may also lend connotations of **strength** and hence **masculinity**. Thus **fine/ showy bird**, a reference to the **male bird** (which generally has the finer plumage) and hence **male** in general.

Mnemonic: **MALE BIRD HAS STRONG ARMS AND ELBOWS?!**

1870 YŪ, sasou
INVITE, TEMPT, LEAD
14 strokes

誘惑 YŪWAKU　　seduction
誘導 YŪDŌ　　　induction
誘い水 SASOIMIZU
pump priming

言 is words/ speak 274. 秀 is excel/ excellent 1355, here acting phonetically to express **lead** and probably also lending similar connotations. Thus **lead with words**, i.e. **tempt**. Now used in a broad sense.

Mnemonic: EXCELLENT WORDS LEAD TO TEMPTATION

1871 YŪ, urei/eru, ui
GRIEF, SORROW
15 strokes

憂愁 YŪSHŪ　　grief, gloom
憂え顔 UREEGAO　　sad look
物憂い MONOUI　weary, gloomy

Once written 憂, showing **head** 頁/頁/直, 93 (here meaning **mind**), **heart**/ feelings 心/心 147, and **upturned foot** 夂/又 438 q.v. (here meaning **walk slowly**). Head 直, is also believed to act phonetically to express **grief**/ **sadness**. Thus **walk slowly with sad heart and mind**, later **grief**/ **sorrow** in general. Suggest taking 夂 as **sit crosslegged**.

Mnemonic: SIT CROSSLEGGED, HEAD AND HEART FULL OF GRIEF

1872 YŪ, tokeru
DISSOLVE, MELT
16 strokes

融和 YŪWA　　　softening
金融 KINYŪ　　　finance
融通 YŪZŪ finance, versatility

鬲 is **large pot on stand** 1078. 虫 is **insect** 56, here onomatopoeically lending its sound CHŪ to express the sound of **steam being given off** (cf. English hiss). 1872 originally referred to **cooking something vigorously (with steam being given off with a CHŪ sound)**, and can still mean steam in Chinese. **Dissolve/ melt** is taken by some scholars to be a borrowing, and by others to be an associated meaning. Suggest remembering 鬲 by association with **round** 口 228 and **one** 一 1.

Mnemonic: DISSOLVE INSECTS IN ONE ROUND POT ON STAND

1873

YO, ata*eru*
GIVE, CONVEY, IMPART, INVOLVEMENT
3 strokes

与え主 ATAENUSHI giver, donor
関与 KANYO involvement
授与式 JUYOSHIKI
award ceremony

Formerly 與 and earlier 𦥑. The oldest form is 𦥑. 𦥑 shows **four hands**, symbolising **many hands**. 与 is a variant of fangs 牙／牙 434 q.v., and indicates **interlocking** (fangs originally being clarified by the addition of mouth 口 20). Thus **many interlocking hands**, indicating a **joint effort** and hence by association **involvement**. The present main meaning of **give** technically stems from confusion between 与 and 与 following the dropping of mouth 口. 与 is an element combining an old variant 勺 of **ladle** 勺 1342 q.v. with **one** 一 1 and meant **one ladleful**, later coming to mean **give a ladleful** and eventually just **give**. However, the idea of hands together contained in itself an idea of **raising** (e.g. see 1603 and 1793), which conceptually overlaps with **offer/ give**, and thus in one sense give is an extended meaning of hands interlocking 𦥑. **Convey/ impart** is an associated meaning. See also 458 and 652.

Mnemonic: **GIVE ONE LADLEFUL**

1874

YO, homa*re*
HONOR, FAME, PRAISE
13 strokes

名誉 MEIYO honor, fame
栄誉 EIYO honor, fame
誉れ高い HOMARETAKAI
renowned

Formerly 譽. 言 is **words/ speak** 274. 與 is **hands together** 1873, here acting phonetically to express **sing/ shout** and also lending connotations of **together**. Thus **shout out words together**, a somewhat vague reference to people **united in the singing of someone's praise**. **Honor** and **fame** are associated meanings. Suggest taking ⺍ as a **laden table**.

Mnemonic: **FAME BRINGS WORDS OF PRAISE AND LADEN TABLE**

1875

YŌ
ORDINARY, WORK
11 strokes

中庸 CHŪYŌ middle path
凡庸 BONYŌ banality
租庸調 SOYŌCHŌ corvee, labor

Once written 庸, showing a combination of **hands holding pestle** 庚／庸 480 and **use** 用／用 215. The latter also acts phonetically to express **work**. Thus **to work while using a pestle** (to pound rice etc.), which on the one hand came to mean **work** in a broader sense and on the other to symbolise **doing something mundane** and thus **ordinary**. Suggest taking 庚 as **building** 广 114, **hand** 彐, and **stick** ｜.

Mnemonic: **HAND USES STICK TO DO ORDINARY WORK IN BUILDING**

1876

揚

YŌ, *ageru*
RAISE, FRY
12 strokes

揚水 YŌSUI — pumping water
揚げ場 AGEBA — landing stage
揚げ物 AGEMONO — fried food

扌 is **hand** 32. 昜 is **sun rising** 144 q.v., here acting phonetically to express **raise** and also lending its own connotations of **rise/ raise**. Thus to **raise with the hand**, later just **raise**. In Japanese it has also acquired a meaning of **(deep) fry**, felt to be an associated meaning from the idea of lifting something out of a vat.

Mnemonic: HAND RAISED TO RISING SUN MAY GET FRIED

1877

揺

YŌ, *yuru/reru/ragu/suru/suburu*
SHAKE, SWING, ROCK
12 strokes

動揺 DŌYŌ — shaking
揺りいす YURIISU — rocking chair
揺れ止め YUREDOME — stabilizer

Formerly 搖. 扌 is **hand** 32. is a CO character meaning **vase/ pitcher**. Its etymology is rather unclear, though its old form 䍃 reveals **meat** 夕/ 夕/ 月 365 and **can/ vessel** 缶/缶 (here 缶) 1095, and presumably it originally indicated a vessel for storing meat. In compounds it often appears to lend connotations of **sway/ shake/ not be straight**, but the reason for this is not clear. Here it acts phonetically to express **sway/ shake** and may possibly also lend similar connotations of its own. Thus to **shake with the hand**, later **shake/ sway/ rock** in a broad sense. Suggest taking 爫 as **reaching hand** 303.

Mnemonic: SHAKING HANDS REACH FOR CAN

1878

溶

YŌ, *tokeru/kasu*
MELT, DISSOLVE
13 strokes

溶液 YŌEKI — solution
溶解 YŌKAI — melt, dissolve
溶け合う TOKEAU — melt together

氵 is **water** 40. 容 is **contain** 802, here acting phonetically to express **full** and also lending its meaning of **contain**. Thus **(a container) full of water**, which is still 1878's sole meaning in Chinese. The Japanese meaning of **dissolve** is felt by some scholars to be a borrowing, and by others to be an associated meaning from the idea of being immersed in water (with **melt** being a further association). Suggest taking 容 as **valley** 谷 122 and **roof/ house** 宀 28.

Mnemonic: HOUSE DISSOLVES IN VALLEY FULL OF WATER

1879 YŌ, koshi
HIP, LOWER BACK,
BEARING
13 strokes

腰痛 YŌTSŪ   lumbago
腰肉 KOSHINIKU   loin meat
物腰 MONOGOSHI   manner

Need/ vital 要 593 q.v., here in its original meaning of waist, with flesh/ of the body 月 365 added for clarity after its meaning started to change. It now means hip/ lower back rather than the waist specifically. Also used by figurative association to indicate bearing/ manner.

Mnemonic: HIP IS VITAL PART OF BODY

1880 YŌ, odoru
DANCE, LEAP, DOUBLE
14 strokes

踊り子 ODORIKO   dancing girl
舞踊 BUYŌ   dance, dancing
踊り字 ODORIJI   'repeat' sign

足 is foot/ leg 51. 甬 is raised/ break clear 176 q.v., here acting phonetically to express leap high and also lending similar connotations of its own. Thus to leap high (with the legs), with dance being an associated meaning. It is not clear how it also came to acquire its lesser meaning of double. Suggest taking 甬 as a simplification of pass 通 176.

Mnemonic: DANCE, USING FEET IN PASSING

1881 YŌ, kama
KILN, OVEN
15 strokes

窯業 YŌGYŌ   ceramics
窯業家 YŌGYŌKA   ceramist
乾燥窯 KANSŌGAMA
    drying kiln

穴 is hole 849, here meaning pit. 羔 is an NGU character meaning lamb (presumably sheep 羊 986 good for roasting [fire] 灬 8), here acting phonetically to express bake and possibly lending similar connotations of its own. Thus baking pit, i.e. oven, with kiln being an associated meaning.

Mnemonic: SHEEP-ROASTING-PIT CAN BE KILN AS WELL AS OVEN

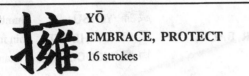

1882	YŌ	擁護 YŌGO	protection, help
	EMBRACE, PROTECT	擁立 YŌRITSU	support
	16 strokes	抱擁 HŌYŌ	embrace

Of confused evolution and somewhat obscure as a result. Once written 㨽雈 ⺙/扌 is hand 32, here meaning **arm**. 雝 comprises **bird** 隹/隹 216 and 邕/邕. The latter is a CO character meaning **union** and **harmony**. Its etymology is not fully clear, but it comprises **village** 邑 355 and **river** 川 /巛 48/ 680, and may have come to symbolise harmony through the naturalness of a village being located beside a river. The role of bird 隹 is not clear, but it should be noted that in Chinese 雝 exists as a character that can be interchanged with 邕 to mean union/ harmony. It also has an additional meaning of marsh, suggesting that it was originally an entirely separate character meaning water (near village) where birds gather before becoming confused with 邕. To add to the confusion, 雍 also exists as a character in Chinese, interchangeable with 邕 but not 雝, despite the fact that it is obviously a simplification of 雝 rather than 邕! It is known that in the case of 1882 雍 acts phonetically to express **envelop/ wrap** (as well as possibly lending connotations of union and hence coming together), to give **wrap with the arms/ embrace** and by association **protect**. (Note that it is thus very similar to embrace/ envelop with the arms 抱 1794, though the latter lacks the associated meaning of protect.) Suggest taking 幺 as a variant of (short) **thread** 幺 111 and 亠 as **top**.

Mnemonic: **HAND PROTECTS BIRD WITH THREAD-LIKE CREST ON TOP**

1883	YŌ, utai, uta*u*	謡曲 YŌKYOKU	Noh chant
	NOH CHANT, SONG	民謡 MINYŌ	folk song
	16 strokes	謡本 UTAIBON	Noh text

Formerly 謡. 言 is **words/ speak** 274. 㡭 is the somewhat unclear 'meat vessel' element seen in 1877 q.v., here acting phonetically to express **sway** and possibly also lending similar connotations of its own. **Swaying words** referred to a **modulated rendition of a noh text** or a **lilting song** (usually with little or no musical accompaniment). Suggest taking ⺈ as **reaching hand** 303 and 缶 as **can** (variant 缶 1095).

Mnemonic: **HAND REACHES FOR CAN, UTTERING WORDY CHANT**

1884 抑 **YOKU, osa*eru***
RESTRAIN, PRESS DOWN
7 strokes

抑止 YOKUSHI deterrent
抑圧 YOKUATSU suppression
抑制 YOKUSEI restraint

Originally written ㄅヨ, being a mirror-image variant of **hand pressing down on bending person** ヒ九/印 425 q.v. (with bending person 九 39 being replaced by bending/ crouching person ㄅ/巴 145). It similarly came to mean **press down** in a general sense, with **restrain** being a figurative association. A further **hand** 扌 32 was added later, and press down 印 was miscopied as raise 卬 1173 q.v. (literally bending person 卩 and a further person 𠂉). Suggest taking 卩 as **bending person** and 𠂉 as a reinforcing symbol of **bending**.

Mnemonic: **HAND PRESSES DOWN ON PERSON TILL DOUBLY BENT**

1885 翼 **YOKU, tsubasa**
WING
17 strokes

右翼 UYOKU right wing
翼端 YOKUTAN wingtip
翼竜 YOKURYŪ pterodactyl

羽 is **wings** 812. 異 is **differ** 807, here acting phonetically to express **wing** but of unclear semantic role. Thus **wing(s)**.

Mnemonic: **DIFFERENT WINGS, BUT WINGS NONETHELESS**

1886 裸 **RA, hadaka**
NAKED, BARE
13 strokes

裸身 RASHIN nudity
赤裸裸 SEKIRARA frankness
裸馬 HADAKAUMA bareback

衤 is **clothes** 420. 果 is **fruit**/ result 627, here acting phonetically to express **peel** but of unclear semantic role. Thus to **peel off clothes/ become naked.**

Mnemonic: **PEEL CLOTHES, LIKE FRUIT, AND BECOME NAKED**

1887 羅 **RA**
GAUZE, NET, INCLUDE
19 strokes

羅列 RARETSU marshalling
羅典 RATEN Latin
網羅的 MŌRATEKI comprehensive

An ideograph combining the three elements of **thread** 糸 27, **net** 罒 193, and **bird** 隹 216, to give a meaning of **bird-net made of thread**. Now **net** in broad sense, including the figurative one of bring into one's fold/ **include**. **Gauze** is an associated meaning.

Mnemonic: **BIRD-NET OF THREAD, FINE AS GAUZE**

1888

RAI, kaminari
THUNDER, LIGHTNING
13 strokes

雷雨	RAIU	thunderstorm
雷名	RAIMEI	renown
魚雷	GYORAI	torpedo

Once written 靁. 雨 is **rain** 3, here in an extended sense of **atmospheric conditions**. 畾 is **three fields** 1419 (**field** 田 59), here acting phonetically to express **reverberate** and possibly also lending connotations of quantity/ repetition. Thus **atmospheric conditions that reverberate (repeatedly?)**, a reference to **thunder**. By association it can also mean **lightning**.

Mnemonic: **RAIN FALLS ON FIELD AMID THUNDER AND LIGHTNING**

1889

RAI, tano*mu/moshii*, tayo*ru*
REQUEST, RELY
16 strokes

信頼	SHINRAI	trust
頼り無い	TAYORINAI	unreliable
頼み	TANOMI	favor, trust

Formerly 賴 and earlier 頼. A combination of shell/ **money** 貝 90 and 剌/剌/剌. The latter is an NGU character meaning **be opposed**, but in Chinese it can also mean **cut/ slash**. It comprises **bundle** 朿/束 1535 and **sword/ cut** 刀/刀/刂 181, and presumably originally meant **cut open a bundle**. Here it acts phonetically to express **profit** (but any semantic role unclear), combining with **money** 貝 to give **profit financially**. It was later borrowed to express **entreat**, giving by extension **request** and **rely**. Note that in compounds it sometimes appears to lend connotations of divide, probably as a result of the presence of cut open 剌| in earlier forms. The modern form shows a miscopying of sword 刀 and money 貝 as **head** 頁 93.

Mnemonic: **RELY ON HEAD TO REQUEST A BUNDLE**

1890

RAKU, kara*mu/maru*
ENTWINE, CONNECT
12 strokes

連絡	RENRAKU	contact
絡み合う	KARAMIAU	intertwine
絡み付く	KARAMITSUKU	entwine

糸 is **thread** 27. 各 is **each** 438 q.v., here acting phonetically to express **tangle** and possibly also lending an idea of impeded progress/ stopping through its upturned foot element 夂. Thus **tangled threads** (which cause a halt in proceedings?), leading to **entwine** and by association **connect**.

Mnemonic: **EACH THREAD IS ENTWINED AND THUS CONNECTED**

1891 **RAKU**
CURD, DAIRY PRODUCE
13 strokes

酪農 RAKUNŌ　dairy farming
酪酸 RAKUSAN　butyric acid
乾酪 KANRAKU　cheese

酉 is **wine jar** 302, here indicating **fermentation**. 各 is **each** 438 q.v., here acting phonetically to express **solidify** and possibly also lending connotations of **stop moving** (freely). Thus **that which ferments and solidifies**, originally a reference to **curd** but now used of **dairy produce** in a broad sense.

Mnemonic: **EACH JAR OF DAIRY PRODUCE CONTAINS CURD**

1892 濫 **RAN**
FLOOD, OVERDO,
WANTON
18 strokes

濫用 RANYŌ　abuse
濫費 RANPI　extravagance
はん濫 HANRAN　inundation

氵 is **water** 40. 監 is **supervise** 1111, here acting phonetically to express **overflow** and possibly also loosely lending connotations of **water filling a container** from its literal meaning of staring at one's reflection in a bowl of water. Thus **water overflowing**, later **overflow/ flood** and by association **overdo**. **Wanton** is also an associated meaning, from the idea of excessive.

Mnemonic: **WANTON SUPERVISION OF FLOODING WATER**

1893 欄 **RAN**
COLUMN, RAILING,
SPACE
20 strokes

欄干 RANKAN　railing
空欄 KŪRAN　blank space
欄外 RANGAI　page margin

Formerly 欄. 木 is **wood/ tree** 69. 闌 is a confusing NGU character meaning height, climax, and be well advanced, while in Chinese it means rather decline, finished, evening, overdo, wanton, fence, and door screen. Its etymology is unclear, though it clearly comprises **door/ gate** 門 211 and **select/ remove from a bundle** 東 608 q.v. In the case of 1893 it is known to have acted phonetically to express **encircle** (as well as lending a meaning of fence?), to give **encircling wood**, namely **fence/ railing(s)**. Encircling fence came to indicate **delineated area/ fixed space**, including by association **column** (i.e. fixed space in a text [and of late newspaper]). Suggest taking 東 as **east** 184.

Mnemonic: **WOODEN RAILINGS ENCLOSE SPACE BY EASTERN GATE**

1894 **RI**
OFFICIAL
6 strokes

吏員 RIIN   official
能吏 NŌRI   able official
吏臭 RISHŪ   'red tape'

Once written 叓, being an early form of **thing** 事 293 q.v. and having the latter's early meaning of **work**. It came by association to mean **person at work**, and in particular to mean **official**. Note however that the addition of person 亻 39 gives use/ servant 使 287 q.v. It is not fully clear how and why 293, 287, and 1894 came to evolve along separate paths. Suggest taking 吏 as a combination of **hand** 乂, **box** ▽, and **ten** 十 33.

Mnemonic: **OFFICIAL'S HAND HOLDS TEN BOXES**

1895 **RI**
DIARRHOEA
12 strokes

下痢 GERI   diarrhoea
赤痢 SEKIRI   dysentery
疫痢 EKIRI   infant diarrhoea

疒 is **sickness** 381. 利 is **profit** 596, here acting phonetically to express **diarrhoea** (itself phonetically associated with a term meaning **pour forth**) but of unclear semantic role. Thus the **sickness of diarrhoea** (the **'pouring forth sickness'**).

Mnemonic: **DIARRHOEA CAN BE A PROFITABLE SICKNESS?!**

1896 **RI, ha**ku
WEAR (ON FEET), WALK,
FOOTWEAR, ACT
15 strokes

履歴 RIREKI   personal history
履行 RIKŌ   performance
履き物 HAKIMONO
               footwear, clog

Once written 𩔉, showing that **again**/ return 復 782 q.v. is a miscopying of 復. This is a now defunct character meaning **walk slowly in clogs**. It comprises **movement (along a road)** ㄔ/彳 118, **upturned foot** ㄆ/夂 438 q.v. (here indicating **slow progress**), and **boat** 月/舟 1354 (here indicating a type of **wooden clog** likened to a boat). **Slumped figure/ corpse** ⊃/尸 236 was added both for its sound, to express **drag**, and for its own suggestion of **inertia/ lack of vitality**. Thus 1896 originally meant **walk slowly in clogs, dragging (the feet) lifelessly**. This gave both **walk** and **wear on the feet** (and occasionally **footwear**), with **act** being an associated meaning (originally do something slowly and reluctantly but do it nonetheless, now act in a broader sense).

Mnemonic: **CORPSE WALKS AGAIN, WEARING FOOTWEAR: SOME ACT!**

1897 RI, hana*reru*/*su*   分 離 BUNRI   separation
SEPARATE, LEAVE   離 陸 RIRIKU   take-off
18 strokes   乳 離 れ CHIBANARE   weaning

隹 is **bird** 216. 离 is a CO character meaning **bright/ glossy** and **oppose**. Its etymology is not fully clear but an old form 离 suggests it is a variant of scorpion 离/萬 392, presumably a type with glossy body and also associated with defiance. In the case of 1897 离 acts phonetically to express the name of a bird (a type of **oriole**) and probably also lends connotations of **bright (colored)**. Thus the **oriole bird (a bird of bright plumage?)**. 1897 can still mean oriole in Chinese. Its main meaning of **separate/ leave** is generally taken to be a borrowing, but it is possible that the oriole may itself have symbolised parting through some migratory pattern (a view supported by the fact that in Chinese 1897 can also mean pass through). Suggest taking 凵 as a **box** 凵 with contents × (i.e. **full**) and **lid** 亠, and 禸 as an 'odd' version of **insect** 虫 56.

Mnemonic: **SEPARATE BIRD FROM LIDDED BOX FULL OF ODD INSECTS**

1898 RYŪ, yanagi   柳 糸 RYŪSHI   willow branch
WILLOW, WILLOWY   花 柳 界 KARYŪKAI   demimonde
9 strokes   川 柳 SENRYŪ   comic verse

木 is **tree** 69. 卯 is a variant of horse's bit 㧖/卯 805 q.v., here acting phonetically to express **flow** and possibly also graphically suggesting drooping. Thus **tree (whose branches) flow (and droop?)**, a reference to the **willow**. Suggest remembering 卯 as a symbol indicating **back to back**.

Mnemonic: **WILLOW TREES BACK TO BACK?!**

1899 RYŪ, RYŌ, tatsu   恐 竜 KYŌRYŪ   dinosaur
DRAGON   竜 神 RYŪJIN   dragon god
10 strokes   竜 巻 TATSUMAKI   whirlwind

Of confused graphic evolution. Formerly 龍. The earliest form 龍 shows a **four-legged creature with long tail, pointed nose, and large ears**. This then appears to have been stylised as 龍 with ✐ felt to indicate pointed head and ears, ○ the body, ⌢ the legs, and ∿ the tail. A later form 龍 (the prototype of the semi-modern 龍) shows the pointed head and ears ✐ replaced (it is not clear whether deliberately or in error) by **needle/ sharp** 辛 1432, the body and legs 月 replaced by **flesh/ of the body** 月 365, and the tail ∿ reshaped as ㇄ with the addition of ⸗ (spikes/ tailplates?). The modern form 竜 derives from the 靑 part of 龍. Suggest remembering it as **stand** 立 73 and **electricity** 巴 (simplification of 電 180).

Mnemonic: **TRY TO GET DRAGON TO STAND ON ELECTRICITY**

1900

RYŪ, tsubu
GRAIN, PARTICLE
11 strokes

粒子 RYŪSHI   particle
一粒 HITOTSUBU   one grain
粒粒 RYŪRYŪ   assiduously

米 is **rice** 201. 立 is **stand** 73, here acting phonetically to express **grain** but of unclear semantic role. Thus **grain of rice**, now **grain/ particle** in a general sense.

Mnemonic: **RICE STANDS IN GRAINS**

1901

隆

RYŪ
HIGH, PEAK, PROSPER
11 strokes

隆盛 RYŪSEI   prosperity
隆起 RYŪKI   upthrust
興隆 KŌRYŪ   prosperity, rise

Formerly 隆 and earlier 䡏. 㞢/生 is **life/ growing plant** 42, here symbolising **upward growth**. 䧐 is an old form of **descend** 降 863 q.v. (later simplified to 阝⽋ and 阝夂), here acting phonetically to express **height** and also lending its own similar connotations (from its literal meaning of descend from a high hill). Thus **grow upward to a (great) height**, leading to **peak** and **high**, with **prosper** being an associated meaning. (Some scholars feel rather that its original meaning was **high hill**, with the 阝 of 䧐 being taken literally as **hill** 229 q.v.[now 阝].) Suggest taking 阝 as **hill**, and 夂 as **sit crosslegged**.

Mnemonic: **PROSPER IN LIFE AND SIT CROSSLEGGED ON PEAK OF HIGH HILL**

1902

RYŪ
SULFUR
12 strokes

硫酸 RYŪSAN   sulfuric acid
硫黄 IŌ*   sulfur
硫化銀 RYŪKAGIN silver sulfide

石 is **rock/ stone** 45, here meaning **mineral**. 㐬 is **newborn child** 409 q.v., here acting phonetically to express **fragile** and possibly also lending similar connotations of its own. Thus **fragile mineral**, a rather vague reference to **sulfur**. Suggest remembering 㐬 as a 'waterless' version of **flow** 流 409 (氵 being **water** 40).

Mnemonic: **SULFUR IS ROCK THAT FLOWS, WITHOUT WATER**

1903	虜	RYO, toriko **CAPTIVE, CAPTURE** 13 strokes	虜囚 RYOSHŪ	captive
			捕虜 HORYO	prisoner of war
			ふ虜 FURYO	prisoner of war

Formerly 虜 and earlier , showing that the modern form 男 is not **man/ male** 男 54 -- though this may be a useful mnemonic -- but a derivative of a combination of **strength** 力 74 and 毌. The latter is a simplification of pierce 貫 1102, here symbolising **gathering**/ putting together (from its literal meaning of threading items [/money] together). Thus 努 means **gather strength/ muster strength**. 虎/虍 is **tiger** 281, here acting phonetically to express **seize** and probably lending similar connotations of its own. 1903 originally meant to **seize something by mustering one's strength** (i.e. **by force**), and later came to mean **seize/ capture** in a broad sense. It was also used of capturing human beings (possibly partly as a result of the similarity of muster strength 努 and man 男), and by association was also used to refer to the **captive**.

Mnemonic: **MAN CAPTURES TIGER**

1904	慮	RYO **THOUGHT, CONCERN** 15 strokes	遠慮 ENRYO	reserve
			考慮 KŌRYO	consideration
			無慮 MURYO	as many as

思 is **think** 131. 虍 is **tiger** 281, here acting phonetically to express **count** but of unclear semantic role. Thus to **think and count**, i.e. **ponder/ calculate**. This eventually came to mean **serious thought/ concern** in a broad sense, though the original association with numbers is still very occasionally encountered (see muryo above).

Mnemonic: **THINK CONCERNED THOUGHTS ABOUT TIGER**

1905	了	RYŌ **FINISH, COMPLETE,** **UNDERSTAND** 2 strokes	了解 RYŌKAI	understanding
			了承 RYŌSHŌ	understanding
			終了 SHŪRYŌ	finish

Originally written , showing an **armless child** 孑/子 25. This was a representation of a **child unable to use its limbs due to paralysis** (presumably as a result of infantile paralysis/ poliomyelitis). The present meanings are borrowings.

Mnemonic: **UNDERSTAND THAT CHILD NEEDS ARMS TO BE COMPLETE**

1906 RYŌ, suzu*mu*/*shii*   涼味 RYŌMI   coolness
COOL   涼み台 SUZUMIDAI   bench
11 strokes   涼風 SUZUKAZE   cool breeze

氵 is **water** 40. 京 is **capital** 99, here acting phonetically to express **cool** but of unclear semantic role. Thus **cool water**, now **cool** rather of ambient temperature.

Mnemonic: **WATER IN CAPITAL IS COOL**

1907 RYŌ   猟師 RYŌSHI   hunter
HUNTING   猟銃 RYŌJŪ   hunting gun
11 strokes   渉猟 SHŌRYŌ

extensive reading

Formerly 獵 and earlier 獥, 犾/犭 is **dog** 17. 巤/鼠 is a CO character of somewhat unclear etymology meaning **mane/ bristles** (conveyed in Japanese by an NGU character 鬣, which adds hair 長彡 1706). 甾 appears similar to brain and hair 甾 954, but lacks the upper stroke ノ of brain 囟 and is possibly here body and hair. 𡰪 shows legs/ claws, and ㇈ presumably a tail. Thus 鼠 appears to have originally depicted a **hairy animal**. Here it acts phonetically to express **leap**, and almost certainly lends a meaning of **animal**. 1907 originally referred to a **hunting dog leaping on its prey**, and later came to symbolise **hunting** in general. Suggest taking 巤 as **claws** ⸲⸲ and **use** 用 (variant 用 215).

Mnemonic: **DOG PUTS CLAWS TO USE IN HUNTING**

1908 RYŌ, misasagi   陵墓 RYŌBO   imperial tomb
IMPERIAL TOMB, MOUND   丘陵 KYŪRYŌ   hill, hillock
11 strokes   御陵 GORYŌ   imperial tomb

Somewhat obscure. 阝 is **hill/ mound** 229. 夌 (once written 夌) is an unclear element but is known to have once meant **high hill**. ㄆ/ 夂 is **upturned foot** 夂 438 q.v., which could mean descend from above and thus imply height (e.g. 863). 㐱 appears to combine high 兀 509 with growing plant 屮/生 9/42, which could also mean upward growth and thus height (see 隆 1901, with which 1908 seems to share considerable semantic and etymological common ground). In the case of 1908 夌 lends a meaning of **high hill** and is also believed to lend its sound to express **big**. Thus **(big?) high hill/ mound**, later used in particular to refer to an **imperial burial mound**. Suggest taking 夌 as **ground** 土 60 and **out of** ハ 66.

Mnemonic: **UPTURNED FOOT STICKS OUT OF GROUND ON MOUND OF IMPERIAL TOMB**

1909 僚 RYŌ
COLLEAGUE, OFFICIAL
14 strokes

同僚 DŌRYŌ　　colleague
僚友 RYŌYŪ　　colleague
官僚 KANRYŌ　　bureaucrat

亻 is **person** 39. 尞 is a CO character meaning **fuel used in sacrifices**. Its etymology is not fully clear, but an early form 尞 (later 尞) clearly shows **fire** 火 8 and **tree/wood** 木／朩 69. may possibly indicate sap/ resin (see 1334), and ö may possibly indicate either puffs of smoke or combustible material (see 120). In the case of 1909 its semantic role is unclear, but it is known to act phonetically to express **work**. Thus **working person**, which later came to refer in particular to an **official** as well as to a **workmate/ colleague**. Suggest taking 尞 as **big** 大 53, **away** 丶 66, **day** 日 62, and **little** 小 36.

Mnemonic: **PERSON AWAY ON BOTH BIG DAYS AND LITTLE DAYS IS OFFICIALLY A COLLEAGUE**

1910 寮 RYŌ
HOSTEL, DORMITORY
15 strokes

寮生 RYŌSEI boarding student
寮歌 RYŌKA dormitory song
寮長 RYŌCHŌ head of hostel

宀 is **building/ house** 28. 尞 is **fuel used in sacrifices** 1909 q.v., here acting phonetically to express **window** and possibly also lending connotations of a (smoking) **fire**. 1910 originally referred to a **window (cum smoke vent?) in a house**. Its meaning later changed rather to **house with a window**, and then to **small building**. In Chinese it now means hut, but in Japanese has come to be applied to a larger building, specifically a **dormitory/ hostel**. Suggest remembering 寮 by association with **colleague** 僚 1909, without the **person** 亻 39 element (i.e. 'impersonal').

Mnemonic: **COLLEAGUE STAYS IN IMPERSONAL HOSTEL BUILDING**

1911 療 RYŌ
CURE, HEAL
17 strokes

療法 RYŌHŌ　　remedy
療養 RYŌYŌ　　recuperation
医療班 IRYŌHAN　medical team

疒 is **sickness** 381. 尞 is **fuel used in sacrifices** 1909, here acting phonetically to express **make good** and possibly also lending connotations of supplication to the gods. Thus **make good an illness** (while praying to the gods?), i.e. **cure/ heal**. Suggest taking 尞 as an 'impersonal' variant of **colleague** 僚 1909 (i.e. without **person** 亻 39).

Mnemonic: **COLLEAGUE'S SICKNESS HEALED BY IMPERSONAL CURE**

1912 RYŌ, RŌ, kate

PROVISIONS, FOOD

18 strokes

食糧 SHOKURYŌ provisions
兵糧 HYŌRŌ army provisions
糧道 RYŌDŌ supplies

米 is rice 201, here symbolising food in general. 量 is quantity 600 q.v., here acting phonetically to express road and also lending its original meaning of sack full of something. Thus sacks full of food for the road, namely provisions for a journey. Later provisions in a broader sense.

Mnemonic: QUANTITY OF RICE MAKES UP PROVISIONS

1913 RIN

RIN, TINY AMOUNT

9 strokes

厘毛 RINMŌ a trifle
二厘 NIRIN two rin
一分一厘 ICHIBUICHIRIN tiny bit

Formerly written 釐. 𠩺 is a CO character meaning pound wheat (striking hand 攵 101, wheat 来 [variant 来 217] and building 厂 [variant 广 114]). 里 is village 219, here acting phonetically to express separate but of unclear semantic role. Thus to pound wheat and separate (wheat from chaff). This led on the one hand to sort/ arrange (still one of 1913's meanings in Chinese) and on the other to small bit(s). By association with small bit, 1913 is used both in Chinese and Japanese to refer to a small coin (one thousandth of a yen in Japanese), and can also be used of a small measurement (0.3 mm. in Japanese). Suggest taking 厂 as cliff 45.

Mnemonic: TINY VILLAGE BELOW CLIFF VALUED AT A MERE RIN

1914 RIN

PRINCIPLES, ETHICS

10 strokes

倫理 RINRI ethics
人倫 JINRIN morality
絶倫 ZETSURIN no peerless

亻 is person 39. 侖 is align neatly 601 q.v., here acting phonetically to express put in proper order and also lending similar connotations of its own. Thus the proper order which a person should observe, a reference to correct principles of behavior/ morality. Ethics is an associated meaning.

Mnemonic: PERSON ALIGNED ACCORDING TO ETHICAL PRINCIPLES

1915

RIN, tonari
NEIGHBOR, ADJOIN
16 strokes

隣室 RINSHITSU   next room
隣接 RINSETSU   adjacency
隣り合う TONARIAU *   adjoin

Of confused evolution. Correctly written 鄰, i.e. with **village** 阝 355 rather than **hill** 阝 229. Moreover, old forms such as 粦 show that **rice** 米 210 is a miscopying of **flame** 炎 1024 (double fire 火 8). Both 粦 and 粦 exist as interchangeable CO characters meaning **flitting light/ will-o'-the-wisp** (the correct 粦 comprising flame/ light 炎 and opposed feet 舛 1211, here believed to lend a meaning of stop and start [normally associated with the related concept of upturned feet -- see 438], and thus meaning light that stops and starts). In the case of 1915 粦 / 粦 acts phonetically to express **row/ line**, and may possibly also lend connotations of **flickering lights**. 1915 originally referred to a **row (of houses along a road) forming a village** (their flickering lights indicating habitation?), a row of five houses or more being the legal definition of a village in ancient China. This gave rise to the present meanings of **neighbor** and **adjoin**. Suggest taking 夕 as **night** 44 and 丯 as a variant of **well** 井 1470.

Mnemonic: **NEIGHBORS WASH RICE NIGHTLY AT WELL ADJOINING HILL**

1916

RUI, namida
TEAR
10 strokes

涙管 RUIKAN   tear duct
涙雨 NAMIDAAME   light rain
空涙 SORANAMIDA
    crocodile tears

Formerly also written 淚. 氵 is **water** 40. 戾/戻 is **return** 1920, here acting phonetically to express **drop** but of unclear semantic role. **Drop of water** is a rather vague reference to a **tear**. Tear is sometimes conveyed by an informal character 泪, using water 氵 and eye 目 72, which is seemingly simpler and more meaningful.

Mnemonic: **WATER RETURNS AS TEARS**

1917 累

RUI
ACCUMULATE, INVOLVE
11 strokes

累計 RUIKEI   sum total
累積 RUISEKI   accumulation
係累 KEIRUI   dependents

Formerly 纍. 糸 is **thread** 27. 畾 is three fields 1419 q.v. (**field** 田 59), here acting phonetically to express **bind** and probably also lending connotations of quantity/ repetition. Thus to **bind with thread** (voluminously?), leading to **bind** in a broad sense (still a meaning in Chinese). Bind led to **bring together** and hence the figurative **involve**. **Accumulate** is also felt to derive from the idea of bringing together, and may at the same time have been suggested by the accumulation of fields in 畾.

Mnemonic: **THREADS ACCUMULATE IN FIELD**

1918 　RUI　　　　　　　　　　　土塁 DORUI　　earthwork
　　　　　　　　　　FORT, BASEBALL BASE　　敵塁 TEKIRUI　enemy fort
　　　　　　　　　　12 strokes　　　　　　　　塁審 RUISHIN　base umpire

Formerly 壘. 土 is **earth** 60. 畾 is three fields 1419 q.v. (**field** 田 59), here acting phonetically to express **build up** and probably also lending its own connotations of accumulation. Thus **built up earth**, a reference to an **embankment** and by association **fort/base**. Also used nowadays of a base in baseball. Suggest taking 丷 as a symbol of **four**.

Mnemonic: **FOUR EARTHEN BASES IN FIELD**

1919 　REI, hage*mu/masu*　　　　精励 SEIREI　　　diligence
　　　　　　　　　　ENCOURAGE, STRIVE　　　奨励金 SHŌREIKIN　bounty
　　　　　　　　　　7 strokes　　　　　　　　励み合う HAGEMIAU　vie

Formerly 勵 and earlier 萬力. 力 is **strength/ effort** 74. 萬 is **scorpion** 392 q.v., here acting phonetically to express **strive** but of unclear semantic role (though it may possibly suggest prick/ sting/ goad). Thus **strive with effort. Encourage** is the causative equivalent. The later addition of **cliff** 厂 45 is believed to result from confusion with a CO character 厲, meaning whetstone (厂 being an abbreviation of stone 石 45, with scorpion 萬 acting phonetically to express grind and probably also lending connotations of sharp). The modern form uses the substitute for 萬, namely **ten thousand** 万 (see 392).

Mnemonic:**STRONGLY ENCOURAGE TO CLIMB TEN THOUSAND CLIFFS**

1920 　戻　 REI, modo*ru/su*　　　　戻し税 MODOSHIZEI　tax refund
　　　　　　　　　　RETURN, BRING BACK,　返戻 HENREI　　　return
　　　　　　　　　　REBEL, BEND, VOMIT 戻しそう MODOSHISŌ　feel sick
　　　　　　　　　　7 strokes

Obscure. Formerly 戾, showing **door** 戸/戸 108 and **dog** 犬 17. 1920 is believed by some authoritative Japanese scholars to have originally referred to a **dog crouching to pass under a door**. Crouching/ bending the back led to **bend** in a broader sense (now a minor meaning in Japanese). The associated idea of **crouching then returning to a normal stance** is believed to have come by further association to mean **return** in a broad sense, including return to a place. **Give back/ bring back** (including in the sense of **vomit**) is the transitive version. **Rebel** and **be perverse** (minor meanings in Japanese, but major meanings in Chinese) are seen as associated meanings with bend, from the idea of not being straight/ proper. The dog under a door theory does not seem convincing, with many of the interpretations appearing forced, and it seems equally likely that the core meaning of return stems simply from a **dog returning to its home and appearing at the door**. However, in such case it is not clear how the meaning of bend (and thus its derivatives) was acquired. Suggest taking 大 as **big** 53.

Mnemonic: **RETURN TO BIG DOOR TO VOMIT**

1921	鈴	REI, RIN, suzu (SMALL) BELL, CHIME 13 strokes	電鈴 DENREI	electric bell
			風鈴 FŪRIN	wind chime
			鈴生り SUZUNARI*	cluster

Also written 鈴. 金 is **metal** 14, here meaning **metal item**. 令/令 is **order** 603, here acting phonetically to express **tongue** but of unclear semantic role. Thus **metal item with a tongue**, a reference to a **bell**.

Mnemonic: **ORDER METAL BELL TO CHIME**

1922	零	REI, kobo*reru* ZERO, TINY, FALL 13 strokes	零細 REISAI na	small
			零下 REIKA	below zero
			零落 REIRAKU	downfall

Also written 零, and earlier 霝. 雨/雨 is **rain** 3, while ᵛᵛᵛ indicates **drops**. Thus **raindrops**. Note that 霝 still exists as a CO character with this meaning. **Order** 令/令 603 was later used as an alternative to ᵛᵛᵛ, lending its sound to express **fall** but of unclear semantic role. Thus **falling rain**, now **fall** in a broader sense (though it can still mean specifically falling rain in Chinese). Originally 零 could, like 霝, also mean raindrops, and this came to mean **drop** in general and by association **something tiny**. **Zero** is a further association (in Japanese only), from the idea of something being so tiny as to be to all intents and purposes non-existent.

Mnemonic: **ORDER RAINFALL TO BE ZERO**

1923	霊	REI, RYŌ, tama SPIRIT, SOUL 15 strokes	幽霊 YŪREI	ghost
			悪霊 AKURYŌ	evil spirit
			霊屋 TAMAYA	mausoleum

Formerly 靈. 霝 is **raindrops** 1922, here with an extended meaning of **falling/ descending from heaven**. 巫 is an NGU character meaning **sorceress/ shamaness/ temple maiden** (etymology unclear, but an old form 巫 suggests **people** {勹/从 39 at work 工 113). 1923 originally referred to a **shamaness in a state of possession**, i.e. with the **gods/ spirits having descended upon her from heaven**. By association it came to refer to the **spirits** themselves. (Note that gods and spirits/ souls of the dead conceptually overlap as a result of ancestor worship.) Suggest taking 雨 as **rain** 3 and 亚 as a variant of **line (up)** 並 1775.

Mnemonic: **SPIRITS LINE UP IN RAIN -- HARDY SOULS**

1924 隸 REI
SLAVE, PRISONER
16 strokes

奴隷制 DOREISEI — slavery
隷従 REIJŪ — slavery
隷属 REIZOKU — subordination

Formerly also 隸. 隶 is **seize by the tail** 1547, here meaning simply **seize/ obtain.**
柰/柰 is the rather awkward supplication to the gods/ earnest wish element seen in 1108
q.v., here acting phonetically to express **pledge** but of unclear semantic role. 1924 originally meant **obtain something pledged** (i.e. pawned). It came to refer in particular to
obtaining a pledged slave, partly because 柰/柰 could also phonetically express bind
and by association bound person/ slave, and eventually 1924 came to refer to the **slave**
himself/ herself. **Prisoner** is an associated meaning with slave/ bound person. Suggest
taking 柰 as **samurai** 士 494 and **show** 示 695.

Mnemonic: SAMURAI SEIZED AND SHOWN AS SLAVE

1925 齢 REI
AGE
17 strokes

年齢 NENREI — age, years
妙齢 MYŌREI — youth
高齢 KŌREI — great age

Formerly 齡. 歯/齒 is **teeth** 290. 令/令 is **order** 603, here acting phonetically to
express **count** but of unclear semantic role. 1925 originally meant to **count teeth and
thereby assess age** (believed to have been used of humans rather than animals), and later came to mean **age.**

Mnemonic: ORDER TEETH-COUNT TO ASSESS AGE

1926 REI, uruwa*shii*
BEAUTIFUL
19 strokes

麗人 REIJIN — a belle, beauty
美麗 BIREI — beauty
秀麗 SHŪREI na — beautiful

鹿 is **deer** 1204. 丽 is a now defunct character indicating **plurality** (from 丽, believed
to indicate two adzes), and also acts here phonetically to express **group.** Thus **group/
herd of deer. Beautiful** is technically a borrowed meaning, though it should be noted
that the deer was itself a symbol of grace and beauty, and thus herd of deer could be reinterpreted symbolically as **much beauty.** Suggest taking 丽 as **hoofprints.**

Mnemonic: HOOFPRINTS LEFT BY BEAUTIFUL DEER

| 1927 | | REKI, koyomi CALENDAR, ALMANAC 14 strokes | 暦年 REKINEN calendar year
西暦 SEIREKI Anno Domini
花暦 HANAGOYOMI floral calendar |

Formerly 曆. 日 is **sun/ day** 62, here indicating **passage of time**. 厤/厤 is a simplification of **history/ regular path** 歷/歴 606 q.v. Thus **(that which shows) regular path of time**, a reference to a **calendar** or **almanac**. Suggest remembering 厤 as **history** 歴 minus its **foot/ stop** element 止 129.

Mnemonic: **CALENDAR RECORDS NON-STOP HISTORY OF DAYS**

| 1928 | | RETSU, otoru BE INFERIOR 6 strokes | 卑劣 HIRETSU baseness
劣情 RETSUJŌ lust
劣等 RETTŌ inferiority |

Strength 力 74 and **few/ little** 少 143. **Little strength** indicated **inferiority**.

Mnemonic: **THOSE WITH LITTLE STRENGTH ARE INFERIOR**

| 1929 | | RETSU FIERCE, INTENSE 10 strokes | 烈火 REKKA raging fire
烈女 RETSUJO heroine
烈風 REPPŪ gale |

灬 is **fire** 8. 列 is **row/ line** 414, here acting phonetically to express **destroy** and possibly also lending a suggestion of **spreading**. Thus **destructive fire** (that spreads?), symbolising something **fierce/ intense**.

Mnemonic: **ROW OF FIERCE FIRES**

| 1930 | 裂 | RETSU, saku/keru SPLIT, RIP, REND 12 strokes | 破裂 HARETSU bursting
分裂 BUNRETSU splitting
裂け目 SAKEME rip, crack |

衣 is **clothes** 420. 列 is **row/ line** 414 q.v., here with its literal meaning of **cut up in sequence**. 1930 originally referred to the **careful cutting of cloth in order to make clothes**, but later came to mean **cut in a destructive sense** (i.e. **rip/ rend**), possibly partly because its sound could also express **destroy**.

Mnemonic: **ROW OF RIPPED CLOTHES**

1931		REN, koi, koi*shii* LOVE, BELOVED 10 strokes	恋愛 RENAI	love
			失恋 SHITSUREN	lost love
			恋人 KOIBITO	lover

Formerly 戀 . 心 is **heart/ feelings** 147, while 緣 is **tied together** 581. **Hearts tied together** is a reference to **love**. Some scholars believe that 緣 also acts phonetically to express **attract**. Suggest taking 亦 as a 'sort of' variant of **red** 赤 46.

Mnemonic: LOVE SYMBOLISED BY A SORT OF RED HEART

1932		REN HONEST, CHEAP, ANGLE 13 strokes	廉直 RENCHOKU	integrity
			廉価 RENKA	cheap price
			破廉恥 HARENCHI	impudence

Formerly 廉 . 广 is **building** 114. 兼/兼 is **combine** 850, here acting phonetically to express **steep/ sheer** but of unclear semantic role. 1932 originally referred to an **impressive building with towering steep walls**, such as a **hall** or **temple**, but this meaning has now disappeared. It came to acquire the lesser meaning of **angle/ angular** as a result of being used instead of a now defunct character 磏 , which shows **stone/ rock** 石 45 and **combine** 兼 and presumably originally meant **assemblage of rocks** or similar (with **angular** being an associated meaning). **Honest** and **cheap** are also borrowed meanings.

Mnemonic: CHEAP BUILDING COMBINES ANGLES

1933		REN, ne*ru* REFINE, TRAIN, DRILL 16 strokes	錬金術 RENKINJUTSU	alchemy
			錬成 RENSEI	training
			錬り金 NERIGANE	
				tempered steel

Formerly 鍊 . 金 is **metal** 14. 柬 is **select/ remove from bundle** 608 q.v., here acting phonetically to express **heat** and probably also lending an idea of **selecting the best/ removing impurities**. Thus to **heat metal (to remove impurities?)**, a reference to **refining** it. Now also used by association of **training/ drilling** people. Suggest taking 柬 as **east** 184.

Mnemonic: GO EAST FOR TRAINING IN METAL REFINING

1934

炉

RO
FURNACE
8 strokes

炉辺 ROHEN/ ROBE　fireside
暖炉 DANRO　fireplace, stove
原子炉 GENSHIRO
　　　　　　　nuclear reactor

Formerly 爐 . 火 is **fire** 8. 盧 is an NGU character confusingly listed (without illustration) as meaning hut, but in Chinese it has a range of meanings centered on **receptacle/ container**. It comprises **dish/ vessel** 皿 1307, **basket** 田 399 (now usually 由 -- see also 1757), and **tiger** 虍 281. The role of tiger 虍 is not clear, but vessel 皿 and basket 田 clearly indicate **containers**. Thus **fire container**, i.e. **hearth** and later **furnace**. The modern form uses **door** 戸 108 as an essentially graphic simplification (despite wide criticism as lacking balance), though it also has some semantic relevance.

Mnemonic: **FURNACE HAS FIRE DOOR**

1935

RO, RŌ, tsuyu
DEW, REVEAL,
SMALL, RUSSIA
21 strokes

露出 ROSHUTSU　exposure
夜露 YOTSUYU　evening dew
露店 ROTEN　　street stall

雨 is **rain** 3, here meaning **rain-like**. 路 is road 415, here acting phonetically to express **round/ globular** and possibly also lending an idea of tread. Thus **round rain-like things** (on which one treads?), a reference to **dew(drops)**. Since a dewdrop was a symbol of something **small** and/or **transient** 1935 is also sometimes used in these senses. It is not fully clear how it also came to mean **reveal/ make open**. This does not seem to be a borrowing, and is believed to stem from the idea of dew appearing openly for all to see. 1935 was later borrowed for its sound to refer to **R**ussia.

Mnemonic: **'RAIN' ON RUSSIAN ROAD REVEALED TO BE DEW**

1936

郎

RŌ
MAN, HUSBAND
9 strokes

新郎 SHINRŌ　bridegroom
郎等 RŌDŌ　　retainers
太郎 TARŌ　　male name

Formerly 郞 . 阝 is **village** 355. 良/艮 is **good** 598. 1936 was originally used as a proper noun to refer to a certain village in ancient China (literally **Good Village**). Its present meanings result from its being used as an expedient simplification of the term 良人. This combines good 良 with person 亻 39 and was used by women to address their **husband**. Hence also **man** in a broader sense, and its frequent use in **male names**.

Mnemonic: **HUSBAND IS MAN FROM GOOD VILLAGE**

| 1937 | | RŌ, nami
WAVE, DRIFT, WASTE
10 strokes | 波浪 HARŌ
浪費 RŌHI
浪人 RŌNIN | waves, surge
waste
ronin, drifter |

氵 is **water/ river** 40. 良 is **good** 598. 1937 was originally used as a proper noun to refer to a **certain river** in ancient China (literally **Good River**), and was later used instead of a complex character meaning **wave**. **Drift** and **waste** are both associated meanings (from the idea of lacking direction).

Mnemonic: **DRIFT ON WAVES ON STRETCH OF GOOD WATER**

| 1938 | | RŌ
CORRIDOR, WALKWAY
12 strokes | 廊下 RŌKA
画廊 GARŌ
回廊 KAIRŌ | corridor
picture gallery
corridor |

Formerly 廊 . 广 is (large) **roof/ building** 114, here meaning **roof**. 郎 /郞 is **man/ husband** 1936, here acting phonetically to express **space** but of unclear semantic role. 1938 originally referred to the **space under the overhang of a roof**, i.e. **veranda/ walkway**, and by association later came to mean **corridor**. Suggest remembering 郎 by association with the name **Tarō** (see 1936).

Mnemonic: **TARŌ IS IN CORRIDOR OF BUILDING**

| 1939 |  | RŌ
TOWER
13 strokes | 鐘楼 SHŌRŌ
望楼 BŌRŌ
楼閣 RŌKAKU | bell tower
watchtower
multi-storied building |

Formerly 樓 . 木 is **wood** 69. 婁/娄 is **tie/ shamaness** 151 q.v., here acting phonetically to express **build up** and possibly also lending connotations of linking/ assembling. Thus **wooden item that is built up**, a reference to a **tower**. Suggest taking 米 as **rice** 201 and 女 as **woman** 35.

Mnemonic: **WOMAN PREPARES RICE IN WOODEN TOWER**

1940 RŌ, mor*u*/rer*u*/ras*u*
LEAK
14 strokes

漏電 RŌDEN   short circuit
漏出 RŌSHUTSU   leakage
雨漏り AMAMORI   leak in roof

Once simply 屚. 尸 is **corpse 236**, here acting as a simplification of **building** 屋 **236**. 雨 is **rain 3**. Thus **rain on building**, a somewhat awkward reference to **rain <u>entering</u> building** and hence **leak**. **Water** 氵 **40** was added later, presumably to draw attention to the rain rather than the building, but it is not clear why a more semantically relevant element such as **hole** 穴 **849** or **enter** 入 **63** (or some phonetic substitute) was not used.

Mnemonic: **RAINWATER LEAKS ONTO CORPSE**

1941 WAI, makana*u*
BRIBE, PROVIDE,
BOARD
13 strokes

収賄 SHŪWAI   taking bribe
贈賄 ZŌWAI   bribery
賄い付き MAKANAITSUKI   with board

貝 is **shell/ money 90**. 有 is **exist/ have 401 q.v.**, here acting phonetically to express **give** and possibly also lending an idea of possession. Thus **to give (someone) money** (i.e. into their possession?), meaning **to provide for someone**. **Board** and **bribe** are associated meanings.

Mnemonic: **HAVE MONEY THANKS TO BRIBE**

1942 惑 WAKU, mado*u*
BE CONFUSED
12 strokes

迷惑 MEIWAKU   trouble
惑星 WAKUSEI   planet
戸惑い TOMADOI   bewilderment

心 is **heart/ feelings 147**. 或 is **a certain 809 q.v.**, here acting phonetically to express **doubt** but of unclear semantic role. Confusingly, 或 normally means **delineated area**, which might be felt to suggest the opposite of doubt/ uncertainty, but since it technically means <u>roughly</u> **delineated area** (from the idea of crude markers -- see also 698) it may possibly focus on the idea of knowing something approximately but not with absolute certainty. Nevertheless, its choice as a phonetic seems very inappropriate. Thus **doubt in the heart/ feelings of doubt**, leading by association to **confusion**. Suggest taking 戈 as **halberd/ lance 493**, and 口 as a variant of **one/ single** 一 **1** and **opening/ entrance** 口 **20**.

Mnemonic: **CONFUSED FEELINGS OVER LANCE AT SINGLE ENTRANCE**

1943 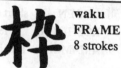 waku
FRAME
8 strokes

枠組 WAKUGUMI framework
枠無し WAKUNASHI frameless
枠内 WAKUNAI within limits

A 'made in Japan' character. 木 is **wood** 69. 卆 is usually the abbreviated form of soldier 卒 537, but is here an abbreviation of rate 率 803 q.v., here with its literal meaning of **devices for twisting threads into rope**. Thus 1943 originally meant **wooden device(s) for twisting threads into rope,** with **frame** being an associated meaning. Suggest taking 九 as **nine** 12 and 十 as **ten** 33.

Mnemonic: **FRAME MADE OF NINETEEN PIECES OF WOOD**

1944 WAN
BAY, GULF
12 strokes

港湾 KŌWAN harbor
湾入 WANNYŪ inlet
東京湾 TŌKYŌWAN Tokyo Bay

Formerly 灣. 氵 is **water** 40. 彎 is an NGU character meaning **bowed/ curved,** comprising **bow** 弓 836 and **tied together** 䜌 581 (i.e. the shape of a strung bow). Thus **water in a bowed shape,** i.e. a **bay/ gulf.** Suggest taking 亦 as a variant of **red** 赤 46, namely **reddish.**

Mnemonic: **REDDISH WATER CHARACTERISES BOW-SHAPED BAY**

1945 WAN, ude
ARM, ABILITY
12 strokes

腕章 WANSHŌ armband
手腕 SHUWAN ability
細腕 HOSOUDE
thin arms, slender means

Formerly also written 捥, i.e. with hand/ **arm** 扌 32 instead of meat/ (of the) **body** 月 365. 宛 is an NGU character now used to mean **addressed to,** but in Chinese it can mean **bending, soft, yield,** and **obliging/ polite** (the latter clearly a figurative association with yielding, and presumably leading by further association to addressed to). It comprises **roof/ house** 宀 28 and 㸳, which is a CO character meaning **turn in one's sleep** (**night** 夕 44 and **slumped/ bent body** 㔾 768). 宛 may have originally been merely an embellished variant of 㸳, meaning turn in one's sleep at home, but it clearly had dominant connotations of **bending the body.** Confusingly, in the case of 1945 宛 acts phonetically to express **straighten,** but also lends its meaning of **bent.** Thus 捥 means to **straighten a bent arm,** while 腕 means **straighten a bent body.** This came to symbolise a **display of strength,** either in pushing or lifting, and hence came to mean both **strong arm** and **ability.** It is now also used of **arm** in a general sense.

Mnemonic: **BODY SLUMPS NIGHTLY AT HOME, BUT ARMS STILL ABLE**

APPENDICES AND INDICES

COMMONLY OCCURRING ELEMENTS
AND THEIR PRINCIPAL MEANINGS

2 strokes

凵	container, vessel	犭	dog, beast
ト	divination	山	mountain, hill, occ. fire
亻	person	子	child, small
一	person	宀	roof, house, building
人	person	巾	cloth, thread
𠆢	person	阝	(on left) hill, mound, terracing
儿	bending person	阝	(on right) village, town
卩	bending person	夂	upturned foot, slow progress,
勹	bending person		stop, fall, come down
己	slumped person	工	work, measure, occ. big, dog
匕	fallen person	土	soil, earth, ground, plant, man
冫	ice, freeze	士	man, warrior
勹	cover, encircle, protect	扌	hand, arm, manual task
冖	cover, roof, building	女	woman, soft, yield
力	strength, effort	小 / 小	small
ナ	hand	忄	heart, feelings
又	hand, take, help	氵	water, river, liquid
十	ten, many, needle, cut, plant	大	big, man, dog, hands, plants
万	twist, flat, emerge, stop	巛	river
八 / 丷	away, out of, split, oppose	尸	corpse, slumped figure,
八 / 儿	away, out of, split, oppose		buttocks, building
厶	nose, self, vapor, abbrev.	己	twist, bend, thread, rise
刀	sword, cut	巳	twist, bend, serpent, embryo
刂	sword, cut	廾	hands, together, raise, offer
匚	container	口	mouth, say, words, opening,
厂	cliff, rock, stone, roof, home,		hole, round
	building, cloth, oppose	弓	bow, bend, curve, pull
几	table, desk, stool	辶	movement, road
		廴	movement
		彳	road, movement
		亼	lid, cover, cap
3 strokes		囗	enclosure
艹	grass, plants		

624

彡幺寸	hairs, delicate, pattern, attractive
	short, small, thread
	hand, measure, careful action
也弋	twisting, uneven
	stake, measure
夕	evening, night, upturned foot
彐 / ヨ	hand

4 strokes

王	jewel, round, precious
日	sun, day, time, bright, speak, full container
火	fire, heat, burn, roast
灬	fire, heat, burn, roast
艹	grass, plants
木	tree, wood, plants
月	meat, body, moon, boat
犬	dog, beast
王	king, ruler, jewel, stand
戈	halberd, lance, weapon, cut
歹	death, injury, cut, bones
手	hand, arm, manual task
少	few, little
水	water, river, liquid
止	foot, stop, move, occ. plant
巴	bending person
辶	movement
欠	gape, open, mouth
牛	cow, bull, horns
心	heart, feeling
爫	hand, claws, reach
戸	door, building,
礻	altar, gods, show
攵	stick in hand, strike, force, causative
殳	strike, use tool
斤	ax, chop, cut

5 strokes

矢	arrow, measure, speed, straight
疒	sickness, illness, affliction
衤	clothing
田	field, container
石	rock, stone
示	gods, altar, show
立	stand
禾	rice plant, rice, grain, soft
且	pile, accumulate
穴	hole, opening
生	life, birth, plant, growth, emerge
聿	writing, recording, arranging
目	eye, see
四	eye, see, net, dish
皿	dish

6 strokes

糸	thread, cord, bind, tie
尨	fluttering flag
衣	clothing
耳	ear, listen
米	rice, grain, food
羽	wings, flight
艮	stop and stare, look back
虍	tiger
虫	insect, snake
竹	bamboo, wood, plant
肉	meat, body
豆	vessel, food
舟	boat, convey
羊 / 䒑	sheep, fine

7 strokes

車	vehicle

625

APPENDIX OF ELEMENTS

舛	opposed feet, firm, guard, all round
貝	shell, money, valuable item
酉	alcohol, ferment, jar
豕	pig, animal
言	word, say, speak
辛	needle, sharp, pierce, slave, prisoner
豸	clawed beast, beast
豆	vessel, food
足	foot, leg, move
臣	stare, guard

8 strokes

雨	rain, weather, atmosphere
金	metal, money, gold
隹	bird, flight
門	door, gate, building
者	person, many, various
食	food, eat

9 strokes

頁	head, mind, face

10 strokes

骨	bone
馬	horse

11 strokes

魚	fish, sea creature
鳥	bird

626

HIRAGANA AND KATAKANA
AND THEIR SOURCE CHARACTERS

A	あ	from	安	A	ア	from	阿
I	い	from	以	I	イ	from	伊
U	う	from	宇	U	ウ	from	宇
E	え	from	衣	E	エ	from	江
O	お	from	於	O	オ	from	於
KA	か	from	加	KA	カ	from	加
KI	き	from	幾	KI	キ	from	幾
KU	く	from	久	KU	ク	from	久
KE	け	from	計	KE	ケ	from	介
KO	こ	from	己	KO	コ	from	己
SA	さ	from	左	SA	サ	from	散
SHI	し	from	之	SHI	シ	from	之
SU	す	from	寸	SU	ス	from	須
SE	せ	from	世	SE	セ	from	世

627

KANA APPENDIX

	hiragana				katakana		
SO	そ	from	曾	SO	ソ	from	曾
TA	た	from	太	TA	タ	from	多
CHI	ち	from	知	CHI	チ	from	千
TSU	つ	from	州	TSU	ツ	from	州
TE	て	from	天	TE	テ	from	天
TO	と	from	止	TO	ト	from	止
NA	な	from	奈	NA	ナ	from	奈
NI	に	from	仁	NI	ニ	from	二
NU	ぬ	from	奴	NU	ヌ	from	奴
NE	ね	from	禰	NE	ネ	from	禰
NO	の	from	乃	NO	ノ	from	乃
HA	は	from	波	HA	ハ	from	八
HI	ひ	from	比	HI	ヒ	from	比
FU	ふ	from	不	FU	フ	from	不
HE	へ	from	部	HE	へ	from	部

628

hiragana			katakana		
HO	ほ from 保		HO	ホ from 保	
MA	ま from 末		MA	マ from 末	
MI	み from 美		MI	ミ from 三	
MU	む from 武		MU	ム from 牟	
ME	め from 女		ME	メ from 女	
MO	も from 毛		MO	モ from 毛	
YA	や from 也		YA	ヤ from 也	
YU	ゆ from 由		YU	ユ from 由	
YO	よ from 与		YO	ヨ from 与	
RA	ら from 良		RA	ラ from 良	
RI	り from 利		RI	リ from 利	
RU	る from 留		RU	ル from 流	
RE	れ from 礼		RE	レ from 礼	
RO	ろ from 呂		RO	ロ from 呂	
WA	わ from 和		WA	ワ from 和	

hiragana			katakana		
(W)O を	from 遠		(W)O ヲ	from 乎	
N ん	from 无		N ン	from 尔	

Other kana sounds (given in hiragana only)

ga	が	gi	ぎ	gu	ぐ	ge	げ	go	ご
za	ざ	ji	じ	zu	ず	ze	ぜ	zo	ぞ
da	だ	ji	ぢ	zu	づ	de	で	do	ど
ba	ば	bi	び	bu	ぶ	be	べ	bo	ぼ
pa	ぱ	pi	ぴ	pu	ぷ	pe	ぺ	po	ぽ
kya	きゃ	kyu	きゅ	kyo	きょ				
sha	しゃ	shu	しゅ	sho	しょ				
cha	ちゃ	chu	ちゅ	cho	ちょ				
nya	にゃ	nyu	にゅ	nyo	にょ				
hya	ひゃ	hyu	ひゅ	hyo	ひょ				
mya	みゃ	myu	みゅ	myo	みょ				
rya	りゃ	ryu	りゅ	ryo	りょ				
gya	ぎゃ	gyu	ぎゅ	gyo	ぎょ				
ja	じゃ	ju	じゅ	jo	じょ				
bya	びゃ	byu	びゅ	byo	びょ				
pya	ぴゃ	pyu	ぴゅ	pyo	ぴょ				

Sounds ending in 'o' lengthened to 'ō' by adding う (rarely お).

Sounds ending in 'u' lengthened to 'ū' by adding う .

Consonants doubled by preceding with っ .

INDEX OF 'NON GENERAL USE' AND 'CHINESE ONLY' CHARACTERS

1 stroke

丿 537

2 strokes

卜 91
厶 134
丂 281
几 832
匕 910

3 strokes

彡 93
幺 111
也 167
弋 177
夂 438
兀 509
巾 778
于 811

4 strokes

乂 10
云 78
尹 266
夬 271
夭 279
瓜 303
勿 387
屮 392
卍 392
从 463
亢 479
戈 493
曰 688
尤 890
句 1022
卯 1173
宂 1601
壬 1610
丙 1744
瓦 1747
厷 1869

5 strokes

弘 100

乍 127
合 158
牙 434
戍 515
戊 515
旡 688
乎 856
旦 929
圣 1061
它 1341
叅 1440
疋 1477
卉 1770
歺 1945

6 strokes

亦 212
艮 263
臼 350
臼 648
耒 673
圭 819
囱 840
肋 843

亥 865
戗 872
束 873
而 887
亘 913
瓜 1229
夸 1233
互 1251
㐬 1253
此 1320
汲 1343
庄 1406
并 1774
仿 1798

7 strokes

佑 2
邮 52
吾 112
甬 176
戋 177
吕 256
抉 271
酉 302

邑	355	阜	229	閩	1650	酉	927
辰	366	其	251	沓	1657	爰	932
流	409	巷	280	盂	1854	臥	994
米	483	虎	281	肱	1869	兔	1010
兑	524	刲	301	宛	1945	曷	1022
肙	664	具	377			里	1027
夋	689	音	384	**9 strokes**		奂	1103
牡	760	苹	388			俎	1134
旱	825	亞	464	頁	93	臤	1179
沙	869	取	487	彦	93	禺	1184
坕	967	昌	508	昜	144	咨	1325
甫	970	夆	597	亲	148	胥	1477
串	1101	姜	731	咸	246	迹	1485
夾	1164	或	809	胡	276	叟	1516
杓	1342	臾	834	冒	386	凿	1517
妝	1406	苟	846	斿	402	耑	1567
沃	1649	岡	864	枼	405	咎	1651
豕	1670	宓	978	洛	408	酋	1656
孚	1752	厓	1069	条	412	契	1673
窂	1799	卦	1083	眇	516	屏	1777
攸	1866	名	1098	柬	608	剌	1889
巫	1923	斧	1176	迣	613		
		困	1177	段	625	**10 strokes**	
8 strokes		昏	1278	复	782		
		隶	1547	扁	785	袁	79
枙	52	朋	1562	敄	795	哥	84
帚	96	炁	1631	眛	797	盇	237
枰	110	沾	1631	俞	799	矩	342

釘	346	髟	1706	奞	966	馭	1158
秤	388	笆	1719	媚	1025	淵	1369
韋	422	逢	1804	崔	1069	閆	1379
專	564	窏	1815	葛	1089	鈔	1390
軑	637	威	1848	頃	1201	隋	1462
菁	675	蚤	1877	鹿	1204	罨	1498
隼	709	羔	1881	桀	1211	韮	1500
莫	788	邕	1882	啃	1250	疏	1509
眛	797	离	1897	崔	1293	棹	1554
堇	842	梦	1913	斬	1311	犀	1574
兹	881			屑	1435	黍	1680
烝	904	**11 strokes**		捧	1793	詈	1709
象	1030			貶	1805	賁	1770
弱	1078	妻	151	曼	1837	敚	1778
崇	1108	彗	157			徧	1783
莧	1110	剪	159	**12 strokes**		彭	1817
躬	1152	徠	217			羕	1820
奚	1199	萍	388	揣	159	蔡	1909
隻	1202	卥	428	喬	259		
窔	1301	絆	444	爲	297	**13 strokes**	
飲	1322	竟	462	堯	509		
逡	1371	執	470	巽	527	鼎	228
眹	1372	寅	621	絜	659	罩	233
朔	1511	萑	648	戠	698	戡	353
蚤	1530	曾	741	筑	751	蜃	366
虖	1618	商	755	卿	841	僉	475
涂	1637	執	894	僅	842	賈	626
畨	1705	匙	910	烹	894	蜀	744

633

栗	922
譽	929
煖	932
裹	1066
睘	1114
熏	1191
嶢	1199
鷹	1204
敦	1210
舜	1372
楷	1375
鉦	1414
蓑	1456
楚	1512
亶	1571
溥	1699
辟	1733
愈	1863
雍	1882
粦	1915

14 strokes

鳳	198
翟	216
僮	363
誩	463
蓺	470

厭	612
替	688
熊	766
箸	937
蔭	1013
鶿	1014
嘔	1034
賏	1036
赫	1080
貂	1152
噓	1156
聶	1225
爾	1329
踆	1371
趚	1486

15 strokes

僭	929
尉	1004
踦	1123
鋏	1165
嘽	1366
餕	1371
晶	1419
蠅	1420
斷	1659
潘	1721

僻	1781
鋪	1786
甌	1907
粦	1915
厲	1919

16 strokes

彊	100
磬	153
橡	407
諧	698
辨	786
樽	927
擔	929
雅	1057
餒	1058
難	1281
鞘	1298
壁	1733
蹁	1782
盧	1934

17 strokes

糠	480
應	622
鴈	648

濡	887
嬰	1036
臅	1039
禦	1158
縚	1199
濠	1272
縶	1332
駿	1371
鍾	1414
騰	1418
襄	1421
鐵	1500
闌	1893
需	1922

18 strokes

輩	445
謳	1034
義	1140
薰	1266
聶	1489
雝	1882

19 strokes

| 櫟 | 218 |
| 顛 | 514 |

絲	581
辮	786
儌	854
麿	1831

20-26 strokes

辮	786
巖	854
瀨	1745
臚	1757
鸛	634
辯	786
鶴	445
彎	1944
鬖	1907
釁	1745

STROKE COUNT INDEX

1 stroke

一 1
乙 1041

2 strokes

九 12
七 30
十 33
人 39
二 61
入 63
八 66
力 74
刀 181
丁 346
又 1835
了 1905

3 strokes

下 7
口 20
三 23
山 24
子 25
女 35
小 36
上 37
夕 44
千 47
川 48
大 53
土 60
工 113
才 126
万 392
士 494
久 647

干 825
丸 830
弓 836
己 855
寸 909
亡 973
及 1148
勺 1342
丈 1415
刃 1446
凡 1827
与 1873

4 strokes

円 4
王 5
火 8
月 16
犬 17
五 19
手 32
水 40
中 55
天 58
日 62
文 68
木 69
六 76
引 77
牛 97
元 106
戸 108
午 110
今 125
止 129
少 143
心 147
切 156
太 164

父 197
分 199
方 204
毛 210
友 214
化 238
公 277
内 364
反 371
予 403
区 465
欠 471
氏 495
不 572
夫 573
支 691
収 703
比 771
仏 784
尺 884
仁 906
片 969
介 1059
刈 1092
凶 1159
斤 1176
幻 1226
互 1236
孔 1241
升 1386
冗 1416
井 1470
双 1513
丹 1563
弔 1588
斗 1633
屯 1669
匹 1736
乏 1805
匂 1858

厄 1859

5 strokes

右 2
左 22
四 26
出 34
正 41
生 42
石 45
田 59
白 65
本 70
目 72
立 73
外 91
玉 102
古 109
広 114
市 130
台 166
冬 182
半 195
母 203
北 205
用 215
去 258
兄 267
号 281
仕 285
写 297
主 299
申 322
世 327
他 334
打 335
代 338
皮 374
氷 378

平 388
由 399
礼 413
以 419
央 429
加 431
功 477
史 496
司 497
失 501
必 568
付 574
辺 580
包 583
末 587
民 590
令 603
圧 612
永 615
刊 636
旧 648
句 655
示 695
犯 768
布 778
弁 786
未 794
可 816
穴 849
冊 874
処 896
庁 938
矢 981
幼 985
凹 1032
且 1091
甘 1093
丘 1149
巨 1153
玄 1227

巧	1242	池	168	好	859	**7 strokes**		完	440
甲	1243	竹	170	至	875	花	9	希	447
込	1275	当	183	存	926	見	18	求	455
札	1304	同	187	宅	928	車	31	芸	470
皿	1307	米	201	仲	934	赤	46	告	481
囚	1353	毎	206	兆	939	足	51	材	485
汁	1361	安	223	弐	950	村	52	初	507
召	1387	曲	261	羊	986	男	54	臣	512
斥	1480	血	270	扱	1000	町	57	折	522
仙	1490	向	278	芋	1011	何	80	低	548
占	1491	死	286	汚	1031	貝	90	努	555
奴	1638	次	292	汗	1094	汽	94	兵	578
凸	1667	式	295	缶	1095	近	103	別	579
尼	1674	守	300	企	1120	形	104	利	596
払	1766	州	304	吉	1142	谷	122	良	598
丙	1773	全	330	朽	1150	作	127	冷	604
矛	1843	肉	365	叫	1160	社	137	労	610
		有	401	仰	1173	図	150	応	622
6 strokes		両	411	刑	1193	声	153	快	631
		列	414	江	1244	走	161	技	644
気	11	衣	420	旨	1312	体	165	均	653
休	13	印	425	芝	1335	弟	177	災	680
糸	27	各	438	朱	1346	売	192	志	692
字	28	共	460	舟	1354	麦	194	似	696
耳	29	成	515	充	1362	来	217	児	697
先	49	争	529	旬	1373	里	219	序	710
早	50	伝	553	巡	1374	医	225	条	716
虫	56	灯	556	如	1383	角	243	状	717
年	64	老	609	匠	1388	究	253	判	769
百	67	因	614	尽	1447	局	262	防	791
名	71	仮	625	迅	1448	君	266	余	800
回	86	件	660	壮	1514	決	271	壱	810
会	87	再	679	吐	1634	言	274	我	817
交	115	在	684	肌	1704	住	310	系	844
光	116	舌	732	伐	1707	助	314	孝	860
考	117	団	749	帆	1711	身	323	困	868
行	118	任	764	妃	1724	対	336	私	876
合	121	宇	811	伏	1763	投	357	否	962
寺	133	羽	812	忙	1806	坂	372	批	963
自	134	灰	818	朴	1819	返	389	忘	974
色	145	危	831	妄	1851	役	397	乱	989
西	152	机	832	吏	1894	位	421	卵	990
多	163	吸	837	劣	1928	囲	422	亜	997
地	167	后	858			改	435	戒	1060

肝	1096	扶	1748	受	303	妻	681	拠	1155
含	1118	芳	1791	所	312	舎	700	享	1162
岐	1121	邦	1792	注	344	述	707	況	1163
忌	1122	坊	1807	定	351	招	712	屈	1188
却	1145	妨	1808	波	367	承	713	茎	1194
狂	1161	没	1823	板	373	制	722	肩	1212
吟	1182	妙	1841	表	379	性	723	弦	1228
迎	1207	抑	1884	服	385	版	770	拘	1249
呉	1237	励	1919	物	387	肥	772	肯	1250
坑	1245	戻	1920	放	391	非	773	昆	1276
抗	1246			味	393	武	781	刺	1314
攻	1247	**8 strokes**		命	394	延	814	枝	1315
更	1248			油	400	沿	815	祉	1316
克	1272	雨	3	和	416	拡	820	肢	1317
佐	1283	学	10	委	423	泣	838	侍	1326
伺	1313	金	14	英	426	供	839	邪	1340
寿	1351	空	15	芽	434	径	845	叔	1367
秀	1355	青	43	官	441	呼	856	尚	1392
床	1389	林	75	季	448	刻	865	昇	1393
抄	1390	画	85	協	461	若	886	松	1394
肖	1391	京	99	固	476	宗	889	沼	1395
伸	1431	国	123	刷	487	垂	907	炊	1453
辛	1432	知	169	参	490	担	929	枢	1464
吹	1452	長	173	姉	498	宙	935	姓	1471
杉	1467	店	178	周	504	忠	936	征	1472
即	1534	東	184	卒	537	届	948	斉	1473
束	1535	歩	202	治	544	乳	951	昔	1481
妥	1538	妹	207	底	549	拝	956	析	1482
択	1551	明	208	的	551	宝	971	拙	1487
沢	1552	門	211	典	552	枚	976	阻	1505
但	1559	夜	212	毒	559	依	1001	卓	1553
沖	1583	育	227	念	561	炎	1024	拓	1554
沈	1601	泳	232	府	575	押	1033	抽	1584
廷	1610	岸	248	法	584	欧	1034	坪	1609
呈	1611	岩	249	牧	586	殴	1035	抵	1612
豆	1640	苦	264	例	605	佳	1044	邸	1613
尿	1675	具	265	易	618	怪	1061	泥	1623
妊	1676	幸	279	往	623	拐	1062	迭	1627
忍	1677	使	287	価	626	劾	1068	到	1641
把	1682	始	288	果	627	岳	1082	突	1668
伯	1694	事	293	河	628	奇	1123	杯	1685
抜	1708	実	296	居	649	祈	1124	拍	1695
伴	1712	者	298	券	661	宜	1134	泊	1696
尾	1734	取	301	効	671	拒	1154	迫	1697

彼	1725	風	198	飛	566	姻	1012	荘	1515
披	1726	屋	236	変	581	疫	1019	促	1536
泌	1737	界	240	便	582	卸	1042	耐	1542
苗	1740	活	244	約	591	架	1045	怠	1543
怖	1749	客	252	勇	592	悔	1063	胎	1544
附	1750	急	254	要	593	皆	1064	胆	1564
侮	1760	級	255	逆	646	垣	1073	衷	1585
沸	1767	係	268	限	665	括	1085	挑	1589
併	1774	研	272	故	668	冠	1097	勅	1600
並	1775	県	273	厚	672	軌	1125	珍	1602
奉	1793	指	289	査	678	虐	1147	亭	1614
抱	1794	持	294	祝	706	糾	1151	貞	1615
泡	1795	拾	305	政	724	峡	1164	帝	1616
房	1809	重	311	祖	736	挟	1165	訂	1617
肪	1810	昭	315	則	742	狭	1166	怒	1639
奔	1825	乗	320	退	746	契	1195	逃	1642
抹	1836	神	324	独	763	孤	1229	洞	1661
岬	1840	送	331	保	787	弧	1230	峠	1663
免	1849	待	337	迷	797	枯	1231	卑	1727
茂	1850	炭	341	映	813	恆	1251	赴	1751
盲	1852	柱	345	革	821	洪	1252	封	1762
炉	1934	直	349	巻	826	荒	1253	柄	1776
枠	1943	追	350	看	827	郊	1254	胞	1796
		度	356	皇	861	香	1255	某	1811
		畑	369	紅	862	侯	1256	冒	1812
9 strokes		発	370	砂	869	拷	1269	盆	1828
		美	376	姿	877	恨	1277	幽	1865
音	6	秒	380	城	903	砕	1287	柳	1898
科	81	品	382	是	910	削	1298	厘	1913
海	88	負	383	宣	913	咲	1303	郎	1936
計	105	面	395	専	914	施	1318		
後	111	洋	404	泉	915	狩	1347	10 strokes	
思	131	胃	424	洗	916	臭	1356		
室	136	栄	427	染	917	柔	1363	校	21
首	139	紀	449	奏	918	俊	1371	夏	82
秋	140	軍	466	俗	925	盾	1375	家	83
春	141	型	468	段	931	叙	1384	記	95
食	146	建	473	派	955	净	1417	帰	96
星	154	昨	486	背	957	侵	1433	原	107
前	159	信	513	肺	958	津	1434	高	119
草	162	省	516	律	993	甚	1449	紙	132
茶	171	浅	525	哀	998	帥	1454	時	135
昼	172	相	530	威	1002	牲	1474	弱	138
点	179	単	542	為	1003	窃	1488	書	142
南	190								

通	176	格	633	華	1046	逝	1475	剖	1813
馬	191	訓	656	蚊	1056	隻	1483	紡	1814
員	228	個	669	核	1074	扇	1492	埋	1833
院	229	耕	673	陥	1098	栓	1493	眠	1842
荷	239	財	685	既	1126	租	1506	娘	1846
起	250	蚕	688	飢	1127	捜	1516	耗	1853
宮	256	師	693	鬼	1128	挿	1517	紋	1857
庫	275	修	704	恐	1167	桑	1518	竜	1899
根	282	除	711	恭	1168	泰	1545	倫	1914
酒	302	称	714	脅	1169	託	1555	涙	1916
消	316	素	737	恵	1196	恥	1572	烈	1929
息	332	造	739	倹	1213	致	1573	恋	1931
庭	352	特	760	剣	1214	畜	1577	浪	1937
島	358	能	766	軒	1215	逐	1578		
配	368	破	767	娯	1238	秩	1580	11 strokes	
病	381	俵	775	悟	1239	朕	1603		
勉	390	容	802	貢	1257	逓	1618	魚	98
流	409	留	805	剛	1270	哲	1628	強	100
旅	410	株	824	唆	1284	途	1635	教	101
案	418	胸	840	宰	1288	倒	1643	黄	120
害	437	兼	850	栽	1289	凍	1644	黒	124
挙	458	降	863	剤	1296	唐	1645	雪	157
郡	467	骨	867	索	1299	桃	1646	船	158
候	478	座	870	桟	1308	透	1647	組	160
航	479	射	882	脂	1319	胴	1662	鳥	174
差	482	従	891	疾	1331	匿	1664	野	213
殺	488	純	895	酌	1343	悩	1680	理	220
残	493	将	899	殊	1348	梅	1689	悪	222
借	502	笑	900	珠	1349	畔	1713	球	257
真	514	針	905	准	1376	般	1714	祭	283
席	520	値	933	殉	1377	疲	1728	細	284
倉	531	展	944	徐	1385	被	1729	終	306
速	534	討	945	宵	1396	姫	1738	習	307
孫	538	党	946	症	1397	浜	1743	週	308
帯	539	納	953	祥	1398	敏	1746	商	317
徒	554	俳	959	辱	1430	瓶	1747	章	318
倍	563	班	960	唇	1435	浮	1752	深	325
粉	577	秘	964	娠	1436	紛	1768	進	326
脈	589	陛	967	振	1437	捕	1784	族	333
浴	595	朗	995	浸	1438	浦	1785	第	339
料	599	悦	1020	陣	1450	俸	1797	帳	347
連	607	宴	1025	粋	1455	倣	1798	転	354
益	619	桜	1036	衰	1456	峰	1799	都	355
恩	624	翁	1037	畝	1468	砲	1800	動	362

部	384	務	795	啓	1197	陳	1604	道	188
問	396	率	803	揭	1198	偵	1619	買	193
貨	432	略	804	渓	1199	笛	1624	番	196
械	436	異	807	蛍	1200	添	1631	飲	230
救	456	域	809	控	1258	悼	1648	運	231
健	474	郷	841	婚	1278	盗	1649	温	237
康	480	済	871	紺	1279	陶	1650	開	241
菜	483	視	878	彩	1290	豚	1670	階	242
産	491	捨	883	斎	1291	軟	1673	寒	245
宿	505	釈	885	崎	1297	粘	1679	期	251
唱	508	推	908	惨	1309	婆	1684	軽	269
清	517	窓	919	執	1332	排	1686	湖	276
側	535	探	930	赦	1336	培	1690	港	280
停	550	著	937	斜	1337	陪	1691	歯	290
堂	557	頂	940	蛇	1341	舶	1698	集	309
敗	562	脳	954	寂	1345	販	1715	暑	313
票	570	閉	968	渋	1364	描	1741	勝	319
副	576	訪	972	淑	1368	猫	1742	植	321
望	585	密	978	粛	1369	符	1753	短	342
陸	597	訳	982	庶	1381	偏	1782	着	343
移	613	郵	983	渉	1399	崩	1801	湯	359
液	620	欲	987	紹	1400	堀	1824	登	360
眼	640	翌	988	訟	1401	麻	1829	等	361
基	641	尉	1004	剰	1418	猛	1854	童	363
寄	642	逸	1010	紳	1439	唯	1864	悲	375
規	643	陰	1013	酔	1457	悠	1866	遊	402
許	650	菓	1047	崇	1465	庸	1875	葉	405
経	658	涯	1069	据	1466	粒	1900	陽	406
険	662	殻	1075	盛	1476	隆	1901	落	408
現	666	郭	1076	惜	1484	涼	1906	覚	439
混	677	掛	1083	旋	1494	猟	1907	喜	450
採	682	喝	1086	措	1507	陵	1908	給	457
授	702	渇	1087	粗	1508	累	1917	極	464
術	708	乾	1099	掃	1519			景	469
常	718	勘	1100	曹	1520	12 strokes		結	472
情	719	患	1101	巣	1521			最	484
責	728	貫	1102	袋	1546	森	38	散	492
接	730	偽	1135	逮	1547	雲	78	順	506
設	731	菊	1141	脱	1560	絵	89	焼	509
断	750	脚	1146	淡	1565	間	92	然	528
張	752	虚	1156	窒	1581	場	144	象	533
得	761	菌	1177	彫	1590	晴	155	隊	540
貧	777	偶	1185	眺	1591	朝	175	達	541
婦	779	掘	1189	釣	1592	答	185	貯	546

博 564	補 970	焦 1404	帽 1816	想 532
飯 565	棒 975	硝 1405	愉 1861	続 536
費 567	握 999	粧 1406	猶 1867	置 545
筆 569	偉 1005	詔 1407	裕 1868	腸 547
満 588	詠 1016	畳 1419	雄 1869	働 558
量 600	越 1021	殖 1426	揚 1876	解 632
営 616	援 1026	診 1440	揺 1877	幹 637
過 629	奥 1038	尋 1451	絡 1890	義 645
賀 630	渦 1048	遂 1458	痢 1895	禁 654
検 663	喚 1103	随 1462	硫 1902	群 657
減 667	堪 1104	婿 1477	塁 1918	絹 664
衆 705	換 1105	疎 1509	裂 1930	鉱 674
証 715	敢 1106	訴 1510	廊 1938	罪 686
税 727	棺 1107	喪 1522	惑 1942	資 694
絶 733	款 1108	葬 1523	湾 1944	準 709
善 735	閑 1109	装 1524	腕 1945	損 745
測 743	幾 1129	堕 1539		墓 788
属 744	棋 1130	惰 1540	**13 strokes**	豊 790
貸 747	欺 1136	替 1548		預 801
提 753	喫 1143	棚 1562	遠 79	勧 828
程 754	距 1157	弾 1570	新 148	源 853
統 757	御 1158	遅 1574	数 151	署 897
備 774	暁 1174	脹 1593	電 180	傷 901
評 776	琴 1178	超 1594	楽 218	蒸 904
富 780	遇 1186	塚 1607	話 221	聖 911
復 782	隅 1187	堤 1620	暗 224	誠 912
報 789	圏 1216	渡 1636	意 226	暖 932
貿 792	堅 1217	塔 1651	園 234	賃 942
無 796	雇 1232	搭 1652	感 246	腹 965
街 819	慌 1259	棟 1653	業 260	幕 977
割 823	硬 1260	痘 1654	詩 291	盟 979
揮 833	絞 1261	筒 1655	鉄 353	裏 992
貴 834	項 1262	鈍 1671	農 366	違 1006
勤 842	詐 1285	廃 1687	福 386	煙 1027
筋 843	酢 1300	媒 1692	路 415	猿 1028
敬 846	傘 1310	蛮 1722	愛 417	鉛 1029
裁 872	紫 1320	扉 1730	塩 428	虞 1040
策 873	滋 1327	普 1754	漢 442	嫁 1049
詞 879	軸 1330	幅 1764	試 499	暇 1050
就 890	湿 1333	雰 1769	辞 500	禍 1051
創 920	煮 1338	塀 1777	照 510	靴 1052
尊 927	循 1378	遍 1783	勢 518	雅 1057
痛 943	掌 1402	募 1787	節 523	塊 1065
晩 961	晶 1403	傍 1815	戦 526	慨 1070

該	1071	賊	1537	鼻	377	維	1007	膜	1834
較	1077	滞	1549	様	407	隠	1014	慢	1837
隔	1078	滝	1550	緑	412	寡	1053	漫	1838
滑	1088	嘆	1566	管	443	箇	1054	銘	1847
褐	1089	痴	1575	関	444	概	1072	網	1855
寛	1110	稚	1576	旗	451	駆	1183	誘	1870
頑	1119	蓄	1579	漁	459	綱	1264	踊	1880
棄	1131	跳	1595	察	489	酵	1265	僚	1909
詰	1144	艇	1621	種	503	豪	1271	暦	1927
愚	1184	殿	1632	静	519	酷	1273	漏	1940
傾	1201	塗	1637	説	524	獄	1274		
携	1202	督	1665	歴	606	魂	1280	15 strokes	
継	1203	漢	1700	練	608	雌	1323		
傑	1211	鉢	1705	演	621	漆	1334	横	235
嫌	1218	搬	1716	慣	638	遮	1339	線	329
献	1219	煩	1717	境	651	銃	1365	調	348
遣	1220	頒	1718	構	675	塾	1370	億	430
誇	1233	微	1735	際	683	緒	1382	課	433
鼓	1234	飽	1802	雑	687	彰	1410	器	452
碁	1240	夢	1844	酸	689	誓	1478	賞	511
溝	1263	滅	1848	精	725	銑	1496	選	527
債	1292	誉	1874	製	726	漸	1503	談	543
催	1293	溶	1878	銭	734	遭	1526	熱	560
歳	1294	腰	1879	総	738	憎	1532	標	571
載	1295	裸	1886	像	740	駄	1541	養	594
搾	1301	雷	1888	増	741	奪	1561	輪	601
嗣	1321	酪	1891	態	748	端	1567	確	634
飼	1322	虜	1903	適	755	嫡	1582	歓	639
慈	1328	鈴	1921	銅	758	徴	1596	潔	659
愁	1357	零	1922	徳	762	漬	1608	賛	690
酬	1358	廉	1932	複	783	摘	1625	質	699
奨	1408	楼	1939	綿	798	滴	1626	敵	756
詳	1409	賄	1941	領	806	稲	1656	導	759
飾	1427			閣	822	寧	1678	編	785
触	1428	14 strokes		疑	835	髪	1706	暴	793
寝	1441			誤	857	罰	1709	遺	808
慎	1442	歌	84	穀	866	閥	1710	劇	848
睡	1459	語	112	誌	880	碑	1731	権	851
跡	1485	算	128	磁	881	漂	1739	熟	894
摂	1489	読	189	需	887	腐	1755	諸	898
践	1495	聞	200	障	902	慕	1788	蔵	923
禅	1502	鳴	209	層	921	暮	1789	潮	941
塑	1511	駅	233	認	952	僕	1820	論	996
僧	1525	銀	263	模	980	墨	1821	慰	1008

影	1017	踏	1657	燃	765	縫	1804	膳	1658
銳	1018	輩	1688	輸	799	膨	1817	頻	1745
調	1022	賠	1693	憲	852	謀	1818	翼	1885
閲	1023	箱	1703	鋼	864	磨	1831	療	1911
緣	1030	範	1719	樹	888	諭	1862	齡	1925
稼	1055	盤	1723	縱	892	融	1872		
餓	1058	罷	1732	操	922	擁	1882	**18 strokes**	
潟	1084	賓	1744	糖	947	謠	1883		
監	1111	敷	1756	奮	966	賴	1889	顏	93
緩	1112	膚	1757	緯	1009	隣	1915	曜	216
輝	1132	賦	1758	憶	1039	隸	1924	題	340
儀	1137	舞	1761	穩	1043	鍊	1933	觀	445
戲	1138	噴	1770	壞	1066			驗	475
窮	1152	墳	1771	懷	1067	**17 strokes**		類	602
緊	1179	憤	1772	獲	1079			額	635
勳	1191	幣	1778	憾	1113	講	676	織	720
慶	1204	弊	1779	還	1114	謝	701	職	721
擊	1209	舖	1786	凝	1175	績	729	簡	829
稿	1266	褒	1803	薰	1192	嚴	854	難	949
撮	1305	撲	1822	憩	1205	縮	893	臨	994
暫	1311	摩	1830	激	1210	優	984	穫	1081
賜	1324	麩	1839	賢	1221	覽	991	騎	1133
趣	1350	默	1856	衡	1267	嚇	1080	襟	1181
潤	1379	憂	1871	墾	1281	轄	1090	繭	1223
導	1380	窯	1881	錯	1302	環	1115	顕	1224
衝	1411	履	1896	諮	1325	擬	1139	鎖	1286
純	1420	慮	1904	儒	1352	犧	1140	瞬	1372
嘱	1429	寮	1910	獸	1366	矯	1170	繕	1504
審	1443	靈	1923	壞	1421	謹	1180	礎	1512
震	1444			孃	1422	謙	1222	騷	1530
穗	1460	**16 strokes**		錠	1423	購	1268	贈	1533
請	1479			薪	1445	懇	1282	懲	1599
潛	1497	親	149	錘	1461	擦	1306	鎮	1605
遷	1498	頭	186	薦	1499	爵	1344	闘	1659
槽	1527	館	247	濁	1558	醜	1359	藩	1721
諾	1557	橋	259	壇	1571	償	1412	覆	1765
誕	1568	整	328	篤	1666	礁	1413	癖	1781
鑄	1586	薬	398	曇	1672	繊	1500	翻	1826
駐	1587	機	453	濃	1681	鮮	1501	癒	1863
澄	1597	積	521	薄	1699	燥	1528	濫	1892
墜	1606	録	611	縛	1701	霜	1529	離	1897
締	1622	衛	617	繁	1720	濯	1556	糧	1912
徹	1629	興	652	避	1733	鍛	1569		
撤	1630	築	751	壁	1780	聴	1598	**19 strokes**	

願 446	驚 1172			
鏡 462	襲 1360			
識 698				
警 847	**23 strokes**			
臓 924				
韻 1015	鑑 1117			
繰 1190				
鶏 1206				
鯨 1208				
壁 1329				
髄 1463				
瀬 1469				
藻 1531				
覇 1683				
爆 1702				
譜 1759				
簿 1790				
霧 1845				
羅 1887				
麗 1926				

20 strokes

議 454	
競 463	
護 670	
響 1171	
懸 1225	
鐘 1414	
譲 1424	
醸 1425	
籍 1486	
騰 1660	
欄 1893	

21 strokes

艦 1116	
顧 1235	
魔 1832	
躍 1860	
露 1935	

22 strokes

645

READINGS INDEX

Note: 1. English alphabetical order
2. Stems and endings not differentiated
3. Where ending can be varied to make more than one word, only one is given (e.g. moru but not moreru or morasu).

A	亜	997	amai	甘	1093	aru	有	401
abareru	暴	793	amaneku	普	1754	aru	在	684
abiru	浴	595	amaneku	遍	1783	aruku	歩	202
abunai	危	831	amaru	余	800	asa	朝	175
abura	油	400	amatsusae	剰	1418	asa	麻	1829
abura	脂	1319	ame	雨	3	asai	浅	525
ada	徒	554	ami	網	1855	ase	汗	1094
aete	敢	1106	amu	編	785	asebamu	汗	1094
agameru	崇	1465	AN	行	118	aseru	焦	1404
agaru	上	37	AN	安	223	ashi	足	51
ageru	挙	458	AN	暗	224	ashi	脚	1146
ageru	揚	1876	AN	案	418	asobu	遊	402
AI	愛	417	ana	穴	849	ataeru	与	1873
ai-	相	530	ana	孔	1241	atai	価	626
AI	哀	998	anadoru	侮	1760	atai	値	933
aida	間	92	ane	姉	498	atama	頭	186
aji	味	393	ani	兄	267	atarashii	新	148
ajiwau	味	393	ano	彼	1725	atari	辺	580
akagane	銅	758	aogu	仰	1173	ataru	当	183
akai	赤	46	aogu	扇	1492	atatakai	温	237
akarui	明	208	aoi	青	43	atatakai	暖	932
akatsuki	暁	1174	arai	荒	1253	ateru	充	1362
akeru	明	208	arai	粗	1508	ato	後	111
akeru	開	241	arasou	争	529	ato	跡	1485
aki	秋	140	arata	新	148	atou	能	766
akinau	商	317	aratameru	改	435	ATSU	圧	612
aku	空	15	arau	洗	916	atsui	暑	313
AKU	悪	222	arawareru	現	666	atsui	熱	560
AKU	握	999	arawareru	顕	1224	atsui	厚	672
aku	飽	1802	arawasu	表	379	atsukau	扱	1000
ama-	雨	3	arawasu	著	937	atsumaru	集	309
ama-	天	58	are	彼	1725	au	会	87
ama	尼	1674	areru	荒	1253	au	合	121

au	遭	1526	BAN	晩	961	BŌ	妨	1808
awa	泡	1795	BAN	伴	1712	BŌ	房	1809
awai	淡	1565	BAN	蛮	1722	BŌ	肪	1810
awaremu	哀	998	BAN	盤	1723	BŌ	某	1811
awaseru	併	1774	BATSU	末	587	BŌ	冒	1812
awateru	慌	1259	BATSU	伐	1707	BŌ	剖	1813
ayakaru	肖	1391	BATSU	抜	1708	BŌ	紡	1814
ayamachi	過	629	BATSU	罰	1709	BŌ	傍	1815
ayamaru	謝	701	BATSU	閥	1710	BŌ	帽	1816
ayamaru	誤	857	BE	部	384	BŌ	膨	1817
ayashii	怪	1061	be	辺	580	BŌ	謀	1818
ayatsuru	操	922	BEI	米	201	BŌ	矛	1843
ayaui	危	831	-beki	可	816	BŌ	妄	1851
ayumu	歩	202	BEN	勉	390	boko	凹	1032
azamuku	欺	1136	BEN	便	582	BOKU	木	69
azayaka	鮮	1501	BEN	弁	786	BOKU	目	72
aze	畔	1713	beni	紅	862	BOKU	北	205
azukaru	預	801	BETSU	別	579	BOKU	牧	586
ba	場	144	BI	美	376	BOKU	朴	1819
BA	馬	191	BI	鼻	377	BOKU	僕	1820
BA	婆	1684	BI	備	774	BOKU	墨	1821
baba	婆	1684	BI	尾	1734	BOKU	撲	1822
BACHI	罰	1709	BI	微	1735	BON	煩	1717
BAI	売	192	BIN	便	582	BON	凡	1827
BAI	買	193	BIN	貧	777	BON	盆	1828
BAI	倍	563	BIN	敏	1746	BOTSU	没	1823
BAI	梅	1689	BIN	瓶	1747	BU	分	199
BAI	培	1690	BO	母	203	BU	部	384
BAI	陪	1691	BO	墓	788	BU	不	572
BAI	媒	1692	BO	模	980	BU	武	781
BAI	賠	1693	BO	募	1787	BU	無	796
BAI	某	1811	BO	慕	1788	BU	侮	1760
bakeru	化	238	BO	暮	1789	BU	舞	1761
BAKU	麦	194	BO	簿	1790	BU	奉	1793
BAKU	博	564	BŌ	望	585	BUN	文	68
BAKU	暴	793	BŌ	防	791	BUN	分	199
BAKU	幕	977	BŌ	貿	792	BUN	聞	200
BAKU	漠	1700	BŌ	暴	793	BUN	蚊	1056
BAKU	縛	1701	BŌ	亡	973	buta	豚	1670
BAKU	爆	1702	BŌ	忘	974	BUTSU	物	387
BAN	番	196	BŌ	棒	975	BUTSU	仏	784
BAN	板	373	BŌ	乏	1805	BYŌ	秒	380
BAN	万	392	BŌ	忙	1806	BYŌ	病	381
BAN	判	769	BŌ	坊	1807	BYŌ	平	388

BYŌ	苗	1740	CHO	貯	546	CHŪ	鋳	1586
BYŌ	描	1741	CHO	著	937	CHŪ	駐	1587
BYŌ	貓	1742	CHO	緒	1382	DA	打	335
CHA	茶	171	CHŌ	町	57	DA	蛇	1341
CHAKU	着	343	CHŌ	長	173	DA	妥	1538
CHAKU	嫡	1582	CHŌ	鳥	174	DA	堕	1539
chi	千	47	CHŌ	朝	175	DA	惰	1540
CHI	地	167	CHŌ	重	311	DA	駄	1541
CHI	池	168	CHŌ	丁	346	DAI	大	53
CHI	知	169	CHŌ	帳	347	DAI	台	166
chi	血	270	CHŌ	調	348	DAI	弟	177
CHI	治	544	CHŌ	腸	547	DAI	代	338
CHI	置	545	CHŌ	張	752	DAI	第	339
CHI	質	699	CHŌ	提	753	DAI	題	340
CHI	値	933	CHŌ	庁	938	DAI	内	364
chi	乳	951	CHŌ	兆	939	DAKU	諾	1557
CHI	恥	1572	CHŌ	頂	940	DAKU	濁	1558
CHI	致	1573	CHŌ	潮	941	daku	抱	1794
CHI	遅	1574	CHŌ	弔	1588	damaru	黙	1856
CHI	痴	1575	CHŌ	挑	1589	DAN	男	54
CHI	稚	1576	CHŌ	彫	1590	DAN	談	543
chichi	父	197	CHŌ	眺	1591	DAN	団	749
chichi	乳	951	CHŌ	釣	1592	DAN	断	750
chigau	違	1006	CHŌ	脹	1593	DAN	段	931
chigiru	契	1195	CHŌ	超	1594	DAN	暖	932
chiisai	小	36	CHŌ	跳	1595	DAN	弾	1570
chijimu	縮	893	CHŌ	徴	1596	DAN	壇	1571
chikai	近	103	CHŌ	澄	1597	dasu	出	34
chikara	力	74	CHŌ	聴	1598	DATSU	脱	1560
chikau	誓	1478	CHŌ	懲	1599	DATSU	奪	1561
CHIKU	竹	170	CHŌ	塚	1607	DE	弟	177
CHIKU	築	751	CHOKU	直	349	DEI	泥	1623
CHIKU	畜	1577	CHOKU	勅	1600	deko	凸	1667
CHIKU	逐	1578	CHŪ	中	55	DEN	田	59
CHIKU	蓄	1579	CHŪ	虫	56	DEN	電	180
CHIN	賃	942	CHŪ	昼	172	DEN	伝	553
CHIN	沈	1601	CHŪ	注	344	DEN	殿	1632
CHIN	珍	1602	CHŪ	柱	345	deru	出	34
CHIN	朕	1603	CHŪ	仲	934	DO	土	60
CHIN	陳	1604	CHŪ	宙	935	DO	度	356
CHIN	鎮	1605	CHŪ	忠	936	DO	努	555
chiru	散	492	CHŪ	沖	1583	DO	奴	1638
CHITSU	秩	1580	CHŪ	抽	1584	DO	怒	1639
CHITSU	窒	1581	CHŪ	衷	1585	DŌ	同	187

DŌ	道	188	EN	園	234	FŪ	富	780
DŌ	動	362	EN	塩	428	FŪ	封	1762
DŌ	童	363	EN	演	621	fuchi	縁	1030
DŌ	堂	557	EN	延	814	fuda	札	1304
DŌ	働	558	EN	沿	815	fude	筆	569
DŌ	銅	758	EN	炎	1024	fue	笛	1624
DŌ	導	759	EN	宴	1025	fueru	増	741
DŌ	洞	1661	EN	援	1026	fueru	殖	1426
DŌ	胴	1662	EN	煙	1027	fukai	深	325
dobu	溝	1263	EN	猿	1028	fukeru	老	609
DOKU	読	189	EN	鉛	1029	fukeru	更	1248
DOKU	毒	559	EN	縁	1030	FUKU	服	385
DOKU	独	763	erabu	選	527	FUKU	福	386
DON	鈍	1671	erabu	択	1551	FUKU	副	576
DON	曇	1672	erai	偉	1005	FUKU	復	782
doro	泥	1623	eru	得	761	FUKU	複	783
E	会	87	eru	獲	1079	FUKU	腹	965
E	絵	89	ETSU	悦	1020	fuku	吹	1452
e	重	311	ETSU	越	1021	FUKU	伏	1763
E	依	1001	ETSU	謁	1022	FUKU	幅	1764
E	恵	1196	ETSU	閲	1023	FUKU	覆	1765
e	江	1244	FU	父	197	fuku	噴	1770
e	柄	1776	FU	負	383	fukumu	含	1118
eda	枝	1315	FU	不	572	fukuramu	脹	1593
egaku	描	1741	FU	夫	573	fukuramu	膨	1817
EI	泳	232	FU	付	574	fukuro	袋	1546
EI	英	426	FU	府	575	fumi	文	68
EI	栄	427	FU	布	778	fumu	践	1495
EI	永	615	FU	婦	779	fumu	踏	1657
EI	営	616	FU	富	780	FUN	分	199
EI	衛	617	FU	扶	1748	FUN	粉	577
EI	映	813	FU	怖	1749	FUN	奮	966
EI	詠	1016	FU	附	1750	FUN	紛	1768
EI	影	1017	FU	赴	1751	FUN	雰	1769
EI	鋭	1018	FU	浮	1752	FUN	噴	1770
EKI	駅	233	FU	符	1753	FUN	墳	1771
EKI	役	397	FU	普	1754	FUN	憤	1772
EKI	易	618	FU	腐	1755	funa-	船	158
EKI	益	619	FU	敷	1756	funa-	舟	1354
EKI	液	620	FU	膚	1757	fune	船	158
EKI	疫	1019	FU	賦	1758	fune	舟	1354
emu	笑	900	FU	譜	1759	fureru	触	1428
EN	円	4	FŪ	風	198	furu	降	863
EN	遠	79	FŪ	夫	573	furu	振	1437

furui	古	109	GATSU	月	16	GO	護	670
furuu	奮	966	gawa	側	535	GO	誤	857
furuu	震	1444	GE	下	7	GO	后	858
fusa	房	1809	GE	夏	82	GO	御	1158
fusegu	防	791	GE	外	91	GO	互	1236
fushi	節	523	GE	解	632	GO	呉	1237
fusu	伏	1763	GE	華	1046	GO	娯	1238
futa	二	61	GEI	芸	470	GO	悟	1239
futa-	双	1513	GEI	迎	1207	GO	碁	1240
futatabi	再	679	GEI	鯨	1208	GŌ	強	100
futoi	太	164	GEKI	劇	848	GŌ	合	121
futokoro	懐	1067	GEKI	撃	1209	GŌ	業	260
FUTSU	仏	784	GEKI	激	1210	GŌ	号	281
FUTSU	払	1766	GEN	元	106	GŌ	郷	841
FUTSU	沸	1767	GEN	原	107	GŌ	拷	1269
fuyu	冬	182	GEN	言	274	GŌ	剛	1270
GA	画	85	GEN	限	665	GŌ	豪	1271
GA	芽	434	GEN	現	666	GOKU	極	464
GA	賀	630	GEN	減	667	GOKU	獄	1274
GA	我	817	GEN	源	853	GON	言	274
GA	雅	1057	GEN	厳	854	GON	権	851
GA	餓	1058	GEN	嫌	1218	GON	厳	854
GAI	外	91	GEN	幻	1226	-goto	毎	206
GAI	害	437	GEN	玄	1227	gotoku	如	1383
GAI	街	819	GEN	弦	1228	GU	具	265
GAI	劾	1068	GETSU	月	16	GU	虞	1040
GAI	涯	1069	GI	議	454	GU	愚	1184
GAI	慨	1070	GI	技	644	GŪ	宮	256
GAI	該	1071	GI	義	645	GŪ	偶	1185
GAI	概	1072	GI	疑	835	GŪ	遇	1186
GAKU	学	10	GI	宜	1134	GŪ	隅	1187
GAKU	楽	218	GI	偽	1135	GUN	軍	466
GAKU	額	635	GI	欺	1136	GUN	郡	467
GAKU	岳	1082	GI	儀	1137	GUN	群	657
GAN	顔	93	GI	戯	1138	GYAKU	逆	646
GAN	元	106	GI	擬	1139	GYAKU	虐	1147
GAN	岸	248	GI	犠	1140	GYO	魚	98
GAN	岩	249	GIN	銀	263	GYO	漁	459
GAN	願	446	GIN	吟	1182	GYO	御	1158
GAN	眼	640	GO	五	19	GYŌ	形	104
GAN	丸	830	GO	午	110	GYŌ	行	118
GAN	含	1118	GO	後	111	GYŌ	業	260
GAN	頑	1119	GO	語	112	GYŌ	仰	1173
gara	柄	1776	GO	期	251	GYŌ	暁	1174

GYŌ	凝	1175	hajimeru	創	920	HAN	藩	1721
GYOKU	玉	102	hajiru	恥	1572	HAN	凡	1827
GYŪ	牛	97	haka	墓	788	hana	花	9
ha	歯	290	hakarigoto	謀	1818	hana	鼻	377
HA	波	367	hakaru	計	105	hana	華	1046
ha	葉	405	hakaru	図	150	hanahada	甚	1449
HA	破	767	hakaru	量	600	hanareru	離	1897
ha	羽	812	hakaru	測	743	hanasu	話	221
HA	派	955	hakaru	諮	1325	hanasu	放	391
ha	刃	1446	hakaru	謀	1818	hane	羽	812
ha	端	1567	hako	箱	1703	haneru	跳	1595
HA	把	1682	hakobu	運	231	hara	原	107
HA	覇	1683	HAKU	白	65	hara	腹	965
haba	幅	1764	HAKU	博	564	haramu	妊	1676
habamu	阻	1505	haku	掃	1519	harau	払	1766
haberu	侍	1326	haku	吐	1634	harawata	腸	547
habuku	省	516	HAKU	伯	1694	harawata	臓	924
HACHI	八	66	HAKU	拍	1695	hareru	晴	155
HACHI	鉢	1705	HAKU	泊	1696	hari	針	905
hada	肌	1704	HAKU	迫	1697	haru	春	141
hada	膚	1757	HAKU	舶	1698	haru	張	752
hadaka	裸	1886	HAKU	薄	1699	hasamu	挾	1165
haeru	生	42	HAKU	簿	1790	hashi	橋	259
haeru	栄	427	haku	履	1896	hashi	端	1567
haeru	映	813	hama	浜	1743	hashira	柱	345
hagane	鋼	864	HAN	半	195	hashiru	走	161
hagemu	励	1919	HAN	反	371	hata	畑	369
hageshii	激	1210	HAN	坂	372	hata	旗	451
haha	母	203	HAN	板	373	hata	機	453
HAI	配	368	HAN	飯	565	hata	端	1567
HAI	敗	562	HAN	犯	768	hatake	畑	369
hai	灰	818	HAN	判	769	hataraku	働	558
HAI	拝	956	HAN	版	770	hatasu	果	627
HAI	背	957	HAN	班	960	hate	果	627
HAI	肺	958	HAN	帆	1711	HATSU	発	370
HAI	俳	959	HAN	伴	1712	hatsu-	初	507
HAI	杯	1685	HAN	畔	1713	HATSU	法	584
HAI	排	1686	HAN	般	1714	HATSU	鉢	1705
HAI	廃	1687	HAN	販	1715	HATSU	髪	1706
HAI	輩	1688	HAN	搬	1716	HATSU	伐	1707
hairu	入	63	HAN	煩	1717	hayai	早	50
haji	恥	1572	HAN	頒	1718	hayai	速	534
hajimaru	始	288	HAN	範	1719	hayai	迅	1448
hajime	初	507	HAN	繁	1720	hayashi	林	75

651

hazukashimeru	辱	1430	HI	秘	964	hisoka	窃	1488
hazumu	弾	1570	HI	妃	1724	hisomu	潜	1497
hazusu	外	91	HI	彼	1725	hitai	額	635
hebi	蛇	1341	HI	披	1726	hitasu	浸	1438
hedataru	隔	1078	HI	卑	1727	hito-	一	1
HEI	病	381	HI	疲	1728	hito	人	39
HEI	平	388	HI	被	1729	hitori	独	763
HEI	兵	578	HI	扉	1730	hitoshii	等	361
HEI	陛	967	HI	碑	1731	hitoshii	均	653
HEI	閉	968	HI	罷	1732	hitoshii	斉	1473
HEI	坪	1609	HI	避	1733	HITSU	必	568
HEI	丙	1773	HI	泌	1737	HITSU	筆	569
HEI	併	1774	hibiku	響	1171	HITSU	匹	1736
HEI	並	1775	hidari	左	22	HITSU	泌	1737
HEI	柄	1776	hieru	冷	604	hitsugi	棺	1107
HEI	塀	1777	higashi	東	184	hitsuji	羊	986
HEI	幣	1778	hiideru	秀	1355	HO	歩	202
HEI	弊	1779	hijiri	聖	911	HO	保	787
HEKI	壁	1780	hikaeru	控	1258	HO	補	970
HEKI	癖	1781	hikari	光	116	ho	穂	1460
hekomu	凹	1032	hikaru	光	116	ho	帆	1711
HEN	返	389	hiki	匹	1736	HO	捕	1784
HEN	辺	580	hikiiru	率	803	HO	浦	1785
HEN	変	581	hiku	引	77	HO	舗	1786
HEN	編	785	hiku	弾	1570	HŌ	方	204
HEN	片	969	hikui	低	548	HŌ	放	391
HEN	偏	1782	hima	暇	1050	HŌ	包	583
HEN	遍	1783	hime	姫	1738	HŌ	法	584
herikudaru	謙	1222	himeru	秘	964	HŌ	保	787
heru	経	658	HIN	品	382	HŌ	報	789
heru	減	667	HIN	貧	777	HŌ	豊	790
hi	火	8	HIN	浜	1743	HŌ	宝	971
hi	日	62	HIN	賓	1744	HŌ	訪	972
HI	皮	374	HIN	頻	1745	HŌ	封	1762
HI	悲	375	hiraku	開	241	HŌ	芳	1791
hi	陽	406	hiratai	平	388	HŌ	邦	1792
hi	灯	556	hiro	尋	1451	HŌ	奉	1793
HI	飛	566	hiroi	広	114	HŌ	抱	1794
HI	費	567	hirou	拾	305	HŌ	泡	1795
HI	比	771	hiru	昼	172	HŌ	胞	1796
HI	肥	772	hiru	干	825	HŌ	俸	1797
HI	非	773	hirugaeru	翻	1826	HŌ	倣	1798
HI	否	962	hisashii	久	647	HŌ	峰	1799
HI	批	963	hisoka	密	978	HŌ	砲	1800

HŌ	崩	1801	I	意	226	imo	芋	1011
HŌ	飽	1802	I	以	419	imōto	妹	207
HŌ	褒	1803	I	衣	420	imu	忌	1122
HŌ	縫	1804	I	位	421	IN	音	6
hō	朴	1819	I	囲	422	IN	引	77
hodo	程	754	I	委	423	IN	員	228
hodokosu	施	1318	I	胃	424	IN	院	229
hogaraka	朗	995	I	移	613	IN	飲	230
hoka	外	91	I	易	618	IN	印	425
hoka	他	334	I	異	807	IN	因	614
hoko	矛	1843	I	遺	808	IN	姻	1012
hokoru	誇	1233	I	依	1001	IN	陰	1013
HOKU	北	205	I	威	1002	IN	隠	1014
homare	誉	1874	I	為	1003	IN	韻	1015
homeru	褒	1803	I	尉	1004	ina	否	962
hōmuru	葬	1523	I	偉	1005	ina	稲	1656
HON	本	70	I	違	1006	inamu	否	962
HON	奔	1825	I	維	1007	ine	稲	1656
HON	翻	1826	I	慰	1008	inochi	命	394
hone	骨	867	I	緯	1009	inoru	祈	1124
honō	炎	1024	i	井	1470	inu	犬	17
hora	洞	1661	I	唯	1864	ireru	入	63
hori	堀	1824	ICHI	一	1	ireru	容	802
horobiru	滅	1848	ichi	市	130	iro	色	145
horu	掘	1189	ICHI	壱	810	irodoru	彩	1290
horu	彫	1590	ichijirushii	著	937	iru	要	593
hoshi	星	154	idaku	抱	1794	iru	居	649
hoshii	欲	987	idomu	挑	1589	iru	射	882
hosoi	細	284	ie	家	83	iru	鋳	1586
hosu	干	825	ikaru	怒	1639	isagiyoi	潔	659
hotaru	蛍	1200	ike	池	168	isamashii	勇	592
hotoke	仏	784	iki	息	332	ishi	石	45
HOTSU	発	370	IKI	域	809	ishizue	礎	1512
HYAKU	百	67	iki	粋	1455	isogashii	忙	1806
HYŌ	氷	378	ikidōru	憤	1772	isogu	急	254
HYŌ	表	379	ikioi	勢	518	ita	板	373
HYŌ	票	570	ikiru	生	42	itadaki	頂	940
HYŌ	標	571	ikou	憩	1205	itadaku	頂	940
HYŌ	兵	578	iku	行	118	itai	痛	943
HYŌ	俵	775	IKU	育	227	itamu	傷	901
HYŌ	評	776	iku-	幾	1129	itamu	悼	1648
HYŌ	拍	1695	ikusa	戦	526	itaru	至	875
HYŌ	漂	1739	ima	今	125	itaru	到	1641
I	医	225	imashimeru	戒	1060	itasu	致	1573

653

itazura	徒	554	JIKI	直	349	JŌ	醸	1425
ito	糸	27	JIKU	軸	1330	JŌ	盛	1476
itonamu	栄	616	JIN	人	39	JŌ	娘	1846
ITSU	一	1	JIN	神	324	JOKU	辱	1430
itsu-	五	19	JIN	臣	512	JU	受	303
ITSU	逸	1010	JIN	仁	906	JU	授	702
ITSU	乙	1041	JIN	刃	1446	JU	需	887
itsukushimu	慈	1328	JIN	尽	1447	JU	樹	888
itsuwaru	偽	1135	JIN	迅	1448	JU	就	890
iu	言	274	JIN	甚	1449	JU	寿	1351
iwa	岩	249	JIN	陣	1450	JU	儒	1352
iwau	祝	706	JIN	尋	1451	JŪ	十	33
iya	嫌	1218	jireru	焦	1404	JŪ	拾	305
iyashii	卑	1727	JITSU	日	62	JŪ	住	310
iyasu	医	225	JITSU	実	296	JŪ	重	311
iyasu	癒	1863	JO	女	35	JŪ	従	891
izumi	泉	915	JO	助	314	JŪ	縦	892
JA	邪	1340	JO	序	710	JŪ	汁	1361
JA	蛇	1341	JO	除	711	JŪ	充	1362
JAKU	弱	137	JO	如	1383	JŪ	柔	1363
JAKU	若	886	JO	叙	1384	JŪ	渋	1364
JAKU	寂	1345	JO	徐	1385	JŪ	銃	1365
JI	字	28	JŌ	上	37	JŪ	獣	1366
JI	耳	29	JŌ	場	144	JUKU	熟	894
JI	寺	133	JŌ	乗	320	JUKU	塾	1370
JI	自	134	JŌ	定	351	JUN	順	506
JI	時	135	JŌ	成	515	JUN	準	709
JI	地	167	JŌ	静	519	JUN	純	895
JI	仕	285	JŌ	条	716	JUN	旬	1373
JI	次	292	JŌ	状	717	JUN	巡	1374
JI	事	293	JŌ	常	718	JUN	盾	1375
JI	持	294	JŌ	情	719	JUN	准	1376
ji	路	415	JŌ	城	903	JUN	殉	1377
JI	辞	500	JŌ	蒸	904	JUN	循	1378
JI	治	544	JŌ	丈	1415	JUN	潤	1379
JI	示	695	JŌ	冗	1416	JUN	遵	1380
JI	似	696	JŌ	浄	1417	JUTSU	述	707
JI	児	697	JŌ	剰	1418	JUTSU	術	708
JI	除	711	JŌ	畳	1419	KA	下	7
JI	磁	881	JŌ	縄	1420	KA	火	8
JI	侍	1326	JŌ	壌	1421	KA	花	9
JI	滋	1327	JŌ	嬢	1422	-ka	日	62
JI	慈	1328	JŌ	錠	1423	KA	何	80
JI	璽	1329	JŌ	譲	1424	KA	科	81

KA	夏	82	KAI	回	86	KAKU	革	821
KA	家	83	KAI	会	87	KAKU	閣	822
KA	歌	84	KAI	海	88	KAKU	核	1074
KA	化	238	KAI	絵	89	KAKU	殻	1075
KA	荷	239	kai	貝	90	KAKU	郭	1076
KA	加	431	KAI	界	240	KAKU	較	1077
KA	貨	432	KAI	開	241	KAKU	隔	1078
KA	課	433	KAI	階	242	KAKU	獲	1079
KA	仮	625	KAI	改	435	KAKU	嚇	1080
KA	価	626	KAI	械	436	KAKU	穫	1081
KA	果	627	KAI	快	631	kakureru	隠	1014
KA	河	628	KAI	解	632	kama	缶	1095
KA	過	629	KAI	灰	818	kama	窯	1881
KA	可	816	KAI	街	819	kamau	構	675
KA	佳	1044	KAI	介	1059	kame	瓶	1747
KA	架	1045	KAI	戒	1060	kami	上	37
KA	華	1046	KAI	怪	1061	kami	紙	132
KA	菓	1047	KAI	拐	1062	kami	神	324
KA	渦	1048	KAI	悔	1063	kami	髪	1706
KA	嫁	1049	KAI	皆	1064	kaminari	雷	1888
KA	暇	1050	KAI	塊	1065	kamosu	醸	1425
KA	禍	1051	KAI	壊	1066	KAN	間	92
KA	靴	1052	KAI	懐	1067	KAN	寒	245
KA	寡	1053	kaiko	蚕	688	KAN	感	246
KA	箇	1054	kakaeru	抱	1794	KAN	館	247
KA	稼	1055	kakageru	掲	1198	KAN	完	440
ka	蚊	1056	kakari	係	268	KAN	官	441
ka	香	1255	kakaru	架	1045	KAN	漢	442
kabe	壁	1780	kakaru	掛	1083	KAN	管	443
kabu	株	824	kakaru	懸	1225	KAN	関	444
kado	門	211	kakawaru	拘	1249	KAN	観	445
kado	角	243	kakeru	駆	1183	KAN	刊	636
kaerimiru	省	516	kaki	垣	1073	KAN	幹	637
kaerimiru	顧	1235	kakomu	囲	422	KAN	慣	638
kaeru	帰	96	KAKU	画	85	KAN	歓	639
kaeru	換	1105	kaku	書	142	KAN	干	825
kaeru	替	1548	KAKU	角	243	KAN	巻	826
kaesu	返	389	KAKU	客	252	KAN	看	827
kaette	却	1145	KAKU	各	438	KAN	勧	828
kagami	鏡	462	KAKU	覚	439	KAN	簡	829
kagayaku	輝	1132	kaku	欠	471	KAN	甘	1093
kage	陰	1013	KAKU	格	633	KAN	汗	1094
kage	影	1017	KAKU	確	634	KAN	缶	1095
kagiru	限	665	KAKU	拡	820	KAN	肝	1096

KAN	冠	1097	karamu	絡	1890	katsu	且	1091
KAN	陥	1098	kare	彼	1725	katsugu	担	929
KAN	乾	1099	kareru	枯	1231	kau	買	193
KAN	勘	1100	kari	仮	625	kau	飼	1322
KAN	患	1101	kariru	借	502	kawa	川	48
KAN	貫	1102	karu	刈	1092	kawa	皮	374
KAN	喚	1103	karu	駆	1183	kawa	側	535
KAN	堪	1104	karu	狩	1347	kawa	河	628
KAN	換	1105	karui	軽	269	kawa	革	821
KAN	敢	1106	kasa	傘	1310	kawaku	渇	1087
KAN	棺	1107	kasanaru	重	311	kawaku	乾	1099
KAN	款	1108	kasegu	稼	1055	kawaru	代	338
KAN	閑	1109	kashikoi	賢	1221	kawaru	変	581
KAN	寛	1110	kashira	頭	186	kawasu	交	115
KAN	監	1111	kasu	貸	747	kayou	通	176
KAN	緩	1112	kasuka	幽	1865	kazaru	飾	1427
KAN	憾	1113	kata	方	204	kaze	風	198
KAN	還	1114	kata	型	468	kazoeru	数	151
KAN	環	1115	kata	片	969	kazu	数	151
KAN	艦	1116	kata	潟	1084	KE	気	11
KAN	鑑	1117	kata	肩	1212	KE	家	83
KAN	甲	1243	kata(chi)	形	104	ke	毛	210
kana-	金	14	katai	固	476	KE	化	238
kanaderu	奏	918	katai	難	949	KE	希	447
kaname	要	593	katai	堅	1217	KE	景	469
kanarazu	必	568	katai	硬	1260	KE	仮	625
kanashii	悲	375	kataki	敵	756	KE	怪	1061
kanbashii	芳	1791	katamari	塊	1065	KE	懸	1225
kane	金	14	katamuku	傾	1201	ke(da)mono	獣	1366
kane	鐘	1414	katana	刀	181	kegareru	汚	1031
kaneru	兼	850	kataru	語	112	KEI	京	99
kanete	予	403	katawara	傍	1815	KEI	形	104
kangaeru	考	117	katayoru	偏	1782	KEI	計	105
kangamiru	鑑	1117	kate	糧	1912	KEI	兄	267
kanmuri	冠	1097	KATSU	合	121	KEI	係	268
kano	彼	1725	KATSU	活	244	KEI	軽	269
kao	顔	93	katsu	勝	319	KEI	競	463
kaori	薫	1192	KATSU	割	823	KEI	型	468
kaoru	香	1255	KATSU	括	1085	KEI	景	469
kara	空	15	KATSU	喝	1086	KEI	境	651
kara	殻	1075	KATSU	渇	1087	KEI	経	658
kara	唐	1644	KATSU	滑	1088	KEI	系	844
karada	体	165	KATSU	褐	1089	KEI	径	845
karai	辛	1432	KATSU	轄	1090	KEI	敬	846

KEI	警	847	KEN	繭	1223	KI	鬼	1128
KEI	刑	1193	KEN	顕	1224	KI	幾	1129
KEI	茎	1194	KEN	懸	1225	KI	棋	1130
KEI	契	1195	kesu	消	316	KI	棄	1131
KEI	恵	1196	KETSU	血	270	KI	輝	1132
KEI	啓	1197	KETSU	決	271	KI	騎	1133
KEI	掲	1198	KETSU	欠	471	KI	崎	1297
KEI	渓	1199	KETSU	結	472	KI	肌	1704
KEI	蛍	1200	KETSU	潔	659	KI	姫	1738
KEI	傾	1201	KETSU	穴	849	kibishii	厳	854
KEI	携	1202	KETSU	傑	1211	KICHI	吉	1142
KEI	継	1203	kewashii	険	662	kieru	消	316
KEI	慶	1204	kezuru	削	1298	ki(iro)	黄	120
KEI	憩	1205	KI	気	11	kiku	聞	200
KEI	鶏	1206	ki	木	69	kiku	利	596
kemui	煙	1027	KI	汽	94	kiku	効	671
kemuri	煙	1027	KI	記	95	KIKU	菊	1141
KEN	犬	17	KI	帰	96	kiku	聴	1598
KEN	見	18	KI	起	250	kimaru	決	271
KEN	間	92	KI	期	251	kimi	君	266
KEN	研	272	KI	希	447	kimo	肝	1096
KEN	県	273	KI	季	448	kimo	胆	1564
KEN	建	473	KI	紀	449	KIN	金	14
KEN	健	474	KI	喜	450	KIN	近	103
KEN	験	475	KI	旗	451	KIN	今	125
KEN	件	660	KI	器	452	KIN	均	653
KEN	券	661	KI	機	453	KIN	禁	654
KEN	険	662	KI	基	641	KIN	勤	842
KEN	検	663	KI	寄	642	KIN	筋	843
KEN	絹	664	KI	規	643	KIN	斤	1176
KEN	兼	850	KI	危	831	KIN	菌	1177
KEN	権	851	KI	机	832	KIN	琴	1178
KEN	憲	852	KI	揮	833	KIN	緊	1179
KEN	肩	1212	KI	貴	834	KIN	謹	1180
KEN	倹	1213	KI	己	855	KIN	襟	1181
KEN	剣	1214	ki	樹	888	kinu	絹	664
KEN	軒	1215	KI	企	1120	kirau	嫌	1218
KEN	圏	1216	KI	岐	1121	kiri	霧	1845
KEN	堅	1217	KI	忌	1122	kiru	切	156
KEN	嫌	1218	KI	奇	1123	kiru	着	343
KEN	献	1219	KI	祈	1124	kisaki	后	858
KEN	遣	1220	KI	軌	1125	kishi	岸	248
KEN	賢	1221	KI	既	1126	kisou	競	463
KEN	謙	1222	KI	飢	1127	kita	北	205

kitaeru	鍛	1569	KŌ	交	115	KŌ	郊	1254
kitanai	汚	1031	KŌ	光	116	KŌ	香	1255
KITSU	吉	1142	KŌ	考	117	KŌ	侯	1256
KITSU	喫	1143	KŌ	行	118	KŌ	貢	1257
KITSU	詰	1144	KŌ	高	119	KŌ	控	1258
kiwa	際	683	KŌ	黄	120	KŌ	慌	1259
kiwamaru	窮	1152	KŌ	公	277	KŌ	硬	1260
kiwameru	究	253	KŌ	向	278	KŌ	絞	1261
kiwameru	極	464	KŌ	幸	279	KŌ	項	1262
kiyoi	清	517	KŌ	港	280	KŌ	溝	1263
kizamu	刻	865	KŌ	功	477	KŌ	綱	1264
kizasu	兆	939	KŌ	候	478	KŌ	酵	1265
kizu	傷	901	KŌ	航	479	KŌ	稿	1266
kizuku	築	751	KŌ	康	480	KŌ	衡	1267
ko	子	25	KŌ	格	633	KŌ	購	1268
ko-	小	36	KŌ	興	652	KŌ	岬	1840
ko-	木	69	KŌ	効	671	KŌ	耗	1853
KO	戸	108	KŌ	厚	672	kobamu	拒	1154
KO	古	109	KŌ	耕	673	koboreru	零	1922
KO	去	258	KŌ	鉱	674	koe	声	153
KO	庫	275	KŌ	構	675	koeru	肥	772
KO	湖	276	KŌ	講	676	koeru	越	1021
KO	固	476	KŌ	后	858	koeru	超	1594
ko	粉	577	KŌ	好	859	kogeru	焦	1404
KO	故	668	KŌ	孝	860	kogoeru	凍	1643
KO	個	669	KŌ	皇	861	koi	濃	1681
ko	児	697	KŌ	紅	862	koi	恋	1931
KO	己	855	KŌ	降	863	koishii	恋	1931
KO	呼	856	KŌ	鋼	864	kokono-	九	12
KO	箇	1054	KŌ	較	1077	kokoro	心	147
KO	拠	1155	KŌ	仰	1173	kokoromiru	試	499
KO	虚	1156	KŌ	孔	1241	kokoroyoi	快	631
KO	孤	1229	KŌ	巧	1242	kokorozashi	志	692
KO	弧	1230	KŌ	甲	1243	kokorozasu	志	692
KO	枯	1231	KŌ	江	1244	KOKU	谷	122
KO	雇	1232	KŌ	坑	1245	KOKU	国	123
KO	誇	1233	KŌ	抗	1246	KOKU	黒	124
KO	鼓	1234	KŌ	攻	1247	KOKU	告	481
KO	顧	1235	KŌ	更	1248	KOKU	刻	865
KŌ	口	20	KŌ	拘	1249	KOKU	穀	866
KŌ	校	21	KŌ	肯	1250	koku	扱	1000
KŌ	後	111	KŌ	恒	1251	KOKU	克	1272
KŌ	工	113	KŌ	洪	1252	KOKU	酷	1273
KŌ	広	114	KŌ	荒	1253	komakai	細	284

komaru	困	868	kowai	怖	1749	kuraberu	比	771
kome	米	201	kowareru	壊	1066	kurai	暗	224
komo	薦	1499	koyomi	暦	1927	kurai	位	421
komu	込	1275	kozotte	挙	458	kurenai	紅	862
kōmuru	被	1729	KU	九	12	kureru	呉	1237
KON	金	14	KU	口	20	kureru	暮	1789
KON	今	125	KU	工	113	kurogane	鉄	353
KON	根	282	KU	宮	256	kuroi	黒	124
KON	建	473	KU	苦	264	kuru	来	217
KON	混	677	KU	区	465	kuru	繰	1190
KON	困	868	KU	功	477	kuruma	車	31
KON	献	1219	KU	久	647	kurushii	苦	264
KON	昆	1276	KU	句	655	kuruu	狂	1161
KON	恨	1277	KU	供	839	kusa	草	162
KON	婚	1278	KU	紅	862	kusai	臭	1356
KON	紺	1279	KU	駆	1183	kusari	鎖	1286
KON	魂	1280	KU	貢	1257	kusaru	腐	1755
KON	墾	1281	KŪ	空	15	kuse	癖	1781
KON	懇	1282	kubaru	配	368	kusuri	薬	398
kona	粉	577	kubi	首	139	kutsu	靴	1052
konomu	好	859	kubiki	衡	1267	KUTSU	屈	1188
kōra	甲	1243	kubo	凹	1031	KUTSU	掘	1189
kore	是	910	kuchi	口	20	KUTSU	堀	1824
kōri	氷	378	kuchibiru	唇	1435	kutsugaeru	覆	1765
kōri	郡	467	kuchiru	朽	1150	kutsurogu	寛	1110
koriru	懲	1599	kuda	管	443	kuu	食	146
korogaru	転	354	kudaku	砕	1287	kuwa	桑	1518
koromo	衣	420	kudaru	下	7	kuwadateru	企	1120
korosu	殺	488	kudasaru	下	7	kuwaeru	加	431
koru	凝	1175	kuiru	悔	1063	kuwashii	詳	1409
kōru	凍	1643	kujira	鯨	1208	kuyamu	悔	1063
koshi	腰	1879	kuki	茎	1194	kuyashii	悔	1063
kosuru	擦	1306	kukuru	括	1085	kuzureru	崩	1801
kotaeru	答	185	kumo	雲	78	KYA	脚	1146
koto	言	274	kumoru	曇	1672	KYAKU	客	252
koto	事	293	kumu	組	160	KYAKU	却	1145
koto	琴	1178	kumu	酌	1343	KYAKU	脚	1146
koto	殊	1348	KUN	君	266	KYO	去	258
kotoba	詞	879	KUN	訓	656	KYO	挙	458
kotobuki	寿	1351	KUN	勲	1191	KYO	居	649
kotonaru	異	807	KUN	薫	1192	KYO	許	650
kotowaru	断	750	kuni	国	123	KYO	巨	1153
KOTSU	骨	867	kura	倉	531	KYO	拒	1154
kou	請	1479	kura	蔵	923	KYO	拠	1155

Reading	Kanji	No.	Reading	Kanji	No.	Reading	Kanji	No.
KYO	虚	1156	KYŪ	久	647	maku	巻	826
KYO	距	1157	KYŪ	旧	638	MAKU	幕	977
KYŌ	京	99	KYŪ	弓	836	MAKU	膜	1834
KYŌ	強	100	KYŪ	吸	837	mama-	継	1203
KYŌ	教	101	KYŪ	泣	838	mame	豆	1640
KYŌ	橋	259	KYŪ	及	1148	mamoru	守	300
KYŌ	兄	267	KYŪ	丘	1149	MAN	万	392
KYŌ	共	460	KYŪ	朽	1150	MAN	満	588
KYŌ	協	461	KYŪ	糾	1151	MAN	慢	1837
KYŌ	鏡	462	KYŪ	窮	1152	MAN	漫	1838
KYŌ	競	463	ma-	目	72	manabu	学	10
KYŌ	境	651	ma-	間	92	manako	眼	640
KYŌ	興	652	ma	馬	191	maneku	招	712
KYŌ	経	658	ma	真	514	manukareru	免	1849
KYŌ	供	839	MA	麻	1829	maru	丸	830
KYŌ	胸	840	MA	摩	1830	marui	円	4
KYŌ	郷	841	MA	磨	1831	marui	丸	830
KYŌ	凶	1159	MA	魔	1832	masa	正	41
KYŌ	叫	1160	maboroshi	幻	1226	masa	将	899
KYŌ	狂	1161	machi	町	57	masaru	勝	319
KYŌ	享	1162	machi	街	819	mashite	況	1163
KYŌ	況	1163	mada	未	794	masu	益	619
KYŌ	峡	1164	mado	窓	919	masu	増	741
KYŌ	挟	1165	madou	惑	1942	masu	升	1386
KYŌ	狭	1166	mae	前	159	mata	又	1835
KYŌ	恐	1167	magaru	曲	261	matataku	瞬	1372
KYŌ	恭	1168	magireru	紛	1768	mato	的	551
KYŌ	脅	1169	mago	孫	538	matsu	待	337
KYŌ	矯	1170	MAI	米	201	MATSU	末	587
KYŌ	響	1171	MAI	毎	206	matsu	松	1394
KYŌ	驚	1172	MAI	妹	207	MATSU	抹	1836
KYOKU	曲	261	MAI	枚	976	matsuri	祭	283
KYOKU	局	262	MAI	埋	1833	matsurigoto	政	724
KYOKU	極	464	mairu	参	490	matsuru	祭	283
KYŪ	九	12	majiru	交	115	mattaku	全	330
KYŪ	休	13	majiru	混	677	mau	舞	1761
KYŪ	究	253	makanau	賄	1941	mawari	周	504
KYŪ	急	254	makaru	罷	1732	mawaru	回	86
KYŪ	級	255	makaseru	任	764	mayou	迷	797
KYŪ	宮	256	makeru	負	383	mayu	繭	1223
KYŪ	球	257	maki	牧	586	mazui	拙	1487
KYŪ	求	455	maki	巻	826	mazushii	貧	777
KYŪ	救	456	maki	薪	1445	me	女	35
KYŪ	給	457	makoto	誠	912	me	目	72

me	芽	434	minami	南	190	momo	桃	1646
me	雌	1323	minamoto	源	853	MON	文	68
-me	奴	1638	minato	港	280	MON	閩	200
megumu	恵	1196	mine	峰	1799	MON	門	211
meguru	巡	1374	minikui	醜	1359	MON	問	396
MEI	名	71	minna	皆	1064	MON	紋	1857
MEI	明	208	minoru	実	296	monme	匁	1858
MEI	鳴	209	miru	見	18	mono	者	298
MEI	命	394	miru	視	878	mono	物	387
MEI	迷	797	miru	診	1440	moppara	専	914
MEI	盟	979	misaki	岬	1840	mori	森	38
MEI	銘	1847	misao	操	922	moro	諸	898
mekura	盲	1852	misasagi	陵	1908	moru	盛	1476
MEN	面	395	mise	店	178	moru	漏	1940
MEN	綿	798	mitasu	充	1362	moshi	若	886
MEN	免	1849	mitomeru	認	952	mōsu	申	322
meshi	飯	565	MITSU	密	978	moto	下	7
mesu	雌	1323	mitsugu	貢	1257	moto	本	70
mesu	召	1387	miya	宮	256	moto	元	106
METSU	滅	1848	miyako	都	355	moto	基	641
mezurashii	珍	1602	mizo	溝	1263	moto	許	650
mi-	三	23	mizu	水	40	moto	素	737
mi	実	296	mizukara	自	134	motomeru	求	455
mi	身	323	mizuumi	湖	276	motozuku	基	641
MI	味	393	MO	模	980	motsu	持	294
MI	未	794	mo	喪	1522	MOTSU	物	387
mi-	御	1158	mo	藻	1531	motte	以	419
MI	詔	1839	MO	茂	1850	mottomo	最	484
michi	道	188	MŌ	毛	210	moyōsu	催	1293
michibiku	導	759	MŌ	望	585	mu-	六	76
michiru	満	588	MŌ	亡	973	MU	武	781
midareru	乱	989	MŌ	妄	1851	MU	務	795
midari	妄	1851	MŌ	盲	1852	MU	無	796
midori	緑	412	MŌ	耗	1853	MU	謀	1818
migaku	磨	1831	MŌ	猛	1854	MU	矛	1843
migi	右	2	MŌ	網	1855	MU	夢	1844
mijikai	短	342	mochiiru	用	215	MU	霧	1845
mijime	惨	1309	modoru	戻	1920	mugi	麦	194
miki	幹	637	moeru	燃	765	mugoi	惨	1309
mikotonori	詔	1407	moguru	潜	1497	mukaeru	迎	1207
mimi	耳	29	mōkeru	設	731	mukashi	昔	1481
MIN	民	590	MOKU	木	69	muko	婿	1477
MIN	眠	1842	MOKU	目	72	muku	向	278
mina	皆	1064	MOKU	黙	1856	mukuiru	報	789

muna-	胸	840	nakunaru	亡	973	nemuru	睡	1459
muna-	棟	1653	nama	生	42	NEN	年	64
mune	胸	840	namakeru	怠	1543	NEN	然	528
mune	旨	1312	namari	鉛	1029	NEN	念	561
mune	棟	1653	nameraka	滑	1088	NEN	燃	765
mura	村	52	nami	波	367	NEN	粘	1679
mura	群	657	nami	並	1775	nengoro	懇	1282
murasaki	紫	1320	nami	浪	1937	neru	練	608
mureru	群	657	namida	涙	1916	neru	寝	1441
muro	室	136	NAN	男	54	neru	錬	1933
mushi	虫	56	NAN	南	190	NETSU	熱	560
mushiro	寧	1678	NAN	難	949	NI	二	61
musu	蒸	904	NAN	軟	1673	ni	荷	239
musubu	結	472	nana-	七	30	NI	児	697
musume	娘	1846	naname	斜	1337	NI	仁	906
muzukashii	難	949	nani	何	80	NI	弐	950
MYAKU	脈	589	nanigashi	某	1811	ni	丹	1563
MYŌ	名	71	nao	尚	1392	NI	尼	1674
MYŌ	明	208	nao	猶	1867	nibui	鈍	1671
MYŌ	命	394	naoru	直	349	NICHI	日	62
MYŌ	苗	1740	naosu	治	544	nigai	苦	264
MYŌ	貓	1742	narabu	並	1775	nigeru	逃	1642
MYŌ	妙	1841	narau	習	307	nigiru	握	999
na	名	71	narau	倣	1798	nigoru	濁	1558
na	菜	483	nareru	慣	638	NIKU	肉	365
NA	納	953	naru	鳴	209	nikumu	憎	1532
nado	等	361	naru	成	515	NIN	人	39
nae	苗	1740	nasake	情	719	NIN	任	764
nagai	長	173	nasu	為	1003	NIN	認	952
nagai	永	615	natsu	夏	82	NIN	妊	1676
nagameru	眺	1591	NATSU	納	953	NIN	忍	1677
nagareru	流	409	natsukashii	懐	1067	ninau	担	929
nageku	嘆	1566	nawa	縄	1420	niru	似	696
nageru	投	357	nawa	苗	1740	niru	煮	1338
nagoyaka	和	416	nayamu	悩	1680	nise	偽	1135
naguru	殴	1035	nazumu	泥	1623	nishi	西	152
nagusamu	慰	1008	ne	音	6	niwa	庭	352
NAI	内	364	ne	根	282	niwatori	鶏	1206
nai	無	796	ne	値	933	no	野	213
naka	中	55	nebaru	粘	1679	NŌ	農	366
naka	仲	934	negau	願	446	NŌ	能	766
nakaba	半	195	NEI	寧	1678	NŌ	納	953
naku	鳴	209	neko	貓	1742	NŌ	脳	954
naku	泣	838	nemui	眠	1842	NŌ	悩	1680

NŌ	濃	1681	Ō	王	5	okoru	起	250
noberu	述	707	Ō	黄	120	okoru	興	652
nobiru	延	814	Ō	横	235	okoru	怒	1639
nobiru	伸	1431	Ō	央	429	okotaru	怠	1543
noboru	上	37	Ō	応	622	OKU	屋	236
noboru	登	360	Ō	往	623	OKU	億	430
noboru	昇	1393	Ō	皇	861	oku	置	545
nochi	後	111	Ō	凹	1032	oku	奥	1038
nogareru	逃	1642	Ō	押	1033	OKU	憶	1039
noki	軒	1215	Ō	欧	1034	okureru	後	111
nokoru	残	493	Ō	殴	1035	okureru	遅	1574
nomu	飲	230	Ō	桜	1036	okuru	送	331
nori	典	552	Ō	翁	1037	okuru	贈	1533
nori	則	742	Ō	奥	1038	omo	主	299
noru	乗	320	obi	帯	539	omo	面	395
noru	載	1295	obiru	帯	539	omoi	重	311
nottoru	則	742	obiyakasu	脅	1169	omomuki	趣	1350
nozoku	除	711	oboeru	覚	439	omomuku	赴	1751
nozomu	望	585	ochiiru	陥	1098	omomuro	徐	1385
nozomu	臨	994	ochiru	落	408	omori	錘	1461
nugu	脱	1560	odayaka	穏	1043	omote	表	379
nuku	抜	1708	odokasu	嚇	1080	omote	面	395
numa	沼	1395	odokasu	脅	1169	omou	思	131
nuno	布	778	odoroku	驚	1172	ōmune	概	1072
nuru	塗	1637	odoru	躍	1860	ON	音	6
nushi	主	299	odoru	踊	1880	ON	温	237
nusumu	窃	1488	odosu	威	1002	ON	恩	624
nusumu	盗	1649	odosu	嚇	1080	ON	穏	1043
nuu	縫	1804	odosu	脅	1169	on-	御	1158
NYO	女	35	ogamu	拝	956	onaji	同	187
NYO	如	1383	ōgi	扇	1492	oni	鬼	1128
NYŌ	女	35	oginau	補	970	onna	女	35
NYŌ	尿	1675	ogosoka	厳	854	ono(-ono)	各	438
NYŪ	入	63	ōi	多	163	onore	己	855
NYŪ	乳	951	oiru	老	609	ori	折	522
NYŪ	柔	1363	oka	丘	1149	oriru	下	7
o-	小	36	okasu	犯	768	oriru	降	863
O	悪	222	okasu	侵	1433	oroka	愚	1184
O	和	416	okasu	冒	1812	oroshi	卸	1042
O	汚	1031	oki	沖	1583	orosu	卸	1042
o-	御	1158	ōkii	大	53	oru	折	522
o	緒	1382	okina	翁	1037	oru	居	649
o	尾	1734	okiru	起	250	oru	織	720
o-	雄	1869	okonau	行	118	osaeru	抑	1884

osameru	治	544	RAN	卵	990	RIN	鈴	1921
osameru	収	703	RAN	覧	991	RITSU	立	73
osameru	修	704	RAN	濫	1892	RITSU	率	803
osameru	納	953	RAN	欄	1893	RITSU	律	993
osanai	幼	985	REI	礼	413	RO	路	415
ōse	仰	1173	REI	令	603	RO	炉	1934
oshieru	教	101	REI	冷	604	RO	露	1935
oshimu	惜	1484	REI	例	605	RŌ	老	609
osoi	遅	1574	REI	励	1919	RŌ	労	610
osore	虞	1040	REI	戻	1920	RŌ	朗	995
osoreru	恐	1167	REI	鈴	1921	RŌ	糧	1912
osou	襲	1360	REI	零	1922	RŌ	露	1935
osu	推	908	REI	霊	1923	RŌ	郎	1936
osu	押	1033	REI	隷	1924	RŌ	浪	1937
osu	雄	1869	REI	齢	1925	RŌ	廊	1938
oto	音	6	REI	麗	1926	RŌ	楼	1939
otoko	男	54	REKI	歴	606	RŌ	漏	1940
otoroeru	衰	1456	REKI	暦	1927	ROKU	六	76
otoru	劣	1928	REN	連	607	ROKU	緑	412
otōto	弟	177	REN	練	608	ROKU	録	611
otozureru	訪	972	REN	恋	1931	RON	論	996
OTSU	乙	1041	REN	廉	1932	RU	流	409
otto	夫	573	REN	錬	1933	RU	留	805
ou	追	350	RETSU	列	414	RUI	類	602
ou	負	383	RETSU	劣	1928	RUI	涙	1916
ou	逐	1578	RETSU	烈	1929	RUI	累	1917
ou	被	1729	RETSU	裂	1930	RUI	塁	1918
ōu	覆	1765	RI	里	219	RYAKU	略	804
owaru	終	306	RI	理	220	RYO	旅	410
oya	親	149	RI	利	596	RYO	虜	1903
ōyake	公	277	RI	裏	992	RYO	慮	1904
oyobu	及	1148	RI	吏	1894	RYŌ	両	411
oyogu	泳	232	RI	痢	1895	RYŌ	漁	459
oyoso	凡	1827	RI	履	1896	RYŌ	良	598
RA	裸	1886	RI	離	1897	RYŌ	料	599
RA	羅	1887	RICHI	律	993	RYŌ	量	600
RAI	来	217	RIKI	力	74	RYŌ	令	603
RAI	雷	1888	RIKU	陸	597	RYŌ	領	806
RAI	頼	1889	RIN	林	75	RYŌ	竜	1899
RAKU	楽	218	RIN	輪	601	RYŌ	了	1905
RAKU	落	408	RIN	臨	994	RYŌ	涼	1906
RAKU	絡	1890	RIN	厘	1913	RYŌ	猟	1907
RAKU	酪	1891	RIN	倫	1914	RYŌ	陵	1908
RAN	乱	989	RIN	隣	1915	RYŌ	僚	1909

RYŌ	寮	1910	SAI	災	680	sameru	覚	439
RYŌ	療	1911	SAI	妻	681	sameru	冷	604
RYŌ	糧	1912	SAI	採	682	samui	寒	245
RYŌ	霊	1923	SAI	際	683	samurai	士	494
RYOKU	力	74	SAI	財	685	samurai	侍	1326
RYOKU	緑	412	SAI	済	871	SAN	三	23
RYŪ	立	73	SAI	裁	872	SAN	山	24
RYŪ	流	409	SAI	砕	1287	SAN	算	128
RYŪ	留	805	SAI	宰	1288	SAN	参	490
RYŪ	柳	1898	SAI	栽	1289	SAN	産	491
RYŪ	竜	1899	SAI	彩	1290	SAN	散	492
RYŪ	粒	1900	SAI	斎	1291	SAN	蚕	688
RYŪ	隆	1901	SAI	債	1292	SAN	酸	689
RYŪ	硫	1902	SAI	催	1293	SAN	賛	690
SA	左	22	SAI	歳	1294	SAN	桟	1308
SA	作	127	SAI	載	1295	SAN	惨	1309
SA	茶	171	saiwai	幸	279	SAN	傘	1310
SA	差	482	saka-	酒	302	sara	更	1248
SA	査	678	saka	坂	372	sara	皿	1307
SA	再	679	sakaeru	栄	427	saru	去	258
SA	砂	869	sakai	境	651	saru	猿	1028
SA	佐	1283	sakana	魚	98	sasaeru	支	691
SA	唆	1284	sakarau	逆	646	sasou	誘	1870
SA	詐	1285	sakaru	盛	1476	sasu	指	289
SA	鎖	1286	sakazuki	杯	1685	sasu	差	482
sabaku	裁	872	sake	酒	302	sasu	刺	1314
sabi	寂	1345	sakebu	叫	1160	sasu	挿	1517
sabishii	寂	1345	sakeru	避	1733	sato	里	219
sachi	幸	279	sakeru	裂	1930	satoru	悟	1239
sadameru	定	351	saki	先	49	satosu	諭	1862
saegiru	遮	1339	saki	崎	1297	SATSU	刷	487
sagaru	下	7	saki	岬	1840	SATSU	殺	488
sagasu	探	930	SAKU	作	127	SATSU	察	489
sagasu	捜	1516	SAKU	昨	486	SATSU	冊	874
sageru	提	753	SAKU	策	873	SATSU	札	1304
saguru	探	930	SAKU	削	1298	SATSU	撮	1305
SAI	才	126	SAKU	索	1299	SATSU	擦	1306
SAI	西	152	SAKU	酢	1300	sawa	沢	1552
SAI	切	156	SAKU	搾	1301	sawagu	騒	1530
SAI	祭	283	SAKU	錯	1302	sawaru	障	902
SAI	細	284	saku	咲	1303	sawaru	触	1428
SAI	菜	483	sakura	桜	1036	sazukeru	授	702
SAI	最	484	sama	様	407	SE	世	327
SAI	再	679	samatageru	妨	1808	se	背	957

SE	施	1318	SEKI	積	521	SETSU	切	156
se	畝	1468	SEKI	責	728	SETSU	雪	157
se	瀬	1469	SEKI	績	729	SETSU	殺	488
SECHI	節	523	SEKI	尺	884	SETSU	折	522
SEI	正	41	SEKI	潟	1084	SETSU	節	523
SEI	生	42	SEKI	寂	1345	SETSU	説	524
SEI	青	43	SEKI	斥	1480	SETSU	接	730
SEI	西	152	SEKI	昔	1481	SETSU	設	731
SEI	声	153	SEKI	析	1482	SETSU	拙	1487
SEI	星	154	SEKI	隻	1483	SETSU	窃	1488
SEI	晴	155	SEKI	惜	1484	SETSU	摂	1489
SEI	世	327	SEKI	跡	1485	SHA	車	31
SEI	整	328	SEKI	籍	1486	SHA	社	137
SEI	成	515	semai	狭	1166	SHA	写	297
SEI	省	516	semaru	迫	1697	SHA	者	298
SEI	清	517	semeru	責	728	SHA	舎	700
SEI	勢	518	semeru	攻	1247	SHA	謝	701
SEI	静	519	SEN	千	47	SHA	砂	869
SEI	情	719	SEN	川	48	SHA	射	882
SEI	制	722	SEN	先	49	SHA	捨	883
SEI	性	723	SEN	船	158	SHA	赦	1336
SEI	政	724	SEN	線	329	SHA	斜	1337
SEI	精	725	SEN	浅	525	SHA	煮	1338
SEI	製	726	SEN	戦	526	SHA	遮	1339
SEI	済	871	SEN	選	527	SHAKU	石	45
SEI	聖	911	SEN	銭	734	SHAKU	赤	46
SEI	誠	912	SEN	宣	913	SHAKU	借	502
sei	背	957	SEN	専	914	SHAKU	尺	884
SEI	歳	1294	SEN	泉	915	SHAKU	釈	885
SEI	井	1470	SEN	洗	916	SHAKU	勺	1342
SEI	姓	1471	SEN	染	917	SHAKU	酌	1343
SEI	征	1472	SEN	仙	1490	SHAKU	爵	1344
SEI	斉	1473	SEN	占	1491	SHAKU	昔	1481
SEI	牲	1474	SEN	扇	1492	SHI	子	25
SEI	逝	1475	SEN	栓	1493	SHI	四	26
SEI	盛	1476	SEN	旋	1494	SHI	糸	27
SEI	婿	1477	SEN	践	1495	SHI	止	129
SEI	誓	1478	SEN	銑	1496	SHI	市	130
SEI	請	1479	SEN	潜	1497	SHI	思	131
SEKI	夕	44	SEN	遷	1498	SHI	紙	132
SEKI	石	45	SEN	薦	1499	SHI	自	134
SEKI	赤	46	SEN	繊	1500	SHI	仕	285
seki	関	444	SEN	鮮	1501	SHI	死	286
SEKI	席	520	seru	競	463	SHI	使	287

SHI	始	288	shibui	渋	1364	SHIN	浸	1438
SHI	指	289	SHICHI	七	30	SHIN	紳	1439
SHI	歯	290	SHICHI	質	699	SHIN	診	1440
SHI	詩	291	shigeru	繁	1720	SHIN	寝	1441
SHI	次	292	shigeru	茂	1850	SHIN	慎	1442
SHI	士	494	shiitageru	虐	1147	SHIN	審	1443
SHI	氏	495	shikaru	然	528	SHIN	震	1444
SHI	史	496	SHIKI	色	145	SHIN	薪	1445
SHI	司	497	SHIKI	式	295	SHIN	請	1479
SHI	姉	498	SHIKI	識	698	shina	品	382
SHI	試	499	SHIKI	織	720	shinobu	忍	1677
SHI	支	691	shikiri	頻	1745	shinu	死	286
SHI	志	692	shiku	敷	1756	shio	塩	428
SHI	師	693	shima	島	358	shio	潮	941
SHI	資	694	shimaru	閉	968	shiraberu	調	348
SHI	示	695	shimaru	締	1622	shirizokeru	斥	1480
SHI	至	875	shimeru	絞	1261	shirizoku	退	746
SHI	私	876	shimeru	湿	1333	shiro	城	903
SHI	姿	877	shimeru	占	1491	shirogane	銀	263
SHI	視	878	shimesu	示	695	shiroi	白	65
SHI	詞	879	shimiru	染	917	shiru	知	169
SHI	誌	880	shimo	下	7	shiru	汁	1361
SHI	矢	981	shimo	霜	1529	shirushi	印	425
SHI	旨	1312	shimobe	僕	1820	shirushi	標	571
SHI	伺	1313	SHIN	森	38	shirushi	徴	1596
SHI	刺	1314	SHIN	心	147	shita	下	7
SHI	枝	1315	SHIN	新	148	shita	舌	732
SHI	祉	1316	SHIN	親	149	shitagau	従	891
SHI	肢	1317	SHIN	申	322	shitashii	親	149
SHI	施	1318	SHIN	身	323	shitataru	滴	1626
SHI	脂	1319	SHIN	神	324	shitau	暴	1788
SHI	紫	1320	SHIN	深	325	SHITSU	室	136
SHI	嗣	1321	SHIN	進	326	SHITSU	失	501
SHI	飼	1322	SHIN	臣	512	SHITSU	質	699
SHI	雌	1323	SHIN	信	513	SHITSU	疾	1331
SHI	賜	1324	SHIN	真	514	SHITSU	執	1332
SHI	諮	1325	SHIN	針	905	SHITSU	湿	1333
SHI	漬	1608	SHIN	伸	1431	SHITSU	漆	1334
shiawase	幸	279	SHIN	辛	1432	shizuka	静	519
shiba	芝	1335	SHIN	侵	1433	shizuku	滴	1626
shibaraku	暫	1311	SHIN	津	1434	shizumaru	鎮	1605
shibaru	縛	1701	SHIN	唇	1435	shizumu	沈	1601
shiboru	絞	1261	SHIN	娠	1436	SHO	書	142
shiboru	搾	1301	SHIN	振	1437	SHO	所	312

667

SHO	暑	313	SHŌ	肖	1391	SHU	修	704
SHO	初	507	SHŌ	尚	1392	SHU	衆	705
SHO	処	896	SHŌ	昇	1393	SHU	朱	1346
SHO	署	897	SHŌ	松	1394	SHU	狩	1347
SHO	諸	898	SHŌ	沼	1395	SHU	殊	1348
SHO	且	1091	SHŌ	宵	1396	SHU	珠	1349
SHO	庶	1381	SHŌ	症	1397	SHU	趣	1350
SHO	緒	1382	SHŌ	祥	1398	SHŪ	秋	140
SHŌ	小	36	SHŌ	渉	1399	SHŪ	州	304
SHŌ	正	41	SHŌ	紹	1400	SHŪ	拾	305
SHŌ	生	42	SHŌ	訟	1401	SHŪ	終	306
SHŌ	青	43	SHŌ	掌	1402	SHŪ	習	307
SHŌ	少	143	SHŌ	晶	1403	SHŪ	週	308
SHŌ	声	153	SHŌ	焦	1404	SHŪ	集	309
SHŌ	星	154	SHŌ	硝	1405	SHŪ	周	504
SHŌ	昭	315	SHŌ	粧	1406	SHŪ	収	703
SHŌ	消	316	SHŌ	詔	1407	SHŪ	修	704
SHŌ	商	317	SHŌ	奨	1408	SHŪ	衆	705
SHŌ	章	318	SHŌ	詳	1409	SHŪ	祝	706
SHŌ	勝	319	SHŌ	彰	1410	SHŪ	宗	889
SHŌ	唱	508	SHŌ	衝	1411	SHŪ	就	890
SHŌ	焼	509	SHŌ	償	1412	SHŪ	執	1332
SHŌ	照	510	SHŌ	礁	1413	SHŪ	囚	1353
SHŌ	賞	511	SHŌ	鐘	1414	SHŪ	舟	1354
SHŌ	省	516	SHŌ	井	1470	SHŪ	秀	1355
SHŌ	清	517	SHŌ	姓	1471	SHŪ	臭	1356
SHŌ	相	530	SHŌ	荘	1515	SHŪ	愁	1357
SHŌ	象	533	SHŌ	装	1524	SHŪ	酬	1358
SHŌ	招	712	SHOKU	色	145	SHŪ	醜	1359
SHŌ	承	713	SHOKU	食	146	SHŪ	襲	1360
SHŌ	称	714	SHOKU	植	321	SHUKU	宿	505
SHŌ	証	715	SHOKU	織	720	SHUKU	祝	706
SHŌ	性	723	SHOKU	職	721	SHUKU	縮	893
SHŌ	政	724	SHOKU	殖	1426	SHUKU	叔	1367
SHŌ	精	725	SHOKU	飾	1427	SHUKU	淑	1368
SHŌ	将	899	SHOKU	触	1428	SHUKU	粛	1369
SHŌ	笑	900	SHOKU	嘱	1429	SHUN	春	141
SHŌ	傷	901	SHU	手	32	SHUN	俊	1371
SHŌ	障	902	SHU	首	139	SHUN	瞬	1372
SHŌ	升	1386	SHU	主	299	SHUTSU	出	34
SHŌ	召	1387	SHU	守	300	SO	組	160
SHŌ	匠	1388	SHU	取	301	SO	想	532
SHŌ	床	1389	SHU	酒	302	SO	祖	736
SHŌ	抄	1390	SHU	種	503	SO	素	737

SO	且	1091	SŌ	箱	1703	SŪ	数	151
SO	阻	1505	soba	側	535	SŪ	枢	1464
SO	租	1506	sodatsu	育	227	SŪ	崇	1465
SO	措	1507	soko	底	549	su	巣	1521
SO	粗	1508	sokonau	損	745	sube	術	708
SO	疎	1509	SOKU	足	51	suberu	統	757
SO	訴	1510	SOKU	息	332	suberu	滑	1088
SO	塑	1511	SOKU	速	534	subete	総	738
SO	礎	1512	SOKU	側	535	sude	既	1126
SŌ	早	50	SOKU	則	742	sue	末	587
SŌ	走	161	SOKU	測	743	sueru	据	1466
SŌ	草	162	SOKU	即	1534	sugata	姿	877
SŌ	送	331	SOKU	束	1535	sugi	杉	1467
SŌ	争	529	SOKU	促	1536	sugiru	過	629
SŌ	相	530	somaru	染	917	sugu	直	349
SŌ	倉	531	somuku	背	957	sugureru	優	984
SŌ	想	532	SON	村	52	SUI	水	40
SŌ	総	738	SON	孫	538	SUI	垂	907
SŌ	宗	889	SON	損	745	SUI	推	908
SŌ	奏	918	SON	存	926	SUI	吹	1452
SŌ	窓	919	SON	尊	927	SUI	炊	1453
SŌ	創	920	sonaeru	具	265	SUI	帥	1454
SŌ	層	921	sonaeru	備	774	SUI	粋	1455
SŌ	操	922	sonaeru	供	839	SUI	衰	1456
SŌ	双	1513	sono	園	234	SUI	酔	1457
SŌ	壮	1514	sora	空	15	SUI	遂	1458
SŌ	荘	1515	soreru	逸	1010	SUI	睡	1459
SŌ	捜	1516	sōrō	候	478	SUI	穂	1460
SŌ	挿	1517	soru	反	371	SUI	錘	1461
SŌ	桑	1518	sosogu	注	344	suji	筋	843
SŌ	掃	1519	sosonokasu	唆	1284	sukoshi	少	143
SŌ	曹	1520	sosoru	唆	1284	sukoyaka	健	474
SŌ	巣	1521	soto	外	91	suku	好	859
SŌ	喪	1522	SOTSU	卒	537	suku	透	1647
SŌ	葬	1523	SOTSU	率	803	sukunai	少	143
SŌ	装	1524	sou	沿	815	sukuu	救	456
SŌ	僧	1525	sou	添	1631	sumi	炭	341
SŌ	遭	1526	sozoro	漫	1838	sumi	隅	1187
SŌ	槽	1527	SU	子	25	sumi	墨	1821
SŌ	燥	1528	SU	数	151	sumiyaka	速	534
SŌ	霜	1529	SU	守	300	sumu	住	310
SŌ	騒	1530	su	州	304	sumu	済	871
SŌ	藻	1531	SU	素	737	sumu	澄	1597
SŌ	贈	1533	su	酢	1300	SUN	寸	909

suna	砂	869	TAI	待	337	tamawaru	賜	1324
sunawachi	即	1534	TAI	代	338	tame	為	1003
suppai	酸	689	TAI	帯	539	tameru	矯	1170
suppai	酢	1300	TAI	隊	540	tamesu	試	499
suru	刷	487	TAI	退	746	tami	民	590
suru	為	1003	TAI	貸	747	tamotsu	保	787
suru	擦	1306	TAI	態	748	TAN	炭	341
suru	摩	1830	TAI	耐	1542	TAN	短	342
surudoi	鋭	1018	TAI	怠	1543	TAN	反	371
susumeru	勧	828	TAI	胎	1544	TAN	単	542
susumeru	薦	1499	TAI	泰	1545	TAN	担	929
susumu	進	326	TAI	袋	1546	TAN	探	930
sutaru	廃	1687	TAI	逮	1547	TAN	堪	1104
suteru	捨	883	TAI	替	1548	TAN	但	1559
suteru	棄	1131	TAI	滞	1549	TAN	丹	1563
suu	吸	837	taira	平	388	TAN	胆	1564
suwaru	座	870	taka	高	119	TAN	淡	1565
suzu	鈴	1921	takai	高	119	TAN	嘆	1566
suzushii	涼	1906	takara	宝	971	TAN	端	1567
ta	田	59	take	竹	170	TAN	誕	1568
TA	多	163	take	岳	1082	TAN	鍛	1569
TA	太	164	take	丈	1415	TAN	壇	1571
TA	他	334	taki	滝	1550	tana	店	178
taba	束	1535	takigi	薪	1445	tana	棚	1562
tabaneru	束	1535	TAKU	度	356	tanagokoro	掌	1402
taberu	食	146	TAKU	宅	928	tane	種	503
tabi	度	356	taku	炊	1453	tani	谷	122
tabi	旅	410	TAKU	択	1551	tanomu	頼	1889
-tachi	達	541	TAKU	沢	1552	tanoshii	楽	218
tada	唯	1864	TAKU	卓	1553	taoreru	倒	1643
tadachi	直	349	TAKU	拓	1554	tareru	垂	907
tadashi	但	1559	TAKU	託	1555	tariru	足	51
tadashii	正	41	TAKU	濯	1556	tashika	確	634
tadayou	漂	1739	takumi	巧	1242	tasukeru	助	314
taeru	絶	733	takuwaeru	貯	546	tatakau	戦	526
taeru	堪	1104	takuwaeru	蓄	1579	tatakau	闘	1659
taeru	耐	1542	tama	玉	102	tatami	畳	1419
tagai	互	1236	tama	球	257	tatamu	畳	1419
tagayasu	耕	673	tama	魂	1280	tate	縦	892
TAI	大	53	tama	弾	1570	tate	盾	1375
TAI	太	164	tama	霊	1923	tatematsuru	奉	1793
TAI	体	165	tamago	卵	990	tateru	建	473
TAI	台	166	tamashii	魂	1280	tatoeru	例	605
TAI	対	336	tamau	給	457	tatsu	立	73

TATSU	達	541	TEKI	摘	1625	TŌ	党	946
tatsu	経	658	TEKI	滴	1626	TŌ	糖	947
tatsu	絶	733	TEN	天	58	TŌ	納	953
tatsu	断	750	TEN	店	178	TŌ	豆	1640
tatsu	裁	872	TEN	点	179	TŌ	到	1641
tatsu	竜	1899	TEN	転	354	TŌ	逃	1642
tattobu	尚	1392	TEN	典	552	TŌ	倒	1643
tattoi	貴	834	TEN	展	944	TŌ	凍	1644
tattoi	尊	927	TEN	添	1631	TŌ	唐	1645
tawamureru	戯	1138	TEN	殿	1632	TŌ	桃	1646
tawara	俵	775	tera	寺	133	TŌ	透	1647
tayori	便	582	teru	照	510	TŌ	悼	1648
tayoru	頼	1889	TETSU	鉄	353	TŌ	盗	1649
tazuneru	訪	972	TETSU	迭	1627	TŌ	陶	1650
tazuneru	尋	1451	TETSU	哲	1628	TŌ	塔	1651
tazusawaru	携	1202	TETSU	徹	1629	TŌ	搭	1652
te	手	32	TETSU	撤	1630	TŌ	棟	1653
TEI	体	165	TO	土	60	TŌ	痘	1654
TEI	弟	177	to	戸	108	TŌ	筒	1655
TEI	丁	346	TO	図	150	TŌ	稲	1656
TEI	定	351	TO	都	355	TŌ	踏	1657
TEI	庭	352	TO	登	360	TŌ	謄	1658
TEI	低	548	TO	徒	554	TŌ	闘	1659
TEI	底	549	TO	斗	1633	TŌ	騰	1660
TEI	停	550	TO	吐	1634	tobira	扉	1730
TEI	提	753	TO	途	1635	toboshii	乏	1805
TEI	程	754	TO	渡	1636	toboso	枢	1464
TEI	廷	1610	TO	塗	1637	tobu	飛	566
TEI	呈	1611	tō	十	33	tobu	跳	1595
TEI	抵	1612	TŌ	刀	181	todokōru	滞	1549
TEI	邸	1613	TŌ	冬	182	todoku	届	948
TEI	亭	1614	TŌ	当	183	toge	刺	1314
TEI	貞	1615	TŌ	東	184	tōge	峠	1663
TEI	帝	1616	TŌ	答	185	togeru	遂	1458
TEI	訂	1617	TŌ	頭	186	togu	研	272
TEI	逓	1618	TŌ	道	188	tōi	遠	79
TEI	偵	1619	TŌ	投	357	tojiru	閉	968
TEI	堤	1620	TŌ	島	358	tokeru	融	1872
TEI	艇	1621	TŌ	湯	359	tokeru	溶	1878
TEI	締	1622	TŌ	登	360	toki	時	135
TEKI	的	551	TŌ	等	361	toko	床	1389
TEKI	適	755	TŌ	灯	556	tokoro	所	312
TEKI	敵	756	TŌ	統	757	TOKU	読	189
TEKI	笛	1624	TŌ	討	945	toku	説	524

671

toku	解	632	tsubasa	翼	1885	tsumu	詰	1144
TOKU	特	760	tsubo	坪	1609	tsumu	錘	1461
TOKU	得	761	tsubu	粒	1900	tsumu	摘	1625
TOKU	徳	762	tsuchi	土	60	tsumugu	紡	1814
toku	釈	885	tsuchikau	培	1690	tsuna	綱	1264
TOKU	匿	1664	tsugeru	告	481	tsune	常	718
TOKU	督	1665	tsugi	次	292	tsune	恆	1251
TOKU	篤	1666	tsugu	次	292	tsuno	角	243
tomaru	止	129	tsugu	接	730	tsunoru	募	1787
tomaru	留	805	tsugu	継	1203	tsura	面	395
tomaru	泊	1696	tsugu	嗣	1321	tsurai	辛	1432
tomo	友	214	tsugunau	償	1412	tsuraneru	連	607
tomo	共	460	TSUI	対	336	tsuranuku	貫	1102
tomo	供	839	TSUI	追	350	tsureru	連	607
tomonau	伴	1712	tsui	遂	1458	tsuru	弦	1228
tomu	富	780	TSUI	墜	1606	tsuru	釣	1592
tomurau	弔	1588	tsuide	序	710	tsurugi	剣	1214
TON	団	749	tsuiyasu	費	567	tsutaeru	伝	553
TON	屯	1669	tsuka	束	1535	tsutanai	拙	1487
TON	豚	1670	tsuka	塚	1607	tsutomeru	努	555
tonaeru	唱	508	tsukaeru	仕	285	tsutomeru	務	795
tonari	隣	1915	tsukamu	捕	1784	tsutomeru	勤	842
tori	鳥	174	tsukaneru	束	1535	tsutsu	筒	1655
toriko	虜	1903	tsukareru	疲	1728	tsutsumi	堤	1620
tōru	通	176	tsukaru	漬	1608	tsutsumu	包	583
toru	取	301	tsukasadoru	司	497	tsutsushimu	謹	1180
toru	採	682	tsukau	使	287	tsutsushimu	慎	1442
toru	撮	1305	tsukau	遣	1220	tsuyoi	強	100
toru	執	1332	tsuki	月	16	tsuyu	露	1935
toru	把	1682	tsukiru	尽	1447	tsuzuku	続	536
toru	捕	1784	tsuku	着	343	tsuzumi	鼓	1234
toshi	年	64	tsuku	付	574	U	右	2
tōtoi	貴	834	tsuku	就	890	U	雨	3
tōtoi	尊	927	tsuku	突	1668	U	有	401
totonoeru	整	328	tsukue	机	832	U	宇	811
totonoeru	調	348	tsukurou	繕	1504	U	羽	812
TOTSU	凸	1667	tsukuru	作	127	ubau	奪	1561
TOTSU	突	1668	tsukuru	造	739	uchi	内	364
totsugu	嫁	1049	tsuma	妻	681	ude	腕	1945
tou	問	396	tsumamu	撮	1305	ue	上	37
TSU	都	355	tsumamu	摘	1625	ueru	植	321
tsu	津	1434	tsumetai	冷	604	ueru	餓	1058
TSŪ	通	176	tsumi	罪	686	ueru	飢	1127
TSŪ	痛	943	tsumu	積	521	ugoku	動	362

ui	憂	1871	utsu	打	335	waza	業	260
uji	氏	495	utsu	討	945	waza	技	644
ukagau	伺	1313	utsu	撃	1209	waza	態	748
ukeru	受	303	utsukushii	美	376	wazawai	災	680
ukeru	請	1479	utsuru	移	613	wazawai	禍	1051
uketamawaru	承	713	utsuru	映	813	wazurau	患	1101
uku	浮	1752	utsuru	遷	1498	wazurau	煩	1717
uma	馬	191	utsusu	写	297	ya-	八	66
umai	旨	1312	utsuwa	器	452	ya	家	83
umaru	埋	1833	uttaeru	訴	1510	ya	谷	122
ume	梅	1689	uwa-	上	37	YA	夜	212
umi	海	88	uyamau	敬	846	YA	野	213
umu	生	42	uyauyashii	恭	1168	ya	屋	236
umu	産	491	uzu	渦	1048	ya	矢	981
UN	雲	78	uzumaru	埋	1833	yabureru	敗	562
UN	運	231	WA	話	221	yaburu	破	767
unagasu	促	1536	WA	和	416	yado	宿	505
unaji	項	1262	wa	輪	601	yadoru	宿	505
une	畝	1468	wa	我	817	yaiba	刃	1446
uo	魚	98	wa	環	1115	yakko	奴	1638
ura	裏	992	-wa	把	1682	YAKU	役	397
ura	浦	1785	WAI	賄	1941	YAKU	薬	398
uramu	憾	1113	wakai	若	886	yaku	焼	509
uramu	恨	1277	wakareru	別	579	YAKU	約	591
uranau	占	1491	wakaru	分	199	YAKU	益	619
urawashi	麗	1926	wake	訳	982	YAKU	訳	982
ureeru	愁	1357	wakeru	分	199	YAKU	疫	1019
ureeru	憂	1871	waku	沸	1767	YAKU	厄	1859
uro	虚	1156	WAKU	惑	1942	YAKU	躍	1860
uru	売	192	waku	枠	1943	yama	山	24
uru	得	761	wameku	喚	1103	yamai	病	381
uruou	潤	1379	WAN	湾	1944	yameru	辞	500
urushi	漆	1334	WAN	腕	1945	yamu	病	381
ushi	牛	97	warabe	童	363	yanagi	柳	1898
ushinau	失	501	warau	笑	900	yani	脂	1319
ushiro	後	111	ware	我	817	yaru	遣	1220
usui	薄	1699	wari	割	823	yasashii	易	618
uta	歌	84	waru	割	823	yasashii	優	984
uta	謡	1883	warui	悪	222	yashinau	養	594
utagau	疑	835	wasureru	忘	974	yashiro	社	137
utage	宴	1025	wata	綿	798	yasui	安	223
utau	歌	84	watakushi	私	876	yasui	易	618
utau	謡	1883	wataru	渡	1636	yasumu	休	13
utoi	疎	1509	watashi	私	876	yatou	雇	1232

yatsu	奴	1638	yome	嫁	1049	yue	故	668
yawaragu	和	416	yomu	読	189	YUI	遺	808
yawarakai	柔	1363	yomu	詠	1016	YUI	唯	1864
yawarakai	軟	1673	yorokobu	喜	450	yuka	床	1389
yo-	四	26	yorokobu	歓	639	yuki	雪	157
yo	夜	212	yoroshii	宜	1134	yuku	行	118
yo	世	327	yoru	夜	212	yuku	逝	1475
yo	代	338	yoru	選	527	yume	夢	1844
YO	予	403	yoru	因	614	yumi	弓	836
YO	余	800	yoru	寄	642	yuru	揺	1877
YO	預	801	yoru	依	1001	yurui	緩	1112
YO	与	1873	yoru	拠	1155	yurusu	許	650
YO	誉	1874	yoru	択	1551	yutaka	豊	790
YŌ	用	215	yoshi	由	399	yutaka	裕	1868
YŌ	曜	216	yosōu	裂	1524	yuu	結	472
YŌ	洋	404	you	酔	1457	yuzuru	譲	1424
YŌ	葉	405	yowai	弱	138	ZA	座	870
YŌ	陽	406	yu	湯	359	ZAI	材	485
YŌ	様	407	YU	由	399	ZAI	在	684
YŌ	要	593	YU	油	400	ZAI	財	685
YŌ	養	594	YU	遊	402	ZAI	罪	686
YŌ	容	802	YU	輸	799	ZAI	剤	1296
YŌ	幼	985	YU	愉	1861	zama	様	407
YŌ	羊	986	YU	諭	1862	zama	態	748
YŌ	庸	1875	YU	癒	1863	ZAN	残	493
YŌ	揚	1876	YŪ	右	2	ZAN	惨	1309
YŌ	揺	1877	yū	夕	44	ZAN	暫	1311
YŌ	溶	1878	YŪ	友	214	ZATSU	雑	687
YŌ	腰	1879	YŪ	由	399	ZE	是	910
YŌ	踊	1880	YŪ	有	401	ZEI	税	727
YŌ	窯	1881	YŪ	遊	402	ZEN	前	159
YŌ	擁	1882	YŪ	勇	592	ZEN	全	330
YŌ	謡	1883	YŪ	郵	983	ZEN	然	528
yobu	呼	856	YŪ	優	984	ZEN	善	735
yogoreru	汚	1031	YŪ	幽	1865	ZEN	禅	1502
yoi	良	598	YŪ	悠	1866	ZEN	漸	1503
yoi	善	735	YŪ	猶	1867	ZEN	繕	1504
yoi	宵	1396	YŪ	裕	1868	zeni	銭	734
yoko	横	235	YŪ	雄	1869	ZETSU	舌	732
YOKU	浴	595	YŪ	誘	1870	ZETSU	絶	733
YOKU	欲	987	YŪ	憂	1871	ZŌ	象	533
YOKU	翌	988	YŪ	融	1872	ZŌ	雑	687
YOKU	抑	1884	yubi	指	289	ZŌ	造	739
YOKU	翼	1885	yudaneru	委	423	ZŌ	像	740

ZŌ	増	741
ZŌ	蔵	923
ZŌ	臓	924
ZŌ	曹	1520
ZŌ	憎	1532
ZŌ	贈	1533
ZOKU	族	333
ZOKU	続	536
ZOKU	属	744
ZOKU	俗	925
ZOKU	賊	1537
ZON	存	926
ZU	図	150
ZU	頭	186
ZU	事	293
ZU	豆	1640
ZUI	随	1462
ZUI	髄	1463
zuku	銑	1496

GENERAL PRINCIPLES OF STROKE ORDER

1. Top to bottom.

three 一 二 三

word 、 一 亠 言 言

guest 宀 字 客

2. Left to right.

province 、 丿 爿 州 州 州

faction 氵 汈 沠 派

example 亻 仴 伢 例

3. Horizontal strokes usually precede vertical strokes when crossing.

ten 一 十

earth 一 十 土

till 三 丰 耒 耒 耕

4. However, in a few cases vertical strokes precede horizontal ones.

king 一 丁 干 王

field 冂 冂 田 田

bend 冂 曲 曲 曲

5. Center usually precedes left and right where latter do not exceed two strokes each.

small 亅 小 小

water 亅 水 水 水

receive 了 手 承 承 承

Note that the two exceptions are the heart radical 忄 (丶 忄) and fire 火 (丶丷 火).

6. Outer frame first, but bottom line last.

country　　　门　国　国

sun　　　　门　日　日

moon　　　门　月　月

Note the order of 匚 , with the left hand stroke joined to the bottom (e.g. 一 ア 匠).

7. Right-to-left diagonal stroke precedes left-to-right.

person　　　ノ　人

father　　　ソ　父

again　　　フ　又

8. Central vertical line last.

middle　　　口　中

vehicle　　　一　車　車

thing　　　一　事　事

9. Strokes which cut through come last.

woman　　　女　女

child　　　了　子

boat　　　舟　舟

Note that the only exception is 世 (一 廿 世).

The following pointers should also be observed.

a. squares are written with three strokes not four (丨 冂 口)
b. vertical strokes should not slope (e.g. 中 not 中)
c. horizontal strokes may slope, but should be parallel (e.g. 羊)
d. characters should be of uniform size.